PENGUIN CLASSICS

THE AGE OF ALEXANDER

PLUTARCH (c. AD 45–120) was a Greek philosopher from the small town of Chaeronea in Boeotia. He lived at the height of the Roman Empire and is author of one of the largest collections of writings to have survived from Classical antiquity. His work is traditionally divided into two: the *Moralia*, which include a vast range of philosophical, scientific, moral and rhetorical works, and the Lives or biographies. Almost fifty such biographies survive, most from his collection of *Parallel Lives*, in which biographies of Greek and Roman statesmen are arranged in pairs. Plutarch's philosophical and moral interests are apparent in the Lives, as are his considerable literary talent, his vast knowledge of the ancient world and his careful research. Both the Lives and *Moralia* have been extremely influential since they were first translated in the Renaissance.

IAN SCOTT-KILVERT was Director of English Literature at the British Council and editor of *Writers and Their Works*. He also translated Cassius Dio's *The Roman History* as well as Plutarch's *The Rise and Fall of Athens: Nine Greek Lives* and *Makers of Rome* for Penguin Classics. He died in 1989.

TIMOTHY E. DUFF is Reader in Classics at the University of Reading. He is author of *Plutarch's Lives: Exploring Virtue and Vice* (1999) and the *Greek and Roman Historians* (2003) and has published extensively on Plutarch.

CHRISTOPHER PELLING is Regius Professor of Greek at Oxford University. He has published a commentary on Plutarch's *Life of Antony* (1988) and a commentary on Plutarch's *Life of Caesar* (2011). His other books include *Literary Texts and the Greek Historian* (2000). Most of his articles on Plutarch were collected in his *Plutarch and History* (2002).

The Age of Alexander

Ten Greek Lives by Plutarch

Artaxerxes · Pelopidas · Dion · Timoleon
Demosthenes · Phocion · Alexander · Eumenes
Demetrius · Pyrrhus

Revised edition

Translated by
IAN SCOTT-KILVERT *and* TIMOTHY E. DUFF

Introductions and Notes by
TIMOTHY E. DUFF

With Series Preface by
CHRISTOPHER PELLING

PENGUIN BOOKS

PENGUIN CLASSICS

Published by the Penguin Group
Penguin Books Ltd, 80 Strand, London WC2R ORL, England
Penguin Group (USA) Inc., 375 Hudson Street, New York, New York 10014, USA
Penguin Group (Canada), 90 Eglinton Avenue East, Suite 700, Toronto, Ontario,
Canada M4P 2Y3 (a division of Pearson Penguin Canada Inc.)
Penguin Ireland, 25 St Stephen's Green, Dublin 2, Ireland (a division of Penguin Books Ltd)
Penguin Group (Australia), 250 Camberwell Road, Camberwell, Victoria 3124, Australia
(a division of Pearson Australia Group Pty Ltd)
Penguin Books India Pvt Ltd, 11 Community Centre, Panchsheel Park, New Delhi – 110 017, India
Penguin Group (NZ), 67 Apollo Drive, Rosedale, Auckland 0632, New Zealand
(a division of Pearson New Zealand Ltd)
Penguin Books (South Africa) (Pty) Ltd, Block D, Rosebank Office Park, 181 Jan Smuts Avenue,
Parktown North, Gauteng 2193, South Africa

Penguin Books Ltd, Registered Offices: 80 Strand, London WC2R ORL, England

www.penguin.com

This translation first published 1973
This edition first published in Penguin Classics 2011

025

Translation copyright © Estate of Ian Scott-Kilvert, 1973
Revisions to these translations and translations of *Artaxerxes* and *Eumenes* © Timothy E. Duff, 2012
Introductions and Notes copyright © Timothy E. Duff, 2012
Series Preface copyright © Christopher Pelling, 2005
All rights reserved

The moral right of the translators and editor has been asserted

Set in 10.25/12.25 pt PostScript Adobe Sabon
Typeset by Jouve (UK), Milton Keynes
Printed in England by Clays Ltd, Elcograf S.p.A.

ISBN: 978-0-140-44935-8

www.greenpenguin.co.uk

Contents

THE AGE OF ALEXANDER

Penguin Plutarch

The first Penguin translation of Plutarch appeared in 1958, with Rex Warner's version of six Roman Lives appearing as *Fall of the Roman Republic*. Other volumes followed steadily, three of them by Ian Scott-Kilvert (*The Rise and Fall of Athens* in 1960, *Makers of Rome* in 1965 and *The Age of Alexander* in 1973), and then Richard Talbert's *Plutarch on Sparta* in 1988. Several of the moral essays were also translated by Robin Waterfield in 1992. Now only fourteen of the forty-eight Lives remain. It is planned to include these remaining Lives in a new edition, along with revised versions of those already published.

This is also an opportunity to divide up the Lives in a different way, although it is not straightforward to decide what that different way should be. Nearly all Plutarch's surviving biographies were written in pairs as *Parallel Lives*: thus a 'book' for Plutarch was not just *Theseus* or *Caesar* but *Theseus and Romulus* or *Alexander and Caesar*. Most, but not all, of those pairs have a brief epilogue at the end of the second Life comparing the two heroes, just as many have a prologue before the first Life giving some initial grounds for the comparison. Not much attention was paid to this comparative technique at the time when the Penguin series started to appear, and it seemed natural then to separate each Life from its pair and organize the volumes by period and city. The comparative epilogues were not included in the translations at all.

That now looks very unsatisfactory. The comparative technique has come to be seen as basic to Plutarch's strategy, underlying not only those brief epilogues but also the entire pairings. (It is true, though, that in the last few years scholars have become increasingly alert to the way that *all* the Lives, not just the pairs, are crafted to complement one another.) It is very tempting to keep the pairings in this new series in a way that would respect Plutarch's own authorial intentions.

After some agonizing, we have decided nevertheless to keep to something like the original strategy of the series, though with some refinement. The reason is a practical one. Many, perhaps most, readers of Plutarch will be reading him to see what he has to say about a particular period, and will wish to compare his treatment of the major players to see how the different parts of his historical jigsaw fit together. If one kept the pairings, that would inevitably mean buying several different volumes of the series; and if, say, one organized those volumes by the Greek partner (so that, for instance, *Pericles–Fabius, Nicias–Crassus* and *Coriolanus–Alcibiades* made one volume), anyone primarily interested in the Roman Lives of the late Republic would probably need to buy the whole set. That is no way to guarantee these finely crafted works of art the wide reading that they deserve. Keeping the organization by period also allows some other works of Plutarch to be included along with the Lives themselves, for instance the fascinating essay *On the Malice of Herodotus* along with the Lives of Themistocles and Aristides and (as before) several Spartan essays along with the Spartan Lives.

Of course the comparative epilogues must now be included, and they will now be translated and printed along with the second Life of each pair, just as the prologues are conventionally printed before the first Life. Each volume will now also usually include more extended introductions to each Life, which will draw attention to the importance of the comparison as well as other features of Plutarch's technique. This is a compromise, and an uncomfortable one; but it still seems the better way.

The volumes will, however, sort the Lives into more logical groups. The early Roman figures will now be grouped together in a single volume entitled *The Rise of Rome*; the life of Agesilaus will migrate from the *The Age of Alexander* to join the rest of the Spartan Lives, and the *Life of Artaxerxes* will join the *The Age of Alexander* collection; the rest of the new translations of

Roman Lives will join those of the Gracchi, Brutus and Antony in a new *Rome in Crisis* volume. The introductions and notes will be revised where necessary. In due course we hope to include the *Moral Essays* in the project as well.

In a recent bibliometric study (*Ancient Society*, 28 (1997), 265–89), Walter Scheidel observed that the proportion of scholarly articles devoted to most classical authors had remained more or less constant since the 1920s. The one author to stand out with an exceptional rise was Plutarch. That professional pattern has been matched by a similar surge in the interest in Plutarch shown by the general reading public. The Penguin translations have played a large part in fostering that interest, and this new, more comprehensive project will surely play a similar role in the future.

Christopher Pelling
2004

Preface to the Revised Edition

This volume was first published in 1973. In that first edition Ian Scott-Kilvert was responsible for the translations and notes and G. T. Griffiths for the Introduction. For the new edition I have completely rewritten the General Introduction and the explanatory Notes (now printed as endnotes), added new introductions and bibliographies to each Life, and partly revised the Chronology, Historical Events and Biographical Notes. I have also added translations of two Lives which were not included in the original collection: *Artaxerxes* and *Eumenes*. To make way for them, *Agesilaus* has now been moved to Penguin's *Plutarch on Sparta*.

All the Lives included here except *Artaxerxes* are from Plutarch's collection of *Parallel Lives*. In that collection the Lives are arranged in pairs, one Greek figure with one Roman; many pairs are preceded by a prologue, which introduces both men, and most are followed by a brief comparison of the two. This and other Penguin volumes do not reproduce this 'parallel' structure, but instead arrange Lives according to historical period. In the 1973 edition the comparisons were simply discarded and the prologues printed, as they usually are, as part of the first Life. In this new edition, I have added translations of the comparisons which follow the two second Lives included here (*Timoleon* and *Eumenes*); I have numbered the chapters of these comparisons separately, though giving the conventional numeration in brackets. I have also attempted to distinguish more clearly between the prologues and the start of the Lives which follow them, though in this case I have retained the conventional chapter numbering system, as to do otherwise would have meant interfering with the numeration of the whole Life. Finally, I have deleted the prologue to *Aemilius and Timoleon*, which in the first edition was wrongly placed at the start of *Timoleon*; it now appears in its rightful place at the start of *Aemilius* in Penguin's *The Rise of Rome*.

I have left Scott-Kilvert's translations largely unchanged, except that I have corrected mistakes or omissions where I found them, removed inconsistencies and occasionally brought the translation closer to Plutarch's own wording. I have also altered the layout of poetic quotations: brief verse quotations are now marked simply by italics rather than being inset on separate lines. This communicates better the feel of the original, where such quotations are integrated into the syntax of Plutarch's prose. The other consistent change I have made concerns the links between episodes. Scott-Kilvert's translation had a tendency to insert at the start of new episodes or paragraphs markers of time, such as 'next', 'later' or 'after this', where they did not appear in Plutarch's Greek; the result was to give a false sense of chronological progression. I have in such cases attempted to give a rendering which better reflects the logic of Plutarch's original.

Finally, I wish to express my thanks to the Alexander von Humboldt Foundation for the award of a fellowship at the Freie Universität Berlin during which I completed much of this volume, and especially to Bernd Seidensticker of the Institut für Griechische und Lateinische Philologie for his unfailing hospitality and support during my stay. I am also grateful to Christopher Pelling for his advice on this project and on much else; to Monica Schmoller and all at Penguin for their patience in seeing this volume through to press; and to the following friends and colleagues who generously read and commented on drafts of some or all of the Lives in this volume: Emma Aston, Eftychia Bathrellou, Jeffrey Beneker, Alastair Blanshard, Marc Domingo Gygax, Lucy Fletcher, Richard Talbert and Pat Wheatley. They are not, of course, responsible for any mistakes that may remain.

Timothy E. Duff
2011

Abbreviations

ANRW   Haase, W., and Temporini, H. (eds.), *Aufstieg und Niedergang der Römischen Welt* (Berlin and New York: De Gruyter, 1972–)

Austin   Austin, M. M. (ed.), *The Hellenistic World from Alexander to the Roman Conquest: A Selection of Ancient Sources in Translation* (Cambridge: Cambridge University Press, 1981)

Bergk   Bergk, T. (ed.), *Poetae Lyrici Graeci*, 3 vols. (4th edn; Leipzig: Teubner, 1878–82)

CAH vi   Lewis, D. M., Hornblower, S., and Ostwald, M. (eds.), *The Cambridge Ancient History*, vol. vi, *The Fourth Century BC* (2nd edn; Cambridge: Cambridge University Press, 1994)

CAH vii   Walbank, F. W., Astin, A. E., Frederiksen, M. W., and Ogilvie, R. M. (eds.), *The Cambridge Ancient History*, vol. vii, *The Hellenistic World* (2nd edn; Cambridge: Cambridge University Press, 2 vols., 1984–9)

CQ   *Classical Quarterly*

De Falco   De Falco, V. (ed.), *Demades Oratore: Testimonianze e Frammenti* (2nd edn; Collana di Studi Greci 25, Naples: Libreria Scientifica Editrice, 1954)

FGrHist   Jacoby, F. (ed.), *Die Fragmente der Griechischen Historiker*, 3 vols. (Berlin: Werdmann, 1923–30; Leiden: Brill, 1940–58)

Harding   Harding, P. (ed.), *From the End of the Peloponnesian War to the Battle of Ipsus* (Cambridge: Cambridge University Press, 1985)

K–A   Kassel, R., and Austin, C. (eds.), *Poetae Comici Graeci*,

8 vols. (Berlin and New York: De Gruyter, 1983–2001)

Maehler   Maehler, H., and Snell, B., *Pindari carmina cum fragmentis*, 2 vols. (Leipzig: Teubner, 1987–9)

Page   Page, D. L. (ed.), *Poetae Melici Graeci* (Oxford: Clarendon Press, 1962)

Pfeiffer   Pfeiffer, R. (ed.), *Callimachus*, 2 vols. (Oxford: Clarendon Press, 1949–53)

PSI   *Papiri Greci e Latini: Pubblicazioni della Società Italiana per la Ricerca dei Papiri Greci e Latini in Egitto* (Florence: Tipografia Ariani, 1912–)

R&O   Rhodes, P. J., and Osborne, R. (eds.), *Greek Historical Inscriptions 404–323 BC* (Oxford: Oxford University Press, 2003)

Rose   Rose, V. (ed.), *Aristotelis qui ferebantur Librorum Fragmenta* (Leipzig: Teubner, 1886)

TrGF   Snell, B., Kannicht, R., and Radt, S. (eds.), *Tragicorum Graecorum Fragmenta*, 5 vols. (Göttingen: Vandenhoeck & Ruprecht, 1971–2004)

Voigt   Voigt, E.-M. (ed.), *Sappho et Alcaeus* (Amsterdam: Athenaeum, 1971)

West   West, M. L. (ed.), *Iambi et Elegi Graeci ante Alexandrum cantati*, 2 vols. (2nd edn; Oxford: Clarendon Press, 1989–92)

General Introduction

This volume contains a selection of ten Lives, written by the Greek biographer and philosopher Plutarch and covering the period from the start of the fourth century BC to early in the third. It includes Plutarch's biographies of some of the most famous and important figures in Greek history, such as Demosthenes and Alexander the Great. It also includes some less well-known figures such as Dion of Syracuse or Eumenes, Alexander's secretary. All the Lives included here are extremely important historical sources. They also provide a vivid picture of the Greek world and beyond at a crucial period, which saw the collapse of Spartan power, the eclipsing of the city-states of mainland Greece by Macedonia, the conquests of Alexander the Great and the establishment of a series of Macedonian kingdoms in the wake of those conquests.

Plutarch and his Works

Plutarch lived when the Roman Empire was at its height (c. AD 45–120), and more of his work survives than of almost any other author from Classical antiquity. About Plutarch's life we know almost nothing except what he himself tells us in his writings, but from those we can learn a good deal. He seems to have travelled widely, including to Rome, and to have been acquainted with many important Roman figures. But his home was in the small Greek city of Chaeronea in Boeotia, some 60 miles north-west of Athens, where he was a member of the governing elite. Plutarch's writings contain many references to the dinner parties and philosophical conversations held at his house, and give us a lively picture of the intellectual and social life of his circle. In one famous passage he complains of the difficulties of accessing books in Chaeronea, far away from the main urban centres like Athens: 'I ... live in a small city', he declares, 'and choose to stay there to prevent its becoming even smaller' (*Demosthenes* 2).

Plutarch's works, all written in Greek, are traditionally divided into two categories: *Moralia* and Lives. *Moralia* means literally 'ethical works', but in fact this title, which does not seem to be Plutarch's own, is rather misleading: the *Moralia* are much broader in nature than the title implies, and the Lives, as we shall see, are also in their own way concerned with ethics. Over seventy different works survive in the *Moralia*; they range in content from practical treatises, such as *On control of one's anger* or *How to profit from one's enemies*, to heavyweight philosophical works, such as commentaries on Plato or polemics against the doctrines of the Stoic or Epicurean philosophies. The *Moralia* also include a number of works of political theory and guidance, such as *Political advice*, an open letter to a young aristocrat about to enter public life in the city of Sardis in Asia Minor. Most of these works are steeped in quotation and allusion to earlier Greek literature and display an immense erudition. Many also show the influence of Plato, especially in the latter's understanding of human psychology, and a concern for morality: that is, for the art of living properly and well.

Plutarch's other great literary achievement was his biographies. A series of *Lives of the Caesars* was written first. Unfortunately, only two short Lives of the emperors Galba and Otho survive, but the series as a whole seems to have covered the Roman emperors from Augustus to Vitellius (roughly from *c.* 31 BC to AD 69). This series preceded Suetonius' better-known Latin *Lives of the Caesars* by a generation, and it is a great pity that it has largely been lost. Plutarch also wrote a few stand-alone Lives, such as that of the Persian King Artaxerxes II, which is included in this volume. But his most famous and influential work is the *Parallel Lives*, a series of paired biographies of

Greek and Roman statesmen, and it is from that collection that all the other biographies translated in this volume are drawn.

Parallel Lives

The *Parallel Lives* include many of the great names of Greek and Roman history. Even not counting the few Lives of mythical or semi-mythical figures, such as Theseus and Romulus, the supposed founders of Athens and Rome respectively, they span some six centuries, from Archaic and Classical Greece and the early Roman Republic to the Greek kings of the Hellenistic period and the dynasts of the later Roman Republic, such as Pompey, Julius Caesar and Mark Antony. The *Parallel Lives* were written between about AD 96 and 120, that is after most of the works of the *Moralia*, and are often regarded as the pinnacle of Plutarch's achievement. They were used as a source by Shakespeare, and have since the Renaissance exerted a great influence on both writers and statesmen; in the eighteenth century no other work from Classical antiquity was so widely read.

The *Parallel Lives* owe their name to their unique structure. They were designed to be read not as individual biographies but in *pairs*, each pair consisting of the biography of a Greek statesman or general and the biography of a Roman, usually but not always in that order. Thus, for example, the *Life of Alexander* is paired with the *Life of Caesar*, and the *Life of Demosthenes* with the *Life of Cicero*. Many pairs of Lives begin with a prologue, which introduces both men and sets out some of the factors which led Plutarch to pair them. In addition, most pairs of Lives are followed by a 'Comparison' (in Greek, *syncrisis*), where the two subjects are weighed up against each other. Together these elements – prologue (where it exists), first Life, second Life, and Comparison – form a single Plutarchan 'book'.

Twenty-two such books survive. Some of the men whom Plutarch paired, such as those just mentioned, had already been compared with each other by writers before Plutarch; in other cases the pairing seems to have been of Plutarch's own devising. But the paired or 'parallel' structure was plainly of great importance to Plutarch's design. It encourages the reader to think not just about a particular individual and the specifics of his career, or about the period or society in which he lived; rather, we are encouraged to compare and contrast, to think about common character traits or experiences shared by the two men or differences between them, and about similarities or differences between the two men's societies. Many modern readers approach the *Parallel Lives* primarily as sources for history, and most modern editions, such as this one, dispense with the parallel structure and group Lives for convenience by theme or by period. But it is important to keep in mind that Plutarch's Lives were not designed to be read one by one in chronological order, nor was Plutarch's aim simply to provide a historical narrative of any particular period. Rather, the reader was expected to read both Lives of a pair together and to read the second directly after reading the first. Furthermore, the comparative element implied in the structure of the *Parallel Lives* is central to their meaning: they were supposed to be an exercise in cultural and biographical comparison, and to read one Life without its partner, or without the common prologue or comparison which weld the two Lives together, is to miss much that was of importance to Plutarch and his original readers.

The Purpose of the *Parallel Lives*

Plutarch himself tells us something of the purposes of his work and its main concerns in the prologues which introduce many pairs of Lives. Perhaps the most famous is the prologue to the *Lives of Alexander and Caesar*. After naming the two subjects of the book ('Alexander, the king, and ... Julius Caesar, the conqueror of Pompey'), Plutarch warns his readers not to expect large-scale historical narrative. The deeds of Alexander and Caesar will not, he claims, be narrated in detail:

> For I am writing Lives not history, and the truth is that the most
> brilliant exploits often tell us nothing of the virtues or vices of the

men who performed them, while on the other hand a chance remark or a joke may reveal far more of a man's character than battles where thousands die, huge troop deployments or the sieges of cities. When a portrait painter sets out to create a likeness, he relies above all upon the face and the expression of the eyes and pays little attention to the other parts of the body: in the same way it is my task to dwell upon those details which illuminate the workings of the soul, and to use these to create a portrait of each man's life, leaving to others their great exploits and battles.

(Alexander 1)

Two related points stand out here. First, Plutarch's focus is on the character of his subjects. Secondly, in order to pursue this interest in character, Plutarch self-consciously declares that he will be selective in his choice of material. He will not offer a narrative of historical events per se, and will not attempt to cover all the subject's known actions. Instead, just as a portrait painter concentrates particular attention on the face because it is there that his subject's character is most evident, so Plutarch will choose material that will most bring out character; indeed, he will often, he says, prefer a revealing anecdote or saying to a detailed narrative of political and military events.

An interest in character is central to all Plutarch's Lives. But by 'character' Plutarch meant something slightly different from what a modern biographer might mean by the term. Today we tend to think of character as having to do with what makes a person distinctly themselves; the unique collection of traits which sets them apart from others. In antiquity, however, character was conceived in *moral* terms. Thus, when Plutarch talks here about his concern to bring out the character of his subjects, the focus is on judging them according to accepted standards of behaviour (hence the reference to 'virtues or vices'). Furthermore, in ancient thought a person's character was only revealed through his deeds. Thus Plutarch's Lives do not concern themselves with the inner world of the individual or what we might call his 'private' life (a concept that would scarcely have made sense to Plutarch's readers) but with his behaviour, by which character is actualized and made manifest.

This focus on the character of the subject is meant to have for the reader a practical moral benefit. Plutarch explains in another prologue, that to the *Lives of Aemilius and Timoleon* (one of the few pairs of Lives in which the Roman Life precedes the Greek):

> When I first took up the writing of these Lives I did it for the sake of others, but now I find that I have grown fond of the task and continue it for my own pleasure, endeavouring somehow in the mirror of history to adorn my life and make it like the virtues of these men. It is as though we could talk with them and enjoy their company every day. We receive each one of them in turn and welcome him as our guest, when they visit us through history, and examine '*how great he was and of what kind*' [Homer, *Iliad* 24.630], taking from his deeds the most important and most beautiful to know. '*Ah! What greater joy than this could you obtain*' and what more effective for the improvement of character?
>
> (*Aemilius* 1)

Plutarch imagines himself and his readers communing with the great men of the past, learning from them and imitating them; trying, as he puts it, 'to adorn my life and make it like the virtues of these men'. He compares this process to looking in the 'mirror' of history. This is a very significant metaphor. Plutarch imagines himself and his readers not only observing the actions of the statesmen of the past, assessing their behaviour and judging it on a moral scale, but also comparing themselves with those great men: by looking in the mirror of history one sees oneself reflected, good points and bad, and considers one's own behaviour in the light of that of the great men of history. Such self-examination, Plutarch explains, with a quotation from a now lost play of Sophocles (*TrGF* IV fragment 636), is pleasurable but also 'effective for the improvement of character'. A central goal, then, of the *Parallel Lives* is the moral improvement of the reader.

We should not confuse Plutarch's moral aims with his being 'moralistic', or imagine that in the *Parallel Lives* Plutarch lectures his readers on good or bad behaviour. In fact, Plutarch very rarely goes in for overt moralizing, but tends to shape his work so that moral issues appear to emerge directly from his narrative, and trusts his reader to notice them. Furthermore, as well as providing examples of good or bad behaviour, the Lives also seem to highlight difficult moral problems or dilemmas. To take an example from the Lives in this volume, when Dion of Sicily sanctions the assassination of his troublesome opponent Heracleides, the Syracusans, though at first annoyed, soon recognize that the city would have had no peace with both men alive (*Dion* 53). This might suggest that the reader should approve. But earlier Plutarch has had Dion himself argue that murdering Heracleides would be an act of moral weakness (ch. 47). So was the murder a necessary evil essential to ensuring the greater good or a lamentable failure of moral nerve? Plutarch draws his readers' attention to the problem, but does not resolve it.

Finally, Plutarch never paints his subjects as black-and-white heroes and villains. It may be easy to label some of their actions as more or less good or bad, but Plutarch presents whole Lives rather than isolated stories, and in all of his Lives there are many grey areas and much food for thought. To take just one example, Alexander the Great combines great bravery and drive, and his conquests are presented as glorious and praiseworthy. But he also murders his friends and dies from heavy drinking, superstitious and embittered. This is not a model for simple adulation or imitation; rather, Plutarch's *Alexander* encourages the reader to think deeply about moral issues: what makes a good leader? what makes a good life? It is exactly in this capacity of the Lives to make the reader *think* that their moral power lies.

Plutarch's Historical Selectivity

We have already noticed how in the prologue to *Alexander and Caesar* Plutarch declares that he will be selective in the events he chooses to narrate. He relates this selectivity not only to his moral focus but also to the fact that he is 'writing Lives not history' (*Alexander* 1). This was a more controversial and striking claim to his original readers than it now seems to us, as political biography in Plutarch's time was only gradually developing

an identity as a separate genre. At any rate, Plutarch declares
that his aim is not to give a complete or consistent coverage of
a particular historical period, but to focus on his biographical
subject and to give only such background material as the reader
may need to understand him.

Plutarch's selectivity can sometimes be frustrating for the
modern historian. He tends to assume knowledge of the basic
narrative, which forms the background against which the
actions of the subject of the particular Life are set. Furthermore,
Plutarch does not attempt to give a full coverage even of the
events in which the subject was involved; instead he tends to
select for special treatment episodes which he considers particularly revealing of the subject's character and to explore them at
length, while ignoring or passing quickly over other events or
periods of the subject's life entirely. This selectivity means that,
although we can often fill in the gaps from other ancient sources,
there are times when Plutarch assumes knowledge of the wider
period that we simply do not possess. For example, the first
third or so of *Phocion* consists largely of anecdotes designed to
bring out Phocion's character. As a result, much remains unclear
in the early career of Phocion, and neither this Life nor that of
Demosthenes enables us to understand fully Athenian foreign
policy in the decades leading up to Chaeronea in 338 BC. Similarly, *Eumenes* concentrates almost exclusively on the last six
years of Eumenes' life, and even then focuses mainly on his difficulties in dealing with his Macedonian subordinates, and on
his betrayal by his troops, rather than on giving a clear narrative of the hugely important events which convulsed Greece
and the Near East in the years after Alexander's death and in
which Eumenes played a major role. In both cases Plutarch certainly had access to sources which would have informed him of
the wider narrative; his decision not to repeat this narrative is
a deliberate one.

Also challenging for the historian is Plutarch's tendency to
be sympathetic to the subject of whichever Life he is writing.
This is perfectly understandable in a biographer, and in Plutarch
never involves a white-wash. But it does mean that in each
Life Plutarch tends to adopt something of the point of view of

the subject of that Life. As a result, different Lives give quite radically different presentations of the same events or period. For example, *Pelopidas* portrays the events of the 370s and 360s BC from a Theban point of view, whereas *Agesilaus* portrays them from a Spartan one. Similarly, *Demosthenes* and *Phocion* give very different 'takes' on the question of Athenian resistance to or collaboration with Macedonia. In neither case are the differences explicable in terms of Plutarch's access to information or of his own personal beliefs; rather they flow naturally from his single-minded biographical focus. This tendency to focalize through the subject of each Life can be seen particularly clearly in *Artaxerxes*, the one stand-alone Life in this volume (i.e., the only one which is not part of the *Parallel Lives*); here the Greeks are mere bit-players, seen from the point of view of the Persian court (though the terms in which Plutarch analyses that court, and the assumptions he brings, are themselves thoroughly Greek).

Plutarch and his Sources

One of the reasons for Plutarch's selectivity must have been that for all the periods of Greek history about which he wrote, including the period covered in this volume, there already existed large-scale histories to which many of his readers had access. For the fourth- and third-century BC Greek Lives collected in this volume this included, among many others, the works of Xenophon, Ephorus, Timaeus and Hieronymus of Cardia. All of these historians had by Plutarch's day attained the status of classics, though unfortunately only Xenophon's work now survives. Plutarch's aim is not to repeat what these historians said or to compete with them, but to give a new, distinctive version of history, focused tightly on the individual subject and his character.

Plutarch makes explicit his desire to avoid direct competition with earlier historians in the prologue to another pair of Lives, *Nicias and Crassus*. Nicias was commander of Athens' ill-fated expedition to Sicily in 415 BC, and he died, like most of his men, in the slaughter which followed the Athenian retreat from Syracuse. All this had been dealt with by the great fifth-century historian Thucydides, whose account had become a classic, as well as by the Sicilian historian Philistus. Plutarch announces in his prologue that he will not try to compete with either work. He continues:

> But in order not to appear totally careless or lazy, I have run through briefly and without unnecessary detail those deeds which Thucydides and Philistus described, since it is impossible to pass them by, containing as they do indications of the man's character and disposition, which are revealed in the midst of great sufferings. I have also tried to bring together those incidents which escape the majority and which have been mentioned in scattered locations by others, or have been found either on votive offerings or in old decrees. My aim is not to gather a useless mass of material, but rather material that contributes to an understanding of character and temperament.
>
> *(Nicias* 1)

The basic narrative covered by earlier historians will not, Plutarch claims, be ignored: after all, a man's deeds, especially when he is placed in situations of great stress, can throw light on his character. But Plutarch will supplement the narrative he found in the major historians with material from other sources. The purpose, he maintains, in a claim which is meant to set him apart from writers of standard historiography, is not mere narration; gathering material for its own sake could so easily be 'useless' erudition. Rather, his focus will be the 'character and temperament' of his subjects, an analysis of which, he implies, might be useful for his readers.

Plutarch certainly drew on a vast range of sources, and names literally hundreds of writers whose work he used. As well as the large-scale narrative histories, he cites as sources of information comedies, speeches and letters, and where relevant the work of Latin historians, as well as collections of inscriptions, oral tradition, and occasionally his own knowledge of the terrain or its landmarks. In many cases, and especially in the Lives collected in this volume, these sources are now lost, and Plutarch's own citations have become important evidence for the content of these works. But where Plutarch's sources do survive, it is clear that he has exercised a considerable degree of flexibility in the use he made of them. While he occasionally sticks close to the wording of his source, he more often rewrites the material entirely, transforming its tone and the use to which it is put, either by combining it with material from other sources or simply by adapting it for his own purposes or to suit his own concerns.

In fact, Plutarch uses and cites earlier writers not simply as sources of information. His Lives are peppered with references to and quotations of the classics of Greek literature, especially Homer, the tragedians and Plato. Many of these allusions have no direct relevance to the subject or period about which Plutarch is writing. Sometimes they merely add literary colour to Plutarch's prose. But in many cases we can see that readers who knew the original passage and could call to mind its context would find additional meaning in such quotations or allusions. For example, when Plutarch discusses the Theban general Pelopidas' simplicity of life in *Pelopidas* 3, he quotes two lines of Euripides' *Suppliant Women*: 'Like Capaneus in Euripides' play, he possessed "*Abundant wealth, but in that wealth no pride*".' This quotation is no mere ornament. In Euripides' play, these lines were spoken in praise of Capaneus, after he had been killed in battle. To readers who know the original passage, Plutarch's quotation of it both reinforces the sense of Capaneus' noble character and provides a hint to think forward to Pelopidas' rash death in battle, which had itself just been discussed at length in the prologue (*Pelopidas* 1–2). Similarly, when Plutarch has Pyrrhus declare to his men, as they prepare to assault Argos (*Pyrrhus* 29), '*One omen is best, to fight for Pyrrhus!*', readers who recognize that this is an adaptation of Hector's words in the *Iliad*, and that Hector's death soon followed, will understand that Pyrrhus too will die in the forthcoming battle. In such cases we should not talk about Plutarch's use of 'sources' but about his use of intertextual allusion.

Chronology and Structure

Each Life has a broadly chronological structure, but Plutarch does not always follow chronological order; indeed, his interest in character almost guarantees that he will from time to time interrupt his narrative and gather into one place material which illustrates or reveals particular character-traits. Such sections usually include one or more self-contained stories, or anecdotes; these anecdotes may have no chronological relationship to each other or to the context into which they are inserted, but are selected because of the light they throw on the subject's character. In such cases it would be wrong to say that Plutarch is imprecise or unconcerned about chronology; he is in fact often in the Lives very precise about chronological matters, giving exact dates or making comments of the kind 'But this happened later'. But chronological considerations are not the only ones which guide Plutarch in his selection or deployment of material: at times thematic considerations may trump the chronological and the links between episodes may be logical rather than chronological. It is important to keep this in mind. Modern readers tend to expect narrative and to assume that the order in which events are mentioned must correspond with the order in which they happened or the order in which the author thought they happened. But Plutarch may follow a train of thought or argument and group together various incidents which have a bearing on a particular theme. As a result, unless he states it clearly, we should never assume that the order in which Plutarch introduces his material must necessarily correspond to the chronological order of events, or to what Plutarch believed to be the chronological order.

There is one part of the Life which is almost never chronological: the start. A very few Lives, notably *Timoleon* and *Pyrrhus*, begin with some general historical background before introducing the subject, possibly because in these cases Plutarch was dealing with geographical areas (Sicily, Epirus) whose history was less known to his readers. But the openings of most Lives include material on a fairly uniform set of themes, such as the subject's family, appearance and character. Stories from the subject's childhood may be included here, but, if they are, they are often placed alongside stories from later in life. Thus early sections of Lives do not necessarily or exclusively deal with the early part of a man's life. The truth is that Plutarch is not much interested in investigating the childhood of his subjects in its own right, and there is only rarely any *narrative* of childhood, or sense that the child is developing or changing. This is all very different from how a modern biographer might work. The latter will often look to childhood influences or experiences to explain the way a person developed as they did. Plutarch, on the other hand, usually includes stories from childhood merely to confirm or illustrate a point about adult character or to provide early indications of that adult character. Accordingly, he tends to begin the narrative proper with the subject's first actions as an adult on the public stage.

Plutarch's Lives do not, then, normally narrate the subject's life from birth. Nor do they tend to finish with his death. Many Lives continue the story to look briefly at the fate of the subject's body, and at his reputation after death: any posthumous honours, for example. Others look at the fate of his descendants or opponents, and many Lives give some sort of summing up of the man and his life. Thus Plutarch's literary Life tends not to be co-terminous with the life of the subject.

One feature of Plutarch's narrative technique which deserves special mention is his variation of narrative 'speed'. Plutarch will often pass quickly over long periods, perhaps several years or more, especially if the subject did not himself play a major role in the wider events of that time. On the other hand, Plutarch often slows the narrative down to create dramatic scenes, described at length and in great detail, in which the subject of the Life and his actions form the focal point. This variation in narrative speed gives Plutarch's Lives an 'episodic' or even 'cinematic' feel, as the narrative fragments into a series of self-contained vignettes or tableaux. This prevents the writing from becoming monotonous, and also serves to create meaning by throwing emphasis on these large scenes and on the characteristics of the subject which emerge from them, and away from other events which are brushed over quickly.

Plutarch and his Period

Plutarch's *Parallel Lives* were written at the height of the Roman Empire, some four to five centuries after the men whose Lives are included in this volume. They are dedicated to a powerful Roman, Sosius Senecio (see *Dion* 1 and *Demosthenes* 1 and 31), but several features make it likely that they were written with a mainly Greek audience in mind. First, and most obviously, the Lives were written in Greek. Secondly, Plutarch seems to assume that his readers have a much greater background knowledge of Greek history than of Roman, as he includes much more basic historical narrative in his Roman Lives than he does in his Greek ones. Finally, in his Lives of both Greek and Roman figures, Plutarch constantly quotes and alludes to the classics of Greek literature, both prose and verse, but rarely makes reference to Latin literature, except for the immediate sources which he is following.

It is important to keep in mind that Plutarch and his Greek readers lived in a world far removed from the one he was writing about. Peace and stability had been imposed on Greece, with some interruptions, two centuries before Plutarch's birth, and Roman power was now unchallenged across the Mediterranean world. For the Greeks of the mainland, the era of conquest and warfare was, for the moment, over. So was the era of competing kings, of shifting alliances, of mercenaries and the sacking of cities. Furthermore, even though in Plutarch's time many cities called their constitutions 'democracies', in reality power lay firmly in the hands of the landed elites, whose own power was underwritten by the might of Rome.

Thus Plutarch is in no sense a contemporary witness or source of the events or people he describes. Indeed, some features of the Lives, especially the ways in which the politics of the *polis* are portrayed, reflect Plutarch's own political and social context. For example, while Plutarch, like many writers of his day, idealizes Classical Athens in general, its democracy, like that of Syracuse, is not presented in a particularly positive light. The masses are consistently presented in the Lives as a dangerous force which must be carefully managed and controlled; popular leaders, in Plutarch's projection, can easily become demagogues, who stir up the masses. Similarly, while Plutarch and his wealthy contemporaries maintained a deep, personal attachment to their own *polis*, they were also used to a world in which the *polis* had long been subsumed within much wider political and geographic entities, and in which a broader, over-arching concept of Greekness had more traction than it had in the Classical period. It was thus much more natural for Plutarch to present the conquest of the states of mainland Greece by Macedonia as a natural, perhaps inevitable, development and to take seriously Alexander's pan-Hellenic propaganda, just as it was for him to accept the incorporation of the mainland Greek cities first into the Hellenistic kingdoms and then into the Roman Empire. Indeed, the decision to pair Greek subjects with Roman ones is itself, at the very least, a recognition of the importance of Roman culture, and perhaps suggests a bipartite vision of history, in which the Mediterranean world is made up of two dominant civilizations, comparable and yet separate: a Latin-speaking West and a Greek-speaking East.

But for all that we should not overstate Plutarch's distance from the periods about which he writes. Roman control did not mean the end of the Greek city-states, such as Plutarch's own city of Chaeronea. Governing councils still met, magistrates were still appointed, inscriptions put up and festivals with their athletic contests still held. Plutarch's own writing in the *Moralia*, especially his *Political advice*, gives a lively picture of political life within these cities, where the well-to-do competed among themselves for power and prestige. Thus, although Roman power meant that freedom of action in foreign policy was now more limited, the structures and rhythms of *polis* life were little changed. Furthermore, although the Greek language had evolved and changed, Plutarch still spoke essentially the same language as had been spoken in the Classical period, and worshipped the same gods at the same shrines. He also had the benefit of reading hundreds of ancient authors now lost. So although not a contemporary source, Plutarch's choices and the way he presents his material are always worth taking very seriously. This is the case not least in his ability to recreate for us the *atmosphere* of the ancient world, whether he is describing the palace of Dionysius II in Sicily, a meeting of the Athenian assembly, Alexander's banquets or the clash of two Hellenistic armies on the great plains of Asia.

Plutarch's Language

Plutarch's Greek is difficult. This is partly because the Greek language itself had changed since the Classical period, and Plutarch had open to him a much wider range of linguistic and stylistic choices than were available to Classical authors such as Thucydides or Demosthenes. His style is mildly 'Atticizing', that is, he utilizes the grammatical forms and syntactical structures of the Classical Athenian writers. But his sentences are more loosely constructed and his vocabulary, drawing on the new coinages of the Hellenistic period, wider and more abstract.

His Greek provides some particular problems for the translator. Some sentences are very long and cannot be reproduced in English without tiring the reader. Plutarch also has a tendency to put in subordinate clauses those important political or military events in which the subject of the Life was not involved, sometimes at length, reserving the main clause for the subject himself. This has the effect of presenting such events as background, against which to set the activity of the subject of the Life. The modern translator must in most cases break such sentences down into smaller units and use more main clauses, thereby losing the grammatical and thematic hierarchization of Plutarch's prose.

A particular characteristic of Plutarch's style is his use of 'doublets': that is, to express a single concept or action, Plutarch will often use pairs of almost, but not quite, synonymous nouns, adjectives or verbs. The translator may try to reproduce these doublets in English, where this can be done naturally. But often one must translate with just a single term and risk losing some of the richness of Plutarch's style.

Finally, a particular problem is caused to the translator by Plutarch's assumption that his readers will be well versed in the Classics of Greek literature. He frequently quotes and alludes to earlier Greek authors (especially Plato, Homer and the tragedians), often without making it explicit that he is doing so. In order to understand fully Plutarch's point, the reader must recognize and call to mind the passage to which he alludes. The modern reader, who is dependent on endnotes to explain such allusions, inevitably misses much of the allusive or 'literary' quality of Plutarch's prose.

List of Surviving Lives
by Plutarch

Lives included in this volume are marked with an asterisk.

PARALLEL LIVES

Theseus and Romulus
Lycurgus and Numa
Solon and Publicola
Themistocles and Camillus
Aristides and Cato Major
Cimon and Lucullus
Pericles and Fabius
Nicias and Crassus
Coriolanus and Alcibiades
Lysander and Sulla
Agesilaus and Pompey
Pelopidas* and Marcellus

Dion* and Brutus
Aemilius and Timoleon*
Demosthenes* and Cicero
Phocion* and Cato Minor
Alexander* and Caesar
Sertorius and Eumenes*
Demetrius* and Antony
Pyrrhus* and Marius
Agis & Cleomenes and Tiberius
& Caius Gracchus (a double
pair)
Philopoemen and Flamininus

STAND-ALONE LIVES

Artaxerxes*
Aratus

LIVES OF THE CAESARS

Galba
Otho

Further Reading

Recommended reading specific to each Life is given in the endnotes.

Plutarch

All the *Parallel Lives* are now available in English translation in this and the other volumes of Penguin Classics (see the list at the end of this volume). Oxford University Press has also published two volumes of selected Lives (*Greek Lives* and *Roman Lives*), translated by R. Waterfield and with introduction and notes by P. A. Stadter. Both the Penguin and the Oxford translations dispense with the paired structure and treat Greek and Roman Lives separately, arranging individual Lives by period. To read the Lives in their original pairs one must use either the rather old translation by John Dryden, revised in the nineteenth century by Arthur Clough and still in print in numerous editions, or B. Perrin's 11-volume edition for the Loeb Classical Library, which presents the Greek text with a facing English translation (*Plutarch's Lives*, Cambridge, Mass.: Harvard University Press, 1914–26).

The standard Greek text of the Lives is K. Ziegler's *Plutarchi Vitae Parallelae*, 4 vols. (Stuttgart and Leipzig: Teubner, 1st edn 1914–39, 2nd edn 1957–71, further editions of some volumes). A Greek text with facing French translation is provided in the Budé edition (R. Flacelière et al., *Plutarque Vies*, 16 vols. (Paris: Les Belles Lettres, 1957–83)). A Greek text with facing Italian translation, and very useful introduction and notes, is now available for most Lives, in a series published by the Biblioteca Universale Rizzoli (Milan, 1987–); some Lives have also been published, with longer Italian commentaries, by the Fondazione Lorenzo Valla (Milan, 1987–).

There are recent commentaries in English on *Alexander* (J. R. Hamilton, 1969; 2nd edn, 1999), *Antony* (C. B. R. Pelling, 1988), *Aristides and Cato Major* (D. Sansone, 1989), *Pelopidas* (A. Georgiadou, 1997), *Cicero* (J. M. Moles, 1988), *Pericles* (P. A. Stadter, 1989), *Sertorius* (C. F. Konrad, 1994) and *Themistocles* (J. L. Marr, 1998).

There are older commentaries by H. A. Holden on *Themistocles, Pericles, Nicias, Timoleon, Demosthenes, Gracchi* and *Sulla* (1885–94); these are out of date on historical matters but still useful on Plutarch's language and style.

Introductions to Plutarch's Lives

Duff, T. E., *Plutarch's Lives: Exploring Virtue and Vice* (Oxford: Oxford University Press, 1999).

Duff, T. E. (ed.), *Oxford Readings in Ancient Biography* (Oxford: Oxford University Press, forthcoming).

Humble, N. (ed.), *Parallelism in Plutarch's Lives: Parallelism and Purpose* (London: Duckworth, and Swansea: Classical Press of Wales, 2010).

Lamberton, R., *Plutarch* (New Haven and London: Yale University Press, 2001).

Mossman, J. M. (ed.), *Plutarch and his Intellectual World: Essays on Plutarch* (London: Duckworth, and Swansea: Classical Press of Wales, 1997).

Pelling, C. B. R., *Plutarch and History: Eighteen Studies* (London: Duckworth, and Swansea: Classical Press of Wales, 2002).

Russell, D. A., *Plutarch* (London: Duckworth, 1973; 2nd edn, London: Bristol Classical Press, 2001).

Scardigli, B. (ed.), *Essays on Plutarch's* Lives (Oxford: Oxford University Press, 1995).

Stadter, P. A. (ed.), *Plutarch and the Historical Tradition* (London and New York: Routledge, 1992).

Fourth- and Third-Century BC Greek History
Ancient Texts

Translations of most important ancient texts are available in the Loeb Classical Library series. Other useful translations are:

Xenophon, *Hellenica*: translated as *Xenophon: A History of my Times* (Penguin Classics, 1966).

Xenophon, *Anabasis*: translated as *Xenophon: The Persian Expedition* (Penguin Classics, 1972) and *Xenophon: The Expedition of Cyrus* (Oxford: Oxford University Press, 2009).

The speeches of Demosthenes and Aeschines: a selection (*On the crown* and *On the false embassy*) is translated as *Demosthenes and Aeschines* (Penguin Classics, 1975); all the speeches are translated in the University of Texas Press's Oratory of Classical Greece series (Austin, Tex., 1998).

Diodorus: Books 11–14.34 are translated as *Diodorus Siculus: The Persian Wars to the Fall of Athens* (Austin, Tex.: University of Texas Press, 2010). The Greek text and English translation of all surviving books are published in the Loeb Classical Library (Cambridge, Mass., and London: Harvard University Press, 1933–67).

Cornelius Nepos: Latin text and English translation published in the Loeb Classical Library (Cambridge, Mass., and London: Harvard University Press, 1984).

Arrian's *Anabasis*: translated as *The Campaign of Alexander* (Penguin Classics, 1971).

Curtius Rufus: translated as *Curtius Rufus: The History of Alexander* (Penguin Classics, 1984).

Justin: translated as *Justin: Epitome of the Philippic History of Pompeius Trogus* (Atlanta, Ga.: Scholars Press, 1994; Oxford: Oxford University Press, 2001).

Collections of Ancient Source-Material

Austin, M. M. (ed.), *The Hellenistic World from Alexander to the Roman Conquest: A Selection of Ancient Sources in Translation* (Cambridge: Cambridge University Press, 1981).

Crawford, M., and Whitehead, D. (eds.), *Archaic and Classical*

Greece: A Selection of Ancient Sources in Translation (Cambridge: Cambridge University Press, 1983).

Dillon, M., and Garland, L. (eds.), *Ancient Greece: social and historical documents from Archaic times to the death of Alexander the Great* (3rd edn, London: Routledge, 2010).

Harding, P. (ed.), *From the End of the Peloponnesian War to the Battle of Ipsus* (Cambridge: Cambridge University Press, 1985).

Rhodes, P. J., and Osborne, R. (eds.), *Greek Historical Inscriptions 404–323 BC* (Oxford: Oxford University Press, 2003).

Modern Introductions

Errington, R. M., *A History of the Hellenistic World, 323–30 BC* (Blackwell: Oxford, 2008).

Green, P., *Alexander to Actium: The Hellenistic Age* (Berkeley: University of California Press; corr. edn, 1993).

Habicht, C., *Athens from Alexander to Antony* (Cambridge, Mass.: Harvard University Press, 1997).

Hammond, N. G. L., Griffith, G. T., and Walbank, F. W. (eds.), *History of Macedonia* (Oxford: Oxford University Press, 3 vols., 1972–88).

Hansen, M. H., *The Athenian Democracy in the Age of Demosthenes: Structure, Principles and Ideology* (Oxford: Blackwell, 1991; rev. edn, London: Bristol Classical Press, and Norman, Okla.: University of Oklahoma Press, 1999).

Heckel, W., *The Marshals of Alexander's Empire* (London and New York: Routledge, 1992).

Heckel, W., *Who's Who in the Age of Alexander the Great: Prosopography of Alexander's Empire* (Oxford: Blackwell, 2006).

Hornblower, S., *The Greek World 479–323 BC* (3rd edn, London and New York: Routledge, 2002).

Lewis, D. M., Hornblower, S., and Ostwald, M. (eds.), *The Cambridge Ancient History*, vol. vi, *The Fourth Century BC* (2nd edn, Cambridge: Cambridge University Press, 1994).

Mossé, C., *Athens in Decline 404–86 BC* (London: Routledge, 1973).

Osborne, R. (ed.), *Classical Greece 500–323 BC* (Oxford: Oxford University Press, 2000).

Pritchett, W. K., *The Greek State at War*, 5 vols. (Berkeley: University of California Press, 1974–91).

Rhodes, P. J., *A History of the Classical Greek World 478–323 BC* (Oxford: Blackwell, 2006).

Roisman, J., and Worthington, I. (eds.), *A Companion to Ancient Macedonia* (Oxford: Wiley-Blackwell, 2010).

Shipley, G., *The Greek World After Alexander, 323–30 BC* (London: Routledge, 2000).

Tritle, L. A. (ed.), *The Greek World in the Fourth Century: From the Fall of the Athenian Empire to the Successors of Alexander* (London: Routledge, 1997).

Walbank, F. W., *The Hellenistic World* (London: Fontana Press, 1980; corr. edn 1986).

Walbank, F. W., Astin, A. E., Frederiksen, M. W., and Ogilvie, R. M. (eds.), *The Cambridge Ancient History*, vol. vii, *The Hellenistic World* (2nd edn, Cambridge: Cambridge University Press, 2 vols., 1984–9).

The Age of Alexander

ARTAXERXES

INTRODUCTION TO ARTAXERXES

[died 359/8 BC]

Artaxerxes II was Achaemenid Great King of Persia from 405 BC to his death in 359. Soon after ascending to the throne he was confronted with a revolt fomented by his younger brother Cyrus, who in 401 led an army, which included a large force of Greek mercenaries, to overthrow him. The two men met in battle at Cunaxa, some 45 miles north of Babylon, and Cyrus was defeated and killed. Sparta, which had lent tacit support to Cyrus, continued to oppose Persian influence in Asia Minor, and it was not until 394 that Artaxerxes was able to drive Spartan troops out of Asia and reassert Persian control of Asia Minor. That control was confirmed in 386 by a treaty negotiated at Susa between the king and the Spartan commander Antalcidas and known to the Greeks as the King's Peace or Peace of Antalcidas. This treaty, to which the other Greek states then at war with Sparta reluctantly agreed, gave Artaxerxes undisputed overlordship of Asia Minor and Cyprus, and at the same time underwrote Spartan dominance in Greece.

In addition to the Greeks, Artaxerxes had to face various other threats to his empire. Throughout the 380s and 370s he attempted, unsuccessfully, to regain control of Egypt, which had revolted when he came to the throne. There were almost certainly other wars in this period; we know, for example, of several campaigns against the Cadusii in the north. But the Greek sources, on whom we are almost entirely dependent, have little to say on events away from the western fringes of the Empire. The final years of Artaxerxes' reign saw the so-called 'Satraps' Revolt' in Asia Minor (c. 366–360); it is not clear whether this was merely a set of purely local squabbles among

the dynasties of western Asia Minor, in which some Greek cities
involved themselves, or whether it was a more widespread and
organized rebellion. At any rate, Artaxerxes weathered that
storm and died in 359.

Plutarch's *Life of Artaxerxes* is remarkable on various levels.
Unlike the other Lives in this volume, it did not form part of
the collection of *Parallel Lives*, but is rather a stand-alone Life.
Secondly, its subject is neither Greek nor Roman but a Persian.
Plutarch thus allows his readers to delve into what he presents
as a foreign, exotic world of palace intrigues, concubines, hor-
rific tortures and strange customs. There was a long tradition
in Greek literature of interest in the East, going back to Herodotus in the late fifth century, who began his account of the
Persian invasions of Greece by tracing the history of Persia and
describing its customs. Similarly, Xenophon's fourth-century
Education of Cyrus gave a fictionalized account of the upbringing and training of Cyrus the Great, the founder of the Persian
Empire and ancestor of Artaxerxes. Both Herodotus and Xenophon, in different ways, used Persia as a means of reflecting on
Greek society: what had led to the Persians' initial success in
making themselves masters of such a huge empire? Were Persian
virtues like those of the Greeks? Why was it that the Greeks had
been able to beat the Persians in the Persian Wars of the early
fifth century? In the same way, Plutarch in this Life performs
two related tasks: he gives his readers an exciting and exotic tale
of Eastern despotism; and at the same time, by analysing the
Persian court and the characteristics of its ruler, with the same
conceptual tools that he applies to his Greek and Roman figures, he invites his readers to compare and contrast.

Artaxerxes' power-struggle with his brother Cyrus domi-
nates the first half of the Life. By comparison with the rash and
impetuous Cyrus, Artaxerxes is presented as calm and mild; a
series of anecdotes illustrates this mildness (chs. 2–5). He is
also brave: after some initial wavering, he acquits himself courageously in the battle of Cunaxa and meets Cyrus face to face
in combat (chs. 7–10). But once Cyrus is defeated, Artaxerxes
becomes vainglorious and vindictive, punishing horribly any
who threaten to diminish his own glory by claiming to have

had a hand in Cyrus' death. The middle part of the Life is a catalogue of the methods of execution and torture used against Artaxerxes' victims. The focus here is on the king's household and its intrigues, and Plutarch demonstrates how Artaxerxes is manipulated by members of this household, especially his mother, who is even more bloodthirsty than him. The Life ends with strife among Artaxerxes' sons over who would succeed him. For Plutarch's readers the inner world of the court will have stood in stark contrast to the public nature of Greek politics, centred on the assembly and agora. The difference in setting and the murderous intrigues which abound in this Life might have suggested to them an important truth (as they would have seen it) about the way monarchies, especially the Persian one, worked.

As often in the Lives, Plutarch's narrative in *Artaxerxes*, though broadly chronological, does not always stick to chronological order, especially in the later part of the Life. For example, the execution of Tissaphernes, satrap of Lydia and Caria, which took place in 395, is placed immediately after the peace conference in Susa of 367 (chs. 22–3). This is followed by the failed attempt of Pharnabazus and Iphicrates to reconquer Egypt for Persia in 374/3, and by Artaxerxes' own campaign against the Cadusii, which may have happened in the 380s (chs. 24–5). Plutarch is arranging his material here thematically, dealing first with Artaxerxes' relationship with the Greeks, then with his campaigns elsewhere, before turning to the troubles within his own house (ch. 26 onwards).

Plutarch refers by name to his three most important sources, Xenophon, Ctesias and Deinon. For the sections on Cyrus, he used Xenophon's work, *Anabasis* or *March inland*. Xenophon was himself one of the Greek mercenary commanders who fought with Cyrus. The early part of the *Anabasis* describes Cyrus' preparations, the march inland, the battle of Cunaxa, and its aftermath, all from the point of view of the Greek participants on Cyrus' side; the bulk of the *Anabasis* then describes the tribulations of these Greeks as they fought their way north to the coast. Plutarch mentions Xenophon several times in *Artaxerxes*, and in chapter 8 speaks admiringly of his skills as a vivid narrator and disavows any attempt to go over the same ground. Plutarch avoids mere repetition of Xenophon's material in two ways. First, he shifts perspective and tells the story of the conflict between Cyrus and Artaxerxes from the Persian point of view. Second, he supplements Xenophon with additional material. A good example of this supplementing can be seen in the opening chapter, where Plutarch echoes the opening words of the *Anabasis* ('Darius and Parysatis had two sons, of whom Artaxerxes was the elder, and Cyrus the younger'). But Plutarch, though sticking almost word for word to the Xenophontic original, speaks not of two but of four children, and provides the missing names.

Here and elsewhere Plutarch must be dependent on other sources, now lost to us. One of these was the *Persica* or *Persian affairs* of Ctesias. Ctesias claimed to have been a Greek doctor present at the Persian court in the early part of Artaxerxes' reign; his work covered Persian history from early times to part way through the reign of Artaxerxes. He seems to have focused particularly on the scandals of court life and to have had a tendency to the sensational. His work had a reputation in antiquity as unreliable and exaggerated, and this impression is not dispelled by examination of the quotations or summaries of his work which survive in Plutarch and in other authors such as Diodorus, Nicolaus of Damascus and the Byzantine writer Photius. Plutarch refers to Ctesias frequently in *Artaxerxes*, though he often expresses caution about his reliability or even downright rejects his claims (e.g., chs. 1, 6, 11, 13, 18). Plutarch also drew on the *Persica* of another Greek historian, Deinon, whom he cites frequently. We know less about Deinon than about Ctesias, but he also seems to have had a tendency to the sensational; he wrote some time in the fourth century BC and was father of Cleitarchus, one of the historians of Alexander the Great.

As *Artaxerxes* is not part of the *Parallel Lives*, it is not paired with any other Life, nor is there any prologue or concluding comparison. The Life ends with a reference to Artaxerxes' age and a statement that he 'had the reputation of being a mild and benevolent ruler not least because of his son Ochus, who surpassed all in savagery and bloodthirstiness' (ch. 30). This neatly recalls the opening words of the Life which refer to Artaxerxes I, the subject's grandfather, 'who surpassed all other Persian kings in mildness and magnanimity'. Similarly, the power-struggles which plague the court of Artaxerxes in his old age, and lead to the deaths of all but the most wicked and ruthless of his sons (chs. 26–30), recall the power-struggle between Artaxerxes and his brother with which the Life began. Thus Artaxerxes is sited within a series of other kings, with a suggestion that violent palace intrigue was endemic, and that the worst was yet to come. For Plutarch's Greek readers, who knew that within thirty years of Artaxerxes' death Alexander would have swept away the Persian royal family and its palace politics, this would all have been very suggestive.

LIFE OF ARTAXERXES

1. The first Artaxerxes,[1] who surpassed all other Persian kings in mildness and magnanimity, was nicknamed Macrochir ('long-hand'), because his right hand was longer than his left. He was the son of Xerxes.[2] The second Artaxerxes, the subject of this work, was nicknamed Mnemon ('mindful'), and was the son of the first Artaxerxes' daughter, Parysatis. For Darius[3] and Parysatis had four sons, of whom Artaxerxes was the eldest, then Cyrus, and then the youngest Ostanes and Oxathres.[4] Cyrus was named after the earlier Cyrus, and it is reported that the latter took his name from the sun, since *cyrus* is said to be the Persian word for sun.[5] Artaxerxes was at first called Arsicas. Deinon[6] gives the name as Oarses, but Ctesias[7] is more trustworthy here, since, even though in general he fills his books with a miscellaneous jumble of wild and incredible tales, it is unlikely that he did not know the name of the king at whose court he spent his time, acting as doctor to him, his wife, mother and children.

2. Now Cyrus was intense and impetuous from his youth, while Artaxerxes seemed milder in all things and was by nature gentler in his impulses. Artaxerxes married a beautiful and noble wife in accordance with his parents' bidding, and kept her against their wishes. For his father, the king, had her brother killed and wanted to do away with her too. But throwing himself on his mother's mercy and supplicating her with many tears, Arsicas (as he was then called) in the end succeeded in persuading them not to kill his wife nor to insist on a separation.

But their mother loved Cyrus more than his brother and

wanted him to be king. So when their father was ill Cyrus was immediately summoned from the coast and began journeying inland, in full expectation that his mother had arranged for him to be declared successor to the throne.[8] Indeed his mother did have a plausible argument, the same one that the elder Xerxes had used on the advice of Demaratus: that she had given birth to Arsicas when her husband was a private individual, but to Cyrus when he was a king.[9] However, she could not persuade Darius, and the elder of the two was proclaimed king under the new name Artaxerxes,[10] while Cyrus was proclaimed satrap of Lydia and commander of the coastal provinces.[11]

3. Shortly after Darius' death, the new king rode to Pasargadae in order that the initiation ceremony marking his accession to the throne might be carried out by the Persian priests. There is a shrine there to a warrior goddess, whom one might liken to Athena.[12] The candidate for the royal initiation has to enter this shrine and lay aside his own robes and put on those worn by the elder Cyrus before he became king. Then he should eat a cake of figs, chew some terebinth and drink a cup of sour milk.[13] Whether they do anything else in addition is unclear to outsiders. Artaxerxes was on the point of doing these things when Tissaphernes arrived with one of the priests. This priest had supervised Cyrus' boyhood studies when he was undergoing the traditional Persian education[14] and had taught him the wisdom of the Magi,[15] and had seemed more distressed than any other Persian when Cyrus was not declared king. As a result he was given considerable credence when he made an accusation against Cyrus. He claimed that Cyrus was intending to lie in wait in the shrine; as soon as the king started taking off his clothes, he would attack and kill him. Some people say that Cyrus' arrest followed this denunciation; others, however, maintain that Cyrus had actually entered the shrine and his hiding place was betrayed by the priest. He was almost put to death, but his mother threw her arms round him, entwined him with her hair and held him close, and with loud laments and entreaties succeeded in averting his death and had him conveyed down to the coast again. But Cyrus was not content with

his command there and kept in mind not his release but his arrest; he seethed with rage and his determination to obtain the throne grew all the greater.

4. Some people say that Cyrus revolted against the king because he was not satisfied with the revenue he received for his daily meals.[16] But that is ridiculous. For whatever else he might have lacked, he had his mother, and she could supply freely from her own wealth whatever he wanted. Evidence of his wealth is also provided by the mercenary troops that were maintained for him by his friends and allies, as Xenophon has reported.[17] He did not bring these together into one body, as he was still trying to conceal his preparations, but he had agents scattered in different places recruiting troops for him on a variety of pretexts. Meanwhile at court his mother worked to allay the king's suspicions, and Cyrus himself always wrote to Artaxerxes in an obsequious manner, sometimes requesting favours, sometimes making counter-accusations against Tissaphernes, as though his jealous rivalry were directed wholly against the latter.

Artaxerxes was by nature rather indecisive, though most people took this as clemency. At the beginning he seemed eager to emulate the mildness of his namesake, the first Artaxerxes. He was pleasant to deal with and gave greater honours and favours than their recipients really deserved,[18] while from all punishment he took away the element of humiliation or sadistic pleasure. And whether he received favours or gave them, he appeared equally gracious and kind both to givers and recipients. No gift was too small for him to accept eagerly. Indeed, when a certain Omises presented him with a single pomegranate of surpassing size, he said, 'By Mithras, this man could even transform a city from small to great, if it were entrusted to his care.'

5. Once, when Artaxerxes was on a journey and was being presented with a variety of gifts, a peasant who had not had time to find any suitable gift ran down to the river, scooped up some water in his hands and offered it to him.[19] Artaxerxes was so delighted that he sent him a gold cup and 1,000 darics.[20] On

another occasion when Eucleidas of Sparta was haranguing him at length in an arrogant manner, Artaxerxes told his vizier to say to him, 'You may have the power to say what you like, but I have the power to back up my words with action.' Once on a hunt, Tiribazus pointed out that Artaxerxes' robe was torn, and Artaxerxes asked what should be done. Tiribazus replied, 'Put another one on and give that one to me.' So the king did so, saying, 'I am giving this one to you, Tiribazus, but I forbid you to wear it.' But Tiribazus took no notice – not because he was wicked, but because he lacked judgement and was prone to act without thinking. He at once put on the king's robe and decked himself out with golden necklaces of royal splendour. At this, all the others began to grow angry as this was not permitted.[21] But the king simply laughed and said, 'I grant you the right to wear the gold trinkets like a woman and the royal robe like a madman!' And whereas traditionally none shared the king's table except his mother and his wedded wife, the former sitting higher up than him, the latter lower down, Artaxerxes used to invite his younger brothers Ostanes and Oxathres to the same table as him. But what most pleased the Persians was the sight of his wife Stateira's carriage, since she always travelled with the curtains open, thus allowing the common women to approach and greet her. For this reason the queen was held in great affection by the masses.[22]

6. However, those who were inclined towards revolution and intrigue thought that affairs were crying out for Cyrus, whom they credited with a dazzling character, exceptional skill in war and loyalty to his friends. The magnitude of the empire, they claimed, required a bold and ambitious king. So with no less confidence in his friends at court than in those around him, Cyrus began to prosecute the war. He even corresponded with the Spartans, requesting them to help him by sending out men to join his expedition, promising that he would give horses to any infantrymen who came along and chariots to any horsemen; if they had farms, he would give them villages, if villages, cities. Those who marched with him, he claimed, would have their pay weighed out to them rather than counted! He made

many extravagant claims about himself, including that he had a sturdier heart than his brother, was more of a philosopher, was better versed in the wisdom of the Magi and could drink more and hold his wine better. His brother, he declared, was such a coward and a weakling that he could not keep his seat on a horse in a hunt or on the throne in times of danger. Accordingly, the Spartans sent out a dispatch-roll[23] to Clearchus[24] ordering him to assist Cyrus in every way possible.

Cyrus began making his way inland against the king with a huge force of barbarians and nearly 13,000 Greek mercenaries. Meanwhile, he kept up a continual barrage of excuses to explain his expedition.[25] But he did not manage to keep secret the real purpose of his mission for long, since Tissaphernes went to the king in person and reported it. The palace was filled with uproar; Parysatis was held most to blame for the war and her friends were regarded with suspicion and discredited. What mortified Parysatis most of all was Stateira, the king's wife, who was outraged at the war and kept crying out, 'Where are those pledges of yours now? Where are your pleas for mercy? You saved him when he was plotting against his brother and now have embroiled us in war and suffering!' As a result Parysatis began to hate Stateira. Parysatis was by nature sullen and barbarous in her anger and resentment and so she now began plotting to kill Stateira. Deinon says that her plot was carried out during the course of the war, but Ctesias says that it was later; and it is scarcely likely that the latter was unaware of the chronology since he was actually present at the events and had no reason to want to shift the execution of the deed out of its proper time in his narration. (That is a common failing of his work, which is often diverted from the truth into the fantastic and dramatic.) Accordingly this event at least will keep the place assigned to it by Ctesias.[26]

7. As Cyrus advanced, rumours and reports kept on reaching him that Artaxerxes had decided not to fight at once and was in no hurry to rush into combat with him; rather, he had decided to wait in Persia until forces could be gathered there from all parts. And in fact there was some truth in this. For

Artaxerxes had dug a ditch 60 feet wide and 60 feet deep for 45 miles across the length of the plain, and yet he let Cyrus penetrate this and get within a short distance of Babylon itself.[27] According to tradition it was Tiribazus who first dared to suggest that Artaxerxes should not avoid battle nor abandon Media and Babylon and Susa and take refuge in Persia;[28] he had a force many times bigger than Cyrus' and innumerable satraps and generals, all better able to think and fight than Cyrus. At these words, Artaxerxes resolved to fight it out with Cyrus as quickly as possible. First he made a sudden appearance at the head of an army of 900,000 men, all brilliantly arrayed. The enemy, who in their confidence and disdain of their opponents were marching along in disorder and without their weapons at hand, were thrown into such confusion and consternation that, what with the deafening noise and the shouting, Cyrus was scarcely able to form them up for battle. Then Artaxerxes led his troops forward slowly in silence, causing great surprise among the Greeks at their discipline; for, given the enemy's huge numbers, they were expecting his ranks to be confused and lacking in cohesion, with much raucous shouting and prancing. In addition, Artaxerxes cleverly drew up the sturdiest of his scythed chariots[29] opposite the Greeks and in front of his own phalanx, with the aim that by the shock of their charge they would cut open the ranks of the Greeks before hand-to-hand combat actually began.

8. This battle has been reported by many writers, but Xenophon's account[30] is so vivid that he all but makes his audience share the passion and danger of those present, and feel not that the events had taken place in the past but that they are actually happening before their eyes.[31] In view of this there is no sense in going through it all again, except for any points of interest which may have escaped Xenophon's mention.

The place where the two armies deployed is called Cunaxa and is 55 miles from Babylon. It is reported that Clearchus begged Cyrus to stay behind the lines and not expose himself to danger, but he replied, 'What are you talking about, Clearchus? Are you telling me that though I aspire to kingship I am unworthy of it?' It is true that Cyrus made a grave mistake in plunging headlong into the midst of the fray and not taking account of the danger; but Clearchus made no less a mistake, and perhaps a greater one, in refusing to draw up the Greeks opposite the king and insisting on keeping his right flank in contact with the river to prevent an encirclement. For if safety and the avoidance of harm was his main object, then he should have stayed at home. He had marched under arms 1,100 miles inland under no compulsion but with the purpose of setting Cyrus on the royal throne, and he now started looking about for the location in which to draw up his troops which would enable him not to ensure the salvation of his leader and employer, but to fight safely and at his ease. Thus, through fear of present danger, he cast off all rational considerations for overall success and abandoned the purpose of the expedition. Events themselves proved that none of those drawn up around Artaxerxes could have withstood an assault by the Greeks. They would have been driven back and the king would either have fled or fallen on the field; and Cyrus would thus have triumphed and won not only his life but the throne as well. For this reason, Clearchus' caution is more to blame than Cyrus' rashness for the destruction of both Cyrus and his cause. For if Artaxerxes himself were looking out for a place where he might deploy the Greeks so that they would pose the least threat to him, he could have found no better position than that which was furthest away from him and his own troops. Indeed, Artaxerxes had no inkling that he had been defeated on that part of the field, and Cyrus was cut down before he could make any use of Clearchus' victory. Yet Cyrus was not ignorant of what ought to be done and ordered Clearchus to take up his position in the centre. The latter replied that he was taking care that all would turn out for the best, but then went and ruined everything.

9. For the Greeks had no difficulty in beating the barbarians, and advanced a long way in their pursuit. But Cyrus, mounted on a high-bred but unruly and high-spirited horse called (according to Ctesias) Pasacas, was confronted by Artagerses, the ruler of the Cadusii, who rode up to him and cried out, 'You disgrace

the name of Cyrus, that most noble of names among the Persians. You are the most wicked of men and the stupidest, coming here with damnable Greeks on a damnable journey to seize the good things of Persia. You hope to kill your own brother and master, who has countless thousands of slaves who are better men than you – as you will experience this instant, for you will lose your own head here before you see the king's face.' With these words Artagerses hurled a javelin at him. Cyrus' breastplate resisted the blow firmly and Cyrus himself was not wounded, but he reeled under the heavy blow. Artagerses turned his horse aside and Cyrus threw his javelin and hit him, and drove the point through his neck near the collar-bone.

Almost everyone agrees that Artagerses was killed by Cyrus. But the death of Cyrus himself gets only a simple and brief mention by Xenophon, since he was not actually present. Perhaps, then, there is nothing to stop me recounting Deinon's version of it, followed by that of Ctesias.

10. Deinon says that, when Artagerses had fallen, Cyrus charged furiously into the troops stationed in front of the king, wounded his horse and knocked Artaxerxes to the ground. Tiribazus quickly helped Artaxerxes onto another horse and said, 'My king, remember this day; it should not be forgotten.' Again Cyrus spurred his horse forward and hurled the king to the ground. But on the third assault the king could bear it no longer and, saying to those around him that he would rather die than sit and wait, galloped forward to meet Cyrus, who was charging rashly and without caution into a hail of missiles. The king himself took aim at Cyrus with a javelin, as did those around him, and Cyrus fell, according to some hit by the king, but according to others, struck down by a Carian. As a prize for this exploit the king gave the latter the privilege of henceforth carrying on campaign a golden cock on his spear in front of the line. For the Persians call the Carians themselves cocks on account of the crests with which they adorn their helmets.

11. Ctesias' narrative, on the other hand, to give it in a much abbreviated form, goes something like this. When Cyrus had

killed Artagerses he began riding towards Artaxerxes himself
and Artaxerxes towards him, both men in silence. Cyrus' friend
Ariaeus managed to throw his javelin first but did not wound the
king. Artaxerxes launched his spear and missed Cyrus but hit
and killed Satiphernes, a trusted and noble follower of Cyrus.
Cyrus threw his javelin and pierced the king's breastplate and
wounded him in the chest, the javelin penetrating to a depth of
two fingers, and the king fell off his horse with the blow. The
king's guard were thrown into confusion and fled; but Artaxerxes got to his feet and with a small party, Ctesias included,
made it to a hill nearby and lay low there.

Meanwhile, Cyrus was in the thick of the enemy and was
carried forward a long way by his horse, whose blood was up.
As it was now dark, the enemy did not recognize him and his
own men were unable to find him. But elated at his victory and
full of rage and daring, he rode on through the enemy shouting,
'Out of the way, you scum.' He shouted this many times in Persian and some did get out of the way, prostrating themselves
before him. But his tiara fell from his head and a young Persian
called Mithridates, ignorant of who he was, hit him with a javelin in the forehead, near the eye. Dizzy and bleeding copiously
from the wound, Cyrus fainted and fell to the ground. His
horse escaped and wandered about, and his saddle-blanket,
which had slipped off, was captured by the attendant of the
man who had hit him, covered in blood as it was. As Cyrus
began with great difficulty to come round from the blow, a few
of his eunuchs[32] who happened to be present tried to put him
on another horse and convey him to safety. But he wanted to
walk on his own feet, weak as he was, and so they supported
him and helped him along, his head spinning and his feet stum-
bling as he went. He was under the impression that victory was
his, since he heard the enemy fugitives addressing him as king
and begging to be spared. Meanwhile, some Caunians, poor
and destitute men, who were accompanying the king's army as
camp-followers to do menial tasks, by chance joined Cyrus'
company thinking they were on the same side. But when finally
they made out that the tunics over their breastplates were
crimson – whereas all the king's soldiers wore white – they real-

ized that they had fallen in with the enemy. So one of them, unaware at whom he was aiming, ventured to throw a javelin at Cyrus from behind. The blow pierced an artery behind his knee and he fell over, hitting his already wounded temple against a rock, and died. That is Ctesias' account, in which he kills Cyrus off slowly, as though with a blunt dagger.

12. After Cyrus had died, Artasyras, the King's Eye,[33] happened to pass by on horseback. Recognizing the eunuchs who were lamenting, he asked the most trusted of their number, 'Who is this, Parisca, over whom you sit mourning?' He replied, 'Don't you see, Artasyras? It is Cyrus, dead.' In amazement, Artasyras encouraged the eunuch to have no fear and guard the body, while he himself rode off at a gallop to Artaxerxes, who had by now given up his cause as lost and was in a bad way physically, on account both of thirst and of his wound, and told him with great joy that he had seen Cyrus' body. Artaxerxes' first impulse was to set out at once to see for himself and he told Artasyras to lead him to the place. But since there was a good deal of fearful talk about the Greeks, who were said to be carrying all before them in their victorious pursuit, he decided to send a larger party to see the body. So a group of thirty men with torches was dispatched. Artaxerxes himself was almost dead with thirst and Satibarzanes the eunuch began running about looking for something for him to drink, since the place had no water and was far from the camp. Finally, he came across one of the destitute Caunians who happened to have in a miserable skin some foul, dirty water amounting to about four pints, which he took and brought to the king and gave to him. When Artaxerxes had drunk it all, Satibarzanes asked him if the water did not utterly turn his stomach. But Artaxerxes swore by the gods that neither wine nor the freshest and cleanest water had ever tasted so pleasant.[34] 'So', he declared, 'if I cannot find and repay the man who gave you this, I pray that the gods will bless him and make him rich.'

13. Meanwhile, the party of thirty came riding up beaming with joy and reported to Artaxerxes the unexpected good fortune.

He was already beginning to take heart from the number of men who were flocking to him and forming up, and he began to descend from the hill amid a blaze of torches. When he reached the corpse, and its head and right hand had been cut off in accordance with Persian law,[35] he ordered the head to be brought to him and, grasping it by its thick and luxuriant hair, he began to display it to those who were still doubtful and in flight. They were amazed and started prostrating themselves before him, and soon 70,000 soldiers had rallied to him and marched back with him to the camp.

According to Ctesias, Artaxerxes had led 400,000 men out to battle, but Deinon and Xenophon put the number of combatants much higher.[36] Ctesias says that the number of dead reported to Artaxerxes was 9,000, but that in his estimation they numbered not less than 20,000. That matter, then, is open to dispute. But it is certainly a flagrant lie on Ctesias' part when he says that he himself was sent to negotiate with the Greeks, along with Phalinus of Zacynthus and some others. For Xenophon was well aware that Ctesias was in attendance upon the king; after all, he mentions him and has clearly read this part of his work. So if Ctesias had really come and acted as interpreter in such momentous events, Xenophon would hardly have left him nameless and specified only Phalinus of Zacynthus. But Ctesias, as it seems, is incredibly vain of his own honour, and no less biased towards Sparta and Clearchus, and always finds space for himself in his narratives, and there takes the opportunity to talk of Clearchus and the Spartans at length and in the highest terms.

14. After the battle Artaxerxes distributed gifts. The largest and finest were sent to the son of Artagerses, who had fallen at Cyrus' hand, but he also honoured Ctesias and the others generously. He searched out the Caunian who had given him the water-skin and raised him from obscurity and poverty to honour and wealth. He also took great care over the punishment of those who had done wrong. For example, a certain Arbaces, a Mede who had deserted to Cyrus during the battle and then, after Cyrus' death, had changed back, was charged with cowardice

and weakness rather than with treachery or even ill-intent; his punishment was to carry a naked prostitute around the market-place on his shoulders for a whole day. Another man who, besides deserting, had also declared falsely that he had felled two of the enemy, was ordered to have his tongue pierced with three needles.

Artaxerxes thought – and wished everyone else to think and say – that he himself had killed Cyrus. So he sent gifts to Mith-ridates, who had been the first to hit Cyrus, and told the bearers to say 'The king honours you with these gifts because you found Cyrus' saddle-blanket and brought it to him.' Further-more, when the Carian who had struck Cyrus the fatal blow behind the knee also started asking for a gift, Artaxerxes told those who gave it to him to say 'The king gives these things to you as a second prize for bringing good news. For Artasyras was the first and you the second to report the death of Cyrus.' Now Mithridates, despite his disappointment, withdrew in silence. But the wretched Carian in his folly was overcome by a passion that is all too common. For he was corrupted, so it seems, by the good things that lay before him and convinced that he should claim what lay beyond him, and refused to accept the gifts as rewards for bringing good news. Instead, he began crying out angrily and protesting that he and no other had killed Cyrus and that he was being unjustly stripped of his glory. When the king heard this he was incensed and gave orders that the man should be beheaded. But the king's mother, who was present, said, 'Do not rid yourself of this wretched Carian like that, but let him receive from me the fitting reward for his outrageous words.' The king handed him over and Parysatis ordered the executioners to stretch the man on the rack for ten days and then gouge his eyes out and pour molten bronze into his ears until he died.

15. A short while later Mithridates too met a bad end as a result of the same folly. He was invited to a dinner at which some eunuchs belonging to the king and his mother were pres-ent, and came decked out in the clothing and gold jewellery which he had received from the king. When it came to the time

for drinking, the most powerful of Parysatis' eunuchs said to him, 'What fine attire is this that the king has given you, Mithridates, what fine necklaces and bracelets, and what a valuable dagger![37] Without a doubt, the king has made you happy, the object of all men's admiration!' Mithridates, who was already drunk, said, 'Sparamizes, what does all this add up to? My services to the king on that day deserved greater and finer gifts than these!' With a smile Sparamizes said, 'No one would begrudge you them, Mithridates. But since the Greeks say that there is truth in wine,[38] tell me, my dear fellow, what is so great or glorious in finding a saddle-blanket which has slipped off and bringing it to the king?' Sparamizes opened this line of conversation not because he was ignorant of what had happened, but because he wanted to expose Mithridates to all those present. So he slyly played upon the vanity of the man, seeing that on account of the wine he had become talkative and was not in control of himself. Accordingly, Mithridates spoke out without restraint: 'You can talk as much as you like about saddle-blankets and other such rubbish. But I tell you plainly that it was by this hand here that Cyrus was slain. I did not, like Artagerses, waste my throw, but I hit him in the temple, just missing the eye, and pierced it, and brought the man down. He died as a result of that wound.' The guests could already see the end of Mithridates and his unhappy fate, and bowed their faces to the ground. But their host said, 'Mithridates, my friend, for the present time let us drink and feast, and do obeisance before the king's guardian spirit,[39] and let us not concern ourselves with talk that is too weighty for us.'

16. Afterwards the eunuch reported to Parysatis what Mithridates had said, and she reported it to the king. The king was enraged, thinking that he was being exposed as a liar and was losing the finest and sweetest part of his victory. For he wanted everyone, barbarian and Greek alike, to believe that, when he had charged at Cyrus and engaged him in hand-to-hand combat, he had both given and received a blow, and, while he himself had been wounded, he had actually killed Cyrus. So he ordered Mithridates to die the death of the troughs. The death

of the troughs is as follows. Two troughs are taken, designed to fit over one another exactly, and in one of them the man to be tortured is made to lie on his back. Then the other trough is fitted over the first and adjusted, so that the man's head, hands and feet are left outside and the rest of his body is covered. They then give the man food to eat and if he refuses they force him by pricking his eyes. When he has eaten they pour a mixture of milk and honey into his mouth for him to drink and they slop it over his face. Then they keep his eyes constantly turned towards the sun, so that swarms of flies settle on his face and hide it completely. Since inside the trough he does what men must do when they have eaten and drunk, worms and maggots swarm up from the foul mess of excrement, consuming his body and burrowing their way inside. When at last the man is obviously dead, the upper trough is removed and the man's flesh can be seen to have been eaten away and at his entrails are swarms of the animals I have mentioned, clinging and devouring his flesh. This was the manner in which Mithridates finally died, after wasting away for seventeen days.

17. Parysatis had one target remaining: the man who had cut off the head and hand of Cyrus, Masabates, one of the king's eunuchs. So, as the latter did not himself provide any stranglehold for her to use against him, Parysatis contrived a plot against him along the following lines. She was a gifted woman and particularly good at dice. Accordingly, before the war she often used to play dice even with the king. After the war, when she had been reconciled with him, she did not try to avoid demonstrations of affection, but actually joined in his amusements and shared in his love-affairs, often being present and lending her assistance. In short, she left his wife Stateira only the smallest of opportunities to see him or spend time with him, since she hated Stateira more than anyone and wanted to wield the most influence herself. So one day, when Parysatis found Artaxerxes with nothing to do and in a state of agitation, she challenged him to a game of dice for 1,000 darics. First, she allowed him to win and paid over the gold. Then, pretending to be upset at the loss and eager to win herself, she challenged him to another

game, this time for a eunuch, and he consented. They agreed on the following rules: that each should put out of the reckoning their five most trusted eunuchs, but that from the rest the loser had to give whichever the winner might choose. So they began dicing on these terms. Parysatis took the matter very seriously and threw herself in earnest into the game, and since the dice this time seemed to favour her, won the game and took possession of Masabates, for he was not on the list of those set aside. Before the king's suspicion was roused, she delivered him into the hands of the executioners and ordered them to flay him alive, impale his body sideways on three stakes and nail out his skin separately. When this was carried out, the king was filled with resentment and anger against her. But she said with an innocent laugh, 'My dear, you are so silly to get upset at one wicked old eunuch, when I happily accept the loss of 1,000 darics without complaining.' So the king, although he regretted the way he had been deceived, did not make a fuss. But Stateira, who was clearly opposed to Parysatis in general, took this particularly badly, as she could see that Parysatis was lawlessly and with great cruelty destroying the king's faithful retainers on account of Cyrus.

18. When Clearchus and the other generals had been tricked by Tissaphernes,[40] and contrary to a sworn truce had been arrested and sent up country in chains, Ctesias says that Clearchus asked him to supply him with a comb.[41] He got it and attended to his hair and was so appreciative of the gift that he gave Ctesias his ring; Ctesias could show it to Clearchus' relatives and friends in Sparta as a token of their friendship. The engraving on the seal-stone was of Caryatids dancing.[42] Ctesias also reports that the rations that were sent to Clearchus were being continually pilfered and consumed by the soldiers who were in prison with him, and who gave Clearchus only a very small part. He says that he remedied the matter by seeing to it that not only were Clearchus' rations increased but also separate rations were given to the soldiers, and he adds that he performed this service to please Parysatis and with her full approval. He says also that a side of ham was sent in each day

to Clearchus to supplement his rations and that the latter begged him, and told him that it was his duty, to smuggle in a small knife concealed in the meat and not to allow his end to be dependent on the king's cruelty. But Ctesias says that he was afraid and refused. He also says that the king's mother implored Artaxerxes not to kill Clearchus and that he agreed and swore an oath to that effect, but later was persuaded by Stateira and had them all killed, except for Menon. This was the reason, according to Ctesias, that Parysatis plotted against Stateira and contrived to poison her. But this is not a very plausible story and is totally illogical as a motive, if we are to believe that Parysatis carried out such a dreadful crime, and put herself in such danger, for the sake of Clearchus – daring to kill the king's lawfully wedded wife and the mother by him of children reared for the throne. But it is quite obvious that Ctesias adds this melodramatic detail out of respect for the memory of Clearchus, since he also says that after they had been executed, the bodies of the other generals were torn apart by dogs and birds, but not that of Clearchus; his corpse was buried by a sandstorm, which formed a great mound of earth and hid his body. Some dates were scattered there and in a short time a wonderful grove of trees grew up and covered the site with its shade, so that even the king was filled with deep regret for having put Clearchus to death, believing that he was a man dear to the gods.

19. Now Parysatis had from the beginning nurtured a secret hatred for Stateira and looked upon her as a rival. But when she saw that her own influence was based on the king's respect and honour, whereas Stateira's influence was based on the king's love and trust, and so was firm and solid, she hatched a plot against her and ventured all, she thought, for the highest stake. Parysatis had a trusted maidservant called Gigis, whom she valued highly. It was this Gigis, according to Deinon, who assisted in the poisoning. But Ctesias says that she was merely complicit in the plot, and that against her will. Ctesias gives the name of the man who actually administered the poison as Belitaras, Deinon as Melantas.

Parysatis and Stateira had put aside their earlier suspicion and made up their differences and had begun to frequent the same places and take their meals together. But they were still afraid and on their guard, and so were careful to partake of the same food from the same dishes. Now the Persians have a little bird, called the *rhyntaces*. It produces no excrement but is packed full of fat inside, so that they think the creature actually lives on wind and dew. Ctesias says that Parysatis cut one of these birds in half with a small knife, on one side of which she had smeared the poison. She thus wiped the poison on one half of the bird but not on the other. She put the safe, clean half in her own mouth and began to eat it and gave the poisoned part to Stateira. Deinon, however, says that it was not Parysatis but Melantas who used the knife to cut the bird in half and placed the meat before Stateira. As Stateira lay dying in great pain and with violent convulsions, she began to realize what had happened; and the king too became suspicious of his mother, well aware as he was of her savagery and implacability. So he rushed at once to investigate the matter and arrested his mother's servants and waiters and tortured them on the rack. But Gigis was for a long time kept hidden in her palace by Parysatis, and when the king demanded her surrender, Parysatis refused. Later, however, when Gigis asked to be allowed to go home one night, the king got word of it and set an ambush for her, seized her and condemned her to death. By Persian custom poisoners are put to death in the following way: they place the head on a certain flat stone and then strike and crush it with another stone until the head and face are beaten to a pulp. So Gigis died in this way. But Artaxerxes took no action either in word or in deed against Parysatis. He merely sent her away, at her own request, to Babylon, declaring that as long as he lived he would never set eyes on that city. Such, then, was the state of affairs in the king's household.

20. Artaxerxes was no less eager to capture the Greeks who had marched inland with Cyrus than he had been to overcome Cyrus and secure his throne. But he failed and, although they had lost Cyrus and their own generals, they managed to escape,[43] as it were, from the palace itself. They thus made it

plain for all to see that the Persian empire and its king abounded
in gold, luxury and women, but was otherwise an arrogant
façade with no substance.[44] The whole of Greece accordingly
took heart and looked with disdain on the barbarians, and the
Spartans thought that it would be a disgrace not to liberate
from slavery the Greeks living in Asia and to put an end to their
humiliation at the hands of the Persians. To fight this war they
appointed first Thibron, then Dercyllidas, neither of whom
achieved anything remarkable. Then they entrusted its conduct
to Agesilaus, their king. As soon as he had made the crossing to
Asia, he at once fell to the task with great energy and began to
build up a wide reputation for himself. He beat Tissaphernes in
a pitched battle and proceeded to start winning over the Greek
cities.[45] At this point, Artaxerxes realized how the war should
be waged and sent Timocrates of Rhodes to Greece with a large
sum of gold and orders to use it to bribe the leading figures in
the Greek cities and so open up a Greek front against Sparta.
Timocrates set about doing this, and the largest cities began
conspiring together against the Spartans, and the Peloponnese
descended into turmoil.[46] The result was that the authorities
were forced to recall Agesilaus[47] from Asia. Tradition has it
that, as he was leaving, Agesilaus remarked to his friends that
the king was driving him out of Asia with 30,000 archers – for
Persian coins had an archer depicted on them.

21. Artaxerxes also drove the Spartans from the sea by employing Conon the Athenian as his commander, in conjunction with
Pharnabazus. For Conon had taken refuge in Cyprus after the
sea-battle at Aegospotami.[48] But he was not content merely to
have found a safe refuge; rather he was biding his time and
waiting for the direction of affairs to change, like the wind at
sea. And seeing that he lacked the power to put his own plans
into effect, while the king lacked a shrewd commander to direct his power, Conon sent a letter to the king in which he
explained his intentions. He told the bearer of the letter to do
all in his power to pass it to the king via Zenon of Crete, a dan-
cer, or Polycritus of Mende, a doctor. If they were not there, he
should pass it via Ctesias the doctor. It is said that Ctesias took

this letter and added to Conon's recommendations a clause requesting that Ctesias be sent to Conon as he would likely be of use in matters down on the coast. Ctesias, however, says that the king gave him this new duty of his own accord.

Anyway, through the agency of Pharnabazus and Conon, Artaxerxes won the sea-battle off Cnidus and stripped the Spartans of their hegemony at sea.[49] He thus made all Greece dependent on himself and so was able as arbitrator to dictate the terms of the infamous peace-treaty known as the Peace of Antalcidas.[50] Antalcidas was a Spartan, the son of Leon. Acting in collaboration with the king he succeeded in making the Spartans abandon to Artaxerxes all the Greek cities of Asia and the islands off the Asian coast;[51] they would henceforth be subject to his authority and taxation. Peace was also imposed on the Greeks – if one can call 'peace' the mockery and betrayal of Greece, a peace more ignominious than the end of any war ever was to the conquered.

22. For this reason, although Artaxerxes detested all the rest of the Spartans and thought, as Ctesias tells us, that they were the most shameless of all men, he showed remarkable affection to Antalcidas when the latter travelled up from the coast. Once he even took a garland of flowers, dipped it in perfume of the most expensive kind and sent it to Antalcidas after dinner, and all were amazed at the gesture. But Antalcidas was a fit person, so it seems, to enjoy such luxury and receive such a garland, since he had danced away among the Persians the fame of Leonidas and Callicratidas.[52] It is true that when someone said to Agesilaus, 'Alas for Greece when the Spartans medize,' he is said to have replied, 'No, it is rather the Medes who are laconizing.' But this clever turn of phrase did not take away the shame of what was actually happening. Indeed, although it was after their disastrous performance at the battle of Leuctra that the Spartans lost their hegemony,[53] the honour of Sparta had already been lost through this peace-treaty.

Now as long as Sparta reigned supreme, Artaxerxes continued to treat Antalcidas as his guest and call him his friend. But when they were defeated and brought low at Leuctra and in need of money, and sent Agesilaus out to Egypt, Antalcidas travelled up to Artaxerxes to ask him to help the Spartans.[54] But Artaxerxes so ignored, slighted and rejected him that when he had travelled back to the coast, he was laughed at by his enemies and, in fear of the ephors,[55] starved himself to death.

Ismenias and Pelopidas the Thebans, the latter of whom had just won the battle of Leuctra, also travelled up to the king.[56] Pelopidas did nothing to be ashamed of, but when Ismenias was ordered to prostrate himself before the king, he threw his ring down on the floor in front of him and then stooped to pick it up, thus giving the impression that he was doing obeisance.[57] As for Timagoras the Athenian,[58] when he sent in a secret note via the king's secretary Belouris, Artaxerxes was so pleased with him that he gave him 10,000 darics and, as Timagoras had to drink cow's milk on account of illness, the king ordered that eighty dairy cows accompany him wherever he went. He also sent him a bed, together with bedclothes and servants to make the bed – on the grounds that Greeks did not know how to make beds properly – as well as bearers to carry him down to the coast in his weak condition. In addition, when Timagoras was at court, Artaxerxes had wonderful banquets sent to him,[59] so that Ostanes, the king's brother, remarked, 'Timagoras, remember this meal. For it is not for free that such a marvellous spread is laid before you' – an insulting insinuation that he was a traitor rather than a reminder to appreciate the favour he was enjoying. At any rate, Timagoras was condemned to death by the Athenians for accepting bribes.

23. Now Artaxerxes, in return for all the anguish which he caused the Greeks, did bring them one item of joy, when he executed Tissaphernes, their most bitter enemy. He killed him on account of false charges made against him which his mother, Parysatis, seconded.[60] For the king's anger with her did not last very long and he was soon reconciled with her and sent for her to return to court. He could see that her intellect and pride were those befitting a queen, and that there was now no longer any reason for them to hold each other in suspicion or upset each other when they were together. In consequence, she endeavoured

to please the king in all things, and by finding fault with nothing that he did she gained great influence over him and obtained whatever she wanted. She realized that he was madly in love with one of his own two daughters, Atossa. Some writers say that he was trying to keep it a secret, not least on his mother's account, and to keep his passion in check, though he had already had secret meetings with the young girl. So when Parysatis became suspicious, she began to treat the girl with greater affection than before and to praise her beauty and character to Artaxerxes, saying that she was truly royal and majestic. In the end she persuaded him to marry the girl and declare her his lawful wife, thus ignoring the principles and customs of the Greeks and presenting himself to the Persians as the embodiment of divinely appointed law and arbitrator of right and wrong. Furthermore, some historians, including Heracleides of Cyme, say that Artaxerxes did not marry just one of his daughters, but also a second, called Amestris, of whom we shall have more to say later. At any rate, he was so fond of his consort Atossa that when her body became covered with leprosy, he was not in the least disgusted but prayed on her behalf to Hera, and prostrated himself and touched the earth with his hands – something he would do for no other deity. Furthermore, at his bidding, his satraps and friends sent so many gifts to the goddess that the road between the temple and the palace, a distance of two miles, was lined with gold, silver, purple and horses.

24. He waged war on Egypt, but failed when his commanders, Pharnabazus and Iphicrates, fell out with one another.[61] He campaigned in person against the Cadusii with 300,000 infantry and 10,000 cavalry.[62] But the country which he invaded was rough and hard and prone to mist; it produced no grain whatsoever, although it did produce pears and apples and other such fruit, which sustained a warlike and spirited people. Thus, without realizing, he found himself in an extremely difficult and dangerous situation. For it was impossible to find food in the country itself or to bring it in from outside. His men were reduced to butchering their pack animals, so that a donkey's head fetched as much as 60 drachmas. The royal banquets

were abandoned, and only a few horses were left, as they had consumed the rest.

At this point Tiribazus, a man whose bravery had often set him in the front rank but whose stupidity had equally often led to his being spurned, and who at this time was despised and overlooked,[63] saved the king and his army. For the Cadusii had two kings who were encamped at some distance from each other. Tiribazus had a meeting with Artaxerxes and explained his plans, and then went in person to one of the two kings and sent his son secretly to the other. Each of them managed to fool the king to whom he had gone by saying that the other king was sending envoys to Artaxerxes and trying to secure friendship and alliance for himself alone; each of them, if he had any sense, they argued, should arrange a meeting with Artaxerxes before the other one did. They themselves promised to lend help in any way they could. Both kings were persuaded by this and, under the impression that they were stealing a march on the other, sent off delegations to Artaxerxes, accompanied respectively by Tiribazus and Tiribazus' son. But as time dragged on, suspicions and attacks on Tiribazus began to reach Artaxerxes' ears. He himself was pessimistic about the whole thing and beginning to regret that he had trusted Tiribazus, and this gave encouragement to Tiribazus' rivals to malign him. But finally Tiribazus arrived, and his son arrived too, bringing with them the Cadusian envoys. A peace-treaty was agreed with both parties and Tiribazus, now an influential and splendid figure, began to march for home with Artaxerxes.

It was on this occasion that the king made it clear that cowardice and lack of moral fibre do not spring from luxury and extravagance, as most people suppose, but from an abject and ignoble nature under the influence of wicked sentiments. For the king was not prevented by his gold, his fine robes or the 12,000 talents' worth of jewellery which always adorned his person, from undergoing the toils and hardships of the journey like anyone else. He dispensed with his horse and, with his quiver strapped to his back and shield in hand, personally led the column on foot as it marched through mountainous and precipitous country. This had such an effect on the rest of the

army that they felt they had grown wings and had their bur-
dens lifted, seeing as they did his determination and strength.
Indeed, he accomplished marches of 25 miles a day or more.

25. Finally, Artaxerxes descended from the high ground and
reached a royal travelling-lodge, which was equipped with
wonderful parks,[64] beautifully tended. This stood in striking
contrast to the bare and treeless country round about. Since it
was cold, he gave the soldiers permission to cut down trees
from the gardens for firewood, sparing neither pine nor cypress.
When they hesitated and were inclined to spare the trees on
account of their size and beauty, he himself took up an axe and
cut down the largest and most beautiful one. After this, the
men procured the firewood they needed and lit numerous fires
and thus passed the night comfortably. Nevertheless, he lost
many good men on that march and nearly all the horses, and
when he arrived back he became suspicious of the chief men,
thinking that they despised him because of the disastrous failure of the expedition. Indeed, he executed many of them in
anger and was afraid of even more. For it is fearfulness which
is the most murderous thing in tyrannies, whereas confidence
makes the tyrant merciful, gentle and unsuspicious. It is the
same with animals: the wildest horses and those which are
most difficult to train are the most fearful and frightened of
noise, whereas the noble ones are more trusting because of
their courage and do not recoil from friendly advances.

26. Artaxerxes was now advanced in years, and he realized
that his sons were competing for influence among his friends
and those who wielded power in order to secure the succession
for themselves. For men of sense thought that, just as Artaxerxes had himself received the throne by virtue of seniority, so
he would leave it to Darius as the eldest of his sons. But his
youngest son, Ochus, who was of an extreme and violent disposition, had gathered a good number of supporters at court
and was also confident of winning his father over through the
agency of Atossa. For he cultivated her by saying that after the
death of his father he would marry her and that she would rule

alongside him. There is even a report that he had relations with her secretly while Artaxerxes was still alive. At any rate, although Artaxerxes was unaware of this latter matter, he was eager to disabuse Ochus of his expectations swiftly, so that he would not try the same thing as Cyrus has done and plunge the kingdom again into war and conflict. So he proclaimed Darius, who was then fifty years old,[65] king and gave him permission to wear upright the so-called 'tiara'.[66]

Now it was a Persian custom that the one designated as successor could ask for a favour, and that the one who so designated him should, if at all possible, give him whatever he asked for. Accordingly, Darius asked for Aspasia,[67] who had been Cyrus' special favourite and was now a concubine of the king. She was a native of Phocaea in Ionia, the child of free parents and had had a decent upbringing. This woman had been brought in with a group of other women at one of Cyrus' dinners. The rest of them sat down near him and he began to amuse himself and touch them and make jokes, all of which they accepted with good grace. But Aspasia stood by the couch in silence and paid no heed when Cyrus called her over. When his valets wanted to lead her over to him, she said, 'If any of them lays hands on me he will regret it.' Those present thought she was ungracious and uncouth, but Cyrus was amused and laughed and said to the man who had brought in the women, 'Do you see? This is the only free and unblemished woman, you have brought me!' From this time on Cyrus was devoted to her; he was more attached to her than to any other woman and gave her the name 'Wise'. She was captured after Cyrus' death in the battle, when his camp was plundered.

27. It was this woman that Darius asked for, thus upsetting his father. For barbarian society is terribly prone to sexual jealousy, so that it is punishable by death not only to come up and touch one of the royal concubines, but also, while travelling, to ride past or overtake the carriages in which they are conveyed.[68] And yet despite this, Artaxerxes had relations with Atossa, whom he had married out of love, contrary to the law, and he also maintained in addition 360 concubines of surpassing

beauty.[69] However, since he had been asked for Aspasia, he said that she was a free woman and told Darius to take her, if she was willing, but not to force her against her will. So Aspasia was summoned, and when against the king's expectations she chose Darius he was forced by custom to give her to him. But shortly after he had given her he took her away. For he declared her priestess of Artemis of Ecbatana, whom they call Anaïtis,[70] in order that she might remain chaste for the rest of her life, thinking that in this way he would take a mild and rather amusing revenge on his son. But the latter did not take it at all mildly, whether because he was passionately in love with Aspasia or because he thought he had been humiliated and ridiculed by his father.

When Tiribazus realized that Darius felt like this, he sought to embitter him all the more, seeing in Darius' plight his own grievance, which was as follows. The king had quite a number of daughters, and he declared that he would give Apama in marriage to Pharnabazus, Rodogune to Orontes and Amestris to Tiribazus. Although he kept his word to the other two, he broke it in Tiribazus' case, and married Amestris himself, and in her place betrothed to him his youngest daughter, Atossa. But when he fell in love with her too and married her, as has been mentioned, Tiribazus, who in general did not have a stable character but was unpredictable and impetuous,[71] became utterly hostile to him. For he was one moment in the highest regard and the next moment out of favour and treated with contempt, and he could bear neither change of circumstance with moderation. When he found himself held in honour he was offensive in his vanity, and when he had his wings clipped he could not take it humbly or quietly, but was bitter and arrogant.

28. So when Tiribazus attached himself to the young Darius[72] it was like adding fire to fire. Tiribazus kept on repeating that a tiara standing upright on the head was of no help at all to those who did not seek by their own efforts to stand upright in affairs of state, and that Darius was stupid if he thought that his succession to the throne was secure, while his brother was insinuating himself into the affairs of state by means of the harem, and while

his father was so fickle and unstable in character. For there was no way that someone who was ready to set at nought an inviolable custom of the Persians for the sake of a mere Greek girl could be trusted to live up to his promises when it came to matters of the greatest importance. It was not the same thing, he said, for Ochus to fail to get the throne as it was for Darius to be deprived of it. For there was nothing to stop Ochus from living a happy life in a private station, whereas he, once he had been proclaimed heir, must either take up the throne or lay down his life. Now perhaps in general, as Sophocles says, '*Swiftly treads persuasion unto evil conduct.*'[73] For smooth and downward sloping is the path towards what we desire,[74] and most people desire what is bad for them through ignorance and inexperience of what is good. However, in this case it was the size of the kingdom and Darius' fear of Ochus that provided Tiribazus with material, although, since Aspasia had been taken away, '*Cypriote Aphrodite was not altogether blameless*'[75] either.

29. So Darius surrendered himself to Tiribazus' influence, and as the number of conspirators grew, a eunuch betrayed to the king both the nature of the plot and the manner in which it was to be carried out. He had detailed knowledge that they had decided to burst into the king's bedroom at night and kill him in his sleep. When Artaxerxes heard this he decided that it would be a serious mistake to ignore such a great danger and pay no heed to the report; on the other hand, he thought it an even more serious mistake to believe it without any investigation. So he put into effect the following plan. He told the eunuch to stick close by the conspirators wherever they went. Meanwhile, he had the wall of his bedroom behind the bed cut away and a doorway added and covered with a hanging. When the hour was at hand and the eunuch reported the exact time for the assassination, he kept his place on the bed and did not jump up until he had seen the faces of his assailants and recognized each one clearly. When he saw them rushing at him with drawn daggers, he raised the hanging and retreated into the inner chamber and slammed the door with a cry. The assassins had been seen by him but had accomplished nothing, and fled

through the doors and told Tiribazus and his friends to make their escape as the plot was revealed. The rest of the conspirators scattered and fled, but Tiribazus killed many of the king's bodyguards as they tried to arrest him. Finally, he was struck by a javelin thrown from a distance and fell.

Darius together with his children was brought before the king and consigned to trial before the royal judges. The king was not himself present at the trial, as others brought the prosecution, but he ordered his servants to write down the decision of each judge and to bring it to him. The judges were unanimous in their decision and condemned Darius to death. So the servants seized him and took him to a nearby chamber, and the executioner was summoned and arrived carrying a razor with which the heads of the condemned are cut off. But when he saw Darius he was dumbfounded and retreated towards the doors with head averted, saying that he had neither the power nor the courage to murder a king. Outside, however, the judges began to threaten and exhort him, so he turned round and, grasping Darius' hair with one hand and pulling him down, slit his throat with the razor. Some say that the sentence was passed in the presence of the king himself and that Darius, when he was overwhelmed with proofs, fell prostrate before him and begged for mercy. But the king jumped up in anger, drew his dagger and stabbed at him until he died. Then he went forth into the courtyard and did obeisance to the sun and declared: 'Depart joyfully, Persians, and tell all you meet that those who contrived a wicked and unlawful plot have been punished by the great Oromazes.'[76]

30. Such then was the end of the conspiracy. Ochus was already full of hopeful expectation and buoyed up by Atossa, but he still feared Ariaspes, the only other surviving legitimate son, and Arsames, who was illegitimate. For Ariaspes was considered by the Persians worthy of the throne, not because he was older than Ochus but because he was mild, straightforward and humane. Arsames was also considered wise and Ochus was quite aware of how dear he was to his father. So he plotted against both, and since he was at the same time both devious

and bloodthirsty, he indulged the savagery of his nature against Arsames and his malice and cunning against Ariaspes. For to the latter he surreptitiously sent eunuchs and friends of the king, who kept on telling him of various threats and terrifying utterances, implying that his father had decided to kill him in a cruel and humiliating way. They pretended that these daily reports were secret and kept repeating that now the king was delaying or now he was on the point of acting, and they so terrified the man and thrust him into such anxiety, confusion and despondency that he procured a fatal poison and by drinking it rid himself of the need to go on living. When the king learnt of the manner of Ariaspes' death, he mourned him and also had suspicions as regards the real cause. But being utterly incapable on account of his age of seeking out and convicting the guilty, he became even more attached to Arsames and clearly placed great trust in him and spoke freely in his presence. Therefore Ochus did not postpone the deed but assigned it to Arpates, the son of Tiribazus, and through him killed the man.

Already by that time Artaxerxes had only a tenuous grip on life due to his old age, and so when on top of all else news of the fate of Arsames reached him, he could hold out no more but at once expired out of grief and despondency. He had lived ninety-four years and reigned for sixty-two.[77] He had the reputation of being a mild and benevolent ruler not least because of his son Ochus,[78] who surpassed all in savagery and bloodthirstiness.

PELOPIDAS

PELOPIDAS

INTRODUCTION TO
PELOPIDAS

[c. 410–364 BC]

The career of the Theban general Pelopidas coincides with the period of Thebes' greatest influence and success, and correspondingly with the collapse of Spartan power. Thebes, the largest city in the region of Boeotia, was also the most powerful city in the Boeotian Confederacy. In the Peloponnesian War (431–404 BC) most of Boeotia had been allied with Sparta against Athens, but, as the war ended, tensions between the former allies escalated. Thebes gave refuge to Athenian democrats who fled Athens in 404 after Sparta abolished its democracy, and fear of the now untrammelled power of Sparta led Boeotia to fight against Sparta and on the side of Athens and Corinth in the Corinthian War of 395–387. Sparta was not slow to take revenge. The Peace of Antalcidas of 386 disbanded the Boeotian Confederacy, and in 382 Spartan troops seized the acropolis of Thebes and set up a pro-Spartan oligarchy in the city.

Pelopidas was among a group of aristocratic Thebans who fled across the border to Athens. In 379 he took part in a dramatic coup, which assassinated many of the oligarchs, expelled the Spartan garrison from Thebes and re-established the Boeotian Confederacy. In the following year Pelopidas was elected Boeotarch, one of the chief officials of the Confederacy, a position to which he was re-elected almost every year until his death. He played an important role in military operations against the Spartans and was present, as commander of the Theban Sacred Band, at the decisive battle of Leuctra in 371, where Boeotian troops under Epaminondas unexpectedly inflicted a crushing defeat on Sparta. In 370 Pelopidas and Epaminondas led Theban troops into the Peloponnese, where they liberated Messenia from Spartan control, founded the new city of Messene and so changed the balance of power in mainland Greece for ever. In the years that followed, Pelopidas led Boeotian troops on several expeditions to Thessaly against Alexander, the tyrant of Pherae. In 368 he was captured by Alexander but later freed when Epaminondas threatened a renewed attack; in 364 he was killed while fighting Alexander at the battle of Cynoscephalae.

Plutarch's *Life of Pelopidas* presents Pelopidas in a favourable light throughout. He lays special stress on the friendship and cooperation between Pelopidas and his contemporary, Epaminondas; Plutarch presents this as a model of harmony and cooperation against which so many other famous leaders of the past fell short (chs. 3–4; cf. 23–4). Pelopidas is also presented as a brave man and a skilful leader, and as a champion of freedom against oppression. Those qualities are first in evidence in the narration of the liberation of Thebes (chs. 7–13), which forms the centrepiece of the first half of the Life (this was plainly a story which interested Plutarch; he also tells it, at greater length, in his *On the sign of Socrates*). Pelopidas' courage and love of freedom are also evident in his opposition towards Alexander of Pherae, which forms the focus of the second half of the Life. As Plutarch presents it, Pelopidas' motivation for intervening in Thessaly is to defend the Thessalians (chs. 26–7); Plutarch also emphasizes the barbarity and cruelty of the tyrant in order to play up by contrast Pelopidas' reasonableness, even showing how the tyrant was hated by his own wife, who finally plotted to murder him (Pelopidas. 28, 35). The fact that after Pelopidas' death the Thessalians are griefstricken and accord him a magnificent funeral shows for Plutarch the love and loyalty Pelopidas had won. 'While engaged', Plutarch concludes, 'in a heroic action aimed at the destruction of a tyrant, he sacrificed his life for the freedom of Thessaly' (ch. 34).

Plutarch's *Pelopidas* covers some of the same material as Xenophon does in his *Hellenica* Books 6 and 7 and in his encomium of the Spartan King Agesilaus, and Xenophon was plainly an important source for this Life. But Xenophon is consistently anti-Boeotian and in his complete works only deigns to mention Pelopidas in a single passage (*Hellenica* 7.1.33–40, discussing the embassy to Persia of 367). Indeed, in the *Hellenica* he fails to mention at all both the battle of Tegyra, which Plutarch saw as a precursor to Leuctra (ch. 16), and the liberation of Messenia from Spartan control, despite the importance of the latter as a turning-point in Greek history. *Pelopidas*, on the other hand, not only gives generous treatment to Boeotian achievements, but presents the great events of the mid-fourth century from a Boeotian point of view. Thus the liberation of Thebes forms an exciting and dramatic mini-narrative of its own and Plutarch presents it as parallel to Athens' own liberation from Sparta and the restoration of Athenian democracy in 403 (ch. 13).

Plutarch must, then, have had other sources in addition to Xenophon, which were rather more favourable to the Boeotian side. In fact, Plutarch is reticent as to the identity of these other sources. Comparison with Diodorus Book 15 (15.50–88) suggests that Plutarch may have used the now lost fourth-century historian Ephorus, who was Diodorus' main source for this period. He probably also used Aristotle's nephew Callisthenes, whose *Hellenica* seems to have covered the period from the Peace of Antalcidas to the mid-350s. Plutarch names both Ephorus and Callisthenes once (ch. 17). There were probably other sources too, perhaps local Boeotian ones. Plutarch was himself Boeotian and had almost certainly visited in person the sites of some of the events in *Pelopidas* (see his descriptions in chs. 16 and 20).

Whatever the exact identity of the sources used by Plutarch, he was certainly aware of traditions that were less favourable to Pelopidas. For example, in chapter 25 Plutarch deals with the trial in Thebes of Pelopidas and Epaminondas in 369 for holding on to their command longer than the twelve-month term allowed by law. Plutarch presents the prosecution as motivated by envy, remarks on Epaminondas' fortitude and spends most time on Pelopidas' successful counter-prosecution of one of their most ardent detractors. But in Plutarch's treatise *On inoffensive self-praise* (540d–e), Pelopidas' performance at the trial is presented in a much less favourable light: in contrast to the confident dignified bearing of Epaminondas, Pelopidas 'cringed and begged'. The positive presentation of Pelopidas in the Life, then, is not simply a result of Plutarch reproducing unthinkingly the emphasis of his sources and must, partly at least, be a deliberate choice.

The *Life of Pelopidas* is paired with the *Life of Marcellus*. M. Claudius Marcellus (consul 222 BC) was famous as victor over the Gauls, conqueror of Syracuse and above all veteran of Rome's long struggle against Hannibal in the Second Punic War (218–201 BC). In the prologue which forms an introduction to both Lives and immediately precedes the *Pelopidas*, Plutarch draws attention to one similarity between them in particular: 'both were careless of their own lives and recklessly threw them away'. Plutarch returns to the point in the Comparison of the two men which follows the *Life of Marcellus*.

Other similarities are built into Plutarch's account of the two men. For example, the trials of Pelopidas and Epaminondas find their parallel in Marcellus' trials before the Senate (*Marcellus* 23, 27). But there are also some differences. Whereas Pelopidas always cooperates harmoniously with Epaminondas, Marcellus' cooperation with his colleague Fabius Maximus is less than perfect (see esp. *Marcellus* 24). Similarly, whereas Pelopidas' anger against Alexander of Pherae is presented as a result of a laudable love of freedom and hatred of tyranny, Marcellus' desire to defeat Hannibal is portrayed partly at least as a result of an obsessive personal ambition (esp. *Marcellus* 28). Finally, the threat posed by Alexander of Pherae, and the brutality of his character, is played up, whereas the threat posed by Hannibal is played down. Unusually, then, in this pair of Lives, the Greek subject seems to be treated more favourably than the Roman. Or, to put it another way, the Greek subject provides a more straightforward model against which to read the more complex Roman one.

PROLOGUE TO THE LIVES
OF PELOPIDAS AND
MARCELLUS

1. When the elder Cato[1] once heard some people praising a man who was unreasonably reckless and daring in war, he observed that there was a difference between valuing courage highly and life cheaply, and his remark was just. At any rate, there is a story of one of Antigonus' soldiers,[2] a man who was apparently quite fearless, but who suffered from weak health and a wretched physique. When the king asked him what was the reason for his pallid colour, he admitted that he was afflicted with a little-known disease. The king took the matter to heart and gave orders to his physicians that if any remedy could be found, they should give him their utmost skill and care. The result was not only that the man was cured, but that he immediately ceased to risk his life and lost all the fire and dash which had distinguished him on the battlefield, so that even Antigonus reproved him and expressed his amazement at the change. The soldier made no attempt to conceal the reason for his behaviour, but said, 'It is you, sire, who have taken away my courage, because you have freed me from the miseries that made me hold life cheap.' The same point was once made by a citizen of Sybaris,[3] who remarked that it was no great sacrifice for the Spartans to lay down their lives fighting if this meant an escape from the innumerable hardships and generally wretched existence that they endured. Of course to the Sybarites, a people completely enervated by their soft and luxurious way of living, it was natural to suppose that these men, whose ambition and ardent desire for renown had banished the fear of death, could only feel as they did because they hated life; but the truth was that the valour of the Spartans gave them happiness both in living

and in dying, as the following epitaph shows us. These men died, it says,

> Not seeing death or life in itself as the object of striving,
> But to accomplish both nobly, this they considered true honour.[4]

For there is no disgrace in avoiding death, so long as a man does not cling to life dishonourably; but neither is there any special virtue in meeting it if this is done out of contempt for life. It is for this reason that Homer always brings his bravest and most warlike heroes into battle splendidly and effectively armed, and that the Greek lawgivers punish a man for throwing away his shield, but not his sword nor his spear: their object was to teach him that his first duty is to protect himself from harm rather than inflict it on the enemy, and this is most of all true for a man who governs a city or commands an army.

2. The Athenian general Iphicrates[5] once compared the light-armed troops to the hands, the cavalry to the feet, the main body of infantry to the chest and breast-plate, and the general to the head: thus if the commander is over-impetuous and takes undue risks, he endangers not only his own life but those of all the others, whose safety or destruction depend on him. This is why Callicratidas, although in other respects a great man, was wrong in the answer he gave to the diviner who urged him to take care since the sacrificial omens before the battle foretold his death. 'Sparta', he retorted, 'does not depend on one man!'[6] It is true of course, that when he was fighting, or at sea, or serving under the orders of another, Callicratidas was one man, but as general he combined in his own person the strength of all the rest, so that in this sense he was certainly not one man, when his death involved the destruction of so many others.

A better answer was given by Antigonus the old when he was about to engage in a sea-battle off Andros[7] and somebody told him that the enemy's fleet was far stronger than his own, to which he answered, 'How many ships do I count for?' In saying this, he was implying that leadership is a great thing, as indeed it is, when it is combined with courage and experience, and it is its first duty to protect the man who holds the fate of all the others in his hands. In the same way, when Chares was once showing the Athenians his wounds and his shield which had been transfixed by a spear, Timotheus was right in saying, 'For my part I was ashamed at the siege of Samos whenever an arrow passed near me, because I was afraid I was behaving more like an impetuous youth than a general in charge of such a great force.'[8] To sum up, we might say that where the whole issue of a battle may turn upon the general's exposing himself to danger, there he must use hand and body unsparingly, and disregard those who say that a general should die in old age, if not of old age. But where the advantage to be gained from success is small, and all is lost if he fails, no one demands that a general should risk his life fighting like an ordinary soldier.

These things occurred to me to say by way of preface as I write the Lives of Pelopidas and Marcellus, both of them great men who fell in battle unexpectedly. For they were both formidable in hand-to-hand fighting, both won honour for their countries in brilliant campaigns and both were faced with the most formidable opponents of their times. Marcellus, it is said, was the first to rout Hannibal, who had hitherto proved invincible, while Pelopidas, in a pitched battle, defeated the Spartans, who at that time were supreme on land and sea. Yet both were careless of their own lives and recklessly threw them away at the very moment when there was the most pressing need that men of their calibre should be alive and hold command. These are the points of resemblance which they share and which have led me to write their Lives in parallel.

LIFE OF PELOPIDAS

3. Pelopidas, the son of Hippoclus, was descended, like Epaminondas, from an illustrious Theban family. He grew up surrounded by riches, and having succeeded while he was still a young man to a splendid inheritance, he made it his business to relieve the condition of men who both needed and deserved his help, so as to prove that he was truly the master of his wealth and not its slave. Most rich men, according to Aristotle, either make too little use of their wealth through miserliness, or too much through extravagance, and so live in perpetual slavery, the one class to their business and the other to their pleasures.[9] At any rate, many Thebans were glad to benefit from Pelopidas' kindness and generosity, and of all his friends it was only Epaminondas who could not be persuaded to share his wealth. Instead, Pelopidas shared Epaminondas' poverty and took pride in the simplicity of his dress, the austerity of his diet, his readiness to endure hardships and the thoroughness of his performance of military service. Like Capaneus in Euripides' play, he possessed 'Abundant wealth, but in that wealth no pride',[10] and he was ashamed that anyone should suppose that he enjoyed more personal luxury than the poorest citizen of Thebes. Epaminondas, who had been born to poverty and was thus accustomed to it, made it more endurable by his philosophy of life and by choosing from the beginning to remain single. Pelopidas, on the other hand, married into a noble family and had children born to him, but nevertheless, by devoting all his time to public duties, he neglected to make money for himself and suffered losses to his estate. When his friends found fault with him for this and reminded him that money, even though he chose to

ignore it, was still a necessity of life, he replied, 'A necessity I dare say – for example, for Nicodemus here!' and he pointed to a man who was both lame and blind.

4. Both men were by nature equally fitted to pursue every kind of excellence, except that Pelopidas took more pleasure in cultivating the body and Epaminondas the mind, so that the one gave his leisure hours to the wrestling arena and the hunting field, and the other to listening to and discussing philosophy. Both had many claims to renown, but the greatest of these in the opinion of the wise was the unquestioned good faith and friendship which endured between them from first to last, throughout a multitude of political crises, campaigns and public actions. For if anyone considers the political careers of Themistocles and Aristides, or of Cimon and Pericles, or of Nicias and Alcibiades,[11] and how full they were of mutual dissensions, jealousies and rivalries, and then contrasts these with the honour and consideration with which Pelopidas treated Epaminondas, he will see that they can in the fullest sense be called colleagues in government and in command, which cannot be said of those who were constantly striving to get the better of one another rather than of the enemy. The true reason for the superiority of the two Thebans is to be found in their virtue; because of this their actions were not undertaken to obtain personal glory or wealth, which always arouse bitter envy and strife. Instead, they were both fired from the beginning by a divine ardour to see their country raised to the heights of power and prestige in their own lifetime and through their own efforts, and to this end each treated the other's successes as if they were his own.

However, most people think that their close friendship began during the campaign at Mantineia,[12] where they served in a contingent sent from Thebes to support the Spartans, who at that time were still their friends and allies. In this battle the two were stationed side by side among the hoplites and fought against the Arcadians. When the wing of the Lacedaemonian army where they were posted gave way and most of their companions were put to flight, they locked their shields together and drove back their opponents. Pelopidas received seven wounds in the front of his body, and at last sank down upon a heap of corpses, in which friend and foe lay dead together, but Epaminondas, although he thought his comrade had been killed, stood in front of him to defend his body and his arms and fought desperately, holding a host of attackers at bay single-handed, for he was determined to die rather than leave Pelopidas lying there. It was not long before Epaminondas was in deadly danger himself, for he had received a spear-thrust in the chest and a sword-cut on the arm, but at last Agesipolis, the Spartan king, came to his rescue from the other wing, and when hope was almost gone saved the lives of both men.

5. After this, the Spartans made a show of treating the Thebans as friends and allies, but the truth was that they were suspicious of the city's power and of her ambitious spirit; above all they hated the grouping led by Ismenias and Androcleidas and to which Pelopidas belonged, which was believed to be devoted to the cause of liberty and of government by the people. Consequently Archias, Leontidas and Philip, who were rich members of the oligarchic faction and whose ambitions were not restrained by any scruples, entered into negotiations with Phoebidas the Spartan as he was passing through Theban territory with a body of troops.[13] They proposed that he should seize the Cadmeia[14] by a surprise attack, banish the party that opposed them and, by establishing an oligarchy, ensure that the regime would be subservient to Sparta. Phoebidas allowed himself to be persuaded, timed his assault upon the Thebans when they were least expecting it in the midst of the festival of the Thesmophoria and seized the acropolis.[15] Ismenias was arrested, carried off to Sparta and soon afterwards executed, while Pelopidas, Pherenicus, Androcleidas and many others escaped from the city and were proclaimed outlaws. Epaminondas was allowed to remain, for he was not considered to be a man of action on account of his interest in philosophy, nor to be of any danger to the regime on account of his poverty.

6. The Spartans proceeded to deprive Phoebidas of his command and fined him 100,000 drachmas, but they nevertheless

continued to occupy the Cadmeia with a garrison: in this way they made all the rest of Greece marvel at their inconsistency in punishing the offender but approving the offence.[16] As for the Thebans, they had lost their ancestral constitution and became enslaved to the group of Archias and Leontidas; nor was there room for any hope of deliverance from this tyranny which they could see was protected by Sparta's military supremacy and could not be unseated, unless Sparta's ascendancy by land and sea could somehow be broken. But in spite of this apparent security, when Leontidas and his supporters learnt that the Theban refugees were living in Athens and that they were not only welcomed by the common people but honoured by the well-to-do, they plotted against their lives. They sent secret agents to Athens, who contrived to assassinate Androcleidas by treachery but failed in their attempts against the others. The Spartans sent letters to the authorities in Athens requesting them not to harbour or encourage the exiles, but to banish them on the ground that they had been declared public enemies by the allied cities. The Athenians, however, would do no harm to the Thebans in their city, for apart from their traditional and natural instincts of humanity, they had a debt of gratitude to repay to Thebes, who had been jointly responsible for the restoration of their own democracy, since at that time they had passed a decree that if any Athenians marched through Boeotia on their way to attack the tyrants,[17] no Boeotian should see or hear them.[18]

7. Although Pelopidas was one of the youngest of the exiles, he took the initiative in encouraging each of his companions privately. Besides this, whenever they met together, he would argue that it was utterly wrong and dishonourable to allow their native city to remain garrisoned and enslaved by foreigners, and for themselves to think of nothing but their personal safety and survival, to depend upon the decrees of the Athenians and to cultivate and fawn upon whichever orators could sway the people in their favour. They should play for the highest stakes and take the courage and idealism of Thrasybulus as their model, and just as he had started out from Thebes and

overthrown the tyrants in Athens, so they in their turn should set forth from Athens and deliver Thebes. After a while the exiles were won over by these arguments; they secretly resumed contact with their supporters in Thebes and told them what they had resolved. Their friends approved of these plans and Charon, one of the leading citizens of Thebes, agreed to put his house at their disposal, while Phillidas contrived to have himself appointed secretary to Archias and Philip, the two polemarchs. Meanwhile, Epaminondas had already communicated his own ideals to the younger generation of Thebans. He urged them whenever they trained in the gymnasium to challenge the Spartans and wrestle with them. Then, when he saw them elated by their victories in these bouts, he would scold them and tell them that such triumphs ought rather to make them feel ashamed; for since they so much exceeded their opponents in physical strength, it could only be their cowardice which kept them enslaved to them.

8. When a day had been fixed for the attempt, the exiles decided that the main body led by Pherenicus should wait in the Thriasian plain,[19] while a few of the youngest men undertook the dangerous mission of going on ahead into the city; if these were surprised by their enemies, the rest should see to it that neither their children nor their parents should be left in want. Pelopidas was the first to volunteer for this task, followed by Melon, Damocleidas and Theopompus: each of these men belonged to the leading families in Thebes, they were attached to each other by the closest ties of friendship and were rivals only in the pursuit of valour and reputation. A group of twelve volunteers was made up, they embraced those who were to stay behind and sent a messenger ahead to warn Charon. They set out[20] in short cloaks and took with them hounds and hunting-nets, so that anybody who met them on the road should have no suspicion of their purpose, but should take them for hunters ranging the countryside in search of game.

When the messenger arrived and reported that they were on their way, Charon, although the hour of danger was now at hand, in no way faltered in his determination, but acted as a man of his word and made his house ready to receive them. But there was another conspirator, Hipposthenidas, by no means an unprincipled man, indeed a patriot and a sympathizer with the exiles, but one who did not possess the intrepid spirit which the urgency of the moment and the nature of the attempt demanded. The importance of the enterprise, which was now so close at hand, threw him into a panic, especially when he realized that in attempting to overthrow the occupying garrison they were in a sense trying to shake off the hegemony of Sparta, and that for this ambitious purpose they had put their trust in the hopes of refugees who had no resources behind them. Hipposthenidas went quietly home and dispatched one of his friends to Melon and Pelopidas urging them to postpone their plans for the present, return to Athens and wait for a more favourable opportunity. The man he sent was called Chlidon, and he hurried to his house, led out his horse and asked for the bridle. His wife was at her wits' end because she could not find it for him and made the excuse that she had lent it to a neighbour. They began to quarrel, then to curse one another and finally his wife uttered a prayer that his journey might prove fatal to him and whoever had sent him. By that time Chlidon had wasted a great deal of the day in this squabble; he decided that what had happened was a threatening omen, gave up all idea of the journey and turned his attention to other business. We may reflect how near at the very outset the greatest and most glorious enterprises have sometimes come to missing their opportunity.

9. Meanwhile, Pelopidas and his party exchanged clothes with some peasants, separated and entered the city from different directions while it was still daylight. The weather had begun to change, there was a strong wind blowing and some flurries of snow, and it was easy for them to remain unobserved because many people had already gone indoors to shelter from the storm. However, those who were in on the plot received them as they arrived and immediately led them to Charon's house: together with the exiles there were forty-eight men in the conspiracy.

As for the tyrants, the situation was as follows. Their secretary Phillidas had for some time been taken into the confidence of the conspirators, as I have mentioned, and was working hand in hand with them. Some while before, he had proposed a drinking-party for Archias and his friends, to which they were to invite a number of married women: his plan was to get them under the influence of wine and thoroughly relaxed in their pleasures, and then to deliver them into the hands of their attackers. But the drinking had scarcely got under way when a report was brought in, which, although true, was unconfirmed and vague in its details, to the effect that the exiles were hidden somewhere in the city. Phillidas did his best to change the subject, but Archias sent one of his attendants to Charon with orders that he should come at once. By then it was evening and Pelopidas and his companions were making themselves ready in Charon's house; they had already buckled on their breast-plates when suddenly a knock was heard at the door. Somebody ran to it, was told by the messenger that he had come from the polemarchs to fetch Charon and in a state of great agitation gave his news to the rest. All the conspirators at once concluded that the plot had been discovered and that they were lost before they could achieve anything worthy of their courage.

However, they agreed that Charon must obey the summons and appear before the polemarchs as though he suspected nothing. Charon was a man of courage and of stern resolution in the face of danger, but on this occasion he was anxious and his determination was undermined on account of his friends; moreover, he feared that if so many brave citizens were to lose their lives, he could scarcely escape the suspicion of treachery. So just before he left the house, he sent for his son, who was still no more than a boy, but handsomer and stronger than others of his age: he fetched the youth from the women's quarters and handed him over to Pelopidas, saying that if they discovered any treachery or deceit in the father, they must treat the son as an enemy and show him no mercy. Many of the conspirators wept at Charon's noble spirit and at the concern which he showed for them, and all were indignant that he

should think any of them so demoralized by the present danger
and so mean-spirited as to suspect or blame him in any way.
They implored him not to involve his son with them, but to
send him out of harm's way so that he might escape the tyrants
and live to avenge the city and his friends. But Charon refused
to take his son away and asked them, 'What life or what safety
could be more honourable for him than to die a noble death in
the company of his father and of so many friends?' Then he
offered up a prayer to the gods, embraced and encouraged
them all and went off, striving to compose his expression and
control his voice so as to yield no hint of the part he was really
playing.

10. When he reached the door of the polemarch's house, Archias came out with Phillidas and said to him, 'Charon, I have
heard that a number of men have arrived and have hidden
themselves in the city, and that some of the citizens are in league
with them.' Charon was alarmed at first, but he began by asking who these men were and who was helping to conceal them.
He soon saw that Archias had no exact information and that
what he had heard did not come from any of those who knew
the truth. 'You must take care', he said, 'not to let yourself be
misled by idle rumour. But in any case I will make inquiries. We
must not neglect any report of this kind.' Phillidas, who was
standing next to him, approved of this answer and thereupon
led Archias back into the house, plied him with wine and did
his best to spin out the drinking with assurances that the women
would soon arrive.

When Charon returned to his house he found the conspirators fully prepared; they had given up any hope that they
would succeed in their attempt, or even survive it, but they
were determined to die gloriously and kill as many of their
enemies as possible. And so it was only to Pelopidas that he
confided the truth; for the rest he made up a story that Archias
had talked about other matters. But even before this first storm
had blown over, fortune soon brought another in its train. A
messenger arrived from Athens, sent by Archias the priest to
his namesake and close friend Archias of Thebes. He brought

with him a letter which contained, as was afterwards discovered, no mere vague or imaginary suspicion, but a clear and detailed account of the conspiracy. The messenger was taken to Archias, and handed him the letter saying, 'The man who sent this said that you must read it immediately: it concerns very serious matters.' Archias was by that time so drunk that he merely smiled and answered, 'Serious matters for tomorrow!' Then he took the letter, put it under his pillow and returned to whatever he had been talking about with Phillidas. This phrase has become a proverb which is current in Greece down to this day.[21]

11. Now that the moment of opportunity seemed to have arrived, the conspirators set out in two parties. One, led by Pelopidas and Damocleidas, was to attack Leontidas and Hypates, who lived near one another; the other, under Charon and Melon, went to Archias and Philip. The men had put on women's gowns over their breast-plates and wore thick garlands of pine and fir which shaded their faces.[22] For this reason, when they first came through the door of the dining-room, the company shouted and clapped their hands, imagining that the long-awaited women had at last arrived. The conspirators looked carefully around the party, took note of each one of the guests as they reclined and then, drawing their swords, they threw off their disguises and made a rush for Archias and Philip. Phillidas prevailed upon a few of the guests to stay quiet; the rest who staggered to their feet and tried to defend themselves and help the polemarchs were so drunk that they were easily dispatched.

Pelopidas and his party were faced with a harder task, for Leontidas, whom they had marked out as their victim, was sober and a formidable adversary, and they found his house shut up as he was already asleep. They knocked for a long time before anyone answered, but at last the attendant heard them, and began to come out and draw back the bolt. As soon as the door gave way and opened, they burst in all together, knocked down the servant and rushed to the bedroom. Leontidas, when he heard the noise and the sound of running feet, guessed what was happening, leaped from his bed and drew his dagger. But he forgot to throw down the lamps so as to make the men stumble over one another in the darkness. The consequence was that when he moved to the door of his bedroom and struck down Cephisodorus – the first man who entered – he came into full view of his attackers. As Cephisodorus fell dead, Leontidas grappled with Pelopidas who was immediately behind. There was a violent struggle between them, in which their movements were hampered by the narrowness of the doorway and by the dead body of Cephisodorus which lay under their feet. At last Pelopidas got the upper hand and, after killing Leontidas, he at once hurried on with his companions to attack Hypates. They broke into his house in the same way, but Hypates instantly guessed why they had come and fled for shelter to his neighbours. The conspirators followed close on his heels, caught him and killed him.

12. Having carried out their mission, they joined Melon's party, and sent a message to the main body of exiles whom they had left in Attica. They also called upon the citizens of Thebes to fight for their liberty, and armed all who came to them, taking down the spoils and trophies of war which hung in the porticoes and breaking open the shops of the spearmakers and swordsmiths in the neighbourhood. Epaminondas and Gorgidas joined them with a band of armed followers consisting of young men and the most active of the older men. By this time the whole city was in an uproar, the air was filled with shouting, lights were lit in the houses and men ran frantically here and there. The people, however, did not yet gather in a body. They were frightened by the turn which events had taken, but as they had no clear idea of what was happening they waited for daylight. Here the Spartan commanders seem to have blundered in not making a sortie and attacking them immediately, for their garrison numbered some fifteen hundred men, and many people ran out of the city to take refuge with them. But they too were alarmed at the shouting, the watch-fires and the din which reached them from all directions, and so they took no action but merely stood at arms on the Cadmeia. At daybreak, the exiles from Attica marched into the city fully armed and a general assembly of the people was summoned. Then

Epaminondas and Gorgidas led forward Pelopidas and his companions surrounded by priests who carried garlands in their hands, and called upon the citizens to fight for their country and their gods. At the sight of these men, the whole assembly rose and with shouts and loud applause welcomed them as their saviours and benefactors.

13. After this Pelopidas was elected Boeotarch,[23] and together with Melon and Charon he at once blockaded the Cadmeia and attacked it on every side, for he was anxious to drive out the Lacedaemonians and free the acropolis before an army could arrive from Sparta. He succeeded in his object, but with so little time to spare that after the Spartans had surrendered on terms and had been allowed to depart, they had gone no further than Megara before they met Cleombrotus marching against Thebes with a large army. Of the three men who had been harmosts or military governors in Thebes, the Spartans condemned and executed Herippidas and Arcesus, while the third, Lysanoridas, was heavily fined and afterwards went into exile.

This exploit so closely resembled the liberation of Athens,[24] not only in the courage displayed and the dangers and ordeals endured by the men who took part in it, but also in the fact that their success was crowned by good fortune, that the Greeks came to refer to it as the sister of Thrasybulus' achievement. It would be hard to find another instance in which so small a group of men with such weak resources overcame so numerous and powerful an enemy by virtue of sheer courage and determination, or conferred greater blessings on their country by so doing. And, indeed, the change which they brought about in the political situation made their action even more glorious. It can truly be said that the war which destroyed Sparta's prestige and put an end to her supremacy by land and sea began with that night on which Pelopidas, not by surprising any fortress, wall or acropolis but simply by entering a private house with eleven other men, loosened and broke in pieces, if we may express the truth in a metaphor, the fetters of Spartan domination which until then had seemed adamantine and indissoluble.

14. The Spartans then invaded Boeotia[25] with a large army, and at this the Athenians took fright and denounced their treaty of alliance with the Thebans. They went on to impeach all those who supported the Boeotian cause, executed some of them and fined or banished others; and as nobody offered to help the Thebans, their situation began to appear desperate. However, Pelopidas, who was Boeotarch, together with Gorgidas, found a way to embroil the Athenians once more with the Spartans by means of the following ruse. There was a Spartan named Sphodrias who enjoyed a high reputation as a soldier, but who lacked judgement and was apt to be misled by vain hopes and reckless ambitions; this officer had been left at Thespiae with a number of troops to help and act as a rallying-point for those Thebans who had been exiled because they favoured the Spartans. Pelopidas and Gorgidas arranged for one of their friends who was a merchant to visit Sphodrias secretly and to unfold a scheme which proved even more attractive to him than money. The idea was that he should attempt an ambitious operation and capture Piraeus[26] by a surprise attack when the Athenians were off their guard. Nothing, the merchant explained to him, would please the Spartans so much as the seizure of Piraeus, and at that moment the Athenians could expect no help from the Thebans, who were angry with them and regarded them as traitors. At length, Sphodrias allowed himself to be persuaded, put his force under arms and made a night march into Attica. He advanced as far as Eleusis, but there his soldiers lost heart and his attempt was discovered; at this he withdrew to Thespiae, but his action was to involve the Spartans in a serious and difficult war.

15. As a result of this raid, the Athenians eagerly renewed their alliance with Thebes and began operations by sea; they travelled around and invited and accepted the alliance of any Greeks that were disposed to revolt.[27] Meanwhile, the Thebans on their own account continually engaged the Spartans in battle in Boeotia. These actions were no more than skirmishes, but such frequent encounters gave them invaluable training and practice and had the effect of raising their spirits, strengthening

their bodies through hardship and adding to their experience and courage. This is why they say that Antalcidas the Spartan, when King Agesilaus returned from Boeotia with a wound, remarked to him, 'You taught the Thebans the art of war when they did not want to fight, and now, I see, they have paid you handsomely for your tuition!' However, the truth was that it was not Agesilaus who had taught them, but those of their own leaders who, with reasoned planning and an eye to the right moment, would skilfully unleash the Thebans against their enemies just like young hounds. They allowed them to get a taste of victory and of the self-confidence which goes with it, and then would bring them back again to safety. And of these leaders the chief honour was due to Pelopidas. From the moment when his countrymen first chose him as their commander, there was not a single year in which they did not elect him to office, either as captain of the Sacred Band[28] or more often as Boeotarch, so that he remained continuously on active service until the time of his death.

During these years the Spartans were defeated and routed at Plataea; at Thespiae Phoebidas, the man who had originally seized the Cadmeia, was killed; and at Tanagra a large Spartan force was put to flight, and Panthoidas, the military governor, lost his life. These actions however, although they gave courage and confidence to the victors, by no means broke the spirit of the vanquished. They were not pitched battles, nor were the combatants drawn up in open or in regular formation: the Thebans gained their successes by making well-judged attacks and by adopting flexible tactics, according to which they might retire and break off the action, or pursue and come to close quarters with the enemy.

16. However, the battle of Tegyra,[29] which provided as it were a prelude to the Theban victory at Leuctra, greatly increased Pelopidas' reputation, for on this occasion none of his fellow commanders could claim a share in the success, nor had the enemy any excuse for their defeat. The city of Orchomenus[30] had taken the side of Sparta and had received two Spartan battalions[31] to protect it. Pelopidas kept it under observation and

watched carefully for his opportunity. When he heard that the Spartan garrison had made an expedition into Locris, he took the Sacred Band and a small detachment of cavalry, and marched against the city, hoping to catch it defenceless. When he approached it he discovered that the garrison had been relieved by fresh troops from Sparta, and so he led his force back to Thebes through the district of Tegyra. This was a roundabout route which skirted the foot of the mountains, but it was the only one he could take, for the River Melas, which spreads out from its source into marshes and quagmires, made the centre of the plain completely impassable.

A little below the marshes stands the temple of Apollo of Tegyra, whose oracle had been abandoned comparatively recently. It flourished down to the time of the Persian Wars, when Echecrates served as priest and prophet there. According to the legend it was here that the god was born, and the mountain which overlooks the temple bears the name of Delos; at its foot the Melas contracts into its channel, while behind the temple flow two springs, whose water is much praised for its sweetness, coolness and abundance. One of these is called the Palm and the other the Olive to this day, as though the goddess Leto had borne her children not between two trees[32] but between two fountains. Close by is Mount Ptoon, from which it is said that a wild boar suddenly appeared and terrified the goddess, and in the same way the legends of the dragon Python and the giant Tityus[33] which belong to this locality also lend some support to the tradition that the god was born here. However, I shall pass over most of the evidence on this subject, since according to our ancestral tradition Apollo is not to be ranked among those deities who were born in a mortal state and later changed into an immortal one, as for example Heracles and Dionysus, who through their virtues were enabled to cast off mortality and suffering. Apollo is one of those deities who are eternal and unbegotten, if we may be guided by the testimony which the oldest and wisest men have uttered on these matters.

17. It was in the neighbourhood of Tegyra, then, that the Thebans met the Spartans, as they were returning in the opposite

direction from Locris. As soon as the Thebans caught sight of the Spartans emerging from the narrow defiles in the hills, one of them ran to Pelopidas and cried out, 'We have fallen into our enemy's hands!' 'Why not the enemy into our hands?' retorted Pelopidas. He immediately ordered his whole cavalry force to ride up from the rear and to prepare for a charge, and he drew up his hoplites, who numbered three hundred, in close formation: his hope was that wherever the cavalry charged, this point would offer him the best chance to break through the enemy who outnumbered him. There were two battalions of Spartans, each consisting of five hundred men according to Ephorus, although Callisthenes gives their strength as seven hundred, and other writers, Polybius among them, put it at nine hundred. The Spartan polemarchs Gorgoleon and Theopompus felt certain of victory and advanced against the Thebans. There was a furious clash as the two lines met, the fighting being fiercest at the point in the line where the two commanders were stationed, and it was there that the Spartan polemarchs engaged Pelopidas and were both killed. Then, when the Spartans around them were also cut down, panic began to spread through the army, and they parted their ranks to make a passage for the Thebans, supposing that they wanted to force their way to the rear and escape. However, Pelopidas used the corridor which was thus opened to attack the formations which were still holding their ground, and he cut his way through them with great slaughter, until finally the entire Spartan force turned and fled.

The Thebans did not press the pursuit far, because they were afraid of being counter-attacked by the Orchomenians, whose city was close at hand, or by the relieving force from Sparta. Nevertheless, they had succeeded in defeating the enemy outright and forcing their way through the whole of the beaten army; so they set up a trophy,[34] stripped the Spartan dead and returned home triumphantly. For in all the wars that had been fought between Greeks and barbarians, the Lacedaemonians, it appears, had never been beaten by an army smaller than their own, nor for that matter in a pitched battle in which the numbers were equal. For this reason they possessed an invincible

spirit and when they came to close quarters their mere reputation was enough to give them an ascendancy over their enemies,
since other men could not believe that they were a match for
the same number of Spartans. So it was this battle which first
proved to the rest of Greece that it was not only the Eurotas,
nor the country between Babyce and Cnacion,[35] which bred
brave and warlike soldiers. The truth is that if the youth of a
nation is ashamed of disgrace, is ready to dare anything in a
noble cause and shrink from dishonour rather than from danger, these soldiers prove the most terrible to their enemies.

18. The Sacred Band, we are told, was originally founded by
Gorgidas. It consisted of three hundred picked men, who were
given their training and lodging by the city and were quartered on the Cadmeia. This was why they were called the city
regiment, because at that time the acropolis was known as the
city. But according to some accounts, this force was composed
of lovers and beloved, and a joke of Pammenes has come down
to us in which he remarks that Homer's Nestor was paying
little attention to tactics when he urged the Greeks to arrange
their military formations by clans and tribes, *'That clans should
stand shoulder to shoulder with clans, and tribes aid one
another,'*[36] and that he ought instead to have posted lovers side
by side. Tribesmen or clansmen do not feel any great concern
for their kinsfolk in time of danger, but a band which is united
by the ties of love is truly indissoluble and unbreakable, since
both lovers and beloved are ashamed to be disgraced in the
presence of the other, and each stands his ground at a moment
of danger to protect the other. We need not be surprised at this,
since men are more anxious to earn the good opinion of their
lovers, even when these are absent, than that of others who are
present: there is the case of a man who, when his enemy was
about to kill him as he lay on the ground, implored the other to
run him through the breast, 'so that my beloved may not see
me lying dead with a wound in my back and be ashamed of
me'. The legend has it, too, that Iolaus, who was beloved by
Heracles, accompanied him during his labours and shared
them with him, and Aristotle says[37] that even down to his own

times, the tomb of Iolaus was a place where lovers exchanged their vows.

It was natural, therefore, that the Band was termed Sacred for the same reason that Plato describes the lover as a friend 'inspired by God',[38] and it is said that it was never defeated until the battle of Chaeronea.[39] The story goes that when King Philip of Macedon was inspecting the dead after the fighting, he stood at the place where the three hundred had faced the long pikes of his phalanx and lay dead in their armour, their bodies piled one upon the other. He was amazed at the sight, and when he learnt that this was the band of lovers and beloved, he wept and exclaimed, 'A curse on those who imagine that these men ever did or suffered anything shameful!'

19. Speaking generally of love between men, it was not, as the poets have reported, the passion of Laius for the young Chrysippus which first set the fashion for this kind of relationship in Thebes.[40] Its origins are rather to be traced to their lawgivers who wished to soften and tone down the hot-tempered and violent element in the Theban character, beginning from earliest boyhood, and for this reason they paid great attention to the flute, both in their education and their recreation. They gave this instrument especial prominence and value, and at the same time gave the emotions of love a place of honour in the wrestling-school and the gymnasium, and in this way they tempered, like steel, the characters of their young men. It was for the same reason that they established in their city the worship of the goddess Harmony, who is said to have been the child of Ares and Aphrodite: they believed that where the courage and aggressive qualities of the soldier are blended and mingled with eloquence and the social graces, there all the elements of communal life are harmonized, so that they produce the most perfect consonance and order.

When Gorgidas founded the Sacred Band, he originally distributed its members among the front ranks of the entire Theban hoplite phalanx. The result was that their exceptional courage was made inconspicuous, and their striking power was not exploited in any way which could benefit the whole army, because it was dissipated and diluted with that of a large body of inferior troops. But after the Band had distinguished themselves so brilliantly at Tegyra, where they had fought as an individual formation around Pelopidas' own person, he saw to it that they were never afterwards separated from one another or broken up; instead, he treated them as a single unit and gave them the place of danger in his greatest battles. Just as horses gallop faster when they are harnessed to a chariot than when they are ridden singly – not because they travel through the air more rapidly as a result of their combined weight, but because their mutual rivalry and competition kindles their spirits – so Pelopidas believed that brave men are at their most ardent in a common cause and give of their best when they strive to outdo one another in valour.

20. When the Spartans concluded a common peace with the rest of Greece,[41] they continued to wage war against Thebes alone, and Cleombrotus their king invaded Boeotia with a force of 10,000 hoplites and 1,000 cavalry. The Thebans found that they had to face a new danger, that of being completely displaced from their native land, and a fear such as they had never experienced before now spread through the whole of Boeotia. It was at this time, just as Pelopidas was leaving his house, that his wife followed him on his way, weeping and entreating him to take care of his life. 'My dear,' he said to her, 'this is very good advice for private citizens, but generals need to be told to take care of the lives of others.' When he reached the camp, he found that the Boeotarchs disagreed as to what should be done; he at once gave his support to Epaminondas and voted in favour of engaging the enemy. Pelopidas did not then hold the office of Boeotarch, but he was commander of the Sacred Band and highly trusted, as was only right for a man who had given his country such tokens of his devotion to liberty.

Accordingly, the decision was taken to risk a battle and the Thebans pitched camp opposite the Spartan army at Leuctra. Here Pelopidas had a dream which disturbed him deeply. In the plain of Leuctra are the tombs of the daughters of Scedasus. These girls are known as the Leuctridae, because it was here that they were buried after they had been raped by some Spartan strangers. Their father could obtain no satisfaction from the Spartans for this brutal and lawless outrage, and so, after solemnly cursing the Spartan race, he killed himself on the tombs of his daughters, and hence forever after prophecies and oracles continually warned the Spartans to beware of the vengeance of Leuctra. Most of them, however, did not fully understand the allusion and were also uncertain as to the place it concerned, since there is a small town in Laconia near the sea which is also named Leuctra, and another near Megalopolis in Arcadia. This atrocity, of course, took place long before the battle.

21. As Pelopidas slept in the camp, he dreamt that he saw the girls weeping over their tombs and calling down curses on the Spartans, and also that Scedasus urged him to sacrifice a red-haired virgin to his daughters if he wished to conquer his enemies. Pelopidas thought this a terrible and impious command, but nevertheless he rose and began describing his dream to the diviners and the generals. Some of these insisted that he must not neglect or disobey the order, and they quoted a number of precedents: from ancient times, Menoeceus the son of Creon, and Macaria the daughter of Heracles; and from more recent times, the case of Pherecydes the wise, who was put to death by the Spartans and whose skin was preserved by their kings on the instructions of some oracle; of Leonidas, the Spartan king, who, in a sense, was obeying the command of the oracle when he sacrificed his life at Thermopylae to save the rest of Greece; and of the Persian youths, who were sacrificed by Themistocles to Dionysus the eater of flesh before the sea-battle at Salamis.[42] In all these instances the sacrifices were vindicated by the successes that followed. On the other hand, when Agesilaus was setting out on an expedition from the same place and against the same enemies as Agamemnon, he had the same vision as he lay asleep at Aulis, in which the goddess Artemis demanded his daughter as a sacrifice, but he was too tender-hearted to give her up, and thus ruined his expedition, which ended unsuccessfully and ingloriously.[43] Others took the

opposite view and argued that such a barbarous and impious sacrifice could not be pleasing to the powers above, because it is not the Typhons or Giants or other monsters who rule in heaven, but the Father of gods and men. They argued that it is probably foolish in any case to believe that there are deities who delight in bloodshed and in the slaughter of men, but, that if they exist, we should disregard them and treat them as powerless, since it is only weak and depraved minds that could conceive or harbour such cruel and unnatural desires.

22. While the Theban leaders debated this problem, and Pelopidas in particular was at a loss what to do, a filly suddenly broke away from a herd of horses, galloped through the camp and stopped at the very spot where the conference was taking place. The other spectators admired above all the colour of her glossy mane, which was a fiery chestnut, the vigour of her movements and the strength and boldness of her neighing, but Theocritus the prophet, with a sudden flash of understanding, cried out to Pelopidas, 'The gods are with you! Here is your victim. Let us not wait for any other virgin, but take the gift the god has provided for you.' At this they caught the filly and led her to the tombs of the girls. There they crowned her with garlands, consecrated her with prayers and joyfully offered up the sacrifice. Then they explained to the whole army the details of Pelopidas' dream and the reasons for the sacrifice.

23. During the battle, Epaminondas kept edging his phalanx diagonally to the left in order to draw away the right wing of the Spartans as far as possible from the rest of the Greeks, and to drive Cleombrotus back and overwhelm him by launching a massive attack in column. The enemy perceived his intention and began to change their formation, extending their right wing and starting an encircling movement so as to outflank and envelop Epaminondas. But at this point Pelopidas dashed forward from his position and, advancing at the run with his band of three hundred, attacked before Cleombrotus could either deploy his wing or bring it back to its previous position and close up his ranks. His charge caught the Spartans in some disarray

and confusion. And yet of all men the Spartans were consummate experts in matters of war, and in their training they paid
special attention to not falling into disorder or confusion when
their formation was disrupted; they were all accustomed to
take any of their comrades as neighbours in the battle-line, and,
wherever danger might threaten, to concentrate on that point,
knit their ranks and fight as effectively as ever. But now when
Epaminondas' main phalanx bore down on them alone and
ignored the rest of their army, and Pelopidas with a charge of
extraordinary speed and daring had already hurled himself
upon them, their spirit faltered, their courage deserted them
and there followed a rout and a slaughter of the Spartans such
as had never before been seen. Therefore Pelopidas, although
he was not one of the generals and commanded only a few
men, won as much fame for the victory and the triumph of
Theban arms as Epaminondas, who was the Boeotarch in command of the whole army.

24. However, when the Thebans invaded the Peloponnese,[44]
both men held the office of Boeotarch. In this campaign, they
won over most of the peoples of the region and detached from
the Lacedaemonian alliance the states of Elis, Argos, the whole
of Arcadia and most of Laconia itself. By this time the winter
solstice was approaching, so that only a few days of the latter
part of the last month of the year remained. The law ordained
that as soon as the first month of the new year began, other
officials must take their places, and that those who refused to
give up their offices could incur the death penalty. The other
Boeotarchs were in a hurry to withdraw the army and march
home, not only because they feared the law, but also because
they wished to escape the hardships of winter. But Pelopidas
was the first to support Epaminondas in urging a contrary resolution: he joined him in appealing to the Thebans to follow
them, and led the army into Sparta and across the Eurotas. He
captured many of the enemy's cities and ravaged their territory
as far as the coast. The army he led numbered 70,000, of whom
the Thebans formed less than a twelfth part. Yet the reputation
of the two men was such that they did not need a formal decree,

but were able to persuade all the allies to follow wherever they led, without a murmur. The first and supreme law, it would seem, which is a law of nature, makes the man who wishes to be saved submit to the authority of the man who can save him; in the same way, men sailing on a calm sea or lying at anchor near the shore may treat their captain insolently or rebelliously, but as soon as a storm blows up or danger threatens, they look up to him and place all their hopes in him. Similarly, the Argives and Eleans and Arcadians would argue and dispute with the Thebans in their joint assemblies as to who should lead the allies, but at times of crisis, and when battles had to be fought, they obeyed the Theban generals and followed them of their own free will. In this campaign the allies united the whole of Arcadia into one state,[45] freed the territory of Messenia from the Spartans who had annexed it, recalled the former inhabitants of Messenia and established them in their ancient capital of Ithome.[46] On their way home, as they marched through Cenchreae,[47] they defeated the Athenians when they tried to hinder their passage in a series of skirmishes in the passes.

25. After these achievements, the rest of the Greeks idolized the two men for their valour and marvelled at their success. But as their fame grew, so did the envy of their compatriots, who now prepared for them a reception as disgraceful as it was undeserved. On their return, both Pelopidas and Epaminondas were put on trial for their lives, the charge being that they had not resigned the office of Boeotarch, as the law required, in the first month of the new year (which the Thebans call Boucation), but had extended their terms by four months, during which time they had carried out their campaign in Messenia, Arcadia and Laconia. It was Pelopidas who was tried first, and so ran the greater risk of being condemned, but both men were acquitted.

Epaminondas bore this attempt to slander him with patience, for he believed that a man of true courage and magnanimity should be forbearing when he comes under political attack. But Pelopidas, who was more hot-tempered by nature and was encouraged by friends to avenge himself upon his enemies, seized

the opportunity to retaliate, and he did it as follows. The orator Menecleidas had been one of the conspirators who had
accompanied Pelopidas and Melon from Athenian territory to
Charon's house in Thebes. After the liberation of Thebes from
the Spartans, he was not held in so much honour as the other
conspirators, and since he was an able speaker but a man of
little self-control and of a malevolent disposition, he employed
his eloquence in slandering and attacking the reputations of
those who were in power, and he continued to do this even
after the trial.

In this way, Menecleidas succeeded in preventing Epaminondas from holding the office of Boeotarch and in weakening his
influence in affairs for a long while. But he was not strong
enough to damage Pelopidas' reputation in the eyes of the
people, and so he attempted to stir up trouble between him and
Charon. It is often a comfort to the envious to make out those
whom they cannot surpass to be in some way inferior to others,
and so in all his speeches to the people Menecleidas made a
point of magnifying Charon's achievements and lavishing
praise on his campaigns and victories. In particular, he tried to
have a public monument set up to commemorate the victory
which the Theban cavalry had won at Plataea under Charon's
command, some time before the battle of Leuctra. Androcydes
of Cyzicus had been commissioned by the city to paint a picture of another battle and had been engaged on the work at
Thebes. Before he could complete the painting, the city had
revolted from Sparta and the Thebans were left with the unfin-
ished work on their hands. So Menecleidas tried to persuade the
people to set up this picture with Charon's name inscribed on
it as victor, and he hoped in this way to overshadow the fame
of Pelopidas and Epaminondas. It was an absurd piece of pretension to single out for praise one action and one victory – in
which we are told that an obscure Spartan named Gerandas
and forty other soldiers were killed, but nothing else of any
importance was accomplished – and to ignore the many great
battles won by the other two men. At any rate, Pelopidas
attacked this decree as unconstitutional and contended that it
was against the traditions of the Thebans to honour any man

individually, but that the whole city should share equally in the glory of a victory. All through the trial which followed, he paid generous tribute to Charon, but he argued that Menecleidas was an unscrupulous slanderer and repeatedly asked the Thebans whether they themselves had never before done anything worthy of note. The outcome was that Menecleidas was heavily fined, and, as he could not pay because the amount was so large, he tried at a later date to overthrow the government and bring about a revolution. These events, then, throw some light on Pelopidas' life.

26. Alexander the tyrant of Pherae[48] was openly at war with many of the Thessalian cities and was plotting against all of them. These communities, therefore, sent a delegation to Thebes to ask for a body of troops and a general. Pelopidas knew that Epaminondas was fully occupied in the Peloponnese[49] and so he offered his services to the Thessalians, partly because he could not bear to let his military skill and talents remain unused and partly because he believed that wherever Epaminondas was, there could be no need for another general. So he led the expedition into Thessaly and immediately captured Larissa; then, when Alexander came to him and begged for peace, he tried to convert him from a tyrant into a mild ruler and to persuade him to govern the Thessalians according to their laws. But on closer acquaintance, Alexander turned out to be incorrigibly brutal and given to savage cruelty, and so, since he received frequent complaints of the man's insolence and greed, Pelopidas treated him harshly and severely, whereupon Alexander departed in a rage, taking his bodyguard with him.

Pelopidas left the Thessalians secure against the threat of the tyrant, and after he had united them in harmony he set out for Macedonia. Here, Ptolemy was at war with Alexander, the king of Macedon,[50] and on this occasion both parties had invited Pelopidas to act as arbitrator, judge between their claims and then give his help and support to whichever party proved to have been wronged. He came and settled their dispute, and after he had restored the exiles to their homes he took Philip,[51] the king's brother, and thirty other sons of the leading men in the state and brought them to Thebes as hostages. He did this to show the Greeks how far the prestige of Thebes had advanced: his action not only demonstrated her power but also the confidence which men placed in the justice of her decisions.

This was the same Philip who was later to make war upon the Greeks and deprive them of their freedom, but at this time he was no more than a boy and was quartered in Thebes with Pammenes. It was for this reason that he was believed to have become a devoted disciple of Epaminondas. It may be that Philip was quick to appreciate the Theban's efficiency in the art of war and generalship, which represented no more than one of his virtues; as for the qualities of moderation, justice, magnanimity and clemency which constituted the true greatness of his character, Philip had no share of these by nature, nor did he choose to imitate them.

27. After this[52] the Thessalians again appealed for help because Alexander of Pherae was threatening their cities. Pelopidas and Ismenias were sent to them as ambassadors, but as no fighting was expected, they brought no troops with them from Boeotia and so Pelopidas was forced to make use of the Thessalians to deal with the emergency. It so happened that at this moment Macedonia was also in a state of disorder. For the king had been murdered by Ptolemy, who had then seized power, and the dead ruler's friends had appealed to Pelopidas to intervene. Pelopidas wished to support their cause and, as he had no troops of his own, he recruited some mercenaries on the spot and took the field against Ptolemy. As the two forces converged, Ptolemy was able to subvert the mercenaries and bribe them to come over to his side, but as he was afraid of Pelopidas' mere name and reputation, he went to pay his respects to him. At their meeting he greeted Pelopidas as his superior, begged for his favour and agreed to act as regent for the brothers of the dead king and to conclude an alliance with the Thebans; to confirm these undertakings, he handed over as hostages his own son Philoxenus and fifty of his followers. Pelopidas sent this party off to Thebes. But he was also angry at the treachery

of his mercenaries and he now discovered that their wives and children and most of their possessions had been sent to Pharsalus for safety; he decided to punish them for their affront to him and so he gathered a number of Thessalian troops and marched upon the town. But he had hardly arrived when Alexander the tyrant of Pherae appeared before the city with his own forces. Pelopidas and Ismenias supposed that he had come to justify his conduct, and so they went of their own accord to meet him. They knew that he was a depraved creature, who had often been guilty of bloodshed, but they expected that their own dignity and reputation and the prestige of Thebes would protect them. However, when the tyrant saw them approaching unattended and unarmed, he at once arrested them and took possession of Pharsalus. This step aroused horror and dismay among his subjects, who concluded that after committing an act of such flagrant injustice he would spare nobody, but would behave on all occasions and to all persons like a man who had by now given up all hope for his own life.

28. The Thebans were enraged when they heard the news and at once dispatched an army, but Epaminondas was temporarily out of favour and they appointed other commanders. As for Pelopidas, the tyrant brought him back to Pherae and at first allowed him to be visited by anyone who wished to speak to him, imagining that he had been crushed by his misfortunes and would become an object of pity. But when the Pheraeans visited him to lament his plight, Pelopidas urged them to take heart, since they could now be sure that the tyrant would be punished for his crimes. He also sent a message to Alexander himself telling him that it made no sense to torture and murder unhappy and innocent citizens every day but to spare him, the man who he knew would surely take his revenge if he escaped. Alexander was amazed at his fearless spirit and asked, 'Why is Pelopidas in such haste to die?' to which Pelopidas replied, 'So that you may become even more hateful to the gods than you are now, and die all the sooner.' After this the tyrant forbade anybody but his personal attendants to visit the prisoner.

Alexander's wife, Thebe, who was a daughter of Jason of

Pherae, had heard from Pelopidas' jailers of his courageous and noble conduct and was seized with an impulse to see him and speak to him. When she visited him she did not at once recognize the greatness of his nature in the midst of his misfortunes, but at the sight of his hair, his ragged clothes and his meagre diet, she supposed, as was natural for a woman, that he was suffering anguish from these indignities which were hard to bear for a man of his position, and she burst into tears. Pelopidas, who at first did not know who she was, watched with amazement, but when he understood, he addressed her as a daughter of Jason, since he knew her father well. When she said, 'I pity your wife,' he replied, 'So do I pity you, for you are not a prisoner, and yet you are compelled to endure Alexander.' Thebe was touched by this speech, since she detested Alexander not only for his cruelty and arrogance, but also for the fact that he had seduced her youngest brother. She came to see Pelopidas frequently, and during these visits she spoke openly of her sufferings: the result was that these conversations filled her with courage and with a burning hatred of Alexander.

29. The Theban generals invaded Thessaly but accomplished nothing, and finally either through inexperience or misfortune they beat an ignominious retreat. The state fined each of them 10,000 drachmas and then dispatched Epaminondas with another army.[53] This news immediately aroused great excitement among the Thessalians and their hopes rose high because of Epaminondas' reputation. Alexander's generals and supporters, on the other hand, were so overcome by fear, and his subjects were so eager to revolt and so overjoyed by the prospect of his impending punishment, that the tyrant's cause seemed to be tottering at the very brink of destruction. Epaminondas, however, was more concerned for Pelopidas' safety than for his own fame. He was afraid that if the country were allowed to fall into disorder, Alexander would be driven to despair and would then turn upon his prisoner like a wild beast, and so he played a waiting game and advanced only in a roundabout fashion. He hampered and circumscribed the tyrant's movements by his own preparations and apparent intentions in

such a way that he neither encouraged him to take reckless or precipitate action, nor provoked the harsh and violent element in his disposition. For Epaminondas had heard of his cruelty and his contempt for right and justice, how he buried men alive or clothed them in the skins of wild boars or bears and set his hunting-dogs upon them, and tore them apart or shot them down; and how in the case of Meliboea and Scotusa, two cities which were on friendly terms with him, he had surrounded them with his guards while the popular assembly was in session and slaughtered the inhabitants from the youths upward. He had also consecrated the spear with which he had killed Poly-phron, his uncle, and hung garlands on it, and he used to sacrifice to it as to a god and call it 'Tychon'.[54] On another occasion, when he was watching a tragedian perform Euripi-des' *Trojan Women*, he left the theatre suddenly and sent a message to the actor telling him not to lose heart or to relax his efforts because of his departure: it was not out of contempt for his acting that he had left the theatre, but rather because he was ashamed to let the citizens see him, who had never pitied any of the men he had done to death, shedding tears over the suffer-ings of Hecuba and Andromache. But it was this same tyrant who was so terrified by the name and fame of Epaminondas and the very appearance of an expedition led by him that '*He cowered slave-like, as a beaten cock that lets its feathers droop*'[55] and hurriedly sent a deputation to excuse his actions. However, Epaminondas would not tolerate the suggestion of making a treaty of peace and friendship with such a man; he merely concluded a truce of thirty days and, after Pelopidas and Ismenias had been handed over, he returned home.

30. The Thebans discovered that Sparta and Athens had both sent ambassadors to the king of Persia to negotiate an alliance. They therefore dispatched Pelopidas on a similar mission,[56] a choice which proved well justified because of the great pres-tige he had won. In the first place, his reputation had already preceded him: as he travelled through the provinces of the Per-sian empire he attracted universal attention, for the fame of his battles against the Spartans had by no means been muted nor

had it been slow to circulate among the Persians, and no sooner had the report of the battle of Leuctra become known abroad than it was echoed time and again by the news of some fresh exploit which penetrated to the remotest parts of the interior. All the satraps, generals and officers who met him at the king's court spoke of him with wonder as the man who had expelled the Lacedaemonians from land and sea, and had confined between Mount Taygetus[57] and the Eurotas that same Sparta which only a few years before had made war upon the great king under the leadership of Agesilaus and fought the Persians for the possession of Susa and Ecbatana.[58] King Artaxerxes was naturally pleased on this account: he admired Pelopidas for his reputation and paid him exceptional honours, since he wished to create the impression that he was courted and highly regarded by the greatest men of every country. But when Artaxerxes saw Pelopidas face to face and understood his proposals, which were more trustworthy than those of the Athenians and more honest than those of the Spartans, his pleasure was even greater, and using his kingly prerogative to display his sentiments he made no secret of the admiration he felt for Pelopidas and allowed the ambassadors to see that he stood the highest in his favour. And yet of all the Greeks it was to Antalcidas[59] that Artaxerxes seems to have shown the greatest honour, since he took off the garland which he had worn at a banquet, had it steeped in perfume and presented it to him. He did not favour Pelopidas with refinements of this kind, but sent him the richest and most magnificent of the gifts which were customary on such occasions, and granted his requests. These were that the Greeks should be independent, Messene inhabited and the Thebans regarded as the king's hereditary friends.[60]

With these answers, but without accepting any of the gifts save those which were simply intended as pledges of friendship and goodwill, Pelopidas set out for home, and it was this action which more than anything else brought the other ambassadors into discredit. At any rate, Timagoras was condemned and executed by the Athenians, and if this was on account of the vast quantity of gifts which he accepted, then the sentence was just: these had included not merely gold and silver, but an expensive bed, complete with slaves to make it up, since, according to him, Greeks were not capable of doing this, and also eighty cows with their herdsmen, since, as he claimed, he needed cows' milk for some ailment. Finally, he was carried down to the coast in a litter and the king gave him four talents to pay the bearers. However, it was apparently not so much the fact that he accepted these gifts which enraged the Athenians. His shield-bearer Epicrates at once admitted that his master had received gifts from the king, and had spoken of putting forward a proposal to the assembly that instead of electing nine archons, they should choose nine of the poorest citizens as ambassadors to the king so that they could benefit from his bounty and become rich men, and at this suggestion the people burst out laughing. The real cause of the Athenians' anger was that the Thebans had been granted all their requests. They did not stop to think that in the eyes of a ruler who had always shown most regard for a militarily strong people, Pelopidas' reputation counted for far more than any amount of skill in oratory.

31. The success of Pelopidas' mission, and his achievement in ensuring the foundation of Messene and the independence of the rest of the Greeks, earned him much goodwill on his return. Meanwhile, however, Alexander of Pherae had reverted to his former ways. He had destroyed several of the cities of Thessaly and had installed garrisons in the territory of the Achaeans of Phthiotis and of the people of Magnesia. So when the cities learnt that Pelopidas had returned, they at once sent ambassadors to Thebes to ask for an army to be dispatched to them and for him to command it. The Thebans enthusiastically passed a decree to this effect, preparations were quickly made and the commander was about to set out when there was an eclipse of the sun and darkness descended on the city in the middle of the day. Pelopidas saw that all the Thebans were dismayed by this phenomenon and decided that it would be wrong to coerce men whose courage and hopes had deserted them or to risk the lives of 7,000 citizens. So he offered his own services to the

Thessalians, took with him a detachment of three hundred cavalry who belonged to other cities and had volunteered for the
expedition, and set out: in this he was defying the advice of the
seers and the wishes of the rest of the people, who considered
that the eclipse must be a portent sent from heaven and must
refer to some great man. For his own part he was enraged
against Alexander when he remembered the humiliations he
had suffered, and his earlier conversations with Thebe led him
to hope that the tyrant's family was already divided within itself
and hostile to its head. But above all else, it was the glory of the
enterprise which spurred him on. At this moment the Spartans
were sending out generals and governors to help Dionysius the
tyrant of Syracuse, while the Athenians who were in Alexander's pay were setting up a bronze statue of him as a benefactor,
and so Pelopidas was eager to show the Greeks that it was only
the men of Thebes who took up arms for the cause of the
oppressed and who dethroned those dynasties in Greece which
relied on violence and defied the rule of law.

32. Accordingly, when he arrived at Pharsalus he assembled his
forces and marched at once against Alexander.[61] The tyrant
saw that there were only a few Thebans with Pelopidas and
that his own hoplites outnumbered the Thessalians' by more
than two to one, and set out to meet him near the shrine of
Thetis. When Pelopidas was told that Alexander was advancing against him with a large force, he remarked, 'All the better,
as there will be more for us to conquer.'

At the place which is known as Cynoscephalae, or the Dogs'
Heads, a number of steep and lofty hills project into the middle
of the plain, and both sides advanced to occupy these with their
infantry. Pelopidas possessed a large force of cavalry of excellent quality, and launched them against the enemy's cavalry;
these they routed and pursued into the plain. But Alexander
got possession of the high ground first, and when the Thessalian hoplites came forward later and tried to force their way
up the steep slopes, he attacked and killed the leading ranks,
and the rest took heavy casualties and were unable to achieve
anything. When Pelopidas saw this, he sent orders recalling the

cavalry and ordering it to attack the enemy where they still held together, while he himself took up his shield and ran to join the fighting on the hills. He forced his way through the rear and quickly inspired the front ranks with such courage and vigour that the enemy imagined they were being attacked by reinforcements who were fresh in body and spirit. They succeeded in resisting two or three attacks, but when they saw that infantry were coming on resolutely and the cavalry were now returning from their pursuit, they gave way and fell back step by step.

Pelopidas looked down from the heights and saw that the enemy, although not yet routed, were beginning to waver and fall into disorder. He stood there and cast about looking for Alexander. At last he saw him on the right wing encouraging and rallying his mercenaries. All Pelopidas' hatred flared up at the sight, his rage overwhelmed his reason, and, surrendering both his own safety and his responsibility as a general to his passion, he ran out far in front of his own men and rushed towards the tyrant, shouting and challenging him to fight. Alexander did not stand his ground and await his adversary's attack, but fled for refuge back to his bodyguard and hid there. The front ranks of the mercenaries came to close quarters with Pelopidas and were beaten back by him, and some were killed; but most of them kept their distance and set about attacking him with their javelins, which pierced his armour and riddled his body with wounds, until the Thessalians, in great anxiety for his safety, rushed down the hill to rescue him; but by then he had already fallen. Meanwhile, the cavalry launched a charge and routed the whole of the enemy's phalanx. They pursued them to a great distance, cut down more than three thousand of them, and left the countryside strewn with corpses.

33. It was no wonder that those of the Thebans who were present at Pelopidas' death should have been plunged into grief and called him their father, their saviour and their teacher of all that was best and noblest. But the Thessalians, too, and their allies went further than this:[62] not only did they surpass in their decrees the highest honours that are rightly paid to human valour, but

by their sorrow they demonstrated even more conspicuously the gratitude which they felt for their deliverer. It is said that the soldiers who took part in the battle neither took off their breast-plates, nor unbridled their horses, nor even bound up their wounds when they heard of his death, but still wearing their armour and hot from the fighting they came first to Pelopidas' body, as if he were still conscious, then they piled around it the arms of their slain enemies, sheared their horses' manes and cut off their own hair. After they had dispersed to their tents, many of them neither lit a fire, nor ate any supper; instead, a melancholy silence reigned throughout the camp, as if they had been defeated and enslaved by the tyrant instead of having won a great and glorious victory over him.

When the news reached the cities of Thessaly, the magistrates, accompanied by priests, young men and boys, came out in procession to take up the body, and they carried trophies, wreaths and suits of golden armour in its honour. Then when the body was to be taken out for burial, the leading citizens of Thessaly begged the Thebans to grant them the privilege of burying it themselves, and one of them spoke as follows: 'Friends and allies, we ask of you a favour which we shall consider an honour to us in our great misfortune and a comfort in our grief. We Thessalians can never escort a living Pelopidas again, nor render him honours which he can see and hear. But if we may have his body to touch, to adorn and bury, we shall be able to show you, we believe, that this is an even greater loss for Thessaly than it is for Thebes. For you have lost only a good commander, but we both a commander and our freedom. For how can we dare to ask of you another general when we have failed to give you back Pelopidas?' This request the Thebans granted.

34. There has never been a more splendid funeral, at least in the estimation of those who do not believe that splendour necessarily demands a profusion of ivory, gold and purple: as Philistus[63] does when he gives a rapturous description of the funeral of Dionysius, which brought down the curtain in grandiose style upon the great tragedy of his tyranny. In the same

fashion, Alexander the Great, when Hephaestion died, not only cut off the manes of his horses and mules, but even demolished the battlements of city walls in order to show the cities in mourning and make them present a shorn and dishevelled appearance in place of their former beauty.[64] But these tributes represented the commands of despots, they were carried out under duress and they excited envy against those who received them and hatred against those who enforced them; they were not prompted either by gratitude or by true regard for the dead, and they expressed only a barbaric pomp and an arrogant luxury which was characteristic of men who squandered their superfluous wealth on vain and paltry ostentation. The fact that a mere commoner, dying in a strange country far from his wife and children, should be borne forth and escorted and crowned, with so many peoples and cities vying with one another to show him honour, and yet with nobody demanding or compelling this, surely demonstrates that he attained the height of good fortune. To die in the hour of triumph is not, as Aesop calls it, a most cruel stroke of fate, but a most happy one, since it secures beyond all mischance the enjoyment of the blessings a man has earned and places them beyond the reach of fortune.[65] Therefore better advice was given by a Spartan, when he greeted Diagoras, who was not only an Olympic victor but had lived to see his sons and grandsons crowned there besides. 'Die now, Diagoras,' he said. 'You cannot ascend Mount Olympus!'[66]

Yet I do not suppose that anyone would compare all the Olympian and Pythian victories put together with a single one of Pelopidas' achievements. He accomplished many of these and every one successfully, he spent the greater part of his life surrounded with honour and renown and finally, after being appointed Boeotarch for the thirteenth time and while engaged in a heroic action aimed at the destruction of a tyrant, he sacrificed his life for the freedom of Thessaly.

35. Pelopidas' death caused great sorrow to his allies, but it brought them even greater advantages. When the Thebans learnt the news, they made immediate preparations to avenge his fate, and at once dispatched an army consisting of 7,000 hoplites and

700 cavalry under the command of Malecidas and Diogeiton. They found that Alexander was weakened and that his forces had suffered heavy losses, and they forced him to restore the cities he had taken from the Thessalians, to set free the Magnesians and the Achaeans of Phthiotis and withdraw his garrisons from those territories, and to guarantee to the Thebans that he would proceed against any enemy they might require him to attack. The Thebans were satisfied with these terms, but soon after this the gods took their own revenge for Pelopidas' death in a manner which I shall now describe.

As mentioned earlier, Pelopidas had taught Thebe, the tyrant's wife, not to be afraid of Alexander's display of outward pomp and splendour, since these depended entirely on force and the security of his bodyguards. For her own sake she feared his untrustworthiness and dreaded his cruelty, and she now entered into a plot with her three brothers Tisiphonus, Pytholaus and Lycophron to kill him in the following way. The rest of the palace was patrolled by sentries who were on duty all night, but the bedchamber in which she and Alexander slept was on an upper floor and was guarded on the outside by a chained dog, which would attack anyone except his master and mistress and the one servant who fed him. When Thebe was ready to make the attempt, she kept her brothers hidden in a nearby room all through the day, and at night went into Alexander alone, as was her custom. She found him already asleep, and soon afterwards came out and ordered the servant to take the dog outside, explaining that his master wished to sleep undisturbed. Next she covered the stairs with wool to prevent them creaking as the young men climbed them, brought up her brothers safely with their swords drawn and posted them outside the bedroom door. Then she went inside herself, took down the sword which hung over her husband's head and showed it to them as a sign that he was fast asleep. When she found that the young men were terrified and could not bring themselves to strike, she scolded them and swore in a rage that she would waken Alexander and tell him of the plot. After this she led them into the room, still unnerved, but by now filled with shame, placed them round the bed and brought the lamp. Then one of them seized the tyrant's feet and held them down, another dragged his head back by the hair and the third ran him through with his sword. The swiftness of the killing gave him a more painless death than he perhaps deserved. Nevertheless, he was the first and perhaps the only tyrant to die at the hands of his own wife, and since his body was outraged after his death, thrown out of doors and trampled underfoot by the Pheraeans, it may be judged that he suffered a fate to match his own lawless crimes.[67]

DION

INTRODUCTION TO DION

[*c.* 408–354 BC]

In *Dion* and *Timoleon* Plutarch turns to the history of the Greek cities of Sicily, specifically Syracuse. Syracuse, the largest of the Sicilian cities, was a democracy at the end of the fifth century and had endured a long siege by Athens (415 to 413 BC). But in 405, in the face of invasion by Carthage, power was seized by the young Dionysius I, who made himself tyrant and ruled Syracuse until his death in 367. By that time he had brought much of Sicily and parts of southern Italy under his control, and had access to vast wealth and resources, including the service of a mercenary army.

Dion, the subject of Plutarch's Life, was closely related to the family of Dionysius I, and was a trusted adviser. He was also at some level a Platonist, having met Plato when the latter visited Syracuse in 388. When the young Dionysius II, son of the former tyrant, came to power in 367, Dion tried to influence him towards Platonic philosophy and had Plato again invited to court. The results, however, were rather disappointing and Plato, by now in fear for his life, was in the end expelled (365). In the meantime, Dion had been accused of entering into private negotiations with Carthage, and was himself banished (366). After nine years in exile in Greece, and now convinced that he would not be recalled, Dion gathered a force of mercenaries and landed in Sicily with the aim of overthrowing the tyranny (357). He was greeted as a liberator and succeeded first in cooping up Dionysius and his family in Ortygia, the fortified headland of Syracuse, and ultimately in expelling his forces entirely. But politically he was less successful. His political instincts were oligarchic and he had no intention of restoring democracy. He was thus forced to rely on his mercenary troops in an increasingly violent struggle with the democratic forces in Syracuse, which culminated in the murder of the democratic leader, Heracleides. In 354 Dion was himself assassinated, after which Syracuse endured a series of short-lived rulers before Dionysius II returned to power in 346.

Plutarch's *Life of Dion* is idealized and politically one-sided. There is little sympathy for the Syracusan democratic leaders. Heracleides is presented as self-serving, ungrateful and a demagogue, flattering the common people and stirring them up against Dion. Dion is by contrast presented as reasonable and moderate, refusing to bow to popular demands such as the redistribution of land. Plutarch hurries over the murder of Heracleides, emphasizing Heracleides' destabilizing effect on Syracuse and the fine funeral Dion gave him, while implying that Dion himself did not give the orders but merely failed to restrain the assassins (ch. 53). All of this could have been presented very differently, with Dion seen as a would-be tyrant, relying on the support of his mercenaries, and Heracleides as a champion of popular freedom. Plutarch's own anti-democratic biases, as much as those of his sources, are probably at work here.

Plutarch's main narrative sources for *Dion* are lost. He several times cites the work of Timonides, a member of the Platonic Academy who accompanied Dion on his expedition, and the Sicilian historian Timaeus (*c.* 350–260 BC), whose long work on the history of Sicily was highly regarded in antiquity. Both are lost, but quotations of Timaeus in later writers show that he was almost certainly unfavourable to the tyrants. Plato's *Letters* were also an important source in this Life, especially his Seventh Letter, which purports to have been written shortly after Dion's death and is addressed to Dion's friends and associates. In it Plato (if the letter is genuinely by him) defends and justifies his own involvement in Sicily, and discusses Dion's actions at length. Plutarch refers to and paraphrases this letter frequently, and in general plays up the influence of Plato on Dion; in particular, he presents Dion's political programme, especially his concern to reorganize the Syracusan constitution after the fall of the tyranny, as an attempt to put Plato's ideas into practice. In his *Republic* and *Laws* Plato had described a utopian state in which philosophers would rule as kings. Plutarch presents Dion's constitutional aims for Syracuse as modelled on this idealized city-state (see esp. ch. 53). He also has Dion refer in discussions with his friends to his time spent studying with Plato and has him holding forth to them on the nature of virtue (ch. 47). This almost certainly exaggerates the influence of Plato on Dion. But Plutarch, himself a committed Platonist, found in the story of Dion an opportunity to explore what it would be like to apply Plato's doctrines to a real city. The theme was also topical: Greek intellectuals of Plutarch's period were fascinated by the idea that a single wise man might be able to influence a man of power, be he a tyrant, a governor or a Roman emperor, and Plutarch himself wrote a treatise on this subject called *Philosophers and men in power*.

For all the idealization of Dion and his political programme in this Life, however, Dion does not emerge as wholly admirable. Despite his personal virtues, Dion is unable to impose either by force or by persuasion his political vision. His liberation of Syracuse plunges the city into chaos and civil war; and although he is able to expel the tyrant, he is unable to handle the masses. Indeed, it is this inability which forms the one point of criticism which Plutarch makes. Plutarch comments early in the Life on Dion's haughty and severe demeanour (chs. 8, 17), and remarks towards the end that Dion continued his aloofness in dealing with the common people, 'even though the times called for a more gracious demeanour' (ch. 52). His murder, when it comes, has a certain inevitability to it.

For Plutarch, then, Dion was virtuous and guided by right principles, but he lacked that quality of flexibility and the ability to get on with people essential to success in politics. The same can be said for Brutus, whose Life is paired with that of Dion. Brutus too is presented as a man of philosophic principles, with a strong commitment to liberty and hatred of tyranny. It is these virtues which motivate him to overthrow the regime of Julius Caesar, which Plutarch presents in *Brutus* as parallel to the tyranny of the Dionysii. But Brutus, too, is unable to win popular support for his ideals; he dies, along with the Republic he attempted to restore, on the field of Philippi. These two Lives together, then, both idealize the notion of the philosopher in politics, but also suggest that correct philosophical principles and a virtuous character are not enough to succeed.

Two other extant writers deal with Dion. One is the first-century BC historian Diodorus, also of Sicily, who covers this period in his Book 16. The contrast with Plutarch's picture of Dion is striking: Diodorus is uninterested in Dion's philosophical commitments, and much more favourable to Heracleides, the democratic leader ultimately assassinated by Dion. His work, probably based on the fourth-century historian Ephorus, gives us a glimpse into another tradition which was much less biased in Dion's favour. There is also the brief biography of Dion by the first-century BC Roman writer Cornelius Nepos, which, while it presents Dion in glowing terms at the start, shows him to be an autocrat by the end. Both of these accounts are important counterweights to Plutarch's Life, showing how idealized, how politically biased and how imbued with Platonic conceptions it is.

PROLOGUE TO THE LIVES
OF DION AND BRUTUS

1. The poet Simonides tells us, Sosius Senecio,[1] that Troy bears no grudge against the men of Corinth for having fought against her on the side of the Greeks, since Glaucus, one of the very staunchest of her allies, was also, as it happened, a Corinthian.[2] In the same way, it is unlikely that either the Romans or the Greeks will find fault with the Academy, since in this book, which presents the Lives of Dion and of Brutus, each nation receives equal treatment. Dion was a disciple of Plato who knew the philosopher personally, while Brutus was nurtured on his doctrines, so that both men were trained in the same wrestling school, one might say, to take part in the greatest struggles. There is a remarkable similarity in many of their actions, and so we should not be surprised that they confirm the conviction of their teacher in virtue, namely that wisdom and justice must be accompanied by power and good fortune if a man's political actions are to possess both nobility and substance.[3] For Hippomachus the trainer used to say that he could always pick out his pupils from afar, even if they were only taking home meat from the market-place, and in the same way it is natural that where men have been trained in a similar way, reason should likewise guide their conduct and confer a certain grace, harmony and propriety upon all their actions.

2. These two men's lives resemble each other in their fortunes, that is in those events which were the result of chance rather than of deliberate choice. Both of them were cut off in the prime of life and so failed to accomplish the purposes to which

they had devoted such long and arduous efforts. But the strangest thing of all is that both of them were warned by the gods
of their approaching death in the form of a malevolent and
threatening spectre which appeared to each of them alike.
Those who utterly deny the existence of such phenomena maintain that no man in his right senses has ever set eyes on a ghost
or apparition sent by the gods. They insist that it is only little
children or women or people under the stress of sickness through
some bodily disorder or mental aberration who have indulged
in such imaginings, because they have within themselves the evil
spirit of superstition.[4] But Dion and Brutus were men of solid
understanding and philosophical training, whose judgement was
not easily deceived nor their composure shaken, and yet each
of them was so affected by an apparition that they actually
described what they had seen to others. So in the light of their
experience we may be compelled to give credit to the strangest
theory of ancient times, namely that there exist certain mean
and malevolent spirits who envy good men. They strive to frus-
trate their actions, to confuse and terrify them, shaking and
tripping up their virtue: all this is done to hinder them from
continuing their upright and blameless progress along the path
of honour, which would enable them to win a happier lot after
death than the envious spirits themselves.[5] However, this subject must be left for discussion elsewhere, and in this, the
twelfth book[6] of my *Parallel Lives*, let us bring on to the stage
first the life of the older man.

LIFE OF DION

3. Dionysius the elder, as soon as he had made himself master of Syracuse,[7] married the daughter of Hermocrates the Syracusan. But before the tyranny had been securely established, the people of Syracuse rose in revolt and violated her in such a cruel and barbarous fashion that she took her own life. Dionysius then recovered control, and once he had asserted his supremacy he married two wives. One of these was a woman of Locri named Doris; the other, Aristomache, was the daughter of Hipparinus, one of the most prominent citizens of Syracuse, who had been a colleague of Dionysius when he had been appointed commander-in-chief of the army, with unlimited powers to carry on the war against Carthage. It is said that he married both these women on the same day, and that nobody ever knew with which one he first consummated the marriage, but that afterwards for the rest of his life he spent an equal share of his time with each: it was his custom to dine with both of them together, and at night they shared his bed in turn. The Syracusans, however, were anxious that their own countrywoman should take precedence over the foreigner, but it was Doris' good fortune to be the first to become a mother, and thus by presenting Dionysius with his eldest son[8] she was able to offset her foreign birth. Aristomache, on the other hand, remained barren for a long time, although Dionysius passionately desired that she should bear him children, and he even went so far as to accuse the mother of his Locrian wife of giving her drugs to prevent conception, and had her put to death.

4. Dion was Aristomache's brother, and at first he was treated with honour because of his sister's position; but after a while he was able to give proof of his ability and earned the tyrant's regard on his own account. Besides the other privileges which Dion enjoyed, Dionysius instructed his treasurers to give the young man anything he asked for, but to inform him of the amounts on the same day. Now, from the very beginning Dion had shown a high-principled, generous and manly character, and these qualities became even more strongly developed in him when, by a providential accident, Plato arrived in Sicily.[9] This event was certainly not the work of any human agency, but it seems that some supernatural power was already preparing, far in advance of the time, the means to liberate the Syracusans and overthrow the tyranny, and to this end brought Plato to Syracuse and introduced him to Dion. Dion was then a young man of twenty, but of all Plato's followers he was by far the quickest to learn and the most ready to respond to the call of the virtuous life. Plato himself has written of him in these terms and events bear out his judgement.[10] Although Dion had been brought up to accept the habit of submission to tyrannical rule and had been steeped in an atmosphere of servility and intimidation on the one hand, and of ostentatious adulation and tasteless luxury on the other – a way of life which has no higher aspirations than pleasure and the love of gain – yet at the first taste of philosophic reason and of a doctrine which requires obedience to virtue, his spirit was instantly fired with enthusiasm. Then, because he himself was so quickly won over by these ideals, he assumed with all the innocence of youth that Dionysius would respond just as readily to the same arguments, and so he set to work and finally persuaded the tyrant that when he was at leisure he should meet Plato and listen to his ideas.

5. At this encounter the general theme of the conversation was human virtue, and most of the discussion centred upon the topic of courage. Here, Plato took the line that of all mankind the tyrant possesses the smallest share of this quality, and then turning to the subject of justice, he maintained that the life of the just is happy, while the life of the unjust is full of misery.[11]

Dionysius would not hear out this argument, since it implied a direct reproach to himself, and he grew exasperated with the audience when he saw how much they admired the speaker and were charmed by his doctrines. At last he lost his temper and angrily demanded of Plato why he had come to Sicily. Plato replied that he had come in search of a man of virtue, whereupon Dionysius retorted, 'Indeed! Then, by the gods, you do not seem to have found one yet!'

Dion and his friends supposed that this was the end of the tyrant's anger and that nothing more would come of it. Accordingly, as Plato was by then anxious to leave Sicily, they arranged passage for him on a trireme which was taking Pollis the Spartan envoy back to Greece. But Dionysius secretly approached Pollis and asked him to have Plato killed on the voyage if this could be arranged, or, if not, at least to sell him into slavery. This, he argued, would not do Plato any harm, since according to his own doctrines he would, as a just man, be equally happy even if he became a slave.[12] Pollis, therefore, took Plato to Aegina, so we are told, and sold him into slavery, for the people of Aegina were at war with Athens[13] and had passed a decree that any Athenian who was caught on the island should be sold as a slave.

In spite of this, Dion enjoyed the same honour and confidence in the eyes of the tyrant as before, and he was entrusted with the most important diplomatic missions: in particular he was sent to Carthage, where his achievements won great admiration. Dionysius even tolerated his habit of frank speech, and indeed, Dion was almost the only man who was left free to express his opinions, as, for example, when he reproved Dionysius for what he had said about Gelon.[14] The tyrant was sneering at Gelon's government, and when he said that Gelon had become the laughing-stock[15] of Sicily, the other courtiers pretended to admire the joke, but Dion was indignant and retorted, 'You might remember that the reason why you are our tyrant today is that people trusted you because of the example that Gelon set. After what you have said, nobody will be trusted because of your example.' The truth is that Gelon seems to have succeeded in making the spectacle of a city under absolute rule

appear admirable, whereas Dionysius could only make it appear
detestable.

6. Dionysius had three children by his Locrian wife, Doris, and
four by Aristomache: two of the latter were girls, Sophrosyne
and Arete. Sophrosyne married her half-brother, Dionysius the
younger, and Arete the tyrant's brother Thearides. Then, after
Thearides died, Arete married Dion, who was her uncle. When
the elder Dionysius fell sick and it was considered certain
that he would die, Dion tried to speak to him on behalf of Aristomache's children, but the physicians, who were anxious to
ingratiate themselves with the heir to the throne, refused to
allow this. Indeed, according to Timaeus,[16] when Dionysius
asked for a sleeping-draught, they gave him a drug which made
him completely insensible, so that he died without ever regaining
consciousness.[17]

At the first council which the young Dionysius held with his
friends, Dion summed up the political situation and the immediate needs of the state with such authority that the rest of
the company gave the impression of being mere children, while
his frankness of speech made them appear by comparison the
merest slaves of the tyranny, who could only offer in the most
timorous and servile fashion the kind of advice which was calculated to please the young man. But what impressed the
council most of all – since they were greatly disturbed by the
danger from Carthage[18] which threatened the empire – was
Dion's undertaking that if Dionysius wanted peace, he would
sail at once to Africa and put an end to the war on the best
terms he could obtain; but that if he was set on war, Dion would
supply fifty fast triremes and maintain them at his own expense.

7. Dionysius was greatly astonished at his magnanimity and
delighted at his public spirit. But the other members of the
council felt that this display of generosity reflected on them and
that they were humiliated by Dion's power, and so they at once
began a campaign in which they seized every opportunity to
turn the young ruler against Dion. They accused him of trying
to manoeuvre himself into the position of tyrant through the

authority which he exercised over the fleet, and of using the ships to place the control of the state in the hands of Aristomache's children, who were his own nephews and nieces. However, the strongest and most obvious reasons for their hatred of him lay in the difference between his way of life and their own, and in his refusal to mingle with others. From the very beginning they made it their business to cultivate the friendship of the young and ill-educated tyrant and to become intimate with him by devising all kinds of flatteries and pandering to his amusements. They continually drew him into love-affairs, crowded his leisure with entertainments, complete with wine and women, and contrived many other dissipations for him. In this way, the tyranny was gradually softened like iron in the fire. To its subjects it may have seemed to have become more benevolent and its inhumanity to have abated, but if the edge of cruelty had been blunted, this was really due to the tyrant's indolence rather than to any genuine clemency. Thus little by little, the laxity of the young ruler increased, until those 'adamantine chains',[19] by which the elder Dionysius had claimed to have left the monarchy secured, were dissolved and destroyed. The story goes that the young man once kept a drinking party going for ninety days in succession, and that during the whole of this time no person of consequence was admitted or business discussed, while the court was given over to carousing, scurrilous humour, singing, dancing and every kind of buffoonery.

8. It was therefore only natural that Dion should seem offensive, since he never indulged in any pleasure or youthful folly,[20] and so they tried to destroy his reputation. In particular, they excelled at finding plausible ways of misrepresenting his virtues as vices; for example, they described his dignity as arrogance and his frankness of speech as presumption. When he gave good advice, they made out that he was denouncing them, and when he refused to join in their misdemeanours, that he was looking down on them. And indeed, it was true that there was a certain haughtiness in his character together with an austerity which made him difficult to approach and unsociable in conversation. In fact it was not only a young man like Dionysius

whose ears had been corrupted by flattery who found him a disagreeable and tiresome companion: many of his closest friends who loved the simplicity and nobility of his disposition still blamed him for his manner, because he behaved with unnecessary harshness or discourtesy towards those who sought his help in public life. Later on Plato also wrote to him on this subject, with a foresight that was to prove prophetic, and warned him to guard against stubbornness, the companion of solitude.[21] And yet even at this time, although through force of circumstances he was regarded as the most important man in the state and the only, or at least the principal, bulwark of the storm-tossed tyranny, he knew very well that his prominence owed nothing to the tyrant's goodwill, but was actually contrary to his wishes and rested simply on the fact that he was indispensable.

9. Dion believed that this situation resulted from the tyrant's lack of education, and so he tried to interest him in liberal studies and to give him a taste of literature and science, in the hope of forming his character, delivering him from the fear of virtue, and accustoming him to take pleasure in high ideals. Dionysius did not belong by nature to the worst class of tyrants. He had suffered from his father's fear that if he acquired a judgement of his own and associated with men of good sense, he would plot against him and deprive him of his power. In consequence, he had been kept closely shut up at home, and there, because of the lack of company and his ignorance of affairs, he had spent his time making little wagons and lamp-stands and wooden chairs and tables. Indeed, the elder Dionysius had been so obsessed by his fears and so distrustful and suspicious of all and sundry that he would not even allow his hair to be cut with a barber's instruments, but arranged for one of his workmen to come and singe his hair with a live coal. Neither his brother nor his son was admitted to his apartment in the dress they happened to be wearing, but everyone was obliged to strip, to be inspected naked by the guard and to put on other clothes before entering.

On one occasion, when his brother Leptines was describing

to him the nature of some place, he took a spear from one of the guards and drew a sketch on the floor; Dionysius immediately flew into a rage against his brother and had the man who had given him the spear put to death. He used to say that he was on his guard against all those of his friends who were intelligent, because he felt sure that they would rather be tyrants themselves than a tyrant's subjects. He also executed a Sicilian named Marsyas whom he had himself promoted to a position of authority, because the man had had a dream in which he saw himself killing the tyrant. He could only have experienced the dream, Dionysius argued, because he had conceived and planned the action in his waking hours. So much had he become the prey of his own fears and the victim of all the miseries brought on by cowardice, and yet it was he who had been angry with Plato because Plato did not consider him to be the bravest man alive.[22]

10. Dion, as was said earlier, recognized that the son's character had been warped and stunted by lack of education, and so he urged him to apply himself to study and to use every means to persuade Plato, the most eminent of living philosophers, to visit Sicily. With Plato in Syracuse, Dionysius should submit himself to his teaching, and so aided, his character might accept the discipline imposed by virtue and form itself upon the fairest and most divine of models, in obedience to whose direction the universe moves from chaos towards order. In this way, he would not only win great happiness for himself, but would also ensure it for his people. He would find that the spirit of indifference in which they now obeyed him under compulsion would change to one of goodwill in response to his own justice and moderation, once these qualities were expressed in a benevolent and fatherly mode of government.[23] In short, he would become a king instead of a tyrant.[24] The celebrated adamantine chains which secured the state were not, as his father used to say, forged out of fear and force, a great fleet and a host of barbarian bodyguards, but rather out of the goodwill, the loyalty and the gratitude which are engendered by the exercise of virtue and justice. These forces, although they are more pliant than the stiff,

harsh bonds of absolute rule, are the ties which prove the strongest in enabling the leadership of one man to endure. And apart
from these considerations, so Dion argued, it showed a mean
and ignoble spirit in a ruler to clothe his body magnificently and
decorate his home with fine and luxurious furniture but to
achieve no greater dignity in his conversation and in his dealings
with others than any ordinary man, and to neglect to adorn the
royal palace of his soul in a manner worthy of a king.

11. Dion repeatedly pressed this advice on the young man and
skilfully introduced some of Plato's own ideas into his arguments, until Dionysius became impatient, indeed almost obsessed
with the desire to acquaint himself with Plato's teachings and
to enjoy his company. Before long he was writing letter after
letter to Athens, while at the same time Plato received further
advice from Dion, as well as from a number of Pythagorean
philosophers in Italy. All of these last urged him to make the
journey, establish his influence over this youthful soul, which
was now being tossed and buffeted about as if it were on the
seas of great power and absolute rule, and steady it with his
balanced reasonings. So Plato yielded to these requests, though
he did so rather out of a sense of shame, as he has written,[25] so
as to dispel the impression that he was only interested in theory
and was unwilling to put it to the test of action.[26] At the same
time, he hoped that if he could purify the mind of this ruler,
who seemed to dominate all the Sicilians, he might be able to
cure the disorders of the whole island.

Dion's enemies, however, became alarmed at this transformation in Dionysius, and they persuaded him to recall Philistus[27]
from exile. This man was well versed in literature and possessed long experience of the ways of tyrants, and by this move
the courtiers hoped to offset the influence of Plato and his philosophy. Philistus had played a most active part in establishing
the tyranny from the beginning, and for a long time he had
commanded the garrison which guarded the acropolis. There
was also a story that he had been the lover of the mother of the
elder Dionysius and that the tyrant had not been entirely
ignorant of this. But when Leptines, who had two daughters by

a woman whom he had seduced while she was living with another man, gave one of his daughters in marriage to Philistus, Dionysius, who had not been told of the matter, became angry, and had Leptines' wife[28] put in chains, imprisoned Philistus and later banished him. He took refuge with some friends on the Adriatic and there, it seems, wrote the greater part of his history during his enforced leisure. He remained in exile for the rest of the tyrant's lifetime, but after the latter's death, as I have explained, the envy which the other courtiers felt towards Dion prompted them to arrange his recall, since they saw in Philistus a man whom they could count on to serve their purposes and to be a staunch supporter of autocratic rule.

12. Accordingly, as soon as Philistus returned, he began to work closely with the supporters of the tyranny. At the same time, others began to lodge accusations and slanders against Dion, and in particular they charged him with having plotted with Theodotus and Heracleides to overthrow the government. It seems he had hopes that with the help of Plato's presence the autocratic and arbitrary nature of the tyranny could gradually be relaxed and Dionysius transformed into a moderate and constitutional ruler. On the other hand, he had made up his mind that if Dionysius resisted his efforts and refused to be softened, he would depose him and restore power to the hands of the Syracusan people. This was not because he was in favour of democracy in itself, but because he considered it in every way preferable to a tyranny in the absence of a stable aristocracy.

13. This was the state of affairs when Plato arrived in Sicily,[29] and at first he was received with wonderful demonstrations of kindness and respect. One of the royal chariots, magnificently decked out, was waiting to receive him as he stepped ashore, and the tyrant offered up a sacrifice of thanksgiving for the great blessing which had been granted to his government. The sobriety of the royal banquets, the decorous tone of the court and the tolerance displayed by Dionysius himself in his dealings with the public, all combined to inspire the citizens with

wondrous hopes of change. The study of letters and philosophy became all the fashion, and it is said that so many people
began to study geometry that the very palace was filled with
dust.[30] There is a story that a few days later, one of the customary sacrifices was held in the grounds of the palace and that
the herald, according to the usual formula, intoned a prayer
that the tyranny might remain unshaken for many years, whereupon Dionysius cried out, 'Stop cursing us!' This greatly
disturbed Philistus and his party, who concluded that if Plato
had already brought about such a change in the young man's
ideas, even after this brief association, his influence would
become irresistible if he were allowed the time to get to know
Dionysius intimately.

14. And so the courtiers no longer abused Dion singly and in
secrecy, but attacked him all together and quite openly. They
declared that he had caused the tyrant to be charmed and
bewitched by Plato's doctrines, and that his motives for doing
so were now transparent: his plan was to persuade Dionysius
to give up his authority of his own accord, after which Dion
would assume power and hand it over to Aristomache's children, whose uncle he was. Some of them pretended to be deeply
indignant at the idea that the Athenians, who had once invaded
Sicily with a great military and naval expedition and had perished utterly before they could take Syracuse,[31] should now
succeed in overthrowing the tyranny of Dionysius[32] through
the efforts of a single sophist. Plato would persuade the young
man to shun his 10,000 bodyguards, give up his fleet of 400
triremes and his 10,000 cavalry and many times more hoplites,
and all this in order to pursue the ineffable good[33] in the Academy, to make geometry his guide to happiness and to hand over
the blessings of power, of wealth and of luxury so that they
could be enjoyed by Dion's nephews and nieces. The result of
these tactics was that Dionysius at first became suspicious and
then began to show his displeasure and anger more openly. At
this point a letter was secretly brought to him which Dion had
written to the representatives of Carthage. In it he advised them

that whenever they opened their negotiations for peace with Dionysius, they should not hold their conference without his being present: he assured them that with his help there would be no possibility of mishap in obtaining a settlement. According to Timaeus, Dionysius read this letter over to Philistus, and after taking his advice deceived Dion by pretending to be reconciled with him. He made out that he harboured no extreme feelings and that their differences were at an end, and then, after he had led Dion alone down to the sea below the acropolis, he showed him the letter and accused him of plotting with the Carthaginians against him. When Dion tried to defend himself, the tyrant refused to listen, but immediately forced him to board a small boat just as he was, and ordered the sailors to put him ashore on the Italian coast.[34]

15. When this became known, Dionysius was considered to have acted very harshly, and the women of his household went into mourning. But the spirits of the rest of the Syracusans rose and they began to look forward to a revolution and a speedy change of government, partly because the treatment of Dion had caused such a stir, and partly because others would now feel distrustful of the tyrant. Dionysius took fright at this and tried to pacify Dion's friends and the women by making out that he had not banished him, but merely sent him out of harm's way, for fear that he himself might be provoked by the man's stubbornness into doing him some mischief if Dion remained at home. He also put two ships at the disposal of Dion's family and told his kinsmen to embark any servants or possessions of his that they might choose, and have them sent to the Peloponnese. Now Dion was very rich, and his house and style of living were kept up on an almost royal scale, and so his friends collected his valuables and sent them to him. Besides his own property, the women of the court and his supporters also sent him many gifts: in this way, so far as wealth and possessions were concerned, he cut a brilliant figure among the Greeks, and the riches he displayed, even as an exile, gave some hint of the power and resources of the tyrant.

16. Dionysius at once transferred Plato to the acropolis, and here under the pretext of hospitality he arranged to give him a guard of honour: the object of this was to prevent him from sailing away to join Dion and revealing to the world how badly Dion had been treated. But as time passed and their association continued, Dionysius learnt to tolerate Plato's company and conversation, much as a wild animal becomes accustomed to the presence of a human being, and he developed a passion for him which was characteristic of a tyrant: he demanded that Plato should respond to his love alone and admire him above all others, and he even offered to hand over the tyranny to him on condition that Plato would not prefer Dion's friendship to his. This passion of Dionysius was a great misfortune for Plato, since, like most lovers, the tyrant was violently jealous, would often fly into a rage and then soon afterwards beg to be forgiven. He was also extravagantly eager to listen to Plato's theories and take part in his philosophical discussions, but he felt ashamed of them when he was in the company of those who wanted him to break off his studies on the grounds that they would corrupt him.[35]

Meanwhile a war had broken out, and Dionysius sent Plato away, promising that he would recall Dion in the following summer.[36] He promptly broke his promise, but he continued to send Dion the revenues from his property and asked Plato to excuse his change of plan concerning Dion's return, which was occasioned by the war. As soon as peace was concluded, he would send for Dion; Dionysius asked Dion to stay quiet and to refrain from making any revolutionary attempts or speaking ill of him among the Greeks.

17. Plato tried to carry out these requests. He turned Dion's attention to philosophy and kept him with him in the Academy. Dion was living in Athens at the house of Callippus, one of his friends, but he also bought a house in the country for pleasure, and later when he sailed for Sicily he gave it to Speusippus,[37] who was Dion's closest friend and most frequent companion in Athens. Plato was anxious that Dion's austere disposition should be mellowed and sweetened by the company of men

who possessed some social charm and whose wit was good-
natured and well timed. Speusippus was a man of this kind: he
is referred to in Timon's *Lampoons*[38] as being good at making jokes. Besides this, when Plato himself was called upon to
provide a chorus of boys for a public festival, Dion undertook
both the training and the expense. Plato encouraged him to
earn this distinction in the eyes of the Athenians, because he
was more concerned to create goodwill for Dion than fame for
himself.

Dion also travelled to a number of other cities in Greece,
where he visited their nobility and political leaders and took
part in their recreations and festivities. During these visits he
never showed himself in any way boorish, arrogant or effeminate: his behaviour was always conspicuous for its moderation,
virtue, courage and a becoming devotion to literature and philosophy. By this means he earned the goodwill and admiration
of all he met, and many cities decreed him public honours. The
Lacedaemonians even made him a citizen of Sparta and disregarded any offence which this might cause to Dionysius, who
was at that time their staunch ally against the Thebans.[39] On
another occasion, it is said that Dion was invited to visit
Ptoedorus the Megarian and went to his house. This man, it
appears, was one of the most wealthy and influential citizens
of Megara, and so when Dion saw that there was a crowd of
people at his door and that the number of visitors made it difficult to approach him, he turned to his friends who seemed
indignant at this hindrance, and asked them, 'Why should we
blame this man? We ourselves used to do exactly the same thing
in Syracuse.'

18. As time went on Dionysius began to grow jealous of Dion,
and to fear the popularity which he was creating for himself
among the Greeks. He stopped remitting the revenues from his
property and handed over Dion's estates to his own officials.
However, he was anxious to efface the bad reputation he had
earned among the philosophers because of his treatment of
Plato, and he therefore gathered at his court a number of men
with some pretensions to learning. But as he was ambitious to

outshine them all in discussion, he was obliged to make use, often incorrectly, of ideas he had picked up from Plato but had only half digested. So he began once more to long for Plato's company and reproached himself for not having made the best use of him when he was in Sicily or paid more attention to his admirable lessons. And since, like so many tyrants, he was erratic in his impulses and impatient to obtain whatever he desired, he at once set his heart on bringing Plato back. He was ready to try anything to get his way, and so he persuaded Archytas[40] and his fellow Pythagoreans to send the invitation to Plato and to guarantee his offer, for it was through Plato that he had first entered into friendly dealings with these philosophers. They sent Archedemus to Plato, and Dionysius also dispatched a trireme and several of his friends to beg Plato to return. The tyrant also wrote to Plato in clear and explicit terms, telling him that there would be no concessions or favours for Dion unless the philosopher agreed to come to Sicily, but that much could be expected if he did.[41] Dion was also pressed by his wife and sister to urge Plato to let the tyrant have his way and not provide any excuse for treating him still more harshly. It was in this way that Plato ventured for the third time, as he describes it, into the straits of Scylla and *shaped his course yet again within reach of the deadly Charybdis*.[42]

19. Plato's coming filled Dionysius with great joy and filled Sicily with high hopes. The Sicilians all earnestly prayed that Plato should prevail over Philistus and philosophy prove stronger than tyranny. The women too, especially Aristomache and Arete, gave Plato their support, and Dionysius bestowed on him a special mark of confidence which nobody else enjoyed – the privilege of coming into his presence without being searched. The tyrant also pressed gifts of money on him, repeatedly offering him large sums, but Plato would accept none of them. At this, Aristippus of Cyrene,[43] who was present on one of these occasions, remarked that Dionysius' generosity was of the safest kind: he offered small sums to men such as himself who wanted more, and large ones to Plato, who refused everything.

After the first formal courtesies had been exchanged, Plato

raised the subject of Dion. Dionysius first put off the discussion, and later there were reproaches and quarrels. Nobody else knew of these, since Dionysius was careful to conceal them, and by paying honours and assiduous attention to Plato he tried to draw him away from his friendship for Dion. Plato at first kept silent about the tyrant's treachery and double-dealing, endured it as best he could, and played the part that was required of him. Then, while they were on these terms and imagined that nobody else knew of this situation, Helicon of Cyzicus, one of Plato's close friends, predicted an eclipse of the sun.[44] This duly took place, as he had forecast, whereupon the tyrant expressed his admiration and presented him with a talent of silver. At this Aristippus put on a bantering tone towards the other philosophers and declared that he, too, had a remarkable event to predict. When they pressed him to tell them what it was, he replied, 'Well then, I predict that in a short while Dionysius will fall out with Plato.'

Finally, Dionysius sold Dion's property and kept the money for himself. He then removed Plato from his quarters in the gardens of the palace and lodged him among his mercenaries. The soldiers hated him and wanted to kill him because they believed that he was trying to persuade Dionysius to give up the tyranny and live without a bodyguard.

20. As soon as Archytas and his friends learnt that Plato was in such danger, they immediately sent a galley with messengers to demand that Dionysius should send him back, and they reminded the tyrant that they had guaranteed Plato's safety when he had agreed to sail to Syracuse. Dionysius did his best to disguise his hostility towards Plato by giving banquets in his honour and doing him various kindnesses before his departure, but he could not resist letting fall a remark to this effect: 'I dare say, Plato, that you will have many things to say against me to your fellow philosophers,' to which Plato answered with a smile, 'God forbid that we should have so little to talk about in the Academy that we need mention your name at all.' It was on these terms, so it is said, that they parted, but Plato's own version does not entirely agree with this account.[45]

21. Dion had already been angered by these events, but it was the treatment of his wife that soon afterwards turned him into an open enemy of Dionysius. Plato also referred enigmatically to this subject in a letter to Dionysius.[46] What had happened was the following. After Dion's banishment and at the time when Dionysius was sending Plato back to Athens for the first time, he asked Plato to sound Dion as to whether he would object to his wife being married to another man. There had been rumours, which may have been true or may have been fabricated by Dion's enemies, that his marriage had not been happy and that he did not live harmoniously with his wife. After Plato had returned to Athens and had discussed the subject at length with Dion, he sent a letter to Dionysius. Part of this concerned other matters and was phrased in a manner which would be clear to everybody, but on this particular topic he used allusive language, which only Dionysius could understand: he mentioned that he had spoken about the affair with Dion, who, it was clear, would be furious if Dionysius carried out any such plan. For a time, then, as there were still hopes that a reconciliation was possible, Dionysius did nothing to change his sister's situation, but allowed her to continue to live with Dion's young son. But when it became clear that the breach between the two men was irreparable and Plato, who had come to Sicily again, had incurred the tyrant's displeasure and been sent away, then Dionysius compelled Arete against her will to marry one of his friends named Timocrates.

In this action, at least, Dionysius fell short of the tolerance shown by his father. For the elder Dionysius had, so it seems, made an enemy of Polyxenus, the husband of his sister Theste. Polyxenus feared for his life, escaped from Sicily and fled into exile, whereupon Dionysius sent for his sister and reproached her because she had known of her husband's plan to escape but had told her brother nothing about it. Theste was quite undismayed and answered him confidently, 'Do you think, Dionysius, that I am such a mean and cowardly wife that if I had known beforehand that my husband was planning to escape I would not have sailed away with him and shared his fortunes? The truth is that I knew nothing of it. If I had, it would have been

more honourable for me to have been called the wife of Polyxenus the exile than the sister of Dionysius the tyrant.' It is said
that Dionysius admired her for speaking out so boldly, and the
Syracusans also greatly respected her for her courage, so much
so that even after the tyranny had been overthrown, they continued to treat her with the honour and deference that they
paid to royalty, and when she died, the citizens by public consent walked in procession at her funeral. This is a digression,
but the story is relevant to my subject.

22. From this point onwards Dion began to prepare for war.[47]
Plato himself refused to take any part in such an attempt, partly
out of respect for the bond of hospitality between Dionysius
and himself and partly because of his age.[48] However, Speusippus and Dion's other friends rallied to his support and urged
him to liberate Sicily, which they said beckoned to him and was
ready to receive him with open arms. It seems that during Plato's
stay in Syracuse, Speusippus and his friends had circulated
among the people and made it their business to discover their
feelings. At first the Syracusans had been alarmed by the frankness of Speusippus' talk and suspected that this was a trap set
by the tyrant to test their loyalty, but after a time they came to
trust him. On every side Speusippus heard the same story: they
all begged and entreated Dion to come, not to bring ships or
cavalry or hoplites, but simply to step into an open boat and
lend the Syracusans his name and his person in their struggle
against Dionysius. Dion was heartened by this news from
Speusippus, and through the agency of others he began secretly
to recruit mercenaries, taking care to conceal his plans. Many
statesmen and philosophers gave him their help, including
Timonides of Leucas and Eudemus of Cyprus, concerning whom
after his death Aristotle wrote his dialogue On the Soul.[49] They
also engaged Miltas of Thessaly, a soothsayer who had studied
in the Academy. Yet of all the Syracusans who had been exiled
by the tyrant – and there were no less than a thousand of
them – only twenty-five joined the expedition: the remainder
played the coward and shrank from it.[50] The starting-point was
the island of Zacynthus, and here the soldiers assembled.[51]

Their total strength was less than eight hundred, but these were all men of some note who had gained a reputation from their service in many great campaigns. They were in superb physical condition, for experience and daring they had no equals in the world, and they were fully capable of rousing and inspiring to action the thousands whom Dion expected to rally to him in Sicily.

23. When these men learnt that the expedition was directed against Dionysius and Sicily, they were at first dismayed and condemned the whole enterprise. They could only suppose either that Dion was being driven on like a madman in some wild fit of rage, or else that he had lost all rational hopes of success. There seemed to be no other reason to throw himself into such a desperate undertaking, and they were furious with their commanders and recruiting-officers for not having warned them of the object of the war at the very beginning. But then Dion addressed them, explained in detail the weakness and rottenness of Dionysius' regime and announced that he was taking them not merely as fighting troops but as leaders of the Syracusans and the rest of the Sicilians who had long been ripe for rebellion. He was followed by Alcimenes, one of the most influential and distinguished of the Achaeans serving with the expedition, who spoke to the same effect, and finally the men were convinced and their doubts set at rest.

It was now midsummer,[52] the Etesian winds[53] were blowing steadily at sea and the moon was at the full. Dion prepared a magnificent sacrifice to Apollo and marched in solemn procession to the temple with his troops, who paraded in full armour. After the ceremony he entertained them to a banquet at the stadium of the Zacynthians. Here, as they reclined on their couches, they marvelled at the splendour of the gold and silver drinking-vessels and of the tables which far exceeded the means of a private citizen, and they reflected that a man who possessed such wealth and was by then past middle life, as in Dion's case,[54] would never attempt such a risky undertaking unless he had solid hopes of success and could count upon friends on the spot who could offer him unlimited resources.

24. No sooner had the libations and the customary prayers been offered than there followed an eclipse of the moon. Dion and his friends found nothing surprising in this, since they knew that eclipses recurred at regular intervals, and also that the shadow which is projected upon the moon is produced by the interposition of the earth between it and the sun.[55] But as the soldiers were dismayed at the portent and needed to be reassured, Miltas the diviner rose to his feet in the midst of the company and urged them to take heart. He assured them that the expedition would succeed, since through this portent the gods were foretelling that something which was then at the height of its splendour would be eclipsed. There was no regime whose splendour exceeded that of Dionysius' tyranny, and it was its light that they would extinguish as soon as they arrived in Sicily. Miltas made public his interpretation of the eclipse to all and sundry. But as for the phenomenon of the bees, which were seen to be settling in swarms on the sterns of the ships, he told Dion and his friends privately he feared this might signify that their expedition would prosper at the start, but that after flourishing for a short while, it would wither away. It is said that Dionysius also witnessed a number of prodigies at this time. An eagle snatched a spear from one of his guards, flew up into the air with it and then let it fall into the sea. Besides this, the sea-water which washes against the base of the acropolis of Syracuse became sweet and drinkable for a whole day, as all those who tasted it could perceive. Also, a number of pigs were born within his realm, which were perfectly formed in other respects but possessed no ears. This was interpreted by the diviners as a sign of rebellion, since it indicated that the people would no longer obey the tyrant's commands. The sweetness of the sea-water, so they said, heralded a change from harsh and oppressive times to more agreeable circumstances. As for the eagle, this bird, they said, is a servant of Zeus, while the spear is the symbol of power and sovereignty, and hence the portent indicated that the greatest of the gods intended to remove and annihilate the tyranny. This at any rate is the account which we have from Theopompus.[56]

25. It required no more than two merchant vessels to accommodate Dion's troops, and they were accompanied by a third small transport and two thirty-oared galleys. Besides the arms which the soldiers carried, Dion took with him 2,000 shields, great quantities of spears and other missiles and ample stocks of provisions, so that there should be no risk of running short during the voyage, since they were putting themselves at the mercy of wind and waves and sailing across the open sea: they were afraid to hug the coast, because they had learnt that Philistus was lying in wait for them with a fleet off Iapygia.[57] For twelve days they sailed with a light and gentle breeze and on the thirteenth they were off Pachynus, a headland of Sicily. Here Protus their pilot urged them to disembark without any delay, since if they were once driven off shore and did not take advantage of this landfall they would be tossed about in the open sea for many days and nights while they waited for a southerly wind in the summer season. Dion was afraid to disembark so near the enemy and wished to land further along the coast, and so he sailed past Pachynus. Soon afterwards a violent northerly gale swept down on them, whipped up the sea and drove the squadron away from Sicily: at the same time the sky was filled with flashes of lightning, peals of thunder and sheets of torrential rain, the storm coinciding with the rising of Arcturus.[58] The sailors were dismayed and had quite lost their reckoning, until they discovered that their ships were being driven by the waves upon the island of Cercina[59] off the coast of Africa, at a point where the cliffs present a craggy, precipitous face that falls sheer to the water. After they had narrowly escaped being driven ashore and dashed to pieces against the rocks, they heaved and thrust their way along with great difficulty, using their punting-poles until the storm gradually abated, when they learnt from a vessel they hailed that they had arrived at what were known as the 'heads' of the Great Syrtis.[60] They were by now disheartened to find themselves becalmed and were drifting helplessly up and down the coast when a gentle breeze sprang up from the south, which was so little expected that they could scarcely believe in the change. Gradually the wind freshened and gathered strength, and so

they set all the sail they could, offered up prayers to the gods, and skimmed across the open sea from Africa towards Sicily. For five days, they ran on at full speed and finally dropped anchor at Minoa, a small coastal town in the western part of Sicily, which was controlled by the Carthaginians.

It so happened that Synalus, the Carthaginian commander of the region, was a guest-friend[61] of Dion's, but as he knew nothing of the expedition nor of Dion's presence there, he tried to prevent the troops from landing. The Greeks charged ashore fully armed, and although in obedience to Dion's orders they did not kill a single man, they routed their opponents, entered the town on their heels and seized possession of it. But as soon as the two commanders had met and greeted one another, Dion handed back the town to the Carthaginian without any damage having been done, while for his part Synalus treated the soldiers hospitably and supplied Dion with all the stores he needed.

26. What gave them the greatest encouragement of all was the lucky accident of Dionysius' absence from Syracuse at that moment, for it so happened that he had just set off for Italy with a fleet of eighty ships. So although Dion urged his men to rest and recover after the hardships of their long voyage, they would have none of it but were eager to seize the opportunity and clamoured for him to lead them on to Syracuse. He therefore stored his surplus arms and baggage at Minoa, asked Synalus to send them on to him when opportunity offered and set out for Syracuse. As he marched, he was joined first by two hundred horsemen from Acragas who lived near Ecnomum, and then by a contingent from Gela.

The news of his movements was quickly brought to Syracuse. There Timocrates, who had married Dion's wife, the sister of Dionysius, and was the most prominent of Dionysius' friends who had remained in Syracuse, at once sent off a messenger with letters reporting Dion's arrival. At the same time he took measures to forestall any disturbances or uprisings in the city. All the Syracusans were excited at the news of the invasion, but they remained quiet because they were as yet uncertain what to believe and were afraid of the outcome. But an extra-ordinary mischance befell the bearer of the letters. After crossing the straits to Italy, he passed through the territory of Rhegium, and as he was hurrying on to Dionysius at Caulonia, he fell in with an acquaintance who was carrying a sacrificial victim which had just been slaughtered. His friend gave him a piece of the meat and he continued his journey with all speed. Then after he had walked for part of the night, he was obliged by sheer exhaustion to take a little sleep and lay down just as he was in a wood by the roadside. As he slept, a prowling wolf, attracted by the scent, came up, seized the meat which had been fastened to the wallet containing the letters and made off with both. When the man awoke and saw what had happened, he spent a long time wandering about and searching in vain for the lost wallet, but as he could not find it, he decided not to go to the tyrant without the letters, but to run off and stay out of harm's way.

27. So Dionysius was to learn that war had broken out in Sicily from other sources and only after some time had passed. Meanwhile, as Dion advanced, the people of Camarina came over to him, and large numbers of the peasants in the districts surrounding Syracuse rose in revolt and attached themselves to him. Next, Dion sent a false report to the Leontines and Campanians who were garrisoning the plateau west of Syracuse, which is known as Epipolae; he informed them that he intended to attack their cities first, with the result that they deserted Timocrates and went off to help their compatriots. When the news of their movements was brought to Dion at his camp at Acrae, he roused his troops while it was still dark and advanced to the River Anapus, which flows a little over a mile from the city. There he halted and offered sacrifice to the river, addressing his prayers to the rising sun. Immediately, the diviners announced that the gods would grant him victory. His followers had noticed that Dion was wearing a wreath on his head while he was sacrific-ing, and straightaway with a single impulse they all crowned their heads with garlands. No fewer than 5,000 men had joined him on the march, and although these were wretchedly equipped

and carried only such improvised weapons as they could find, their spirit made up for their lack of arms, so that when Dion ordered the advance, they ran forward with shouts of joy, encouraging one another to regain their freedom.

28. As for the townsfolk of Syracuse, the most prominent and best educated of the citizens put on clean clothes and went to meet the invaders at the gates, while the populace set upon the tyrant's supporters and seized the informers. These were an abominable race, detested by gods and men alike, who made it their business to circulate among the citizens and report on their opinions and conversations to the tyrant. They were the first to suffer for their misdeeds and were beaten to death by any of the townspeople who found them. Timocrates was unable to join the garrison within the acropolis and so took a horse and galloped out of the city; in his flight he created panic and confusion by spreading exaggerated reports of Dion's strength, for he was anxious to avoid the suspicion of having surrendered the city to an insignificant force. Meanwhile, Dion was close at hand and presently came into view, marching at the head of his troops, clad in splendid armour and flanked by his brother Megacles on one side and Callippus the Athenian on the other, both of them crowned with garlands. After them came a bodyguard of a hundred mercenaries and next the officers leading the rest of the army in good order. The Syracusans looked on and welcomed the troops as if this were a sacred and religious procession to celebrate the return to the city of liberty and popular government after an absence of forty-eight years.

29. Dion entered the city by the Temenitid gate and here he ordered his trumpets to be sounded so as to quieten the shouting. Then his herald proclaimed that Dion and Megacles had come to overthrow the tyranny and that they declared the Syracusans and the rest of the Sicilians to be free of the rule of Dionysius. Next, as he wished to address the people himself, he marched through the quarter of Achradina, while on each side of the street the Syracusans set out tables, sacrificial victims and bowls of wine, and each group as Dion passed strewed

flowers before him and hailed him with prayers and vows as if he were a god. Below the acropolis and the Five Gates, there stood a tall and conspicuous sun-dial, built by Dionysius. Dion sprang up on this, addressed the citizens and urged them to defend their liberty. Then the people in an ecstasy of joy and gratitude appointed Dion and Megacles generals with absolute powers, and besides this, at the two men's own request, they elected twenty colleagues, half of whom were chosen from the exiles who had returned with Dion. The diviners found it a most happy omen that Dion, while he was addressing the people, should have placed his feet on the tyrant's pretentious monument; but because it was a sun-dial on which he was standing at the moment when he was elected general, they were afraid that his cause might suffer some swift change of fortune.

After this Dion went on to capture Epipolae and release the citizens who were imprisoned there, and he cut off the acropolis by building a wall.[62] Then on the seventh day after Dion's arrival, Dionysius entered the acropolis by sea, and wagons began reaching Dion with the arms and armour he had left with Synalus. He distributed these as far as possible among the citizens, while the rest armed themselves as best they could and eagerly offered to serve as hoplites under him.

30. At first Dionysius sent emissaries privately to Dion in the hope of making terms with him. Dion's reply was that any negotiations with the Syracusans must be carried out publicly, because they were a free people. The tyrant's envoys then returned with a generous offer, in which he promised a reduction of taxes and an easing of the burden of military service, subject to the people's vote of consent. But the Syracusans only laughed at these proposals, and Dion told the envoys that Dionysius was not to continue negotiations with the people unless he formally renounced his sovereignty: if he agreed to this, Dion would guarantee his personal safety and obtain any other reasonable concession that was in his power, bearing in mind that they were related. Dionysius accepted these conditions and again sent his representatives to invite some of the Syracusans to come to the acropolis: he proposed to discuss

with them a general settlement for the common benefit, with concessions to be made by both sides. Dion chose the delegates, who were at once sent to meet the tyrant, and rumours began to reach the Syracusans from the acropolis that Dionysius really intended to abdicate, and would do this to claim the credit for himself, rather than let Dion enjoy it.

All this, however, was nothing but a treacherous pretence on Dionysius' part, which had been carefully devised to trick the Syracusans. He promptly arrested the delegates who came to him from the city, issued a ration of neat wine to his mercenaries and ordered them to make a sortie at dawn to attack the siege-works which had been erected so as to cut off the acropolis. The manoeuvre achieved complete surprise. The barbarians[63] set to work boldly and with loud shouts to demolish the wall; then they attacked the Syracusans so fiercely that no one had the courage to stand his ground, except for a number of Dion's mercenaries who were the first to hear the commotion and ran to the rescue. Even these troops were at first uncertain as to how they could help, and unable to hear what was being said to them, for the Syracusans were shouting wildly, running back in panic through the midst of the mercenaries and breaking their ranks. In the end Dion, when he saw that he could not make his orders heard, determined to show by his own example what ought to be done, and charged into the midst of the enemy.

A fierce and bloody battle raged around him, since he was as well known to the enemy as he was to his own troops, and both sides converged on him at the same moment, shouting at the top of their voices. He had reached an age at which he was no longer agile enough for this kind of hand-to-hand fighting, but his courage and vigour enabled him to stand his ground and cut down all his attackers, until he was wounded in the hand by a spear. By then, too, his breast-plate had been so battered that it could hardly give protection against the thrusts and missiles which rained upon him; finally, he was wounded by a number of spears and lances which had pierced his shield, and when these were broken off, he fell to the ground. His soldiers carried him away and he ordered Timonides to take command of the front-line, while he himself mounted his horse and rode round the city, rallying the Syracusans who had fled. He ordered up a detachment of his mercenaries who had been posted to guard the quarter of Achradina, and began leading these troops, who were fresh and eager, against the flagging barbarians, who had already begun to despair of victory. Dionysius' troops had counted on overrunning and capturing the whole city at their first onslaught, but now that they had unexpectedly come up against men who knew how to fight and counterattack, they began to fall back towards the acropolis. As soon as they gave ground, the Greeks pressed them all the harder, and finally they turned tail and took refuge within the walls of the acropolis. They had killed seventy-four of Dion's men and lost many of their own.

31. This was a brilliant victory for Dion, and the Syracusans presented his mercenaries with a hundred minas,[64] while the mercenaries honoured Dion with a crown of gold. Soon after some heralds arrived from Dionysius bringing letters to Dion from the women of his family. One of these was addressed 'To his father from Hipparinus', which was the name of Dion's son, although according to Timaeus he was named Aretaeus after his mother Arete; but for these details I think we should accept the evidence of Timonides, since he was a friend and comrade of Dion. At any rate, the letters from the women, which were full of supplications and entreaties, were read aloud to the Syracusans, but they did not wish the letter which purported to be from Dion's son to be opened in public. However, Dion overruled them and insisted on reading it aloud. It turned out to be from Dionysius, who was nominally addressing himself to Dion, but in reality was appealing to the Syracusan people. On the face of it, the writer was pleading his case and justifying his actions, but the letter was really intended to bring discredit on Dion. It recalled how devotedly Dion had worked for the tyranny, and at the same time it threatened the persons of those dearest to him, his sister, his child and his wife. It combined importunate demands with lamentations, and, what angered him most of all, with the proposal that far from abolishing the tyranny, Dion should carry it on himself.

The writer urged him not to set free a people who hated him and would never forget the wrongs done them, but to wield power himself and so ensure the safety of his friends and his family.

32. When these letters had been read aloud, it did not occur to the Syracusans, as it should have done, to admire Dion's altruism and magnanimity in upholding the ideals of honour and justice against the claims of his personal loyalties. Instead, they became alarmed that he might come under strong pressure to spare the tyrant, and so they at once began to look around for other leaders, and they were particularly excited at the news that Heracleides was just putting into the harbour. This man was one of those who had been exiled by Dionysius. He possessed some experience as a soldier and had gained a reputation through the commands he had held under the tyrants, but he was a man of erratic and unstable disposition and not at all reliable as a colleague in an enterprise in which power and prestige were at stake. He had already fallen out with Dion in the Peloponnese and had determined to sail against the tyrant with an expedition under his own command.[65] But when he arrived in Syracuse with a squadron of seven triremes and three transports, he found Dionysius once more blockaded and the Syracusans elated at their victory. He, therefore, immediately set out to ingratiate himself with the masses. He possessed a natural facility for winning over and swaying the emotions of the populace, which loved to be courted, and he was able to gain his ends and draw the people to his side all the more easily because they were repelled by Dion's grave and serious manner. They found this too austere and quite out of place in a public man: the power they had suddenly acquired had made them careless and arrogant, and they expected populist measures before they had become a people.

33. Accordingly, they first summoned the assembly on their own initiative and elected Heracleides admiral. At this, Dion came forward and protested that by conferring this appointment upon Heracleides they had abolished the command which

they had previously entrusted to him, for it was impossible to regard himself as a commander-in-chief with absolute powers if another officer wielded authority over the fleet. The Syracusans then reluctantly cancelled Heracleides' appointment. Dion afterwards summoned him to his house and mildly reproved him, pointing out that he was acting neither honourably nor even sensibly in starting a quarrel concerning a matter of prestige at a moment of crisis, when the least false step might ruin their cause. He then summoned a fresh assembly, nominated Heracleides as admiral and prevailed upon the citizens to allow him a bodyguard, such as he possessed himself. Heracleides then professed great respect for Dion, so far as his words and his manner went, acknowledged his indebtedness and obeyed his orders with a great show of humility, but in secret he undermined the loyalty of the populace, stirred up the revolutionaries and, by distracting him with disturbances on every side, manoeuvred him into a most difficult position. If he were to urge the people to let Dionysius leave the acropolis under a truce, he would be accused of sparing and protecting the despot, while if he took care not to give offence in this way and merely continued the siege, he would appear to be deliberately prolonging the war in order to keep himself in command and overawe the citizens.

34. Now there was a man named Sosis, who, simply through his audacity and lack of principle, had gained a certain reputation in Syracuse, where people imagined that liberty was inseparable from the kind of licence of speech which he enjoyed. This man, who was secretly plotting against Dion, first of all stood up one day in the assembly and abused the Syracusans for failing to understand the fact that they had merely exchanged an imbecile and drunken tyrant for a vigilant and sober one; then, having thus openly shown himself an enemy of Dion's, he left the assembly. The next day he was seen running through the city naked, with his head and face covered with blood, as though he were fleeing from some pursuers. He rushed into the market-place in this condition, cried out that he had been attacked by Dion's mercenaries and showed his wounded head

to the spectators. He found many who were ready to share his grievances and take his side, and who declared that Dion was guilty of a monstrous act of tyranny if he was attempting to deprive the citizens of freedom of speech by acts of murder or threats against their lives. A noisy and disorderly meeting of the assembly then gathered, but in spite of their riotous mood Dion came before them and spoke in his own defence. He pointed out that Sosis was a brother of one of Dionysius' guards and had been persuaded by him to stir up dissensions and disturbances, since Dionysius' only hope of safety now lay in the chance of making the citizens distrust and quarrel with one another. Meanwhile, some physicians examined Sosis' wound and discovered that it had been made by a glancing rather than a vertical stroke. A blow dealt by a sword leaves a wound which is deepest in the middle, because of the weight of the blade, but the gash on Sosis' head was shallow throughout its length; besides this it was not one continuous cut, as it would be had it been inflicted with a single stroke, but there were a number of incisions, as one would expect if he had left off because of the pain and begun again. Apart from this evidence, a number of well-known citizens brought a razor to the assembly and testified that as they were walking along the street Sosis had met them all covered in blood and explained that he was running away from Dion's mercenaries, who had just wounded him; the witnesses at once ran after the alleged attackers, but could find nobody. What they did find, however, was a razor lying under a hollow stone near the place from which Sosis had been seen coming out.

35. By this time Sosis' case had been almost completely discredited, and when in addition to all these proofs his servants gave evidence that he had left his house while it was still dark, alone and carrying a razor, Dion's accusers dropped their charges and the people condemned Sosis to death and were reconciled with Dion.

They continued to be as suspicious as ever of the mercenaries, all the more so since most of the operations against Dionysius were now carried on by sea: this was because of the arrival of Philistus, who had sailed over from Iapygia with a large fleet of triremes to help Dionysius. As the mercenaries were hoplites, the Syracusans concluded that there would be no further need for them in the war: indeed, they actually imagined that these troops depended to some extent upon the citizens for their protection, since the Syracusans themselves were seamen and their power lay in their fleet. Their spirits rose still higher after a successful action at sea: here they defeated Philistus[66] and then proceeded to treat him in a most inhuman fashion. Ephorus,[67] it is true, says that Philistus killed himself when his ship was captured, but Timonides, who was present with Dion throughout these events, from the very beginning, describes in a letter to Speusippus how Philistus was taken alive when his trireme ran aground. The Syracusans then stripped off his breast-plate and humiliated him in his old age by exposing his naked body. After this they beheaded him and handed over his corpse to the boys of the city, with orders to drag it through the quarter of Achradina and throw it into the stone quarries. Timaeus gives more details of these outrages, and says that when Philistus was dead the boys tied a rope to his lame leg and hauled his body through the streets, while all the Syracusans looked on and jeered. They laughed at the spectacle of this man being dragged about by the leg, since it was he who had once told Dionysius that he must not try to escape from his tyranny with a swift horse, but must wait until he was pulled down from it by the leg. Philistus, however, has said that this advice was given to Dionysius by someone else, not by him.

36. Certainly, Philistus was to blame for the fervour and devotion he showed on behalf of the tyranny, but Timaeus takes advantage of this by fabricating slanders against him. It was perhaps excusable for those who were actually wronged by Philistus in his lifetime to express their hatred of him, even to the point of maltreating his lifeless body. But those who came to write the history of the period many years afterwards, and who suffered nothing from his actions while he lived but have made use of his writings, owe it to his reputation not to attack him with vulgar and insolent abuse for his misfortunes, which

fate may inflict upon even the best of men. On the other hand, Ephorus is also at fault in showering praises on Philistus; for although Philistus shows infinite resource in inventing flattering motives for unjust actions and unscrupulous characters, and finding decorous names for both, the fact remains that for all his ingenuity, he cannot escape the charge of having been the most devoted supporter of tyrants alive and, more than any other man, a fervent admirer of the luxury they enjoyed, their power, their wealth and their marriage alliances. At any rate, the man who neither praises Philistus' conduct, nor exults over his misfortunes, makes the most appropriate judgement.

37. After Philistus' death, Dionysius approached Dion with an offer to hand over the acropolis, all the weapons it contained and the mercenaries, for whom he provided five months' full pay. In return he asked that he should be allowed to depart unharmed to Italy, and that while he lived there he should enjoy the revenues of Gyarta,[68] a large and fertile area of Syracusan territory which stretched from the sea to the interior of the island. Dion refused these terms, but told him that he must address himself to the Syracusans, and as they hoped to capture Dionysius alive, they dismissed the envoys. At this, the tyrant handed over the acropolis to Apollocrates, his eldest son; meanwhile he embarked all the persons and possessions that he valued most dearly, and, watching his opportunity for a fair wind, managed to elude the blockade of Heracleides the admiral, and make his escape.

The Syracusans angrily blamed Heracleides for this blunder; he thereupon persuaded Hippo, one of the popular leaders, to lay before the people a scheme for the distribution of land, using the argument that equality is the source of freedom, while poverty reduces those who have no possessions to a state of slavery. Heracleides spoke in support of his motion, placed himself at the head of a faction which overruled Dion's opposition and prevailed upon the Syracusans to pass this measure, and not only this one but others to deprive the mercenaries of their pay, to elect other generals and thus to rid themselves of Dion's allegedly oppressive authority. After such a long period of tyranny, the Syracusans were in the position of a man who tries at the end of a long illness to stand immediately on his feet, and so in attempting to act the part of a free people before they were ready for it, they stumbled in their efforts. At the same time they resented the attentions of Dion, who, like a good physician, tried to impose a strict and temperate course of treatment.

38. When the Syracusans summoned their assembly to elect new commanders it was midsummer,[69] and there occurred a succession of extraordinary thunderstorms and other ominous portents which continued for fifteen days consecutively; these prodigies were enough to disperse the people, and their superstitious fears prevented them from electing any other generals. The popular leaders, however, bided their time, at last found a fine, clear day and proceeded to hold the elections. But on this occasion a draught ox, which was quite tame and accustomed to crowds, for some reason became enraged with its driver, broke away from its yoke and made a dash towards the theatre. The people immediately scattered and took to their heels in a disorderly rout, and the beast then ran on, leaping and throwing everything into confusion, and it traversed just that quarter of the city which the enemy afterwards occupied. However, the Syracusans paid no attention to all this, but elected twenty-five generals, one of whom was Heracleides. They also secretly approached Dion's mercenaries and tried to persuade them to desert him and transfer their allegiance to the Syracusans, in return for which they offered them equal rights with the rest of the citizens. The mercenaries refused to listen to these proposals. Instead, they showed their courage and their loyalty to Dion by taking up their arms, placing him in their midst and escorting him out of the city. They did no harm to anyone on their march, but reproached the citizens they met for their shameful and ungrateful behaviour. The Syracusans treated them with contempt because they were so few in number and had shown no disposition to attack, and so when a crowd had gathered together which outnumbered the mercenaries, they set upon them, expecting that they would easily be

able to overpower them and kill them all before they could escape from the city.

39. Dion thus found himself compelled by fortune to make a most painful choice: either to fight against his fellow-citizens or to die with his mercenaries. He pleaded with the Syracusans, stretched out his hands to them and pointed to the acropolis, crammed as it was with their enemies who were looking down from the battlements to watch the spectacle below. But the mob was in no mood to respond to entreaty, and the city was at the mercy of the demagogues, like a ship buffeted by winds at sea, and so Dion ordered his mercenaries not to charge the crowd but to advance towards them brandishing their weapons. When this was done, not one of the Syracusans stood his ground: they took to their heels and fled through the streets, although nobody followed them in pursuit, for Dion immediately ordered his men to turn about and led them in the direction of Leontini.

This affair made the Syracusan commanders a laughing-stock in the eyes of the women of the city, and so in an effort to wipe out their disgrace they armed the citizens again and set out in pursuit of Dion. They caught up with him just as he was crossing a river and some of their horsemen rode up to his troops in skirmishing order. But the moment they saw that Dion would no longer treat their provocations indulgently and in a paternal fashion, but was angrily ordering his men to turn about and drawing them up in battle-order, they beat a hasty and even more ignominious retreat, and returned to the city with the loss of a few men.

40. The people of Leontini welcomed Dion and accorded him exceptional honours. They engaged his mercenaries on full pay, granted them civil rights and also sent a delegation to the Syracusans demanding that they should do justice to these men, to which the Syracusans replied by sending envoys to denounce Dion. Later, when all the allies[70] had assembled at Leontini and discussed the question, it was decided that the Syracusans were in the wrong. For their part the Syracusans repudiated this verdict: they had become arrogant and full of their own importance

because they had no one to rule them, and also because they employed generals who acted like slaves and lived in perpetual fear of the people.

41. After this, a squadron of triremes arrived at Syracuse under the command of Nypsius of Naples.[71] It had been sent by Dionysius, and brought food and pay for the besieged troops in the acropolis. There followed a naval battle in which the Syracusans gained the day and captured four of the tyrant's ships. The victory quite turned their heads, so that casting aside all sense of discipline they fell to celebrating their triumph with banquets and carousals. In this mood they became so oblivious to their real interests that at the very moment when they imagined that the acropolis was within their grasp, they lost it and the city besides. Nypsius had taken note that there was no sign of order or control to be found among his opponents, that the masses had abandoned themselves to music-making and drinking from dawn till midnight, and that their generals welcomed these revels and shrank from using force to recall the drunken troops to their duty. He, therefore, seized his opportunity and attacked the siege-wall. Then, having captured and demolished it, he let loose his barbarians into the city, giving them leave to deal as they chose with everyone they met. The Syracusans quickly perceived their plight, but they had been so much taken by surprise that it was only slowly and with difficulty that they could organize any resistance. What was now happening was nothing less than the sack of their city. The men were being slaughtered, the walls torn down, the women and children dragged screaming into the acropolis, while the generals gave up all for lost and were helpless to rally the citizens against the enemy, who by then were everywhere in their midst and inextricably mingled with them.

42. With the city in this plight and the quarter of Achradina in imminent danger of being captured, there remained one man alone upon whom the entire population's hopes were fixed: Dion's name was in everyone's thoughts, but nobody dared to

mention it because they were ashamed of the folly and ingratitude with which they had treated him. But sheer necessity left them no choice, and at last some of their allies and their horsemen raised the cry to send for Dion and his Peloponnesians from Leontini. As soon as someone had nerved himself to do this and Dion's name was again heard, the Syracusans shouted aloud and wept for joy. They prayed for Dion to appear before them and longed for the sight of him, for they remembered the courage and strength which he had shown in time of danger, and how he was not only undaunted in himself, but could make them share his fearless confidence when they engaged their enemies. So they immediately dispatched to his camp a party, consisting of Archonides and Telesides to represent the allies, and Hellanicus with four others from the cavalry. They set off at full gallop and arrived at Leontini just as the sun was setting. Their first action was to leap from their horses and throw themselves at Dion's feet, and then with tears in their eyes they told him of the disasters the Syracusans had suffered. Presently, some of the Leontines came up and a crowd of the Peloponnesians gathered around Dion, for they had guessed from the speed of the men's arrival and the imploring tone of their voices that something extraordinary had happened. Dion immediately led the messengers to the place of assembly and the people eagerly gathered there. Then Archonides and Hellanicus briefly described to them the catastrophe which had befallen the city, and begged the mercenaries to forget the wrongs that had been done to them and to come to the rescue of the Syracusans, since those who had committed the injustice had suffered a punishment even harsher than their victims would have expected to inflict on them.

43. As soon as the envoys had finished their appeal, a dead silence fell upon the theatre. As Dion rose to speak, his voice was choked with sobs, but his mercenaries who shared his feelings urged him to take heart. So when he had mastered his emotions somewhat, he said to them, 'Peloponnesians and allies, I have brought you here to decide how you should now act. For myself

I cannot think of my own interests while Syracuse is on the brink of destruction, but if I cannot save her, I shall return to bury myself in her ruins and make the flames that consume her my funeral pyre. As for you, if you can find it in your hearts after all that has passed to come to the rescue of us Syracusans, who are the most ill-advised and ill-fated of mankind, then I beg you to rescue once more this city of ours which was founded by your own fellow-countrymen.[72] But if you condemn the Syracusans and decide to abandon them to their fate, I pray that at least the gods will grant you a just reward for the courage and the loyalty you have shown towards me, and that you will remember Dion as a man who did not desert you when you were wronged, nor his own fellow-citizens in their hour of misfortune.'

While Dion was still speaking, the mercenaries leaped to their feet, interrupted him with shouts and clamoured for him to lead them immediately to the rescue. The envoys from Syracuse threw their arms around the soldiers and embraced them with joy, calling upon the gods to bless Dion and his men. Then when the uproar had subsided, Dion dismissed his troops to their quarters and ordered them to make ready to march, take their supper and reassemble with their arms in the same place, for he was determined to march to relieve the city during the night.

44. Back in Syracuse, Dionysius' generals continued to wreak havoc on the city so long as daylight lasted; then as soon as it was dark, they withdrew to the acropolis, having lost a few of their men. At this point the demagogues again recovered their spirits; their hope was that the enemy would rest content with what they had achieved, and so they once more urged the people to have nothing to do with Dion. If he approached with his mercenaries, they should not let him in; they must not regard his troops as superior to themselves in courage, but should make up their minds to save the city and defend their liberty by their own efforts. In consequence, further emissaries were sent out to Dion, some from the generals forbidding his advance, and others from the cavalry and the more prominent citizens, exhorting

him to hasten it, and these contradictory messages caused him to proceed more slowly but with more determination. As the night wore on, Dion's opponents seized possession of the gates to prevent him from entering the city, but at the same time Nypsius led a sortie from the acropolis. This time, he attacked in greater strength and with still more confidence, with the result that he at once demolished the whole of the siege-wall and overran and pillaged the city. He went on to massacre not only many of the male citizens but also women and children; few prisoners were taken and the Syracusans were slaughtered without discrimination. Dionysius[73] had evidently come to despair of his prospects, and as he was consumed with hatred of the Syracusans, he had resolved to bury his falling tyranny in the ruins of the city. His soldiers were determined to forestall Dion's arrival and so sought out the quickest way to annihilate everything before them, that is by reducing the city to ashes: anything that was close at hand they set alight with the torches and firebrands they carried, and anything further away they shot at with blazing arrows. As the Syracusans fled from the destruction, some of them were overtaken and butchered in the streets, while those who sought refuge in houses were forced out by the flames, for many buildings were now ablaze and collapsed upon the fugitives as they ran past.

45. It was this catastrophe above all which caused the citizens to unite in opening the gates to Dion. When he had first received the news that the enemy had shut themselves into the acropolis, he had slackened the pace of his march. But as the day went on, first some of the cavalrymen met him with the news that the city had been captured a second time; then even some of those who had opposed his coming arrived to beg him to hasten his advance. Next, as the situation grew desperate, Heracleides dispatched his brother and finally Theodotes his uncle to entreat Dion to help them; the report said that resistance was at an end, that Heracleides was wounded and that almost the whole of the city was in ruins or in flames. When this terrible news reached Dion, he was still seven miles from the city gates. He at once explained to his troops the danger in which the city stood,

spoke encouragingly to them and then led them forward, no longer marching but at the double, while one messenger after another met him and implored him to hasten. The mercenaries responded with a sudden burst of speed, and advancing with tremendous ardour Dion broke through the gates into the area known as the Hecatompedon. At once he ordered his light-armed troops to charge the enemy, so that the Syracusans might take heart from the sight. Meanwhile, he began drawing up his hoplites in order of battle and included with them those of the citizens who kept running up to join him; he divided these formations into separate commands and grouped them in columns, so as to create greater alarm among the enemy by attacking from several points at once.

46. When he had made these preparations and offered up a prayer to the gods, the sight of him leading his troops through the city to attack the enemy caused the Syracusans to raise a great shout of joy; in the clamour that then arose were mingled battle-cries, prayers and supplications, as the citizens hailed Dion as their saviour and their god[74] and his mercenaries as their brothers and fellow-citizens. Certainly at that moment of crisis there was not a man so selfish or so cowardly that he did not value Dion's life more dearly than his own or those of all the rest, as he marched at their head to meet the danger, forcing his way through blood and fire and the heaps of corpses which littered the streets.

It is true that the enemy presented a terrifying appearance, for the fighting had made them savage and they had posted themselves along the demolished siege-wall in a position which was awkward to approach and hard to force; but the dangers caused by the fire distracted Dion's troops more and created further obstacles to their advance. They were surrounded on all sides by the glare of the flames as the conflagration spread from house to house. Every step they took was upon burning ruins and whenever they ran forward they risked their lives, as great fragments of buildings came crashing down; they struggled on through clouds of dust and smoke, always striving to keep together and not break their formation. When they came to grips with the enemy, the approach was so narrow and uneven that only a few men could engage at a time, but the Syracusans urged them on with shouts of encouragement, and at last Nypsius and his men were overcome. Most of them managed to save themselves by escaping into the acropolis which was close by, but those who were left outside and scattered in different directions were hunted down and killed by the mercenaries. However, in the city's desperate situation the Syracusans had no time to relax and enjoy their victory, or to indulge in the rejoicing and congratulations which such an achievement deserved. Instead, they devoted their efforts to saving their houses, and by dint of toiling all night they succeeded in putting out the fires.

47. When daylight came, not one of the popular leaders dared to remain in the city: all of them condemned themselves by taking flight. Heracleides and Theodotes came of their own accord and surrendered themselves to Dion. They openly admitted that they had done wrong and implored him to treat them more justly than they had treated him. But it was only right, they pleaded, that Dion, who surpassed them in every other good quality, should also show that he was more capable of controlling his anger than these ungrateful men who had now come to confess that he excelled them in the very quality in which they had disputed his superiority, that is in virtue. Heracleides and Theodotes pleaded with Dion in this way, but his friends urged him not to spare such unprincipled and envious rascals; instead, he should hand over Heracleides to the soldiers and deliver the state from the habit of pandering to the mob, a disease scarcely less pernicious than tyranny itself.

Dion did his best to appease their anger and pointed out that while other generals devoted most of their training to the handling of weapons and the fighting of battles, he had spent a long time in the Academy studying how to overcome anger, envy and the spirit of rivalry. To show moderation only to one's friends and benefactors is no proof of having acquired such self-control: the real test is for a man who has been wronged to be able to show compassion and clemency to the evil-doers.

Besides, he wished it to be seen that he excelled Heracleides not so much in power or in statesmanship as in virtue and justice, for these are the qualities in which true superiority resides. After all, fortune can always claim some of the credit for successes in war, even when no other man has a share in them. And if Heracleides had been led by envy into base and treacherous conduct, that was no reason for Dion to sully his virtue by giving way to anger, for although taking revenge for a wrong is more justifiable in the eyes of the law than committing the wrong without provocation, yet in the nature of things both actions spring from the same weakness.[75] What is more, although baseness is a deplorable thing in a man, yet it is not so savage and intractable a defect that it cannot be overcome by repeated kindness and transformed by a sense of gratitude.

48. On the strength of arguments such as these, Dion released Heracleides and Theodotes. Next he turned his attention to the siege-wall. He ordered every Syracusan citizen to cut a stake and lay it down near the siege-works. Then he set the mercenaries to work all night while the citizens were resting and fenced off the acropolis with a palisade, so that when day dawned both the Syracusans and the enemy were amazed to see how quickly the work had been finished. He also buried the Syracusans who had been killed in the fighting, ransomed those who had been captured – although there were at least two thousand of these – and summoned a meeting of the assembly, at which Heracleides came forward with a motion that Dion should be elected general with absolute powers both on land and sea. The wealthy citizens supported the proposals and urged that the motion should be put to the vote, but the mob of sailors and labourers raised an uproar. They were angry that Heracleides should lose his position as admiral, and even though he was worthless in other respects, they regarded him as more of a friend of the people than Dion. On this issue Dion gave way and reinstated Heracleides in command of the fleet, but when the people pressed for the redistribution of land and houses, he incurred great unpopularity by opposing them and annulling the earlier decrees. Seeing this, Heracleides promptly resumed

his intrigues. When he was stationed at Messana, he addressed
the soldiers and sailors who had sailed there with him and tried
to rouse them against Dion, whom he accused of plotting to
make himself tyrant; at the same time he entered into secret
negotiations with Dionysius with the help of Pharax the Spartan. The nobility of Syracuse suspected that these moves were
in progress and violent dissension broke out in his camp, which
led to a severe shortage of provisions and much distress in the
city. Dion was at his wits' end about what to do and was bitterly reproached by his friends for having allowed a man so
unprincipled and so corrupted by envy to build up a position of
strength against him.

49. Pharax the Spartan was encamped near Neapolis in the territory of Acragas, and Dion, who led out the Syracusan forces
against him, did not wish to engage him on this occasion but to
bide his opportunity. However, Heracleides and his sailors
raised a clamour against these tactics and made out that Dion
had no wish to finish the campaign by a battle, but was content
to make it last indefinitely so as to keep himself in command.
He was, therefore, forced to fight and suffered a defeat. Since
this was by no means a serious reverse, but was due to the confusion created by his men's lack of discipline rather than to the
enemy's efforts, Dion once more prepared to engage, drew up
his order of battle and spoke to his men to raise their spirits. But
that evening he received a report that Heracleides had weighed
anchor and was making for Syracuse with the fleet, intending to
seize possession of the city and shut out Dion and his troops.
He at once gathered together the most active and devoted of his
men, rode all through the night and was at the gates of the city
by about nine o'clock the next morning, having covered some
80 miles.

Heracleides, although he had made the best speed he could,
arrived too late and stood out to sea again. For a while he was
at a loss as to what to do next, and then by chance he fell in
with Gaesylus the Spartan, who informed him that he was sailing from Sparta to take command of the Sicilians, just as
Gylippus had done before him.[76] Heracleides gladly took up

with this man; he displayed him to the allies, attached him to himself as it were like a talisman against the influence of Dion and secretly dispatched a herald to Syracuse with orders that the citizens should accept the Spartan as their commander. Dion sent back the answer that the Syracusans had quite enough commanders, and that if the situation demanded the presence of a Spartan, then he himself was the man, since he had been made a citizen of Sparta. When Gaesylus learnt this, he gave up any claim to command, sailed to meet Dion and arranged a reconciliation between him and Heracleides. He made Heracleides swear oaths and give the most solemn pledges, and he himself vowed that he would avenge Dion and punish Heracleides if the latter broke his word.

50. After this the Syracusans disbanded their fleet; by then it was of no further use to them, required large outlays to pay the crews and was a constant cause of dissension among the commanders. But at the same time they tightened the blockade of the acropolis and completed the encircling wall that enclosed it. No attempt was made from any quarter to raise the siege, the garrison's provisions were running out and the mercenaries were on the verge of mutiny; in these circumstances Dionysius' son gave up all hope and came to terms with Dion. He surrendered the acropolis, together with all the arms and warlike stores it contained, and then, after embarking his mother and sisters, and taking five triremes, he sailed away to his father. Dion allowed him to depart unmolested and the spectacle of his departure was watched by every Syracusan in the city; in fact, they even invoked those of their fellow-countrymen who were absent and pitied them because they could not witness that day and see the sun rise upon a free Syracuse. Even to this day the expulsion of Dionysius is still cited as one of the most spectacular examples of the vicissitudes of fortune, and so we may imagine what joy and pride the Syracusans must then have felt at having overthrown with the most meagre resources the greatest tyranny that had ever been established.

51. After Apollocrates had sailed off and Dion was on his way to the acropolis, the women could no longer bear to wait for him to enter the fortress but ran out to the gates. Aristomache was leading Dion's son, while Arete came behind her in tears, quite unsure as to how she should greet and address her husband after she had lived with another man. Dion first embraced his sister, and next his young son, and then Aristomache led Arete forward and said, 'We lived in misery, Dion, all through the years when you were in exile. But now that you have come back to us, your victory has taken away our sorrows – for all of us except Arete, whom I had the misfortune to see forced to take another husband while you were still alive. Now that fate has made you our lord and master, how will you judge what she was compelled to do? How is she to greet you: as her uncle or as her husband?' These words of Aristomache made Dion weep, and he threw his arms around his wife fondly, put his son's hand in hers and bade her come to his house; there he continued to live after he had handed over the acropolis to the people of Syracuse.

52. Now that all his plans had been successfully accomplished, Dion did not think it right to enjoy his good fortune before he had first shown his gratitude to his friends, rewarded his allies – especially those with whom he had been associated in Athens – and bestowed some special mark of honour and recognition upon his mercenaries; but here his generosity outran his resources. For his own part, he continued to live in a modest and frugal style, using only his own private means, and this was a matter for wonder to the whole world. His successes had captured the attention not only of Sicily and of Carthage, but of all Greece: all these peoples considered his achievements the greatest of his age and him a commander who combined a degree of courage and good fortune which none could rival, and yet he was so unassuming in the style of his dress, his household and his table that he might have been dining with Plato in the Academy, not sitting down with commanders and mercenaries and hired soldiers, who compensate themselves for the toils and dangers of their profession by keeping up a lavish

standard of eating and drinking and other pleasures. Plato, indeed, wrote to remind him that the eyes of the whole world were now fixed upon him,[77] but Dion himself, it would seem, kept his eyes fixed upon that one spot in one city, namely the Academy. He believed that those who watched him from there were not so much impressed by feats of arms or courage or battles won, but judged his conduct only according to whether he had used his good fortune with moderation and wisdom, and behaved with due restraint after he had reached the heights of power. Nevertheless, he made a point of maintaining the same gravity in his bearing and the same formality of manner in dealing with the people, even though the times called for a more gracious demeanour; he did this in spite of the fact, as I have mentioned earlier, that Plato wrote and tried to warn him that 'stubbornness is the companion of solitude'.[78] However, Dion possessed the kind of temperament which finds it difficult to unbend, and besides this he thought it important to curb the behaviour of the Syracusans, who were accustomed to too much luxury and too little self-discipline.

53. For Heracleides was opposing him again. First of all, when Dion invited him to become a member of his council he declined to come, declaring that as a private citizen he would only go to the public assembly with his fellow-citizens. Next, he publicly attacked Dion for not having demolished the acropolis, for having prevented the people from breaking open the tomb of Dionysius the elder and casting out his body,[79] and for having insulted his fellow-countrymen by sending a request to Corinth to provide a number of advisers and colleagues for the government. It was quite true that he had appealed to the Corinthians, but this was precisely because he hoped that their participation in the government would make it easier to establish the constitution he had planned. Through this plan he intended to put a curb upon unrestrained democracy, which he did not regard as a constitution at all, but rather as a kind of market of constitutions – to use Plato's phrase[80] – and to introduce a blend of democracy and monarchy on the Spartan and Cretan model.[81] According to this system, it is an oligarchy which is in control of affairs

and decides the most important issues; at any rate, Dion saw that the government of Corinth was inclined towards oligarchy and that very little public business was handled in the popular assembly.

At this point, since he expected that Heracleides would take the lead in opposing these measures, and since the man was unstable and a born trouble-maker and rabble-rouser, Dion at last gave way to those who had long ago wished to kill him but whom he had hitherto restrained, and so they forced their way into Heracleides' house and murdered him. The Syracusans were deeply indignant at his death, but when Dion gave him a spectacular funeral and escorted his body to the grave with his troops and afterwards made a speech to them, they recognized that the city could never have been at peace so long as Dion and Heracleides were both engaged in political life.

54. One of Dion's companions was a man named Callippus, an Athenian who, according to Plato,[82] had become an intimate friend of Dion, not as a fellow-student of philosophy, but because they were both initiated into the Mysteries[83] and were therefore regularly in each other's company. He had taken part in the expedition from the beginning and had distinguished himself brilliantly in action. Dion accorded him special honours and at their entry into Syracuse had placed him by his side at the head of their companions wearing a wreath on his head. By this time many of the noblest and best of Dion's friends had died on the battlefield, and since Heracleides was also now dead, Callippus perceived that the Syracusans were without a leader, and that he himself had more influence than anyone else with Dion's troops. So like the detestable creature that he was, Callippus calculated that he could make Sicily his prize in return for killing his friend, while some writers say that he accepted 20 talents from Dion's enemies as his reward for the murder. At any rate, he bribed a number of Dion's mercenaries to form a conspiracy against him and he set his plot working in a peculiarly mean and treacherous manner. He made a practice of reporting to Dion any seditious remarks uttered by the soldiers against him, sometimes using words he had actually heard and

sometimes making them up, and in this way he won Dion's confidence and was authorized to hold clandestine meetings and talk freely with the men against him, in order that none of those who were secretly disaffected should remain undiscovered. As a result, Callippus quickly succeeded in identifying and bringing together all the most unscrupulous and discontented elements; at the same time, if any man refused his overtures and reported them, Dion was not at all disturbed and showed no anger, but simply assumed that Callippus was carrying out his orders.

55. While this conspiracy was being hatched, Dion saw a phantom of gigantic size and terrible appearance. As he was sitting late in the day in the portico of his house, by himself and lost in thought, he suddenly heard a noise at the far end of the colonnade. He looked up and in the twilight he saw a tall woman, whose face and dress were exactly like those of one of the Furies on the stage,[84] sweeping the house with a kind of broom. He started violently, and finding himself shaking with terror, he sent for his friends, described to them what he had seen and begged them to stay and spend the night with him, for he was almost beside himself with fear and was afraid that if he were left alone the apparition might return. This did not happen, but a few days later his only son, who was by then almost grown up, flew into a passion on account of some trivial grievance, threw himself headlong from the roof and was killed.

56. While Dion was in this state of distress, Callippus made all the more progress with his conspiracy and spread a rumour among the Syracusans that Dion, now that he was childless, had decided to send for Dionysius' son Apollocrates – who happened to be at once his wife's nephew and his sister's grandson – to make him his successor. By this time, both Dion and his sister had begun to suspect what was afoot, and information about the plot was reaching them from all sides. But it seems that Dion was tormented by the death of Heracleides, and the memory of his murder continually weighed upon and depressed his mind, since he regarded it as a stain upon his own life and actions. He declared that he was ready to die many

times over, and that he would let any man cut his throat if the alternative was to be obliged to live in perpetual fear not only of his enemies but even of his friends.

At this point Callippus, who had noticed that the women were becoming very inquisitive to discover what was going on, took fright and came to them in tears; he denied vehemently that there was any plot and offered to give any pledge of his loyalty they wanted. At this, they demanded that he should swear the great oath, which was done in the following manner. The giver of the pledge goes down into the precinct of Demeter and Persephone and there, after certain ceremonies have been performed, he puts on the purple robe of the goddess, takes a lighted torch in his hand and recites the oath. Callippus performed all these ceremonies and repeated the oath, but treated the gods with such contempt that he actually waited for the festival of the goddess by whom he had sworn, and on that day committed the murder.[85] But it may be that he paid no attention to the day, for he must have known that he was committing just as outrageous a sacrilege when he, as an initiating priest, shed the blood of an initiate, no matter which day he chose to do it.

57. There were many people in the plot, and as Dion was sitting with his friends in a room furnished with several couches, some of the conspirators surrounded the house outside, while others guarded the doors and the windows. The murderers, who were all from Zacynthus, entered the room in their tunics and without swords. Then, at the same moment, those outside shut the doors and held them fast, while those in the room threw themselves upon Dion and tried to strangle and crush him. When they could not succeed in this, they called for a sword, but nobody dared to open the door. There were many of Dion's friends in the room, but each of them seemed to imagine that if he left Dion to his fate, he could save his own skin, and so no man had the courage to help him. After a long delay, Lycon the Syracusan handed a dagger through the window and with this they cut his throat, like a victim at a sacrifice: he had for a long while been overpowered and was trembling as he waited for the blow. The conspirators at once took away his wife, who

was pregnant, and threw her into prison. She endured a most wretched confinement and gave birth to a boy in the jail: the women ventured to rear the child and found it easy to obtain the permission of the jailers, because Callippus was already embroiled in troubles of his own.

58. At first after the murder of Dion, Callippus enjoyed great prestige and was in complete control of Syracuse. He even sent letters to the city of Athens, the place for which he should have felt most dread, second only to that which he felt for the gods, since he had brought such a terrible pollution on himself. But it seems to have been truly said of Athens that the good men she breeds are the best of their kind, and the worst the most abominable, just as her soil brings forth the sweetest honey and the deadliest hemlock. At any rate, Callippus did not long survive as a reproach to fortune and the gods – as though they could overlook the impiety of a man who had won position and power by committing such an outrage. Instead, he soon paid the penalty he deserved. For when he made an expedition to capture Catana, he at once lost Syracuse, after which he is said to have remarked that he had lost a city and gained a cheese-grater.[86] Next, he attacked Messana, and here many of his soldiers were killed, among them the murderers of Dion. Then, as no city in Sicily would admit him, but all showed how they hated and abhorred him, he seized possession of Rhegium. There he found his resources so much reduced that he could not pay his mercenaries and was murdered by Leptines and Polyperchon, who, by a twist of fate, used the same dagger as the one with which Dion is said to have been killed. It was recognized by its size, which was very short, after the Spartan fashion, and also by the style of its workmanship, for it was finely and elaborately chased.

Such was the retribution which overtook Callippus. As for Aristomache and Arete, when they were released from prison, they were received by Hicetas the Syracusan, who had been a friend of Dion and who had at first seemed to treat them loyally and honourably. But later, at the instigation of some of Dion's enemies, he provided a ship for them and made out that they were to be sent to the Peloponnese; then, once they were at sea, he ordered the sailors to cut their throats and throw their bodies overboard. According to another version, however, they were thrown into the sea alive and their little boy with them. But Hicetas also suffered a fitting punishment for his crimes. He was captured by Timoleon and put to death, and the Syracusans killed his two daughters in revenge for the murder of Dion. These events I have described at length in my *Life of Timoleon*.[87]

TIMOLEON

INTRODUCTION TO
TIMOLEON
[died *c.* 336 BC]

The *Life of Timoleon* picks up almost exactly where the *Life of Dion* leaves off, and mutual cross-references suggest the two were composed at around the same time (*Dion* 58; *Timoleon* 13 and 33). Dion was murdered in 354 BC, and Syracuse endured a period of instability until in 346 Dionysius II established himself as tyrant once again. Some of those in Syracuse opposed to the tyranny appealed to Corinth, the city whose colonists had originally founded Syracuse, and in early 344 the Corinthians dispatched a small force under the leadership of Timoleon to assist the Syracusans against the tyrant. Timoleon quickly succeeded in persuading Dionysius to leave Syracuse, and in the following years ended the tyrannies in several other Sicilian cities. He also campaigned against the Carthaginians who controlled the west of Sicily and won a decisive victory against superior numbers at the River Crimisus in *c.* 340. After the battle of Crimisus, Timoleon concluded a treaty with the Carthaginians which restricted Carthaginian influence to the western part of the island. During this time, Timoleon seems to have been granted exceptional powers; that he did not make himself tyrant but stepped down from office contributed to the adulation with which he seems to have been regarded. He died around 336.

This is one of Plutarch's most idealized Lives. It is perhaps for this reason that Timoleon does not emerge very clearly as an individual. There is almost no criticism, and very few anecdotes or sayings to individuate him or give a sense of his character. Indeed, the Life begins not with Timoleon himself, but with an account of the state of Sicily in the years following

Dion's death (chs. 1–2). In fact, Plutarch tells us almost nothing about Timoleon until he is selected at an advanced age for the expedition to liberate Sicily. The one detail Plutarch does give us is that he was devoted to his brother, Timophanes, and saved his life in battle, but later killed him when he tried to make himself tyrant of Corinth (chs. 3–4). This story sets out at the start of the Life the two most important features of Plutarch's Timoleon: his valour and his hatred of tyranny.

Two factors contribute to the extremely positive presentation of Timoleon. The first is that Timoleon managed to settle the internal dissension that had plagued Syracuse since the Athenian invasion. The *Life of Timoleon* therefore provides for Plutarch an example of the ideal relationship of people and leader: the people respect Timoleon and do not listen to demagogues, and he guides them wisely; furthermore, he is not corrupted by power and does not try to extend his term in office. Secondly, Timoleon's military victories were chiefly against non-Greeks (that is, Carthaginians) or tyrants. Elsewhere in his work, Plutarch laments the fact that Greek history was mainly a tale of Greeks fighting Greeks (e.g., *Flamininus* 11); Timoleon's liberation of Sicily is presented in comparison as a glorious, patriotic event. Plutarch begins the Life with a picture of Sicily as a land overrun by barbarians. And after his great victory at the Crimisus, Plutarch comments: 'His ambition was that in Corinth ... men should see the most conspicuous temples adorned not with the spoils taken from Greek states ... but decked with ornaments won from the barbarians and bearing honourable inscriptions which testified to the justice as well as the courage of the victors' (ch. 29).

The *Life of Timoleon* is paired with that of the Roman L. Aemilius Paullus, who was famous for his victory over the Macedonians at the battle of Pydna in 168 BC. Unusually in this pair it is the Roman Life which comes first; Plutarch's readers would therefore have approached *Timoleon* only after reading *Aemilius*. In the prologue, which precedes both Lives, Plutarch dwells on the moral benefit to be obtained from studying biography, and concludes by presenting Aemilius and

Timoleon as the 'finest of examples', that is, as models of good conduct (*Aemilius* 1).

In both Lives fortune plays a prominent role. But in *Aemilius*, while fortune providentially favours Rome, it often seems to work against Aemilius personally (e.g., chs. 3, 22, 26–7), most spectacularly at the end of his life, where his two sons die prematurely (chs. 34–6). In *Timoleon*, on the other hand, fortune is always on Timoleon's side. Timoleon's taking of Dionysius' stronghold, Ortygia in Syracuse, is attributed to good fortune (ch. 13); so are the safe arrival of reinforcements from Corinth (ch. 19), his survival of a plot against his life (ch. 16; cf. ch. 37) and his overwhelming victories against Hicetas and against the Carthaginians (ch. 30). Fortune in this Life is not merely luck, nor the fickle deity of *Aemilius*; it is a providential power, the outworking of the divine will. The idea of a providential care for Sicily was already present in *Dion* (chs. 4, 50), but it is particularly prominent in *Timoleon* and is confirmed by numerous omens and divine signs.

Such a stress on the favour of providence, in contrast to the fickle fortune with which Aemilius had to deal, might have suggested that Timoleon's own personal qualities were less important, that he was merely the tool by which providence freed Sicily. Indeed, Plutarch himself, at the end of the prologue, raises the question of 'whether the greatest of their achievements were due to their wisdom or their good fortune' (*Aemilius* 1). In fact, the issue of the relative roles played by fortune and by virtue in a great success was one of profound interest in the ancient world. Plutarch himself wrote a work examining the issue in relation to Alexander the Great (his *On the fortune or virtue of Alexander*). There, Plutarch played down the good luck that Alexander enjoyed, arguing instead that fortune was really *against* Alexander, in order to demonstrate that all Alexander's successes were the result of his own virtue. In *Timoleon* Plutarch takes a different approach: Timoleon's successes were due to what he calls 'virtue reinforced by fortune' (ch. 36), that is, to Timoleon's own courage assisted by fortune. Providence played a role in directing events, but

Timoleon's own personal virtue was indispensable. It goes without saying that in emphasizing Timoleon's personal virtue and the blessings of providence, Plutarch ignores other factors in his success, whether military or financial, and does not address the Carthaginian perspective at all.

Plutarch plainly found positive accounts of Timoleon in his main source, the Sicilian historian Timaeus. His work is now lost, but Timaeus' father was a supporter of Timoleon (see ch. 10), and Timaeus' account of Timoleon seems also to have influenced Diodorus' Book 16 and Nepos' brief *Life of Timoleon*. Both of these writers also give favourable pictures of Timoleon, though neither places such emphasis on the role of fortune.

LIFE OF TIMOLEON[1]

1. The situation in Syracuse before Timoleon's expedition arrived in Sicily was as follows. Soon after Dion had driven out the tyrant Dionysius, he was treacherously murdered,[2] and the men who had joined him to free the Syracusans were divided among themselves. The city had passed through a period during which it repeatedly exchanged one tyrant for another,[3] and as a result of all the misfortunes it had suffered, was in an almost derelict condition. As for the rest of Sicily, some districts had been ravaged and their cities completely depopulated as a result of the wars. Most cities were in the hands of barbarians of various races and of disbanded soldiers, who because they had no regular pay were ready to accept any change of ruler. At last Dionysius, after spending ten years in exile, recruited a force of mercenaries, drove out Nisaeus who was at that time the ruler of Syracuse, recovered control of affairs and re-established himself as tyrant. He had unexpectedly been dislodged by a very small force[4] from the most powerful tyranny that ever existed and now, more unexpectedly still, he had raised himself from the condition of a lowly exile to become the master of those who had banished him. Those of the Syracusans who remained in the city found themselves the slaves of a tyrant who had always been oppressive and had now become even more inhuman as a result of the misfortunes he had suffered. But the most prominent and influential of the citizens turned to Hicetas, the ruler of Leontini, placed themselves under his protection and elected him their general for the war. This man was no better than any other of the acknowledged tyrants, but the citizens had no other refuge and they were prepared to trust a man who

belonged to a Syracusan family and commanded a force which could match that of Dionysius.

2. Meanwhile, the Carthaginians appeared with a powerful fleet and hovered off the coast of Sicily, awaiting their opportunity to intervene. Their approach struck terror into the Sicilians and they resolved to send a delegation to Greece and appeal for help to Corinth. This was not only on account of their kinship with the Corinthians[5] and of the many services they had received from them in the past, but because they knew that Corinth had always upheld the cause of freedom, that she detested tyranny and that she had fought most of her wars – and the greatest ones at that – not to acquire an empire or make herself more powerful, but to defend the liberty of Greece.[6] Hicetas, on the other hand, when he accepted the command had no intention of freeing the Syracusans but, rather, of bringing them under his own tyranny, and he had already entered into secret negotiations with the Carthaginians. But in public he praised the Syracusan plan and supported the decision to send a delegation to the Peloponnese. He was not at all anxious to see an allied army arrive from that quarter. He hoped that if, as seemed likely, the Corinthians refused to send help, on account of the troubled state of Greece and of their own commitments at home,[7] he could more easily sway the course of events so as to favour the Carthaginians: he planned to use them as allies and auxiliaries, either against the Syracusans or against Dionysius. These intentions were exposed not long afterwards.

3. When the delegation from Syracuse arrived, the Corinthians eagerly voted in favour of sending help. They were always concerned for the interests of their colonies overseas and especially for those of Syracuse, and by a happy chance there were no distractions to divert their attention either in Greece or within their own frontiers, where they were enjoying peace and leisure. Then, when the question arose of choosing a commander for the expedition, and while the magistrates were writing down the names of those citizens who wished to be considered for this honour and nominating them for election, a man from

the crowd rose to his feet and proposed Timoleon, the son of
Timodemus. Timoleon was not at this time active in politics
and had no intention of standing for the command or expectation that he would be appointed to it. But some god, it would
seem, inspired the proposer to put forward his name, because
fortune immediately revealed herself to be on his side; this
became evident not only by the ease with which he was elected,
but also in a peculiar grace which attended all his subsequent
actions and enhanced his personal virtues.

Timoleon's parents, Timodemus and Demariste, both belonged
to noble families, and he himself was an ardent patriot and a man
of gentle disposition, except only for his hatred of tyrants and of
base behaviour in any form. As a soldier his abilities were so
finely and evenly balanced that he proved himself exceptionally
astute in the exploits of his youth and no less daring in those of
his old age. He had a brother named Timophanes who was older
but possessed a completely different temperament. Timophanes
was headstrong and was dominated by a fatal passion for absolute power, which was encouraged by a circle of worthless friends
and foreign military adventurers with whom he spent all his time.
He enjoyed the reputation of being a furious fighter in war and of
having a positive craving for danger: for this reason many of the
Corinthians thought highly of him as a soldier and man of action
and he was appointed to senior commands. Timoleon helped him
to obtain these and did his best to cover up or extenuate his faults,
while at the same time he praised and made the most of those
virtues which nature had given him.

4. In the battle which the Corinthians fought against the Argives
and the people of Cleonae,[8] Timoleon happened to be serving
with the hoplites, but Timophanes, who was in command of
the cavalry, suddenly found himself in great danger. His horse
was wounded and threw him while he was surrounded by the
enemy. Some of his companions scattered and fled in panic, and
the few who stood fast were fighting against greatly superior
numbers and could scarcely hold their ground. When Timoleon
saw what was happening, he ran to the rescue and covered
Timophanes with his shield as he lay on the ground. He received

a hail of blows to his body and armour both from the javelins that were hurled at him and in the hand-to-hand fighting, but he succeeded at last in driving back the enemy and in saving his brother.

When the Corinthians became alarmed that their city might once more be captured because of the treachery of their allies,[9] they passed a decree to maintain a force of four hundred mercenaries and placed Timophanes in command of it.[10] The immediate result was that Timophanes put aside all considerations of justice and honour, took steps to seize power, executed a large number of the leading citizens without trial and proclaimed himself tyrant. Timoleon was outraged by these actions, but since he regarded his brother's crimes as his own misfortune, he tried to reason with him, and begged him to abandon his insane and ill-starred ambition and make amends for the wrong he had done to his fellow-citizens. Timophanes contemptuously rejected all his appeals, whereupon Timoleon called together his kinsman Aeschylus, who was Timophanes' brother-in-law, and his friend the diviner Satyrus: at least this was his name according to Theopompus, but Ephorus and Timaeus refer to him as Orthagoras. Timoleon waited a few days and then went up again to see his brother. Here the three men surrounded Timophanes and made a final appeal, urging him even now to listen to reason and change his mind. Timophanes at first laughed at them, but then flew into a violent rage. At this Timoleon stepped a little way aside, covered his face and wept, while the other two drew their swords and straightaway killed him.

5. When the news became known, the leading Corinthians praised Timoleon for his hatred of wrongdoing and his greatness of soul. They saw that although he was a kindly man who loved his family, he had nevertheless placed his country before his own flesh and blood, and the cause of honour and justice before expediency. When his brother was fighting valiantly for his country, Timoleon had saved his life, but after he had plotted against her and enslaved her, Timoleon had killed him. On the other hand, those who could not bear to live in a democracy,

and were accustomed to pay court to whoever was in power, pretended to rejoice at Timophanes' death but nevertheless reviled Timoleon for having committed an impious and detestable action, and their abuse reduced him to a state of deep dejection. When he heard that his mother's grief had turned to hatred and that she had uttered the most terrible denunciations and curses against his name, he went to try to console her; but she could not bear to see his face and shut him out of her house. Then his grief overcame him completely, he became distracted and determined to starve himself to death. His friends, however, would not stand by and allow this, and brought every kind of pressure and entreaty to bear on him, until finally he resolved to live by himself, apart from the world. He withdrew completely from public life and for the first years of his retirement did not even return to the city, but spent his time wandering in great agony of mind in the most deserted parts of the country.

6. So true is it that men's judgements are unstable and may easily be swayed and carried away by casual praise or blame and forced from their own rational thoughts, unless they acquire strength and steadiness of purpose from philosophy and reason. It is not enough, it seems, that our actions should be noble and just: the conviction from which they spring must be permanent and unchangeable, if we are to approve our own conduct. Otherwise we may find ourselves becoming prey to despondency, or to sheer weakness, when the vision of the ideal which inspired us fades away, just as a glutton who devours cloying delicacies with too keen a pleasure soon loses his appetite and becomes disgusted with them. Remorse may cast a sense of shame over even the noblest of actions, but the determination which is founded upon reason and understanding is not shaken even if the outcome is unsuccessful. The case of Phocion the Athenian is a good example. Phocion had opposed the course of action taken by Leosthenes, and when Leosthenes' policy seemed to have triumphed, and the Athenians were seen to be sacrificing and exulting over their victory, Phocion remarked that he could have wished the success had been his, but that he was glad to have given the advice that he did.[11] And

Aristides the Locrian, who was one of Plato's companions, put the matter even more forcefully when he was asked by Dionysius the elder for the hand of one of his daughters in marriage. He said that he would rather see the girl dead than the wife of a tyrant; but when a little while later, Dionysius put Aristides' sons to death, and then asked him scornfully whether he had changed his opinion about giving his daughters in marriage, Aristides replied that he was grieved at what Dionysius had done, but did not repent of what he had said. Such sayings as these are perhaps the mark of a greater, a more perfect, virtue than is found in ordinary men.

7. In the case of Timoleon his grief, whether it arose out of pity for his dead brother or the reverence which he bore his mother, so crushed and overwhelmed his spirit that it was almost twenty years before he could again engage in any important public enterprise.[12] So when he had been named as the commander of the expedition and the people had gladly accepted him and given him their votes, Telecleides, who was at that time the most distinguished and influential man in Corinth, rose and appealed to Timoleon to show all his valour in the enterprise he was undertaking. 'If you fight bravely,' he said, 'we shall think of you as the man who destroyed a tyrant, but otherwise as the man who killed his brother.'

While Timoleon was making ready for his voyage and collecting his troops, letters from Hicetas were brought to the Corinthians which clearly revealed that he had changed sides and betrayed them. For as soon as he had sent off his ambassadors to Corinth, he openly attached himself to the Carthaginians and joined forces with them so as to expel Dionysius from Syracuse and make himself tyrant instead. And in fear that he might miss his opportunity if a general and an army were to arrive from Corinth too soon, he sent a letter to the Corinthians pointing out that there was no need for them to incur the trouble, the expense and the danger of sending a force to Sicily. Because of their delay, he had been obliged to make an alliance with the Carthaginians against the tyrant, and his new allies forbade the Corinthians to send an expedition and were on the watch to intercept it with a large fleet. These letters were read out in public, and if any of the Corinthians had previously been lukewarm about the operation, they were now roused to fury against Hicetas and eagerly contributed to support the expedition and help Timoleon prepare for his voyage.

8. After the fleet had been made ready and the soldiers completely equipped, the priestesses of Persephone dreamed that they saw the goddess and her mother preparing for a journey and heard them say that they intended to sail with Timoleon to Sicily. Therefore the Corinthians fitted out a sacred trireme and named it after the two goddesses. Moreover Timoleon himself travelled to Delphi and offered sacrifice to Apollo there. As he descended into the chamber where the oracular responses were delivered, he was the witness of a portent. Among the votive offerings which were hung up there, a wreath, which had crowns and figures of victory embroidered on it, slipped down and fell directly on his head, and thus gave the impression that he was being sent forth upon his enterprise crowned with success by the god.

So Timoleon set sail[13] with seven ships from Corinth, two from Corcyra and a tenth supplied by the people of Leucas. That night when he had reached the open sea and was sailing with a fair wind, suddenly the heavens seemed to burst open above his ship and pour down a flood of brilliant fire. Out of this fire a torch, like one of those which are carried in the procession of the Mysteries, rose up before them, and, moving in the same direction as his vessel, descended upon exactly that part of Italy towards which the pilots were shaping their course. The diviners declared that this apparition confirmed the dreams of the priestesses, and that the goddesses were displaying this light from heaven to show that they were taking part in the expedition, for Sicily, they said, was sacred to Persephone: it was the scene of her mythical rape by Hades, and the island was presented to her as a wedding gift.

9. These divine portents greatly encouraged the expedition; the fleet made its best speed across the open sea and sailed down

the coast of Italy. However, the news which they then received
from Sicily perplexed Timoleon and disheartened his men.
Hicetas, they learnt, had defeated Dionysius in battle, and captured most of the outlying districts of Syracuse; he had then
driven the tyrant into the acropolis, known as 'the island',[14]
and was blockading him there. At the same time he had ordered
the Carthaginians to prevent Timoleon from landing in Sicily.
The Corinthian expedition was to be driven off, so that Hicetas
and the Carthaginians could then divide the island between
them at their leisure. Accordingly, the Carthaginians dispatched
twenty triremes to Rhegium carrying envoys from Hicetas to
Timoleon. The proposals they brought with them were as deceit-
ful as the rest of his actions: they consisted of specious overtures
and declarations which concealed treacherous designs. The
envoys requested that Timoleon should, if he wished, join Hicetas, who would treat him as his adviser and partner in all his
successes, but that he should send his ships and his soldiers back
to Corinth. They claimed that the campaign against Dionysius
was virtually finished, and that the Carthaginians were prepared
to oppose his passage and fight him if he attempted to force the
issue. So when the Corinthians arrived at Rhegium, they met the
ambassadors and saw the Carthaginian fleet riding at anchor
close by. They were filled with indignation at the insult they
had suffered,[15] with rage against Hicetas and with fear for the
people of Sicily, since it was evident that they were being
handed over to Hicetas as a prize for his treachery and to the
Carthaginians for their help in making him tyrant. It seemed to
the Corinthians quite impossible that they could overcome
both the barbarians, who faced them with a fleet twice the size
of their own, and Hicetas' army in Syracuse, of which they had
expected to take command.

10. However, after Timoleon had met the envoys and the Carthaginian commanders, he calmly informed them that he would
comply with their demands – for what would he achieve by
refusing? He added that he wished to have their proposals and
his answer discussed before they parted in the presence of the

people of the city of Rhegium, since this was a city which was friendly to both parties. This arrangement, he pointed out, would help to justify his action before his own countrymen, while for their part the envoys and commanders would be the more bound to carry out their promises concerning the Syracusans if the people of Rhegium were made the witnesses to the agreement. This proposal was in fact a trick to enable him to cross the straits, and the people of Rhegium gave him their help because they were anxious that the Sicilian Greeks should come under the protection of Corinth and were afraid of having the barbarians as neighbours. They therefore summoned an assembly of the people and closed the gates to ensure that the citizens should not engage in any other business. Then they came forward and addressed the populace with lengthy speeches, one man handing on the same topic to his successor; they took care not to reach any conclusion but spun out the time, apparently to no purpose, until the Corinthian triremes had put to sea. In this way the Carthaginians were kept in the assembly: they suspected nothing because Timoleon was present and gave the impression that he was on the point of rising to address the people. Then somebody unobtrusively brought him word that the rest of the Corinthian triremes were under way and that his ship alone remained behind and was waiting for him. The Rhegians who were standing around the platform helped to screen him so that he could slip through the crowd unnoticed, and he hurried down to the sea and sailed away at full speed.

The squadron put in at Tauromenium in Sicily. They had been invited some while before and were now warmly received by Andromachus, the ruler of the city. This man was the father of Timaeus the historian. He had made himself by far the most powerful of the rulers of Sicily of that time, and he not only observed the principles of law and justice in governing his people, but made no secret of the fact that he was constantly and implacably hostile to tyrants.[16] For this reason he allowed Timoleon to make Tauromenium his base of operations, and prevailed upon the citizens to join the Corinthians in their campaign to liberate Sicily.

11. When the assembly at Rhegium was dissolved and Timoleon's escape was discovered, the Carthaginians were beside themselves with rage, though the people of Rhegium were greatly amused, not only to have defeated them in this battle of wits, but also to hear them complaining bitterly of deceit, despite their being Phoenicians.[17] So the Carthaginians sent a trireme to Tauromenium with an envoy on board. This man held a long conversation with Andromachus, in which he threatened the Greek in insulting and barbaric fashion if he did not immediately send the Corinthians away. Finally, he stretched out his hand with the palm upwards, and then, turning it downwards, declared that he would overturn the city in the same way. Andromachus merely laughed and made no reply, except to hold out his hand and repeat the gesture, showing his palm first upwards and then downwards. Then he ordered the envoy to sail off at once, if he did not want to see his ship capsized in the same fashion.

As soon as Hicetas heard that Timoleon had made the crossing, he became alarmed and sent for a strong fleet of Carthaginian triremes, but for their part the Syracusans were in despair that they could ever be rescued. They saw their harbour controlled by the Carthaginians, their city in the hands of Hicetas and their acropolis occupied by Dionysius. Timoleon, on the other hand, seemed to have no more than a foothold on the edge of Sicily, in the little city of Tauromenium, with little hope of success and only a slender force to support him. Apart from his thousand soldiers, for whom he had barely enough supplies, he possessed no resources whatever. The cities of Sicily showed little confidence in him, for they were beset with troubles of their own, and were particularly exasperated against all those who claimed to lead armies to liberate them. These feelings were the result of the treachery of Callippus[18] and of Pharax,[19] the first an Athenian and the second a Spartan. Both of these men had declared that they had come to fight for the freedom of Sicily and overthrow her despots, but in fact they had caused the rule of the tyrants to appear like a golden age compared to their own, and led the people to believe that those who had died in slavery were happier than those who had survived to witness her so-called independence.

12. The cities therefore did not expect that the Corinthian liberator would turn out to be any better than his predecessors. They feared that the same enticements and sophistries would be held out, and that they would be offered fair hopes and generous promises to make them docile enough to accept a new master. In consequence, all the cities were suspicious of the overtures made by the Corinthians and rejected them, with the exception of the people of Adranum.[20] They lived in a small city dedicated to Adranus, a god who is held in the highest honour throughout Sicily. At this time they were divided against each other: one party had called in Hicetas and the Carthaginians, while another had sent an invitation to Timoleon. As fortune would have it, both generals hurried to answer the summons and arrived at the same moment, with the difference that while Hicetas came with 5,000 soldiers, Timoleon's force numbered no more than twelve hundred. He started with these from Tauromenium, which is 38 miles from Adranum, and on the first day covered only a short distance before pitching camp for the night. On the second, he quickened his march and after passing through difficult country, received news late in the day that Hicetas had just reached the little town and was pitching his camp.

Timoleon's officers halted the vanguard in order to rest and feed the men and make them ready and eager for battle. But when Timoleon arrived, he begged them not to wait but to press on as fast as they could so as to fall upon the enemy while they were in disorder, as they were likely to be when they had just finished their march and were engaged in pitching their tents and preparing a meal. With these words he snatched up his shield, put himself at the head of the column and marched on as if he were leading his troops to certain victory. Inspired by his example, the men followed him and quickly covered the three and a half miles which separated them from Hicetas. Their attack achieved complete surprise and the enemy fled as soon as they saw the Corinthians advancing upon them. For this reason no more than three hundred of them were killed, but twice as many were taken prisoner and their camp was captured. Thereupon, the people of Adranum opened their gates to

Timoleon and gave him their allegiance. They also told him
with awe and wonder that at the very beginning of the battle
the sacred doors of the temple had flown open of their own
accord, the spear of the god was seen to quiver at its point and
drops of sweat ran down the face of his image.

13. These portents, it seems, foretold not only Timoleon's immediate victory, but also his future exploits to which this battle
was an auspicious prelude. Other cities immediately sent envoys
to Timoleon and began to attach themselves to his cause, and
in particular Mamercus, the tyrant of Catana, a warlike and
wealthy ruler, came forward as an ally. But most important was
the fact that Dionysius himself had by now lost all hope of success and was almost at the end of his resistance. He despised
Hicetas for his shameful defeat, but was full of admiration for
Timoleon, and sent messengers with an offer to surrender both
himself and the acropolis to Timoleon and the Corinthians.

Timoleon welcomed this unexpected stroke of good fortune
and sent a detachment of four hundred soldiers to the acropolis
under two Corinthian officers, Eucleides and Telemachus. He
could not send them openly nor all together, since the Carthaginian fleet was blockading the harbour, but infiltrated them
in small groups. These soldiers took possession of the acropolis
and of the tyrant's palace, together with all its equipment and
military stores, for the place contained many horses, all kinds of
artillery and siege-weapons, great quantities of missiles and
arms and armour for 70,000 men, all of which had been kept
there for many years. Dionysius also had with him 2,000 soldiers, whom he handed over to Timoleon with the stores. Then
gathering together a few friends and his treasure, he put to sea
and passed through Hicetas' lines unnoticed. After this he was
brought to Timoleon's camp, where he was seen for the first
time in the humble dress of a private citizen, and as such he was
sent with a single ship and a small allowance of money to Corinth. Dionysius had been born and bred under a tyranny which
was the greatest and most celebrated of all tyrannies. He had
wielded this power for ten years, but then for the next twelve,
ever since the time of Dion's expedition against him, he had

been continually harassed by wars and political struggles, during which his personal sufferings had far outweighed all his acts
of tyranny.[21] He had lived to see his sons die in their early manhood, his daughters violated, and his wife, who was also his
sister, subjected to the brutal lusts of his enemies and finally
murdered with her children and thrown into the sea. These episodes have been fully described in my *Life of Dion*.[22]

14. When Dionysius arrived in Corinth there was hardly a man
in Greece who did not feel the desire to see and speak to him.
Some, who rejoiced in his misfortunes, came for the pleasure of
trampling on a man who had been cast down by fate; others,
who were more interested in the change in his situation and
who sympathized with him, saw in his destiny a convincing
proof of the potency with which divine and invisible causes
operate in the midst of human and visible circumstances. Certainly, that age produced no example either in nature or in art
which was so striking as this change of fortune – namely, the
sight of the man who had not long before been tyrant of Sicily
whiling away his time at Corinth in the food-market, sitting in
a perfumer's shop, drinking diluted wine in the taverns, bandy-
ing jokes in public with prostitutes, correcting music-girls in
their singing or earnestly arguing with them about songs for
the theatre or the melodies of hymns. Some people thought that
Dionysius indulged in these undignified pastimes out of sheer
idleness, or because he was naturally easy-going and fond of
pleasure, but others considered that he acted deliberately so
that the Corinthians should despise him rather than fear him:
they believed that he wished to dispel any suspicion that he was
oppressed by the change in his way of living or that he still
hankered after power, and that by making a parade of these
trivial amusements he was acting out a part that was foreign to
his nature.

15. For all that, some of his sayings have come down to us,
from which it appears that there was nothing ignoble about the
way in which he adapted himself to his changed situation.
When he arrived at Leucas, which, like Syracuse, had originally

been colonized by the Corinthians, he said that he had the same feelings as young men who have managed to disgrace themselves. They pass their time gaily with their brothers, but are ashamed to meet their fathers, and in the same way he would gladly settle in Leucas, but felt ashamed to live in her mother-city, Corinth. Again, when in Corinth some stranger made a cheap joke about the conversations with philosophers in which he used to take pleasure during the days of his power, and finally asked him what good was Plato's wisdom to him now, he replied, 'Do you really think that I gained nothing from Plato, when I can bear as I do the changes of fortune that I have suffered?' On another occasion, when Aristoxenus the musician and others asked him what fault he had found with Plato and for what reason, Dionysius replied that there were many evils inherent in absolute power but by far the greatest was the fact that of all a tyrant's so-called friends not one will speak his mind, and that it was through such people that he had lost Plato's goodwill. Another man, who thought himself witty, tried to make fun of Dionysius by shaking out his cloak when he came into his presence, as is the custom before a tyrant: Dionysius turned the joke against him by asking him to do the same thing before leaving, to make sure that he had not taken anything from the house away with him. And when Philip of Macedon at a banquet began to sneer at the lyrics and tragedies which Dionysius the elder had left behind him, and expressed surprise as to how a ruler could find so much time for writing, Dionysius smartly retorted, 'He can do it in the hours which you and I and all those whom we call happy fritter away over the wine-bowl.'[23]

Plato had already died by the time that Dionysius arrived in Corinth.[24] But when Diogenes of Sinope[25] met Dionysius for the first time, he remarked, 'How little you deserve to live in this way, Dionysius.' The former tyrant stopped and answered, 'It is kind of you, Diogenes, to sympathize with me in my misfortunes.' 'What do you mean?' retorted Diogenes. 'You surely do not suppose that I am sympathizing with you. I am only angry that a slave such as you, a man who deserved to have grown old and died surrounded by tyranny, as your father did,

should now be sharing the luxury and the wit of our society.'
When I compare these sayings of Dionysius with the lamentations which Philistus poured out about the daughters of
Leptines, and how they had fallen from the splendours of tyrannical power to a humble station in life,[26] they sound to me
like the complaints of a woman who pines for her alabaster
caskets, purple dresses and golden trinkets. At any rate, these
details are relavant, it seems to me, to the writing of my Lives,
and may be useful to readers who are not in too much haste or
absorbed in other concerns.

16. If Dionysius' misfortunes appeared extraordinary, Timoleon's good fortune had something almost miraculous about it.
Fewer than fifty days had passed since his first landing in Sicily
before he had accepted the surrender of the acropolis of Syracuse and had dispatched Dionysius to the Peloponnese. The
Corinthians were so encouraged by this success that they sent
him a reinforcement of 2,000 hoplites and 200 cavalry. This
expedition reached Thurii, but found it impossible to cross into
Sicily, as the straits were patrolled by a strong Carthaginian
fleet. They were therefore obliged to remain there quietly and
await their opportunity, but they took advantage of this
enforced idleness to perform a most noble action. For when the
Thurians left their country on an expedition against the neighbouring people of Bruttium, the Corinthians took charge of
their city and guarded it as faithfully and scrupulously as if it
had been their own.

Meanwhile, Hicetas was blockading the acropolis of Syracuse and preventing any food from reaching the Corinthians by
sea. He also engaged two foreigners to assassinate Timoleon
and sent them to Adranum. Timoleon had never kept a bodyguard about him, and at this time in particular he felt so much
confidence in the protection of the god Adranus that he spent
his time there in a carefree fashion, without fear for his security. The two agents learnt by chance that he was about to offer
a sacrifice, and so they made their way into the sacred precinct
with daggers concealed under their cloaks, mingled with the
crowd that stood around the altar and gradually edged nearer

to Timoleon. Then, at the very moment that they were about to give the signal to attack, a man struck one of them on the head with his sword and cut him down. Neither the assailant nor the surviving assassin stood his ground. The first fled to a lofty rock and sprang onto it still clutching his sword, while the other laid hold of the altar and begged for Timoleon's pardon on condition that he revealed the plot. When he had been promised his safety, he confessed that he and his dead accomplice had been sent to assassinate Timoleon. In the meantime, others dragged down the man who had climbed the rock, who kept crying out that he had done no wrong, but had taken a just revenge for the death of his father, whom the other had murdered some while before at Leontini. Several of the bystanders confirmed the truth of his story, and they marvelled at the ingenious workings of fortune, how she makes one thing the cause of another, brings the most incongruous elements into conjunction, interweaves events which appear to have no relation or connection with one another and so makes use of their respective beginnings and endings to serve her purpose.

The Corinthians gave this man a reward of 10 minas because he had put his just resentment at the service of the deity who was guarding Timoleon. Besides this, he had not, on an immediate impulse, expended the wrath which had long burned within him, but for personal reasons had bided his time and put off the desire to avenge his injury until fortune availed herself of it to preserve the general's life. This stroke of fortune had consequences which stretched beyond the present, since it raised the Corinthians' hopes as they looked to the future, encouraging them to revere and protect Timoleon and regard him as a minister of the gods who had come with a divinely appointed mission to avenge the wrongs of Sicily.[27]

17. When Hicetas had failed in this attempt on Timoleon's life and saw that more and more Sicilians were going over to him, he began to blame himself for not having taken full advantage of the strong Carthaginian forces which were at hand. Hitherto, he had only used them secretly and in small detachments, introducing the troops of his allies by stealth, as though he were

ashamed of their presence, but now he appealed to the Carthaginian commander Mago to join him with all the forces at his
disposal. So Mago, with a formidable fleet of a hundred and
fifty ships, sailed in and took possession of the harbour. At the
same time he landed 60,000 of his infantry and quartered them
in the city, so that it seemed to everyone that the subjugation of
Sicily by the barbarians, which had so long been talked of and
expected, had finally come to pass. For never before in all their
many campaigns in Sicily had the Carthaginians actually captured Syracuse, but now Hicetas had opened the gates and
handed over the city, and men could see that it had been transformed into a barbarian camp. In the meantime, the Corinthian
troops who were holding out in the acropolis were in a position
of great difficulty and danger: their food was running short
because the harbours were blockaded, and they were constantly obliged to divide their forces to beat off skirmishes and
assaults upon the walls and to counter every ploy and every
sort of siege strategy employed by the attacking army.

18. However, Timoleon came to their rescue by sending them
grain from Catana, which was carried in small fishing boats
and other light craft. These vessels could run the gauntlet of the
Carthaginian fleet, especially in heavy weather, by stealing in
between the barbarian triremes, which could not keep together
because of the roughness of the sea. Mago and Hicetas soon
became aware of these operations and determined to capture
the Corinthians' source of supply at Catana, and so they sailed
out of Syracuse with the best of their troops. But Neon, the
Corinthian officer in command of the garrison, noticed from
the acropolis that the enemy's forces left behind had relaxed
their attention and were off their guard. He launched a sudden
attack, caught them dispersed, killed a number of them, routed
others and then stormed and occupied the district known as
Achradina. This was the strongest and most impregnable part
of Syracuse, which is a city consisting of several townships
joined together. Neon was now in possession of large supplies
of grain and of money. Accordingly, he did not withdraw or go
back to the acropolis but fortified the perimeter of Achradina,

and, by linking it to the defences of the acropolis, succeeded in holding both areas at once. Meanwhile, Mago and Hicetas had almost arrived at Catana when a courier from Syracuse overtook them and reported the capture of Achradina. They were alarmed at the news and returned at full speed, so that in the end they not only failed to capture the objective for which they had set out, but lost the position they had originally held.

19. In these successes, foresight and courage might very well claim to have played as important a part as fortune, but the success which followed must be entirely credited to good fortune. The Corinthian reinforcements had all this time been waiting at Thurii, partly for fear of the Carthaginian triremes which were lying in wait for them under the command of Hanno, and partly because of a storm which had lasted for many days and had made the sea too rough for them to attempt the crossing; they now set out to travel over land through Bruttium. They used a combination of force and persuasion to make their way through this barbarian territory, and began descending to Rhegium, where a violent storm was still raging at sea. But the Carthaginian admiral had formed the conclusion that the Corinthians would never venture out and that there was thus no object in his continuing to keep watch for them. So he devised, as he imagined, a masterly ruse. He ordered his sailors to crown themselves with garlands, decked out his triremes with scarlet battle-flags and Greek shields, and sailed off towards Syracuse. As he sailed past the acropolis at full speed, his crews clapped their hands and laughed, and he shouted out that he had just defeated and captured the Corinthian reinforcements as they were attempting to cross the straits, imagining that in this way he would make the besieged garrison despair of relief. But while he was engaged in this foolish attempt at deception, the Corinthians, after passing through Bruttium, had already arrived in Rhegium. There they found nobody to bar their passage, and as the gale had unexpectedly died down and left the sea completely calm and smooth, they quickly embarked in the ferry boats and fishing craft which they found at hand and crossed to Sicily; indeed, there was

such a dead calm that they were able to make their horses swim alongside and tow them by their reins.

20. As soon as they had all crossed, Timoleon came to meet them and immediately took possession of Messana. There the reinforcements were united with his other troops and the whole army marched on Syracuse. In taking the offensive in this way, he was relying more on the good fortune and success he had so far enjoyed than on the strength of his army, for his entire force numbered no more than four thousand. However, when Mago learnt of his approach he became alarmed and perplexed, and his suspicions were increased by the following circumstance. In the marshes around the city, which receive much fresh water from springs and rivers flowing to the sea, there lived great numbers of eels which could always be caught by anybody who cared to fish for them, and whenever there was a pause in the fighting, the mercenary soldiers of both sides used to fish there together. As they were all Greeks and had no reason to hate each other personally, these men would bravely risk their lives in battle, but at times of truce they would meet and converse in the friendliest fashion. So on this occasion, as they fished, they spoke enthusiastically of how rich the sea was in fish and of the character of the city and the neighbourhood. Then one of the Corinthian garrison said, 'You are Greeks like us. Can it be that you really want to hand over a great city such as this with all its riches and amenities to the barbarians? Do you really want to plant the Carthaginians, who are the cruellest and wickedest people on earth, so much nearer to our country? You ought to pray that there were many more Sicilies to stand between them and Greece. Or do you imagine that these men have gathered an army from the Pillars of Heracles[28] and the Atlantic to risk their lives for the sake of Hicetas and his family? If Hicetas possessed the judgement of a real ruler, he would not be trying to drive out the founders of his city, or leading his country's enemies against her, when he could be enjoying the honour and authority which would be his by right if he allied himself to Timoleon and the Corinthians.' The news of these talks quickly spread through the mercenaries' camp and implanted in Mago's

mind the suspicion that a plot was being hatched against him; he was all the more ready to believe this because he had long been searching for a pretext to leave the island. So although Hicetas begged him to remain and tried to convince him how far superior his forces were to the enemy's, Mago preferred to believe that Timoleon's courage and good fortune more than compensated for his weakness in numbers. And so he weighed anchor at once and sailed for Africa, thus allowing Sicily to slip out of his hands to his own discredit and against all human logic.

21. On the day after Mago's departure, Timoleon drew up his troops to attack. But when the Corinthians learnt of Mago's flight and saw the docks completely empty of ships, they could not help laughing at his cowardice, and sent a crier round the city to offer a reward for anyone who could tell them to where the Carthaginian fleet had slunk off. In spite of this, Hicetas still put on a bold front and showed no sign of relaxing his grip on the city; instead, he held on tenaciously to those quarters which were well fortified and difficult to attack. Accordingly, Timoleon divided his forces. He himself led the assault along the River Anapus, where the fighting was likely to be fiercest, and ordered another force under Isias the Corinthian to advance on the city from Achradina. A third assault was directed against Epipolae by Deinarchus and Demaretus, the officers who had brought the reinforcements from Corinth. The attack was launched from all three quarters at once, and Hicetas' troops were soon overwhelmed and routed. To have captured the city by storm and gained control of it so quickly once the enemy had been driven out was undoubtedly due to the valour of the soldiers and the skill of their general, but the fact that not a single Corinthian was killed or even wounded can only be ascribed to Timoleon's luck: this good fortune of his seemed to rival his own personal courage, so as to make those who learn of his story marvel even more at the providence which smiled on all his undertakings than at his own achievements. His fame now spread not only over Sicily and Italy, but within a few days the news of his success was echoing through

every state in Greece; and in Corinth, where the people were still in doubt as to whether the second expedition had reached Sicily, the news of its safe crossing and of its victory arrived at the same moment. The triumph of his campaign was complete and fortune added a special lustre to his achievements because of the extraordinary speed with which they were accomplished.

22. When Timoleon had captured the acropolis, he did not repeat Dion's mistake of sparing the place because of the beauty of its architecture or the money it had cost to build.[29] He was determined not to arouse the suspicions which had brought first discredit and finally disaster upon his predecessor, and so he had it proclaimed that any Syracusan who wished could come with a crowbar and help to cast down the bulwarks of tyranny. Thereupon, the whole population went up to the fortress, and taking that day and its proclamation to mark a truly secure foundation for their freedom, they overthrew and demolished not only the acropolis but also the palaces and tombs of the tyrants. Timoleon immediately had the site levelled and built the courts of justice over it, thus delighting the Syracusans by displaying the supremacy of democracy over tyranny.

But once he had captured the city, Timoleon found it empty of citizens. Many of the Syracusans had perished in the various wars and uprisings, while others had escaped from the rule of the tyrants into exile. The population had declined so rapidly that the market-place of Syracuse had become thickly over-grown, and horses were pastured in the midst of it, while their grooms stretched out beside them on the grass. In the other cities, almost without exception, deer and wild boar roamed at large, and those who had leisure could hunt them in the streets and around the walls. Those citizens who had established themselves in castles and strongholds were unwilling to obey any summons or venture down to the city, and they had come to regard the market-place, political activity and public speak-ing with fear and horror, because they had so often proved the breeding-ground for their tyrants. Accordingly, Timoleon and the Syracusans decided to write to the Corinthians and urge them to send settlers from Greece. One reason for this was that the land would otherwise be doomed to lie uncultivated, and another was that they expected a great invasion from Africa. They had learnt that Mago had committed suicide, that the Carthaginians in their rage at his mishandling of the expedition had impaled his dead body and that they were gathering a great force with the intention of crossing into Sicily in the following summer.

23. When these letters from Timoleon were delivered at Corinth, they were accompanied by delegates from Syracuse, who begged the Corinthians to take the city under their protection and become its founders once again. For their part, the Corinthians would not take any advantage of this opportunity to enrich themselves, nor did they appropriate the city for themselves. Instead, in the first place they visited the sacred games in Greece and the principal religious festivals, and had it publicly proclaimed that they had overthrown the tyranny in Syracuse and driven out the tyrant; they now invited former citizens of Syracuse and any other Sicilian Greeks who wished to settle in the city to go and live there as free and independent men and divided the land among them on just and equal terms. Secondly, they dispatched messages to Asia Minor and to the islands, where they had learnt that most of the scattered groups of exiles were living. These men they invited to come to Corinth, and they promised that the Corinthians would at their own expense provide them with leaders, ships and a safe passage to Syracuse. Through these proclamations, the city of Corinth won for herself the most well-deserved praise and the noblest fame for her actions in liberating the country from its tyrants, rescuing it from the barbarians and restoring it to its legitimate citizens.

However, even when all the exiles had assembled at Corinth their numbers were still too few, and so they begged to be allowed to invite colonists from Corinth and from the rest of Greece. Then, after they had raised their numbers to as many as 10,000, they sailed for Syracuse.[30] But in the meantime multitudes of people from Italy and Sicily had now also flocked to Timoleon, and when he found that the total number of immigrants had risen to 60,000, according to Athanis,[31] he sold the houses in the city for 1,000 talents. This measure secured for the original owners the right to buy back their houses, and at the same time raised a large sum of money for the benefit of the community. Before this the public funds had sunk so low, not only for any civil requirements but also for the financing of the war, that the community had been obliged to put up the public statues for auction. A meeting of the assembly had been held and a vote taken on the case of each statue, as if they had been officials submitting their accounts. It was on this occasion, so the story goes, that the Syracusans voted to save the statue of Gelon, their former tyrant – although they condemned all the rest to be sold – because they admired and honoured him for the victory he had won over the Carthaginians at Himera.[32]

24. Now that the city was beginning to revive and its population to be replenished as citizens poured in from every quarter, Timoleon resolved to set the other Sicilian cities free and to root out every tyrant on the island. He therefore invaded the territory of these rulers,[33] and compelled Hicetas to abandon his alliance with the Carthaginians and to agree to pull down his fortresses and live as a private citizen in Leontini. And when Leptines,[34] the tyrant who ruled Apollonia and a number of other small towns, saw that he was in danger of being captured and he surrendered voluntarily, Timoleon spared his life and sent him to Corinth. He considered that it would be an admirable lesson for the Sicilian tyrants to live in the mother-city which had colonized Sicily and where the Greeks could see them leading the humble life of exiles. Besides this, he was anxious that his own mercenaries should not remain idle but should have the opportunity to enrich themselves by plundering enemy territory. He then returned to Syracuse in order to supervise the remodelling of the constitution and to help Cephalus and Dionysius, the lawgivers who had come from Corinth, to embody its most important provisions in the most satisfactory form. But at the same time he sent out an expedition under Deinarchus and Demaretus into the western districts of Sicily, which were controlled by the Carthaginians. Here

they persuaded many cities to revolt against the barbarians, and not only secured great quantities of plunder for themselves, but succeeded in raising money from the spoils to finance the war.

25. Meanwhile,[35] the Carthaginians landed at Lilybaeum[36] with an army of 70,000 men, 200 triremes and 1,000 transports. These ships carried siege-engines, four-horse chariots, abundant supplies of food and other military stores. The Carthaginians had had enough of the minor operations of earlier campaigns and were determined to drive the Greeks out of Sicily in a single offensive, and indeed their force was quite enough to overwhelm all the Sicilian Greeks, even if the latter had not been disunited and weakened by their own internal quarrels. When the Carthaginians learnt that the territory they controlled was being ravaged by the Corinthians, they were enraged and immediately sent an expedition against them under the command of Hasdrubal and Hamilcar. The news quickly reached Syracuse and the people were so alarmed by the reports of the size of the enemy's forces that Timoleon could only with difficulty prevail upon 3,000 men out of the many tens of thousands of able-bodied Syracusans to take up arms and march out with him. His force of mercenaries was only four thousand strong, and of these about a thousand lost heart as they neared the Carthaginians and slunk back to Syracuse. They protested that Timoleon must be out of his wits and that the judgement one should expect of a general of his years had obviously deserted him. Not only was he advancing with 5,000 infantry and 1,000 cavalry against an enemy force of 70,000, but he was leading his troops on a march of eight days away from Syracuse. This would make it impossible for any fugitives from the battle to escape, and those who fell on the battlefield could expect no burial. For his part, Timoleon thought it an advantage that these men had revealed their cowardice before the fighting began. As for the rest, he encouraged them and led them by forced marches to the banks of the River Crimisus,[37] where he had heard that the Carthaginians were concentrating their forces.

26. Timoleon was climbing a hill, from the crest of which they expected to gain a view of the enemy's troops and their camp, when quite by chance he met a convoy of mules laden with parsley. The soldiers thought that this was an unlucky omen, because it is our custom to place wreaths of this herb upon tombs – hence the saying concerning anyone who is dangerously ill, that he 'needs his parsley'. Timoleon was anxious to get rid of their superstitious fears and raise their spirits, and so he ordered a halt and made a short speech to meet the occasion. He made a point of telling them that the crown of victory had of its own accord fallen into their hands before the battle. He was referring to the fact that it is this very herb which the Corinthians use to crown their victors at the Isthmian Games, since they regard parsley as the sacred wreath of their country. For at that date parsley was still used at the Isthmian as it is now at the Nemean Games,[38] for it is only quite recently that the pine was introduced at Corinth. So when Timoleon had finished speaking, he took some parsley and crowned himself with it, whereupon the officers and soldiers around him all followed his example. Besides this, the diviners noticed two eagles flying towards them, one of which was clutching a snake in its talons, while the other uttered a loud and inspiring cry as it flew.[39] The diviners pointed these out to the soldiers, and the whole army with one accord began to pray and call upon the gods.

27. The time of year was the early summer; the month of Thargelion was nearing its end and the summer solstice was approaching. A thick mist hung over the river, which at first completely enveloped the plain, so that nothing could be seen of the enemy: a confused and indistinguishable noise which echoed up to the brow of the hill was the only indication that their huge army was on the move. When the Corinthians had reached the summit, they halted, laid down their shields and rested. Meanwhile, the sun was climbing towards the meridian and drawing the mist into the upper air. The thick haze began to gather together and drift towards the heights, so that it hung in clouds over the mountain crests, while the lower parts of the

valley became clear and open; the River Crimisus came into view and the enemy could be seen crossing it. First came the four-horse chariots formidably arrayed for battle, and next a body of 10,000 hoplites with white shields. These the Corinthians supposed to be Carthaginians, judging by the brilliance of their armour and the slow pace and strict discipline of their advance. After them the troops of other nationalities were surging forward, making the crossing in a confused and disorderly fashion. Timoleon grasped the fact that it was the river which controlled the speed of the enemy's advance and gave the Greeks the opportunity of cutting off and engaging whatever numbers of the enemy they chose. He pointed out to his men how the enemy's phalanx had been divided by the river: some had already crossed, while others were still awaiting their turn. So he ordered Demaretus to take the cavalry and charge the Carthaginians, so as to throw their ranks into confusion before they could take up their battle formation. He then marched down into the plain and drew up his own order of battle, for which he placed the Sicilian Greeks on the wings, distributed a few of his mercenaries among them and massed the Syracusans and the best of his mercenary troops in the centre. Then he waited a little to watch the effect of the cavalry charge. He saw that the horsemen could not get to close quarters with the Carthaginians, because the chariots drove up and down and protected their front. The horsemen were compelled to wheel about continually, in order to prevent their own formation from being broken up, and to charge in short rushes whenever the opportunity offered. So Timoleon snatched up his shield and called upon the infantry to take heart and follow him. His voice seemed to them to have taken on a superhuman strength and volume, whether it was from emotion that he raised it so high because of the intensity of the fighting and the enthusiasm which it inspired, or whether, as most of his men felt at the time, some god were speaking through his lips. His troops instantly responded with encouraging shouts, and urged him to lead them on and not wait a moment longer. Thereupon, he ordered the cavalry to ride round the line of chariots and attack the enemy from the flank; at the same time he made his own front ranks close up and lock their shields, and then with the trumpet sounding the charge he bore down upon the Carthaginians.

28. The enemy resisted his first attack courageously, and thanks to the protection of their iron breast-plates and helmets and the great shields which they held in front of them, they were able to ward off the spear-thrusts of the Greeks. But when they closed for sword-fighting and the struggle became a matter of skill no less than of strength, suddenly a tremendous storm burst upon them from the hills, with deafening peals of thunder and brilliant flashes of lightning. The dark clouds which until then had hovered over the mountain peaks descended upon the battlefield, mingled with sudden gusts of wind, rain and hail. The tempest enveloped the Greeks from behind and beat upon their backs, but it struck the barbarians in the face, while the lightning dazzled their eyes as the storm swept violently along with torrents of rain and continual flashes darting out from the clouds. These were terrible disadvantages, especially to inexperienced troops, and above all, it seems, the roar of the thunder and the beating of the rain and hail upon the men's armour prevented them from hearing their officers' commands. Besides this, the mud also proved a great hindrance to the Carthaginians – who were not lightly equipped, but clad in full armour, as has been said – and so did the water which filled the folds of their tunics and made them heavy and unwieldy in combat. It was easy for the Greeks to fell them, and once on the ground it was impossible for them to rise again from the mud because they were encumbered by their armour. For in fact the Crimisus, which had already been swollen to a torrent by the rain, overflowed its banks because the great numbers who were crossing it impeded its course. At the same time, the surrounding plain, into which many ravines and hollows ran down from the hills, was flooded with rivulets which poured over the ground unconfined to any channels, and among these the Carthaginians floundered and could move only with great difficulty.

At last, as the storm still beat upon them and the Greeks had broken their front line of four hundred men, the main body

turned and fled. Many were overtaken in the plain and cut
down as they ran, many were caught by the river and swept
away as they became entangled with those who were trying to
cross, but most of the slaughter was done by the Greek light-
armed troops who intercepted the fugitives and dispatched
them as they made for the hills. At any rate, it is said that of the
10,000 who fell on the battlefield 3,000 were Carthaginians, a
fearful loss to the city, for these men had no superiors in birth,
in wealth or in military prowess. Nor is there any record of so
many Carthaginians ever having fallen in a single engagement
before; this was because they generally employed Libyans,
Iberians and Numidians to fight their battles, so that when
they were defeated the loss was borne by other nations.

29. The Greeks discovered the exalted rank of those who had
fallen through the richness of the spoils. They crossed the river
and seized the Carthaginian camp, and those who stripped the
bodies paid little attention to bronze or iron, so great was the
abundance of silver and gold. A great many prisoners were
secreted away by the soldiers,[40] but even so 5,000 were delivered into the public stock and 200 of the four-horsed chariots
were also captured. But the most glorious and magnificent
spectacle of all was Timoleon's tent, which was surrounded by
piles of booty of every kind, among them being 1,000 breast-
plates of particularly fine workmanship and 10,000 shields.
There was only a small number of men to strip so many bodies,
and the quantities of plunder which they found were so
immense that it was not until the third day after the battle that
they erected a trophy.[41]

Timoleon sent home to Corinth the handsomest pieces of the
captured armour, together with the dispatch announcing his
success, for he wished his native city to be the envy of the whole
world. His ambition was that in Corinth, alone of Greek cities,
men should see the most conspicuous temples adorned not
with the spoils taken from Greek states, melancholy offerings
obtained by the slaughter of men of their own race and blood,
but decked with ornaments won from the barbarians and bearing honourable inscriptions which testified to the justice as well

as the courage of the victors: in this instance, the memorial proclaimed that the Corinthians and their general Timoleon freed the Greeks living in Sicily from the yoke of Carthage and thus dedicated these thank-offerings to the gods.[42]

30. After the battle, Timoleon left his mercenaries to plunder the Carthaginian dominions in the west of the island and returned to Syracuse. There he expelled from Sicily the thousand mercenaries who had deserted him before the battle, and compelled them to leave Syracuse before sunset. These men crossed into Italy and there they were treacherously massacred by the Bruttians: such was the vengeance that the gods took upon them for their betrayal of Timoleon.

But Mamercus of Catana and Hicetas – either because they were jealous of Timoleon's successes or because they feared him as an implacable enemy who would never trust a tyrant – once more formed an alliance with the Carthaginians and urged them to send a general and an army if they did not wish to be driven out of Sicily altogether. Accordingly, Gisco sailed across with a fleet of seventy ships. His force also included a contingent of Greek mercenaries: the Carthaginians had never employed Greek soldiers before, but by now they had come to admire them, thinking that no one could withstand their attack and believing them to be the most warlike men anywhere to be found. Mamercus and Hicetas joined forces in the territory of Messana and there killed four hundred of Timoleon's mercenaries who had been sent to reinforce the local inhabitants; next they laid an ambush near the place named Hierae, which was situated in the part of the island controlled by Carthage, and annihilated the force of mercenaries commanded by Euthymus of Leucas. These apparent reverses, however, made Timoleon's good fortune especially famous. For this band of mercenaries included some of the men who, under the command of Philomelus the Phocian and Onomarchus, had seized Delphi and taken part in the plundering of the sacred treasures.[43] This act of sacrilege caused them to be universally detested and shunned as men who had put themselves under a curse. For some time they roamed about the Peloponnese and there they were recruited by Timoleon, who at that time was unable to enlist any other troops. Since they had come to Sicily they had been victorious in every action they had entered under his command, but after his greatest battles had been fought, he had sent them out to help the other Sicilian peoples and there they had perished to a man, not all at once but in a succession of engagements. Thus justice exacted her penalty, while at the same time Timoleon's good fortune was sustained through a stroke of retribution[44] which ensured that no harm should come to the good through the punishment of the wicked.[45] In short, the favour which the gods showed towards Timoleon was a cause for wonder just as much in his apparent reverses as in his successes.

31. However, the people of Syracuse were angry at the insults which the tyrants heaped upon them after these defeats. Mamercus, who had a high opinion of himself as a writer of poems and tragedies, boasted of his victory over the mercenaries, and when he dedicated their shields to the gods, he composed the following insulting inscription:

> These gilded shields of purple with amber and ivory inlaid
> Proved no match in the field for our cheap little shields.[46]

Afterwards, while Timoleon was engaged in an expedition to Calauria,[47] Hicetas made a raid on Syracusan territory, carried off much plunder and caused a great deal of wanton damage. On his return, he marched past Calauria to show his contempt for Timoleon, who only had a small force with him. Timoleon allowed him to pass, but then pursued him with cavalry and light-armed troops. When Hicetas learnt that he was being followed, he crossed the River Damurias[48] and halted on the far side to receive the enemy; he was encouraged to do this by the difficulty of the crossing and the steepness of the river banks. This caused an astonishing outburst of rivalry among the officers of Timoleon's cavalry, which delayed the attack. Not one of them was willing to follow behind his comrades in crossing the river, but each demanded the honour of leading the charge himself. As it was certain that their crossing would be disorderly if they crowded and tried to push their way past one another, Timoleon decided to settle the order of precedence by lot. He, therefore, took a seal-ring from each of the commanders, dropped them all into his cloak, mixed them up, and held up to them the first one that came out, which, as luck would have it, displayed as its device a trophy of victory. When the young officers saw this, they gave a shout of delight and, without waiting for the other rings to be drawn, all made their way across the river-bed and closed with the enemy. Their charge proved irresistible and Hicetas' troops fled: they all threw away their arms and left a thousand dead upon the field.

32. A little later, Timoleon invaded the territory of Leontini and captured Hicetas alive, together with his son Eupolemus, and Euthymus the commander of his cavalry. The soldiers bound the three of them and led them into Timoleon's presence. Hicetas and his young son were put to death as tyrants and traitors, and Euthymus, although he was a man of exceptional courage, who had shown great daring in battle, was likewise executed without mercy, because of an insult which he was accused of having uttered against the Corinthians. It was alleged that when the Corinthians were marching against Leontini, Euthymus had made a speech to the people telling them that they had nothing to fear if 'Corinthian women have come out from their homes'.[49] In the same way, the great majority of mankind are more offended by a contemptuous word than by a hostile action, and find it easier to put up with an injury than an insult. An act of self-defence is tolerated from an enemy as a matter of necessity, while insults are regarded as springing from an excess of hatred or spite.

33. On Timoleon's return the Syracusans put the wives and daughters of Hicetas on trial before the assembly and executed them. This seems to have been the most unpleasant action in Timoleon's career, for if he had opposed the sentence it would not have been carried out. But apparently he chose not to interfere, and to abandon the victims to the fury of the citizens and

their desire to avenge the wrongs done to Dion, who had driven out Dionysius. For it had been Hicetas who had had Dion's wife Arete, his son, who was still a boy, and his sister Aristomache thrown into the sea alive – as has been recorded in my *Life of Dion*.[50]

34. After this, Timoleon marched to Catana against Mamercus, defeated and routed his army in a pitched battle near the River Abolus, and killed over 2,000 of his troops, many of whom were Carthaginian auxiliaries sent him by Gisco. The result of this victory was that the Carthaginians sued for peace and a treaty was negotiated.[51] The terms were that they should keep the territory west of the River Lycus,[52] that any of the inhabitants of this region who so wished should be allowed to emigrate to Syracusan territory with their families and property and that they should renounce their alliances with the tyrants. This agreement reduced Mamercus to despair, and he sailed to Italy to try to form an alliance with the Lucanians against Timoleon and the Syracusans. But he was deserted by his followers, who put their triremes about, sailed back to Sicily and handed over Catana to Timoleon, so that Mamercus was obliged to seek refuge with Hippo, the tyrant of Messana. Timoleon followed him and blockaded Messana by land and sea, and Hippo was captured as he tried to escape by ship. The people of Messana brought him to the public theatre and summoned their children from the schools to witness that most exemplary of spectacles, the punishment of a tyrant; they then tortured him and put him to death. As for Mamercus, he surrendered to Timoleon on condition that he should be put on trial before the people of Syracuse and that Timoleon should not be his accuser. He was taken to Syracuse, and when he was brought before the assembly, he tried to deliver a speech which he had prepared a long while before. But he was continually shouted down, and when he saw that the assembly was inexorably hostile to him, he threw away his cloak, rushed across the theatre and dashed his head against one of the stone steps in an effort to kill himself. However, he was not lucky enough to die as a result but was taken away while he was still alive and executed like a common thief.

35. In this way, Timoleon rooted out all the tyrannies in Sicily and put an end to the wars between her rulers. When he had first arrived, he found that the island had been reduced almost to a wilderness by its troubles and had grown hateful to its inhabitants. But he transformed it into a country so civilized and so desirable in the eyes of the rest of the world that foreigners came from across the sea to settle in the places from which the native inhabitants had fled before. Acragas and Gela, for example, two great cities which had been left desolate by the Carthaginians after the war with Athens,[53] were now repopulated, the first by Megellus and Pheristus from Elea, and the second by Gorgus who sailed from Ceos and brought back with him a number of the original citizens. To all these colonists, Timoleon offered not only security and tranquillity while they were establishing themselves after many years of war, but also supplied their wants and took especial pleasure in assisting them, so that they cherished him as a founder. These feelings were shared by every other city on the island, so that no peace could be concluded, no laws laid down, no land divided between colonists and no constitutional changes made to the general satisfaction, unless Timoleon took a hand in them: he was, as it were, the master-craftsman[54] who, when a building is nearing completion, adds a final touch of his artistry which makes the work pleasing to gods and men.

36. At any rate, although in Timoleon's lifetime there were many Greeks, such as Timotheus,[55] Agesilaus,[56] Pelopidas and Epaminondas (Timoleon's especial model), who rose to positions of great power and accomplished great things, yet there was in these men's achievements an element of violence and of laborious effort which detracts from their lustre, and which in some instances caused their authors to be blamed or to regret what they had done. But in the whole career of Timoleon – if we set aside his treatment of his brother, which was forced upon him by circumstances – there is not a single action to which we could not fittingly, as Timaeus says, apply the words of Sophocles, 'O gods, what deity of love, what desire had a part in this?'[57] For the poetry of Antimachus and the paintings of Dionysius (both of them men of Colophon), for all their

strength and energy, leave us with an impression of something strained and forced about them; on the other hand, the paintings of Nicomachus[58] and the verses of Homer, in addition to the power and grace which they possess, strike us as having been executed with an extraordinary ease and spontaneity. In the same way, if we contrast the generalship of Epaminondas and of Agesilaus – both of whom faced great difficulties and had to overcome tremendous odds – with that of Timoleon, the glories of his achievements seem to have been accomplished almost without effort, and his success appears, if we consider the matter justly and carefully, to be the product not of fortune but of virtue reinforced by fortune. And yet Timoleon himself put down all his successes to fortune, for in his letters to his friends in Corinth and in his public speeches to the Syracusans he often remarked that he was grateful to the divine power which had evidently determined to save Sicily and had designated him as its liberator. Indeed, he built in his house a shrine to Automatia, the goddess of Chance, and dedicated the whole building to the divine spirit.

The house he lived in had been chosen for him by the Syracusans as a prize for his achievements in the field, and they presented him with the pleasantest and most beautiful estate in their territory; here he spent most of his leisure with his wife and children after he had brought them from Corinth. For he never returned to his native land, nor did he play any part in the troubles of Greece at this time, nor expose himself to political envy, the rock upon which so many generals have been wrecked because of their insatiable pursuit of honours and power.[59] Instead, he remained in Sicily, enjoying the blessings which he himself had brought about, the greatest of which was the spectacle of so many cities and tens of thousands of people whose happiness was due to his efforts.

37. However, just as every lark, according to Simonides, grows a crest,[60] so every democracy produces, it seems, a false accuser, and even Timoleon found himself attacked by two of the Syracusan demagogues, Laphystius and Demaenetus. When Laphystius tried to make him pay surety to appear at a trial, Timoleon refused to allow the people to shout the man down or prevent

his action; he told them that he had willingly endured all the trials and dangers of his campaigns for just this object: that any Syracusan who wished could have recourse to the laws. And when Demaenetus launched an outspoken attack in the assembly on Timoleon's generalship, he offered him no reply but said that he was grateful to the gods for having granted his prayer that he might live to see the Syracusans in possession of the right of free speech.

Timoleon had indeed accomplished what were universally regarded as the greatest and most glorious achievements of any Greek of his time, and he was the only man who had actually performed those exploits which the orators in their speeches at the great festivals were constantly exhorting his countrymen to attempt.[61] His good fortune had removed him from the troubles which befell his native land and saved him from staining his hands with the blood of his compatriots. He had shown courage and resourcefulness against barbarians and tyrants, and justice and moderation towards the Greeks and his friends; he had set up most of his trophies without causing tears to be shed or mourning to be worn by his fellow-citizens of Syracuse or of Corinth, and in less than eight years he had restored Sicily to its inhabitants, delivered from the strife and disorders which had constantly plagued it in the past.

As he was now old, his sight failed him, and then after a little while he became completely blind. He had done nothing himself to bring on this condition, nor was he the victim of any wanton trick of fortune, but this impairment of his vision was hereditary, it seems, and came upon him with advancing years: it is said that several of his kindred lost their sight in the same way after it had been weakened by old age. But Athanis records that, while the war against Hippo and Mamercus was still ongoing, Timoleon's sight was obscured by glaucoma when he was in camp at Mylae, and he says that it was clear to everybody that Timoleon was going blind; however, he did not abandon the siege for this reason, but persevered until he had taken the tyrants prisoner. Then, as soon as he returned to Syracuse, he laid down his post of commander-in-chief and begged the Syracusans to relieve him of it, since the war had been successfully concluded.

38. It was to be expected that Timoleon would endure his misfortune without complaint, but what was more remarkable was the honour and gratitude which the Syracusans showed him in his affliction. They frequently visited him in person and would often bring to his town or country house any strangers who might be staying in the city, so as to let them set eyes on the benefactor of Syracuse. They were delighted and intensely proud of the fact that he had chosen to spend the rest of his life among them, and had disregarded the brilliant reception which had been prepared for him in Greece in consequence of his successes. And of all the many decrees that were passed and ceremonials enacted in his honour, none is more impressive than the resolution voted by the Syracusans that whenever they engaged in a war against a foreign enemy, they would employ a Corinthian as their commander. They also honoured Timoleon in the procedure which they adopted in the meetings of their assembly, for whereas they would discuss ordinary business among themselves, as soon as any important debate was impending, they would send for Timoleon. On these occasions, he would be driven through the market-place in a carriage drawn by mules to the theatre where their assemblies were held. The carriage would then be ushered in and the people would greet him all in unison and call upon him by name. He would return their greeting and allow a short pause for their salutations and applause, after which he would listen carefully to the subject of the debate and finally give his own opinion. When this had been confirmed by a vote, his attendants would escort his carriage out of the theatre, the citizens would cheer and applaud him on his way and would then proceed at once to dispatch the rest of their business by themselves.

39. Such was the honour and affection with which Timoleon was cherished in his last years. He had come to be regarded as the father of the whole people, and at last a mild illness combined with old age to end his life.[62] A period of several days was decreed for the city to prepare his funeral and for the inhabitants of the country districts and foreign visitors to assemble. The ceremony was performed with great splendour and the bier,

superbly decorated, was carried by a group of young men, chosen by lot, over the ground where the palace of Dionysius had stood before Timoleon had had it pulled down. The bier was followed by many thousands of men and women, all of them crowned with garlands and dressed in white, so that their appearance suggested a festival rather than a funeral. Their tears and their lamentations, which mingled with their praises of the dead man, clearly showed that this was no merely formal tribute nor a ceremony enacted in obedience to a decree, but a true expression of their sorrow and gratitude. At last, when the bier was placed upon the funeral pyre, a man named Demetrius, who possessed the most powerful voice of any herald of his time, read out the following announcement:

> The people of Syracuse have decreed the burial of Timoleon the Corinthian, son of Timodemus, at public cost of two hundred minas. They resolve to honour his memory for all time with annual contests of music, horse-racing and athletics, because he overthrew the tyrants, subdued the barbarians, repopulated the largest of the devastated cities and then restored their laws to the people of Sicily.

They buried him in the market-place,[63] and later surrounded the area with a colonnade and built wrestling-schools; they set the site apart as a gymnasium for their young men and named it the Timoleonteum. They continued to apply the laws and the constitution which Timoleon had established, and lived for a long time[64] in happiness and prosperity.

COMPARISON OF AEMILIUS
AND TIMOLEON

1(40). After this narrative of the two men's lives, it is clear that a comparison will not find many differences or dissimilarities between them. Both men fought wars against notable opponents, one against Macedonians, the other against Carthaginians. Both won famous victories, one taking Macedonia and putting an end to the royal line of Antigonus in its seventh generation,[65] the other annihilating all the tyrannies in Sicily and liberating the island – unless one wants to argue that, whereas Perseus was in full strength and had inflicted a defeat on the Romans when Aemilius encountered him, Dionysius was altogether worn down and desperate when Timoleon encountered him. On the other hand, one might argue in Timoleon's favour that he defeated many tyrants and vanquished the formidable might of Carthage with an army hastily got together. Aemilius had at his disposal a force of well-disciplined and experienced soldiers, while Timoleon's men were ill-disciplined mercenaries who had got into the habit of pleasing themselves on campaign. For when equal success is won from unequal resources, the credit must go to the commander.

2(41). Both men were just and incorruptible in their conduct of affairs. But Aemilius seems to have been prepared for this from the outset by the laws of his country, whereas Timoleon's integrity was self-generated. Evidence for this can be found in the fact that the Romans of that time were all humbly obedient to their traditions, fearing both the laws and their magistrates, whereas there was no other Greek leader or general, save only Dion, who was not corrupted by contact with Sicily. Yet even

Dion some people suspect of craving monarchy and dreaming of a Spartan-style kingship. In addition, Timaeus says that the Syracusans dismissed Gylippus and sent him away in disgrace because they found him guilty of avarice and greed in command.[66] And many have written about the laws and treaties which Pharax the Spartan and Callippus the Athenian violated in their hope of ruling Sicily.[67] Yet who were they and what were their resources that they entertained such hopes? Pharax paid court to Dionysius after the latter had been banished from Syracuse, and Callippus was one of Dion's mercenary captains. But Timoleon was sent out as general with full powers at the urgent request of the Syracusans; he did not seek power, but needed only to hold on to that power which they gladly gave him. And yet he ended his own command and stepped down from office as soon as he had dissolved the unlawful power of others.

It is admirable of Aemilius that, though he subdued such a great kingdom, he enriched himself by not a single drachma. He neither looked upon nor touched the treasures he seized, and yet he bestowed large amounts on others.[68] I do not say that Timoleon is to be blamed because he accepted a fine house and an estate; accepting in such circumstances is not shameful. But not accepting is better and reveals an abundance of virtue, which shows itself in not wanting what one lawfully might have. A body that can endure either heat or cold is weaker than one which can endure both extremes. In the same way, a soul only possesses complete vigour and strength if it is neither corrupted and enervated by success nor humbled by misfortune. On this reckoning, Aemilius is more perfect, since in the grievous misfortune and great sorrow brought on him by the death of his sons he displayed no less greatness and dignity than he did in the midst of his successes. But Timoleon, though he performed a noble deed in killing his brother, could not use his reason to help him face his sorrow but was cast down with regret and grief and could not endure the sight of the agora or speakers' platform. One should avoid and shun shameful conduct; but over-sensitivity to every kind of ill-report suggests a character which is kind and delicate but not truly great.[69]

DEMOSTHENES

INTRODUCTION TO
DEMOSTHENES

[*c.* 384–322 BC]

Demosthenes was regarded by later generations as Athens' most accomplished orator. He also came to symbolize Athens' unequal struggle against Philip of Macedon; his speeches advocating resistance to Philip, or defending this policy in retrospect, were later regarded as classics. His suicide in 322 BC, after he had encouraged the Athenians to an unsuccessful attempt to throw off the Macedonian yoke, coincided with the end both of a fully independent Athenian foreign policy and of full democracy.

Demosthenes was born about 384. He began his career as an orator at the age of twenty-one with a successful prosecution of the guardians to whom his dead father had entrusted his estate. Numerous law-court speeches followed, in which Demosthenes acted as speech-writer for others; he also launched prosecutions in his own right against leading political figures. From the late 350s, Demosthenes became a powerful voice in the popular assembly, warning that the growing power of Macedonia posed a threat to Athens. Macedonia had long been regarded as a rather backward and unstable region on the fringes of the Greek world. But it was now united under Philip II, who showed every sign of expansionist aims. Demosthenes argued that Macedonian power ought to be checked as soon as possible, and as far from Athens as possible. The case was put most forcefully in his *Olynthiac speeches* of 349, where Demosthenes called upon the Athenians to send military aid to the city of Olynthus in the Chalcidice. In 346 Demosthenes was a member of the negotiating team that agreed a treaty between Philip and Athens, which the Athenians called the Peace of Philocrates. But Demosthenes later repudiated the treaty and distanced himself from it, and, in a series of speeches known since antiquity as the *Philippics*, denounced Philip and urged bold military action. War became inevitable in 340 when Philip laid siege to Byzantium and threatened Athens' access to grain from the Black Sea. Finally in 338, as Philip advanced southwards, Demosthenes engineered an alliance with Athens' neighbour Thebes and mobilized an army to meet Philip in Boeotia near the town of Chaeronea.

The result was a crushing defeat for the allies. Demosthenes, who was present at the battle, was later accused by his enemies of abandoning his shield and running away. But despite this accusation, and despite the failure of his policy, he evidently stood high in Athenian public opinion at this time, as he was chosen to deliver the funeral oration over the Chaeronea war-dead. Furthermore, in 336, when the danger had receded, he was also voted an honorific crown in recognition of his services to Athens. In that same year, Philip was assassinated and his son, the young Alexander, then only twenty years old, acceded. Thebes saw an opportunity to revolt from Macedon, and Demosthenes encouraged the Athenians to do the same. But Athens remained neutral, Thebes was destroyed and Demosthenes was lucky not to have been surrendered to Alexander in the aftermath. At this time Demosthenes delivered one of his most famous and most successful speeches, *On the crown*. In this speech, technically a defence of Ctesiphon, the man who had moved the motion to vote Demosthenes his gold crown after Chaeronea, Demosthenes set out a defence and justification of his whole policy of opposition to Philip.

The final act of Demosthenes' life came when news of Alexander's death in Asia in 323 reached Athens. Demosthenes had shortly before been forced into exile on a charge of receiving a bribe; now he returned to the city and lent his support to Athens' attempt to shake off Macedonian domination. The forces of Athens and Aetolia besieged Antipater, Alexander's regent, in Lamia in Thessaly, in what became known as the Lamian War. But Antipater was finally relieved, and in the battle of Crannon in 322 he defeated Athens and her allies decisively. Demosthenes fled to Calauria in the Peloponnese, where he committed suicide rather than fall into Antipater's hands. Antipater imposed on Athens a garrison at Munychia, and insisted that the poorest Athenians be stripped of their political rights.

Plutarch pairs Demosthenes with the Roman statesman and orator Cicero. The pairing was well established before Plutarch. Both men were considered masters of oratory in their respective languages and models for later orators and stylists; both employed their oratorical powers in ultimately unsuccessful struggles against autocracy: Demosthenes against Philip, Cicero against first Julius Caesar, then Octavian and finally Mark Antony, who had him murdered. Furthermore, Cicero himself seems to have cultivated the comparison with Demosthenes; he even used the name 'Philippics' for a series of his own speeches in which he denounced Mark Antony.

Plutarch sets out some of the similarities he saw between the two men in the prologue to the two Lives which immediately precedes *Demosthenes*. First he notes similarities in character: 'the same personal ambition, the same love of liberty and the same lack of courage in the face of war or physical danger'. Then he lists similarities in fortunes: they were both orators from humble beginnings 'who opposed kings and tyrants, who each lost their daughters, who were exiled from their native cities, recalled with honour, forced to seek refuge again, were finally captured by their enemies and lost their lives at the same time as their fellow-countrymen lost their liberty' (ch. 3). Plutarch also declares in the prologue that he will not compare the two men as orators but as statesmen. In reality the two spheres of their activity are not so easily separated; this Life has much on Demosthenes' education and development as a speaker, and uses his own words as a source for his actions and intentions. In this respect, *Demosthenes* has much in common with biographies of poets and philosophers, a popular form of writing in the ancient world, which gave much attention to training and development and which ransacked an author's works for details of his life.

Plutarch is particularly interested in this Life in the tension between Demosthenes' power as a speaker to inspire others to action and his own personal cowardice and failure, most notably at the battle of Chaeronea. This weakness of character is evident early on: his voice is weak, he is laughed at in his first attempts at public-speaking and demoralized because of it; he has to learn by dint of good technique to carry conviction (chs. 6–7). Later, Plutarch remarks on Demosthenes' consistency of policy and concern to speak the truth and not pander to his audience, but notes that he was let down by lack of courage and financial dishonesty (ch. 13). However, despite the accusations of cowardice at Chaeronea, even Philip, in the aftermath of his victory, is forced to acknowledge the power of Demosthenes' oratory, which 'had forced him to risk his supremacy and his life on the outcome of a small part of a single day' (ch. 20). And if, in Plutarch's account, Demosthenes' cowardice at Chaeronea, and his later acceptance of a bribe, marred his career, he dies nobly and bravely, refusing to submit to his enemies or to beg for his life. He kills himself by secretly taking poison, which he has hidden in his pen – a fitting end, Plutarch seems to imply, for a man whose words had been so powerful. The Life thus finishes on a high note and Demosthenes, for all his failings, ends as a man of deep moral courage, who finally matched his deeds to his words.

Demosthenes' own speeches, especially his *On the crown*, formed one of Plutarch's most important sources of information for this Life. Many of these are still extant and we can see that Plutarch refers to and quotes from Demosthenes' speeches frequently; indeed, sometimes, as at the start of chapters 18 and 19, Plutarch's narrative is very close to Demosthenes' own wording and seems to recall it deliberately. Plutarch also used Aeschines' speech *Against Ctesiphon*, which attacked Demosthenes and was delivered on the same occasion as Demosthenes' *On the crown*; but Plutarch is aware of Aeschines' bias and warns against it on two occasions (chs. 4, 22). He also cites the historians Theopompus (c. 371–287 BC) and Douris of Samos (c. 340–260), as well as philosophers such as Theophrastus, Hermippus and Panaetius. Finally, Plutarch several times refers to information drawn from Demetrius of Phaleron; the latter, a philosopher and pro-Macedonian governor of Athens after Demosthenes' death, can be assumed, like the other writers, to have been hostile to Demosthenes and to have presented him in a rather poor light; but Demosthenes' own speeches will have put the case for the defence. Most of these writers are now lost, and Plutarch's *Demosthenes*, together with his *Phocion* and parts of Diodorus Books 16–18, remain the only narrative accounts of this period of Athenian history. There is some overlap with material in another, shorter *Life of Demosthenes*, which is preserved in a collection of orators' Lives ascribed to Plutarch in the manuscripts (*Lives of the ten orators*). But the style and treatment are so different that the latter text cannot be by Plutarch; it did not influence Plutarch's Life, but rather drew on some of the same sources.

PROLOGUE TO THE LIVES
OF DEMOSTHENES
AND CICERO

1. The author of the poem which celebrates Alcibiades' victory in the chariot race at Olympia (whether it be Euripides, as most people think, or another writer), tells us, Sosius Senecio,[1] that the first necessity for a happy life is to be born a native of a 'famous city'.[2] But in my opinion if a man is to enjoy true happiness, this will depend most of all upon his character and disposition, and consequently it will make no difference if he happens to belong to an obscure and humble city, any more than it need do if he is born the son of a small or a plain-looking woman. For it would be absurd to suppose that Iulis, which is no more than a small town on the little island of Ceos, or Aegina, which a famous Athenian appealed to his country-men to subdue because it was 'the eyesore of Piraeus',[3] should be capable of producing a fine actor or poet[4] but not a man who was just, independent, wise and magnanimous. It is true, certainly, that the arts – since one of their objects is to bring fame and employment to the men who practise them – are likely to wither in cities which are poor and undistinguished; but virtue, on the other hand, like a tough and hardy plant, will take root and flourish in any place where it can lay hold upon a noble nature and a persevering spirit. Therefore, if we fall below the standards which we ought to attain in thought and action, we must not blame the insignificance of our native city, but rather our own shortcomings.

2. However, when a man has undertaken to compose a history, the sources for which are not easily available in his own country, or do not even exist there, the case is quite different. Because

most of his material must be sought abroad or may be scattered among different texts, his first concern must be to base himself in a famous city which is well populated and favourable to the arts. Here he may not only have access to all kinds of books, but through hearsay and personal inquiry he may succeed in uncovering facts which elude writers and are preserved in more reliable form in human memory; and with these advantages he can avoid the danger of publishing a work which is defective in many or even the most essential details. But I, for my part, live in a small city and choose to stay there to prevent its becoming even smaller.[5] When I visited Rome and other parts of Italy, my public duties and the number of pupils who came to me to study philosophy took up so much of my time that I had no leisure to practise speaking the Latin tongue, and so it was not until quite late in life that I began to study Roman literature. When I did I made a surprising discovery, which was nevertheless a genuine one. I found that it was not so much through words that I was enabled to grasp the meaning of things, but rather that it was my knowledge of things which helped me to understand the words that denoted them. To be able to appreciate the beauty and the pithiness of the Roman style, the figures of speech, the oratorical rhythms and the other embellishments of the language would be a most graceful and enjoyable accomplishment. But the study and practice required would be formidable, and I must leave such ambitions to those who have the youth and the leisure to pursue them.

3. Accordingly, in this fifth book[6] of my *Parallel Lives*, which is devoted to Demosthenes and Cicero, I shall examine against each other the nature and the disposition of each in the light of their respective actions and political conduct, but I shall make no critical comparison of their speeches, nor attempt to determine which was the more agreeable or powerful orator. As Ion puts it:[7] 'The dolphin's strength deserts him on dry land'[8] – a saying that Caecilius,[9] who goes to excess in everything, forgot when he rashly ventured to publish a comparison of Demosthenes and Cicero. But if it came easily to every man to

practise the famous imperative 'Know yourself',[10] we should not perhaps think of it as a divine commandment.

Demosthenes and Cicero resemble each other so closely that it seems that god originally fashioned them out of the same mould, and implanted in them many of the similarities in their characters, notably the same personal ambition, the same love of liberty in their political careers and the same lack of courage in the face of war or danger – and many similarities in their fortunes too. History offers us no other parallel, in my opinion, of two orators who raised themselves from small beginnings to positions of authority and power, who opposed kings and tyrants, who each lost their daughters, who were exiled from their native cities, recalled with honour, forced to seek refuge again, were finally captured by their enemies and lost their lives at the same time as their fellow-countrymen lost their liberty. In short, if there were to be a contest between nature and fortune, as between two artists, it would be difficult to decide whether nature made them more alike in their characters or fortune in the circumstances of their lives. But the discussion should begin with the older man first.

LIFE OF DEMOSTHENES

4. Demosthenes' father, who bore the same name, was of a good family, as Theopompus records,[11] and was nicknamed 'Knife-maker', because he owned a large factory and employed slaves who were skilled in this type of manufacture. As for the charge made by Aeschines against Demosthenes' mother, that she was the daughter of a barbarian woman and that her father was a certain Gylon who was exiled from Athens for treason, I cannot say whether this is true or a malicious slander.[12] Demosthenes' father died when he was seven and left him a considerable inheritance, the estate being valued at a little less than 15 talents, but he was disgracefully treated by his guardians, who appropriated part of his patrimony to their own uses, neglected the rest and even failed to pay the boy's tutors.[13] For this reason he seems not to have received the education which a boy of good family should have had. Besides, because he was delicate and physically under-developed, his mother discouraged him from training in the wrestling-school and his tutors did not press him to attend it. He was a skinny and sickly child from the beginning and it is said that it was to make fun of his puny physique that the other boys called him Batalus.[14] According to one account, Batalus was an effeminate flute-player, who was ridiculed for this in a comedy by Antiphanes.[15] Another story has it that Batalus was a poet who wrote sensual lyrics and drinking-songs. It also appears that 'batalus' was a word then used in Attica for a part of the body not decent to name. They say that Demosthenes was also nicknamed 'Argas'. The name may have been given to him on account of his manners, which were savage and harsh, since some of the poets use this word

of the snake. Or it may have referred to his speech which offended the ears of his listeners, since Argas was the name of a composer of scurrilous and disagreeable songs. So much on that score.

5. His desire to become a public speaker is said to have originated as follows. Callistratus, the orator, was due to speak in court on the question of Oropus,[16] and the trial was eagerly awaited, partly because of the eloquence of Callistratus, who was then at the height of his powers, and partly because of the importance of the issue, which was in the forefront of everyone's minds. So when Demosthenes heard several of his teachers and schoolmasters discussing their plans for attending the trial, he begged and implored his own tutor to take him to the hearing. As it happened, this man knew some of the officials who were on duty at the doors of the courts, and secured a seat where the boy could sit and listen without being seen. Callistratus won the case and was extravagantly praised, and when Demosthenes saw him being escorted by a large following and congratulated on all sides, he was seized with the desire to emulate his fame. But what gained his admiration and appealed to his intellect even more strongly was the power of Callistratus' eloquence, which, as he saw, was naturally adapted to tame and subdue all opposition.

As a result he abandoned all other studies and all the normal pastimes of boyhood, and threw himself wholeheartedly into the practice of declamation, in the hope that he would one day take his place among the orators. He employed Isaeus as his teacher in the art of speaking, even though Isocrates was also lecturing at this time; one tradition has it that because he was an orphan, he could not pay Isocrates the required fee of 10 minas, but alternatively he may have preferred Isaeus' style as being more vigorous and effective in actual use. On the other hand, Hermippus says that he discovered an anonymous book of memoirs, according to which Demosthenes was a pupil of Plato and owed his instruction in the art of speaking chiefly to him. He also says that, according to Ctesibius, Demosthenes secretly obtained from Callias the Syracusan and others the treatises on rhetoric of Isocrates and Alcidamas,[17] and learned these thoroughly.

6. However this may be, once Demosthenes had come of age,[18] he began to prosecute his guardians and to compose speeches attacking them.[19] They resorted to various legal evasions and procured retrials, but Demosthenes gained some hard-won experience 'by running risks and sparing no effort',[20] as Thucydides puts it, and finally won his case, though he did not succeed in recovering even the smallest fraction of his inheritance. However, in this way he acquired some practice and assurance in public-speaking and got a foretaste of the distinction and power which forensic eloquence can bring, and so he ventured to come forward and engage in public affairs. We are told that Laomedon of Orchomenus originally took up long-distance running on the advice of his doctors to protect him against some disease of the spleen, and that once he was obliged to go into training in the first place to recover his health, he soon afterwards entered the Olympic Games and became one of the best long-distance athletes of his time. Similarly, Demosthenes was obliged to make his first appearance in the courts in the effort to recover his property; thereafter he developed such skill and power in public debate that in the political championships, so to speak, he outstripped all his rivals among the orators in the public assembly.

And yet, when he first came before the people he was interrupted by heckling and laughed at for his inexperience: this was because his manner of speaking appeared confused and overloaded with long sentences, and his expression contorted by a formality which his audience found harsh and wearisome. It appears, too, that his voice was weak and his utterance indistinct and that he suffered from a shortness of breath, which had the effect of breaking up his sentences and making his meaning difficult to follow. At last, when he had left the assembly and was wandering about the Piraeus in despair, he met another orator named Eunomus of Thriasia, who was by then a very old man. Eunomus reproved him and said: 'You have a style of speaking which is very like Pericles', and yet out of sheer timidity and cowardice you are throwing away your talents. You will neither stand up to the rough and tumble of the assembly, nor train your body to develop the stamina that you need for the law-courts. It is through your own sheer feebleness that you are letting your gifts wither away.'[21]

7. On another occasion,[22] it is said, when he had again been rebuffed by the people and was going home in a state of bewilderment and depression, Satyrus the actor, who knew him well, followed him and accompanied him indoors. Demosthenes then told him, with tears in his eyes, that although he took more trouble than any other orator to prepare his speeches and had almost ruined his health in his efforts to train himself, he never succeeded in gaining the ear of the people: drunken sailors[23] and illiterate louts were listened to with respect and could hold the platform, but he was always ignored. 'What you say is true,' Satyrus told him, 'but I will soon put that right if you will just recite to me a longish speech from Sophocles or Euripides.' Demosthenes did this, whereupon Satyrus repeated the same passage and so enhanced its effect, by speaking it with the appropriate characterization and tone of voice, that the words seemed to Demosthenes to be quite transformed. Now that he could see how much grace and dignity an orator gains from a good delivery, he understood that it is of little or no use for a man to practise declamation if he does not also attend to the arrangement and delivery of what he has to say. After this, we are told, he built an underground study, which, in fact, was preserved intact even up to our own time. Every day, without fail, he would go down to work at his delivery and to train his voice, and he would often remain there for two or three months on end, and would shave only one side of his face, to prevent himself out of shame from going out even if he wanted to.[24]

8. Besides these formal exercises, he took advantage of his interviews, conversations and other dealings with the outside world to give himself further training. For as soon as he was free, he would review in due order everything that had been discussed and the arguments used for and against each course of action. Any speeches that he happened to have heard delivered, he would afterwards analyse by himself and work them up into regular propositions and periods, and he would introduce

all kinds of corrections or paraphrases into speeches that had
been made against him by others, or into his own replies to
them. It was this habit which created the impression that he
was not really an eloquent speaker, but that the skill and the
power of his oratory had been acquired by hard work. There is
strong evidence for this in the fact that Demosthenes was very
seldom heard to make an impromptu speech. The people often
called on him by name, as he sat in the assembly, to speak on
the subject under debate, but he would not come forward
unless he had given thought to the question and could deliver a
prepared speech. For this reason, many of the popular leaders
used to sneer at him, and Pytheas in particular told him mock-
ingly that his arguments smelled of the lamp. Demosthenes had
a sharp retort for this. 'I am sure that your lamp, Pytheas,' he
told him, 'sees very different kinds of goings-on than mine.'
However, to other people he did not entirely deny the charge:
he used to admit that his speeches were prepared, but said that
he did not write them out word for word. Moreoever, he also
used to declare that the man who prepares what he is going to
say is the true democrat, for the fact that he takes this amount
of trouble indicates respect for the people, whereas to speak
without caring what they will think of one's words is the sign
of a man who favours oligarchy and is inclined to rely on force
rather than persuasion. Another fact often cited as a proof that
Demosthenes lacked the confidence to speak on the spur of the
moment is that when he was being shouted down by the people,
Demades[25] would often take his place and make an impromptu
speech in his support, but that Demosthenes never did this for
Demades.

9. How was it then, one might ask, that Aeschines could refer to
him as a man of the most astonishing boldness in his speeches?
Or that Demosthenes was the only man to stand up and refute
Python of Byzantium when he was arrogantly attacking the
Athenians and pouring forth a flood of abuse against them?[26]
Or again, when Lamachus of Myrrhine had composed a pan-
egyric on Philip and Alexander, which was also full of abuse of
Thebes and Olynthus, and was reading it out aloud at Olympia,

how was it that Demosthenes came forward and marshalled a complete array of historical facts to remind the audience of the benefits which the peoples of Thebes and Chalcidice had conferred on Greece and of the misfortunes for which the flatterers of Macedonia had been responsible? With these arguments he worked upon the feelings of his audience so powerfully that the sophist took fright at the uproar which arose against him and slunk away from the festival.[27] The fact is that while Demosthenes did not wish to model himself upon Pericles in every respect, he especially admired and sought to imitate the modulation of his speech and the dignity of his bearing, and also his determination not to speak on impulse or on any subject which might present itself, and he seems to have been persuaded that it was to these qualities that Pericles owed his greatness. For the same reasons, Demosthenes did not aspire to the kind of reputation which is won in a sudden crisis, and he was very seldom willing to expose his oratorical power to the mercy of fortune. However, those speeches which he delivered impromptu displayed more courage and spirit than those which he wrote out, if we are to believe the evidence of Eratosthenes,[28] Demetrius of Phaleron[29] and the comic poets. Eratosthenes tells us that often in his speeches he seemed to be transported into a kind of ecstasy, and Demetrius says that on one occasion he pronounced to the people the well-known metrical oath which runs, 'By earth, by all her fountains, streams and floods',[30] as if he were possessed by some god. As for the comic poets, one of them calls him a 'dealer in petty bombast', and another makes fun of his fondness for antithesis: 'In taking, he retook!' 'That's a phrase Demosthenes would have loved to take up'[31] – unless, by Zeus, Antiphanes intended this too as a dig at Demosthenes' speech on Halonnesus, where he urged the Athenians not to 'take' the island as a gift from Philip, but to 'retake' it as a right.[32]

10. At any rate, it was universally agreed that Demades, when he used his natural gifts, was invincible as an orator, and that when he spoke on the spur of the moment he far excelled Demosthenes' carefully prepared efforts. Ariston of Chios has given

us Theophrastus' verdict on these two orators. When he was asked what kind of orator he considered Demosthenes to be, he replied, 'An orator worthy of Athens,' but of Demades he said, 'He is too good for Athens.' According to the same philosopher, Polyeuctus of Sphettus, one of the leading Athenian politicians, declared that Demosthenes was the greatest orator, but Phocion the most effective, because his speeches packed the greatest proportion of sense into the fewest words. In fact we are told that Demosthenes himself, whenever Phocion rose to answer him, would mutter to his friends: 'Here comes the chopper of my speeches.' It is not clear from the phrase whether Demosthenes felt like this towards Phocion because of his oratory, or because of his life and character, and so was implying that even a single word from a man in whom the people felt so much confidence carries more weight than any number of lengthy periods.

11. Demetrius of Phaleron has described the various exercises which Demosthenes took up to overcome his physical deficiencies, and he says that he learnt of these from the orator himself when he was an old man. He corrected his lisp and his indistinct articulation by holding pebbles in his mouth while he recited long speeches, and he strengthened his voice by running or walking uphill, discoursing as he went, and by reciting speeches or verses in a single breath. Besides this, he kept a large mirror in his house and would stand in front of it while he went through his exercises in declamation.

There is a story that a man once came to Demosthenes, asked him to represent him in court and explained to him at length how he had been physically assaulted. 'But you did not suffer this ill-treatment you are telling me about,' said Demosthenes. At this the man raised his voice, and shouted, 'What do you mean, I did not suffer it?' 'Ah, now', said Demosthenes, 'I can hear the voice of a man who has been attacked and beaten.' So important did he consider the tone and the bearing of a speaker in convincing his audience.

His own manner of speaking was very popular with the general public, but men of sensibility, such as Demetrius of

Phaleron, thought it mean, vulgar and weak. On the other hand, Hermippus tells us that when Aesion, a contemporary of Demosthenes, was asked his opinion of the ancient orators as compared with the moderns, he said that anyone who heard the orators of the past must admire the decorum and the dignity of their manner, but that when we read Demosthenes' speeches, we must admit that they are superior in their construction and more powerful in their effect. It goes without saying that his written speeches contain many harsh and bitter judgements, but in his extempore replies he could also be humorous. For example, when Demades exclaimed, 'Demosthenes teach me? Athena might as well take lessons from a sow!'[33] Demosthenes retorted, 'That was the Athena who was seen the other day in a brothel in Collytus.' When a well-known thief who was nicknamed 'brazen' tried to make fun of the orator's late hours and midnight studies, Demosthenes answered, 'I know my lighted lamp must be a nuisance to you. But you Athenians should not be surprised at the number of thefts that are committed when we have thieves of brass, while the walls of our houses are made only of clay.' There are many more stories of this kind, but his other qualities, and his moral character, are best examined as they emerge from his achievements as a statesman.

12. Demosthenes first began to take an active part in affairs after the outbreak of the Phocian War:[34] we know this partly from his own statements and partly from the speeches he made against Philip. Some of these were delivered after the war had ended, and the earliest of them touch upon matters which were closely connected with it.[35] It is evident that when he was preparing his speech for the prosecution of Meidias, he had reached the age of thirty-two[36] but had not yet acquired any influence or reputation in the political arena. It was his lack of confidence on this score, so it seems to me, which was the principal reason for his dropping the case in return for a sum of money, in spite of his personal animosity towards Meidias. '*For he was not a sweet-tempered man, nor kindly towards his oppon-*

ents,'[37] but sharp and even forceful in avenging any wrongs done to him. However, he recognized that it was no easy task, indeed scarcely within his power, to destroy a man such as Meidias, who was well protected not only by his oratory but by his friends and his wealth, and so he gave way to those who pleaded on his enemy's behalf. I doubt very much whether the 3,000 drachmas he was paid would have appeased the hatred he felt towards Meidias, if he had hoped or felt able to get the better of his enemy.

But, once Demosthenes had found a noble cause to engage his political activity – that is, pleading the cause of the Greeks against Philip – and began fighting for it honourably, he quickly became famous and his reputation was enhanced by the courage of his speeches. The result was that he was admired in Greece and treated with respect by the king of Persia, and King Philip took more notice of him than of any other Athenian statesman, and even his enemies were forced to agree that they were dealing with a man of distinction:[38] both Aeschines and Hypereides admit as much, even in their denunciations of him.

13. For this reason I do not know what evidence Theopompus had for his statement that Demosthenes was of a fickle and unstable disposition and incapable of remaining faithful for any length of time either to the same policies or the same men. On the contrary, it is clear that he remained loyal to the same faction and the same line of policy that he had chosen from the beginning, and indeed he was so far from forsaking these principles during his lifetime that he deliberately sacrificed his life to uphold them. Demades, when he wanted to excuse his change of policy, would plead that he had often said things that were contrary to his former opinions but never contrary to the interests of the state. Melanopus, who was an opponent of Callistratus, was often bribed by him to change sides, and he would then say to the people, 'This man is my personal opponent, but the essential thing is that the public interest should prevail.' Nicodemus the Messenian, who first took the side of Cassander and later supported Demetrius,[39] declared that there was no inconsistency in this, because it is always best to obey

whoever is in power. We cannot bring any of these charges against Demosthenes, nor accuse him of being a man who ever wavered or deviated from his course, in word or deed. He maintained a single unchangeable harmony throughout, and continued in the same key that he had chosen from the start.[40]

Panaetius the philosopher remarks that in most of Demosthenes' speeches, for example in *On the crown*, *Against Aristocrates*, in the one on those who should be exempted from taxation,[41] and in the *Philippics*, we can trace the conviction that honour alone ought to be pursued for its own sake. In all these orations, Demosthenes does not try to persuade his fellow-citizens to do what is most agreeable, or easy, or profitable, but time and again he argues that they ought to place their honour and their obligations before their safety or self-preservation. In short, if only the nobility of his aspirations and the dignity of his words had been matched by an equivalent courage in war and integrity in his other dealings, he would have deserved to be ranked not with orators such as Moerocles, Polyeuctus and Hypereides, but with the men of Athens' greatest days, such as Cimon, Thucydides[42] and Pericles.

14. Among Demosthenes' contemporaries we may say that Phocion, although he championed an unpopular policy and had the reputation of favouring the Macedonians, was considered, by virtue of his courage and integrity, to be a statesman of the calibre of Ephialtes and Aristides and Cimon.[43] Demosthenes, on the other hand, according to Demetrius of Phaleron, could not be relied on when it came to fighting, nor was he altogether immune from taking bribes. He could resist any number of offers from Philip or from Macedon, but he not only yielded to but was finally overwhelmed by the Persian gold, which poured down from Susa and Ecbatana in a torrent.[44] And so while he was admirably fitted to extol the virtues of former generations, he was not so good at imitating them. Yet in spite of these shortcomings, he led a more exemplary life than the other orators of his time. (I leave Phocion out of the reckoning.) And it is undeniable that he went further than any of them in speaking frankly to the people, and that he often opposed the desires of the

majority and continually criticized their faults, as we may see from his speeches. Even Theopompus[45] records that when the Athenians called upon him to impeach a man, and, finding that he refused, began to create an uproar, he rose and declared, 'Men of Athens, I shall continue to give you advice, whether you ask for it or not, but I refuse to become a false accuser, even if you insist on it.' And his conduct in the case of Antiphon[46] was not at all that of a man who courts the favour of the people. Antiphon had been acquitted by the assembly, but Demosthenes had him arrested and brought before the Council of the Areopagus,[47] and, disregarding the affront to the sovereignty of the people which his action implied, he succeeded in proving him guilty of having promised Philip to set fire to the dockyards. As a result, Antiphon was handed over to justice by the Areopagus and later executed. Demosthenes also accused the priestess Theoris of a number of misdemeanours, among them of teaching slaves to cheat their masters. As one of the parties before the court, he was allowed to propose her sentence and caused her to be put to death.

15. Demosthenes is also said to have written the speech which was used by Apollodorus to obtain judgement against Timotheus the general, whom he was suing for debt, and likewise the speeches which Apollodorus used against Stephanus and Phormion.[48] In this instance, Demosthenes was rightly considered to have acted dishonourably, for he had also written Phormion's defence, and was thus, as it were, selling the two adversaries blades from the same knife-shop[49] with which they could fight one another.

Among his public speeches he wrote the *Against Androtion*, *Against Timocrates* and *Against Aristocrates* to be delivered by others; he must have composed these before he had begun his political career, for it appears that these speeches were made public when he was only thirty-two or thirty-three years of age.[50] But he himself delivered the speech *Against Aristogeiton*, as well as the one concerning tax-exemptions. He says that he took up the latter case at the request of Ctesippus, the son of Chabrias, but according to other accounts, he did so because he was wooing the young man's mother. He did not, however, marry her but a Samian woman, as Demetrius of Magnesia tells us in his treatise *On persons of the same name*. As for the speech which was made against Aeschines, entitled *On the false embassy*, it is not certain that this was ever delivered, although Idomeneus[51] has recorded that Aeschines was acquitted by a bare thirty votes. But this is contradicted by the speeches of both Demosthenes and Aeschines, in *On the crown*, for neither of them refers to the case of the embassy as ever having come to court. This is a question I shall leave others to decide.

16. Demosthenes' political position was clear enough even while peace still prevailed, for he allowed no act of Philip's to pass uncriticized, and seized upon every occasion to incite and inflame the Athenians against him. In consequence, nobody was more talked of at Philip's court, and when Demosthenes visited Macedonia as one of a delegation of ten,[52] Philip listened to all their speeches, but took most trouble to answer Demosthenes. As regards other official courtesies or marks of honour, Philip did not pay him so much attention, but singled out Aeschines and Philocrates for his especial favour. So when they complimented Philip as the most eloquent speaker, the handsomest man and the drinker with the biggest capacity in the company, Demosthenes could not refrain from belittling these tributes and retorting sarcastically that the first of these qualities was excellent for a sophist, the second for a woman and the third for a sponge, but none of them for a king.[53]

17. When the course of events began to move inexorably towards war, since Philip was incapable of sitting quietly at home, and the Athenians were constantly being stirred up against him by Demosthenes, first of all Demosthenes urged his countrymen to invade Euboea,[54] which had been subdued and handed over to Philip by its local tyrants; and as a result of the resolution which he proposed, the Athenians crossed over to the island and drove out the Macedonians. Secondly, when Macedonia was at war with the citizens of Byzantium and Perinthus, Demosthenes persuaded the Athenians to lay aside

their grievances and forget the wrongs they had suffered from these peoples in the Social War,[55] and to dispatch a force which succeeded in relieving both cities.[56] Furthermore, he led a number of diplomatic missions throughout Greece, where, through a combination of discussion and exhortation, he succeeded in uniting almost all the Greeks against Philip. The result was that an army of 15,000 infantry and 2,000 cavalry was raised, besides the citizen forces of each city, and the allies readily agreed to pay these mercenaries.[57] It was on this occasion, according to Theophrastus, when the Greek states requested that a quota for their contributions should be fixed, that the demagogue Crobylus remarked, 'War has an appetite that cannot be satisfied by quotas.'

Greece was now wrought up to a high pitch of expectation at the thought of her future, and her peoples and cities all drew together, Euboeans, Achaeans, Corinthians, Megarians, Leucadians and Corcyraeans. But there remained the most important task of all for Demosthenes to accomplish, namely, to persuade Thebes to join the alliance.[58] The Thebans had a common frontier with the Athenians and an army ready to take the field, and at that time they were regarded as the finest soldiers in Greece. But it was no easy matter to persuade them to change sides; moreover, during the recent Phocian War[59] Philip had rendered them a number of services and cultivated their goodwill, and the various petty quarrels which arose because of their proximity to Athens were continually breaking out afresh and exacerbated the relations between the two cities.[60]

18. However, Philip, encouraged by his success in dealing with Amphissa,[61] marched on to take Elateia[62] by surprise and proceeded to occupy Phocis. The news stunned the Athenians. No speaker dared to mount the rostrum, nobody knew what advice should be given, the assembly was struck dumb and appeared to be completely at a loss. It was at this moment that Demosthenes alone came forward and urged the people to stand by the Thebans. Then, in his usual manner, he put heart into his compatriots and inspired them with fresh hopes, and he was sent off with others as an ambassador to Thebes. At the same

time Philip, as we learn from Marsyas the historian, sent Amyntas and Clearchus of Macedonia, Daochus of Thessaly and
Thrasydaeus to oppose the Athenians and put the case for
Macedon. For their part, the Thebans could see clearly enough
where their interests lay, but each of them could also visual-
ize the horrors of war, for the sufferings they had endured
in the Phocian conflict were still fresh in their memories. Yet in
spite of this, Demosthenes' eloquence – so Theopompus tells
us – stirred their courage, kindled their desire to win glory and
threw every other consideration into the shade. As if transported by his words, they cast off all fear, self-interest or thought
of obligation towards Macedon and chose the path of honour.
So complete and so glorious was the transformation wrought
by his oratory that Philip promptly began making overtures for
peace,[63] and Greece, full of expectation, was up in arms to support Demosthenes for the future – so much so that, not only did
the Athenian generals take their orders from him, but also the
Boeotarchs. At this moment he could control all the meetings of
the Theban assembly as effectively as those of the Athenians, he
was beloved by both nations and exercised supreme authority;
moreover, he never used his position unconstitutionally nor did
he go beyond his powers, so Theopompus tells us, but acted
with complete propriety.

19. However, it seems that at that very moment a sort of
divinely ordained fortune or the cyclical course of events was
putting an end to the freedom of the Greeks: this force opposed
all their efforts in the common cause and showed many signs of
what was to come. Among these were the ominous prophecies
uttered by the Pythian priestess, and an ancient oracle which
was quoted from the Sibylline books:[64]

> Let me be far from the battle at Thermodon
> Watching it from high in the clouds, like an eagle.
> The vanquished weep, and the victor has perished.

Now the Thermodon is said to be a small stream near my
native town of Chaeronea, which flows into the River Cephisus.

However, I know of no stream which bears this name today, but my guess is that the one which is now called Haemon ('Blood') was then known as Thermodon. It flows past the Heracleum, where the Greeks pitched their camp, and I imagine that after the battle this river was filled with blood and corpses, and that its present name of Haemon was substituted for the original one. However, Douris[65] writes that the Thermodon was not a river at all, but that some soldiers who were pitching a tent and digging a trench around it found a small stone image with an inscription on it, signifying that this was Thermodon carrying a wounded Amazon in his arms;[66] he also reports that there was current another oracle about it, which ran as follows:

Bide your time for the battle of Thermodon, bird of black pinions;
There you shall find the flesh of mankind to devour in abundance.

20. It is difficult to discover the exact truth about these prophecies, but certainly Demosthenes is said to have had complete confidence in the Greek forces and to have been elated by the strength and spirit of so many men, all of them eager to engage the enemy: in consequence, he would not allow his countrymen to pay attention to the oracles or listen to the prophecies. Indeed, he even suspected that the Pythian priestess was on the side of Philip, and he reminded the Thebans of the example of Epaminondas and the Athenians of Pericles, both of whom acted only on the promptings of reason and regarded prophecies of this kind as mere pretexts for faint-heartedness. Up to this point, then, Demosthenes acted like a brave man, but in the battle[67] which followed, so far from achieving anything honourable, he completely failed to suit his actions to his words. He left his place in the ranks and took to his heels in the most shameful fashion, throwing away his arms in order to run faster, and he did not hesitate to disgrace the inscription on his shield, on which, according to Pytheas, were engraved in letters of gold the words 'With good fortune'.

In the first flush of victory, Philip felt insolently exultant at his success. He went out in a drunken revel to look at the bodies of the dead, and chanted the opening words of the decree which had been passed on Demosthenes' initiative, dividing it up metrically, and beating time: 'Demosthenes, son of Demosthenes, of Paeania, moves as follows . . .' But when he sobered up and understood the magnitude of the dangers that had surrounded him, he trembled to think of the power and skill of the orator who had forced him to risk his supremacy and his life on the outcome of a small part of a single day.[68] For the fame of this speaker had travelled even to the Persian king, who had sent letters to the satraps on the coast ordering them to offer money to Demosthenes and to pay more attention to him than to any other Greek, since he could create a diversion and keep the king of Macedon busy at home by means of the troubles he stirred up in Greece. This intelligence was discovered long afterwards by Alexander, who found in Sardis letters from Demosthenes and papers belonging to the king's generals and containing details of the sums of money which had been given to him.

21. However, at this moment when the news of the disaster to Greece became known, the orators who opposed Demosthenes attacked him and prepared indictments and impeachments against him. But the people not only acquitted him of these charges, but continued to honour him and appealed to him as a loyal citizen to remain in public life. Consequently, when the bones of those who had fallen at Chaeronea were brought home to be buried, they chose Demosthenes to deliver the panegyric in honour of the dead. So far from displaying a cowardly or ignoble spirit in the hour of disaster (as Theopompus implies in his exaggerated description of the scene), they made it clear by the special honour and respect which they paid their counsellor that they did not regret the advice he had given them. So Demosthenes delivered the funeral oration, but henceforth he would not put his own name to any of the decrees he proposed in the assembly: instead, he used those of his friends, one after the other, and avoided his own as being ill-omened and unfortunate, until he once more took courage after Philip's death. And Philip died soon afterwards;[69] in fact he survived his victory at Chaeronea by less than two years, and this it would seem was

foretold in the last verse of the oracle: *'The vanquished weep, and the victor has perished.'*

22. Now Demosthenes had obtained secret intelligence of Philip's death, and in order to inspire the Athenians with hope for the future, he appeared before the Council[70] with an air of high spirits and told them he had had a dream which seemed to presage that some great stroke of good fortune was in store for Athens. Not long afterwards, messengers arrived with the report of Philip's death. The Athenians immediately offered up sacrifices for the good news and voted a crown for Pausanias, the king's assassin, while Demosthenes appeared in public dressed in magnificent attire and wearing a garland on his head, even though his daughter had died only six days before. These details are reported by Aeschines,[71] who attacked him for his action and reviled him as an unnatural father. This only proves the weakness and vulgarity of his own nature, if he considers that the wearing of mourning and an extravagant display of grief are the signs of a tender heart, but finds fault with a man who bears his loss in a serene and resolute fashion.

For my part, I cannot say that the Athenians did themselves any credit in putting on garlands and offering sacrifices to celebrate the death of a king who, when he was the conqueror and they the conquered, had treated them with such tolerance and humanity.[72] For apart from provoking the anger of the gods, it was a contemptible action to make Philip a citizen of Athens and pay him honours while he was alive, and then, as soon as he had fallen by another's hand, to be beside themselves with joy, trample on his body and sing paeans of victory, as though they themselves had accomplished some great feat of arms. On the other hand I praise the behaviour of Demosthenes for leaving his personal misfortunes to be lamented over by the women and devoting himself to the action he thought necessary for his country. I hold it to be the duty of a man of courage and one who wishes to be considered fit to govern never to lose sight of the common good, to find consolation for his private griefs and troubles in the well-being of the state and to conduct himself with a dignity[73] far greater than actors show when they play the

part of kings or tyrants: for these men as we see them in the
theatres do not laugh or weep as their feelings dictate, but as
the subject of the drama demands.

Apart from these considerations, it is our duty not to leave
our neighbour without any consolation in his misfortune, but
to find words which will relieve his sorrow and turn his
thoughts to less distressing subjects, just as those who are suffering from sore eyes are advised to look away from brilliant or
dazzling colours and towards softer or more verdant shades.
And I believe that a man can find no better consolation for his
private griefs than to balance them against the well-being of his
fellow-citizens, when his country's fortunes are prospering,
thus making the happier circumstances of the majority out-
weigh the misfortunes of the individual.[74] I have been led to
offer these reflections because I have noticed how this speech of
Aeschines has melted the hearts of many people and encouraged them to give way to an unmanly tenderness.

23. The cities were again banding together, and Demosthenes
fanned the flames. He helped to provide the Thebans with
arms, and they attacked the Macedonian garrison in their city
and killed many of them,[75] and the Athenians began to prepare
to go to war in their support. Demosthenes now completely
dominated the assembly and he wrote letters to the Macedonian king's generals in Asia inciting them to declare war on
Alexander,[76] whom he referred to as a boy, and compared
to Margites.[77] But as soon as Alexander had established his
authority in his own kingdom and led his army to Boeotia, the
Athenians' courage wilted, Demosthenes' ardour was extinguished, and the Thebans, betrayed by their allies, fought alone
and lost their city.[78] Panic reigned in Athens, and Demosthenes
was chosen with a number of others to form a delegation to
visit Alexander, but he dreaded the king's anger so much that
he turned back at Cithaeron and abandoned his mission.

Alexander at once sent to Athens to demand that ten of
the popular leaders should be surrendered to him. This is the
account given by Idomeneus and Douris, but, according to
most of the more reliable authorities, he only specified eight,

namely Demosthenes, Polyeuctus, Ephialtes, Lycurgus, Moerocles, Demon, Callisthenes and Charidemus.[79] It was on this
occasion that Demosthenes reminded the Athenians of the fable
of the sheep who gave up their watch-dogs to the wolves, and he
compared himself and his colleagues to sheep-dogs who fought
to defend the people, and referred to Alexander as the lone wolf
of Macedon.[80] He added, 'You know how corn-merchants sell
whole consignments of their stock by showing a few grains of
wheat which they carry around with them in a bowl as a sam-
ple. In the same way, if you deliver us up, you are delivering up
yourselves, every one of you.' These details we have from Aristobulus of Cassandreia.[81]

The Athenians debated these demands in the assembly but
could not decide how to reply to them. Then Demades, in return
for five talents which he had been offered by the eight men,
volunteered to go to the king and plead on their behalf: he may
have trusted in his personal friendship with Alexander, or he
may have counted on finding him sated with blood, like a lion
that has been glutted with slaughter. At any rate, Demades persuaded the king to pardon the eight men, and arranged terms
of peace for the city.[82]

24. When Alexander had left, Demades and his confederates
were all-powerful and Demosthenes was completely humbled.
Later, when Agis the Spartan organized a revolt against Macedonia,[83] Demosthenes made a feeble effort to support him,
but then he cowered ignominiously because the Athenians
refused to take part in the uprising, Agis was killed in battle
and the resistance of the Spartans was crushed.

It was at this time too that the indictment against Ctesiphon
on the subject of the crown came up for trial. The case had originally been prepared in the archonship of Chaerondas, shortly
before the battle of Chaeronea, but it did not come into court
until ten years later in the archonship of Aristophon.[84] Although
this was a private suit, no public action ever attracted more
attention, not only on account of the fame of the orators, but
also because of the admirable conduct of the jurors. Demosthenes' accusers were then at the height of their power and

supporters of Macedon, yet the jurors would not bring in a verdict against him but acquitted him so decisively that Aeschines did not obtain a fifth of their votes.[85] The result was that Aeschines immediately left Athens and spent the rest of his life in Rhodes and Ionia as a teacher of rhetoric.

25. Not long afterwards, Harpalus[86] arrived in Athens from Asia. He had fled from the king's service because he knew that he was guilty of many misdeeds committed through his love of extravagance, and because he dreaded his master, who had by then become an object of terror to his friends. He, therefore, sought refuge in Athens and placed himself, his ships and his treasure in the people's hands. The other orators at once rallied to his support and urged the Athenians to receive him as a suppliant and protect him, while at the same time they cast longing eyes upon his wealth. Demosthenes, on the other hand, began by advising the Athenians to turn him away and urged them to beware of involving the city in a war by taking such an unnecessary and unjustifiable action. But a few days later, when an inventory was being made of the treasure, Harpalus noticed that Demosthenes was admiring a cup of Persian manufacture and was examining closely the style and the workmanship of the moulding. He then invited him to balance it in his hand and feel the weight of the gold. Demosthenes was astonished at this and asked how much it would fetch, at which Harpalus smiled and replied, 'It would fetch you 20 talents.' Then as soon as it was dark, he sent the cup and the 20 talents to Demosthenes' house. Harpalus was exceptionally shrewd at discerning the character of a man who had a passion for gold, which he recognized from the expression which passed over his face and the gleam that lit up his eyes. And he was not deceived in this instance, for Demosthenes could not resist the bait, and having once, as it were, admitted a garrison into his house, immediately went over to Harpalus' side.

The next day Demosthenes appeared in the assembly, having first carefully swathed his throat with woollen bandages; then, when he was called upon to rise and speak, he made gestures to signify that he had lost his voice. The wits of the day made fun of him by remarking that the orator had been seized overnight, not with a sore throat, but with a silver one. Afterwards, it became clear to the whole people that he had been bribed, and when he tried to get a hearing to explain his conduct, the people showed their indignation by raising an uproar and shouting him down. At this, someone rose and said sarcastically, 'Men of Athens, won't you give a hearing to the man who has the cup in his hand?'[87] At that time, then, the Athenians sent Harpalus away from the city, and as they were afraid that they might have to account for the money which the orators had received, they organized a thorough search and ransacked all the speakers' houses, except for that of Callicles, the son of Arrhenides. His was the only house which they exempted, because he was newly married and his bride was living there, so Theopompus tells us.

26. But Demosthenes decided to meet the issue squarely and put forward a motion that the matter should be referred for investigation to the Council of the Areopagus, and those whom the Areopagus found guilty should be punished. However, he was himself one of the first whom the Areopagus condemned, and when he was brought to court, he was fined 50 talents and committed to prison in default of payment.

He tells us[88] that he was overcome with shame at these accusations and that since his weak health made it impossible for him to endure imprisonment, he escaped thanks to the negligence of some of his jailers, and the active assistance of others. At any rate, the story goes that he had not fled far from Athens before he discovered that he was being pursued by some of his opponents, and so he tried to hide himself. Presently, they caught up with him, called out to him by name, and begged him to accept some help for his journey. They explained that they had brought money from home for this very purpose and were only pursuing him to put it into his hands, and they urged him to take heart and not let himself be cast down by what had happened. At this Demosthenes broke out into even more anguished cries of grief and exclaimed, 'What comfort can I have at leaving a city where even my enemies treat me with a generosity I shall hardly find among friends anywhere else?'

He showed little strength of character during his exile, but spent much of his time in Aegina or Troezen, looking towards Attica with tears in his eyes. The only sayings of his which have come down to us from this period are quite unworthy of him and quite inconsistent with the bold actions for which he was responsible when he was active in politics. It is said, for example, that as he was leaving the city, he stretched out his hands towards the Acropolis and exclaimed, 'Athena, goddess and guardian of Athens, how can you take pleasure in these three savage and intractable creatures, the owl, the snake[89] and the people?' And when young men came to visit and converse with him, he would try to dissuade them from having anything to do with politics. He told them that if, at the beginning of his political career, he had been offered two roads, the one leading to the rostrum and the assembly, and the other to destruction,[90] and if he could have foreseen the innumerable evils which lie in wait for the politician – the fears, the jealousies, the slanders and the struggles – he would have chosen the path which led directly to death.

27. But while Demosthenes was still in exile, Alexander died,[91] and the Greek states combined yet again to form a league against Macedon. They were encouraged in this action by the gallant exploits of the Athenian general Leosthenes, who had succeeded in driving Antipater into the city of Lamia, where he held him besieged. At this, the orators Pytheas and Callimedon the 'Crayfish' fled from Athens, joined Antipater and travelled about with the latter's supporters and ambassadors, urging the rest of the Greeks not to rebel against Macedon or to ally themselves with Athens. Demosthenes, on the other hand, attached himself to the Athenian envoys, and threw all his energies into helping them incite the various states to attack the Macedonians and drive them out of Greece. Phylarchus[92] tells us that in Arcadia Pytheas and Demosthenes actually met face to face and abused one another in the assembly, the one speaking for Macedon and the other for Greece. Pytheas, so the story goes, argued that just as we can always expect to find sickness in a house when we see asses' milk being carried into it, so a city

must be in a state of decay if it receives an embassy from Athens. Demosthenes then turned his illustration against him, by pointing out that asses' milk is given to restore health and that the Athenians only came to benefit the sick.

At any rate, the people of Athens were so pleased with Demosthenes' efforts that they voted for him to be recalled from exile. The decree was introduced by Demon of Paeania, who was a cousin of Demosthenes, and a trireme was dispatched to Aegina to bring him home. When he landed at Piraeus, every archon and priest was present and the entire citizen-body gathered to watch his arrival and give him an enthusiastic welcome. On this occasion, according to Demetrius of Magnesia, Demosthenes lifted up his hands to heaven and congratulated himself, because he was returning on that day more honourably than Alcibiades had done, for his fellow-citizens had been persuaded, not compelled, to welcome him back.[93] The fine, which had been inflicted on him, however, still remained in force, for it was unconstitutional for the people to abolish a penalty by an act of grace, and so they devised a means to evade the law. It was the custom at the festival of Zeus the Saviour to pay a sum of money to those who prepared and decorated the altar, and so they appointed Demosthenes to make these arrangements for the sum of 50 talents, which had been the amount of his fine.

28. However, Demosthenes did not have long to enjoy his return to his native land as the Greek cause was soon crushed. In the month of Metageitnion the battle of Crannon[94] took place, in Boedromion a Macedonian garrison entered Munychia and in Pyanepsion Demosthenes met his death,[95] in the following way.

When reports came in that Antipater and Craterus were marching upon Athens, Demosthenes and his supporters escaped secretly from the city, and the people condemned them to death on the motion of Demades. Meanwhile, they had split up and fled in different directions, and Antipater sent out troops to scour the country and arrest them: these detachments were under the command of Archias, who was known as 'the exile-hunter'. This man was a citizen of the colony of Thurii in Italy, and it was said that he had at one time been a tragic actor, and that Polus of Aegina, the finest actor of his time, had been a pupil of his. According to Hermippus, however, Archias had been one of the pupils of Lacritus the orator, while Demetrius of Phaleron says that he was a pupil of Anaximenes. At any rate, Archias discovered that Hypereides the orator, Aristonicus of Marathon and Himeraeus the brother of Demetrius of Phaleron had all taken refuge in the sanctuary of Aeacus at Aegina. He then had them dragged out by force and sent to Antipater at Cleonae.[96] There they were put to death, and it is said that Hypereides' tongue was also cut out.

29. When Archias learnt that Demosthenes had taken sanctuary in the temple of Poseidon at Calauria,[97] he crossed over in some small boats, with a detachment of Thracian spearmen, and tried to persuade Demosthenes to leave the sanctuary and go with him to Antipater, assuring him that he would not be harshly treated. It so happened that Demosthenes had experienced a strange dream the night before, in which he had seen himself acting in a tragedy and competing with Archias. But although he acted well and won the applause of the audience, the verdict went against him because of the lack of stage decorations and costumes and the poverty of the production. So when Archias offered him this string of assurances, Demosthenes remained seated where he was, looked him full in the face and said, 'Archias, I was never convinced by your acting, and I am no more convinced by your promises.' Then, when Archias became angry and began to threaten him, he said, 'Ah, before this you were acting a part, but now you are speaking like the genuine Macedonian oracle.[98] Give me a few moments to write a letter to my family.' With these words he retired into the inner part of the temple. There he picked up his tablets as if he were about to write, put his pen to his mouth and bit it, as was his habit when he was thinking out what to say. He kept the reed between his lips for some while, then covered his head with his cloak and bent down. The soldiers who stood at the door jeered at him, because they supposed that he was afraid to

die and called him a faint-hearted weakling, while Archias came near, urged him to get up and began to repeat his assurances about reconciling him to Antipater. By this time Demosthenes recognized from his sensations that the poison was beginning to work upon him and overcome him, and he uncovered his head, looked steadfastly at Archias and said, 'Now you can play the part of Creon as soon as you wish and throw my body to the dogs without burying it.[99] I, my dear Poseidon, will leave your sanctuary while I am still alive, although Antipater and his Macedonians would have been ready to defile it with murder.' With these words he asked to be supported, since by now he was trembling and could scarcely stand, and as they were helping him to walk past the altar, he fell, and with a groan breathed his last.[100]

30. As for the poison, Ariston says that he sucked it from the reed as I have described, but a man named Pappus, from whom Hermippus took his account of the scene, says that when Demosthenes had fallen by the side of the altar, the opening words of a letter were found on his tablets, beginning 'Demosthenes to Antipater' and nothing more. The speed and suddenness of his death astonished everybody, and the Thracian guards who had been standing at the door said that he took the poison into his hand from a cloth, put it to his mouth and swallowed it. They had supposed that what he had swallowed was gold,[101] but the young girl who waited on him told Archias, in answer to his questions, that Demosthenes had long carried this cloth girdle with him as a last resort to protect him against his enemies. Eratosthenes says that Demosthenes carried the poison in a hollow bracelet, which he wore as an ornament upon his arm. There is no need for me to list all the different versions of this scene which have been given by the many authors who have described it. I will mention only that of Demochares, one of his kinsmen, who says that in his opinion Demosthenes did not die from poison but, thanks to the honour and benevolence shown him by the gods, he was delivered from the cruelty of the Macedonians by a swift and painless death. He died on the sixteenth of the month Pyanepsion, the most solemn day of the festival of

the Thesmophoria,[102] which the women observe by fasting in the temple of the goddess.

Soon after his death, the people of Athens paid him fitting honours by erecting his statue in bronze[103] and by decreeing that the eldest member of his family should have the right to dine in the *prytaneum* at public expense.[104] On the base of his statue was carved this famous inscription:

If only your strength had been equal, Demosthenes, to your wisdom,
Never would Greece have been ruled by a Macedonian Ares.[105]

It is of course absurd to say, as some writers have done, that Demosthenes himself composed these lines in Calauria just before he took the poison.

31. A little while before I arrived in Athens,[106] the following episode is said to have occurred. A soldier, who had been summoned by his commanding officer to be tried for some offence, put what little money he had between the hands of this statue which are represented as clasped together. Beside the statue grew a small plane-tree, and the leaves from the tree, whether they were blown there by chance or placed there on purpose by the soldier, piled up over the gold and hid it for a long time. Finally, the soldier returned and found his treasure intact, and later the story spread abroad and became a theme to inspire the wits of the city to compete with one another in their epigrams celebrating the incorruptibility of Demosthenes.

As for Demades, he did not live long to enjoy his infamy. The vengeance of the gods for the part he had played in the death of Demosthenes took him to Macedonia, where he justly met his death at the hands of the people he had so basely flattered. He had for some time already been disliked by the Macedonians, but he now incurred an accusation which it was impossible for him to evade. A letter of his was intercepted in which he had urged Perdiccas to intervene in Macedonia and rescue the Greeks, who he said were attached to it only by an old and rotten thread, by which he meant Antipater.[107] Deinarchus of Corinth accused him of treason, and Cassander was so enraged at his treachery that he killed Demades' son as he stood by his father's side, and then ordered Demades himself to be put to death. Through this terrible fate, he learnt that traitors always betray themselves first, a truth which Demosthenes had often prophesied to him, but which he would not believe.

And so, Sosius, you have the life of Demosthenes, which we have drawn from all that we have read or heard about him.

PHOCION

INTRODUCTION TO PHOCION

[402–318 BC]

Phocion was an Athenian statesman and general. He was almost twenty years older than Demosthenes and outlived him by four years. Plutarch claims that Phocion was elected to the generalship forty-five times over his career, a staggering number and, if true, probably more than any other Athenian. He was present at the battle of Naxos against the Spartans in 376 BC, but the next we hear of him is in the 340s when he led Athenian expeditionary forces to Euboea (348), Megara (?343), Euboea again (341) and Byzantium (340). The latter two of these expeditions, and possibly the second, were directed against Philip of Macedon or his allies. In 338 Phocion commanded a fleet operating against Philip in the Aegean, and in the immediate aftermath of the defeat of Athens and Thebes at Chaeronea in Boeotia organized the defence of Athens. But in the years that followed he pursued a policy of accommodation to Macedonian rule. He advised against Athenian involvement in Thebes' disastrous revolt of 335. He also argued against involvement in the Lamian War of 323–2, though this time unsuccessfully: when news of Alexander's death in Asia arrived in Greece, Athens and a number of allies moved to expel Macedonian forces from southern Greece. The allied forces were defeated at Crannon, and the task fell to Phocion, together with the orator Demades, to negotiate terms with Antipater, Alexander's regent and commander of Macedonian forces in Europe. Under these terms, a Macedonian garrison was installed on the hill of Munychia, thus allowing control of Piraeus, and full political rights were restricted to those with sufficient wealth to pass a new property qualification. The institutions of the democracy themselves continued to function, but the franchise was now much more limited and many poor Athenians were excluded from political life.

Phocion played a prominent role in this reconfigured Athens in the period from 322 to 318 BC. His downfall occurred amid the confused and dramatic events following the death of Antipater in 319. A power-struggle ensued in Macedonia between Cassander, Antipater's son, who might have expected to take over his father's position, and Polyperchon, a hardened general who had seen service under both Philip and Alexander, and whom Antipater had designated as his successor. Phocion collaborated with Cassander's man, Nicanor, commander of the garrison in Munychia, and failed to act against him when he seized Piraeus. Meanwhile Polyperchon, in a bid to win the Athenian masses to his side, called for the restoration of full democracy. The restored assembly, now including again the poor citizens excluded by Antipater, blamed Phocion both for the disenfranchisement of many poor Athenians and for his cooperation with the Macedonian occupation of Piraeus. In scenes which, in Plutarch's telling, have for a modern reader something about them of the Terror following the French Revolution, the assembly condemned Phocion to death by a simple vote, i.e., unconstitutionally and without a trial. He and his associates were executed forthwith. The triumph was short-lived. In the following year (317) Cassander defeated Polyperchon, a property qualification was reimposed on Athens (though this time the bar was set somewhat lower), and the wealthy Athenian Demetrius of Phaleron was installed by Cassander as the leader of a pro-Macedonian regime. One of Demetrius' first acts was to rehabilitate Phocion: he was given a state burial, a statue was erected in his honour and those held chiefly responsible for his execution were killed or driven abroad.

Plutarch paints a very sympathetic picture of Phocion. In Plutarch's telling, he was a brave and skilled general, who put the interests of his country first and who, unlike the popular leaders who flattered and pandered to the whims of the masses, spoke the truth as he saw it, even if it would be unpopular. Cooperation with Macedonia after Chaeronea could so easily have been presented as self-serving and revealing of a lack of principle. But Plutarch is careful to show that Phocion opposed Philip while there was still hope of maintaining Athens' independence, and, indeed, fought bravely; after Chaeronea his cooperation with the Macedonians is presented as sensible and moderate. That Phocion is presented as treading a rational middle course is brought out by comparison both with Demades, who is presented by Plutarch as a disgraceful toady of the Macedonians, and with those politicians who favoured resistance to Macedon even after Chaeronea, and who come across as deluded rabble-rousers. Similarly, the restored democracy of 318, which had Phocion executed, is presented as an unruly mob. The death scene, furthermore, in which Phocion and his companions drink hemlock in prison, is made in Plutarch's telling to recall the death eighty years earlier of the philosopher Socrates, likewise unfairly executed by a restored democracy.

The rather anti-democratic tone of the Life almost certainly owes something to Plutarch's sources, especially Demetrius of Phaleron's own account of his ten-year rule in Athens; although Plutarch never specifies Demetrius as a source in this Life, he was almost certainly used here, as he was for *Demosthenes*. The only other extant version of these events, that in Diodorus, Book 18, is much less favourable to Phocion and presents the democratic leaders in a more positive light. Plutarch's pro-Phocionic stance here may also reflect his own political instincts: like many ancient writers – by definition members of a wealthy elite – he was suspicious about unfettered popular sovereignty. In his treatise entitled *Political advice*, he spends a good deal of time advising how the wealthy should control and guide the people, and he tends in other Lives to take an 'elitist' view of Athenian democracy: it is good when strong leaders, like Pericles or Phocion, control and guide the people; but the masses, when stirred up instead by demagogues, are dangerous and unpredictable.

But we should be careful about assuming that the sympathetic presentation of Phocion and his policies in this Life simply reflects the political views of Plutarch or his sources. In other Lives, notably the *Demosthenes*, which deals with the same period, Plutarch is equally sympathetic to those who, like Demosthenes, resisted Macedon; Demosthenes' death is also moving and noble, and his Life, like Phocion's, ends with a statue being erected in his honour. In general, then, whatever his own political assumptions, Plutarch tends, within each Life, to be rather sympathetic to its subject, and to evaluate them against the background of the political situation with which they were faced. And Plutarch's sympathy does baulk at one act of Phocion: in a rare narratorial intervention in chapter 32, Plutarch criticizes at length Phocion's acquiescence in the seizure of Piraeus by Nicanor's troops.

This Life is a particularly anecdotal one, and there is accordingly less chronological narrative than in many Plutarchan Lives. Plutarch relies on his reader's already knowing the basic outline of the history of this period, perhaps partly through having in mind his own *Demosthenes*. The first eleven chapters, although they do contain some information on Phocion's early commands, are not arranged chronologically but designed rather to give an impression of his character and political conduct over his whole career. Even when chronological narrative gets going in chapter 12, it is often interrupted by short episodes which are not related chronologically to their context. Much space is devoted to the last few years of Phocion's life; indeed, the four years from 322 to 318 fill almost half the Life (chs. 23–37), including the dramatic description of Phocion's condemnation and death (chs. 34–7).

The *Life of Phocion* is paired with the *Life of Cato the Younger*. Cato (95–46 BC) was well known for his uncompromising opposition to Julius Caesar; he famously committed suicide after the destruction of the Republican cause, refusing to accept the pardon which Caesar would most probably have offered him. Like Phocion's, Cato's death is treated at length by Plutarch and forms the focal point of the Life; it is also modelled heavily on Socrates' death in Plato; indeed parallels with Socrates abound in *Cato the Younger*. In the prologue to the two Lives, which immediately precedes *Phocion*, Plutarch remarks on the fact that both men had the misfortune to be statesmen at a time of national defeat. Such times of crisis,

Plutarch explains, provide particular difficulties to the statesman in his dealings with the people: speaking out too boldly
against the popular will can elicit their anger, but flattering
them and speaking only to please can lead to the ruin of all.
The wise statesman will attempt to tread a difficult middle
course, making concessions where necessary 'while demanding
in return an obedience and cooperation which will benefit the
whole community' (ch. 2). Plutarch also makes in the prologue
a distinction between the statesman's personal virtue and the
circumstances with which he was confronted. Phocion and
Cato, then, had to battle against circumstances and their Lives
show how even under the most difficult conditions it is still possible to act virtuously. But, as Plutarch portrays it, there is one
major difference between the two men: Phocion compromised
with Macedonia after resistance became futile, and so, in Plutarch's telling, saved Athens; Cato, on the other hand, refused to
compromise his own personal principles and in doing so harmed
the Republican cause and brought about its destruction. Thus,
by comparison with Cato, Phocion's collaboration with Macedonia appears moderate and reasonable, and the Lives of
Phocion and Cato the Younger could be read as a case-study in
the virtues of moderation and the dangers of extremism.

PROLOGUE TO THE LIVES
OF PHOCION AND CATO
THE YOUNGER

1. Demades the orator,[1] who rose to power in Athens by serving the interests of Antipater and the Macedonians, was in consequence obliged to propose and support many measures which were contrary to the city's dignity and traditions. He often made the excuse that by the time he came to the helm, the ship of state was already a wreck. It may have been an exaggeration for Demades to say this; but it has more of the ring of truth if it is applied to the career of Phocion. Indeed, Demades himself was the mere flotsam of public life: his course of conduct both in personal and in public life was so outrageous as to make Antipater remark of him that in his old age he had become like a victim which has been dismembered for sacrifice – there was nothing left but the tongue and the stomach.[2] It was Phocion's lot, on the other hand, to carry on an unequal struggle against the violent and distressing events through which he lived, when the misfortunes suffered by Greece caused his virtue to be overshadowed and undervalued. For we need not agree with Sophocles' rendering of virtue as weak when he says, 'Reason, my lord, may dwell within a man and yet abandon him when troubles come.'[3] But we must admit that when Fortune is ranged against good men, she prevails to the extent that she often brings upon them slanders and false accusations instead of the honour and gratitude which they deserve, and in this way undermines the world's belief in their virtue.

2. And yet it is often held that a people is more inclined to insult and humiliate its best men when the nation's affairs are going well, because it then feels buoyed up by a sense of

ascendancy and power, but equally the opposite has been known to happen. Misfortunes cause men's dispositions to become bitter, intolerant and ready to take offence at trifles, they grow peevish and unwilling to listen and are angry with any counsellor who gives them forthright advice. If he makes criticisms, they think he is insulting them on account of their misfortunes, and if he speaks his mind freely, they feel that he is despising them. Just as honey can irritate wounded and ulcerated parts of the body, so also does truthful and reasoned advice sting and provoke people who are in trouble, unless it is offered in a kindly and soothing manner. It is no doubt for this reason that Homer uses the word *menoeikes*[4] to signify that which is pleasant because it yields to that part of the soul which experiences pleasure, and does not fight with or oppose it. Just as an eye that is inflamed finds most relief in colours which are subdued and lack lustre, and turns away from those which are brilliant and dazzling, so too a city which is passing through a crisis in its fortunes becomes too timid and sensitive to endure plain-speaking at the very moment that it needs it most badly, because the situation may offer no chance of retrieving the mistakes that have been made. Therefore it is in a state of this kind that political life is most dangerous: here the man who speaks only to please the people may be involved in their ruin, but the man who refuses to indulge them may be destroyed even sooner.

Now the sun, so the mathematicians tell us, does not move in the same path as the rest of the heavenly bodies, nor yet in a completely opposite direction, but pursues an oblique course at a slight angle to theirs: it follows a spiral progression with gentle and easy curves, and by this means all created things are kept in their place, and the most suitable blending of the elements is maintained. So, too, in political affairs, a method of government which is too rigid and opposes the popular will on every occasion will be resented as harsh and overbearing, but on the other hand, to acquiesce in all the demands of the people, and share in their mistakes, is a dangerous, sometimes a catastrophic, policy. The art of wise administration consists in making certain concessions and granting that which will please the people, while demanding in return an obedience and cooperation which will benefit the whole community – and men will cooperate readily and usefully in many ways provided they are not treated harshly and despotically all the time. This is the style of government which ensures the security of the state, but its practice is arduous and beset with difficulties, and it must combine those elements of severity and benevolence which are so hard to balance. But if such a happy mixture can be achieved, it provides the most complete and perfect blending of all rhythms and all harmonies. It is in this fashion, we are told, that God governs the universe, introducing his ultimate purpose not by force but by reason and persuasion.

3. This situation applied also to Cato the Younger. He lacked the power of persuasion, his manner did not endear him to the people and he never attained much popularity in his political career. Cicero tells us that he was defeated when he stood for the consulship because he acted as if he had been living in Plato's republic, not among the dregs of Romulus,[5] but I should rather say that he suffered in the same way as certain kinds of fruit do when they appear out of season: people gaze at them with wonder and delight, but do not eat them. In the same way, when the old style of virtue which had vanished for many years was reincarnated in the person of Cato, amid a general climate of depraved lives and corrupted manners, it won great fame and estimation. But it proved quite unsuited to men's needs: its nature was grand but ponderous, and therefore out of harmony with the age in which he lived. Cato did not find the ship of state already listing dangerously, as Phocion did, but beset by storms and heavy seas. In politics he could serve her only by lending a hand with the sails and ropes, and by giving his support to those with greater influence, since he himself was kept away from the helm, but nevertheless he gave Fortune a hard struggle. It did indeed seize and overthrow the Roman constitution by means of other men, but this only came about slowly, with difficulty, and after a long struggle in which the cause of the Republic almost prevailed through Cato and his virtue.

With Cato's virtue we compare that of Phocion, though not because of their general resemblances in that they were both good men devoted to the public interest. It is certainly true that two men may possess the same attribute in different forms:[6] the courage of Alcibiades differs from that of Epaminondas, the wisdom of Themistocles from that of Aristides, and the justice of Numa from that of Agesilaus. But in the case of Cato and Phocion, it is clear that their virtues bore the same stamp, shape and colour down to the most minute particulars. Both, alike, displayed the same blend of kindness and severity, of caution and daring, of solicitude for the safety of others and disregard for their own; both, alike, abhorred dishonour, but were indefatigable in the pursuit of justice. We shall therefore need a most finely adjusted instrument of reason, so to speak, to discover and define the points of difference between them.

LIFE OF PHOCION

4. It is generally agreed that Cato's origins were noble, as shall be described later,[7] but Phocion's too, so far as I can judge, were by no means lowly or undistinguished. If his father had really been a pestle-maker, as Idomeneus[8] makes out, we may be sure that Glaucippus, the son of Phocion's opponent Hypereides, would not have missed the opportunity of mentioning his humble birth in the speech he composed which cast so many aspersions on Phocion's character. Nor, in that case, would Phocion have enjoyed a life of leisure or the excellent education which enabled him to become a pupil of Plato when he was only a boy, in later life a disciple of Xenocrates in the Academy, and to devote himself to the noblest pursuits from the very beginning of his career. Hardly any Athenian ever saw him laugh or shed tears, so Douris[9] has recorded, nor did he make use of the public bath or take his hand from under his cloak[10] – that is when he wore a cloak. Indeed, whenever he was in the country or on active service, he wore neither shoes nor an outer garment, unless the cold was unendurably bitter, and after a while his soldiers used to make a joke of this habit and say that when Phocion put on his cloak it was the sign of a hard winter.[11]

5. By nature he was one of the kindest and most considerate of men, but his appearance was stern and forbidding, so that those who did not know him intimately were discouraged from talking to him alone. Chares raised a laugh at Phocion's expense in one of his speeches by referring to his lowering brow, whereupon Phocion retorted, 'At least this brow of mine has never

caused you any harm, but the laughter of those who are now sneering at me has given the city plenty to cry about.'

In the same way, Phocion's choice of words brought great benefit to his listeners, since it was full of keen insight which often led to successful action, but it also had a brevity which made his expression peremptory, severe and altogether lacking in charm. Zeno[12] used to say that a philosopher should steep his words in meaning before he utters them, and Phocion's speeches followed this principle, in that they used the fewest possible words to convey the strongest concentration of meaning. This characteristic of his is probably what Polyeuctus of Sphettus had in mind when he said that Demosthenes was the best orator, but Phocion the most effective speaker, for just as the coins which are very small in bulk are those which are very great in value, so effectiveness of speech may be judged by the ability to communicate the maximum of meaning within the smallest possible compass. Indeed, there is a story that once, when the audience was beginning to fill up the theatre, Phocion was seen walking about behind the stage lost in thought. One of his friends remarked, 'You seem to be pondering something, Phocion.' 'Yes,' he said, 'I am thinking out whether I can shorten the speech I am going to make to the Athenians.' Demosthenes himself, who had a very low opinion of the other orators, used to say quietly to his friends whenever Phocion rose to speak, 'Here comes the chopper of my speeches.' But this remark should perhaps be taken as referring to Phocion's character, since a mere word or a nod from a good man carries more weight than any number of elaborate pieces of reasoning or long sentences.

6. As a young man Phocion attached himself to Chabrias,[13] the general, and followed him on his campaigns. In these operations he gained plenty of experience of action, and also on occasion he was able to check the irregularities of Chabrias' temperament, which was both inconsistent and liable to fly to extremes. Normally, Chabrias was phlegmatic and difficult to move, but once in action his spirits would be roused and kindled, and he would rush into the thick of the battle and expose himself unnecessarily. This was in fact what happened at Chios,[14]

where he undoubtedly sacrificed his life by being the first to run his trireme on shore in the effort to force a landing in the face of the enemy. On these occasions Phocion, who knew how to temper courage and initiative with prudence, would urge on Chabrias when he was slow to act, but would restrain his impetuosity when this was out of place. The result was that Chabrias, who was a good-natured and upright man, became much attached to Phocion and promoted him to a number of enterprises and commands. In this way, he was employed in most of the important military operations of the time and his name became known throughout Greece. In particular, on the occasion of the sea-battle off Naxos,[15] he gave Phocion the opportunity to distinguish himself and enhance his reputation: he placed him in command of the left wing, and it was here that the fighting raged most fiercely and the issue was quickly decided.[16] This was the first sea-battle in which the Athenians, on their own, had fought successfully against Greek opponents since the capture of their city,[17] and they were incredibly pleased with Chabrias and came to regard Phocion as a man with the qualities of a leader. The battle was won at the time when the Great Mysteries[18] were being celebrated, and to commemorate this Chabrias made it his custom to provide the Athenians with wine for the festival every year on the sixteenth day of the month of Boedromion.[19]

7. After this, Chabrias sent out Phocion to collect the contributions which were due from a number of islands[20] and gave him an escort of twenty ships. It is said that Phocion commented that if he was being sent to fight the islanders, he would need a larger force, but that if he was visiting them as allies, one ship was enough. He sailed in his own trireme, discussed the purpose of his mission with the cities, dealt in a frank yet considerate manner with their leading men and returned home with a large fleet which the allies themselves dispatched to carry the money to Athens. Phocion not only honoured and showed his regard for Chabrias as long as the older man was alive, but when he died he took good care of his family. He paid particular attention to Chabrias' son Ctesippus, whom he tried

to make into a good man, and although he found the youth stupid and intractable, he persevered in trying to correct and cover up his faults. But on one occasion, when the young man was serving on an expedition, he continually vexed Phocion by asking him tiresome questions and offering him ill-timed advice, as though he were in a position to criticize the general and share in his command. Then at last, Phocion exclaimed, 'O Chabrias, Chabrias, did ever a man show so much gratitude for your friendship as I do in putting up with your son?'

Phocion recognized that the politicians of his time had divided between themselves the duties of the general and of the orator, almost as if they had cast lots for them. Thus, some men such as Eubulus, Aristophon, Demosthenes, Lycurgus and Hypereides did nothing but make speeches before the people and introduce measures, while others such as Diopeithes, Menestheus, Leosthenes and Chares pursued their careers by holding the office of general and directing campaigns. Phocion wished to revive the kind of public service that had been rendered by Pericles, Aristides and Solon, which was at once comprehensive and well-balanced, so that it included both political and military service to the state. For each of these men had proved himself, in the words of Archilochus, '*both a servant of the War-God and skilled in the gift of the lovely Muses*',[21]and Phocion saw that Athena was a goddess of both war and politics, and was addressed as such.[22]

8. Having adopted this principle, Phocion's policies were always aimed at preserving a state of peace; yet, in spite of this, he held the office of general more frequently not only than any of his contemporaries, but even than any of his predecessors. He never sought nor campaigned for the post, but neither did he shun, or decline it when his city called upon him. For it is generally agreed that he held the office of general forty-five times, yet he never once attended the election, but was always absent when the people sent for him and chose him. As a result, people who lack understanding are amazed at the behaviour of the Athenian people, since Phocion opposed their wishes more often than any other leader and never said or did anything to

win their favour. The truth is that just as kings are supposed to call in their flatterers after dinner has been served, so the Athenians would listen to the most sprightly and sophisticated of their demagogues by way of entertainment; but when they wanted a commander, they would switch to a more sober and serious mood and would call upon the wisest and most austere of their citizens, the man who alone, or at least more than all the rest, stood fast in opposing their impulses and wishes. Indeed, when an oracle from Delphi was read out one day in the assembly, which declared that the rest of the Athenians were unanimous in their opinions and that there was only one man who dissented from them, Phocion came forward and told them that they need look no further: he himself was the man in question, for it was only he who disapproved of everything that they did. And on another occasion, when he uttered some sentiment which was greeted with applause and saw that the whole assembly had accepted his argument, he turned to his friends and asked them, 'Can it be that I have been arguing on the wrong side without knowing it?'

9. Once the Athenians were collecting money for a public sacrifice. Everybody else put in their contribution, but Phocion after he had several times been invited to follow suit, remarked, 'I suggest you appeal to these rich men. I should be ashamed to give you anything before I have paid my debt to this man here,' and he pointed to Callicles, the money-lender. On another occasion, when his listeners would not stop clamouring and trying to shout him down, he told them this story: 'A cowardly man was once setting out for a war. Some ravens began to croak around him, whereupon he laid down his arms and sat still. After a while he picked them up and started again. Then, when the ravens croaked once more, he stopped and said, "You may croak to your hearts' content, but you shall never make a meal of me." '23

On another occasion when the Athenians urged him to lead them out against the enemy, and called him a coward and a man of no spirit because he refused, he retorted, 'You cannot make me bold, and I cannot make you cowards. But we know

very well what each of us really is.' Then at a time of crisis for
Athens, when the people were showing great hostility towards
him and demanding an inquiry into his generalship, Phocion's
advice was, 'My friends, first of all make sure of your own
safety.' Again when the people had been humble and submissive during a war, but as soon as peace had been proclaimed
became overbearing and denounced him for having robbed
them of victory, he told them, 'You are lucky to have a general
who knows you – otherwise you would have been ruined long
ago.' When there was a territorial dispute with Boeotia,[24] about
which the Athenians refused to negotiate but insisted on going
to war, he recommended them to fight by using words, in which
they had the advantage, not weapons, in which they were inferior. When he was addressing the assembly and the people
refused to take his advice or even to give him a hearing, he told
them, 'You can make me act against my wishes, but you shall
never make me speak against my judgement.'

When Demosthenes, one of the orators who opposed his policies, said to him, 'The Athenians will kill you,' Phocion replied,
'Yes, if they lose their senses, but they will kill you, if they get
them back again.'[25] Once, on a very hot day, he saw Polyeuctus
of Sphettus urging the Athenians to declare war on Philip of
Macedon. The speaker was gasping as he was a very fat man,
the sweat was pouring off him and he was gulping down great
draughts of water, whereupon Phocion remarked, 'It is most fitting that you should vote for war on the strength of this man's
advice. What sort of figure do you think he will cut when the
enemy are close at hand and he is carrying a shield and a breast-
plate? Even the effort of making a prepared speech to you is
enough to suffocate him!' On another occasion, Lycurgus showered abuse on him in the public assembly, and was particularly
bitter because, when Alexander of Macedon had demanded
that ten orators should be surrendered to him, Phocion had supported the request.[26] Phocion's reply was, 'I have often given
this people good advice, but they will not listen to me.'

10. There was a certain Archibiades who was nicknamed
'Laconist', because he aped the Spartans by growing a huge

beard, wearing a short cloak and going about with a permanent scowl on his face.[27] At a meeting of the Council, Phocion
was greeted with a stormy reception, and so he appealed to this
man to testify in his favour. However, when Archibiades rose to
speak, he merely gave the advice which he thought would
please the Athenians, whereupon Phocion seized him by the
beard and exclaimed, 'Archibiades, you might just as well have
shaved this off!'[28] Aristogeiton the informer was well known in
the assembly as a warmonger who was always trying to urge
the people into action, but when the lists of those to be selected
for military service had to be drawn up, he arrived hobbling
with the aid of a staff and with both legs bandaged. Phocion,
who was on the rostrum, caught sight of him in the distance
and cried out, 'Put down Aristogeiton as lame and unfit for service.' All these sayings of his make it astonishing that a man
who created such a harsh and austere impression should ever
have earned the nickname of 'The Good'.

It is certainly difficult, though not, I think, impossible for the
same man to be at once sweet and sharp, as a wine can be. In
the same way, other men and other wines may at first appear
agreeable, but in the end prove both unpleasant and harmful to
those who use them. And yet we are told that Hypereides once
said to the people: 'Men of Athens, do not ask yourself whether
I am harsh, but whether I am paid to be harsh.' In other words,
his question implied that the populace would only fear or
attack men because they were avaricious, and not because they
used their power to gratify their insolence, their envy, their
anger or their ambition. Phocion, then, never harmed any of
his fellow-citizens out of personal spite, nor did he regard a
single one of them as his enemy; whenever he showed himself
to be harsh or stubborn or inexorable, it was only to the extent
that he was forced to struggle against those who opposed his
efforts to save his country. In all his other dealings, he was
benevolent, accessible and considerate to everyone, indeed he
even came to the rescue of his opponents when they were in
trouble or in danger of being put on trial for their actions.
Once, when his friends reproached him for appearing on behalf
of some worthless individual who had been accused, he retorted

that good men need no defenders. Again, when Aristogeiton the informer had been condemned and begged Phocion to visit him, he responded to the appeal and set out for the prison. His friends tried to prevent him, whereupon he said to them, 'Let me go, my friends: after all, where would one rather meet Aristogeiton than in prison?'

11. Certainly, if the Athenians sent out emissaries under the command of any general other than Phocion, the allies and inhabitants of the islands would always treat them as enemies. They would strengthen their walls, block their harbours, and bring back their herds, their slaves, their wives and their children from the countryside into their cities. But whenever Phocion was in command, they would come far out to sea to meet him in their ships, put garlands on their heads and escort him to their shores with joy.

12. Philip was infiltrating Euboea, bringing troops over from Macedonia and, through his support of tyrants there, bringing its cities into his sphere of influence. Plutarch of Eretria appealed to the Athenians and begged them to save the island from falling under the rule of Macedon; so Phocion was sent out in command of a small expedition on the assumption that the people of the island would rally enthusiastically to his support.[29] But he found that Euboea was in a bad way; it was full of traitors and undermined by bribes, and in consequence Phocion's own situation was extremely dangerous. He occupied a ridge that was separated by a deep ravine from the plains which surrounded the city of Tamynae, and there he established himself and concentrated the best of his troops. As for the disorderly, argumentative and untrustworthy soldiers in his force who were apt to steal out of his lines and desert, he told his officers to make no effort to keep them: he calculated that if they remained in his camp, they would be useless because of their lack of discipline and would only demoralize those soldiers who were reliable, while if they returned to Athens, the memory of their cowardice would make them less likely to denounce him and would deter them from making false accusations.

13. As the enemy advanced, Phocion ordered his men to stand to arms, but to remain quiet until he had finished sacrificing, then waited a long time, possibly because the omens were unfavourable, or because he wanted to draw the enemy closer to his position. At this, Plutarch the Eretrian, who imagined that Phocion's backwardness in engaging was due to cowardice, first charged the enemy at the head of his mercenaries; then when the cavalry saw Plutarch advance, they could not bear to remain idle but at once rode at their opponents, galloping out of the camp in scattered groups and without formation. The result was that first the leading ranks were repulsed, then the whole body of troops broke and Plutarch himself took to his heels. Some of the enemy reached the palisade of Phocion's camp and, imagining that they were masters of the field, started trying to tear up the stakes from which it was built and break through. But the sacrifices had been completed in the meantime and the Athenians attacked and at once drove the enemy from the camp and cut down most of them among the fortifications as they strove to escape. Phocion ordered his phalanx to halt and hold its ground, so that the soldiers who had been scattered in the earlier action could rally to it and re-form; meanwhile, he himself with his picked troops launched a fresh attack on the enemy. There followed a fierce engagement in which all the Athenians fought with great courage and gallantry: on this occasion, Thallus the son of Cineas and Glaucus the son of Polymedes, who fought side by side with Phocion, distinguished themselves most conspicuously. However, Cleophanes also made a name for himself in the battle. It was he who halted the cavalry in their headlong flight, and by shouting at them to rally to their general, who was in great danger, he made them ride back and complete the victory which had been won by the hoplites. After this battle, Phocion expelled Plutarch from Eretria, and he also captured a fortress named Zaretra, which commands the narrowest part of the island where the sea reduces it to a mere neck of land. He also released all his Greek prisoners, for he was afraid that the demagogues at Athens might give way to a fit of anger and persuade the people to pass some cruel sentence on them.

14. After these successes Phocion sailed home, but all too soon the allies were to feel the absence of his high principles and just conduct, and the Athenians the loss of the experience and vigour he had just shown. For his successor, Molossus, carried on the war so ineptly that he was actually captured by the enemy.[30]

When Philip reached the Hellespont[31] with all his forces, he had great hopes of subduing the Chersonese and making himself master of Perinthus and Byzantium at the same time. The Athenians were anxious to help these cities, but thanks to the efforts of the demagogues it was Chares who was appointed to command the expedition. When he arrived there he achieved nothing worthy of the size of his force, and the cities even refused to allow his fleet to enter their harbours. They all regarded him with suspicion and he was reduced to roaming about the country, where he extorted money from the Athenians' allies and was treated with contempt by their enemies. At length, the people in Athens, urged on by the demagogues, became exasperated with him and began to regret that they had ever sent help to the Byzantines. But then Phocion rose in the assembly and declared that they had no right to blame the allies for withholding their trust: the fault lay with their own generals who had failed to inspire it. 'These men', he declared, 'make you feared even by those who need your help to save them.'

The people were so impressed by this speech that they again changed their minds. They ordered Phocion to raise another army and set out to help the allies on the Hellespont. It was this decision, above all, which saved Byzantium. For Phocion's credit already stood high there, but more important still Leon, one of their leading citizens who was well known among the Byzantines for his virtue and who had been a close friend of Phocion's at the Academy, personally guaranteed the Athenian's good faith. The citizens would not let Phocion encamp outside their walls as he had intended, but opened their gates, welcomed the Athenians into their homes and fraternized with them. After this gesture of confidence, the Athenians not only behaved with exemplary discipline and courtesy inside the city but fought with great spirit to defend it. The result was that in this campaign Philip was driven out of the Hellespont and his previous reputation as an unbeatable commander suffered a severe setback. Besides this, Phocion captured several of Philip's ships and recaptured some cities which the Macedonian king had garrisoned. He also made landings at a number of points on Philip's territory, plundered and overran it; finally, when an enemy force was mustered for its defence, he was wounded and sailed back home.

15. On one occasion, the people of Megara appealed secretly to Athens for help.[32] Phocion was afraid that the Boeotians might discover this and prevent the Athenians from sending help, and so he summoned a meeting of the assembly early in the morning and explained the communication from Megara. Then, as soon as the necessary decree had been approved, he had the trumpet sounded, ordered his men to leave the assembly and immediately marched them away under arms. The Megarians received him with enthusiasm, and he proceeded to fortify their harbour at Nisaea and to build two long walls running down to it from the city;[33] in this way, he made Megara's communications with the sea so secure that she had no need to fear her enemies by land and could be connected with Athens by sea.

16. Athens was now in a state of total hostility to Philip, and in Phocion's absence other generals were elected to take charge of the war. However, when Phocion returned with his fleet from the islands, he at first tried to persuade the people not to go to war and to accept Philip's terms, in view of the fact that the king was peaceably inclined and greatly feared the dangers which were likely to ensue from a war. One of the Athenians, who made his living by hanging about the law-courts and acting as an informer, opposed Phocion and asked, 'Do you dare to try to dissuade the Athenians from going to war when they are already under arms?' 'Certainly I do,' retorted Phocion, 'and I am not forgetting that if we go to war, it is I who will be in charge, while if we remain at peace, it will be you.' In the event Phocion could not make his point of view prevail. It was Demosthenes who carried the day and urged the Athenians to engage Philip as far away from Athens as possible.[34] At this

Phocion declared: 'The problem is not where we are going to fight, my good sir, but how we are to win the battle. If we can do that, we shall keep the war at a distance anyhow, but it is the loser who finds that the horrors of war are on his very doorstep.' But when Athens was defeated[35] and the most discontented and revolutionary elements among the people dragged Charidemus to the public platform and clamoured for him to be appointed general, the more reputable citizens were filled with alarm. With the aid of the Council of the Areopagus in the assembly, they managed through tears and entreaties to persuade the Athenians to entrust the city to Phocion.

Phocion considered that the terms which Philip was offering to Athens were generous and humane, and that the Athenians should accept them. But when Demades proposed a motion that the city should associate herself with the common peace and take part in the congress for all the states,[36] Phocion would not support it until he had first discovered what demands Philip would make upon the Greeks. His advice was overruled because of the critical situation in which Athens stood, but as soon as he saw that the Athenians were beginning to regret their choice, because they were being called upon to supply Philip with cavalry and triremes, he said to them, 'This is exactly what I was afraid of when I resisted your proposals, but since you made the choice, you must not allow yourselves to become disappointed or cast down. You must remember that your ancestors sometimes gave the orders, and at other times had to submit to them; but because they acted with honour in both situations, they saved their city and the rest of the Greeks.' When Philip was assassinated,[37] the people's first impulse was to offer up sacrifice for the good news, but Phocion opposed this. He said it would show an ignoble spirit to rejoice at what had happened, and reminded them that the army which had opposed them at Chaeronea had been weakened by the loss of no more than one man.

17. Again, when Demosthenes was speaking abusively of Alexander, even while the king was already advancing upon Thebes, Phocion said to him *Foolhardy man, why seek to provoke a*

man whose temper is savage[38] and who is reaching out after greater glory? Or do you wish, when there is already a fearful conflagration on our borders, to make the flames spread to our city too? My whole object in taking up the burden of office was to prevent this, and I shall not allow my fellow-citizens to destroy themselves, even if they wish it.'

After Thebes had been destroyed,[39] Alexander demanded that Demosthenes, Lycurgus, Hypereides, Charidemus and several others should be handed over to him. When the people heard this proposal, the whole assembly turned their gaze upon Phocion and called upon him repeatedly by name. Phocion then rose to his feet. He beckoned to his side one of his closest friends, whom he loved and confided in above all others, and said, 'These men, whom Alexander has demanded, have brought our city to such a pass that for my part, even if the king were to ask for my friend Nicocles, I should urge you to give him up. And if I myself could sacrifice my life to save you all, I should count this a happy fate. I feel pity too, men of Athens, for the Thebans who have fled here for shelter, but it is enough for Greece to have to mourn the destruction of Thebes. For this reason it is better to ask for mercy and to intercede with the victors, both for you and for them, than to fight.'

It is said that when the first decree was presented to Alexander, he flung it from him, turned his back on the envoys and left the room. But the second decree, which was brought by Phocion, he accepted, since he had learnt from the older Macedonians that Philip had always admired this man. Alexander not only consented to receive Phocion and hear his petition, but he actually listened to his advice, which was as follows. If it was peace that Alexander wanted above all, then he should make an end of the fighting, but if it was glory, then he should transfer the theatre of the war and turn his arms away from Greece and against the barbarians. Phocion spoke at length and his words were well chosen to fit Alexander's character and aspirations, with the result that he quite transformed the king's mood and allayed his resentment against the Athenians.[40] In this frame of mind, Alexander told Phocion that the Athenians ought to watch the course of events with great care, since, if anything happened to him, they were the people who should become the leaders of Greece. In private, too, he welcomed Phocion as his friend and guest, and treated him with greater honour than even most of his closest associates enjoyed. At any rate, the historian Douris tells us that after Alexander had become great and had conquered Darius, he left out the customary word of greeting, *chairein*,[41] in all his letters, except when he wrote to Phocion. For two men alone, Phocion and Antipater, he used the word: this detail is also recorded by Chares.[42]

18. As regards the story of the money offered to Phocion, it is generally agreed that Alexander sent him a present of 100 talents. When this arrived in Athens, Phocion asked those who brought it why, when there were so many Athenians to choose from, Alexander should have singled out him as the recipient of such a huge sum. They answered, 'Because Alexander considers that only you are a good and honourable man.' Phocion's reply was, 'In that case let him allow me to continue in that state and to enjoy that reputation always.' But when the messengers followed him to his house and saw his frugal way of life, how his wife kneaded the bread, while Phocion with his own hands drew water from the well and washed their feet, they were indignant, and pressed him even more insistently to accept the money; they exclaimed that it was monstrous that Phocion, who was an honoured friend of the king, should live in such poverty. Phocion caught sight of a poor old man who was walking by dressed in a squalid cloak, and so he asked them which of the two they thought inferior, himself or the old man. They begged him not to make such a comparison, whereupon Phocion replied, 'Well, this man has less to live on than I have, and yet he finds it quite enough. In other words,' he went on, 'either I make no use of this enormous sum, or if I do, I shall destroy my good name with the Athenians and with the king as well.'

So the treasure went back from Athens to where it had come from, after it had served to prove to the Greeks that the man who did not need such a sum was richer than the man who had offered it. Alexander was annoyed and wrote back to Phocion that he did not consider those who refused to accept anything from him to be his friends. But even then Phocion would not take the money, though he did ask for the release of Echecratides the sophist, Athenodorus of Imbros and two Rhodians, Demaratus and Sparton, who had been arrested on various charges and imprisoned at Sardis. Alexander immediately set these men free, and years later, when he sent Craterus back to Macedonia,[43] he ordered him to make over to Phocion the revenue of whichever one of four cities in Asia he might choose.[44] The cities were Cius, Gergithus, Mylasa and Elaea, and he insisted even more vehemently than before that he would be angry if Phocion did not accept this gift. But Phocion again declined, and soon afterwards Alexander died. Phocion's house, which is in the quarter of Athens known as Melite, can be seen to this day. It is decorated with a number of plates of bronze, but in other respects it is simple and unpretentious.

19. As for Phocion's wives, we have no record of the first, except for the fact that she was a sister of Cephisodotus the sculptor. But his second wife was as celebrated among the Athenians for her modesty and simplicity as was Phocion for his integrity. On one occasion, when the Athenians were watching a performance of some new tragedies, the actor who was to play the part of the queen asked the *choregos*, the sponsor of the festival, to provide him with a large number of women attendants, all of them dressed in expensive costumes. When the sponsor declined to provide these, the actor became indignant and kept the audience waiting by refusing to make his entrance. At this the sponsor, whose name was Melanthius, pushed him onto the stage, shouting out at the same time, 'Don't you see Phocion's wife, who always goes out with only one maidservant to wait on her? Why should you give yourself these airs and turn all our wives' heads with your extravagance?' His words could be heard by the whole audience and were greeted with loud applause. It was Phocion's wife, too, who remarked, when an Ionian woman who was staying with her showed off her gold ornaments and her collars and necklaces glittering with jewels, 'My ornament is Phocion, who is just now serving his twentieth year as a general of Athens.'

20. When Phocion's son Phocus was anxious to take part in the Panathenaic Games as an equestrian acrobat, Phocion gave him permission. This was not because he cared whether or not his son won a prize, but rather because he hoped that the young man would benefit from the exercise and physical training that were needed for the race, for in general Phocus had led a disorderly life and was fond of drinking. He won the race and received many invitations from friends who wished to celebrate his victory in their houses, but Phocion allowed only one host to have this honour, and declined all the other invitations. When Phocion came to the house and saw the magnificence of the preparations, he was particularly struck by the basins of spiced wine which were provided to wash the feet of the guests as they arrived, and he called his son and said, 'Phocus, won't you prevent your friend from spoiling your victory?' Wishing to remove his son altogether from that style of living, he took him to Sparta and placed him among the young men who were undergoing the traditional course of Spartan discipline.[45] This annoyed the Athenians, since it implied that Phocion had a poor opinion of their own customs and institutions, and on one occasion Demades said to him, 'Phocion, why don't we try to persuade the Athenians to adopt the Spartan constitution? If you give me the word, I am quite ready to introduce the necessary legislation.' 'Yes, why not?' replied Phocion. 'With all these exotic perfumes and lotions you put on, you would be just the man to sing the praises of Lycurgus and sell the Athenians the idea of plain food and state-controlled dining halls.'[46]

21. When Alexander wrote requesting the Athenians send him triremes[47] and the other orators opposed the idea, the Council invited Phocion to give his opinion. 'My advice,' he said, 'is that you should either possess superior strength yourselves, or be on good terms with those who do possess it.' When Pytheas, who at that time was just beginning to speak in public, reeled off a long harangue with complete self-confidence, Phocion remarked, 'You had better hold your tongue and remember that you are a slave of the people, and newly bought at that.' Again when Harpalus, Alexander's treasurer,[48] landed in Attica,

and those of the demagogues who were in the habit of trading their political influence rushed to him and vied eagerly for his favours, he scattered a few trifles among them from his hoard to whet their appetite. But he immediately sent a message to Phocion, offered him 700 talents and placed himself and the whole of his property at his disposal in return for his protection. Phocion answered sharply that Harpalus would regret it if he did not give up his attempts to corrupt the city, and for the moment the man was abashed and ceased his efforts. But soon afterwards, when the Athenians met to consider his case, he discovered that those who had accepted money from him were now changing sides and denouncing him to prevent themselves from being found out, while Phocion, who had refused to accept anything, was showing some regard for his safety, if this could be reconciled with the public interest. This encouraged Harpalus to try to ingratiate himself with Phocion a second time, but he found him completely impervious to bribes and as unassailable on every side as a fortress. However, he succeeded in making a friend and associate of Phocion's son-in-law, Charicles: Harpalus trusted him and employed him in all his affairs, with the result that he ruined Charicles' reputation.

22. For example, Harpalus had been passionately in love with the courtesan Pythonice, who had borne him a daughter. When Pythonice died,[49] Harpalus resolved to build a magnificent monument to her memory and entrusted the supervision of the work to Charicles. This was a disreputable enough assignment in itself, but it was made even more so by the appearance of the tomb when it was completed. For the monument can still be seen at Hermeium on the way from Athens to Eleusis, but there is nothing in its character to justify the sum of 30 talents, which Charicles is said to have charged Harpalus for its construction. And yet after Harpalus' death, Charicles and Phocion took his daughter under their protection and educated her with every care. On the other hand, when Charicles was prosecuted for his dealings with Harpalus and appealed to Phocion to appear with him in court and speak on his behalf, Phocion refused and

said, 'When I made you my son-in-law, Charicles, it was only for honourable purposes.'

When Asclepiades, the son of Hipparchus, broke the news of Alexander's death in Athens,[50] Demades urged the people not to believe it: if Alexander were really dead, he declared, the stench of the corpse would have filled the whole world long before. But Phocion, who immediately saw that the people were bent on revolution, tried his utmost to calm them down and restrain them. And when many of them rushed to the public platform and shouted that the report which Asclepiades had brought was true, Phocion merely said, 'Very well then, if he is dead today, he will be dead tomorrow and the day after. We shall have all the more quiet to debate the matter, and all the more safety to decide what we should do.'

23. When Leosthenes had involved the Athenians in the Greek War,[51] and saw that Phocion strongly disapproved of his action, he scornfully asked him what good he had done the city in all the years he had served her as general. 'Do you think it is nothing, then,' retorted Phocion, 'that our citizens are all buried at home in their own tombs?' On another occasion, when Leosthenes was making a boastful and arrogant speech in the assembly, Phocion said, 'Your speeches, young man, remind me of cypress trees. They are towering and stately, but they bear no fruit.' And when Hypereides once rose and demanded of Phocion, 'Will the time ever come when you will advise Athens to go to war?' Phocion retorted, 'Yes, she can go to war when I see the young men willing to observe discipline, the rich to make contributions and the demagogues to refrain from embezzling public funds.' Many people admired the force which Leosthenes had assembled,[52] and they asked Phocion what he thought of the preparations. 'They are good enough for a sprint,' he said; 'but if it is to be a long race, then I fear for Athens, since we have no reserves, either of money, or of ships, or of hoplites.'[53] And events proved him right. At first Leosthenes achieved some brilliant successes, defeating the Boeotians in a pitched battle and driving Antipater into Lamia. At this point, the Athenians are said to have been buoyed up with high hopes and constantly

holding festivals and offering sacrifices to the gods to celebrate the good news. Some of the citizens thought they could prove to Phocion that he had been wrong, and asked him whether he would not have been glad to have achieved these successes. 'Certainly I would,' he said, 'but I am still glad to have given the advice I did.' And again when one dispatch after another arrived, either in writing or by messenger from the camp, he remarked, 'I wonder when we shall stop winning victories.'

24. But when Leosthenes was killed,[54] those who were afraid that, if Phocion were elected general, he would put an end to the war, arranged with an obscure person that he should rise to speak in the assembly. He was to make out that he was a friend and intimate associate of Phocion and urge the people to spare him and keep him safe since they had no one else like him in Athens. They should, therefore, not send him into the field, but appoint Antiphilus to command the army. The Athenians approved his proposal, whereupon Phocion came forward and declared that he had never been associated with the man, and, so far from his being a close friend, he had not the slightest knowledge of him. 'But from this day,' he went on, 'I shall regard you as my friend and companion, for you have given advice which suits me very well.'

When the Athenians were eager to invade Boeotia,[55] Phocion began by opposing the plan, and some of his friends warned him that he would be put to death if he continually came into conflict with his fellow-countrymen. 'That will be an injustice', he said, 'so long as I am acting in their interests; but it will be just if I lead them astray.' Later, when he saw that the people would not give up the project but continued to clamour for it, he ordered the herald to make a proclamation that all Athenian citizens under the age of sixty should take rations for five days and follow him immediately out of the assembly. At this there was an instant uproar, as the older citizens leaped to their feet and shouted their disagreement.[56] 'There is nothing extraordinary about this,' Phocion told them; 'after all, I who am to lead you am in my eightieth year.' For the moment, then, he held them back and persuaded them to give up their intention.

25. When the sea-coast of Attica was being ravaged by Micion, who had landed at Rhamnus[57] with a large force of Macedonians and mercenaries and was overrunning the countryside nearby, Phocion led out the Athenian army against him. As they marched, men kept running up to him from all sides and telling him what to do. One advised him to occupy a hill on this side, another to send his cavalry round that way, a third to launch an attack on the enemy. 'Heracles!' Phocion exclaimed, 'how many generals I see around me and how few soldiers!' Again, when he had drawn up his hoplites in battle, one of his soldiers ran a long way out in front of the ranks, was overcome with fear when an opponent ran out to meet him and raced back again to his position. 'Young man,' said Phocion sternly, 'you ought to be ashamed at deserting your post twice in one day, first the position which I gave you and then the one you gave yourself.' He then immediately attacked the enemy and utterly routed them, killing Micion their commander along with many others. The Greek army in Thessaly also defeated Antipater, although he had been reinforced by Leonnatus and his Macedonian troops from Asia. The Greek infantry were commanded by Antiphilus and the cavalry by Menon the Thessalian: in this battle Leonnatus was killed.

26. A little later, Craterus crossed over from Asia with a large army and another pitched battle was fought at Crannon, in which the Greeks were beaten.[58] This was not a crushing defeat, nor were many men killed. But the Greek commanders were young men and were too lenient to maintain a strict discipline, while at the same time Antipater made tempting offers to a number of the Greek cities from which the confederate army had been drawn: the result was that the troops melted away and disgracefully betrayed the cause of Greek freedom. Antipater at once marched upon Athens, and Demosthenes and Hypereides fled from the city. As for Demades, he had found it impossible to pay any part of the fines which had been imposed on him by the city: he had been convicted of putting forward illegal proposals on seven occasions, had been deprived of his civic rights and was, therefore, disqualified from speaking in

the assembly. But he discovered that at a moment of crisis these disabilities were ignored, and so he brought forward a proposal that delegates should be sent to Antipater with full powers to sue for peace. However, the people were afraid and called upon Phocion, declaring that he was the only man in whom they felt confidence. 'If you had trusted me in the first place,' he reminded them, 'we should not now be debating this question at all.' When the motion had thus been passed, Phocion was sent to Antipater,[59] who was encamped in the Cadmeia,[60] and was preparing to invade Attica at once. Phocion's first request was that Antipater should stay where he was and arrange terms. Craterus protested that it was unfair of Phocion to try to persuade the Macedonians to remain in the territory of a friend and ally, thereby inflicting all the damage which is caused by an occupying army, when they were quite free to plunder the territory of their enemy; but Antipater took his colleague by the hand and said, 'We must grant Phocion this favour.' However, as for the remainder of the terms of peace, Antipater told the Athenians that these must be dictated by the victors: this was exactly what he in his turn had been told by Leosthenes at Lamia.[61]

27. Accordingly, when Phocion returned to Athens and reported these demands, the people accepted them, since they had no choice. Phocion then visited Thebes again with the rest of the Athenian delegation, which had now been reinforced by the philosopher Xenocrates.[62] For Xenocrates' reputation for virtue, together with his fame and prestige, could not fail to command consideration: no man's heart, it was generally believed, could be so full of pride, or anger, or cruelty, that it would not at the mere sight of the man be moved to a feeling of reverence and a desire to do him honour. But in this case the opposite happened, owing to a certain ruthlessness and antagonism to virtue in Antipater's disposition. In the first place, he refused to salute Xenocrates at all, although he greeted the other ambassadors, at which Xenocrates is said to have remarked, 'Antipater does well to feel ashamed before me alone for his ruthless designs towards our city.' Then, when Xenocrates

began to speak, Antipater would not listen to him, brutally interrupted him and reduced him to silence. Finally, after Phocion had spoken, Antipater replied that the Athenians could be admitted to friendship and alliance with him on the following conditions. First, they must deliver up Demosthenes and Hypereides; secondly, they must revert to their ancestral constitution, whereby the franchise was limited to those who possessed a property qualification;[63] thirdly, they must admit a garrison into Munychia;[64] and fourthly, they must pay the whole expense of the war, as well as a fine.

The other delegates considered these terms tolerable, and even humane, but Xenocrates remarked that Antipater was treating the Athenians leniently if he regarded them as slaves, but harshly if as free men. Phocion begged Antipater not to install a garrison in Athens, to which Antipater, so we are told, replied, 'Phocion, we are ready to do you any favour which will not bring ruin on you and on ourselves.' However, some people give a different account. They say that Antipater asked whether, if he made a concession to the Athenians in the matter of the garrison, Phocion could give him a guarantee that the city would abide by the terms of the peace and not stir up trouble. They also report that when Phocion was silent and hesitated as to how to answer, a certain Callimedon,[65] nicknamed 'The Stag-beetle', who was an arrogant man and a hater of democracy, leaped to his feet and shouted out, 'But even if this fellow goes on talking nonsense, Antipater, and gives you his promise, will you believe him and not carry out what you have already decided?'

28. In this way, the Athenians were obliged to admit a Macedonian garrison; it was commanded by Menyllus, who was a fair-minded man and a friend of Phocion. But the posting of a garrison was regarded as a demonstration of power which was deliberately carried out to humiliate the Athenians, and not as the occupation of a strong-point which was dictated by necessity. Moreover, the moment that was chosen for this action was even more galling for the Athenians, for the garrison was installed on the twentieth day of the month of Boedromion,

while the Mysteries were being celebrated.[66] It is on that day that the god Iacchus is conducted from the city to Eleusis,[67] and this disturbance of the ceremony caused the people to compare the present celebration of the rites with those of years gone by. In those earlier days, mystic apparitions had been seen and voices heard, which had coincided with the city's most glorious successes and had struck terror and dismay into the hearts of their enemies.[68] But now, even in the midst of these same observances, the gods apparently looked down unmoved, while the most crushing misfortunes fell upon Greece. So the desecration of this season, which hitherto had been the most hallowed and beloved in the eyes of the Athenians, henceforth made them associate its name with their greatest disasters. And in fact a few years before this, the priestess of Dodona had sent an oracle to Athens warning the people to 'guard the heights of Artemis'[69] and make sure that no strangers should seize them. Again, on this occasion, when they dyed the fillets which are twined around the sacred chests that are carried in the procession, instead of taking on their usual purple colour, they turned a pale and deathly hue; and, more ominous still, all the articles belonging to private individuals which were dyed with them at the same time retained their natural colour. Besides this, one of the initiates, who was washing a pig in the harbour of Cantharus,[70] was seized by a shark, which devoured all the lower parts of his body as far as the belly: by this omen the gods were believed to be making a clear prophecy that the Athenians would lose the lower parts of the city which bordered on the sea, but would keep the upper city.

Now the garrison at Munychia did not harm the citizens in any way, thanks to the influence of Menyllus. But the Athenians who were deprived of the vote because they were too poor to possess the property qualification, numbered more than twelve thousand.[71] Those of them who remained in Athens were considered to have received harsh and humiliating treatment; on the other hand, those who because of this measure left the capital and migrated to the town and the territory which Antipater provided for them in Thrace were regarded as no better than the exiles of a captured city.

29. The death of Demosthenes at Calauria and of Hypereides at Cleonae, which I have described elsewhere,[72] caused the Athenians to look back on the times of Philip and Alexander with regret and almost to long for their return. At a later period, after Antigonus had been killed in battle, and those who had taken his life had begun to oppress and tyrannize their subjects, a peasant in Phrygia who was digging on his farm was asked by a passer-by what he was doing, and replied with a sigh, 'I am searching for Antigonus.' So now the same sentiments occurred to the Athenians, when they recalled the greatness and generosity of those kings, and how these qualities made their anger easy to appease. By contrast, Antipater, although he tried to conceal his power by counterfeiting the appearance of a private citizen who dressed meanly and followed a simple mode of life, was really a harsher and more tyrannical master to those who had to endure his rule. However, by pleading with Antipater, Phocion managed to save many Athenians from banishment, while for those who were obliged to go into exile he obtained the concession of living in the Peloponnese, instead of being banished from Greece to live beyond the Ceraunian mountains or Cape Taenarus, as was the fate of many of those who were expelled from other Greek cities.[73] One of these men was Hagnonides, the informer.

Phocion also succeeded in regulating the city's internal affairs so that government was carried on mildly and in a law-abiding fashion. He found means to keep the men of education and culture continuously in office, while the agitators and busybodies, by the very fact of their being constantly excluded from power, gradually faded into insignificance and ceased to trouble the state; instead, he encouraged such men to find satisfaction in staying at home and cultivating the soil. He noticed that Xenocrates paid tax as a resident alien and offered to enrol him as a citizen, but the philosopher declined, saying that he could not acknowledge a regime the establishment of which he had been publicly delegated to oppose.

30. When Menyllus offered him a gift of money, Phocion replied that Menyllus was no better a man than Alexander, and that

there was no stronger reason for him to accept it now than on the previous occasion when he had refused the present from Alexander. But Menyllus pressed him to accept the money, if only for the benefit of his son Phocus, whereupon Phocion said, 'If Phocus becomes converted to a modest style of living, then his inheritance will be enough for him, but as he is now, nothing will satisfy him.' However, when Antipater wished him to perform some service which he considered dishonourable, Phocion answered him sharply and said, 'Antipater cannot have me as a friend and a flatterer at once.' Antipater himself declared, so we are told, that he had two friends at Athens, Phocion and Demades: he could never influence the one, whatever he offered him, or satisfy the other, whatever he gave him. Indeed, Phocion could point to his poverty as the most conspicuous evidence of his virtue: he had served Athens times without number as a general, he had enjoyed the friendship of kings and now he had reached old age and was still a poor man, whereas Demades prided himself on his wealth and on his contempt for the laws which had enabled him to acquire it. For example, there was a law in force in Athens at this time which forbade the sponsor of a choric festival to include a foreigner in his chorus, on pain of a fine of 1,000 drachmas. So Demades presented a chorus of a hundred, every one of whom were foreigners, and at the same time brought into the theatre the fine of 1,000 drachmas for each of them. Again, on the occasion of the marriage of his son Demeas, he said to him, 'My boy, when I married your mother, not even our next-door neighbours knew about it, but at your wedding you will have presents from kings and princes.'

The presence of the garrison was a standing grievance to the Athenians, and the people plagued Phocion with requests that he should appeal to Antipater to remove it. Whether it was that he had no hope of persuading Antipater to agree, or because he saw that the fear which it inspired obliged the Athenians to conduct their affairs in a more reasonable and law-abiding fashion, at any rate, he continually contrived to put off the task. However, he succeeded in persuading Antipater not to insist on immediate payment of the fine that had been inflicted on the city, but to allow a moratorium. So the people turned to Demades and appealed to him on the subject of the garrison; he willingly accepted the mission and set off for Macedonia, taking his son with him. He arrived, as if by some divine dispensation, at the precise moment when Antipater had fallen sick, and when his son Cassander, who had taken charge of affairs, had just discovered a letter written by Demades to Antigonus in Asia. In this he had urged Antigonus[74] to appear suddenly in Greece and Macedonia, for these territories were hanging by an old and rotten thread, as he scornfully referred to Antipater. So as soon as Cassander saw Demades after his arrival in Macedonia, he placed him under arrest. First of all he had Demades' son slaughtered in his presence: the two were standing so close that the young man's blood poured into the folds of his father's tunic and filled them;[75] then he reviled and abused Demades for his ingratitude and treachery, and dispatched him in the same fashion.

31. Shortly before he died, Antipater appointed Polyperchon commander-in-chief and Cassander second in command.[76] Cassander, however, soon overturned this arrangement and hastened to seize power for himself. He sent out Nicanor[77] with all speed to relieve Menyllus of the command of the garrison in Athens, and ordered him to take over at Munychia before Antipater's death had become publicly known. These orders were carried out, and when the Athenians learnt a few days later that Antipater was dead, they indignantly blamed Phocion, alleging that he had received information in advance, but had kept quiet as a favour to Nicanor. Phocion ignored these accusations and instead held discussions with Nicanor, and secured lenient and considerate treatment for the Athenians; in particular, he persuaded Nicanor to become president of the games and undertake considerable expenditure in that capacity.[78]

32. Meanwhile Polyperchon, who had the king[79] in his personal charge and who was opposing Cassander's schemes, sent a letter to Athens. In this he announced that the king had restored to all the Athenians their democratic form of government and called upon the citizens to exercise their political

rights according to their ancestral constitution. This was a plot designed to destroy Phocion. Polyperchon's plan, as his actions revealed later, was to win over the city to his side. He had little hope of achieving his design unless he could secure Phocion's banishment, but he calculated that this might well come about if the mass of disfranchised citizens overwhelmed the government and the assembly was once more dominated by demagogues and public informers.

Nicanor saw that the Athenians were intensely excited by this communication from Macedon, and he was anxious to address them. A meeting of the Council was held at Piraeus and he appeared before it, his personal safety having been previously guaranteed by Phocion. Dercylus, the Athenian general responsible for the countryside, tried to arrest him, but Nicanor, who had got wind of this in time, eluded the attempt and soon made it clear that he intended to make reprisals against the city. When Phocion was blamed for failing to detain Nicanor and allowing him to escape, he replied that he had confidence in the Macedonian and had no reason to suspect him of any harmful intention, but that in any case he preferred to be seen suffering wrong than doing it. Now, such a sentiment may, on reflection, seem honourable and high-minded if a man is speaking for his own interests alone, but if he endangers his country's safety, especially when he is a commander and magistrate, it seems to me that he violates an even more important and more sacred obligation: that is, his duty towards his fellow-citizens. It is not a good enough defence that Phocion refrained from arresting Nicanor because he was afraid of plunging the city into war, and that he justified his unwillingness to act by his professions of good faith and fair-dealing in the hope that Nicanor would respect these obligations and do no harm to the Athenians. The truth seems to have been that Phocion was firmly convinced that Nicanor was trustworthy: he believed this so strongly that even when many people warned him against the Macedonian and alleged that he was plotting to seize Piraeus, that he had sent mercenary troops over to Salamis and had corrupted a number of the inhabitants of Piraeus, Phocion would not believe the report or even pay any attention to it. Indeed, even

after Philomelus of Lamptrae had introduced a decree that all
Athenians should take up arms and await orders from Phocion,
as their general, he still took no action until Nicanor marched
his troops out of Munychia and began to surround Piraeus
with a trench.[80]

33. When matters had reached this pass, Phocion was willing
to lead out the Athenians, but by now he was shouted down
and treated with contempt. Then Alexander, the son of Polyperchon, arrived with his army. He had come ostensibly to
bring help to the citizens in their struggle against Nicanor, but
his real purpose was to seize the city if he could, now that it
was fatally divided. The exiled Athenians, who had accompanied him when he invaded Attica, quickly made their way
into the city. A horde of foreigners and disfranchised citizens
hurried in to join them, and a motley and disorderly assembly
of the people was held, at which Phocion was removed from
his command and other generals were elected. And but for the
fact that Alexander and Nicanor were seen to be meeting alone
near the walls, and that these conferences were so frequent that
they roused the Athenians' suspicions, the city would not have
escaped the danger in which it stood. The orator Hagnonides[81]
then attacked Phocion and denounced him as a traitor, and this
so much alarmed Callimedon and Charicles[82] that they fled
from the city, while Phocion and those of his friends who
remained loyal to him set out to visit Polyperchon. They were
accompanied out of regard for Phocion by Solon of Plataea and
Deinarchus of Corinth,[83] both of whom were believed to be
close friends of Polyperchon. However, Deinarchus fell sick
and his party was detained for many days at Elateia, and during this time the people of Athens passed a decree, proposed by
Archestratus and supported by Hagnonides, as a result of
which they dispatched a delegation to denounce Phocion. The
two parties reached Polyperchon simultaneously, as he was on
the march with the king and had arrived at a village named
Pharygae in Phocis: this lies at the foot of Mount Acrurium,
which is now known as Galata.

Here Polyperchon set up the throne with the golden canopy

and had the king and his friends seated beneath it. As soon as Deinarchus came forward, he ordered him to be seized, tortured and put to death, and then he gave audience to the delegation from Athens. However, they quickly reduced the interview to chaos by shouting, accusing and contradicting one another in the council, until at last Hagnonides came forward and said, 'Best pack us all into one cage and send us back to Athens to be tried.' At this the king burst out laughing, but the Macedonians and foreigners who happened to be in attendance at the council, and had nothing else to do, were curious to listen, and nodding to the delegates they encouraged both sides to state their case. But in fact the hearing was very far from impartial. When Phocion tried to speak, he was continually interrupted by Polyperchon, until at last he struck the ground with his staff, turned away and did not utter another word. Again, when Hegemon[84] claimed that Polyperchon could testify to his goodwill towards the people, Polyperchon exclaimed angrily, 'Be so good as not to slander me to the king,' while the king himself jumped to his feet and made as if to run Hegemon through with a spear. But Polyperchon quickly threw his arms around the king and the council immediately broke up.

34. Phocion and his companions were placed under guard, and at the sight of this his friends who were standing some way apart covered their faces and made their escape. Cleitus then took the prisoners back to Athens: it was given out that they were to be tried, but in reality they had already been condemned to death. The manner in which this was done created a particularly distressing scene, for they were transported in carts through the Cerameicus[85] to the theatre, where Cleitus kept them in custody until the archons had summoned the assembly. This gathering included slaves, foreigners and those who had recently been disfranchised: all alike, both men and women, were allowed free access to the theatre and the rostrum. First a letter from the king of Macedon was read aloud, in which he declared that he personally was convinced that the men were traitors, but that he left it to their fellow-countrymen to pass judgement upon them, since they were free individuals

governed by their own laws, and then Cleitus led the men in. At the sight of Phocion, the best of the citizens covered their faces, lowered their heads and wept. But one of them rose to his feet and had the courage to say that since the king had entrusted so important a trial to the citizens of Athens, it would be well for all foreigners and slaves to leave the assembly. The mob would not allow this, but shouted out, 'Down with the oligarchs and the enemies of the people.' Nobody tried to speak on Phocion's behalf, but at last he succeeded with great difficulty in making himself heard and asked, 'Do you wish to put us to death justly or unjustly?' and when some voices answered 'Justly!' he rejoined, 'And how will you do that without hearing me?' The people showed no sign of being any more ready to hear him and so, coming closer, he said, 'I admit my own guilt, and I propose the penalty of death for my political actions,[86] but why, men of Athens, should you put to death these others, who have done no wrong?' 'Because they are your friends,' a chorus of voices answered him, and at this Phocion turned away and said no more. Hagnonides then read the motion he had prepared, according to which the people were to decide by a show of hands whether they considered the accused guilty, and the men, if found guilty, were to be put to death.

35. When the decree was read, there were some who demanded an additional clause sentencing Phocion to be tortured before he was put to death, and they urged that the rack should be brought and the executioners summoned. However, Hagnonides saw that even Cleitus was disgusted at this proposal and considered it detestable, and he said, 'Whenever we catch that villain Callimedon, men of Athens, let us put him to the torture, but I will not propose anything of the kind for Phocion.' At this, one of the more scrupulous citizens shouted out, 'And quite right too, for if we are to torture Phocion, what should we do to you?' So it was that the decree was confirmed, and when the show of hands was taken, nobody remained seated but the entire assembly rose to their feet, many of them wearing garlands of flowers, and condemned the men to death. These, besides Phocion, were Nicocles, Thoudippus, Hegemon and

Pythocles, while Demetrius of Phaleron, Callimedon, Charicles and various others were condemned to death in their absence.

36. After the assembly had broken up and the condemned men were being led to the prison, the others walked along lamenting and shedding tears, while their friends and relatives clung about them. As for Phocion, his expression looked exactly the same as it had in the days when he served as general and had often been escorted back from the assembly, and as men gazed at him they marvelled at his grandeur of spirit and composure. But some of his enemies ran along by his side shouting abuse at him, and one even came up and spat in his face. At this, we are told, Phocion turned towards the archons and said, 'Will nobody make this fellow behave himself?' Later, when they were in the prison, Thoudippus, as he watched the executioner crushing the hemlock, grew angry and cried out aloud against his hard fate, protesting that he did not deserve to lose his life with Phocion. 'What then?' the old man asked. 'Is it nothing to you to die in Phocion's company?' And when one of his friends asked if he had any message for his son Phocus, Phocion said, 'Yes, certainly, my message is that he should not hold my death as a grievance against the Athenian people.' When Nicocles, the most loyal of all his friends, begged from him the privilege of drinking the poison first, he replied, 'My friend, that is a hard thing you ask, and it is painful to me to grant it, but since I have never refused you anything in my life, I agree to this too.' But when all the rest had drunk it, the poison ran short, and the executioner refused to crush another portion unless he were paid 12 drachmas, which was the price of the weight that was needed. After some delay, Phocion sent for one of his friends. He remarked that it was hard if a man could not even die at Athens without paying for it, and told him to give the executioner the fee.[87]

37. The day of Phocion's death was the nineteenth of the month of Munychion,[88] and the horsemen who took part in the sacred procession in honour of Zeus had to ride past the prison. Some

of them took off their garlands and others wept as they looked
towards the door of the prison. All those who were still capable
of humanity, and whose better feelings had not been swept
away by rage or jealousy, felt that it was sacrilege not to postpone the execution for a single day and thus preserve the city
from the pollution incurred by carrying out a public execution
while a festival was being celebrated.[89] However, Phocion's
enemies, as if they were still not satisfied with their triumph,
had a resolution passed that Phocion's body should be taken
beyond the frontiers of Attica, and that no Athenian should
provide fire for his funeral. The result was that no friend dared
to touch the body, but a man named Conopion, who was accustomed to provide such services for payment, carried the body
beyond Eleusis, had fire brought from Megarian territory and
burned it. Phocion's wife, who was present at the ceremony
with her maid-servants, raised a mound on the spot and poured
the customary libations on it. Then she took Phocion's bones to
her bosom and brought them back to her house by night. There
she buried them by the hearth with these words: 'To you, my
beloved hearth, I entrust these remains of a good man. Restore
them to the tomb of his fathers when the Athenians recover
their senses.'

38. And, indeed, only a short time elapsed before the course of
events taught the Athenians how great a protector and champion of moderation and justice they had lost. Then they set up
a statue of him and gave his bones a public burial.[90] As for his
accusers, the Athenians themselves condemned Hagnonides
and put him to death, while Epicurus and Demophilus, who
had fled from the city, were tracked down by Phocion son, who
took his revenge on them. This son of Phocion, we are told,
turned out to be a man of little worth in most respects. On one
occasion, he had fallen in love with a girl who earned her living
in a brothel. He happened to have heard a discussion in the
Lyceum in which Theodorus the atheist put forward the argument that if there is no disgrace in ransoming a friend, the
same should be true of a girl-friend: if the principle applies to a

comrade, it applies equally to a mistress. Accordingly, he determined to use the argument to justify his passion and so bought the girl's freedom.

But Phocion's fate reminded the Greeks once more of that of Socrates: they felt that in each case the wrong which the city of Athens had done and the misfortune she had suffered were almost identical.[91]

ALEXANDER

ALEXANDER

INTRODUCTION TO
ALEXANDER

[356–323 BC]

Alexander III of Macedon, later styled 'the Great', came to the
Macedonian throne at the age of twenty, upon the assassination of his father Philip in 336 BC. Philip had done much to
unify and strengthen Macedonia and to extend its power southwards; his successes culminated in the battle of Chaeronea in
338, where he smashed Athenian and Theban resistance to his
domination of the Greek mainland. Shortly afterwards, Philip
sent an expeditionary force to Asia Minor, but whatever aims
he might have had were cut short by his murder.

Alexander's first acts as king included a series of military
victories against the tribes threatening the northern and eastern
frontiers of Macedonia. Meanwhile, a rumour that Alexander
had been killed caused Thebes to revolt and to massacre its
Macedonian garrison. Alexander marched south with frighten-
ing speed; Thebes was brutally sacked and the other Greek
states cowed into submission (335). Alexander had already had
himself declared the leader of Greece in a Panhellenic war
against Persia. He now crossed the Hellespont and defeated the
army of the local satraps at the River Granicus in 334. As he
pressed southwards along the coast of Asia Minor, he was welcomed as a liberator by many of the Greek cities. Alexander
next turned east and, as he attempted to advance into Phoenicia, encountered the forces of Darius III, the Persian king, at
Issus in the autumn of 333; the result was a decisive victory,
due in part to the strength of Alexander's cavalry. After taking
the coastal cities of Phoenicia, vital Persian naval bases, and
securing Egypt, Alexander invaded Mesopotamia, the heartland of the Persian empire, and won a second major victory

against Darius' forces at Gaugamela in 331. Darius fled east-wards, but was soon murdered by one of his own noblemen.

Alexander was now master of the Persian empire, and had achieved a feat that other Greeks had only dreamt of. To manage the conquered territories Alexander had from the start accepted the submission of local ruling dynasties. A key moment came in the winter of 331/30 when Alexander appointed a Persian as satrap of Babylonia and was himself proclaimed king of Persia; from this point on, it is clear that Alexander presented himself to his Persian subjects as successor to the Persian kings rather than destroyer of the Persian empire. He also began adopting some of the protocols of the Persian court and some items of Persian dress, much to the disapproval of some of his Macedonian offi-cers. Tensions began to surface. An attempt to extend to Macedonians and Greeks the Persian custom of obeisance before the king (in Greek, *proskynesis*) – which might involve anything from a bow to full prostration – caused particular offence, as to Greeks and Macedonians such an act suggested divine worship. As these tensions grew, various of Alexander's officers were exe-cuted on charges of treason. Meanwhile, Alexander pushed relentlessly on, fighting campaigns in Central Asia (329–7) and India (327–5), the latter of which lay beyond the boundaries of the Persian empire. Finally, at the River Hyphasis, in the modern Punjab, in the face of stiff resistance and after more than eight years of unceasing campaigning, Alexander's troops refused to go further and he reluctantly turned back. Alexander died of ill-ness, worsened by heavy drinking, in Babylon in 323 BC at the age of only thirty-three. He had conquered a vast empire and changed the world irrevocably, though he left no clear successor and no clear plan of what would become of the territories the Macedonians now controlled.

Alexander's short life spawned numerous literary accounts, including several written by officers who accompanied Alexan-der and took part in his expedition. Plutarch therefore had no shortage of material for his *Life of Alexander*, which is his longest biography. His focus, however, is distinctive. In the pro-logue which precedes the *Life of Alexander* Plutarch asks his readers' indulgence for not giving a detailed narrative of Alexander's campaigns. As he explains, 'the most brilliant exploits often tell us nothing of the virtues or vices of the men who performed them'; more revealing, he continues, can be chance remarks or jokes (ch. 1: see pp. 18–19). The *Life of Alexander*, then, is above all a study in Alexander's character.

Plutarch sets out some features of Alexander's character in chapter 4. His temperament, Plutarch claims, in a passage plainly affected by contemporary medical theories, was hot and fiery, a fact which explained his ruddy appearance, his sweet smell, and 'which made him fond of drinking and energetic' (*thymoeides*). Alexander's heavy drinking emerges frequently in the Life, especially towards the end; Plutarch devotes a whole chapter to it (ch. 23), and also suggests several times, rather mysteriously, that Dionysus, the god of wine, was against Alexander (see esp. ch. 13). Plutarch's application to Alexander of the adjective *thymoeides* is particularly important. This is a term drawn straight from Plato; the *thymos* is the dynamic part of a person's soul which produces those emotions necessary for action, such as ambition, desire or anger. But when not properly controlled, this drive and the emotions to which it gives rise can be dangerous and destructive. It is this energy which, in Plutarch's presentation, motivates Alexander and drives him to conquer Persia. But at the same time it threatens to topple over into megalomania, compulsive ambition, insatiable desire for conquest and harshness and arrogance. One of the themes of Plutarch's *Alexander* is the tension between Alexander's drive for action and his ability to control that drive and direct it in worthy directions.

In the early parts of the Life, Alexander's ambitious drive has only good results. Plutarch illustrates it with various stories, such as the childhood anecdote of his taming of his future warhorse Bucephalas (ch. 6). The courage and confidence that he demonstrates there as a child will be constants in his character. Similarly, his success in controlling an animal that no one else could master will be repeated on a larger scale when he conquers the Persian empire. Immediately after this story, Plutarch discusses Alexander's education by Aristotle, and in the early chapters we are constantly reminded of Alexander's commitment to education and to Greek culture: he carries the *Iliad* with him as his most valued possession (ch. 8), and venerates the tomb of Achilles (15); Homer appears to him in a vision (26); later he even educates Persian boys in Macedonian ways (47). Education in Plutarch's period was associated with self-control, and in the early chapters Alexander is admirably restrained. For example, when Darius' family fall into his hands, he shows his self-mastery by refusing to touch any of the Persian women (ch. 21).

Alexander, then, at the start of Plutarch's Life, is no mere conqueror but a civilized man and a civilizer. But as the Life progresses, and Alexander advances further eastwards, Plutarch suggests a change; Alexander becomes increasingly harsh and suspicious. He sees plots everywhere, has friends and comrades executed (chs. 48–9) and even kills his friend Cleitus with his own hands at a banquet (chs. 50–51). This sense of a moral decline coincides with increasing references to tragedy and to the supernatural, especially the god Dionysus. It is not clear whether the sense of the supernatural at the end of the Life is to be taken literally, or should be seen as a reflection of Alexander's increasingly suspicious and irrational psychology. But by the time Alexander dies, he has become in Plutarch's account a far more troubled and complex figure than at the beginning.

The *Life of Alexander* has a broadly chronological structure: that is, events are presented roughly in chronological order. But as with all Lives, some reservations must be made. Sometimes Plutarch arranges stories or incidents thematically rather than chronologically, i.e., events are placed in a series not because they happened in that order but because they all illustrate a particular theme or a particular trait of character. A good example is seen in the stories in chapters 21–3 which illustrate Alexander's temperance. The fact that they are placed between the battle of Issus and the invasion of Phoenicia should not be taken to imply that this material all relates to that period specifically. Rather, it is placed here because the capture of Darius' opulent tent at Issus provided a convenient starting-point for reflection on the theme of Alexander's own attitudes to wealth and its trappings.

Plutarch's *Life of Alexander* is paired with his *Life of Caesar*. The pairing of Alexander and Julius Caesar was already well established by Plutarch's time, and the reasons for the choice are not hard to find: both men were great conquerors, who changed the world; both died before their time. There is also a personal link: Plutarch records a story of Caesar reading about Alexander and lamenting that at his age Alexander was already king of many peoples (*Caesar* 11). As this anecdote makes clear, Plutarch's Caesar, like his Alexander, is motivated by ambition for glory. Another story about Caesar, placed immediately before the first, tells of how, on passing through a small Alpine village, Caesar declared to his friends that he would rather be first man there than second man in Rome. Caesar's ambition, then, is the driver for his success. But at the end of the Life, after Caesar has been cut down in the senate by his former supporters and by enemies whom he had pardoned, Plutarch comments on the futility of that ambition:

> Caesar died at the age of fifty-six, having outlived [his rival] Pompey by not much more than four years. Of the power and dominion which he had pursued all his life at such risk, he enjoyed nothing except only the name and the glory which awakened the citizens' envy. (*Caesar* 69)

It is unclear here whether Plutarch's point is simply that Caesar did not live long enough to enjoy his successes, or that the very goal of Caesar's ambition was not one which would ever bring happiness (a point he makes forcefully in *Demetrius* and *Pyrrhus*). But this final, pessimistic, statement about Rome's greatest conqueror might also offer a suggestive perspective on Alexander.

Most pairs of Lives end with a Comparison (*syncrisis*) of the two men, where Plutarch looks for differences between the two subjects. There is no surviving comparison to this pair; possibly it has been lost in transmission or it may be that Plutarch simply did not write one. But some obvious differences between Plutarch's Caesar and his Alexander emerge from the two Lives themselves. There is no emphasis in *Caesar* on Caesar's education or a civilizing mission; instead, many of Caesar's campaigns were waged against his own country and his own fellow-citizens. But whereas Alexander destroyed himself, Caesar is destroyed by forces outside himself which he cannot control. Alexander is suspicious and harsh, seeing plots where they do not exist; Caesar is too forgiving of his former enemies and fails to take seriously warnings of a very real plot against his life. Alexander at the end of his life is increasingly superstitious; Caesar is dismissive of omens and warnings. In *Alexander* the precise role, if any, played by the supernatural is left unclear. In *Caesar*, on the other hand, Plutarch is unequivocal that the divine had a hand both in Caesar's murder and in the punishing of his murderers (*Caesar*, chs. 66, 69).

Plutarch cites numerous sources in *Alexander*, including a collection of letters thought to be by Alexander, though their authenticity is now disputed. All of these earlier sources are now lost, but we can get some idea of their nature from the use made of them both by Plutarch and by other extant writers on Alexander, especially Arrian in his *Anabasis* [*March inland*] *of Alexander*, which was written in the early to mid-second century AD, that is, shortly after Plutarch's Life. Both writers made use of works by officers of Alexander. One such was Aristobulus, who accompanied Alexander on his expedition and wrote an account which focused on military narrative and seems to have presented Alexander in a good light throughout. The philosopher Callisthenes, who was later arrested by Alexander, was also the author of a very favourable portrayal to which Plutarch had access. A very different account was left by Cleitarchus, who wrote in Alexandria in the decades after Alexander's death. His work, which influenced Diodorus' account of Alexander in his Book 17, seems to have been much more sensational, presenting Alexander as a heroic figure, performing superhuman tasks, but also subject to fits of rage and cruelty. There was also a distinct philosophical tradition on Alexander, which presented him as an exemplum of anger, a classic illustration of the dangers of drink and lack of self-control combined with absolute power. Out of this disparate material, which probably included many other authors now unknown, Plutarch has managed to create an account which is neither hagiographic nor a partisan attack, but presents a picture of a brilliant man corrupted by his own success.

PROLOGUE TO THE LIVES
OF ALEXANDER AND
JULIUS CAESAR

1. My subject in this book is the life of Alexander, the king, and of Julius Caesar, the conqueror of Pompey. The careers of these men embrace such a multitude of events that my preamble shall consist of nothing more than this one plea: if I do not record all their most celebrated achievements or describe any of them exhaustively, but merely summarize for the most part what they accomplished, I ask my readers not to regard this as a fault. For I am writing Lives not history, and the truth is that the most brilliant exploits often tell us nothing of the virtues or vices of the men who performed them, while on the other hand a chance remark or a joke may reveal far more of a man's character than battles where thousands die, huge troop deployments or the sieges of cities. When a portrait painter sets out to create a likeness, he relies above all upon the face and the expression of the eyes and pays little attention to the other parts of the body: in the same way, it is my task to dwell upon those details which illuminate the workings of the soul, and to use these to create a portrait of each man's life, leaving to others their great exploits and battles.

LIFE OF ALEXANDER

2. On his father's side Alexander was descended from Heracles through Caranus,[1] and on his mother's from Aeacus[2] through Neoptolemus: so much is accepted by all authorities. It is said that his father Philip fell in love with Olympias, Alexander's mother, at the time when they were both initiated into the Mysteries at Samothrace. He was then a young man and she an orphan, and after obtaining the consent of her brother Arybbas, Philip betrothed himself to her.[3] On the night before the marriage was consummated, the bride dreamt that there was a crash of thunder, that her womb was struck by a thunderbolt and that there followed a blinding flash from which a great sheet of flame blazed up and spread far and wide before it finally died away. Then, some time after their marriage, Philip saw himself in a dream in the act of sealing up his wife's womb, and upon the seal he had used there was engraved, so it seemed to him, the figure of a lion. The soothsayers treated this dream with suspicion, since it seemed to suggest that Philip needed to keep a closer watch on his wife. The only exception was Aristander of Telmessus,[4] who declared that the woman must be pregnant, since men do not seal up what is empty, and that she would bring forth a son whose nature would be bold and lion-like. At another time a snake was seen stretched out at Olympias' side as she slept, and it was this more than anything else, we are told, which weakened Philip's passion and cooled his affection for her, so that from that time on he seldom came to sleep with her. The reason for this may either have been that he was afraid she would cast some evil spell or charm upon him

or else that he recoiled from her embrace because he believed that she was the consort of some higher being.

However there is another version of this story, that from very ancient times all the women of this region have been initiates of the Orphic religion and involved in the orgiastic rites of Dionysus. For this reason they were known as Klodones and Mimallones[5] and they followed many of the observances of the Edonian and Thracian women who live around Mount Haemus, from whom, it seems, the word *threskeuein*[6] has come to denote the celebration of extravagant and superstitious ceremonies. It was Olympias' habit to enter into these states of possession and surrender herself to the inspiration of the god with even wilder abandon than the others, and she would introduce into the festal procession numbers of large snakes, hand-tamed, which terrified the male spectators as they raised their heads from the wreaths of ivy and the sacred winnowing-baskets, or twined themselves around the wands and garlands of the women.

3. At any rate, after Philip had seen this apparition, he dispatched Chaeron of Megalopolis to Delphi to consult the oracle of Apollo. In reply, the god commanded him to sacrifice to Zeus Ammon and to revere him above all other deities; but he also warned Philip that he was fated to lose the eye with which he had peered through the chink of the half-open door on the night when he saw the god in the form of a snake sharing his wife's bed. According to Eratosthenes, Olympias, when she sent Alexander on his way to lead his great expedition to the East, confided to him and to him alone the secret of his conception and urged him to show himself worthy of his divine parentage. But other authors maintain that she repudiated this story and used to say, 'Will Alexander never stop making Hera jealous of me?'[7]

However this may be, Alexander was born on the sixth day of the month of Hecatombaeon, which the Macedonians call Loüs, the same day on which the temple of Artemis at Ephesus was burned down.[8] It was this coincidence which inspired Hegesias of Magnesia to utter a pronouncement which was wet enough to have put the fire out: he said it was no wonder the temple of Artemis was destroyed, since the goddess was busy attending to the birth of Alexander.[9] But those of the Magi[10] who were then at Ephesus interpreted the destruction of the temple as the portent of a far greater disaster, and they ran through the city beating their faces and crying out that that day had brought forth a great scourge and calamity for Asia.

At that moment, Philip had just captured the city of Potidaea, and he received three messages on the same day. The first was that his general Parmenion had overcome the Illyrians in a great battle, the second that his racehorse had won a victory in the Olympic Games and the third that Alexander had been born. Naturally he was overjoyed at the news, and the soothsayers raised his spirits still higher by assuring him that the son whose birth coincided with three victories would himself prove invincible.

4. Alexander's physical appearance is seen most clearly in the statues sculpted by Lysippus, the only artist whom Alexander considered worthy to represent him. Alexander possessed a number of individual features which many of his successors and friends later tried to reproduce, for example the poise of the neck which was tilted slightly to the left, or a certain melting look in his eyes, and the artist has exactly caught these peculiarities. On the other hand, when Apelles painted Alexander wielding a thunderbolt, he did not reproduce his colouring at all accurately. He made Alexander's complexion appear too dark-skinned and swarthy, whereas we are told that he was fair-skinned, with a ruddy tinge that showed itself especially upon his face and chest.[11]

I have read in Aristoxenus' memoirs that Alexander's skin was fresh and sweet-smelling, and that his breath and the whole of his body gave off a peculiar fragrance which permeated the clothes he wore.[12] The cause of this may have been the blend of elements in his body, which was particularly hot and fiery. For fragrance, according to Theophrastus' ideas,[13] is generated by the action of heat upon moist humours. This is why the hottest and driest regions of the earth produce the finest and most numerous spices, for the sun draws up the moisture which abounds in vegetable bodies and causes them to decay. In Alexander's case, it was this same warmth of temperament which made him fond of drinking[14] and energetic.[15]

While he was still a boy, he gave plenty of evidence of his powers of self-control. In spite of his vehement and impulsive nature, he showed little interest in the pleasures of the body and indulged in them only with great moderation, but his passionate desire for fame implanted in him a pride and a grandeur of vision which went far beyond his years. For it was by no means every kind of glory that he sought, and, unlike his father, he did not seek it in every form of action. Philip, for example, was as proud of his powers of eloquence as any sophist, and took care to have the victories won by his chariots at Olympia stamped upon his coins. But Alexander's attitude is made clear by his reply to some of his friends, when they asked him whether he would be willing to compete at Olympia, since he was a fine runner. 'Yes,' he answered, 'if I have kings to run against me.' He seems in fact to have disapproved of athletes as a whole. At any rate, although he founded a great many contests of other kinds, including not only tragic drama and performances on the flute and the lyre, but also the reciting of poetry, fighting with the quarter-staff and various forms of hunting, yet he showed no interest in offering prizes either for boxing or for the pancration.[16]

5. On one occasion some ambassadors from the king of Persia arrived in Macedonia, and since Philip was absent, Alexander received them in his place. He talked freely with them and quite won them over, not only by the friendliness of his manner, but also because he did not trouble them with any childish or trivial inquiries, but questioned them about the distances they had travelled by road, the nature of the journey into the interior, the character of the king, his experience in war, and the military strength and prowess of the Persians. The ambassadors were filled with admiration. They came away convinced that Philip's celebrated astuteness was as nothing compared to the adventurous spirit and lofty ambitions of his son. At any rate, whenever he heard that Philip had captured some famous city or won an

overwhelming victory, Alexander would show no pleasure at the news, but would declare to his friends, 'Boys, my father will forestall me in everything. There will be nothing great or spectacular for me with your help to show the world.' He cared nothing for pleasure or wealth but only for deeds of valour and glory, and this was why he believed that the more he received from his father, the less would be left for him to conquer. And so every success that was gained inspired in Alexander the dread that another opportunity for action had been squandered on his father. He had no desire to inherit a kingdom which offered him riches, luxuries and the pleasures of the senses: his choice was a life of struggle, of wars, and of unrelenting ambition.

It was natural, of course, that a great number of tutors, teachers and supervisors were appointed to take part in his upbringing, but the man who supervised them all was Leonidas, a severe disciplinarian, who was also a relative of Olympias. He himself did not disdain the title of attendant,[17] since his duties were important and honourable, but because of his natural dignity and his connection with the queen's family, other people referred to him as Alexander's tutor and mentor. The person who took on both the title and the role of attendant was an Acarnanian named Lysimachus. He was neither an educated nor a cultivated man, but he managed to ingratiate himself by calling Philip Peleus, Alexander Achilles, and himself Phoenix,[18] and he held the second place in the prince's household.

6. Once when Philoneicus the Thessalian brought Philip a horse named Bucephalas, which he offered to sell for 13 talents,[19] the king and his friends went down to the plain to watch the horse's trials. But they came to the conclusion that he was wild and quite unmanageable, for he would allow no one to mount him, nor would he endure the shouts of Philip's grooms, but reared up against anyone who approached him. The king became angry at being offered such a vicious animal unbroken, and ordered it to be led away. But Alexander, who was standing close by, remarked, 'What a horse they are losing, and all because they don't know how to handle him, or dare not try!' Philip kept quiet at first, but

when he heard Alexander repeat these words several times and saw that he was upset, he asked him, 'Are you finding fault with your elders because you think you know more than they do, or can manage a horse better?' 'At least I could manage this one better,' retorted Alexander. 'And if you cannot,' said his father, 'what penalty will you pay for being so impertinent?' 'I will pay the price of the horse,' answered the boy. At this the whole company burst out laughing, and then as soon as the father and son had settled the terms of the bet, Alexander went quickly up to Bucephalas, took hold of his bridle and turned him towards the sun, for he had noticed that the horse was shying at the sight of his own shadow as it fell in front of him, and constantly moved whenever he did. He ran alongside the animal for a little way, calming him down by stroking him, and then, when he saw he was full of spirit and courage, he quietly threw aside his cloak and with a light spring vaulted safely on to his back. For a little while he kept feeling the bit with the reins, without jarring or tearing his mouth, and got him collected. Finally, when he saw that the horse was free of his fears and impatient to show his speed, he gave him his head and urged him forward, using a commanding voice and a touch of the foot.

At first Philip and his friends held their breath and looked on in an agony of suspense, until they saw Alexander reach the end of his gallop, turn in full control and ride back triumphant and exulting in his success. Thereupon the rest of the company broke into loud applause, while his father, we are told, actually wept for joy, and when Alexander had dismounted he kissed him and said, 'My boy, you must find a kingdom which is your equal. Macedonia is too small for you.'

7. Philip had noticed that his son was self-willed, and that while it was very difficult to influence him by force, he could easily be guided towards his duty by an appeal to reason, and he therefore made a point of trying to persuade the boy rather than giving him orders. Besides this, he considered that the task of training and educating his son was too important to be entrusted to the ordinary run of teachers of poetry, music and general education: it required, as Sophocles puts it, '*The rudder's guidance*

and the bit's restraint.[20] So he sent for Aristotle,[21] the most famous and learned of the philosophers of his time, and rewarded him with the generosity that his reputation deserved. Aristotle was a native of the city of Stageira, which Philip had himself destroyed. He now repopulated it and brought back all the citizens who had been enslaved or driven into exile.

He gave Aristotle and his pupil the temple of the Nymphs near Mieza as a place where they could study and converse, and to this day they show you the stone seats and shady walks which Aristotle used. It seems clear, too, that Alexander was instructed by his teacher not only in the principles of ethics and politics, but also in those secret and more esoteric studies which philosophers do not impart to the general run of students, but only by word of mouth to a select circle of the initiated. Some years later, after Alexander had crossed into Asia, he learnt that Aristotle had published some treatises dealing with these esoteric matters, and he wrote to him in blunt language and took him to task for the sake of the prestige of philosophy. This was the text of his letter:

> Alexander to Aristotle, greetings. You have not done well to write down and publish those doctrines you taught me by word of mouth. What advantage shall I have over other men if these theories in which I have been trained are to be made common property? I would rather excel the rest of mankind in my knowledge of what is best than in the extent of my power. Farewell.

Aristotle wished to encourage this ambition of his pupil's and so, when he replied to justify his action, he pointed out that these so-called oral doctrines were in a sense both published and not published. For, in truth, his treatise on metaphysics is written in a style which makes it useless for those who wish to study or teach the subject from the beginning: the book serves simply as a memorandum for those who have already been taught its general principles.

8. It was Aristotle, I believe, who did more than anyone to implant in Alexander his interest in the art of healing as well as

that of philosophy. He was not merely attracted to the theory of medicine, but was in the habit of tending his friends when they were sick and prescribing for them various courses of treatment or diet, as one can learn from his letters. He was also devoted by nature to all kinds of learning and was a lover of books. He regarded the *Iliad* as a handbook on the art of war and took with him on his campaigns a text annotated by Aristotle, which became known as 'the casket copy',[22] and which he always kept under his pillow together with his dagger. When his campaigns had taken him far into the interior of Asia and he could find no other books, he ordered his treasurer, Harpalus, to send him some. Harpalus sent him the histories of Philistus,[23] many of the tragedies of Aeschylus, Sophocles and Euripides, and the dithyrambic poems of Telestes and Philoxenus.

At first Alexander greatly admired Aristotle and became, as he himself used to say, more attached to him than to his father, for the one had given him the gift of life, but the other had taught him how to live well. But in later years he came to regard Aristotle with suspicion. He never actually did him any harm, but his friendship for the philosopher lost its original warmth and affection, and this was a clear proof of the estrangement which developed between them. At the same time, Alexander never lost the devotion to and longing for philosophy which had been both innate in him and nurtured from the first by his education: he proved this on many occasions, for example by the honours which he paid to Anaxarchus,[24] the 50 talents which he presented to Xenocrates[25] and the encouragement which he lavished upon Dandamis and Calanus.[26]

9. While Philip was making an expedition against Byzantium,[27] Alexander, although he was only sixteen years old, was left behind as regent of Macedonia and keeper of the royal seal. During this period he defeated the Maedi[28] who had risen in revolt, captured their city, drove out its barbarous inhabitants, established a colony of Greeks assembled from various regions and named it Alexandropolis. He also took part in the battle against the Greeks at Chaeronea,[29] and is said to have been the first to break the line of the Theban Sacred Band.[30] Even in our

own time an oak tree used to be pointed out near the River Cephisus which was known as Alexander's oak, because his tent had been pitched beside it at that time, and not far away is the mass grave of the Macedonians who fell in the battle. Because of these achievements Philip, as was natural, became extravagantly fond of his son, so much so that he took pleasure in hearing the Macedonians speak of Alexander as their king and Philip as their general.

The domestic strife that resulted from Philip's various marriages and love-affairs caused the quarrels which took place in the women's apartments to infect the whole kingdom, and led to bitter clashes and accusations between father and son. This breach was widened by Olympias, a woman of a jealous and vindictive temper, who incited Alexander to oppose his father. Their quarrel was brought to a head on the occasion of the wedding of Cleopatra, a girl with whom Philip had fallen in love and whom he had decided to marry,[31] although she was far too young for him. Cleopatra's uncle Attalus, who had drunk too much at the banquet, called upon the Macedonians to pray to the gods that the union of Philip and Cleopatra might bring forth a legitimate heir to the throne.[32] Alexander flew into a rage at these words, shouted at him, 'Villain, do you take me for a bastard, then?' and hurled a drinking-cup at his head. At this Philip lurched to his feet, and drew his sword against his son, but fortunately for them both he was so overcome with drink and with rage that he tripped and fell headlong. Alexander jeered at him and cried out, 'Here is the man who was making ready to cross from Europe to Asia, and who cannot even cross from one couch to another without losing his balance.' After this drunken brawl Alexander took Olympias away and settled her in Epirus, while he himself went to live in Illyria.

Meanwhile, Demaratus[33] the Corinthian came to visit Philip. He was an old friend of the Macedonian royal family and so was privileged to speak freely. After the formal greetings and courtesies had been exchanged, Philip asked him whether the various city-states of Greece were at harmony with one another. Demaratus retorted, 'It is all very well for you to show so much concern for the affairs of Greece, Philip. How about the disharmony you have brought about in your own household?' This reply sobered Philip to such an extent that he sent for Alexander, and with Demaratus' help persuaded him to return.[34]

10. Pixodarus, the satrap of Caria, tried to form a family union with Philip, hoping by this means to insinuate himself into a military alliance.[35] His plan was to offer the hand of his eldest daughter to Philip's son Arrhidaeus,[36] and he sent Aristocritus to Macedonia to try to negotiate the match. Alexander's mother and his friends sent him a distorted account of this manoeuvre, making out that Philip was planning to settle the kingdom upon Arrhidaeus by arranging a brilliant marriage and treating him as a person of great consequence. Alexander was disturbed by these stories and sent Thessalus, the tragic actor, to Caria to tell Pixodarus that he should pay no attention to Arrhidaeus, who was not only an illegitimate son of Philip but was weak-minded as well; instead, he should offer his daughter's hand to Alexander.

Pixodarus was far more pleased with this suggestion than with his original proposal. When Philip discovered this, he went to Alexander's room,[37] taking with him Philotas the son of Parmenion, one of the prince's friends. There he scolded his son and angrily reproached him for behaving so ignobly and so unworthily of his position as to wish to marry the daughter of a mere Carian, who was no more than the slave of a barbarian king. As for Thessalus, he wrote to the Corinthians ordering them to send him to Macedonia in chains, and at the same time he banished four of Alexander's friends, Harpalus, Nearchus, Erygius and Ptolemy. Later, Alexander recalled all of these men and raised them to the highest honours.

When Pausanias assassinated the king because he had been humiliated by Attalus[38] and Cleopatra and could get no redress from Philip, it was Olympias who was chiefly blamed for the assassination, because she was believed to have encouraged the young man and incited him to take his revenge. It was said that when Pausanias met the young prince and complained to him of the injustice he had suffered, Alexander quoted the verse from Euripides' *Medea*, in which Medea is said to threaten

'*The father, bride and bridegroom all at once*'.[39] However this may be, he took care to track down and punish those who were involved in the plot, and he showed his anger against Olympias for the horrible revenge which she took upon Cleopatra[40] during his absence.

11. Alexander was only twenty years old when he inherited his kingdom, which at that moment was beset by formidable jealousies and feuds, and external dangers on every side. The neighbouring barbarian tribes were eager to throw off the Macedonian yoke and longed for the rule of their native kings; as for the Greek states, although Philip had defeated them in battle, he had not had time to subdue them or accustom them to his authority. He had swept away the existing governments and then, having prepared their peoples for drastic changes, had left them in turmoil and confusion, because he had created a situation which was completely unfamiliar to them. Alexander's Macedonian advisers feared that a crisis was at hand and urged the young king to leave the Greek states to their own devices and refrain from using any force against them. As for the barbarian tribes, they considered that he should try to win them back to their allegiance by using milder methods and forestall the first signs of revolt by offering them concessions. Alexander, however, chose precisely the opposite course, and decided that the only way to make his kingdom safe was to act with audacity and a lofty spirit, for he was certain that if he were seen to yield even a fraction of his authority, all his enemies would attack him at once. He swiftly crushed the uprisings among the barbarians by advancing with his army as far as the Danube, where he overcame Syrmus, the king of the Triballi, in a great battle. Then, when the news reached him that the Thebans had revolted and were being supported by the Athenians, he immediately marched south through the pass of Thermopylae. 'Demosthenes', he said, 'called me a boy while I was in Illyria and among the Triballi, and a youth when I was marching through Thessaly; I will show him I am a man by the time I reach the walls of Athens.'

When he arrived before Thebes,[41] he wished to give the citizens the opportunity to repent of their actions, and so he merely demanded the surrender of their leaders Phoenix and Prothytes, and offered an amnesty to all the rest if they would come over to his side. The Thebans countered by demanding the surrender of Philotas and Antipater and appealing to all who wished to liberate Greece to range themselves on their side, and at this Alexander ordered his troops to prepare for battle. The Thebans, although greatly outnumbered, fought with a superhuman courage and spirit, but when the Macedonian garrison which had been posted in the acropolis of the Cadmeia made a sortie and fell upon them from the rear, the greater part of their army was encircled, they were slaughtered where they stood and the city was stormed, plundered and razed to the ground. Alexander's principal object in permitting the sack of Thebes was to frighten the rest of the Greeks into submission by making this a terrible example. But he also put forward the excuse that he was redressing the wrongs done to his allies, for the Plataeans and Phocians had both complained of the actions of the Thebans against them.[42] As for the population of Thebes, he singled out the priests, a few citizens who had friendly connections with Macedonia, the descendants of the poet Pindar and those who had opposed the revolt to be spared; all the rest were publicly sold into slavery to the number of twenty thousand. Those who were killed in the battle numbered more than six thousand.

12. Among the many outrages and acts of violence which accompanied the sacking of the city, some Thracian troops broke into the house of Timocleia, a woman of noble birth and character. While the soldiers were plundering her property, their leader raped her and then demanded whether she had any gold or silver hidden. She told him that she had, and led him alone into the garden. There she pointed out to him a well, and explained that while the city was being stormed she had thrown into it all her most valuable possessions. Then, as the Thracian leaned over and peered down the shaft, she moved behind him, pushed him in and hurled stone after stone down on him until he was dead. The Thracians seized her, tied her hands and led her to Alexander, who immediately saw from her expression and

from her calm and fearless bearing as she followed her captors
that she was a woman of dignity and spirit. When the king
asked her who she was, she replied, 'I am the sister of Theagenes
who commanded our army against your father, Philip, and fell
at Chaeronea fighting for the liberty of Greece.' Alexander was
filled with admiration not only at her words but at what she
had done, and gave orders that she and her children should be
freed and allowed to depart.

13. Alexander came to terms with the Athenians, in spite of their
open sympathy with the sufferings of the Thebans. For they had
been on the point of celebrating the Mysteries, but abandoned
the festival as an act of mourning, and they treated all the fugitives who reached Athens with the greatest kindness. It may be
that Alexander's fury had been sated with blood, like a lion's, or
perhaps that he wished to efface his cruel and savage treatment
of the Thebans by performing an act of clemency. At any rate, he
not only agreed to overlook the causes of complaint which he
had against the Athenians, but advised them to pay the most
careful attention to their affairs, since if anything should happen
to him, they might once again become the leaders of Greece.
In later years Alexander often felt distressed, we are told, at the
harsh fate of the Thebans, and the recollection of it made him
milder in his treatment of many other peoples. Certainly he used
to claim that the murder of Cleitus, which he committed when
he was drunk, and the cowardly refusal of the Macedonians to
cross the Ganges[43] and attack the Indians, which cut short his
campaign and robbed him of its crowning achievement, were
both caused by the anger and revenge of the god Dionysus.[44]
And of those Thebans who survived, it was remarked that all
who came to him with a request were granted whatever they
asked. So much for Alexander's dealings with Thebes.

14. The Greeks gathered at the Isthmus of Corinth[45] and voted
that they would campaign with Alexander against the Persians,
and he was appointed their leader. Many of the Greek statesmen and philosophers visited him to offer their congratulations,
and he hoped that Diogenes of Sinope, who was at that time

living in Corinth, would do the same. However, since he paid
no attention whatever to Alexander, but continued to live at
leisure in the suburb of Corinth which was known as Craneion,
Alexander went in person to see him and found him basking at
full length in the sun. When he saw so many people approaching him, Diogenes raised himself a little on his elbow and fixed
his gaze upon Alexander. The king greeted him and inquired
whether he could do anything for him. 'Yes,' replied the philosopher, 'you can stand a little to one side out of my sun.'
Alexander is said to have been greatly impressed by this answer
and full of admiration for the hauteur and independence of
mind of a man who could look down on him with such con-
descension. So much so that he remarked to his followers, who
were laughing and mocking the philosopher as they went away,
'You may say what you like, but if I were not Alexander, I
would be Diogenes.'

He visited Delphi because he wished to consult the oracle of
Apollo about the expedition against the Persians. It so happened that he arrived on one of those days which are called
inauspicious, when it is forbidden for the oracle to deliver a
reply. In spite of this he first sent for the prophetess, and when
she refused to officiate and explained that the law forbade her
to do so, he went up himself and tried to drag her by force to
the shrine. At last, as if overcome by his persistence, she
exclaimed, 'You are invincible, my son!' and when Alexander
heard this, he declared that he wanted no other prophecy, but
had obtained from her the oracle he was seeking. When he set
out,[46] many other prodigies attended the departure of the army:
among these was the phenomenon of the statue of Orpheus[47] at
Libethra which was made of cypress wood and was observed
to be covered with sweat. Everyone who saw it was alarmed at
this omen, but Aristander urged the king to take courage, for
this portent signified that Alexander was destined to perform
deeds which would live in song and story and would cause
poets and musicians much toil and sweat to celebrate them.

15. As for the size of his army, the lowest estimate puts its
strength at 30,000 infantry and 4,000 cavalry and the highest

43,000 infantry and 5,000 cavalry.[48] According to Aristobulus, the money available for the army's supplies amounted to no more than 70 talents, Douris says that there were supplies for only thirty days and Onesicritus that Alexander was already 200 talents in debt. Yet although he set out with such slender resources, he would not go aboard his ship until he had discovered the circumstances of all his companions[49] and had assigned an estate to one, a village to another or the revenues of some port or community to a third. When he had shared out and given away almost all the royal property, Perdiccas asked him, 'But your majesty, what are you leaving for yourself?' 'My hopes!' replied Alexander. 'Very well, then,' answered Perdiccas, 'those who serve with you will share those too.' With this, he declined to accept the property which had been allotted to him and several of Alexander's other friends did the same. However, those who accepted or requested rewards were lavishly provided for, so that in the end Alexander distributed among them most of what he possessed in Macedonia. These were his preparations and this was the adventurous spirit in which he crossed the Hellespont.

Once arrived in Asia, he went up to Troy, sacrificed to Athena and poured libations to the heroes of the Greek army. He smeared himself with oil and ran a race naked with his companions, as the custom is, and then crowned with a wreath the column which marks the grave of Achilles; he also remarked that Achilles was happy in having found a faithful friend while he lived and a great poet to sing of his deeds after his death.[50] While he was walking about the city and looking at its ancient remains, somebody asked him whether he wished to see the lyre which had once belonged to Alexander of Troy.[51] He answered that he cared nothing for that lyre but asked for the lyre which Achilles played when he sang of the glorious deeds of brave men.[52]

16. Meanwhile, Darius' generals had gathered a large army[53] and posted it at the crossing of the River Granicus, so that Alexander was obliged to fight at the very gates of Asia if he was to enter and conquer it. Most of the Macedonian officers

were alarmed at the depth of the river and of the rough and
uneven slopes of the banks on the opposite side, up which they
would have to scramble in the face of the enemy. There were
others, too, who thought that Alexander ought to observe the
Macedonian tradition concerning the time of year, according to
which the kings of Macedon never made war during the month
of Daesius. Alexander swept aside these scruples by giving
orders that the month should be called a second Artemisius.[54]
And when Parmenion advised him against risking the crossing at such a late hour of the day,[55] Alexander declared that the
Hellespont would blush for shame if, once he had crossed it,
he should shrink back from the Granicus; then he plunged into
the stream with thirteen squadrons of cavalry. It seemed the act
of a desperate madman rather than of a prudent commander
to charge into a swiftly flowing river, which swept men off their
feet and surged about them, and then to advance through a hail
of missiles towards a steep bank which was strongly defended
by infantry and cavalry. But in spite of this, he pressed forward
and with a tremendous effort gained the opposite bank, which
was a wet treacherous slope covered with mud. There he was
immediately forced to engage the enemy in a confused hand-to-
hand struggle, before the troops who were crossing behind
him could be organized into any formation. The moment his
men set foot on land, the enemy attacked them with loud
shouts, matching horse against horse, thrusting with their
spears and fighting with the sword when their spears broke.
Many of them charged against Alexander himself, for he was
easily recognizable by his shield and by the amazingly tall white
feathers which were fixed upon either side of the crest of his
helmet. The joint of his breast-plate was pierced by a javelin,
but the blade did not penetrate the flesh. Rhoesaces and Spithridates, two of the Persian commanders, then rode at him; he
evaded the charge of the one and struck Rhoesaces, who wore
a breast-plate, with his spear, but the shaft of the weapon
snapped, whereupon he fought with his sword. While he was
engaged with Rhoesaces, Spithridates rode up on the other
side, and rising in his stirrups brought down a barbarian sword
with all his strength upon Alexander's head. The stroke split

the crest of his helmet, sheared away one of his plumes, and all but cleft the head-piece; in fact the edge of the axe penetrated it and grazed the hair on the top of Alexander's head. But just as Spithridates raised his arm for another blow, 'Black' Cleitus[56] struck first and ran him through with a spear, and at the same moment Rhoesaces was cut down by Alexander's sword.

While Alexander's cavalry was engaged in this furious and dangerous action, the Macedonian phalanx crossed the river and the infantry of both sides joined battle. The Persians offered little resistance, but quickly broke and fled, and it was only the Greek mercenaries who held their ground. They rallied together, made a stand on the crest of a hill and sent a message to Alexander asking for quarter. In this instance, he allowed himself to be guided by passion rather than by reason, led a charge against them and lost his horse (not Bucephalas on this occasion), which was pierced through the ribs by a sword-thrust. It was in this part of the field that the Macedonians suffered greater losses in killed and wounded than in all the rest of the battle, since they were fighting at close quarters with men who were expert soldiers and had been rendered desperate.

The Persians are said to have lost 20,000 infantry and 2,500 cavalry, whereas on Alexander's side, according to Aristobulus, only thirty-four soldiers in all were killed, nine of them belonging to the infantry.[57] Alexander gave orders that each of these men should have his statue set up in bronze and the work was carried out by Lysippus. At the same time, he was anxious to give the other Greek states a share in the victory. He therefore sent the Athenians in particular three hundred of the shields captured from the enemy, and over the rest of the spoils he had this proud inscription engraved: 'Alexander, the son of Philip, and the Greeks except the Spartans[58] won these spoils of war from the barbarians who dwell in Asia.' As for the drinking-vessels, purple hangings and other such plunder, he sent it all, with the exception of a few items, to his mother.

17. This battle brought about a great and immediate change in Alexander's situation. Even the city of Sardis, which was the

principal seat of Persian power on the Asiatic seaboard, at once surrendered to him, and the rest of the region likewise made its submission. Only Halicarnassus[59] and Miletus held out, and these cities were stormed and the surrounding territory subdued. At this point Alexander hesitated as to what his next step should be. Time and again he was impelled to seek out Darius and risk everything upon the issue of a single battle, and then as often he would decide that he must build up his strength by securing the coastal region and its resources, and training his army, and only then strike inland against the king.

There is a spring near the city of Xanthus in Lycia, which at this moment is said to have overflowed and cast up from its depths a bronze tablet; this was inscribed with ancient characters which foretold that the empire of the Persians would be destroyed by the Greeks. Alexander was encouraged by this prophecy and pressed on to clear the coast of Asia Minor as far as Phoenicia and Cilicia. His advance through Pamphylia inspired various historians to compose striking and extravagant descriptions of his progress. They claim that through some extraordinary stroke of providence the waves receded to make way for him,[60] although at other times they came flooding in strongly from the open sea, so that the beach of small rocks which lies directly under the steep and broken face of the cliffs was hardly ever left uncovered. Menander alludes to this prodigy in one of his comedies, where he says:

> Like Alexander, if I want to meet
> A man, he's there before me in the street,
> And if I am obliged to cross the sea,
> The waves at once will make a path for me.[61]

Alexander makes no mention in his letters of any such miracle, but says that setting out from Phaselis he made the journey by means of a road he had constructed known as the Climax.[62] It was for this reason that he spent several days in Phaselis, where he noticed in the market-place a statue which had been erected in honour of Theodectas,[63] a former citizen of the place. One evening after dinner when he had drunk well, he had the

impulse to pay a convivial tribute to his association with Aristotle and with philosophy, and so he led a band of revellers to
the statue and crowned it with a garland.

18. Next he marched into Pisidia where he subdued any resistance which he encountered, and then made himself master of
Phrygia. When he captured Gordium,[64] which is reputed to
have been the home of the ancient king Midas, he saw the celebrated chariot which was fastened to its yoke by the bark of the
cornel-tree, and heard the legend, which was believed by all the
barbarians, that the fates had decreed that the man who untied
the knot was destined to become the ruler of the whole world.
According to most people, the fastenings were so elaborately
intertwined and coiled upon one another that their ends were
hidden: in consequence Alexander did not know what to do,
and in the end loosened the knot by cutting through it with his
sword, whereupon the many ends sprang into view. But according to Aristobulus, he unfastened it quite easily by removing
the pin which secured the yoke to the pole of the chariot, and
then pulling out the yoke itself.

After this Alexander won over the peoples of Cappadocia
and Paphlagonia. He also learnt of the death of Memnon,[65] the
general to whom Darius had entrusted the defence of the coast
of Asia Minor, and who, if he had lived, was likely to have
offered the most stubborn resistance to Alexander's advance
and caused him the greatest trouble. This news confirmed his
resolve to invade the interior. By this time Darius was also
marching towards the coast from Susa. He was full of confidence in the strength of his forces, for he was leading an army
of 600,000 men, and he had been encouraged by a dream which
the Magi had interpreted in such a way as to please him rather
than to discover the most likely meaning. He had dreamt that he
saw the Macedonian phalanx encircled with flames and Alexander waiting upon him as a servant and wearing a cloak which
resembled one that Darius himself had once worn when he had
been a royal courier, and that after this Alexander had entered
the temple of Belos and had disappeared. But what God really
intended to prophesy through this dream, it would appear, was

that the Macedonians would accomplish brilliant and glorious exploits, that Alexander would become the ruler of Asia – just as Darius had become its ruler when he rose to be a king from having been a royal courier – and that he would soon die and leave his glory behind him.

19. Darius was encouraged even more by Alexander's long period of inactivity in Cilicia, for he imagined that this was due to cowardice. In fact the delay had been caused by sickness, which some said had been brought on by exhaustion, and others by bathing in the icy waters of the River Cydnus. At any rate, none of his other physicians dared to treat Alexander, for they all believed that his condition was so dangerous that medicine was powerless to help him, and dreaded the accusations that would be brought against them by the Macedonians in the event of their failure. The only exception was Philip, an Acarnanian, who saw that the king was desperately ill, but trusted to their mutual friendship. He thought it shameful not to share his friend's danger by exhausting all the resources of his art even at the risk of his own life, and so he prepared a medicine and persuaded Alexander to drink it without fear, since he was so eager to regain his strength for the campaign. Meanwhile, Parmenion had sent Alexander a letter from the camp warning him to beware of Philip, since Darius, he said, had promised him large sums of money and even the hand of his daughter if he would kill Alexander. Alexander read the letter and put it under his pillow without showing it to any of his friends. Then at the appointed hour, when Philip entered the room with the king's companions carrying the medicine in a cup, Alexander handed him the letter and took the draught from him cheerfully and without the least sign of misgiving. It was an astonishing scene, and one well worthy of the stage – the one man reading the letter and the other drinking the medicine, and then each gazing into the face of the other, although not with the same expression. The king's serene and open smile clearly displayed his friendly feelings towards Philip and his trust in him, while Philip was filled with surprise and alarm at the accusation, at one moment lifting his hands to heaven and pro-

testing his innocence before the gods, and the next falling upon his knees by the bed and imploring Alexander to take courage and follow his advice. At first the drug completely overpowered him and, as it were, drove all his vital forces out of sight: he became speechless, fell into a swoon and displayed scarcely any sign of sense or of life. However, Philip quickly restored him to consciousness, and when he had regained his strength he showed himself to the Macedonians, who would not be consoled until they had seen their king.

20. There was in Darius' army a Macedonian exile named Amyntas, who was acquainted with Alexander's character. When he learnt that Darius was eager to advance and attack Alexander as he marched through the mountain passes, he begged the Persian king to remain where he was in the flat open plains, where his immense numbers would have the advantage in fighting the small Macedonian army. Darius said that he was afraid the enemy might run away before he could come to grips with them, and that Alexander might thus elude him, to which Amyntas retorted: 'Your majesty need have no fears on that score. Alexander will march against you; in fact he is probably on his way now.' Darius refused to listen to Amyntas' advice, but broke camp and advanced into Cilicia, while at the same time Alexander marched against him into Syria. During the night they missed one another and both turned back. Alexander, delighted at his good fortune, hastened to catch his enemy in the narrow defile which leads into Cilicia, while Darius was no less eager to extricate his forces from the mountain passes and regain his former camping-ground in the plains. He already saw the mistake he had made by advancing into country which was hemmed in by the sea on one side and the mountains on the other, and divided by the River Pinarus which ran between them. Here the ground prevented him from using his cavalry, forced him to split up his army into small groups and favoured his opponent's inferior numbers. Fortune certainly presented Alexander with the ideal terrain for the battle, but it was his own generalship which did most to win the victory. For although he was so heavily outnumbered, he not only gave the

enemy no opportunity to encircle him, but leading his own right wing in person he managed to extend it round the enemy's left, outflanked it and, fighting in the foremost ranks, put the barbarians to flight. In this action he received a sword-wound in the thigh: according to Chares, this was given him by Darius with whom he engaged in hand-to-hand combat. Alexander sent a letter to Antipater describing the battle, but made no mention in it of who had given him the wound: he said no more than that he had been stabbed in the thigh with a dagger and that the wound was not a dangerous one.

The result of this battle[66] was a brilliant victory for Alexander. His men killed 110,000 of the enemy, but he could not catch Darius, who had got a start of half a mile or more, although he captured the king's chariot and his bow before he returned from the pursuit. He found the Macedonians busy carrying off the spoils from the enemy's camp, for this contained an immense wealth of possessions, despite the fact that the Persians had marched into battle lightly equipped and had left most of their baggage in Damascus. Darius' tent, which was full of many treasures, luxurious furniture, and lavishly dressed servants, had been set aside for Alexander himself. As soon as he arrived, he unbuckled his armour and went to the bath, saying, 'Let us wash off the sweat of battle in Darius' bath.' 'No, in Alexander's bath, now,' remarked one of his companions. 'The conqueror takes over the possessions of the conquered and they should be called his.' When Alexander entered the bathroom he saw that the basins, the pitchers, the baths themselves and the caskets containing unguents were all made of gold and elaborately carved, and noticed that the whole room was marvellously fragrant with spices and perfumes, and then passing from this into a spacious and lofty tent, he observed the magnificence of the dining-couches, the tables and the banquet which had been set out for him. He turned to his companions and remarked, 'So this, it seems, is what it is to be a king.'[67]

21. As he was about to sit down to supper, word was brought to him that the mother, the wife and the two unmarried daughters

of Darius were among the prisoners, and that at the sight of
the Persian king's bow and chariot they had beaten their breasts
and cried out, since they supposed that he must be dead. When
he heard this Alexander was silent for some time, for he was
evidently more affected by the women's grief than by his own
triumph. Then he sent Leonnatus to tell them that Darius was
not dead and that they need have no fear of Alexander: he was
fighting Darius for the empire of Asia, but they should be provided with everything they had been accustomed to regard as
their due when Darius was king. This kindly and reassuring
message for Darius' womenfolk was followed by still more
generous actions. Alexander gave them leave to bury as many
of the Persians as they wished, taking from the plunder any
clothes and ornaments they thought fit. He also allowed them
to keep the same attendants and privileges that they had previously enjoyed and even increased their revenues. But the most
honourable and truly regal service which he rendered to these
chaste and noble women was to ensure that they should never
hear, suspect nor have cause to fear anything which could disgrace them: they lived out of sight and earshot of the soldiers,
as though they were guarded in some inviolable retreat set
aside for virgin priestesses rather than in an enemy's camp.
This was the more remarkable because the wife of Darius was
said to have been the most beautiful princess of her time, just
as Darius himself was the tallest and handsomest man in Asia,
and their daughters resembled their parents.

But Alexander, so it seems, thought it more worthy of a king
to subdue his own passions than to conquer his enemies, and so
he never came near these women, nor did he associate with any
other before his marriage, with the exception only of Barsine.
This woman, the widow of Memnon, the Greek mercenary
commander, was captured at Damascus. She had received a
Greek education, was of a gentle disposition and could claim
royal descent, since her father was Artabazus who had married
one of the Persian king's daughters. Alexander slept with her,
as, according to Aristobulus, Parmenion had encouraged him
to have relations with a woman of beauty and noble lineage. As
for the other prisoners, when Alexander saw their handsome

and stately appearance, he took no more notice of them than to say jokingly, 'These Persian women are a torment for the eyes.'[68] He was determined to make such a show of his chastity and self-control as to eclipse the beauty of their appearance, and so he passed them by as if they had been so many lifeless images cut out of stone.

22. When Philoxenus, the commander of his forces on the sea-coast, wrote to say that he had with him a slave merchant from Tarentum named Theodorus who was offering two exceptionally handsome boys for sale and asked whether Alexander wished to buy them, the king was furious and angrily demanded of his friends what signs of degeneracy Philoxenus had ever noticed in him that he should waste his time procuring such shameful creatures. He wrote a letter to Philoxenus telling him what he thought of him and ordering him to send Theodorus and his merchandise to the devil. He also sharply rebuked Hagnon, who had written that he wanted to buy as a present for him a young man named Crobylus, whose good looks were famous in Corinth. And when he discovered that Damon and Timotheus, two Macedonian soldiers who were serving under Parmenion, had seduced the wives of some of the Greek mercenaries, he sent orders to Parmenion that if the two men were found guilty, they should be put to death as wild beasts which are born to prey upon mankind. In the same letter he wrote of himself: 'In my own case it will be found not only that I have never seen nor wished to see Darius' wife, but that I have not even allowed her beauty to be mentioned in my presence.' He also used to say that it was sleep and sexual intercourse which, more than anything else, reminded him that he was mortal; by this he meant that both exhaustion and pleasure proceed from the same weakness of human nature.

He was exceptionally temperate in what he ate, as he showed in many different ways, but above all in the answer he gave to Ada,[69] whom he honoured with the official title of 'Mother' and made Queen of Caria. To show her affection for him, she had formed the habit of sending him delicacies and sweetmeats every day, and finally offered him bakers and cooks who were supposed to be the most skilful in the country. Alexander's reply was that he did not need them, because his tutor Leonidas had provided him with better cooks than these: that is, a night march to prepare him for breakfast and a light breakfast to give him an appetite for supper. 'This same Leonidas', he went on, 'would often come and open my chests of bedding and clothes, to see whether my mother had not hidden some luxury inside.'

23. Alexander was also more moderate in his drinking than was generally supposed. The impression that he was a heavy drinker arose because when he had nothing else to do, he liked to linger over each cup, but in fact he was usually talking rather than drinking: he enjoyed holding long conversations, but only when he had plenty of leisure. Whenever there was urgent business to attend to, neither wine, nor sleep, nor sport, nor sex, nor spectacle could ever distract his attention, as they did for other generals. The proof of this is his life, which although so short was filled to overflowing with the most prodigious achievements. When he was at leisure, his first act after rising was to sacrifice to the gods, after which he took his breakfast sitting down.[70] The rest of the day would be spent in hunting, administering justice, planning military affairs or reading. If he were on a march which required no great haste, he would practise archery as he rode, or mounting and dismounting from a moving chariot, and he often hunted foxes or birds, as he mentions in the court journals. When he had chosen his quarters for the night, and while he was being refreshed with a bath or rubbed down, he would ask his cooks and bakers whether the arrangements for supper had been suitably made.

His custom was not to recline on a couch for dinner until it was late and already dark, and he was wonderfully attentive and observant in ensuring that his table was well provided, his guests equally served and none of them neglected. He sat long over his wine, as I have remarked, because of his fondness for conversation. And although at other times his society was more delightful and his manner more full of charm than any king, yet when he was drinking he would sometimes become offensively arrogant and descend to the level of a common soldier, and on these occasions he would allow himself not only to give way to boasting but also to be ridden by his flatterers. These men were an irritation to the more refined members of Alexander's entourage, who had no desire to compete with them in their sycophancy, but were unwilling to be outdone in praising Alexander. The one course they thought shameful, but the other was dangerous. When the drinking was over, it was his custom to take a bath and sleep, often until midday, and sometimes for the whole of the following day.

As for delicacies, Alexander was so restrained in his appetite that often when the rarest fruits or fish were brought him from the sea-coast, he would distribute them so generously among his companions that there would be nothing left for himself. His evening meal, however, was always a magnificent affair, and as his successes multiplied so did his expenditure on it, until it reached the sum of 10,000 drachmas. At this point he fixed a limit and those who entertained Alexander were told that they must not exceed this sum.

24. After the battle of Issus[71] he sent a force to Damascus and there captured the whole of the Persian army's treasure and baggage, together with their wives and children. On this occasion, it was the Thessalian cavalry who obtained the richest share of the plunder. They had particularly distinguished themselves at Issus, and Alexander had deliberately sent them on this expedition to reward them for their courage, but the booty proved so inexhaustible that there was enough to make the whole army rich. It was here that the Macedonians received their first taste of gold and silver and women and of the luxury of the barbarian way of life, and henceforth, like hounds which have picked up a scent, they pressed on to track down the wealth of the Persians.

However, this did not divert Alexander from his strategy of securing the coast before striking inland. The kings of Cyprus promptly visited him to hand over the island, and the whole of Phoenicia surrendered to him except for the city of Tyre. He besieged Tyre for seven months,[72] constructing moles and siege artillery on the landward side, and blockading it with two hundred triremes by sea. During the siege he had a dream in which he saw Heracles stretching out his hand to him from the wall and beckoning him to enter. Many of the Tyrians also dreamt that Apollo appeared to them and announced that he was going to go over to Alexander because he was displeased at what had been done in the city. At this the citizens treated him as if he were a deserter caught in the act of going over to the enemy. They fastened cords to his statue, nailed it to its base and reviled him as a supporter of Alexander. On another occasion, Alexander dreamt that he saw a satyr[73] who mocked at him from a distance and evaded his grasp when he tried to seize him, but who, at last after much coaxing and pursuing, allowed himself to be caught. The soothsayers gave a plausible interpretation of this dream by dividing the word *satyros* into two, to which they gave the meaning 'Tyre will be thine'. To this day the inhabitants show a well, near which they say Alexander dreamt that he saw the satyr.

In the midst of this siege, Alexander led a force against the Arabian tribes who inhabit the mountains of the Anti-Lebanon. During this expedition he risked his life to rescue his tutor Lysimachus, who had insisted on accompanying him, since he claimed that he was neither older nor weaker than Achilles' tutor Phoenix. When the force drew near the mountains, they were obliged to leave their horses and climb the slopes on foot, and the main body pressed far ahead of the rearguard. Lysimachus could not keep up the pace and grew more and more exhausted, but Alexander refused to leave him, since by then it was growing dark and the enemy were close at hand; instead, he tried to encourage him and urge him along. But before he knew it, he found himself separated from the main body with only a handful of men and was forced to spend a night of bitter cold in country which offered him no shelter. In this plight, he saw in the distance a number of scattered watch-fires which belonged to the enemy. It was always his habit in a crisis to encourage the Macedonians by sharing in their dangers, and so, trusting to his speed and agility, he dashed to the nearest camp-fire, dispatched with his dagger the two barbarians who were sitting by it and, snatching up a firebrand, ran back to his own party. They quickly built up a huge fire which frightened some of the enemy into flight, while those who ventured to attack were quickly routed and the Macedonians spent the rest of the night in safety. This is the account of the incident which we have from Chares.

25. The siege finally ended as follows. Alexander was resting the greater part of his army, which was exhausted after the hard fighting it had undergone, but in order to give the enemy no respite he led a small party against the walls. At the same time his diviner Aristander offered up a sacrifice and, after inspecting the omens, confidently announced to all those present that the city would be captured in the course of that month: this pronouncement was greeted with laughter and even some derision because by then it was the last day of the month. The king saw that Aristander was at a loss to explain the omens, and as he was always anxious to uphold the credibility of his prophecies he gave orders that the day should be counted not as the thirtieth of the month, but as the twenty-eighth. The trumpet then sounded the advance and he launched a fiercer attack against the walls than he had originally intended. The fighting grew hotter, until the troops who had been left in camp could not bear to stay inactive, but came running up to join the attackers, and thereupon the Tyrians gave up the struggle. So it came about that Alexander captured the city on that day.

After this he laid siege to Gaza,[74] the most important city in Syria. While he was engaged in these operations, a bird flying overhead let fall a clod of earth which struck him on the shoulder. The bird then perched upon one of the siege-engines and immediately became entangled in the network of sinews which were used to tighten the ropes. On this occasion, too, the portent was fulfilled as Aristander had prophesied: the city was taken and Alexander was wounded in the shoulder. He sent a great part of the spoils captured at Gaza to Olympias, to his sister Cleopatra and to his friends. He also remembered his tutor Leonidas and presented him with 500 talents of frankincense and 100 of myrrh: this was in remembrance of the hopes with which his teacher had inspired him in his boyhood. For it seems that one day when Alexander was sacrificing and was throwing incense on to the altar by the handful, Leonidas had remarked to him, 'Alexander, when you have conquered the countries that produce these spices, you can make as extravagant sacrifices as you like: till then, don't waste what you have!' So now Alexander wrote to him, 'I have sent you plenty of myrrh and frankincense, so that you need not be stingy towards the gods any longer.'

26. One day a casket was brought to him which was regarded by those who were in charge of Darius' baggage and treasure as the most valuable item of all, and so Alexander asked his friends what he should keep in it as his own most precious possession. Many different suggestions were put forward, and finally Alexander said that he intended to keep his copy of the *Iliad* there. This anecdote is supported by many reliable historians, and if the tradition which has been handed down by the Alexandrians on the authority of Heracleides is true, then certainly the poems of Homer were by no means an irrelevant or an unprofitable possession to accompany him on his campaigns. According to this story, after Alexander had conquered Egypt he was anxious to found a great and populous Greek city there, to be called after him.[75] He had chosen a certain site on the advice of his architects and was on the point of measuring and marking it out. Then, as he lay asleep, he dreamt that a grey-haired man of venerable appearance stood by his side and recited these lines from the *Odyssey*:

> Out of the tossing sea where it breaks on the beaches of Egypt
> Rises an isle from the waters: the name that men give it is
> Pharos.[76]

Accordingly, Alexander rose and immediately visited Pharos: at that time it was still an island[77] near the Canopic mouth of the Nile, but since then it has been joined to the mainland by a causeway. When he saw what wonderful natural advantages the place possessed – for it was a strip of land resembling a broad isthmus, which stretched between the sea and a great lagoon, with a spacious harbour at the end of it – he declared that Homer, besides his other admirable qualities, was also a very far-seeing architect, and he ordered the plan of the city to be designed so that it would conform to this site. There was no chalk to mark the ground plan, so they took barley meal, sprinkled it on the dark earth and marked out a semicircle, which was divided into equal segments by lines radiating from the inner arc to the circumference: the shape was similar to that of the *chlamys*, or military cloak, so that the lines proceeded, as it were, from the skirt, and narrowed the breadth of the area uniformly. While the king was enjoying the symmetry of the design, suddenly huge flocks of birds appeared from the river and the lagoon, descended upon the site and devoured every grain of the barley. Alexander was greatly disturbed by this omen, but the diviners urged him to take heart and interpreted the occurrence as a sign that the city would not only have abundant resources of its own but would be the nurse of men of innumerable nations, and so he ordered those in charge of the work to proceed while he himself set out to visit the temple of Ammon.[78]

This was a long and arduous journey, which was beset by two especial dangers. The first was the lack of water, of which there was none to be found along the route for many days' march. The second arises if a strong south wind should overtake the traveller as he is crossing the vast expanse of deep, soft sand, as is said to have happened to the army of Cambyses[79] long ago: the wind raised great billows of sand and blew them across the plain so that 50,000 men were swallowed up and perished. These dangers were present in the minds of almost everyone, but it was difficult to dissuade him from any course once he had set his heart on it. For Fortune, by giving way to his insistence, on every occasion had made his resolve unshakeable, and his passionate nature was carrying his ambition on and making it invincible against all obstacles, so that he was able to overcome not only his enemies but even places and seasons of the year.

27. At any rate, during this journey the examples of divine assistance which he met with in the midst of his difficulties were

more readily believed than the oracles that followed; and in a way it was because of this assistance that the oracles were believed. First of all, the abundant rain and continual showers which fell from heaven relieved the expedition from any fear of thirst, saturated the dry sand so that it became moist and firm to the tread and rendered the air pure and refreshing to breathe. Besides this, whenever the travellers became separated, lost the track or wandered about because the landmarks used by their guides had become obliterated, a number of ravens appeared and proceeded to guide their march, flying swiftly ahead of them when they followed and waiting for them when they marched slowly or lagged behind. And what was most miraculous of all, according to Callisthenes, was that if any of the company went astray in the night, the birds would croak and caw over them, until they had found their way back to the track.

When Alexander had crossed the desert and arrived at the shrine, the high priest of Ammon welcomed him on the god's behalf as a father greeting his son.[80] Alexander's first question was to ask whether any of his father's murderers had escaped punishment. At this the high priest commanded him to speak more guardedly, since his father was not a mortal. Alexander therefore changed the form of his question and asked whether the murderers of Philip had all been punished, and he added another inquiry concerning his own empire, and asked whether he was destined to rule over all mankind. This, the god replied, would be granted to him, and he also assured him that Philip's death had been completely avenged, whereupon Alexander dedicated some magnificent offerings to the god and presented large sums of money to his priests.

This is the account which most writers have given of the oracles pronounced by the god, but Alexander himself, in a letter to his mother, says that he received certain secret prophecies which he would confide to her, and her alone, after his return. Others say that the priest, who wished as a mark of courtesy to address him in Greek with the words 'O, paidion' ['My son'], because of his foreign accent pronounced the last letter as a sigma instead of a nu and said it as 'O, pai Dios' ['son of Zeus'], and that Alexander was delighted at this slip of pronunciation, and hence the legend grew up that the god had addressed him as 'son of Zeus'. It is also said that while he was in Egypt he listened to the lectures of Psammon the philosopher, and especially approved his saying to the effect that all men are ruled by God, because in every case that element which imposes itself and achieves the mastery is divine. Even more philosophical was Alexander's own opinion and pronouncement on this subject, namely that while God is the father of all mankind, it is the noblest and best whom he makes especially his own.

28. In general, Alexander adopted a haughty and majestic bearing towards the barbarians, as a man who was fully convinced of his divine birth and parentage, but towards the Greeks he was more restrained, and it was only on rare occasions that he assumed the manner of divinity. He made an exception when he wrote to the Athenians on the subject of Samos[81] and said, 'I would never have given you that free and glorious city: you received it from your master at that time, who was called my father.'[82] By this he was referring to Philip. But later, when he had been wounded by an arrow and was in great pain, he remarked, 'What you see flowing, my friends, is blood, and not *ichor, which flows in the veins of the blessed gods*.'[83] On another occasion too, when there was a loud crash of thunder and all those in his company were frightened by it, Anaxarchus the sophist asked him, 'Since you are the son of Zeus, could you make a noise like that?' Alexander laughed and replied, 'I have no wish to terrify my friends as you would have me do. It is you who apparently despise my table, because, so you say, what you see on it is merely fish, and not a row of satraps' heads!' For there is a story that this remark had in fact been made by Anaxarchus when he saw a present of small fish that the king had sent to Hephaestion:[84] he seemed to be disparaging and belittling those who undertake immense enterprises and run great risks in pursuit of their ambitions, which in the end leave them no happier or better able to enjoy themselves than other men. At any rate, it is evident from what I have said that Alexander was not at all vain or deluded but rather used belief in his divinity to enslave others.[85]

29. On his return from Egypt to Phoenicia[86] he honoured the gods with sacrifices and solemn processions and arranged contests of dithyrambic choruses and tragedies: these were remarkable not only for the splendour of their presentation but also for the rivalry between those who organized them. Just as at Athens, those who present these spectacles are the *choregoi*, rich citizens chosen by lot from the tribes, so on this occasion the sponsors were the kings of Cyprus, each of whom vied to outdo his competitors in the most spectacular fashion. The keenest contest of all took place between Nicocreon of Salamis and Pasicrates of Soli, who had been given by lot the services of two of the most celebrated actors of the day: Athenodorus was assigned to Pasicrates, and Thessalus, in whom Alexander was particularly interested, to Nicocreon. Alexander did not reveal his preference until Athenodorus had been proclaimed the victor by a majority of the judges' votes. Then, as he was leaving the theatre, it seems, he remarked that he approved of the verdict of the judges, but would gladly have sacrificed a part of his kingdom rather than see Thessalus defeated. However, when Athenodorus, who had been fined by the Athenians for breaking his undertaking to appear at their Dionysiac festival, appealed to the king to write a letter on his behalf, Alexander, although he refused to do this, settled the fine at his own expense. Again, when Lycon of Scarpheia, who was giving a successful performance before Alexander, introduced into the comedy he was playing a line asking for a present of 10 talents, Alexander laughed and gave him the money.

Darius wrote Alexander a letter[87] and sent it by the hand of some of his friends. He appealed to Alexander to accept 10,000 talents as a ransom for his Persian prisoners; he further offered him all the territory west of the Euphrates and the hand of one of his daughters in marriage, and on these terms proposed that they should become friends and allies. Alexander told his companions of this offer, whereupon Parmenion said, 'I would accept those terms if I were Alexander.' 'So would I, by Zeus,' retorted Alexander, 'if I were Parmenion!' In reply, he wrote to Darius that if he would come and give himself up, he would receive every courtesy: if not, Alexander would immediately march against him.

30. However not long after, when Darius' wife died in child-birth, Alexander felt remorse for having written in these terms. It is clear that he was distressed at having lost the chance to show his magnanimity, and he spared no expense to give the queen a magnificent funeral. One of her attendants, a eunuch named Tireos who had been captured with her, escaped from the camp, made his way to Darius on horseback and brought the news of the queen's death. When Darius heard it, he beat his head, broke into lamentations and cried aloud: 'Alas for the god of the Persians! Was it not enough that the king's consort and sister should have become a prisoner while she lived, but she must also be deprived of a royal funeral at her death?' 'As for her burial, sire,' the eunuch replied, 'and all the honours that were due to her state, you have no cause to accuse the evil god of the Persians.[88] To my knowledge neither your queen Stateira while she lived, nor your mother nor your children, lacked any of their former blessings, except for the light of your countenance, which the Lord Oromazes[89] will surely cause to shine again in its former glory. Neither was she deprived of any funeral ornament when she died, but was even honoured with the tears of her enemies. Alexander is as gentle after victory as he is terrible in battle.'

When Darius heard this, his agitation and misery were so great that he was quite carried away and began to entertain the most extravagant suspicions. He took the eunuch aside into a more secluded part of his tent and said: 'If you have not deserted me like the good fortune of Persia and gone over to the Macedonians, and if I, Darius, am still your lord and master, tell me, I charge you as you revere the great light of Mithras and the right hand of the king, was not her death which I am now lamenting the least of Stateira's misfortunes? Did I not suffer an even crueller blow of fate while she was still alive? Would not my unhappy destiny at least have been more honourable if I had met a harsher and more inhuman enemy? For how can a young man's treatment of his enemy's wife be virtuous, if it expresses itself in such tributes?'[90]

While the king was still speaking, Tireos threw himself at his feet and implored him to hold his peace. He should not do

Alexander so much injustice, he told him, nor shame his dead
queen and sister. Nor should he deprive himself of the greatest
consolation left him in his adversity, the belief that he had been
conquered by a man whose powers raised him above the mortal state; indeed, he should admire Alexander for having shown
a restraint towards Persian women which even surpassed the
valour he had shown against their husbands. While the eunuch
reassured the king, he swore the most solemn oaths to attest
the truth of his words, and he described the magnanimity and
self-restraint which Alexander had shown on other occasions.
Then Darius went out to his companions and lifting up his
hands to heaven uttered this prayer: 'You gods of my race and
my kingdom, grant me above all that the fortunes of Persia
may be restored to the prosperity in which I found them. I ask
this so that I may be able to requite Alexander for the favours
I received from him, when I lost everything that is dearest to
me. But if the fated time is at hand when the rule of the Persians
must cease, and if our downfall is a debt we must pay to the
envy of the gods and the laws of change, grant that no other
man but Alexander shall sit upon the throne of Cyrus.' Most
historians agree with this account of what was said and done
on that occasion.

31. After Alexander had subdued the whole region which lay
this side of the Euphrates, he resumed his advance against Darius, who was on his way to meet him with a million men.[91] On
this march one of his companions mentioned to Alexander to
amuse him that the camp-followers had divided themselves for
sport into two armies, and had appointed a general and commander for each, one of whom they had named Alexander and
the other Darius. At first they had only pelted one another with
clods of earth, then they had come to blows with their fists, and
finally, inflamed with the heat of battle, they had fought in
earnest with stones and clubs. More and more men had joined
in, until at last it had become hard to separate them. When
Alexander heard of this, he ordered the leaders to be matched
so as to fight in single combat; he himself gave weapons and
armour to his namesake, and Philotas gave them to the so-

called Darius. The whole army watched this contest and saw in it something of an omen for their own campaign. After a strenuous fight, 'Alexander' finally prevailed, and received as a prize twelve villages and the right to wear the Persian dress. This is the story that Eratosthenes records.

The great battle that was fought against Darius did not take place at Arbela, as the majority of writers say, but at Gaugamela. The word signifies 'the house of the camel': one of the ancient kings of this country escaped the pursuit of his enemies on a swift camel and gave the animal a home there, setting aside various revenues and the produce of several villages to maintain it. It happened that in the month of Boedromion, about the same time as the beginning of the festival of the Mysteries at Athens, there was an eclipse of the moon.[92] On the eleventh night after this, by which time the two armies were in sight of one another, Darius kept his troops under arms and held a review of them by torchlight. Alexander allowed his Macedonians to sleep, but himself spent the night in front of his tent in the company of his diviner, Aristander, with whom he performed certain mysterious and sacred ceremonies and offered sacrifice to the god Fear. Meanwhile, some of the older of his companions and Parmenion in particular looked out over the plain between the River Niphates and the Gordyaean mountains and saw the entire plain agleam with the watch-fires of the barbarians, while from their camp there arose the confused and indistinguishable murmur of myriads of voices, like the distant roar of a vast ocean. They were filled with amazement at the sight and remarked to one another that it would be an overwhelmingly difficult task to defeat an enemy of such strength by engaging them by day. They therefore went to the king when he had performed his sacrifice and tried to persuade him to attack by night, so as to conceal from his men the most terrifying element in the coming struggle, that is, the odds against them. It was then that Alexander gave them his celebrated answer, 'I will not steal my victory.' Some thought this an immature and empty boast on the part of a young man who was merely joking in the presence of danger. But others interpreted it as meaning that he had confidence in his present situation and that he had correctly judged the future. In other words, he was determined that if Darius were defeated he should have no cause to summon up courage for another attempt; he was not to be allowed to blame darkness and night for his failure on this occasion, as at Issus he had blamed the narrow mountain passes and the sea. Certainly, Darius would never abandon the war for lack of arms or of troops, when he could draw upon such a vast territory and such immense reserves of manpower. He would only do so when he had lost courage and become convinced of his inferiority in consequence of an unmistakable defeat suffered in broad day-light.

32. When his friends had gone, Alexander lay down in his tent and is said to have passed the rest of the night in a deeper sleep than usual. At any rate, when his officers came to him in the early morning, they were astonished to find him not yet awake, and on their own responsibility gave out orders for the soldiers to take breakfast before anything else was done. Then, as time was pressing, Parmenion entered Alexander's tent, stood by his couch and called him two or three times by name; when he had roused him, he asked how he could possibly sleep as if he were already victorious, instead of being about to fight the greatest battle of his life. Alexander smiled and said, 'Why not? Do you not see that we have already won the battle, now that we are delivered from roving around these endless devastated plains, and chasing this Darius, who will never stand and fight?' And indeed, not only beforehand, but at the very height of the battle, Alexander displayed the supremacy and steadfastness of a man who is confident of the soundness of his judgement.

For as the action developed, the left wing under Parmenion was driven back and found itself hard pressed by a violent charge from the Bactrian cavalry and by an outflanking move-ment, when Mazaeus sent a detachment of horsemen to ride round the phalanx and attack the troops who were guarding the Macedonian baggage. Parmenion, who was disconcerted by both these manoeuvres, sent messengers to warn Alexander that his camp and his baggage train were lost, unless he could

immediately move strong reinforcements from the front to protect his rear. It so happened that at that moment Alexander was
about to give the signal to the right wing, which he commanded, to attack; when he received this message, he exclaimed
that Parmenion must have lost his wits and forgotten in his agitation that the victors will always take possession of their
enemy's baggage in any event, and that the losers must not concern themselves with their property or their slaves, but only
with how to fight bravely and die with honour.

After he had sent this message to Parmenion, he put on his
helmet. He was already wearing the rest of his armour when he
left his tent – a tunic made in Sicily, which was belted around
his waist, and over this a thickly quilted linen corslet, which
had been among the spoils captured at Issus. His helmet, the
work of Theophilus, was made of steel which gleamed like pol-
ished silver, and to this was fitted a steel neckpiece set with
precious stones. His sword, a gift from the king of Citium, was
a marvel of lightness and tempering, and he had trained himself
to use this as his principal weapon in hand-to-hand fighting.
He also wore a cloak which was more ornate than the rest of
his armour. It had been made by Helicon, an artist of earlier
times, and presented to Alexander as a mark of honour by the
city of Rhodes, and this, too, he was in the habit of wearing in
battle. While he was drawing up the phalanx in formation,
reviewing the troops, or giving out orders, he rode another
horse to spare Bucephalas, who was by now past his prime; but
when he was about to go into action, Bucephalas would be led
up, and he would mount him and at once begin the attack.

33. On this occasion, Alexander gave a long address to the
Thessalians and the other Greeks. They shouted their approval,
urging him to lead them against the barbarians, and at this he
shifted his lance into his left hand, so Callisthenes tells us, and
raising his right he called upon the gods and prayed that, if he
were really the son of Zeus, they should protect and encourage
the Greeks. Then Aristander the diviner, who was wearing
a white robe and a crown of gold, rode along the ranks and
pointed out to the men an eagle which hovered for a while over

Alexander's head and then flew straight towards the enemy. The sight acted as an immediate inspiration to the watching troops, and with shouts of encouragement to one another the cavalry charged the enemy at full speed and the phalanx rolled forward like a flood. Before the leading ranks could engage, the barbarians fell back, hotly pursued, as Alexander drove the retreating enemy towards the centre, where Darius was stationed.

Alexander had sighted his adversary through the ranks of the royal squadron of cavalry, as they waited drawn up in deep formation in front of him. Darius was a tall and handsome man and he towered conspicuously above this large and superbly equipped body of horsemen, who were closely massed to guard the lofty chariot in which he stood. But the horseguards were seized with panic at the terrible sight of Alexander bearing down upon them and driving the fugitives before him against those who still held their ground, and the greater number of them broke and scattered. The bravest and most highly born, however, were slaughtered in front of their king; they fell upon one another and impeded the pursuit, as in their death-throes both horses and men became entangled with their enemy.

As for Darius, all the horrors of the battle were before his eyes and the forces which had been stationed in front of him for his protection were being driven back upon him. It was difficult to turn his chariot round and drive it away, since the wheels were held fast and snarled by heaps of bodies, and the horses which were hemmed in and hidden by the dead began to rear and plunge so that the charioteer could not control them. So Darius abandoned his chariot and his armour, mounted a mare which, so the story goes, had recently foaled and rode away. But it is believed that he would not have escaped at that moment, had not Parmenion sent another party of horsemen begging Alexander to come to his rescue, because he was engaged with a strong enemy force which still held together and would not give way. In this battle, Parmenion is generally accused of having been sluggish and lacking in spirit, either because old age had dulled his courage, or because he had become envious of the authority and pomp, to use Callisthenes' words, which Alexander now displayed. Alexander was vexed by this appeal for help, but at the time he did not reveal to his men the fact that it had been made. Instead, he ordered the recall to be sounded on the ground that it was growing dark and that he wished to bring the slaughter to an end. Then, as he rode back to the part of the field where Parmenion's troops were supposedly threatened, he learnt on his way that the enemy had been utterly defeated and put to flight.

34. After the battle had ended in this way, the Persian empire was regarded as having been completely overthrown. Alexander was proclaimed king of Asia, and after offering splendid sacrifices to the gods, he proceeded to reward his friends with riches, estates and governorships. As he wished to increase his prestige in the Greek world, he wrote to the states saying that all tyrannies had been abolished and that they lived under their own laws.[93] To the Plataeans he wrote specially, telling them to begin rebuilding their city because their ancestors had allowed the Greeks to make their territory the seat of war in the struggle for their common freedom.[94] He also sent a share of the spoils to the people of Croton in Italy in honour of the spirit and valour shown by their athlete Phaÿllus: this man, when the rest of the Greeks in Italy had refused to give any help to their compatriots in the Persian Wars, had fitted out a ship at his own expense and sailed with it to Salamis to share in the common danger.[95] Such was Alexander's desire to pay tribute to any manifestation of courage and to prove himself the friend and guardian of noble actions.

35. In his advance through the whole of Babylonia, which immediately surrendered to him, he was particularly impressed by the fissure in the earth at Ecbatana[96] from which fire continually poured forth as if from a spring, and by the stream of naphtha which gushed out so abundantly that it formed a lake not far from the chasm. This naphtha is in many ways like bitumen, but is so inflammable that a flame can set it alight by its very radiance without actually touching it, and it often kindles all the intermediate air. To demonstrate the nature of the liquid

and the force of its action, the barbarians sprinkled a small quantity along the street which led to Alexander's quarters. Then standing at the far end they applied their torches to the trail of moisture, as it was growing dark. The first drops instantly ignited, and in a fraction of a second, with the speed of thought, the flames darted to the other end and the whole street was ablaze.

Among the attendants who waited upon the king, whenever he bathed and anointed himself, was an Athenian named Athenophanes, who had the task of providing him with diversions and amusements. On one occasion a boy named Stephanus, who possessed an absurdly ugly face but an agreeable singing voice, was also in attendance in the bathroom, and Athenophanes asked the king, 'Would you care for us to try an experiment with the naphtha upon Stephanus? If it catches fire on him and is not immediately put out, then its strength must be extraordinary and irresistible.' Surprisingly, the boy agreed to try the experiment, and no sooner had he touched the liquid and anointed himself with it than the flames broke out and enveloped his body so completely that Alexander was appalled and began to fear for his life. If there had not happened to be many attendants close by holding pitchers of water for the bath, he would have been burned to death before any help could reach him. Even as it was they had great difficulty in putting out the flames, and his whole body was so severely burned that he was in a terrible state afterwards.[97]

It is natural, therefore, that some of those who wish to reconcile legend with fact should say that this was the drug used by Medea when in the tragedy she anoints the crown and the robe which she presents to Creon's daughter.[98] For the fire did not originate from these objects, they explain, nor did it break out of its own accord, but a flame must have been placed near them, with which the liquid was then drawn into contact so quickly that the process was invisible to the naked eye. The rays and emanations which proceed from a flame at a certain distance have no more effect on some substances than to give them light and warmth, but in the case of those which are dry and porous, or possess a sufficiently oily moisture, the heat is concentrated, then bursts into fierce flames and transforms the substance. There has been much dispute as to how naphtha is produced: whether, for example, the liquid combustible matter that feeds the flame flows out from a soil which is naturally oily and inflammable. Certainly the soil of Babylonia is very fiery, so much so that grains of barley are often thrown up out of the earth and bound away, as if the heat of the soil made the ground throb, and in the hottest part of the summer the inhabitants sleep on skins filled with water. When Harpalus, Alexander's treasurer, was left as governor of the province, he was anxious to adorn the royal gardens and walks with Greek plants and shrubs, and he succeeded with all except ivy: the soil would not nourish this, but always killed it.[99] The plant could not endure the temper of the soil which was fiery, whereas ivy loves a cold soil. But perhaps impatient readers will bear with digressions of this kind, so long as they are kept within reasonable limits.

36. After Alexander had made himself master of Susa, he found 40,000 talents of coined money in the palace, besides furniture and other treasures of incalculable value. Among these, it was said, were 5,000 talents of cloth dyed with purple from Hermione, which still kept a fresh and vivid colour even after it had been stored there for 190 years.[100] The reason for this, we are told, is that honey was used in the purple dyes and white olive oil in the white dyes, and each of these substances, it is said, will preserve the lustre and brilliance of the colour and prevent any fading. Deinon[101] also tells us that the kings of Persia had water transported from the Nile and the Danube, and stored among their treasures as a testimony to the extent of their dominions and a proof that they were masters of the world.

37. Persis[102] was difficult to penetrate owing to its mountainous terrain and it was defended by the bravest of the Persians since Darius had fled. In spite of these obstacles, Alexander found a guide who showed him the way by making a short diversion.[103] This man had a Lycian father and a Persian mother and spoke both Greek and Persian, and it was to him, so the story goes, that the Pythian priestess had referred when she prophesied

while Alexander was still a boy that a *lykos* (wolf) would guide him on his march against the Persians. A terrible massacre of prisoners took place there, and Alexander himself writes that he gave orders for them to be slaughtered because he thought that this would help his cause. He found as much gold as he had in Susa, and they say that it required 10,000 pairs of mules and 5,000 camels to carry away the furniture and other treasures that were found there.

When Alexander saw a gigantic statue of Xerxes, which had been toppled from its pedestal and heedlessly left on the ground by a crowd of soldiers as they forced their way into the palace, he stopped and spoke to it as though it were alive. 'Shall I pass by and leave you lying there because of the expedition you led against Greece, or shall I set you up again because of your magnanimity and your virtues in other respects?' For a long while he gazed at the statue and reflected in silence, and then finally went on his way. It was by then winter, and he stayed there for four months to allow his soldiers time to rest. It is said that when he first took his seat on the royal throne under the golden canopy, Demaratus the Corinthian, who was much attached to Alexander, as he had been to his father, began to weep, as old men are apt to do, and exclaimed that any Greek who had died before that day had missed one of the greatest pleasures in life by not seeing Alexander seated on the throne of Darius.

38. After this, when Alexander was about to march against Darius, he happened to get involved in a rowdy drinking party with his companions. Some women were there too, who had come in a drunken revel to see their lovers. The most celebrated of these was Thaïs, an Athenian, the mistress of the Ptolemy who later became the ruler of Egypt. As the drinking went on, Thaïs delivered a speech which was intended partly as a graceful compliment to Alexander and partly to amuse him. What she said was typical of the spirit of Athens, but hardly in keeping with her own situation. She declared that all the hardships she had endured in wandering about Asia had been amply repaid on that day when she found herself revelling luxuriously in the splendid palace of the Persians, but that it would be an

even sweeter pleasure to end the party by going out and setting fire to the palace of Xerxes, who had laid Athens to ashes. She wanted to put a torch to the building herself in full view of Alexander, so that posterity should know that the women who followed Alexander had taken a more terrible revenge for the wrongs of Greece than all the famous commanders of earlier times by land or sea. Her speech was greeted with wild applause and the king's companions excitedly urged him on until at last he allowed himself to be persuaded, leaped to his feet and, with a garland on his head and a torch in his hand, led the way. The other revellers followed, shouting and dancing, and surrounded the palace, and those of the Macedonians who had heard what was afoot delightedly ran up bringing torches with them. They did this because they hoped that the act of burning and destroying the palace signified that Alexander's thoughts were turned towards home, and that he was not planning to settle among the barbarians. According to some writers, it was in this way that the palace was burned down, that is, on impulse, but there are others who maintain that it was an act of deliberate policy. However this may be, it is agreed that Alexander quickly repented and gave orders for the fire to be put out.[104]

39. Alexander was by nature exceptionally generous and became even more so as his wealth increased. His gifts were always bestowed with grace and courtesy, and it is this alone which truly makes the giver's generosity welcome. I shall mention a few instances of this. When Ariston the commander of the Paeonians[105] had killed one of his enemies, he brought the man's head, showed it to Alexander and remarked, 'In my country, sire, a present such as this is always rewarded with a gold cup.' Alexander laughed and replied, 'Yes, but with an empty one. I will drink your health with a cup full of neat wine, and give it you as well.' On another occasion, one of the Macedonian soldiers was driving a mule laden with the king's gold, and when the animal became too exhausted to carry it he took off the load and put it on his own shoulders. When Alexander saw him struggling along in distress and learnt what had happened, he called out as the soldier was about to put down his

burden, 'Hold on, don't give up! Finish your journey and take what you are carrying to your own tent.' Indeed, he was generally more offended with those who refused his gifts than with those who asked for them. He wrote to Phocion telling him that in future he would not regard him as a friend if he declined all his favours,[106] and in the case of Serapion, one of the youths who used to play ball with him, he never gave him anything because he never asked for anything. So one day, whenever the ball came to Serapion, he made a point of throwing it to the others, until the king said, 'Aren't you going to throw it to me?' 'No,' retorted Serapion. 'You never ask for it!' whereupon the king burst out laughing and loaded him with presents.

Then there was Proteas – one of a refined group with whom Alexander used to drink and joke – who seemed on one occasion to have made the king angry. At this, his friends pleaded for Proteas and he begged for forgiveness with tears in his eyes, until Alexander said that he pardoned him. 'Then will you first give me something to prove it?' Proteas asked him, whereupon the king gave orders for him to be presented with five talents. His friends and bodyguards[107] were apt to put on airs as a result of the riches he showered on them, and this is revealed in a letter Olympias once wrote him in which she said, 'I wish you would find other ways of rewarding those you love and honour: as it is, you are making them all the equals of kings and enabling them to make plenty of friends, but leaving yourself without any.' Olympias often wrote to him in this strain, but Alexander kept her letters to himself, with one exception. Hephaestion was in the habit of reading the king's letters with him, and on this occasion his eye fell on a letter which had been opened. The king did not prevent him from reading it, but took the ring from his own finger and pressed the seal to his lips, so much as to tell him to keep silence.

Mazaeus had been the most powerful of Darius' officials, and although his son was already the governor of a province, Alexander now proposed to add an even larger one to it.[108] The young man declined it, however, and said to him, 'In the past, sire, there was only one Darius, but now you have made many Alexanders.' Besides this, he presented Parmenion with the house of Bagoas at Susa, in which it is said clothes were found to the value of 1,000 talents. Alexander also wrote to Antipater, warning him to keep guards around him since he was in danger of plots against his life.[109] He sent a great many presents to his mother, but he would not allow her to interfere in affairs of state or in the management of his campaigns, and when she complained about this he bore her scoldings with great tolerance. But on one occasion, when Antipater had written him a long letter finding fault with her, he exclaimed that Antipater did not understand that one tear shed by his mother would wipe out 10,000 letters such as this.

40. Alexander noticed that those around him had acquired thoroughly luxurious habits and had become vulgar in the extravagance of their way of living. There was Hagnon of Teos, who wore silver nails in his boots; Leonnatus, who had the dust with which he sprinkled his body for wrestling brought by camel-train from Egypt; and Philotas, who hunted with nets that could enclose a space of 11 miles. When his friends bathed, they anointed themselves with myrrh, rather than with plain oil, and were attended by masseurs and personal servants. Alexander reasoned with them and gently reproved them for these excesses. He told them he was amazed to see that men who had fought and conquered in such great battles could have forgotten that those who labour sleep more sweetly than those who are laboured for. Could they not understand, when they compared their style of living with that of the Persians, that there is nothing more slavish than the love of pleasure and nothing more princely than the life of toil? 'How can a man attend to his horse,' he asked them, 'or keep his spear and his helmet clean and bright, if he has lost the habit of using his hands to look after his own precious body? Do you not know that the end and perfection of conquest is to avoid doing the same things as the conquered have done?' And so he exerted himself more strenuously than ever in campaigns and hunting expeditions, exposing himself to hardship and danger, so that an envoy from Sparta, who was by his side when he speared a great lion, remarked, 'Alexander, you fought nobly with this

lion to decide which of you should be king!' Craterus[110] later
had this hunting scene represented in bronze and dedicated it at
Delphi:[111] it showed the figures of the lion, the hounds, the king
fighting with the lion and Craterus advancing to help him.
Some of these sculptures were executed by Lysippus, and some
by Leochares.

41. Alexander made a point of risking his life in this way both
to exercise himself and to inspire others to acts of courage, but
his friends, because of the wealth and pomp with which they
were surrounded, desired only to lead a life of luxury and idleness. They found his expeditions and campaigns an intolerable
burden, and little by little went so far as to abuse and find fault
with the king. Alexander bore this treatment with great tolerance at first, and remarked that it is the lot of a king to do good
to his subjects and be maligned for it. And indeed, even in
the most trivial services which he rendered to his friends, he
revealed the affection and regard which he had for them. I will
give a few examples of this.

He wrote to Peucestas, who had been bitten by a bear, to
complain that he had described his injury to other friends but
had said nothing to Alexander. 'Now,' he went on, 'you must
write to tell me how you are, and whether you were let down
by any of your fellow-huntsmen, so that I can punish them.'
When Hephaestion was absent on some business, Alexander
wrote with the news that while they had been amusing themselves hunting a mongoose, Craterus had accidentally been
wounded in the thighs by Perdiccas' spear. After Peucestas had
recovered from some illness, Alexander wrote to his friend's
physician, Alexippus, congratulating him on the cure. When
Craterus was sick, Alexander had a dream in which he offered
certain sacrifices to the gods on his friend's behalf and told him
to do the same, and he wrote to Craterus' physician, Pausanias,
when the latter wished to treat him with hellebore, expressing
his anxiety and advising him how to use the drug. Ephialtes
and Cissus were the first to bring the news that Harpalus had
deserted,[112] and Alexander had them put in chains because he
believed that they were making a false accusation against the

man. Again, when he was sending home his invalid and super-annuated soldiers, Eurylochus of Aegae contrived to have his name put on the list of the sick, and when it was discovered that there was nothing wrong with him, he confessed that he was in love with a girl named Telesippa and had planned to travel with her on her journey to the coast. Alexander made inquiries about her parentage, and when he found that she was a free-born Greek courtesan, he said, 'I will help you with your love-affair, Eurylochus, but since she is a free woman, you must see whether we can win Telesippa either by presents or by courtship, but not use other means.'

42. It is in fact astonishing that he could find time to write so many letters to his friends. For example, he wrote one ordering a search to be made for a slave belonging to Seleucus, who had run away to Cilicia, and another praising Peucestas because he had caught Nicon, a runaway slave of Craterus, and a third to Megabyzus about a slave who had taken refuge in a sanctuary. In this he told him to try, if possible, to lure the slave outside and then catch him, but not to lay hands on him within the sacred precincts. It is also said that when he was trying a prisoner on a capital charge, he would place a hand over one of his ears while the prosecutor was speaking, so as to keep it free and impartial for listening to the defendant. But later, so many accusations were laid before him that he grew harsh and was inclined to believe even the false charges, because so much that he was told was true. Above all, if anybody spoke ill of him, his judgement was apt to desert him and his mood would become cruel and merciless, since he loved his good name more than his life or his crown.

He was marching against Darius at this time,[113] fully expecting that he would have to fight another battle. However, when he learnt that the king had been arrested by Bessus, the satrap of Bactria, he sent his Thessalian cavalry back to Greece, after first giving them a gratuity of 2,000 talents, besides their regular pay.[114] The pursuit of Darius turned out to be long and exhausting. Alexander covered more than 375 miles in eleven days, and by this time most of his horsemen were on the verge of collapse for lack of water. At this point, he met some Macedonians who were carrying water from a river in skins on the backs of their mules, and when they saw Alexander almost fainting with thirst in the midday heat, they quickly filled a helmet and brought it to him. He asked them for whom they were carrying the water. 'For our own sons,' they told him, 'but so long as your life is safe, we can have other children, even if we lose these.' At this Alexander took the helmet in his hands. But then he looked up and saw the rest of his troops craning their heads and casting longing glances at the water, and he handed it back without drinking a drop. He thanked the men who had brought it, but said to them, 'If I am the only one to drink, the rest will lose heart.' However, no sooner had his men witnessed this act of self-control and magnanimity than they cried out and shouted for him to lead them on boldly. They spurred on their horses and declared that they could not feel tired or thirsty or even like mortal men, so long as they had such a king.

43. All his horsemen were fired with the same enthusiasm, but only sixty of his men, so the story goes, had kept up with Alexander when he burst into the enemy's camp. They rode over great heaps of gold and silver vessels which had been scattered on the ground, passed wagons full of women and children that were moving aimlessly about without their drivers, and at length caught up with the Persian vanguard, imagining that Darius must be among them. At last they found him lying in a wagon, riddled with javelins and at his last gasp. He asked for a drink, and when he had swallowed some cold water, which a Macedonian named Polystratus brought him, he said, 'This is the final stroke of misfortune that I should accept a service from you and not be able to return it, but Alexander will reward you for your kindness, and the gods will repay him for his courtesy towards my mother and my wife and my children. And so through you, I give him my hand.' As he said this, he took Polystratus by the hand and died. When Alexander came up, he showed his grief and distress at the king's death, and unfastening his own cloak, he threw it over the body and covered it. Later, after he had captured Bessus, who had murdered the

king, he had him torn limb from limb. He had the tops of two straight trees bent down so that they met, and part of Bessus' body was tied to each. Then when each tree was let go and sprang back to its upright position, the part of the body attached to it was torn off by the recoil. As for Darius' body, he sent it to his mother to be laid out in royal state, and he enrolled his brother Exathres into the number of the companions.

44. Alexander, with the flower of his army, began to descend into Hyrcania. Here he came in sight of a bay of the open sea which appeared to be as large as the Black Sea and was less salty than the Mediterranean. He could not obtain any certain information about it, but guessed that it was probably an overflow from Lake Maeotis.[115] However, various geographers had already discovered the truth, and many years before Alexander's expedition they had recorded their conclusion that this was the most northerly of four gulfs which ran inland from the outer sea[116] and was called the Hyrcanian or Caspian Sea. In this neighbourhood the barbarians surprised the grooms, who were leading Alexander's horse Bucephalas, and captured him. Alexander was enraged and sent a herald with the threat that unless they gave back his horse he would exterminate the whole tribe, together with their women and children. However, when they returned with the horse and surrendered their cities to him, he treated them all kindly, and even gave a ransom to the men who had captured Bucephalas.

45. From this point he advanced into Parthia, and it was here during a pause in the campaign that he first began to wear barbarian dress. He may have done this from a desire to adapt himself to local habits, because he understood that the sharing of race and of customs is a great step towards softening men's hearts. Alternatively, this may have been an experiment which was aimed at introducing obeisance[117] among the Macedonians, the first stage being to accustom them to accepting changes in his own dress and way of life. However, he did not go so far as to adopt the Median costume, which was altogether barbaric and outlandish, and he wore neither trousers, nor Persian robes,

nor tiara.[118] Instead, he adopted a style which was a compromise between Persian and Median costume, more modest than the
first, and more stately than the second. At first he wore this only
when he was in the company of barbarians or with his intimate
friends indoors, but later he put it on when he was riding or
giving audience in public. The sight greatly displeased the Macedonians, but they admired his other virtues so much that they
considered they ought to make concessions to him in some matters which either gave him pleasure or increased his prestige.
For besides all his other hardships, he had recently been
wounded below the knee by an arrow which splintered the shin-
bone so that the fragments had to be taken out, and on another
occasion he had received such a violent blow on the neck from
a stone that his vision became clouded and remained so for a
long time afterwards. In spite of this, he continued to expose
himself unsparingly to danger: for example, he crossed the River
Orexartes, which he believed to be the Tanaïs, routed the Scythians and pursued them for 11 miles, even though all this while
he was suffering from an attack of dysentery.

46. It was here that he was visited by the queen of the Amazons,
according to the report we have from many writers, among
them Cleitarchus, Polycleitus, Onesicritus, Antigenes and Ister.
On the other hand, Aristobulus, Chares the royal usher, Ptolemy, Anticleides, Philo the Theban and Philip of Theangela,
and besides these Hecataeus of Eretria, Philip the Chalcidian
and Douris of Samos, all maintain that this is a fiction, and this
judgement seems to be confirmed by Alexander's own testimony. In a letter to Antipater, in which he describes the details
of the occasion, he mentions that the king of the Scythians
offered him his daughter in marriage, but he makes no reference
to an Amazon. There is also a story that many years afterwards,
when Onesicritus was reading aloud to Lysimachus,[119] who
was now king, the fourth book of his history, which contained
the tale of the Amazon, Lysimachus smiled and asked quietly, 'I
wonder where I was then.' In any case, our admiration for
Alexander is not diminished if we reject this story, nor increased
if we regard it as true.

47. Alexander was becoming anxious that the Macedonians might refuse to follow him any further in his campaigns. He therefore left the main body where they were and allowed them to rest. He had with him in Hyrcania his best troops, consisting of 20,000 infantry and 3,000 cavalry. These he won over by telling them that up to now the barbarians had watched them as if they were in a dream, but that if they merely threw the whole country into disorder and then retired, the Persians would fall upon them as if they were so many women. He went on to say that he would allow any of them who desired it to go back, but he called on them to witness that at the very moment when he was seeking to conquer the whole inhabited world for the Macedonians, he found himself deserted and left only with his friends and those who were willing to continue the expedition. These are almost the exact words which he used in his letter to Antipater, and he says that after he had spoken in this way the whole of his audience shouted aloud and begged him to lead them to whatever part of the world he chose. Once he had tested the loyalty of these troops, he found no difficulty in winning over the main body, indeed they followed him with a will.

In this way he also began to adapt his own style of living more closely to that of the country and tried to reconcile Asiatic and Macedonian customs; he believed that if the two traditions could be blended and assimilated in this way, his authority would be more securely established when he was far away, since it would rest on goodwill rather than on force. For this reason, he also selected 30,000 boys and gave orders that they should be taught to speak the Greek language and to use Macedonian weapons, and he appointed a large number of instructors to train them. He married Roxane out of love, which began when he first saw her at the height of her youthful beauty taking part in a dance at a banquet, but it also seemed to fit in well with his policy. For the barbarians were encouraged by the feeling of partnership which their marriage created, and they were completely won over by Alexander's moderation and courtesy and by the fact that without the sanction of marriage he would not approach the only woman who had ever conquered him.

Alexander noticed that among his closest friends it was Hephaestion who approved of these plans and joined him in changing his habits, while Craterus clung to Macedonian customs, and he therefore made use of the first in his dealings with the barbarians, and of the second with the Greeks and Macedonians. In general, he showed most affection for Hephaestion and most respect for Craterus, for he had formed the opinion and always said that Hephaestion was a friend of Alexander, while Craterus was a friend of the king. For this reason, a feeling of hostility grew and festered between the two and they often came into open conflict. Once, on the expedition to India, they actually drew their swords and came to blows, and as their friends appeared and began to join in the quarrel, Alexander rode up and publicly reprimanded Hephaestion: he told him that he must be a fool and a madman if he did not understand that without Alexander's favour he was nothing. Then later, in private, he sharply rebuked Craterus. Finally, he called both men together and made them be friends again. He swore by Zeus Ammon and the rest of the gods that these were the two men he loved best in the world, but that if he ever heard them quarrelling again, he would kill them both, or at least the one who began the quarrel. As a result, it is said that afterwards neither of them ever did or said anything to offend the other, even in jest.

48. Philotas, the son of Parmenion, enjoyed a prominent position among the Macedonians.[120] He had a high reputation for courage and for his ability to endure hardship and, after Alexander, he had no equal for generosity and devotion to his friends. At any rate, we are told that when one of his intimate friends asked him for money and his steward replied that he had none to give, he asked the man, 'What do you mean – have I no plate or furniture to sell?' However, Philotas also displayed an arrogance, an ostentation of wealth and a degree of luxury in his personal habits and his way of living which could only cause offence in his position as a private subject. At this time, in particular, his efforts to imitate a lofty and majestic presence carried no conviction, appeared clumsy and uncouth, and succeeded only in provoking envy and mistrust, to such a degree that even

Parmenion once remarked to him, 'My son, do not make so much of yourself.' And, indeed, accusations against Philotas had been reaching Alexander for many years. For when Darius had been defeated in Cilicia and his treasure captured at Damascus, one of the many prisoners who were brought into Alexander's camp was discovered to be a beautiful girl who had been born in Pydna and was named Antigone. She was handed over to Philotas and he – like many a young man who, when he has drunk well, is apt to talk freely to his mistress in the boastful fashion of a soldier – often confided to her that all the greatest achievements in the campaign had been the work of his father and himself. Then he would speak of Alexander as a mere boy who owed his title of ruler to their efforts. Antigone repeated these remarks to one of her friends, and he naturally enough passed them on until they reached the ears of Craterus, who took the girl and brought her privately to Alexander. When the king heard her story, he ordered her to continue visiting Philotas, but to come and report everything that she learnt from him.

49. Philotas had no suspicion of the trap that was being set for him and in his conversations with Antigone he uttered many indiscretions and often spoke slightingly of the king, sometimes through anger and sometimes through boastfulness. Even so, Alexander, although he now had overwhelming evidence against Philotas, endured these insults in silence and restrained himself, either because he had confidence in Parmenion's loyalty, or because he feared the power and prestige of father and son. But meanwhile, a Macedonian from Chalaestra named Dimnus[121] organized a conspiracy against Alexander, and invited a young man named Nicomachus, with whom he was in love, to take part in the plot. Nicomachus refused to be involved, but told his brother Cebalinus of the attempt. Cebalinus then went to Philotas and demanded that he should take them both to Alexander, as they had something of the greatest urgency to tell him. Philotas, however, for some unknown reason, did not arrange the interview, making out that the king was engaged on more important business, and he did this not once but twice. By this time the brothers had become suspicious of Philotas,

and so they turned to somebody else who brought them into the king's presence. First of all they revealed Dimnus' plot and then they made a number of insinuations against Philotas, because he had twice disregarded their requests to see the king.

This news enraged Alexander, and when he learnt that Dimnus had resisted arrest, and had been killed by the men who had been sent to fetch him, he became still more disturbed as he concluded that he had lost the chance to uncover the plot. He felt bitter resentment against Philotas and became all the more ready to listen to those who had long hated his friend. These enemies now said openly that it was folly on the king's part to suppose that a man such as Dimnus, who came from the obscure town of Chalaestra, would ever have undertaken such a daring enterprise on his own account: it was obvious that he was a mere agent, a tool in the hands of somebody of much greater power, and that Alexander must look for the source of the conspiracy among those who had most interest in keeping it concealed. Once the king had begun to listen to these insinuations and suspicions, Philotas' enemies brought innumerable accusations against him. He was arrested, interrogated and tortured in the presence of the king's companions, while Alexander himself listened to the examination from behind a curtain. We are told that when he heard Philotas uttering broken and pitiful cries and pleas for mercy to Hephaestion, he exclaimed, 'Ah, Philotas, if you are so weak and unmanly as this, how could you involve yourself in such a dangerous business?' Philotas was executed, and immediately afterwards Alexander sent messengers to Media and had Parmenion put to death as well. This was a man who had rendered many great services to Philip and who, of all Alexander's older friends, had urged him most strongly to undertake the invasion of Asia; of his three sons he had seen two die in battle and now he was put to death[122] with the third.

These actions made Alexander dreaded by many of his friends, above all by Antipater,[123] and caused him to enter into secret negotiations with the Aetolians and make an alliance with them. The latter were afraid of Alexander, because they had destroyed the city of the Oeniadae, and because the king,

when he heard of it, had said that Aetolians would be punished
not by the sons of the Oeniadae but by him.[124]

50. Not long after this[125] came the killing of Cleitus, whose
treatment, on the bare facts of the case, appears to have been
even more shocking than that of Philotas. However, if we consider both the occasion and the cause, we find that it was a
misfortune rather than a deliberate act, and that it was Cleitus'
evil genius[126] which took advantage of Alexander's anger and
intoxication to destroy him. This was how it came about. Some
men arrived from the coast bringing a present of Greek fruit for
the king. Alexander admired its beauty and ripeness and sent
for Cleitus to share it with him. It so happened that Cleitus was
in the midst of sacrificing, but he at once left the ceremony
and three of the sheep on which libations had been poured followed him. When the king heard of this, he consulted Aristander
his diviner and Cleomantis the Spartan. Since they interpreted
this as an evil omen, he ordered them to offer up a sacrifice at
once for Cleitus' safety. Alexander was all the more disturbed
because two days before he had dreamt a strange dream in
which he saw Cleitus sitting with the sons of Parmenion: they
were dressed in black and all four of them were dead. However,
before the sacrifice offered on Cleitus' behalf was concluded,
he came at once to dine with the king, who had already sacrificed on that day to the Dioscuri. After the company had drunk
a good deal, somebody began to sing the verses of a man named
Pranichus (or Pierion according to another account), which
had been written to humiliate and make fun of some Macedonian commanders who had recently been defeated by the
barbarians. The older members of the party took offence at this
and showed their resentment of both the poet and the singer,
but Alexander and those sitting near him listened with obvious
pleasure and told the man to continue. Thereupon Cleitus, who
had already drunk too much and was rough and hot-tempered
by nature, became angrier than ever and shouted that it was
not right for Macedonians to be insulted in the presence of
barbarians and enemies, even if they had met with misfortune,
for they were better men than those who were laughing at

them. Alexander retorted that in trying to disguise cowardice as misfortune, Cleitus was pleading his own case. At this, Cleitus sprang to his feet and shouted back, 'Yes, it was my cowardice that saved your life, you who call yourself the son of the gods, when you were turning your back to Spithridates' sword.[127] And it is the blood of these Macedonians and their wounds which have made you so great that you disown your father, Philip, and claim to be the son of Ammon!'

51. These words made Alexander furious. 'You scum,' he cried out, 'do you think that you can keep on speaking of me like this, and stir up trouble among the Macedonians and not pay for it?' 'Oh, but we Macedonians do pay for it,' Cleitus retorted. 'Just think of the rewards we get for all our efforts. It's the dead ones who are happy, because they never lived to see Macedonians being beaten with Median rods, or begging the Persians for an audience with our own king.' Cleitus blurted out all this impulsively, whereupon Alexander's friends jumped up and began to abuse him, while the older men tried to calm down both sides. Then Alexander turned to Xenodochus of Cardia and Artemius of Colophon and asked them, 'When you see the Greeks walking about among the Macedonians, do they not look to you like demigods among so many wild beasts?' But Cleitus refused to take back anything and he challenged Alexander to speak out whatever he wished to say in front of the company, or else not invite to his table free-born men who spoke their minds: it would be better for him to spend his time among barbarians and slaves, who would prostrate themselves before his white tunic and his Persian belt. At this Alexander could no longer control his rage: he hurled one of the apples that lay on the table at Cleitus, hit him and then looked around for his dagger. One of his bodyguards, Aristophanes,[128] had already moved it out of harm's way, and the others crowded around him and begged him to be quiet. But Alexander leapt to his feet and shouted out in Macedonian for his corps of guards,[129] a signal that this was an extreme emergency;[130] then he ordered his trumpeter to sound the alarm, and because the man was unwilling to obey, he struck him with his fist. After-

wards, the trumpeter was highly praised for his conduct, because it was chiefly thanks to him that the whole camp was not thrown into a turmoil. Meanwhile, as Cleitus still refused to give way, his friends with great difficulty pushed him out of the banqueting room. But soon afterwards he came in by another door, and, as he did so, recited in a loud and contemptuous voice this line from Euripides' *Andromache*: 'Alas, what evil customs reign in Greece.'[131] At this Alexander seized a spear from one of his guards, faced Cleitus as he was drawing aside the curtain of the doorway and ran him through. With a roar of pain and a groan, Cleitus fell, and immediately the king's anger left him. When he came to himself and saw his friends standing around him speechless, he snatched the weapon out of the dead body and would have plunged it into his own throat if his bodyguards had not forestalled him by seizing his hands and carrying him by force into his chamber.

52. There he spent the rest of the night and the whole of the following day sobbing in an agony of remorse. At last, he lay exhausted by his grief, uttering deep groans but unable to speak a word, until his friends, alarmed at his silence, forced their way into his room. He paid no attention to what any of them said, except that when Aristander the diviner reminded him of the dream he had had concerning Cleitus, and its significance, and told him that these events had long ago been ordained by fate, he seemed to accept this assurance. For this reason they brought to him the philosopher, Callisthenes, who was the great-nephew of Aristotle, and Anaxarchus of Abdera. Callisthenes used a gentle and comforting manner towards the king to relieve his suffering, skirting round the subject and never referring to it directly in order to spare his feelings. Anaxarchus, on the other hand, had always pursued an independent approach to philosophy and had acquired a reputation for despising and looking down on convention. As soon as he entered the room, he exclaimed, 'Here is Alexander, whom the whole world now looks to for an example, and he is lying on the floor weeping like a slave, terrified of the law and of what men will say of him. And yet all the time it should be he who represents the law and

sets up the criterion of justice, since by his victories he has gained the right to govern and command, and need never submit like a slave to the foolish opinions of others. Do you not know that Zeus has Justice and Law seated by his side to prove that everything that is done by the ruler of the world is lawful and just?' By using arguments such as these, Anaxarchus certainly succeeded in relieving Alexander's sufferings, but he made him in many ways more proud and autocratic than before. He also gained great favour for himself and managed to make Callisthenes' company, which had never been very welcome because of his austerity, even more disagreeable to the king.

The story goes that one day at table, when the conversation turned upon the climate and the temperature of the air, Callisthenes, who took the view of those who said it was colder in Persia than in Greece, was contradicted by Anaxarchus in his usual aggressive manner, whereupon he retorted, 'Surely you must admit that it is colder here, for in Greece you used to wear just one cloak all through the winter, while here you are sitting at table with three rugs wrapped around you.' This remark naturally made Anaxarchus dislike him more than ever.

53. Callisthenes also annoyed the other sophists and flatterers of Alexander's court because he attracted the young men by his eloquence and because he was equally admired by the older generation on account of his orderly, dignified and self-sufficient way of life. His behaviour certainly confirmed the reports which were current as to why he had left Greece, namely that he had come to Alexander in the hope of persuading him to resettle his native city of Olynthus.[132] His great reputation naturally exposed him to some envy, but his behaviour at times also made it easy for his detractors to malign him, since he often refused invitations, and when he did appear in company, he was apt to make it plain that he disliked or disapproved of what was going on by sitting wrapped in a morose silence, so that even Alexander said of him that he could not abide 'A wise man who is not wise to his own interests'.[133]

There is a story that on one occasion when a large company

had been invited to dine with the king, Callisthenes was called upon, as the cup passed to him, to speak in praise of the Macedonians. This theme he handled so eloquently that the guests rose to applaud and threw their garlands at him. At this, Alexander quoted Euripides' line, '*On noble subjects all men can speak well.*'[134] 'But now,' he went on, 'show us the power of your eloquence by criticizing the Macedonians so that they can recognize their shortcomings and improve themselves.' So Callisthenes turned to the other side of the picture and delivered a long list of attacks on the Macedonians, pointing out that the rise of Philip's power had been brought about by divisions among the rest of the Greeks, and quoting the verse, '*Once civil strife has begun, even scoundrels may find themselves honoured.*'[135] This speech earned him the implacable hatred of the Macedonians, and Alexander remarked that it was not his eloquence that Callisthenes had demonstrated, but his ill will towards them.

54. According to Hermippus, this is the account which Stroebus, the slave who read aloud for Callisthenes, gave to Aristotle of the quarrel between Callisthenes and Alexander. He also says that when Callisthenes understood that he had antagonized the king, he repeated two or three times, as he was taking his leave, the line, '*Braver by far than yourself was Patroclus, but death did not spare him.*'[136] So Aristotle seems to have come near the truth when he said that Callisthenes possessed great eloquence, but lacked common sense.

But at least in his firm opposition to the practice of obeisance he behaved like a true philosopher, and he was the only man to express in public the resentment which all the oldest and best of the Macedonians felt in private. By persuading the king not to insist on this tribute, he delivered the Greeks from a great disgrace and Alexander from an even greater one, but at the same time he destroyed himself, because he left the impression that he had gained his point by force rather than by persuasion.

Chares of Mitylene says that on one occasion at a banquet Alexander, after he had drunk, passed the cup to one of his friends, who took it and rose so as to face the shrine of the household; next he drank in his turn, then did obeisance to Alexander, kissed him and resumed his place on the couch. All the guests did the same in succession, until the cup came to Callisthenes. The king was talking to Hephaestion and paying no attention to Callisthenes, and the philosopher, after he had drunk, came forward to kiss him. At this Demetrius, who was also called Pheidon, called out, 'Sire, do not kiss him; he is the only one who has not done obeisance to you.' Alexander, therefore, refused to kiss him, and Callisthenes exclaimed in a loud voice, 'Very well then, I shall go away the poorer by a kiss.'

55. As this rift between them developed, it was easy for Hephaestion to be believed when he said that Callisthenes had promised him that he would do obeisance to Alexander and had then broken his word. Besides this, men such as Lysimachus and Hagnon persistently spread the story that the sophist went round giving himself great airs as though he were determined to abolish a tyranny, and that the young men flocked to him and followed him everywhere, as though he were the only free spirit among so many tens of thousands.

These slanders spread by Callisthenes' enemies became all the more plausible when the plot that had been laid against Alexander by Hermolaus and his fellow-conspirators was discovered. According to these accusers, when Hermolaus asked the philosopher how he might become the most famous of men, Callisthenes said, 'By killing the most famous of men,' and further, that when he was encouraging Hermolaus to make the attempt, he told him not to be overawed by Alexander's golden couch, but to remember that he was dealing with a man who was subject to sickness and wounds like anybody else. Yet the fact remains that not one of Hermolaus' accomplices, even under the stress of torture, denounced Callisthenes. Indeed, Alexander himself, in the letters which he immediately wrote to Craterus, Attalus and Alcetas, says that the youths had confessed under torture that the conspiracy was entirely their own and that nobody else knew of it. However, in a letter which he wrote later to Antipater and in which he includes Callisthenes in the general accusation, he says: 'The youths were stoned to death by the Macedonians, but as for the sophist, I shall punish him myself, and I shall not forget those who sent him to me, or the others who give shelter in their cities to those who plot against my life.' In these words, at least, he plainly reveals his hostility to Aristotle, in whose house Callisthenes had been brought up, since he was a son of Hero, who was Aristotle's niece. As for Callisthenes' death, according to some accounts Alexander ordered him to be hanged, but others have it that he was thrown into chains and died of disease. Chares tells us that after his arrest he was kept in prison for seven months in order to be tried by the Council of the League of Corinth in the presence of Aristotle, but that about the time when Alexander was wounded in India he died of excessive corpulence and the disease of lice.

56. These events, however, belong to a later period. Meanwhile Demaratus of Corinth,[137] although he was by now an old man, was eager to visit Alexander, and when the king had received him, Demaratus declared that those Greeks who had died before they could see Alexander seated on the throne of Darius had missed one of the greatest pleasures in the world. However, he did not live long to enjoy the king's friendship, but fell sick and died soon afterwards. He was given a magnificent funeral. The army raised a mound of 80 cubits in height and of a great circumference as a memorial to him, and his ashes were carried down to the coast in a four-horse chariot which was richly adorned.

57. When Alexander was about to cross into India,[138] he saw that his army was over-encumbered with booty and had lost its mobility. So at dawn, after the baggage had been loaded, he burnt first those wagons which belonged to himself and his companions, and then gave orders to set fire to those of the Macedonians. In the event, his decision proved to have been more difficult to envisage than it was to execute. Only a few of the soldiers resented it: the great majority cheered with delight and raised their battle-cry; they gladly shared out the necessities

for the campaign with those who needed them and then they helped to burn and destroy any superfluous possessions with their own hands. Alexander was filled with enthusiasm at their spirit, and his hopes rose to their highest pitch. By this time he was already feared by his men for his relentless severity in punishing any dereliction of duty. For example, he put to death Menander, one of the companions, because he had been placed in command of a garrison and had refused to remain there, and he shot down with his own hand one of the barbarians named Orsodates who had rebelled against him.

When a ewe brought forth a lamb whose head was covered with a substance which in shape and colour resembled the tiara of the king of Persia, with testicles on either side of it, Alexander was revolted by this prodigy and had himself purified by the Babylonian priests, whom he had become accustomed to bring on his campaigns for such purposes. But when he spoke of this portent to his friends, he explained that he was alarmed not for his own sake but for theirs, because he feared that in the event of his death God might allow his power to fall into the hands of some unworthy and feeble successor. However, a more encouraging phenomenon followed, which dispelled his misgivings. The head of Alexander's household servants, a man named Proxenus, was digging a place to pitch the royal tent by the bank of the River Oxus, when he uncovered a spring of a smooth and fatty liquid. When the top of this was strained off, there gushed forth a pure and clear oil which appeared to be exactly like olive oil both in odour and in taste, and was also identical in smoothness and brightness, and this, too, in a country where there were no olive trees. It is said that the water of the Oxus too is extraordinarily soft and gives a glossy texture to the skin of all those who bathe in it. It is clear that Alexander was delighted with this portent, if we may judge from a letter he wrote to Antipater, in which he speaks of it as one of the greatest signs of favour ever granted to him by God. The diviners, however, interpreted the omen as forecasting a campaign which would be a glorious one but also arduous and painful, for oil, they pointed out, was given to men by God as a refreshment for their labours.[139]

58. Alexander encountered many dangers in the battles he fought and was severely wounded, but the greatest losses his army suffered were caused by lack of provisions and by the rigours of the climate. However, he was anxious to prove that boldness can triumph over fortune and courage over superior force; he was convinced that while there are no defences so impregnable that they will keep out the brave man, there are likewise none so strong that they will keep the coward safe. It is said that when he was besieging the fortress of a ruler named Sisimithres,[140] which was situated upon a steep and inaccessible rock, his soldiers despaired of capturing it. Alexander asked Oxyartes whether Sisimithres himself was a man of spirit and received the reply that he was the greatest coward in the world. 'Then what you are telling me', Alexander went on, 'is that we can take the fortress, since there is no strength in its defender.' And in fact he did capture this place by striking terror into Sisimithres. When he was attacking another equally inaccessible stronghold with the younger Macedonians, he said to one of them who was called Alexander, 'You at least will have to prove yourself a brave man to live up to your name.' After this the young man fought with the utmost gallantry and was killed, to the great sorrow of the king. When the Macedonians were hesitating to attack the fortress of Nysa, because there was a deep river in front of it, Alexander halted on the bank and cried out, 'What a wretch I am! Why did I never learn to swim?' and he made ready to ford it, carrying his shield on his arm. After he had ordered a halt in the fighting, ambassadors came from a number of the cities he was besieging to beg for terms, and they were amazed to find him still unkempt and clad in full armour. Then, when a cushion was brought for him, he ordered the most senior of the ambassadors, whose name was Acouphis, to seat himself on it. Acouphis, who was much impressed with his magnanimity and courtesy, asked what he wanted the people to do to earn his friendship. Alexander told him, 'I should like your countrymen to appoint you as their ruler and send me a hundred of their best men.' At this Acouphis laughed and replied, 'I shall rule them better, sire, if I send you the worst men rather than the best.'

59. There was a prince named Taxiles[141] whose territory, we are told, was as large as Egypt and contained good pasturage as well as fertile arable land. He was a wise ruler, and after he had greeted Alexander he asked him, 'Why should we fight battles with one another? You have not come here to rob us of water or of the necessities of life, and these are the only things for which sensible men are obliged to fight. As for other kinds of wealth and property so-called, if I possess more than you, I am ready to be generous towards you, and if I have less, I shall not refuse any benefits you may offer.' Alexander was delighted at this, took his hand and said, 'Perhaps you think that after your kind words and courtesy our meeting will pass off without a contest. No, you shall not get the better of me in this way: I shall fight with you to the last, but only in the services I offer you, for I will not have you outdo me in generosity.' Alexander received many gifts from him, but returned even more, and finally presented him with 1,000 talents in coin. This behaviour greatly annoyed his friends, but it made many of the barbarians far better disposed towards him.

Now, the best fighters among the Indians were mercenaries, whose custom it was to travel from one city to another as they were needed: they defended their clients vigorously and caused Alexander heavy losses. So he concluded a truce with them when they were in one city, allowed them to leave, and then attacked them on the march and annihilated them. This action remains a blot on his career as a soldier: on all other occasions he observed the normal usages of war and behaved like a king. As for the philosophers,[142] they gave him as much trouble as the mercenaries, because they denounced those of the local rulers who went over to him and at the same time encouraged the free peoples to revolt: for this reason he had many of them hanged.

60. The events of the campaign against Porus[143] are described in Alexander's letters. He tells us that the River Hydaspes flowed between the two camps, and that Porus stationed his elephants on the opposite bank and kept the crossing continually watched. Alexander caused a great deal of noise and commotion to be made day after day in his camp and in this

way accustomed the barbarians not to be alarmed by his movements. Then, on a stormy and moonless night, he took a part
of his infantry and the best of his cavalry, marched some distance along the river past the enemy's position and then crossed
over to a small island. Here he was overtaken by a violent
storm of rain accompanied by tremendous bursts of thunder
and lightning. Although he saw that a number of his men were
struck dead by the lightning, he continued the advance and made
for the opposite bank. After the storm, the Hydaspes, which
was roaring down in high flood, had scooped out a deep channel, so that much of the stream was diverted in this direction
and the ground between the two currents had become broken
and slippery and made it impossible for his men to gain a firm
footing. It was on this occasion that Alexander is said to have
exclaimed, 'O you Athenians, will you ever believe what risks I
am running just to earn your praise?'

This is the version which Onesicritus gives of the battle. But
according to Alexander's own account, the Macedonians left
their rafts and waded across the breach in full armour, up to
their chests in water. After making the crossing, Alexander rode
on for more than two miles ahead of the infantry; he calculated
that if the enemy attacked with their cavalry he could overcome
them easily, and that if they moved up their phalanx, there
would still be time for his own to join him. His judgement
proved quite correct. He was attacked by a thousand of the
enemy's cavalry and sixty of their chariots, and killed four
hundred of their horsemen. Then Porus, understanding that
Alexander had crossed, advanced against him with his whole
army, but left behind a force sufficient to prevent the remainder
of the Macedonians from crossing. Alexander, remembering the
threat of the enemy's elephants and their superior numbers,
attacked their left wing and ordered Coenus to charge against
the right. Both flanks of the Indian army were routed, and the
defeated troops fell back upon the elephants and crowded into
the centre. Here they rallied and a stubborn hand-to-hand struggle ensued, so that it was not until the eighth hour that the
enemy was overcome. This, then, is the account we have from
the instigator of the battle himself in one of his letters.

Most historians agree that Porus was about six and a half feet tall, and that his size and huge physique made him appear as suitably mounted upon an elephant as an ordinary man looks on a horse. And yet his elephant, too, was very large and showed an extraordinary intelligence and concern for the king's person. So long as Porus was fighting strongly, it would valiantly defend him and beat off his attackers, but as soon as it recognized that its master was growing weak from the thrusts and missiles that had wounded him, it knelt quietly on the ground for fear that he might fall off, and with its trunk took hold of each spear and drew it out of his body. When Porus was taken prisoner, Alexander asked him how he wished to be treated. 'As a king,' Porus answered, and when Alexander went on to ask whether he had anything more to say, the reply came, 'Those words, "as a king", include everything.' So Alexander not only allowed him to govern his former kingdom, but he also added to it a province which included the territory of the independent peoples he had subdued. These are said to have numbered fifteen nations, five thousand towns of considerable size and innumerable villages. His other conquests embraced an area three times the size of this, and he appointed Philip, one of the companions, to rule it as satrap.

61. After this battle with Porus, Bucephalas also died, not immediately but some while later. Most historians report that he died of wounds received in the battle, for which he was being treated, but according to Onesicritus it was from old age, for by this time he was thirty years old. Alexander was plunged into grief at his death and felt that he had lost nothing less than a friend and a comrade. He founded a city in his memory on the banks of the Hydaspes and called it Bucephalia, and there is also a story that when he lost a dog named Peritas, of which he was very fond and which he had brought up from a puppy, he again founded a city and called it after the dog. The historian Sotion tells us that he learnt this from Potamon of Lesbos.

62. Another consequence of this battle with Porus was that it blunted the edge of the Macedonians' courage and made them

determined not to advance any further into India. It was only with great difficulty that they had defeated an enemy who had put into the field no more than 20,000 infantry and 2,000 cavalry, and so, when Alexander insisted on crossing the Ganges,[144] they opposed him outright. The river, they discovered, was three and a half miles across and one hundred fathoms deep, and the opposite bank swarmed with a gigantic host of infantry, horsemen and elephants. It was said that the kings of the Gandaridae and the Praesii were waiting for Alexander's attack with an army of 80,000 cavalry, 200,000 infantry, 8,000 chariots and 6,000 fighting elephants, and this report was no exaggeration, for Sandrocottus,[145] the king of this territory who reigned there not long afterwards, presented 500 elephants to Seleucus, and overran and conquered the whole of India with an army of 600,000 men.

At first, Alexander was so overcome with disappointment and anger that he shut himself up and lay in his tent. He felt that unless he could cross the Ganges, he owed no thanks to his troops for what they had already achieved; instead, he regarded their having turned back as an admission of defeat. However, his friends set themselves to reason with him and console him, and the soldiers crowded round the entrance to his tent and pleaded with him, uttering loud cries and lamentations, until he relented and gave orders to break camp. But when he did so, he devised a number of ruses and deceptions to impress the inhabitants of the region. For example, he had arms, horses' mangers and bits prepared, all of which exceeded the normal size or height or weight, and these were left scattered about the country. He also set up altars for the gods of Greece,[146] and even down to the present day the kings of the Praesii cross the river and do honour to these and offer sacrifice on them in the Greek fashion. Sandrocottus, who was then no more than a boy, saw Alexander himself, and we are told that in later years he often remarked that Alexander was within a step of conquering the whole country, since the king who ruled it at that time was hated and despised because of his vicious character and his lowly birth.

63. Alexander was now eager to look upon the outer sea. He had a large number of oar-propelled ferries and rafts con-

structed, and was rowed down the rivers on these at a leisurely speed. But his voyage was by no means a peaceful and certainly not a passive affair. As he travelled downstream, he would land, assault the cities near the banks and subdue them all. However, when he attacked the people known as the Malli, who are said to be the most warlike of all the Indians, he nearly lost his life. After the defenders had been driven from the walls by volleys of missiles, he was the first to scramble to the top of the wall by means of a scaling-ladder. The ladder was smashed, so that no more Macedonians could join him, and the barbarians began to gather inside along the bottom of the wall and to shoot at him from below. Finding himself almost alone and exposed to their missiles, Alexander crouched down, leapt into their midst and by good luck landed on his feet. Then, as he brandished his arms, it seemed to the barbarians as if a dazzling sheet of flame suddenly took shape in front of his body,[147] and they scattered and fled. But when they saw that there were only two of his guards accompanying him, they rushed in to attack him. Some of them engaged him hand to hand, and rained blows upon his armour with sword and spear as he strove to defend himself, while another, standing a little way apart, shot at him with a bow. The shaft was so well aimed and struck him with such force that it pierced his breast-plate and lodged in his chest between the ribs. The impact was so violent that Alexander staggered back and sank to his knees; his attacker rushed up with his drawn scimitar in his hand, while Peucestas and Limnaeus threw themselves in front of him. Both men were wounded and Limnaeus was killed, but Peucestas stood firm, while Alexander killed the barbarian with his own hand. But he was wounded over and over again, and at last received a blow on the neck from a club which forced him to lean against the wall, although he still faced his assailants. At this moment the Macedonians swarmed round him, snatched him up as he lost consciousness and carried him to his tent. Immediately, the rumour ran through the camp that he had been killed. Meanwhile, his attendants with great difficulty sawed off the wooden shaft of the arrow and thus succeeded in removing his breast-plate; they then had to cut out the arrow-

head, which was embedded between his ribs and measured, so
we are told, four fingers' width in length and three in breadth.
When it was extracted, the king fainted away and came very
near to death, but recovered. Even when the danger was past,
he remained weak and for a long time needed careful nursing
and was obliged to stick to a strict regimen. Then one day, as
he heard a clamour outside his tent, he understood that the
Macedonians were yearning to see him, and so he took his cloak
and went out to them. After sacrificing to the gods, he once
more boarded his vessel and proceeded down the river, subduing great cities and large tracts of territory as he went.

64. He captured ten of the 'naked philosophers' who had played
the most active part in persuading Sabbas to revolt and had
stirred up most trouble for the Macedonians. These philosophers enjoyed a great reputation for their ingenuity in
devising short pithy answers to questions, and so Alexander
confronted them with a series of conundrums. He had previously announced that he would put to death the first man who
gave a wrong answer, and then the rest in order on the same
principle, and he ordered one of them, the eldest, to act as judge
in the contest. The first was asked which were more numerous,
the living or the dead. 'The living,' he replied, 'since the dead no
longer exist.' The second was asked whether the land or the sea
breeds the larger creatures. 'The land,' he said, 'since the sea is
a part of it.' The third was asked, 'Which is the most cunning
of animals?' and answered, 'The animal which man has not yet
discovered.' The fourth was asked why he had incited Sabbas
to revolt and replied, 'Because I wanted him to live honourably
or to die honourably.' The fifth was asked whether he thought
the day or the night was created first. 'The day,' he replied, 'by
one day.' When he saw that the king was astonished by this
reply, he added that abstruse questions necessarily produce
abstruse answers. Turning to the sixth, Alexander questioned
him on how a man might make himself most beloved. 'If he
possesses supreme power,' he replied, 'and yet does not inspire
fear.' Of the remaining three, one was asked how a man could
become a god, and replied, 'By doing something a man cannot

do.' Another was asked which was stronger, life or death, and replied, 'Life, since it carries so many evils.' The final one was asked how long it was good for a man to live, and replied, 'Until he has stopped regarding death as better than life.' So then Alexander turned to the judge and told him to give his verdict, which was that each of them had answered worse than the one before. 'In that case', Alexander replied, 'you shall be executed first yourself for having given such a verdict.' 'No, your majesty,' replied the judge, 'unless you were lying when you said that you would put to death first the man who gave the worst answer.'

65. Alexander distributed presents to all ten and sent them away unharmed. He then sent Onesicritus to those philosophers who enjoyed the highest reputation but lived a secluded and contemplative life, and invited them to visit him. Onesicritus himself belonged to the school of Diogenes the Cynic, and he tells us that one of the Indians, Calanus, treated him most arrogantly and insolently and told him to take off his clothes and listen to him naked if he wished to hear any of his doctrines, otherwise he would not carry on a conversation, even if the Greek came from Zeus himself. Onesicritus reports that another sage named Dandamis received him more courteously, and when he had spoken at length about Socrates, Pythagoras and Diogenes, Dandamis remarked that they seemed to him to have been men of good natural parts, but to have spent their lives with too submissive an attitude to the laws. According to other writers, however, the only remark which Dandamis made at this meeting was, 'Why did Alexander come all this way to India?' Nevertheless, the prince Taxiles was able to persuade Calanus to visit Alexander. His real name was Sphines, but because he greeted everyone he met not with the Greek salutation *chairete*, but with the Indian word *cale*, the Greeks called him Calanus. It was he, we are told, who first propounded to Alexander the celebrated parable about government, which ran as follows. Calanus threw onto the ground a dry and shrunken piece of hide and put his foot on the outer edge: the hide was thus pressed down at one point on the surface, but rose up at others.

He walked round the circumference and showed that this was what happened whenever he trod on the edge; then finally he put his weight on to the middle, whereupon the whole of the hide lay flat and still. The demonstration was intended to show that Alexander should concentrate the weight of his authority at the centre of his empire and not go wandering around the borders of it.

66. Alexander's voyage down the rivers to the sea occupied seven months. When he reached the ocean[148] with his ships, he sailed out to an island which he himself named Scillustis, while others called it Psiltucis. Here he landed and sacrificed to the gods, and made what observations he could on the nature of the sea and of the coast, as far as it was accessible. Then he offered up a prayer that no man after him might ever pass beyond the bounds of his expedition.

He appointed Nearchus to the supreme command of the fleet, with Onesicritus as its chief pilot, and ordered them to follow the line of the sea-coast, keeping India on their right.[149] Meanwhile, he himself set out by land and marched through the territory of the Oreitae. Here, he endured terrible privations and lost great numbers of men, with the result that he did not bring back from India so much as a quarter of his fighting force. And yet his strength had once amounted to 120,000 infantry and 15,000 cavalry.[150] Some of his men died from disease, some of the wretched food, some of the scorching heat, but most from sheer hunger, for they had to march through an uncultivated region whose inhabitants only eked out a wretched existence. They possessed few sheep and even these were of a stunted breed, and the sea fish on which they subsisted made the animals' flesh rank and unsavoury. It was only with great difficulty that Alexander succeeded in crossing this region in sixty days, but once he reached Gedrosia, he was immediately in a land of plenty, and the satraps and local rulers provided him with all his needs.

67. After resting his force here he set out again and marched for seven days through the territory of Carmania, a march

which soon developed into a kind of Bacchanalian procession. Alexander himself feasted continually, day and night, reclining with his companions on a dais built upon a high and conspicuous rectangular platform, the whole structure being slowly drawn along by eight horses. Innumerable wagons followed the royal table, some of them covered with purple or embroidered canopies, others shaded by the boughs of trees, which were constantly kept fresh and green; these vehicles carried the rest of Alexander's officers, all of them crowned with flowers and drinking wine. Not a single shield, helmet or pike was to be seen, but along the whole line of the march the soldiers kept dipping their cups, drinking-horns or earthenware goblets into huge casks and mixing-bowls and toasting one another, some drinking as they marched, others sprawled by the wayside, while the whole landscape resounded with the music of pipes and flutes, with harping and singing and the cries of women rapt with the divine frenzy. Not only drinking but all the other forms of bacchanalian licence attended this straggling and disorderly march, as though the god himself were present to lead the revels.[151] Then, when Alexander arrived at the palace of Gedrosia,[152] he again allowed the army time to rest and celebrated another festival. It is said that one day, after he had drunk well, he went to watch some contests in dancing and singing and that his favourite, Bagoas, won the prize; thereupon, the young man came across the theatre, still in his performer's costume and wearing his crown as victor, and seated himself beside the king. At the sight, the Macedonians applauded loudly and shouted to Alexander to kiss the winner, until at last the king put his arms around him and kissed him.

68. Here Nearchus came inland and joined him, and Alexander was so delighted with the reports of his voyage[153] that he had the impulse to sail down the Euphrates himself with a large fleet, and then to coast round Arabia and Africa and enter the Mediterranean by way of the Pillars of Heracles. He began to have vessels of many different kinds constructed at Thapsacus and to collect sailors and pilots from all parts. But meanwhile, the difficulties he had encountered during the campaign up-

country, the wound he had received in the battle with the Malli and the heavy losses which his army was reported to have suffered had raised doubts as to his safe return: this combination of events had encouraged the subject peoples to revolt and his various viceroys and satraps to act in an unjust, rapacious and arrogant manner. In short, the whole empire was in turmoil and an atmosphere of instability prevailed everywhere. Even at home, his mother Olympias and his sister Cleopatra had been intriguing against Antipater, and had divided the kingdom between them, Olympias taking Epirus and Cleopatra Macedonia. When Alexander heard of this, he remarked that his mother had made the wiser choice, since the Macedonians would never tolerate being governed by a woman. For these reasons he now sent Nearchus back to sea: his plan was to fill the whole coastline with cities,[154] while he himself would march down and punish those of his officers who had abused their powers. He killed Oxyartes, one of the sons of Abuletes, with his own hands, running him through with a pike, and when Abuletes brought him 3,000 talents in coin instead of the provisions which he ought to have supplied, Alexander ordered the money to be thrown to the horses. Then, when they did not touch it, he asked Abuletes, 'What use are your provisions to us then?' and ordered him to be imprisoned.

69. In Persis Alexander first distributed money to the women: in this he was following the custom of the Persian kings,[155] who, whenever they arrived there, presented each woman with a gold coin. For this reason, it is said, some of the kings seldom visited, and Ochus never set foot there at all:[156] he was mean enough to exile himself from his native land. Secondly, Alexander discovered that the tomb of Cyrus had been plundered and he had the offender put to death, even though he was a prominent Macedonian from Pella named Polymachus. When he had read the inscription on the tomb, he ordered it to be repeated below in Greek characters. The text was as follows:

O man, whoever you are and wherever you come from, for I know you will come, I am Cyrus who won the Persians their empire. Do not therefore grudge me this little earth that covers my body.

These words made a deep impression on Alexander, since they reminded him of the uncertainty and mutability of mortal life.

It was here, too, that Calanus, who had suffered for some while from a disease of the intestine, asked for a funeral pyre to be made ready for him. He rode up to it on horseback, said a prayer, poured a libation for himself and cut off a lock of hair to throw on the fire. Then he climbed on to the pyre, greeted the Macedonians who were present and urged them to make this a day of gaiety and celebration and to drink deep with the king, whom, he said, he would soon see in Babylon.[157] With these words he lay down and covered himself. He made no movement as the flames approached him, and continued to lie in exactly the same position as at first, and so immolated himself in a manner acceptable to the gods, according to the ancestral custom of the wise men of his country. Many years afterwards, an Indian who belonged to the retinue of Augustus Caesar performed the same action in Athens, and the so-called Indian's tomb can be seen there to this day.[158]

70. After Alexander had left the funeral pyre, he invited a number of his friends and officers to dine with him and proposed a contest in drinking neat wine, the winner of which was to receive a crown. The victor was Promachus, who downed four pitchers, or about 12 quarts: the prize was a crown worth a talent, but he lived for only three days afterwards. Of the other competitors, forty-one, according to Chares, died of the effects of the wine: they were seized by a violent chill after the drinking.

Alexander celebrated the marriages of his companions at Susa,[159] he himself marrying Stateira, the daughter of Darius, and assigning the noblest of the Persian women to the bravest of his men. He also invited to a collective wedding-banquet the Macedonians who had already married Persian wives. We are told that 9,000 guests attended this feast and each of them was given a gold cup for the libations. The whole entertainment was carried out on a grand scale and Alexander went so far as to discharge all the debts owed by any of his guests: the outlay for the occasion amounted to 9,870 talents. Antigenes, one of Alexander's officers who had only one eye, contrived to get himself fraudulently enrolled as a debtor. He produced a witness who pretended to have lent him a sum at the bank repaid him the money. Then when the fraud was discovered Alexander deprived him of his command and banished him from the court. But Antigenes had a brilliant military record. While he was still a young man, he had served under Philip at the siege of Perinthus, and when he was hit in the eye by a bolt from a catapult, he had refused to leave the fighting or have the dart extracted until he had helped to drive back the enemy and shut them up in the city. Accordingly, he could not endure the humiliation of his disgrace, and it was clear that he intended to kill himself out of grief and despair. The king was afraid that he would really carry out his intention, and so he pardoned him and told him to keep the money.

71. The 30,000 boys whom he had left behind to be given a Greek education and military training had now grown into active and handsome men and had developed a wonderful skill and agility in their military exercises. Alexander was delighted with their progress, but the Macedonians were disheartened and deeply disturbed for their own future, because they assumed that the king would henceforth have less regard for them. So when he arranged to send the sick and disabled among them to the sea-coast,[160] they protested that he was not only doing them an injustice but deliberately humiliating them. He had first worn them out in every kind of service, and now he was turning them away in disgrace and throwing them upon the mercy of their parents and native cities, no longer the men they were when he recruited them. Why not send them all home and write off the Macedonians as useless, now that he had this corps of young ballet-soldiers, with whom he could go on to conquer the world? These words stung Alexander and he angrily rebuked the Macedonians, dismissed his guards, handed over their security duties to Persians and recruited from these his

royal escort and personal attendants. When the Macedonians saw him surrounded by these men, while they were barred from his presence and treated as being in disgrace, they were greatly humbled, and when they considered the matter, they understood that they had been almost beside themselves with jealousy and rage. Finally, when they had come to their senses, they presented themselves at Alexander's tent unarmed and dressed only in their tunics, and there they cried out and lamented, threw themselves on his mercy and begged him to deal with them as their baseness and ingratitude deserved. Alexander refused to receive them, although he had already begun to relent, but the men would not go away and remained for two days and nights outside his tent weeping and calling him their master. On the third day he came out, and when he saw them reduced to such a forlorn and pitiful state, he himself wept for a while. Then he reproached them gently for their behaviour and spoke to them kindly; afterwards he dismissed those who were no longer fit for service and gave them generous gratuities. Besides this, he sent instructions to Antipater that at all public contests and in the theatres these men should occupy the best seats and wear garlands on their heads. He also gave orders that the orphaned children of those who had died in his service should continue to receive their fathers' pay.

72. When he arrived in Ecbatana in Media[161] and had dealt with the most pressing of his concerns, he once more turned his attention to plays and spectacles, since 3,000 performers had arrived from Greece. About this time, it happened that Hephaestion had caught a fever, and being a young man who was accustomed to a soldier's life he could not bear to submit to a strict regime. No sooner had his physician, Glaucus, gone off to the theatre, than he sat down to breakfast, devoured a boiled fowl and washed it down with a great cooler-full of wine. He took ill and soon afterwards died. Alexander's grief was uncontrollable. As a sign of mourning, he gave orders that the manes and tails of all horses should be shorn,[162] demolished the battlements of all the neighbouring cities, crucified the unlucky physician and forbade the playing of flutes or any other kind of

music for a long time, until finally an oracle came from Ammon, commanding him to honour Hephaestion and sacrifice to him as a hero.[163] To lighten his sorrow he waged war, as if the tracking down and hunting of men might console him, and subdued the tribe of the Cossaeans,[164] massacring the whole male population from the youths upwards: this was termed a sacrifice to the spirit of Hephaestion.[165] He determined to spend 10,000 talents on the funeral and the tomb for his friend, and as he wished the ingenuity and originality of the design to surpass the expense, he was especially anxious to employ Stasicrates, as this artist was famous for his innovations, which combined an exceptional degree of magnificence, audacity and ostentation.

It was Stasicrates who had remarked to Alexander at an earlier interview that of all mountains it was Mount Athos in Thrace which could most easily be carved into the form and shape of a man, and that if it pleased Alexander to command him, he would shape the mountain into the most superb and durable statue of him in the world: its left hand would enfold a city of 10,000 inhabitants, while out of its right would flow the abundant waters of a river which would pour, like a libation, into the sea. Alexander had declined this proposal, but now he spent his time with his engineers and architects planning projects which were even more outlandish and extravagant.

73. While Alexander was on the way to Babylon,[166] Nearchus, who had joined him after sailing through the great sea and into the Euphrates, told him that he had met some Chaldaeans who had advised the king to stay away from Babylon. Alexander paid no attention to this warning and continued his journey, but when he arrived before the walls of the city he saw a large number of ravens flying about and pecking one another,[167] and some of them fell dead in front of him. Next, he received a report that Apollodorus the governor of Babylon had offered up a sacrifice to try to discover what fate held in store for Alexander, and he then sent for Pythagoras, the diviner who had conducted the sacrifice. Pythagoras admitted that this was true, and Alexander then asked him in what condition he had found the victim. When he received the answer that the liver

had no lobe, 'Ah,' Alexander exclaimed, 'that is a powerful omen.' He did Pythagoras no harm and he began to regret that he had not taken Nearchus' advice, and so he spent most of his time outside the walls of Babylon, either in his tent or in boats on the Euphrates. Many more omens now occurred to trouble him. For instance, a tame ass attacked the finest lion in his menagerie and kicked it to death. On another occasion, Alexander took off his clothes for exercise and played a game of ball. When it was time to dress again, the young men who had joined him in the game suddenly noticed that there was a man sitting silently on the throne and wearing Alexander's diadem and royal robes. When he was questioned, he could say nothing for a long while, but later he came to his senses and explained that he was called Dionysius[168] and was a native of Messenia. He had been accused of some crime, brought to Babylon from the coast and kept for a long time in chains. Then the god Serapis had appeared to him, cast off his chains and brought him to this place, where he had commanded him to put on the king's robe and diadem, take his seat on the throne and hold his peace.

74. When he had heard the man's story, Alexander had him put to death, as the diviners recommended. But his confidence now deserted him, he began to believe that he had lost the favour of the gods and he became increasingly suspicious of his friends. It was Antipater and his sons whom he feared most of all. One of them named Iolas was his chief cup-bearer. The other, Cassander, had only lately arrived in Babylon, and when he saw some of the barbarians doing obeisance before the king, he burst into loud and disrespectful laughter, for he had been brought up as a Greek and had never seen such a spectacle in his life. Alexander was furious at this insult, seized him by the hair with both hands and dashed his head against the wall. On another occasion, when Cassander wished to reply to some men who were making accusations against his father, Antipater, Alexander interrupted him and said, 'What do you mean? Are you really saying that these men have suffered no wrong, but have travelled all this way just to bring a false accusation?' When Cassander replied that the very fact of their having trav-

elled so far from those who could contradict them might point to the charges being false, Alexander laughed and said, 'This reminds me of some of Aristotle's sophisms, which can be used equally well on either side of a question; but if any of you are proved to have done these men even the smallest wrong, you will be sorry for it.' In general, we are told, this fear was implanted so deeply and took such hold of Cassander's mind that even many years later, when he had become king of Macedon and master of Greece, and was walking about one day looking at the sculptures at Delphi, the mere sight of a statue of Alexander struck him with horror, so that he shuddered and trembled in every limb, his head swam and he could scarcely regain control of himself.

75. Alexander had become overwrought and terrified in his own mind, and now abandoned himself to superstition. He interpreted every strange or unusual occurrence, no matter how trivial, as a prodigy or a portent, with the result that the palace was filled with soothsayers, sacrificers, purifiers and prognosticators. Thus, disbelief or contempt for the power of the gods is a terrible thing, but superstition is also terrible; like water, it constantly gravitates to a lower level. So unreasoning dread filled Alexander's mind with foolish misgivings, once he had become a slave to his fears.[169] However, when the verdict of the oracle concerning Hephaestion was brought to him, he laid aside his grief and allowed himself to indulge in a number of sacrifices and drinking-bouts. He gave a splendid banquet in honour of Nearchus, after which he took a bath as his custom was, with the intention of going to bed soon afterwards. But when Medius invited him, he went to his house to join a party, and there, after drinking all through the next day, he began to feel feverish. This did not happen after he had drained Heracles' cup, nor did he become conscious of a sudden pain in the back as if he had been pierced by a spear: these are details with which certain historians felt obliged to embellish the occasion,[170] and thus invent a tragic and moving finale to a great action. Aristobulus tells us that he was seized with a raging fever, that when he became very thirsty he drank wine which

made him delirious, and that he died on the thirtieth day of the month of Daesius.[171]

76. According to journals, the course of his sickness was as follows. On the eighteenth day of the month of Daesius he slept in the bathroom because he was feverish. On the next day, after taking a bath, he moved into the bedchamber and spent the day playing dice with Medius. He took a bath late in the evening, offered sacrifice to the gods, dined and remained feverish throughout the night. On the twentieth he again bathed and sacrificed as usual, and while he was lying down in the bathroom he was entertained by listening to Nearchus' account of his voyage, and his exploration of the great sea. On the twenty-first he passed the time in the same way, but the fever grew more intense; he had a bad night and all through the following day his fever was very high. He had his bed moved and lay in it by the side of the great plunge-bath, and there he discussed with his commanders the vacant posts in the army and how to fill them with experienced officers. On the twenty-fourth his fever was still worse and he had to be carried outside to offer sacrifice. He gave orders to the senior commanders to remain on call in the courtyard of the palace and to the commanders of companies and regiments to spend the night outside. On the twenty-fifth day he was moved to the palace on the other side of the river, and there he slept a little, but his fever did not abate. When his commanders entered the room, he was speechless and remained so on the twenty-sixth. The Macedonians now believed that he was dead; they thronged the doors of the palace and began to shout and threaten the companions, who were at last obliged to let them in. When the doors had been thrown open, they all filed slowly past his bedside one by one, wearing neither cloak nor armour. In the course of this day, too, Python and Seleucus were sent to the temple of Serapis to ask whether Alexander should be moved there, and the god replied that they should leave him where he was. On the twenty-eighth, towards evening, he died.

77. Most of this account follows the version that is given in the journals, word for word. Nobody had any suspicion at the time

that Alexander had been poisoned, but it is said that five years afterwards some information was given, on the strength of which Olympias put many men to death and had the ashes of Iolas, Antipater's son, scattered to the winds on the supposition that he had administered the poison.

According to some writers, it was Aristotle who advised Antipater to arrange the murder, and it was entirely through his efforts that the poison was provided. They cite a man named Hagnothemis as their authority: he claimed to have heard the details from Antigonus, and according to this story the poison consisted of ice-cold water drawn from a certain cliff near Nonacris,[172] where it was gathered up like a thin dew and stored in an ass's hoof. No other vessel could hold the liquid, which was said to be so cold and pungent that it would eat through any other substance. But most authorities consider that this tale of poisoning is pure invention, and this view is strongly supported by the fact that during the quarrels between Alexander's commanders, which continued for many days, the body showed no sign of any such corruption but remained pure and fresh, even though it lay for all that time without receiving any special care.

At this time, Roxane was expecting a child and she was therefore held in special honour by the Macedonians. But she was jealous of Alexander's second wife, Stateira, whom she tricked into visiting her by means of a forged letter, which purported to have come from Alexander. When she had thus got her into her power, she had her murdered, together with her sister, threw the bodies into a well and filled it up with earth. In this crime her accomplice was Perdiccas,[173] who, after Alexander's death, at once succeeded in concentrating the greatest power in his hands, using Arrhidaeus as a figure-head for the authority of the royal house. This Arrhidaeus was a son of Philip's by an obscure and humbly born woman named Philinna, and was backward as a result of some disease. This was neither hereditary nor was it produced by natural causes. On the contrary, it is said that as a boy he had shown an attractive disposition and displayed much promise, but Olympias was believed to have given him drugs which impaired the functions of his body and irreparably injured his brain.[174]

EUMENES

INTRODUCTION TO
EUMENES

[*c.* 361–316 BC]

When Alexander died in Babylon in June 323 BC, he left behind him no heir and no clear successor capable of taking control of the vast empire which he had carved out in his short life. An assembly of the army at Babylon declared as his joint-successors his as yet unborn child, Alexander (IV), and his own half-brother, Arrhidaeus, who took the name Philip (III). Neither was able to shoulder the responsibility of rule at once, since Philip Arrhidaeus was widely believed to suffer from some form of mental handicap, and both were to be used as pawns in the power-games that followed. In the meantime, Alexander's general Perdiccas took over the royal armies and assumed control of the empire in the name of 'the kings' (as Philip III and Alexander IV were known). Craterus, another experienced general who happened to have possession of the royal treasury in Cilicia, was given in his absence the vague title of 'protector of the kings', while Antipater, whom Alexander had left to govern Macedon, had his powers there confirmed. Governorships or satrapies (the word was taken over directly from the language of Persian administration) were distributed to, or confirmed for, other leading Macedonians.

However, central power was weak, and the settlement at Babylon was no more than provisional; in the years that followed, a series of power-struggles convulsed both the conquered territories and the old Greek lands, as Alexander's marshals vied for power. Some, such as Ptolemy in Egypt, sought to establish themselves as independent rulers in parts of the old empire; others struggled to keep the empire together, either in the name of the kings or with the hope of becoming sole ruler themselves. It was not until after the battle of Ipsus in 301 that some form of order emerged from the chaos. By this time both of the kings had been murdered, and the competing generals had set themselves up as kings in their own right, each ruling over part of Alexander's former empire. These Hellenistic kingdoms were to define the shape of Greek history for the next few centuries.

Eumenes, a Greek from the city of Cardia in the Thracian Chersonese, played an important role in the struggles of the first years after Alexander's death. He served under Philip and Alexander, and on Alexander's death was assigned the satrapy of Cappadocia in central Anatolia. In the ensuing conflict – the so-called First War of the Diadochi (Successors) – he backed Perdiccas and the central authority against a coalition of other leading generals including Craterus, Antipater, Antigonus Monophthalmus, Lysimachus and Ptolemy, and won several victories in Asia Minor. After Perdiccas' death in Egypt in 321 or 320, Eumenes found himself outlawed at a gathering of the army and facing an attack by Antigonus. In this second war he switched his loyalty to Antipater's successor, Polyperchon, who was busy in Macedonia, and, after enduring a year-long siege by Antigonus' troops in Nora in Cappadocia, withdrew southeastwards into the old heartland of the Persian empire, where he took over command of the satraps there who were still loyal to the central power as represented now by Polyperchon. After an indecisive battle at Paraetacene in autumn 317 (or 316), he was defeated by Antigonus in early 316 (or 315) at Gabiene in Susiana. His own troops handed him over to Antigonus and he was murdered soon afterwards.

The *Eumenes* is the shortest of Plutarch's *Parallel Lives*. It contains almost nothing on Eumenes' upbringing or early years. There is also no narrative of his service under Philip and Alexander, though we know from a passing remark in ch. 1 and from Arrian (*Anabasis* 5.24) that he served in Alexander's campaign in India in 326. Instead, most of the Life, from chapter 3 onwards, deals exclusively with Eumenes' role in the six and a half years between Alexander's death in 323 and his own murder in probably 316. Even this is not narrated systematically, and the battles are reduced to disconnected scenes, selected and grouped for the light they throw on Eumenes' character. All we get, for example, of the campaign against Antigonus in 320–19 is a series of stories about Eumenes' cleverness in finding pay for his troops and his resilience under pressure. Similarly, the battle of Paraetacene is missed out almost entirely; Plutarch reduces it to two anecdotes about how Eumenes' presence, even on his sick-bed, inspired his men with courage for battle (chs. 14–15). This should not be seen as the result of carelessness on Plutarch's part, or be taken to imply that he did not know the basic narrative. Rather, these examples show that Plutarch expected that his readers would already know the rough outline; as he declared at the start of the *Life of Alexander*, his focus is often not on narrating the events themselves but on bringing out what they might reveal of the subject's character.

A particular interest of Plutarch in this Life are Eumenes' personal relationships, both with his men and with the leading Macedonians. This theme is first in evidence in the stories recorded in chapter 2 about his quarrels with Alexander's close friend Hephaestion when both served under Alexander. After Alexander's death it is Eumenes' personal quarrel with Antipater and with Hecataeus, tyrant of Cardia, which motivates him to remain loyal to Perdiccas. Later, we hear a good deal about his ability to inspire his men even in the most difficult of circumstances, about their love and respect for him and about the ruses he employs to maintain the loyalty of the fractious Macedonian commanders serving under him, especially in the final campaign in Susiana. In this campaign, Plutarch focuses not on the military details but on the disloyalty and plots of his fellow-officers and the treachery of his own men. This emphasis must have been found in at least one of Plutarch's sources, as it is found also in Cornelius Nepos' first-century BC *Life of Eumenes* (e.g., ch. 8). But the dangers posed by unruly soldiers without firm leadership is a common concern elsewhere in Plutarch (e.g., in the *Lives of Galba and Otho*). This theme is related to a more general interest in Plutarch in the relationship between the masses and their leader: for Plutarch, Eumenes' story, like Phocion's, illustrates the danger of the masses, military or civilian, turning on their own leader in a time of crisis.

Plutarch's main source for *Eumenes* was probably Hieronymus of Cardia, a contemporary of Eumenes and native of
Eumenes' own city. Hieronymus in fact served under Eumenes,
and after his death went on to serve under Antigonus and his
son Demetrius Poliorcetes. Hieronymus was thus intimately
acquainted with the events and personalities of this period. His
history, which seems to have covered the period from Alexander's death down perhaps to the death of Pyrrhus in 272 BC, is
unfortunately lost, but it formed the basis not only for Plutarch's Life, but also for Diodorus' detailed military and political
narrative of the period from 323 to 302 in his Books 18–20.
Close correspondences between some passages of Diodorus
Book 18 and of Plutarch's *Eumenes* strongly suggest that they
were dependent on the same source. Indeed, it seems likely that
Hieronymus' work also lies behind the other surviving accounts
of Eumenes: Nepos' *Life of Eumenes*, the summary of Pompeius Trogus' first-century AD *Philippic histories*, preserved by
the later writer Justin, and the fragments of Arrian's *Events
after Alexander* (second century AD). These all share common
elements with Plutarch and Diodorus.

The use of Hieronymus might help explain the rather favourable interpretation given to Eumenes' actions in Plutarch's
account: he is presented as a man of principle, a skilful commander who inspired his troops, but who is finally brought low
by ambitious subordinates and treacherous soldiers. In fact
Plutarch is always sympathetic to the subject of each of his
Lives and has plainly reworked his source-material in *Eumenes*;
whereas Diodorus, and presumably Hieronymus, provided a
chronological narrative of the main events, Plutarch instead
provides a series of illustrative tableaux, or scenes, which capture or illustrate Eumenes' character or the dangers he was
facing. The material for some of these stories may have been
derived from the *Macedonian History* of Douris of Samos,
whom Plutarch cites as a source for some details of Eumenes'
early life, and who was known for his emotive and colourful
writing. But the reshaping of the military narrative of his source
into a series of set-piece scenes designed to illustrate character
is probably Plutarch's own.

The *Life of Eumenes* is paired with the *Life of Sertorius*. Sertorius (c. 126–73 BC) was a Roman general, who was proscribed by Sulla in 81 BC and through skilful use of guerrilla tactics operated for a number of years in Spain against Roman forces, until he was finally murdered by an associate. Unusually in this pair of Lives, the Roman Life precedes the Greek (as also with the *Aemilius* and *Timoleon*). In the prologue, which forms the first chapter of *Sertorius*, Plutarch lays out some basic similarities between the two men:

> Both men were born leaders, and both combined a warlike spirit with a genius for outwitting the enemy by deceit: both were banished from their own countries, commanded foreign troops, and suffered a similar violent and unjust stroke of fortune in their deaths, since both were the victims of conspiracy and were assassinated by the very men whom they were leading to victory against their enemies.

On the other hand, in the Comparison, which follows the *Life of Eumenes*, Plutarch emphasizes the *differences* between them. Eumenes had a more difficult task as a Greek commanding Macedonians (a factor Plutarch also mentions in chs. 3 and 8 of the Life). But he is criticized for not having come to terms with Antigonus: 'For Antigonus would gladly have employed Eumenes if only he had been prepared to step aside from struggles for the primacy and been happy to accept the second place.' Indeed, in the Comparison Eumenes becomes an example of a man addicted to warfare, driven by ambition for primacy. This judgement does not seem to arise directly from the Life, where Eumenes has been presented in much more positive terms; but closing comparisons in Plutarch often give a new twist, and this judgement may contain a good deal of sense, as well as giving a hint at an alternative, more negative, view of Eumenes current in some of Plutarch's sources.

LIFE OF EUMENES[1]

1. The father of Eumenes of Cardia,[2] according to Douris,[3] was forced by poverty to work as a cart-driver[4] in the Chersonese, but Eumenes himself had a liberal education in literature and athletics. Douris also says that when Eumenes was still a boy Philip happened to be staying in the vicinity,[5] and having some free time, came to see the wrestling contests held for the young men and boys of Cardia. Philip took a liking to Eumenes, who had had great success and seemed intelligent and brave, so he took him along with him. The version that other historians tell, however, seems more probable. They claim that Eumenes owed his advancement by Philip to the latter's ancestral ties of friendship and hospitality with Eumenes' family.

After Philip's death, Eumenes was thought to be the equal in intelligence and trustworthiness to any in Alexander's circle. For although he was given the title of chief secretary, he was in fact treated with as much honour as Alexander's most intimate friends, so that on the Indian campaign he was actually sent out as general with a force under his own command.[6] He also took over command of Perdiccas' cavalry regiment, after Perdiccas had been promoted to Hephaestion's position on the latter's death.[7] So when, after Alexander's death, Neoptolemus, the commander of the royal guard, remarked that whereas he had followed Alexander with shield and spear, Eumenes had done so with pen and writing-tablets, the Macedonians laughed at him because they knew that Alexander had bestowed many honours on Eumenes and had considered him worthy of becoming his kinsman by marriage. For Barsine, daughter of Artabazus, the first woman with whom Alexander had relations in Asia, and by whom he had a son, Heracles, had two sisters. Of these, Alexander gave one, Apama, to Ptolemy, and the other, Artonis,[8] to Eumenes, at the time when he distributed the other Persian women in marriage to his companions.[9]

2. However, Eumenes also often earned Alexander's displeasure and got himself into danger because of disputes with Hephaestion.[10] In the first place, Hephaestion assigned to the flute-player Evius the quarters which Eumenes' servants had already occupied for him. So Eumenes, accompanied by Mentor, went and started railing angrily at Alexander, saying that it was obviously more advantageous to throw away one's weapons and play the flute or sing in a tragedy. At first, Alexander shared his anger and started rebuking Hephaestion, but soon afterwards he changed his mind and became angry with Eumenes, feeling that the latter's behaviour had been more designed to insult Alexander than to assert his rights against Hephaestion.

On another occasion, when Alexander wanted to send Nearchus out with a squadron of ships to reach the outer sea,[11] he began to ask his friends for money as the royal coffers were empty. Eumenes was asked for 300 talents, but contributed only 100, claiming that his stewards had had great difficulty in collecting even this. Alexander made no criticism and did not take the money, but secretly ordered his slave to set fire to Eumenes' tent in order to prove him a liar when his money was carried out to safety. But the tent burnt down before anything could be salvaged and Alexander regretted what he had done as the papers inside were destroyed. However, the gold and silver melted down by the fire was found to come to more than 1,000 talents. Alexander took none of it but actually wrote to his satraps and generals asking them to send copies of the papers which had been destroyed and ordered Eumenes to take charge of them all.

Eumenes also quarrelled with Hephaestion over some gift, and a good deal of abuse passed between them. At that time, Eumenes held his own, but, when Hephaestion died a little later, the king in his grief became harsh and spoke bitterly to all those who he thought had been jealous of Hephaestion while he lived or who were pleased at his death. He was most suspicious of Eumenes and made frequent reference to those abusive quarrels of his with Hephaestion. But Eumenes was shrewd and persuasive and took steps to ensure that what threatened his ruin would actually be his salvation. For he took refuge in Alexander's generous partiality to Hephaestion by suggesting honours which would contribute most spectacularly to the dead man's memory and by eagerly making lavish contributions for the construction of his tomb.[12]

3. When Alexander died and the infantry fell out with Alexander's companions,[13] Eumenes at heart supported the latter but declared publicly that he saw both points of view and took neither side, saying that as a foreigner it was not right for him to meddle in the disputes of Macedonians.[14] So the rest of the companions withdrew from Babylon, and Eumenes was left behind and tried to placate the infantry and make them more disposed to a reconciliation. But when the generals met and among unprecedented tumult set about distributing satrapies and commands, Eumenes received Cappadocia, Paphlagonia and the southern coast of the Black Sea as far as Trapezus, which was at that time not yet under Macedonian control but was ruled by King Ariarathes. Accordingly, Leonnatus[15] and Antigonus[16] were instructed to escort Eumenes there with a large force and declare him satrap of the region.[17]

Now Antigonus took no notice of Perdiccas' written instructions,[18] as he was already haughty and conceited and looked down on everyone, but Leonnatus marched down to Phrygia from the interior in order to accept the satrapy for Eumenes. But Leonnatus was met by Hecataeus, tyrant of Cardia, who asked him instead to help Antipater and the Macedonians who were besieged in Lamia.[19] Leonnatus was eager to cross over into Greece and urged Eumenes to join their venture and tried to reconcile him with Hecataeus. For they had a hereditary suspicion of each other owing to some political differences, and Eumenes had often denounced Hecataeus in the clearest terms as a tyrant and implored Alexander to grant the people of Cardia their freedom. And now, too, Eumenes declined to go on the expedition against the Greeks, alleging that he feared that Antipater, who had long hated him, might do Hecataeus a favour and have him killed. So Leonnatus took him into his confidence and revealed all his plans to him. Assistance to Antipater, he said, was merely a pretext which he put about for the expedition. In reality, he had decided as soon as he crossed over to begin making a bid for Macedonia, and he showed him letters from Cleopatra[20] in which she invited him to come to Pella and promised to marry him. But Eumenes took his baggage and broke camp during the night, either out of fear of Antipater or because he despaired of Leonnatus as a foolish man full of unstable and rash impulses. He had with him three hundred cavalry and two hundred armed slaves, and gold to the value of 5,000 silver talents. Thus he fled to Perdiccas, revealed Leonnatus' plans and at once gained great influence with him and was made a member of his council; a little while later he was escorted to Cappadocia with a large force which Perdiccas commanded in person. Ariarathes was soon taken prisoner and the country subdued, and Eumenes was declared satrap. He entrusted the cities to his own friends, appointed commanders of the various strongholds and left his own appointees as judges and administrators, without any interference from Perdiccas. Finally, he marched away with Perdiccas, both because he desired to cultivate him and because he did not want to be parted from the kings.[21]

4. However, although Perdiccas was confident that he could carry through his plans by himself, he nevertheless thought that the lands he was leaving behind him required an active and trustworthy guardian. So he sent Eumenes back from Cilicia, ostensibly to his own satrapy, but in reality to get control of neighbouring Armenia which had been thrown into uproar by Neoptolemus.[22] This man Eumenes tried at first to restrain by discussion, even though he knew he was corrupted by an empty and boastful pride. But when he saw for himself how arrogant and insolent the Macedonian infantry under Neoptolemus' command had become, he raised a force of cavalry to oppose them, giving freedom from contributions and taxation

to any of the locals who could ride, and buying horses and distributing them to those of his own entourage whom he could most trust. He incited their spirits with honours and gifts and trained their bodies by exercises and drills. The result was a mixture of shock and increased confidence when the Macedonians saw how in a short time he had gathered around himself a force of not less than 6,300 cavalry.

5. Craterus[23] and Antipater had now subdued the Greeks and were crossing over to Asia to topple Perdiccas from his position of power. They were also reported to be planning to invade Cappadocia.[24] So Perdiccas, who was himself on campaign against Ptolemy,[25] appointed Eumenes commander-in-chief of the forces in Armenia and Cappadocia. He sent letters to this effect, with orders that Alcetas[26] and Neoptolemus should take heed of Eumenes and that Eumenes should handle matters as he himself best saw fit. Alcetas flatly refused to take part in the campaign, saying that the Macedonians under his command were ashamed to fight Antipater and were also well disposed to Craterus and inclined to accept him. Neoptolemus, on the other hand, began plotting against Eumenes. But his schemes did not go unnoticed and, accordingly, when he was summoned before Eumenes, he refused to obey but began deploying his forces for battle.[27] This was the first occasion on which Eumenes got the benefit of his foresight and preparation. For although his infantry was getting the worst of it, he routed Neoptolemus with his cavalry and captured his baggage. He then rode in full force against the enemy phalanx, which had become scattered in its pursuit, and forced its members to lay down their weapons and to exchange oaths with him that they would serve under him.[28]

Now Neoptolemus had collected a small number of his men from the rout and fled to Craterus and Antipater. An embassy had been sent out from these generals asking Eumenes to come over to their side. He would be able to enjoy the satrapies which he had and would gain a larger army and more territory from them if he would just put aside his enmity with Antipater and become his friend, and would keep his friendship with

Craterus and not become his foe on the battlefield. When Eumenes heard this, he declared that his enmity with Antipater was long standing,[29] and he could not now become his friend, when he saw Antipater treating Eumenes' friends as his personal enemies. But as far as Craterus was concerned, he was ready to effect a reconciliation between him and Perdiccas and to bring the two together on fair and equal terms. If either one became greedy,[30] he would aid the wronged party as long as he drew breath, and would rather lay down his body and his life than break his word.

6. When Antipater's staff received this answer, they began to take measured counsel about the whole situation. But then Neoptolemus arrived after his rout and gave a report of the battle and urged them to come to his aid – both of them if possible, but at the least Craterus. For he said that Craterus was much missed by the Macedonians, and should they just see his flat cap[31] and hear his voice they would rush to come over to him, arms and all. It was true that Craterus' name really did stand high with the Macedonian soldiers, and after Alexander's death the majority longed for him; they remembered that he had often incurred Alexander's enmity on their behalf by opposing him in his rush to imitate Persian manners and by defending the Macedonians' ancestral customs, when they were being treated with contempt owing to the spread of luxury and pride.[32] So Craterus at this point began preparations to send Antipater into Cilicia, while he himself together with Neoptolemus started to advance with a large portion of his forces against Eumenes, thinking that he would catch him off his guard as his soldiers celebrated their recent victory in drunken disorder.

Now the fact that Eumenes got prior warning of Craterus' advance and took steps to be ready might be thought merely the mark of sober leadership rather than consummate skill. But it seems to have been an achievement peculiar to Eumenes that he managed not only to keep the enemy from gathering any damaging intelligence but also to launch his own troops at Craterus before they were aware of the identity of their enemy, and to conceal from them the identity of the general who was opposing them. For he put about the story that it was Neoptolemus who was again moving against them, accompanied by Pigres and a force of Cappadocian and Paphlagonian cavalry. Eumenes' plan was to break camp during the night, but he fell asleep and had a strange dream. He thought that he saw two Alexanders getting ready to fight one another, each at the head of his own phalanx. Then Athena came to help one and Demeter the other, and after a stiff fight the one whom Athena was helping was beaten and Demeter plucked corn and wove a garland for the victor. Eumenes immediately conjectured that the vision was in his favour, as he was fighting for a very fertile land which at that time was blessed with an abundance of grain as yet unripe. For the whole country had been sown with grain, giving the impression that it was peace time, and the plains were thickly carpeted with it. He took heart even more when it was reported to him that the enemy were using 'Athena and Alexander' as their password. Accordingly, he began himself to give out to his own men the password 'Demeter and Alexander', and told them all to crown themselves with garlands of corn and wreathe their weapons. Many times he felt the impulse to speak to his commanders and generals and divulge the identity of the enemy whom they would soon face, and not to keep bottled up inside him such a momentous secret. Yet he stood by his decision and trusted his own judgement about the coming danger.

7. He did not deploy any Macedonian troops opposite Craterus but rather two foreign cavalry units led by Pharnabazus the son of Artabazus and Phoenix of Tenedus, who had strict orders to charge the enemy as soon as they were sighted and engage them at close quarters without giving them any chance to withdraw or negotiate, and without receiving any herald they might send. For he was acutely afraid that if the Macedonians recognized Craterus they would desert and go over to him. He himself formed up into a guard three hundred of his strongest cavalry and rode to the right wing, intending to attack Neoptolemus. When Eumenes and his men emerged into sight

over the crest of the hill which lay in between the two armies and launched a swift and furious charge, Craterus was amazed and hurled abuse at Neoptolemus for deceiving him with his claims that the Macedonians would desert. But, instructing his commanders to fight like men, he led a counter-charge. Such was the impact as the two sides crashed into each other that their spears were quickly broken and the fighting was done with the sword. Craterus did not disgrace his years of service with Alexander but killed many of those arrayed against him, and frequently routed them. But finally he was wounded by a Thracian on horseback, who came at him from the side, and he fell from his horse. As he lay on the ground, most of the enemy, ignorant of his identity, rode past him, but Gorgias, one of Eumenes' generals, recognized him, dismounted and set a guard over his body, as he was already in a sorry state and struggling for his life.

Meanwhile, Neoptolemus encountered Eumenes. They had long nursed a mutual hatred and were now enraged towards each other, but they did not spot one another in their first two engagements. They recognized each other, however, in the third, and immediately galloped towards one another with swords drawn, screaming. Their horses smashed into each other, like triremes ramming,[33] and letting go of the reins they clutched at each other, trying to tear off the other's helmet and to rip the breast-plate from his shoulders. As they struggled, their horses bolted from under them and they were pitched to the ground. Immediately they fell upon each other once again and set to grappling and wrestling. Then, as Neoptolemus tried to get up first, Eumenes stabbed him behind the knee and managed to regain his feet before him. Neoptolemus, incapacitated in one knee and supporting himself on the other, continued to put up a strong resistance from below until, after sustaining many more minor wounds, he was finally struck in the neck and fell to the ground, where he lay prone. He still had his sword in his hand, however, and while Eumenes, in the throes of rage and long hatred, was stripping him of his arms and insulting him, Neoptolemus managed to deal him a blow under the breast-plate at the point where it touches the groin. But the blow was rather feeble owing to Neoptolemus' weakness, and it shocked Eumenes more than actually doing him much harm.[34] He completed his despoiling of the body and then, although he was suffering grievously from gashes on his thighs and arms, he mounted his horse and set off at speed for the other wing, where he believed that the enemy were still holding together. But news reached him that Craterus was dead, so he rode out to where he lay. When he saw that Craterus was conscious and still breathing, in tears he dismounted, and, giving him his hand, heaped curses on Neoptolemus and poured out words of pity both for Craterus and his fate and for himself and the necessity which had driven him into conflict with a friend and comrade in which he must kill or be killed.

8. This victory took place almost ten days after the first, and Eumenes' prestige was greatly enhanced by it because he had won it by a combination of wisdom and courage. But he also incurred much envy and hatred from both allies and enemies alike, who saw him as a foreign interloper who, with Macedonian arms and men, had killed their foremost and most renowned commander. Now if Perdiccas had learnt of Craterus' death in time, no one else would have been able to assume the primacy of the Macedonians. But as it was, Perdiccas had been killed in a mutiny in Egypt two days before word of the battle reached the camp, and in their anger his Macedonians at once condemned Eumenes to death. Antigonus was appointed to command in the war against him, in conjunction with Antipater.[35]

When Eumenes came upon the royal herds of horses which were at pasture in the vicinity of Mount Ida,[36] he took as many as he needed but sent a written receipt to the officials in charge. At this, Antipater is said to have declared with a laugh that he admired Eumenes' forethought, since he obviously expected to have to give an account to them of how he had used royal property, or to receive one in turn from them.

Eumenes wanted to give battle near Sardis on the plains of Lydia because he was superior in cavalry and was also eager to display his power to Cleopatra.[37] But she was afraid of giving

Antipater any cause for complaint, so at her request he marched off into Upper Phrygia and prepared to spend the winter at Celaenae. There, Alcetas, Polemon and Docimus engaged him in a struggle for the leadership, leading him to declare, 'As the old saying goes, "No account is made of ruin".' He promised his troops that he would give them their pay within three days, which he accomplished by selling off to them the farmsteads and fortified residences that lay about the country and which were full of people and cattle. Every regular or mercenary commander who bought property was supplied with tools and siege-engines in order to invest it, and the soldiers distributed the booty among themselves to cover their arrears of pay.[38] For this reason Eumenes again stood high in the affections of his men, and once when letters distributed by the enemy commanders came to light in the camp, in which they offered 100 talents and great honours to anyone who would kill Eumenes, the Macedonians were outraged and passed a decree that a thousand crack troops would henceforth act as his permanent bodyguard, standing watch by rotation even during the night. The soldiers followed these orders and were delighted to receive from Eumenes the sort of honours that kings give their friends. For Eumenes was able to distribute purple caps and military cloaks, which among the Macedonians are considered a particularly royal gift.[39]

9. Now success lifts the spirits even of men of inferior natures, so that they appear to have a certain grandeur and dignity about them when they are viewed atop their lofty position. But real greatness and firmness of spirit are revealed more by one's behaviour in failure or misfortune. This was the case with Eumenes. In the first place, when he was defeated through treachery by Antigonus at Orcynia in Cappadocia and was being pursued, he did not allow the traitor to take advantage of the rout and escape to the enemy but arrested and hanged him. Then, as he fled, he changed direction and took the opposite route to that taken by his pursuers, and without them realizing it he doubled back to the place where the battle had been fought and there pitched camp. He collected the dead and, using as

firewood pieces of the doors from the villages in the vicinity, he burned the officers in one pyre and the men in another, and heaped up mounds of earth over the ashes.[40] When Antigonus later came upon the place, he was amazed at Eumenes' audacity and his calm head.

Another example of this resilience in adversity is the time when he came across Antigonus' baggage train. He could easily have captured many free men and a great number of slaves and much wealth, all accumulated over so many wars and so much looting. But he was afraid that his men, if loaded with plunder and booty, would be too weighed down for flight, and too soft to endure their continual movements from place to place and the long-drawn-out campaign. For it was in delaying tactics that he put most of his hopes for the war, thinking that in this way he would see the back of Antigonus. He realized, however, that it would be extremely difficult to deflect the Macedonians from seizing goods that were within such easy reach. So he ordered them to refresh themselves and feed their horses and be prepared to advance upon the enemy. Meanwhile, he sent a secret message to Menander, the officer in charge of the enemy's baggage train, in which he feigned concern for him as an old friend and advised him to be on his guard and withdraw as quickly as possible from the low-lying ground, where he was vulnerable to attack, and make for the higher ground nearby which was impassable to cavalry and could not be surrounded. Menander quickly realized the danger and struck camp, whereupon Eumenes started openly sending out scouts and gave the order to his men to take up their arms and bridle their horses as he was going to lead them into battle. But when the scouts reported that Menander could not be caught as he had taken refuge in rough terrain, Eumenes pretended to be annoyed and withdrew his army. The story goes that, when Menander reported all this to Antigonus, the Macedonians fell to praising Eumenes and began to look upon him in a more friendly way, as he had not taken advantage of the opportunity to enslave their children and outrage their wives. But Antigonus said, 'My good men, it was not in order to spare you that he let slip this opportunity, but because he was afraid of tying himself down at the moment when he needed to flee.'

10. After this, Eumenes kept on the move and sought to elude the enemy. He persuaded many of his soldiers to leave him, either because he was concerned about them or because he was unwilling to drag along with him a group of men who were two few to fight but too many to go unnoticed.[41] Finally, he took refuge in Nora,[42] a small town on the borders of Lycaonia and Cappadocia, at the head of five hundred cavalry and two hundred hoplites. There, too, he sent away with kind words and embraces all the friends who could not endure the deprivations of life in the town and the limited food, and who asked to be dismissed. When Antigonus arrived on the scene, he sent word to Eumenes that before he laid siege to the place he would like to speak to him. But Eumenes replied that while Antigonus had many friends who could take command after he was gone, there was none among those he was fighting for who could take his place if he were killed. So he told Antigonus to send hostages if he wanted to talk to him. And when Antigonus began telling him to address him as a superior, Eumenes replied, 'I count no man my better as long as I am master of my own sword.'[43]

In the end, however, Antigonus sent Ptolemaeus,[44] his nephew, into the town as a hostage, just as Eumenes had demanded. So Eumenes went down, and he and Antigonus embraced each other warmly like friends, since they had formerly had many dealings and close ties. A long discussion ensued in which Eumenes made no mention of his own safety or of a truce, but asked that his satrapies be confirmed and all the gifts granted to him be paid out. This caused amazement in all present and they admired his dignity and confidence. At the same time many of the Macedonians came running in their desire to see what Eumenes was like, for no one had been talked about in the ranks so much since the death of Craterus. Antigonus in fact grew afraid in case Eumenes should come to some harm, and first started shouting to the soldiers not to approach and threw stones at some that rushed forward. Finally, he threw his arms round Eumenes and, keeping off the mob with his body-guard, managed to get him to safety.

11. The aftermath of this was that Antigonus surrounded Nora with a wall and departed, leaving troops to guard it. Eumenes was now under close siege. The town had plenty of grain, abundant water and salt, but no other food, not even anything to go with their bread. Nevertheless, with the meagre resources that he had, he managed to make his companions' life cheerful, inviting everyone by turns to his own table and seasoning their common meal with the charm of his conversation. For he was not like some old veteran, worn down by a life under arms, but was attractive in appearance, refined and youthful. His whole body, with its astonishingly well-proportioned limbs, resembled a carefully composed work of art. He was not an accomplished orator, but agreeable and persuasive, as can be deduced from his letters.

Lack of space was most detrimental to the men besieged with him, as their movements were confined to small houses and an area with a circumference of only a quarter of a mile, with the result that they could take no exercise before eating, and likewise had to feed their horses while the animals stood idle. So, in order not only to relieve the boredom and torpor brought about by this inactivity but also to train them in some fashion for flight, should the opportunity arise, he assigned to the men the biggest house in the town, 20 feet long, as a place to walk, and told them to gradually increase their movements. As for the horses, he attached great straps to the roof and fastened them round the horses' necks, and winched them into the air by means of pulleys so that their hind-legs rested on the ground but the hooves of their fore-legs just touched it. When they were suspended like this, the grooms would stand at their side and urge them on with shouts and blows of the whip, and the horses, full of energy and rage, would leap and jump about on their hind-legs, and would try with their fore-legs, which were dangling in the air, to get a footing and beat the ground. They thus exerted their whole body and sweated profusely – no bad exercise for both speed and strength. The grooms also threw them their barley crushed, so that they might finish it more quickly and digest it better.

12. The siege had been going on for some time, when Antigonus received news that Antipater had died in Macedonia and confusion reigned there owing to the hostility between Cassander and Polyperchon.[45] Antigonus thus set aside his smaller-scale plans and determined to aim at nothing less than complete dominance, and wanted to enlist Eumenes as a friend and partner in his undertakings. So he sent Hieronymus[46] to Eumenes and attempted to conclude a treaty with him, proposing an oath which they were both to swear. But Eumenes made some amendments to the oath and referred it to the Macedonians who were besieging him, asking them to judge which was the fairer version. For although Antigonus had for form's sake mentioned the kings at the start of the oath, the rest referred to himself alone. But Eumenes added at the start the name of Olympias, Alexander's mother, alongside those of the kings. Then he altered the oath so that he would swear devotion and mutual alliance not only to Antigonus but also to Olympias and the kings. This was considered fairer by the Macedonians and so they administered this oath to Eumenes and lifted the siege, and sent word to Antigonus for him also to swear the oath to Eumenes. Meanwhile, Eumenes began releasing all the Cappadocian hostages he had in Nora and received in return horses, baggage-animals and tents from those who came for them. He gathered an army together from those who had been scattered and were wandering across the country after the rout so that he soon had a little short of a thousand cavalrymen. He left with these men, fearing, correctly, Antigonus' reaction. For not only did the latter send orders for Eumenes to be walled up again and the siege continued,[47] but he wrote bitter words to the Macedonians for having accepted the amendment to the oath.

13. In the course of Eumenes' flight, letters were brought to him from those in Macedonia who feared Antigonus' growing power. In some of these letters Olympias urged him to come and take charge of Alexander's son[48] and bring him up, as there

were plots against his life. In others, Polyperchon and King Philip ordered him as commander of their forces in Cappadocia to make war on Antigonus; he could take the 500 talents deposited in Cyinda in order to make good his own losses and use as much of the rest as he wanted for waging war on Antigonus. They had also written on this matter to Antigenes[49] and Teutamus, the commanders of the Silver Shields.[50] When the latter two received these letters, they ostensibly welcomed Eumenes in a friendly manner but were plainly filled with jealousy and rivalry, thinking it beneath them to play second fiddle to him. Eumenes tried to allay their jealousy by not taking the money, claiming that he had no need of it. But against their rivalry and greed for office, which made them incapable of command and unwilling to follow others, he deployed superstition. For he said that Alexander had appeared to him in his sleep and had shown him a tent decked out in royal fashion, with a throne placed inside, and had told him that if they held their councils and transacted their business there he himself would be present; he would lend his assistance to every plan or action if it was done in his name. This easily won over Antigenes and Teutamus, who were unwilling to visit Eumenes, while he himself did not think it right to be seen at the doors of others. They thus pitched a royal tent and placed a throne inside dedicated to Alexander, and made it their practice to assemble there when they deliberated on matters of the highest importance.

As they advanced into the interior, they were met by Peucestas, a friend of Eumenes, together with the other satraps, who joined forces with them,[51] so that the Macedonians were encouraged by the number of their arms and the splendour of the equipment. But the satraps themselves had, since Alexander's death, become unmanageable and soft in their way of living, and they brought with them to their meeting minds corrupted by tyranny and enervated by a barbarian swaggering. They were thus harsh and uncooperative with each other, but indulged the Macedonians with great extravagance, and lavished feasts and sacrifices on them, so that within a short time they made the camp a leisurely place of festive prodigality, a mob to be

manipulated for the election of generals, just like in a democracy.[52] Eumenes perceived that they despised each other but
also that they were afraid of him and were looking out for an
opportunity to kill him. So he pretended to be in need of money
and borrowed many talents from those who hated him most
with the purpose both of winning their confidence and also of
preventing them from taking action against him through their
anxiety about losing their money. Thus it turned out that he
used other people's money as a protection. Normally, people
give money to secure their safety; Eumenes is the only one to
have secured it by taking.

14. However, as long as there was no fighting to be done the
Macedonians continued to take gifts from their corruptors and
to pay court at the doors of these men, who went around with
bodyguards and played at being generals. But when Antigonus
camped near them with a large force[53] and the situation was
almost crying out and demanding a real general, not only did
the rank and file start paying heed to Eumenes, but also each
and every one of those who in the luxury of peace time had
seemed so important now gave in and presented themselves
for duty, keeping the post assigned to him without a murmur.
Indeed, when Antigonus tried to cross the River Pasitigris,[54]
none of the other generals who were meant to be watching his
movements even noticed it. Only Eumenes resisted him; he gave
battle and slew great numbers and filled the river with corpses,
and also took 4,000 prisoners. But it was when Eumenes fell
sick that the Macedonians made it most clear that, while they
considered others capable of laying on magnificent feasts and
celebrations, they considered only Eumenes capable of holding
command and directing the war. For Peucestas, after feasting
them lavishly in Persis and distributing to each man a victim for
sacrifice, had high hopes that he was now the strongest of the
generals. But a few days later,[55] when the soldiers were advancing against the enemy, it happened that Eumenes, who was
dangerously ill,[56] was being carried in a litter outside the ranks
where it was quiet, as he had been unable to sleep. They had
gone a little way forward when suddenly the enemy came into

sight crossing the crest of some hills and descending onto the plain. Their golden weapons[57] glittered from the heights in the sunlight, as their guards regiment rode forward in good formation, and the towers on the backs of their elephants,[58] with the purple hangings which they always wore when they were being led into battle, could clearly be seen. When they caught sight of the enemy, the troops in Eumenes' vanguard halted their march and began shouting for Eumenes and declaring that they would not advance unless he was in command. Grounding their weapons, they exhorted each other to stay where they were and urged their leaders to bide their time and not to fight or to risk battle without Eumenes. When Eumenes heard this, he ordered his bearers to increase their pace to a run and thus came up to the army, drawing back the curtains on both sides of his litter and stretching out his hand in joy. As soon as the soldiers saw him, they at once greeted him in Macedonian, picked up their shields and beat upon them with their pikes and raised a war-cry, challenging the enemy to fight now that they had their leader at hand.

15. Now, Antigonus had heard from prisoners that Eumenes was ill and was being carried around in a sorry state, and he thought that it would be no great trouble to crush the others while their leader was sick. So he hastened to lead his army forward to battle. But when he rode along, as the enemy were deploying, and saw their orderly formation, he halted for some time in amazement. Then he caught sight of the litter being carried from one wing to the other, and with his usual hearty laugh said to his friends, 'That, it seems, is our opposition!' With that he gave the order for his army to retire and pitched camp.

Now that they were able to breathe again, the Macedonians began once more to behave in a disorderly manner, lording it over the leaders. They distributed themselves in winter-quarters through pretty much the whole of Gabiene,[59] so that they were scattered over a distance of about 110 miles. When Antigonus realized this, he set out against them at once by a difficult route on which there was no water to be found but that was short and direct. His hope was that if he could catch them dispersed in their winter-quarters, it would be difficult for the rank and file to join forces with their generals. But once he had entered an uninhabited wilderness, appalling wind and bitter cold ravaged the army and impeded its march. In order to improve their plight they were forced to light many fires, and thus their presence became known to the enemy. For the barbarians who inhabited the mountains overlooking the desert were amazed at the number of fires and sent messengers on camels to warn Peucestas. When he heard the news, he went completely out of his mind with fear, and seeing that the others were in a similar state his impulse was to take urgent steps to mobilize the troops who were billeted along their way and to begin a general withdrawal. Eumenes tried to allay their confusion and fear by promising to check the speed of the enemy advance and delay their expected arrival by three days. They were convinced, and he began sending messengers out with orders that the forces in winter-quarters and all the others should gather as quickly as possible. Meanwhile, he rode out in person in the company of the other commanders and selected a tract of land that was visible a long way off to anyone approaching through the desert, and measured it out. Then he gave orders that a great number of fires be lit at intervals as though it was a camp. Once this had been carried out and the fires on the mountains became visible to Antigonus, the latter was overcome by anxiety and dismay, thinking that the enemy had long perceived his advance and were coming to meet him. His army was exhausted and worn out from the march and so in order to avoid its having to face an enemy who were ready for action and had passed the winter in comfort, he abandoned the direct route and began moving at a slower pace through villages and towns. But when no one appeared to obstruct his advance, as usually happens when an enemy is in close proximity, and the local people reported that no army had been seen but that the place was full of lighted fires, Antigonus realized that he had been out-generaled by Eumenes, and in great annoyance began to lead forward his army to decide the issue in a straight fight.

16. Meanwhile, most of Eumenes' forces had gathered and, in admiration of his intelligence, they demanded that he alone

should lead them. At this, Antigenes and Teutamus, the leaders of the Silver Shields, were so bitter and jealous that they hatched a plot against him. They gathered most of the satraps and generals and discussed when and how they should do away with him. They all agreed that they should exploit his talents in the battle but kill him immediately afterwards. But this decision was secretly reported to Eumenes by Eudamus, the commander of the elephants, and Phaedimus – not out of any goodwill or kindness towards him but because they were worried about losing the money which they had lent to him. Eumenes praised them and withdrew to his tent. There, declaring to his friends that he was surrounded by a horde of wild animals, he wrote a will, and tore up and destroyed his papers, not wishing that after his death accusations and false charges be brought against his correspondents on the basis of the confidential information contained in them. When he had settled this matter, he began to debate whether to surrender victory to the enemy or to withdraw through Media and Armenia and invade Cappadocia. He could come to no final decision in the presence of his friends. But his mind remained versatile despite the reverses of fortune which he had suffered,[60] and, after debating the possibilities for a long time, he finally began to draw up his forces.[61] He urged on the Greeks and barbarians, and was himself likewise exhorted by the phalanx and the Silver Shields to be of good courage, as the enemy would not stand up to their onslaught. For these were the oldest of the troops of Philip and Alexander, and, like athletes of war, they had never yet been defeated or thrown. Many of them were seventy years old and none was younger than sixty. So as they charged Antigonus' forces they shouted, 'It is against your fathers that you sin, you scum!'[62] and falling on them angrily they smashed almost their whole phalanx, as no one stood up to them, but most were cut down at close quarters. At this point, then, Antigonus' forces were being overwhelmed. His cavalry, on the other hand, were getting the upper hand. And since Peucestas fought in such a lax and cowardly manner, Antigonus got control of the whole of Eumenes' baggage train, owing both to his own sober head, despite the dangers, and to the aid afforded by the terrain. For the plain was vast and its earth neither very deep nor hard and firm but sandy and full of a dry, salty substance, which with the trampling of so many horses and men during the battle raised a cloud of lime-like dust, which turned the air white and reduced visibility. For this reason it was all the easier for Antigonus to capture the baggage train unobserved.

17. As soon as the fighting was over, Teutamus sent envoys to discuss the baggage. Antigonus promised that he would not just return their baggage to the Silver Shields but would also treat them with kindness in all other respects, if they would only hand Eumenes over. At this, the Silver Shields hatched a terrible plot, to surrender the man alive into the hands of the enemy. First they gradually approached him without raising his suspicions and kept him under watch, some of them lamenting the loss of the baggage, others telling him to keep his spirits up, as he was the victor, or criticizing the other leaders. Then they rushed at him and, snatching away his dagger, twisted his hands and tied them with his belt. And when Nicanor had been sent by Antigonus to take him into custody, Eumenes asked leave to speak to the Macedonians as he was being led through their ranks: not, he said, to beg or plead for his life but to discuss with them what was to their own advantage. Silence fell and standing in a raised area with his arms stretched out, bound as they were, he said, 'Most disgraceful of Macedonians, could Antigonus ever have dreamt of setting up a trophy over you equal to the one you are yourselves erecting, in handing over your commander as a prisoner? Is it not terrible that, though victorious, you admit defeat for the sake of your baggage, as though victory lay in possessions not in arms, and you send your leader, too, as a ransom for your baggage? For my part, I am led away undefeated, conqueror of my enemies, but victim of my allies. But I implore you, by Zeus the god of armies and by the gods who watch over oaths, to kill me here with your own hands; at all events, even if I am killed over there, it will still be your doing. Antigonus will not blame you; he wants Eumenes dead, not alive. If you are ashamed to put your hands to the job, one of mine, freed of its bonds, will

suffice to do it. And if you do not trust me with a sword, then throw me bound as I am under the feet of the animals. If you do this, I acquit you of all blame for my fate, as men who acted in the most honourable and just way towards their own commander.'

18. As Eumenes was speaking, the rest of the soldiers were overcome with sorrow and some began to weep. But the Silver Shields shouted to take him away and not pay any attention to the nonsense he spouted. For there was nothing terrible, they argued, if a pest[63] from the Chersonese should meet his fate, after embroiling Macedonians in so many countless wars. But it was outrageous if the best of the soldiers of Alexander and Philip should, in their old age, and after so many tribulations, be stripped of their prizes and be dependent on others for their upkeep, and if their wives should sleep for the third night in a row with the enemy.[64] As they said this, they led him along even more quickly. However, Antigonus was afraid of the unruly crowd (for no one had been left behind in the camp) and sent out ten of his strongest elephants and a great number of Median and Parthian spearmen to disperse them. He could not bear to see Eumenes himself on account of their previous friendship and intimacy, and when those who had taken custody of him asked how they should guard him, he replied, 'Just like an elephant or a lion.'

But a little later Antigonus took pity on him and ordered the heaviest of his chains to be removed and one of his personal attendants to be admitted to rub him with oil. He also let in any of his friends who wanted to spend the day with him and bring him anything he needed. He deliberated for a good many days over what to do with him and listened to both speeches and promises, since his own son Demetrius[65] and Nearchus the Cretan[66] were eager to save Eumenes' life, but almost all the others were insistent that he must be killed. It is said that Eumenes asked Onomarchus, his jailor, why on earth, now that Antigonus had a personal enemy in his hands, and one who had taken up arms against him, he did not either get it over with and kill him or make a noble gesture and set him free, to which Onomarchus replied in an altogether insulting way that it was not now but on the field of battle that he should have faced death with such boldness. Eumenes answered, 'By Zeus, I did face it then too. Ask those whom I met in combat. I know that no one I met was my better,' to which Onomarchus replied, 'Since you have now found your better, why do you not wait on his timing?'

19. Finally, Antigonus decided to kill Eumenes and ordered him to be deprived of food. After two or three days without eating, Eumenes began to approach his end. But camp suddenly had to be broken, and someone was sent in to murder him.[67] His body was handed over by Antigonus to Eumenes' friends, who were permitted to burn it and to collect the remains in a silver urn, to be returned to his wife and children.

So died Eumenes. Punishment of the treacherous leaders and soldiers was devolved by the divine on none other than Antigonus. He reviled the Silver Shields as impious and bestial and handed them over to Sibyrtius, the governor of Arachosia,[68] with orders to exterminate and destroy them in every way so that none of them might return to Macedonia or behold the Greek sea.[69]

COMPARISON OF SERTORIUS
AND EUMENES

1(20). These are the points of interest which have come down to us concerning Eumenes and Sertorius.[70] Turning to the comparison, one point they have in common is that while both of them were outsiders, foreigners and exiles, they exercised continual command of a multitude of different nations and of large, war-hardened armies. On the other hand, Sertorius, on account of his reputation, held his command at the behest of all the allies, whereas Eumenes had many rivals for the command and had to keep on seizing the primacy through his deeds. One was followed by those who wished to be under a just ruler; the other was obeyed out of expediency by those who were incapable of ruling. For Sertorius was a Roman in command of Iberians and Lusitanians, who had long been slaves to the Romans; Eumenes came from the Chersonese and yet was in command of Macedonians,[71] who were at that time enslaving all mankind. Furthermore, Sertorius rose to leadership through the admiration he won as senator and commander; Eumenes rose to leadership despite being looked down on as a secretary. Eumenes not only started with fewer resources to get into power, but also encountered greater hindrances to his advancement. For there were many who opposed him directly or plotted against him covertly, whereas no one opposed Sertorius openly, and it was only later that a few of his allies rebelled against him secretly. So for Sertorius danger ended with the defeat of his enemies, whereas for Eumenes it was victory itself which brought danger from those who envied him.

2(21). In their conduct as generals they have much to rival and parallel each other, though in terms of their general dispositions Eumenes was fond of war and fond of winning, whereas Sertorius was naturally a man of peace and tranquillity. For it would have been perfectly possible for Eumenes to have kept to the sidelines and lived peacefully and honourably, but instead he constantly put himself in danger by fighting the powerful. Sertorius, on the other hand, though he had no desire for trouble, had to fight for his own personal safety against enemies that would afford him no peace. For Antigonus would gladly have employed Eumenes if only he had been prepared to step aside from struggles for the primacy and been happy to accept the second place, whereas Pompey would not even permit Sertorius to live in retirement. As a result, one made war of his own free will in the pursuit of power; the other found himself in command against his will, since others were making war on him. Now the man who puts greed before safety actually likes war, whereas the man who through war attempts to win safety is simply skilled in waging it.

As far as their deaths go, Sertorius met his end without seeing it coming, whereas Eumenes both saw it coming and expected it. In Sertorius' case, this was a mark of nobility of heart, since he seems to have trusted his friends; in Eumenes' case, it was a mark of weakness, since he wanted to flee but was arrested. And Sertorius did not besmirch his life by his death, since he suffered at the hands of his allies what none of his enemies had been able to do to him; but Eumenes had the chance to flee before he was captured and wanted to stay alive once he was captured, but neither took proper precautions against death nor faced it well. Rather, by begging and pleading for his life, Eumenes gave the impression that the enemy had conquered his soul as well as his body.[72]

DEMETRIUS

DEMETRIOS

INTRODUCTION TO
DEMETRIUS

[336–282 BC]

Demetrius, nicknamed Poliorcetes ('the Besieger'), was the son
of Alexander's general Antigonus Monophthalmus, and fought
alongside him in the wars that followed Alexander's death. By
316 BC, when he defeated Eumenes in Persia, Demetrius' father
controlled vast tracts of land in Asia. But this success led to war
with the other great dynasts who had emerged from the wreck
of Alexander's empire: Ptolemy, based in Egypt, Lysimachus in
Thrace, and Cassander, who had by then asserted his dominance over Macedonia and mainland Greece. In 312 Demetrius
was defeated by Ptolemy at Gaza; in the following year Seleucus, whom Antigonus had expelled from Babylon several years
earlier, returned and established himself there. A peace treaty
of late 311 officially confirmed Antigonus' power in Asia, as
well as Cassander's in Europe and Ptolemy's in Egypt, but
Antigonus was unable to dislodge Seleucus. Seeing his fortunes
waning in Asia, Antigonus dispatched Demetrius to mainland
Greece with a promise of freedom and autonomy to the cities
which came over from Cassander. Demetrius was welcomed
enthusiastically into Athens in 307, expelled Demetrius of
Phaleron, who had governed Athens for Cassander, and restored
full democracy. In the following year, Demetrius defeated
Ptolemy's fleet in a naval battle off Cyprus. By this time both
Philip Arrhidaeus and Alexander IV, the nominal successors to
Alexander the Great's throne, had been murdered, and in 306
Demetrius and Antigonus took the decisive step of declaring
themselves kings in their own right. Ptolemy, Seleucus and Lysi-
machus followed suit.

This success, however, was not to last. In 301, Demetrius

and Antigonus suffered a crushing defeat at Ipsus in Asia Minor at the hands of an alliance of Cassander, Lysimachus and Seleucus. Antigonus was killed and Antigonid power collapsed almost entirely; Athens, like many other cities, rushed to distance itself from the losing side and expelled Demetrius' garrison. However, an alliance with Seleucus revived Demetrius' fortunes. He took Athens again in c. 295, and was able shortly afterwards to intervene in Macedonia, which after Cassander's death in 297 had been rent by civil war and was now facing invasion by Pyrrhus, king of Epirus. After a brief alliance with Alexander V of Macedon, one of Cassander's sons, Demetrius killed him and seized power. Demetrius ruled Macedonia for seven years, but the other kings again allied against him and in 288 he was expelled from Macedonia and his forces were driven out of almost all of mainland Greece. In 285, campaigning again in Asia Minor, Demetrius was forced to surrender to Seleucus; he died in captivity several years later.

The swift collapse of Demetrius' power after Ipsus, and the equally swift collapse in 288 when he was driven from Macedonia, reveal the great weakness of the position of Antigonus and Demetrius in contrast to that of the other dynasts: geographically speaking, they had no fixed power-base, no central heartland on which to fall back. This also makes Demetrius' career rather difficult to follow, as his field of activity shifts constantly. Some ten years after his death, however, his son Antigonus II Gonatas established himself securely on the throne of Macedon and founded a dynasty to rival the other kingdoms, until it was finally overthrown by the Romans in 168 BC.

Plutarch's *Demetrius* is an important source for the history of this period. Diodorus covers the years from Alexander's death up to just before the battle of Ipsus in his Books 18–20, but his account of the period after this survives only in fragments. Plutarch's is, therefore, the only extant narrative account. His main sources were probably the same as those for *Eumenes*. Hieronymus of Cardia almost certainly supplied the basic historical narrative; parallels between Plutarch's account and that of Diodorus are probably to be explained by their both having used Hieronymus. Douris of Samos may have supplied some of the numerous anecdotes about Demetrius. Plutarch most likely also had an Athenian source, perhaps the local historian Philochorus (c. 340–260 BC), which was responsible for the detailed information about the honours paid to Demetrius by the Athenians and the sufferings in Athens caused by Demetrius' siege of c. 295. He made use of other sources, too, including Athenian inscriptions or a work which recorded them.

Plutarch pairs his Life of Demetrius with that of Mark Antony – Julius Caesar's lieutenant, Cleopatra's husband and the enemy of Octavian. In the prologue to the pair, which immediately precedes *Demetrius*, Plutarch introduces Demetrius and Antony as 'men who conducted themselves in a rather unreflecting way' and who became 'conspicuous by their misconduct', and presents them to his readers as examples of men *not* to imitate. They were 'womanizers, drinkers and soldiers ... open-handed, extravagant and arrogant'. Furthermore, for Plutarch Demetrius and Antony 'illustrate the truth of Plato's saying that great natures produce great vices as well as great virtues'. The reference is to Plato's picture in the *Republic* of how a brilliant, aristocratic man, if not educated properly and if exposed at too early an age to flattery, will grow up unstable and obsessed with fame.

This characterization of Demetrius, as a brilliant man corrupted by flattery, is developed as the Life progresses. Demetrius is presented throughout as a man of great personal charisma and a skilful and brave commander. At the start of Plutarch's Life, his penchant for riotous living does not affect his statesmanship. But power and the adulation of the masses go to his head. The key event for Plutarch is his rapturous welcome in Athens in 307, following which the Athenians vote him extravagant honours (chs. 10–13, 23–7). 'By such absurd flattery', Plutarch comments, 'they further corrupted the man, who even before was not of entirely sound mind' (ch. 13). There is an unhealthy interplay in Plutarch's account between a populace willing to give such meaningless honours and a leader ready to receive them. Plutarch portrays the assumption of the title of 'king' and the accompanying regalia as part of this same process of flattery; significantly, it is the Athenians who first address him as king.

The result, Plutarch says, talking not only of Demetrius but of all the dynasts who styled themselves king at this time, was that this 'introduced an element of arrogance and self-importance into their daily lives and their dealings with others, in the same way as tragic actors, when they put on royal robes, alter their gait, their voice, their deportment and their mode of address' (ch. 18). The reference to tragic actors here is important. Plutarch often compares Demetrius to an actor, or his life to a play. In Plutarch's period, tragedy – and the theatre more generally – were often associated with pompousness, pretension, falseness and 'theatricality'. Here, the comparison suggests the strutting arrogance of Demetrius and of other contemporary rulers, their love of adulation and the hollowness of their royal affectations. Thus, when Demetrius moves against Pyrrhus, Plutarch notes that, whereas the Macedonians saw in Pyrrhus a reminder of Alexander, Demetrius and the other kings were 'like actors on a stage', merely imitating Alexander's 'pomp and outward show of majesty' (ch. 41; cf. 44).

References to tragedy, then, suggest the emptiness and instability of Demetrius' power. They also suggest the mutability of fortune which characterized his life. Plutarch draws attention to this aspect of both Demetrius and Antony in the prologue: 'they met with great triumphs and great disasters, huge conquests and huge losses, unexpected failures and unhoped for recoveries . . .' In the Life itself, Plutarch repeatedly highlights the role of fortune and its constant fluctuations. For example, when, after retaking Athens and winning a victory against Sparta, Demetrius receives news of defeat in Cyprus and the collapse of his support in Asia, Plutarch comments, 'But no other king seems to have undergone such huge and sudden reversals of fortune; and in the career of no other does fortune seem to have been so often transformed, from obscurity to renown, from triumph to humiliation and from abasement to the heights of power' (ch. 35).

The emphasis here on the role of chance works against, of course, an interest in explaining or understanding Demetrius' successes and failures in the way a modern historian might do. Plutarch does suggest that Demetrius' luxurious living and neglect of his subjects embittered the Macedonians to him (ch. 42), but this is not advanced as a cause for his loss of control of the country, nor is his increasingly arrogant and perverse treatment of Athens used as an explanation for his expulsion from that city. Rather, as with the heroes of tragedy, for Plutarch's Demetrius *hybris* and disaster go hand in hand; like them Demetrius is presented as a plaything of forces beyond his control.

PROLOGUE TO THE LIVES
OF DEMETRIUS AND
ANTONY

1. Whoever first conceived the idea that there is a parallel between the arts and our bodily senses seems to me to have grasped one fact very clearly, namely that both possess a power to make distinctions which enables us to perceive opposites, both on the physical and on the aesthetic plane. The arts and the senses have this faculty in common, though they differ as to the goals of their discrimination. For our senses are no better equipped to distinguish black objects than white, or sweet things than bitter, or soft and yielding substances than hard and resistant ones: their function is to register impressions from all objects alike as they occur, and to report the sensation as it has been experienced to our understanding. The arts, on the other hand, function with the help of reason to select and apprehend what is appropriate to them and to avoid and reject what is alien; accordingly, they contemplate the one category of objects for themselves and deliberately, and the other incidentally, in order to avoid them. For example, the art of medicine has incidentally investigated the nature of disease, and the art of music has studied that of discord, in order to produce their opposites. In the same way, the most perfect arts of all – self-control, justice and wisdom – do not make judgements only on what is good, useful and just, but also on what is harmful, disgraceful and unjust; and these arts do not prize that kind of innocence which boasts of its inexperience of evil. On the contrary, they regard it as folly, and as ignorance of all the things that one who intends to lead an upright life most ought to know.

Now the ancient Spartans had the custom of compelling the Helots at their festivals to drink large quantities of neat wine;

then they would bring them into the public dining-halls as an object lesson to their young men of what it was like to be drunk.[1] But I think it is neither humane nor the act of a statesman to try to improve some by perverting others. Perhaps, however, it is not such a bad idea for me to insert into the paradigms of my Lives one or two pairs of men who conducted themselves in a rather unreflecting way and who became in their positions of power, and when they were engaged in great enterprises, conspicuous by their misconduct. My purpose in doing so is not to divert or entertain my readers by giving variety to my writings; I am, rather, following the example of Ismenias the Theban, who when he taught the flute used to point out to his pupils both good and bad performers, and tell them, 'You should play like this one' or 'You should not play like that one'. Similarly, Antigenidas believed that young men would appreciate good flute-players better if they were given experience of bad ones. In the same way, it seems to me that we shall be all the more ready to study and imitate the lives of good men if we know something of those of the wicked and infamous.

This book, then, will contain the lives of Demetrius the Besieger and Antony the Imperator,[2] men whose lives conspicuously illustrate the truth of Plato's saying that great natures produce great vices as well as great virtues.[3] Both men were redoubtable womanizers, drinkers and soldiers, both were open-handed, extravagant and arrogant, and these resemblances were reflected in the similarity of their fortunes. For it was not just that in the rest of their lives they met with great triumphs and great disasters, huge conquests and huge losses, unexpected failures and unhoped for recoveries, but also that the one ended his life as a prisoner of his enemies and the other after narrowly escaping the same fate.

LIFE OF DEMETRIUS

2. According to most accounts, Antigonus[4] had two sons from Stratonice the daughter of Corrhagus. One of them he named Demetrius after his brother, the other Philip after his father. But some writers tell us that Demetrius was Antigonus' nephew, not his son: they say that his father died when he was quite young, and that his mother married Antigonus, who thus came to be regarded as Demetrius' father. Philip, who was a few years the younger, died at an early age. Demetrius grew up to be a tall man, although not so tall as his father, and both in form and in feature he was so strikingly handsome that no painter or sculptor ever succeeded in fashioning a likeness of him. His features combined charm and seriousness, beauty and a capacity to inspire fear, but hardest of all to represent was the blend in his appearance of the eagerness and fire of youth with a heroic aspect and an air of kingly dignity. In his disposition he was equally capable of making himself loved and feared. For he could be the most delightful of companions, and when he had leisure for drinking and luxurious living he was the most dissolute of kings, and yet when action was required, he could show the utmost energy, perseverance and practical ability. It was for this reason that of all the gods he took Dionysus as his particular model, since this god was most terrible when waging war, but also most skilful at exploiting the ensuing peace for the pursuit of pleasure and enjoyment.

3. Demetrius was also deeply attached to his father, and to judge by the devotion he showed to his mother, it was evident that his feeling for Antigonus sprang from genuine affection,

not from mere regard for his power. On one occasion, when Antigonus was giving audience to some foreign envoys, Demetrius happened to come home from hunting. He walked straight up to his father and then sat down beside him in his hunting clothes and with his javelins still in his hand. When the envoys had received their answer and were about to leave his presence, Antigonus called out to them in a loud voice, 'Gentlemen, when you return home, you may also report that this is how my son and I live,' for he felt that this demonstration of the harmony and confidence which prevailed between him and his son was the best proof of the power and stability of his kingdom. So difficult is it to share absolute power and how full it is of ill will and suspicion that the oldest and greatest of the successors of Alexander could make it his boast that he was not afraid of his son, but allowed him to sit close by his side with a spear in his hand. And, indeed, it is a fact that Antigonus' was almost the only royal house whose history remained unsullied by crimes of this kind for many generations; or, to put the matter more precisely, the only one of the descendants of Antigonus who put a son to death was Philip.[5] The history of almost all the other dynasties is full of examples of men who murdered their sons, their mothers or their wives, while the murder of brothers had come to be accepted like a geometrical postulate, as a recognized precaution to be taken by all rulers to ensure their safety.

4. To prove that Demetrius in his early years was by nature humane and loyal to his friends, the following example can be quoted. Mithridates, the son of Ariobarzanes, was the same age as Demetrius and a close friend and companion. He was one of Antigonus' courtiers, but although he enjoyed a well-earned position of trust, he incurred the king's suspicion on account of a dream. Antigonus had dreamt that he was crossing a large and beautiful field and was sowing it with gold-dust. At first a crop of gold immediately sprang up, but when after a little while he returned to the field, he could see nothing but stubble. Then, in his disappointment and vexation he seemed to hear a number of voices saying that Mithridates had gathered

the golden harvest for himself and escaped to the coast of the
Black Sea. The vision preyed on Antigonus, and so he sent for
his son and, after making him take an oath of silence, he
described to him what he had seen and added that he had
decided to rid himself of Mithridates. Demetrius was greatly
distressed at this, but when the young man arrived, as was his
habit, to spend the day with the prince, Demetrius did not dare
to refer to the subject or to warn him of his danger, on account
of the oath he had sworn. Instead, he drew him aside, away
from his friends, and when they were alone together he wrote
on the ground with the butt of his spear as the others watched
him, the words 'Fly, Mithridates!'. Mithridates understood and
made his escape by night to Cappadocia. But not long afterwards, fate caused Antigonus' vision to come to pass. Mithridates
made himself master of a large and prosperous territory, and
founded the dynasty of the kings of Pontus, which was put to
an end some eight generations later by the Romans.[6] At any
rate, the story may serve to illustrate Demetrius' natural tendency to behave in a just and humane fashion.

5. Empedocles[7] tells us that strife produces friction and war
among the elements of the universe, especially among those elements which are adjacent to or in contact with one another. In
the same way, wars continually broke out among the successors of Alexander, and these were particularly violent or bitter
when the rival interests or disputed territories happened to lie
close to one another, as was the case at that time with Antigonus and Ptolemy. Antigonus was in Phrygia, and as soon as he
received the news that Ptolemy had crossed over from Cyprus,
was ravaging Syria and was compelling or subverting the cities
there to transfer their allegiance, he sent his son Demetrius to
oppose him. Demetrius was then twenty-two years of age, and
now found himself for the first time on trial as the supreme
commander of an expedition in which great interests were at
stake.[8] In the event, his youth and inexperience proved no
match for an opponent who had been trained in the school of
Alexander, and who had also fought many great campaigns on
his own account. Demetrius was crushingly defeated near the

city of Gaza,[9] 5,000 of his men were killed, 8,000 taken prisoner and he lost his tent, his money and all his personal possessions. Ptolemy returned all these to him, together with his friends, and added the courteous and humane message that they were not engaged in a struggle for life or death, but only for honour and power. Demetrius accepted this generous gesture; at the same time he uttered a prayer to the gods that he should not remain long in Ptolemy's debt, but should soon repay him in like fashion. He did not react like a young man who has been defeated right at the start, but like an experienced general used to reversals of fortune.[10] Accordingly, he occupied himself with enrolling new troops, preparing fresh supplies of arms, keeping the cities firmly in hand and training his recruits.

6. When the news of the battle reached Antigonus, he remarked that Ptolemy had so far conquered beardless youths, but would now have to fight with grown men; but he was anxious not to crush or humble the spirit of his son and so he granted the young man's request to be allowed to fight again on his own account. Soon after this, Cilles, one of Ptolemy's generals, arrived in Syria. He brought with him a splendidly equipped army, he regarded Demetrius with contempt because of his earlier defeat and his intention was to drive him out of the province altogether. But Demetrius launched a sudden attack and achieved complete surprise. He routed Cilles' troops and seized his camp, generals and all, capturing 7,000 prisoners and a vast quantity of treasure. Demetrius was delighted at this success, not so much for what he had acquired as for what he could give back, and he prized the victory less for the glory and the spoils he had won than for the power it gave him to repay Ptolemy's generosity and return the favours he had received. However, he did not take this action on his own responsibility but wrote first to his father. When Antigonus granted him permission to dispose of the spoils as he pleased, he loaded Cilles and his companions with gifts and sent them back to Ptolemy. This reverse drove Ptolemy out of Syria and brought Antigonus down from Celaenae.[11] He was overjoyed at the victory and eager to see the son who had won it.

7. After this, Demetrius' next mission was to subdue the Arabs known as Nabataeans,[12] and in this campaign he ran great dangers by marching through completely waterless country, but by his cool and resolute leadership he so overawed the barbarians that he captured from them seven hundred camels and great quantities of booty, and returned in safety.

Seleucus,[13] who had earlier been driven out of Babylonia by Antigonus, but had later won back the province and re-established his authority there, made an expedition inland with the intention of annexing the peoples living on the borders of India and the provinces in the neighbourhood of the Caucasus. So Demetrius, calculating that he would find Mesopotamia undefended, suddenly crossed the Euphrates and made a surprise attack on Babylon. He captured one of the two citadels of the capital, drove out the garrison left by Seleucus and replaced it with a force of 7,000 of his own troops. Then he gave orders to his soldiers to seize and plunder everything that they could carry or drive out of the country and march back to the coast. But in the event, his action only left Seleucus more firmly established in possession of his kingdom than before, for by ravaging the country he appeared to admit that it no longer belonged to him and his father. However, he was able to relieve Halicarnassus, which Ptolemy was besieging, by coming swiftly to its rescue.

8. This feat won great renown for Demetrius and Antigonus and fired them with the inspiring ambition to liberate the whole of Greece,[14] which had been enslaved by Cassander and Ptolemy. None of the kings who succeeded Alexander ever waged a nobler or a juster war than this, for Demetrius now took the huge quantities of treasure which they had amassed from their victories over the barbarians and devoted it for their own honour and good name to the cause of delivering the Greeks. They decided to begin their campaign by sailing against Athens, whereupon one of Antigonus' friends remarked that if they captured the city they must keep possession of it, since it was the gangway that led to all the rest of Greece. But Antigonus would not hear of this. He declared that he needed no better or

steadier gangway than a people's goodwill, that Athens was the watch-tower of the whole world and that through her reputation she would swiftly beacon forth his deeds to all mankind.

So Demetrius sailed to Athens with a fleet of two hundred and fifty ships and 5,000 talents. The city was at this time governed by Demetrius of Phaleron[15] as Cassander's deputy, and a force of Macedonians was garrisoned in Munychia. Demetrius arrived on the twenty-fifth day of the month of Thargelion,[16] and through a combination of good fortune and foresight his approach took his opponents completely by surprise. When his ships were first sighted off the coast, everybody took them for Ptolemy's fleet and prepared to receive them. Then, at last, the generals discovered their mistake and hurried down to the shore, where all was tumult and confusion, as is natural when men suddenly find themselves obliged to repel a surprise landing. For Demetrius, as he found the entrances to the harbours undefended, sailed straight in, and was now in full view of all; he then signalled to the citizens from his ship for them to be quiet and allow him a hearing. When silence had been restored, he ordered a herald standing by his side to announce that he had been sent by his father on what he prayed would prove a happy mission for the Athenians, for his orders were to set the city free, to expel the garrison and to restore to the people the use of their laws and their ancestral constitution.[17]

9. When they heard this proclamation, most of the Athenians immediately threw down their shields at their feet and burst into applause. With loud cheers they called upon Demetrius to land, acclaiming him as their benefactor and saviour. The supporters of Demetrius of Phaleron decided that they must at all events receive the conqueror, even if he did not fulfil any of his promises, but they also sent a delegation to beg for his protection. Demetrius received the envoys courteously and sent back with them one of his father's friends, Aristodemus of Miletus. Demetrius of Phaleron was an Athenian, and the political changes which he expected would follow made him more frightened of his fellow-countrymen than of the invader. Demetrius took note of this, and because he admired his opponent's courage

and reputation he granted his request to be sent under safe conduct to Thebes. As for himself, he declared that although he was eager to see the city, he would not do so until he had completed its deliverance by expelling the garrison. He then surrounded the fortress of Munychia with a trench and a palisade, thus cutting off its communications with the rest of the city, and sailed against Megara, where Cassander had also stationed a garrison.

When he learnt that the famously beautiful Cratesipolis,[18] who had been the wife of Polyperchon's son Alexander, and was now living at Patrae,[19] would be glad to pay him a visit, he left his army in the territory of Megara and set off across country, taking only a few light troops with him. When he reached the meeting place, he had his tent pitched apart from his guard so that Cratesipolis could visit him unobserved. Some of the enemy discovered this and made a sudden attack on his camp. In his alarm, he only had time to snatch up a shabby cloak and run for his life. In this disguise he made his escape, but through his inability to control his passion he narrowly avoided being ignominiously captured, and the enemy seized his tent and possessions and carried them off.

When Megara was captured[20] and Demetrius' troops were about to plunder the city, the Megarians were only saved from this fate because the people of Athens pleaded strongly on their behalf. Demetrius also expelled the garrison and gave the city its freedom. While he was engaged in these operations, he remembered Stilpo the philosopher, a man who had become famous because he had chosen a life of tranquillity and study. Demetrius sent for him and asked whether any man had robbed him of anything. 'No,' replied Stilpo, 'I have seen nobody carrying away any knowledge.' However, the soldiers had carried off almost all the slaves in Megara and so when Demetrius once more paid his respects to Stilpo and finally remarked, as he was about to take his departure, 'I leave this a city of free men, Stilpo!' the philosopher retorted, 'You may say that, indeed, for you have not left a single one of our slaves.'

10. After Demetrius had returned to Munychia and encamped before it, he drove out the garrison and demolished the fort-

ress.[21] Then, at last, having fulfilled his promise, he accepted the pressing invitation of the Athenians and made his entry into the city. Here he called the people together and formally restored to them their ancestral constitution. He also promised that his father would supply 150,000 bushels of wheat and enough timber to build a fleet of a hundred triremes.

The Athenians had been deprived of their democratic constitution fourteen years earlier, and in the intervening period since the Lamian War and the battle of Crannon[22] they had in theory been governed by an oligarchy but in practice by a monarchy, because of the power of the Phalerean.[23] Demetrius appeared great and glorious because of his benefactions, but they made him obnoxious by the extravagance of the honours which they voted him. For example, they were the first people in the world to confer upon Antigonus and Demetrius the title of king.[24] Both men had hitherto made it a matter of piety to decline this appellation, which was regarded as the one royal honour which was still reserved for the lineal descendants of Philip and Alexander and which it would be wrong for others to assume or share. The Athenians were also the only people who described them in inscriptions as saviour-gods, and they abolished the ancestral office of the 'eponymous' archon,[25] who gave his name to the year, and began electing annually a priest of the saviour-gods, and put his name on the preambles of decrees and contracts. They also decreed that the figures of Demetrius and Antigonus should be woven into the sacred robe of Athena,[26] together with those of the other gods. They consecrated the spot where Demetrius had first alighted from his chariot and built an altar there, which was known as the altar of the Descending[27] Demetrius. Besides this, they created two new tribes and named them Demetrias and Antigonis, and in consequence changed the composition of the Council from five hundred to six hundred members, since each tribe supplies fifty councillors.[28]

11. The most preposterous of Stratocles' ideas (he was the one who invented these extravagant and sophisticated forms of flattery) was the proposal that any official envoys sent to Antigonus or Demetrius by public decree should be referred to not as

ambassadors but as sacred deputies, like the envoys who conveyed the traditional sacrifices on behalf of the various cities at the great Hellenic festivals at Delphi and Olympia. In other respects, too, this Stratocles was a man of extraordinary effrontery. He lived a shamelessly debauched life and through his vulgarity and scurrilous behaviour he seemed to imitate the familiarity with which Cleon[29] of old had treated the people. He kept a mistress named Phylacion, and one day when she had bought some brains and neck-bones in the market-place for their dinner, he said to her, 'Ah, I see you have brought me the very things that we politicians play ball with!' On another occasion, when the Athenians had suffered a defeat in a naval battle off Amorgos,[30] Stratocles hurried to the city before the news of the disaster had arrived. He then put on a garland and drove through the Cerameicus and, after announcing that a victory had been won, proposed a sacrifice to the gods and had meat distributed at public expense to all the tribes. A little later, when the sailors returned bringing back the wrecks from the battle and the people angrily called him to account for his deception, he faced their clamour with his usual impudence and asked them, 'What harm have I done if for two days you have been happy?' Such was the audacity of Stratocles.

12. However 'there are some things even hotter than fire',[31] as Aristophanes puts it, and there was another Athenian whose servility eclipsed even that of Stratocles. This man proposed that whenever Demetrius visited Athens he should be received with the same divine honours that were paid to Demeter and Dionysus, and that whichever citizen surpassed the rest in the magnificence and lavishness of his arrangements for the festival should be granted a sum of money from the public treasury to enable him to dedicate an offering. Finally, the Athenians changed the name of the month Munychion to Demetrion, gave the name of Demetrias to the last day of the month and renamed the festival of the Dionysia the Demetria.[32] Most of these innovations were greeted with signs of displeasure from the gods. The sacred robe, in which it had been decreed that the

figures of Antigonus and Demetrius should be woven beside those of Zeus and Athena, was struck by a violent gust of wind as it was being carried in procession through the midst of Cerameicus, and was torn in pieces; great quantities of hemlock suddenly sprang up around the altars of the so-called saviour-gods, although there are many parts of the country in which this poisonous herb does not grow at all; on the day of the celebration of the Dionysia, the sacred procession had to be cancelled because of a sudden spell of cold weather which arrived out of season, and this was followed by a heavy frost, which not only blasted all the vines and fig-trees but destroyed most of the corn in the blade. It was for this reason that Philippides, who was an enemy of Stratocles, attacked him in a comedy with these verses:

> It was because of him that frost burnt the vines,
> Because of his impiety the robe was torn down the middle
> Because he converted divine honours into mortal ones.
> Such acts, not comedy, destroy a people.[33]

This Philippides was a friend of Lysimachus[34] and on his account the Athenians received many favours from the king.[35] The latter even believed that it was a good omen if he were to meet or catch sight of Philippides at the start of any expedition or enterprise. Besides this Philippides enjoyed a good reputation, since he was no busybody and had none of the self-important habits of a courtier. One day Lysimachus wished to do him a kindness and asked him, 'Philippides, which of my possessions shall I give you?' 'Whichever you please, sire,' he replied, 'but not one of your secrets.' I have purposely made a comparison of this man with Stratocles, in order to contrast the man of the theatre with the man of the speakers' platform.

13. But the strangest and most exaggerated of all the honours devised for Demetrius was the one proposed by Dromocleides of Sphettus. This man, when the question arose concerning the consecration of the shields at Delphi, put down a motion that the people should obtain an oracular response from Demetrius.[36]

I reproduce the actual words of the motion, which read as follows:

> May it be propitious.[37] It has been decreed by the people that they shall elect one man from the Athenians, who shall go to the saviour-god, and after he has sacrificed and obtained good omens, shall inquire of the saviour-god what is the most reverent, decorous and expeditious manner in which the people may ensure the restitution of the intended offerings to their proper places. And whatsoever answer he shall please to give them, the people shall comply with it.

By such absurd flattery, they further corrupted the man, who even before was not of entirely sound mind.

14. During the months which he spent in Athens at this time, he married a widow named Eurydice. She was descended from the famous Miltiades, had married Ophelas, the ruler of Cyrene, and after his death had returned to Athens. The Athenians chose to regard this marriage as a special mark of favour and as an honour to their city. But in general, Demetrius was very free in his attitude towards marriage and had many wives at the same time. Among these the one who enjoyed most respect and honour was Phila; she owed her privileged position to the fact that she was the daughter of Antipater and had been married to Craterus, the man who of all the successors of Alexander had been remembered with the greatest affection by the Macedonians.[38] Antigonus, it seems, had persuaded Demetrius to marry her when he was quite young, in spite of her being considerably older, and it is said that when Demetrius expressed his reluctance, his father whispered in his ear Euripides' words,[39] '*Where it is profitable, a man should marry against his nature*', bluntly substituting 'marry' for 'serve', as the verse was originally phrased. But such regard as Demetrius showed for Phila or the rest of his wives did not prevent him from keeping many mistresses, not only courtesans, but women of free birth, and in this respect he had the worst reputation of all the rulers of his time.

15. When his father started urging him to take command of operations against Ptolemy for possession of Cyprus, Demetrius had no choice but to obey the order; but he was vexed at having to abandon the war for the liberation of Greece which was a nobler and more glorious enterprise. He, therefore, offered a sum of money to Cleonides, Ptolemy's general who commanded the troops garrisoning Sicyon and Corinth, to evacuate the cities and set them free. But Cleonides refused and so Demetrius hurriedly put to sea and, gathering reinforcements, sailed against Cyprus. There he attacked Menelaus, Ptolemy's brother, and immediately defeated him. But Ptolemy himself appeared on the scene with a large fleet and army, and the two commanders exchanged haughty and threatening messages. Ptolemy called upon Demetrius to sail away before he concentrated all his forces and crushed him, while Demetrius offered to allow Ptolemy to withdraw from Cyprus, on condition that he surrendered Corinth and Sicyon. The battle which then followed[40] was of the greatest moment, not only to the combatants themselves but to all the other rulers, for apart from the uncertainty of the outcome, they believed that the prize was not merely the possession of Cyprus and Syria, but an absolute and immediate supremacy over all their rivals.

16. Ptolemy advanced to the attack with a fleet of a hundred and fifty ships and ordered Menelaus to move out of Salamis with sixty at the moment when the battle was at its height, so as to fall upon Demetrius' fleet from the rear and throw it into disorder. Demetrius detached no more than ten ships to oppose Menelaus' sixty, since these were enough to block the narrow channel which led out of the harbour. He then deployed his land forces in extended order along various headlands which jutted out into the water, and put to sea with a hundred and eighty ships. He bore down upon the opposing fleet with great force and violence and utterly routed Ptolemy, who after his defeat fled with a squadron of eight ships. This was all that remained of his fleet; of the rest, some had been sunk in the battle and seventy had been captured, crews and all. But the whole of Ptolemy's enormous train of attendants, friends and women

who had been embarked in transports near his fleet, all fell into
Demetrius' hands; so, too, did all his arms, money and engines
of war. Demetrius rounded up the entire expedition and
escorted it to his camp. Among these prizes of war was the celebrated Lamia,[41] who had first won fame for her skill as a
flute-player and had later become renowned as a courtesan. By
this time her beauty was on the wane and Demetrius was many
years her junior; in spite of this, her charm took possession of
him to such an extent that he loved only her, even though many
other women loved him.

After the battle, Menelaus too offered no further resistance,
but surrendered Salamis to Demetrius together with his fleet and
his land forces of 1,200 cavalry and 12,000 hoplites.

17. Demetrius added still more lustre to his brilliant victory by
the generosity and humanity which he showed to his opponents: he not only buried the enemy's dead with full honours but
he also set his prisoners free. He then chose twelve hundred
complete suits of armour from the spoils and presented them to
the Athenians.

He sent Aristodemus of Miletus as his personal messenger to
carry the news of the victory to his father. Of all those in
Demetrius' entourage, this man was the arch-flatterer and on
this occasion he set out, it seems, to crown his achievement and
surpass any of his previous efforts. For after he had made the
crossing from Cyprus, he would not allow his ship to approach
the land. Instead, he ordered the crew to cast anchor and to
remain quietly on board, while he had himself rowed ashore in
a small boat and landed alone. Then he continued his journey
to Antigonus, who was awaiting news of the battle in a state of
suspense and with all the anxiety which is natural to a man
who is contending for such high stakes. When he heard that
Aristodemus was on his way, his agitation reached such a pitch
that he could scarcely keep himself indoors, but sent servants
and friends one after the other to discover from Aristodemus
what had happened. Aristodemus refused to utter a word to
anybody, but walked on in complete silence, keeping a measured pace and wearing a grave expression on his face. By this

time Antigonus was thoroughly alarmed and could bear the suspense no longer; he came to the door to meet Aristodemus, who was accompanied by a large crowd which was hastening to the palace. At last, when Aristodemus was near enough, he stretched out his hand and cried in a loud voice, 'Hail, King Antigonus, we have defeated King Ptolemy in a sea-battle. We are the masters of Cyprus and we have taken 16,800 prisoners.' Antigonus replied, 'Hail to you likewise, by Zeus. But you will pay for torturing us for so long. You can wait a while for the reward for your good news.'

18. After this success, the masses for the first time acclaimed Antigonus and Demetrius as kings.[42] Antigonus was immediately crowned, and Demetrius received a diadem from his father with a letter addressing him as king. At the same time, when the news reached Ptolemy's followers in Egypt, they also conferred the title of king on him, so as not to appear unduly cast down by their defeat, and this spirit of rivalry proved infectious among the other successors of Alexander. Lysimachus began to wear a diadem, and Seleucus, who had already assumed royal prerogatives when he gave audience to the barbarians, now adopted the same practice in his interviews with Greeks. Cassander, however, although others addressed him as king both in letters and in speech, continued to sign letters with his own name, as he had always done.

The assumption of such dignities meant something more than the mere addition of a name or a change in appearance. It stirred the pride of these men, raised their ideas to a different plane and introduced an element of arrogance and self-importance into their daily lives and their dealings with others, in the same way as tragic actors, when they put on royal robes, alter their gait, their voice, their deportment and their mode of address.[43] As a result they also became harsher in their administration of justice, and they cast off the various disguises whereby they had previously concealed their power and which had made them treat their subjects more gently and tolerantly. Such was the effect of a single word from a flatterer, which in this way brought about a revolution throughout the world.

19. Antigonus, elated by his son's achievements in Cyprus, immediately launched another expedition against Ptolemy.[44] He himself took command of the land forces, while Demetrius with a large fleet supported his operations from the sea. The outcome of the campaign was foretold to Medius, a friend of Antigonus, in his sleep. He dreamt that Antigonus, together with the whole army, was running in a race in the stadium. Over the first part of the course he ran strongly and swiftly, but then little by little his strength failed him; then, after he had rounded the halfway mark, he became weak, began to pant heavily and could barely recover. As events turned out, Antigonus encountered many difficulties on land, while Demetrius ran into a violent storm and heavy seas and was driven on to a rocky shore which offered no shelter. He lost many of his ships and returned home without having accomplished anything.

Antigonus by this time was almost eighty years old, but it was his corpulence and weight even more than his age which incapacitated him for playing an active part in military operations. He therefore made more and more use of his son, for Demetrius, with the help of experience combined with good luck, was now conducting the greatest enterprises with success, and neither his luxury nor his extravagance nor his drinking habits troubled his father. For although in peace-time Demetrius threw himself headlong into these excesses and devoted his time exclusively to the pursuit of pleasure in the most abandoned and wanton fashion, in time of war he was as sober as those to whom abstinence was the natural way of life. There is a story that when Demetrius was completely under the spell of Lamia, a fact which had become common knowledge, he returned home from abroad and greeted his father with a kiss. Antigonus laughed and said, 'Anybody would think, my boy, that you were kissing Lamia.' On another occasion, when Demetrius had been drinking for several days continuously, he excused his absence by saying that he had been laid up with a severe cold. 'So I heard,' remarked Antigonus, 'but did your cold come from Chios or from Thasos?'[45] Another time after hearing that his son was sick, Antigonus went to visit him and met one of his beautiful mistresses coming away from his room. Antigonus went inside, sat down by his side and felt his pulse. 'The fever has left me now,' Demetrius told him. 'Yes, so I see,' his father replied; 'I met it just now as it was going away.' Antigonus was willing to indulge these faults in his son because of his achievements in other respects. The Scythians have a custom of twanging their bowstrings in the midst of their drinking and carousing, as though they were summoning back their courage at the moment when it melts away in pleasure. Demetrius, on the other hand, was in the habit of surrendering his whole being, now to pleasure and now to action: he succeeded in keeping the two spheres completely separate and never allowed his diversions to interfere with his preparations for war.

20. Indeed, as a general he had the reputation of being more effective in preparing an army than in handling it. He insisted on being abundantly supplied for every eventuality, he had an insatiable ambition to embark upon larger and larger projects, whether in shipbuilding or the construction of siege-engines, and he took an intense pleasure in watching the workings of these creations. For he had a good natural intelligence and a speculative mind and he did not apply his talents to mere pastimes or useless diversions, like some other kings, who played the flute or painted or worked in metal. Aeropus of Macedon, for example, used to devote his leisure to making little tables or lampstands. Attalus Philometer made a hobby of cultivating poisonous herbs, not only henbane or hellebore but also hemlock, aconite or dorycnium. He used to sow and plant these in the royal gardens, and he made it his business to know their various juices and fruits and to gather them at the proper season. The kings of Parthia used to pride themselves on notching and sharpening with their own hands the points of their spears and arrows. But with Demetrius even when he played the workman he did it in regal fashion. He approached his projects on a grand scale and his creations were not only skilfully and inventively conceived, but they bore the marks of a lofty mind and purpose, so that men thought them worthy not only of the

genius and wealth of a king but also of his handiwork. Their sheer size alarmed even his friends, while their beauty delighted even his enemies (and this is true and not just a clever way of putting it). His enemies would stand on the shore and gape in wonder at his galleys of fifteen or sixteen rows of oarsmen as they sailed past, while his 'city-takers',[46] as events actually testify, were a spectacle to the inhabitants of the towns he besieged. For example, Lysimachus, who was the bitterest of Demetrius' enemies among the kings of his time, when Demetrius was besieging the town of Soli in Cilicia[47] and he was in the field against him, sent a message asking to be allowed to see his siege-engines and his ships in motion; after Demetrius had displayed these to him, he expressed his admiration and went away. Likewise, the people of Rhodes, after they had resisted a long siege and had come to terms with Demetrius, asked him for some of his machines which they wished to keep as a memorial of his power and of their own courage.

21. Demetrius went to war with the people of Rhodes[48] because they were allies of Ptolemy, and he moved up against their walls the greatest of his 'city-takers'.[49] This was a siege-tower with a square base, each side of which measured 72 feet at the bottom. It was 99 feet high with the upper part tapering off to narrower dimensions. Inside it was divided into many separate storeys and compartments, the side which faced the enemy being pierced with apertures on each storey, through which missiles could be discharged, and it was manned with troops who were equipped with every kind of weapon. The machine never tottered or leaned in any direction, but rolled forwards firm and upright on its base, advancing with an even motion and with a noise and an impetus that inspired mingled feelings of alarm and delight in all who beheld it.

For this campaign Demetrius was sent two iron coats of mail from Cyprus, each of which weighed only 40 pounds. In order to demonstrate the armour's strength and power of resistance, Zoilus, the maker, had a bolt from a catapult shot at one of them at a range of twenty paces. The armour remained unbroken at the point of impact, and its surface showed nothing more than a small scratch such as might have been made by an engraver. Demetrius wore this suit himself and gave the other to Alcimus the Epirot, the man who combined the greatest physical strength and the most warlike spirit in his army, and the only one whose armour weighed nearly 120 pounds, the others carrying only half this weight. Alcimus was killed at Rhodes in the fighting near the theatre.

22. The Rhodians put up a stout defence and Demetrius achieved no success worth mentioning against them. However, he kept the siege going out of anger against them, because when his wife Phila dispatched a ship carrying letters, bedding and clothing for him, the Rhodians captured the vessel and sent it with all its cargo to Ptolemy. In this matter they did not follow the civilized example set by the Athenians, who, when Philip was at war with them, captured one of his messengers and read all the letters he was carrying except for one written by Olympias: this they did not open but returned to Philip with the seal unbroken. However, although Demetrius was irritated at the Rhodians' action, he did not allow himself to retaliate against them when, a little later, they gave him the opportunity to do so. It happened that they had commissioned Protogenes of Caunus to paint a portrait of Ialysus and that this picture, which was almost finished, had been captured by Demetrius in one of the suburbs of the city. The Rhodians sent a herald and begged him to spare the painting and not destroy it, to which he replied that he would rather burn the statues of his father than a masterpiece which had cost so much labour, for Protogenes was reputed to have worked for seven years on the painting. Apelles tells us that when he first set eyes on it, he was so filled with admiration that he could not utter a word, and that when speech returned to him he exclaimed, 'A tremendous labour and a wonderful achievement,' but he added that it lacked something of the grace which raised his own paintings to the heavens. This picture later shared the fate of many others: crowded together at Rome, it was destroyed by fire.[50]

The Rhodians continued to hold out vigorously and at last Demetrius, who was anxious to find a pretext for abandoning the siege, was persuaded to make terms through the mediation of the Athenians; the treaty which they concluded stipulated that the Rhodians should act as the allies of Antigonus and Demetrius in his wars, but should not take up arms against Ptolemy.

23. The Athenians kept making appeals to Demetrius because their city was being besieged by Cassander,[51] and Demetrius sailed to their rescue with a fleet of three hundred and thirty ships and a large hoplite force. He not only drove Cassander out of Attica but pursued him as far as Thermopylae. There he routed Cassander's army, occupied Heracleia whose citizens came over to him and was joined by 6,000 Macedonians who had deserted from Cassander's army. On his return, he freed from Macedonian rule the Greeks living south of Thermopylae, concluded an alliance with the Boeotians and captured Cenchreae. He also took possession of the strongholds of Phyle and Panactum, fortresses in Attica which had been garrisoned by Cassander, and restored them to the Athenians. Although earlier the people of Athens had exhausted all the honours which could possibly be bestowed upon Demetrius, nevertheless they went on to show that they could still invent new forms of flattery. For they gave him the rear part of the temple of the Parthenon for his quarters, and there he lodged throughout his visit. He was entertained, so the arrangement implied, by his hostess Athena, but it could not be said that he was a well-behaved guest or that he conducted himself under her roof with the decorum that is due to a virgin-goddess. And yet once, when Antigonus had learnt that Demetrius' brother Philip was billeted in a house which was occupied by three girls, he had said nothing to Philip but sent for the officer responsible for requisitioning houses and told him in his son's presence, 'Won't you get my son out of this tight spot.'

24. Demetrius ought to have shown Athena some respect, if for no other reason than that she was his older sister (for that was

what he wanted said). But in fact he abused so many free-born youths and Athenian women, and so filled the acropolis with his outrages, that the place was considered to be unusually pure when his partners in debauchery were Chrysis, Lamia, Demo and Anticyra, those well-known prostitutes. For the sake of the city's good name I ought not to enter into the details of Demetrius' other debaucheries, but it would be wrong to pass over the virtue and modesty of a boy named Democles. He was still young and was known as Democles the Beautiful; indeed the epithet betrayed him, since reports of his good looks soon reached the ears of Demetrius. Democles refused the advances of many who tried to win him by persuasion or gifts or threats, and finally stopped appearing at the public wrestling-schools or gymnasia and used only a private bath. Demetrius watched for his opportunity and one day surprised him there alone. When the boy saw that there was no one to help him and that he had no choice but to yield, he snatched the lid off the cauldron, leapt into the boiling water and killed himself. In this way, he suffered a fate which was certainly undeserved, but he showed a spirit which was worthy both of his personal beauty and of his country. Democles' behaviour may be contrasted with that of Cleaenetus, the son of Cleomedon. This man's father had been sentenced to pay the sum of 50 talents, and in the attempt to obtain a letter from Demetrius remitting the fine he not only disgraced himself but caused great trouble to the city. The people excused Cleomedon from this penalty, but they also passed a resolution that no citizen should ever again bring a letter from Demetrius before the assembly. Demetrius was furious when he heard the news, whereupon the people took fright and not only rescinded the motion but actually put to death some of those who had introduced and supported it and banished others. They even went so far as to pass a further decree to the effect that whatever thing Demetrius might command in future should be regarded as holy in the sight of the gods and just towards all men. One of the better class of citizens remarked on this occasion that Stratocles was mad to propose such a motion, to which Demochares of Leuconoe replied, 'He would certainly be mad if he did not show this kind of madness.' For

Stratocles was amply rewarded for his flattery. Demochares, on the other hand, was publicly charged for this utterance and sent into exile. Such was the fate of the Athenians, who fondly imagined that because they had got rid of the occupying garrison they had become a free people.

25. Demetrius marched into the Peloponnese,[52] where not one of his enemies opposed him, but all abandoned their cities and fled. He accepted the allegiance of the eastern part of the coast, which is known as Acte, and of the region of Arcadia with the exception of Mantineia, and liberated the cities of Argos, Sicyon and Corinth by paying to their garrisons 100 talents to evacuate them. It happened that at Argos the festival of Hera was being held and Demetrius presided over the games, joined in the celebration of the festival with the Greeks who had gathered there and married Deidameia, who was the daughter of Aeacides the king of the Molossians and the sister of Pyrrhus.[53] He told the inhabitants of Sicyon that their city was sited in the wrong place and persuaded them to move to the ground which it now occupies, and he also had its name changed and styled Demetrias instead of Sicyon.

When a congress of the city-states was held at the Isthmus,[54] which was attended by a huge concourse of delegates, Demetrius was proclaimed commander-in-chief of the Greeks, as Philip and Alexander had been before him;[55] in the elation of success and of the power which he enjoyed at that moment he even considered himself by far their superior. At any rate, Alexander had never deprived other kings of their royal title, nor had he proclaimed himself King of Kings, although many other rulers received their style and position from him. Demetrius, on the other hand, mocked and ridiculed those who gave the title of king to anybody other than his father and himself, and at his drinking-parties he loved to hear the guests propose toasts to himself as king, but to Seleucus as master of the elephants, Ptolemy as admiral, Lysimachus as treasurer and Agathocles the Sicilian as lord of the islands. The other kings when they heard of these affectations merely laughed at Demetrius, but Lysimachus was enraged at the idea that Demetrius regarded him as a eunuch, because it was the general custom to appoint eunuchs to the post of treasurer. In fact, it was Lysimachus who of all these rulers felt the bitterest hatred for Demetrius, and on one occasion, when he was sneering at his rival's passion for Lamia, he remarked that this was the first time he had ever seen a whore take part in a tragedy, to which Demetrius retorted that his mistress was a more modest woman than Lysimachus' own 'Penelope'.[56]

26. When Demetrius was preparing to return to Athens, he wrote to inform the people that he wished to be initiated into the Mysteries as soon as he arrived, and to be admitted to every one of the various grades of initiation, from the lowest to the highest, the Epopteia. This request was both unprecedented and unlawful, since the lesser rites were enacted in the month of Anthesterion and the greater in Boedromion, and initiates had to wait at least a year after the greater rites before being admitted to the Epopteia.[57] But when Demetrius' letter was read out, the only man who dared to refuse his request was Pythodorus the torch-bearer,[58] and his opposition achieved nothing. Instead, a motion was proposed by Stratocles that the current month which happened to be Munychion should be declared to be Anthesterion, and during this period the lesser rites at Agra were performed for Demetrius. Next, the month of Munychion was again changed and this time became Boedromion, during which Demetrius passed through the remaining rites of initiation, and was also admitted to the Epopteia. It was for this reason that Philippides poured scorn on Stratocles as the man '*Who cut the year down to a single month*', and with reference to his quartering in the Parthenon talked of Demetrius as the man '*Who treated the Acropolis as an inn, and introduced his mistresses to the virgin-goddess*'.[59]

27. Of all the many outrages and abuses which Demetrius committed at this time, the one that most angered the Athenians was his action in commanding them to levy immediately the sum of 250 talents for his services. The money was then extorted from the people in the harshest and most peremptory

fashion, and when he saw the amount that had been raised, he ordered it to be given to Lamia and his other mistresses to buy soap. What the Athenians resented was not so much the loss of the money as the humiliation of this imposition and the words which accompanied it, although according to some accounts it was not they but the people of Thessaly who were treated in this fashion. Apart from this episode, Lamia also extorted money from many of the citizens when she was preparing to entertain Demetrius, and, indeed, the extravagance of this banquet became so legendary that it was described in full by Lynceus of Samos;[60] it was for this reason that one of the comic poets, with some justification, described Lamia as a 'city-taker'[61] in herself, and Demochares of Soli, called Demetrius Mythos, because he too, like the myth, had his Lamia.[62]

Demetrius' passion for Lamia and the favours which he lavished on her roused the enmity and animosity not only of his other wives but of his friends. At any rate, he once sent some ambassadors to Lysimachus, and one day, when they were at leisure, the king showed them a number of deep scars on his thighs and shoulders which had been made by a lion's claws, and told them of the battle he had fought with the beast when Alexander had shut him in with it. The ambassadors laughed and declared that their own king also carried on his neck the marks of a terrible wild beast, a Lamia. The wonder was that Demetrius, who in the beginning had found fault with Phila because she was older than himself, should now be captivated by Lamia and love her so long when she was well past her prime. At any rate, one evening when Lamia was playing the flute at a banquet, Demetrius asked the courtesan Demo, who was surnamed Mania, what she thought of her. 'Your majesty,' she replied, 'I think she is an old woman.' Another time, when some sweetmeats had been placed on the table, Demetrius remarked to Mania, 'You see how many presents Lamia sends me?' 'My mother', answered Mania, 'will send you many more if you will sleep with her.'

Another story is recorded of what Lamia had to say about the celebrated judgement of Bocchoris.[63] An Egyptian fell in love with Thonis the courtesan, who asked him for a large sum of money in return for her favours. Afterwards, he dreamt that he had enjoyed her, and his passion for her then died away. At this, Thonis brought an action against him for the payment which she claimed was her due. When he had heard the case, Bocchoris ordered the defendant to bring into court in its coffer the exact amount of money which had been demanded from him, and to move it backwards and forwards with his hand; meanwhile, the courtesan was to clutch at its shadow, since the thing which is imagined is the shadow of the reality. Lamia thought this judgement unjust, because although the young man's dream had delivered him from his passion, the shadow of the money did not deliver the courtesan from her desire for it. So much then for Lamia.

28. And now our story, as it traces the fortunes and achievements of my subject, moves from the comic to the tragic stage. For all the other kings formed an alliance against Antigonus and combined their forces.[64] Demetrius sailed away from Greece to join him, and was greatly heartened to find his father full of resolution for the war and buoyed up by a spirit that belied his years. And yet it seems probable that if only Antigonus could have made some small concessions and curbed his passion for extending his rule, he could have retained his supremacy among the successors of Alexander and bequeathed it to his son. But he was by nature imperious and disdainful of others, and as overbearing in his words as in his actions, and he therefore exasperated many young and powerful men and provoked them to act against him: he boasted that he would scatter the alliance they had formed with a single stone and a single shout, as easily as one scares away a flock of birds from a field.

Antigonus took the field with more than 70,000 infantry, and with 10,000 cavalry and 75 elephants, while his opponents had 64,000 infantry, 500 more cavalry than Antigonus, 400 elephants and 120 war chariots. But once Antigonus had drawn near the enemy, a change in his demeanour became noticeable – not in his purpose, but rather in his expectations. For in the past, it had been his custom to show a lofty and aggressive spirit before he went into action; he would speak in a loud

428 THE AGE OF ALEXANDER

voice and use arrogant language, and often by uttering some casual joke or piece of mockery when the enemy was close at hand, he would reveal his own assurance and the contempt he felt for his opponent. But this time he was observed to be thoughtful and silent for the most part. He presented his son to the army and formally pronounced him to be his successor, but what astonished everybody most of all was that he now held a long conference alone in his tent with Demetrius, whereas it had never been his practice in the past to enter into secret consultations even with his son. Instead, he had always relied upon his own judgement, formed his own plans and issued his orders openly. At any rate, there is a story that when Demetrius was still only a boy he had asked his father at what hour he intended to break camp, to which Antigonus retorted roughly, 'Why, are you afraid that you will be the only man who does not hear the trumpet?'

29. At this time, however, they were also disheartened by threatening omens. Demetrius dreamt that Alexander appeared before him in shining armour and asked him what would be their password for the battle. Demetrius told him 'Zeus and victory', whereupon Alexander replied, 'In that case I shall go and join your adversaries: they will certainly receive me,' for he was offended to find that Antigonus had not chosen 'Alexander and victory' for his password.[65] Then, while the phalanx was already forming in order of battle, Antigonus, as he stepped out of his tent, stumbled, fell on his face and hurt himself severely. When he rose to his feet, he stretched out his hands towards heaven and prayed that the gods should either grant him victory or else a painless death before his army was routed.

When the battle began,[66] Demetrius led his strongest and best of his cavalry in a charge against Antiochus, Seleucus' son.[67] He fought brilliantly and put the enemy to flight, but by pressing the pursuit too far and too impulsively he threw away the victory. The enemy placed their elephants in his way to block his return and he was prevented from rejoining the infantry; meanwhile Seleucus, seeing that his opponent's phalanx had been left unprotected by cavalry, altered his tactics accordingly. He did not actually launch a mounted attack but, by riding round Antigonus' infantry and continually threatening to charge, he kept them in a state of alarm and at the same time gave them the opportunity of changing sides. And this, indeed, was what actually happened, for a large group of them who had become separated from the main body came over to him of their own accord and the rest were routed. Then, as great numbers of the enemy bore down on Antigonus, one of his attendants cried out, 'They are making for you, sire,' to which the king replied, 'Yes, what other object could they have? But Demetrius will come to our rescue.' In this hope he persisted to the last and kept looking for his son's approach on every side, until the enemy overwhelmed him with a cloud of javelins and he fell. The rest of his friends and attendants abandoned him, and only Thorax of Larissa remained by his body.

30. After the battle had been decided in this way, the victorious kings proceeded to carve up the realm which Antigonus and Demetrius had ruled, like the carcass of some great slaughtered beast, each of them taking a portion and adding new provinces to those they already possessed. Demetrius got away with 5,000 infantry and 4,000 cavalry and marched straight to Ephesus. Here, everybody supposed that as he needed money he would inevitably plunder the treasures of the temple of Artemis, but, as he was afraid that the troops would do precisely this, he immediately left the city and sailed for Greece. He placed his remaining hopes principally in Athens, for he had left his wife Deidameia there, together with his ships and his treasure, and he believed that his safest refuge in his misfortune lay in the goodwill of the Athenian people. But as he approached the Cyclades, he met a delegation from the city who requested him to keep away, since the people had passed a resolution not to admit any of the kings within their walls; at the same time they informed him that his wife Deidameia had been escorted to Megara with appropriate honours and ceremony. At this Demetrius, who had borne his other trials serenely and who despite the complete reversal in his fortunes had never behaved in a mean or ignoble fashion, was transported with rage and quite lost control of himself. He was cut to the heart at being

unexpectedly disappointed and betrayed in this fashion by the Athenians, and at discovering that their apparent goodwill proved to be empty and false as soon as it was put to the test.

And, indeed, it would seem that the bestowing of extravagant honours is really the least substantial proof of the goodwill of a people towards a king or ruler, for the true value of such tributes lies in the intentions of those who bestow them. They are worthless if they are prompted by fear, for an identical decree may equally well be passed out of motives of fear or of affection. Accordingly, men of sense will consider first of all the substance of their actions and achievements, and only afterwards the statues, paintings or deifications which have been offered to them: they can then judge whether these can be trusted as genuine honours or distrusted as obligatory ones, since it often happens that a people in the very act of conferring honours will hate those who accept them arrogantly and without modesty or respect for the free will of the givers.

31. At any rate, Demetrius thought that he had been shamefully treated by the Athenians, but as he was powerless to avenge the affront he sent them a message in which he courteously protested at their decision and requested that his ships should be returned to him, among them the vessel which had thirteen rows of oarsmen. These were duly handed over to him and he then sailed for the Isthmus of Corinth, where he found that his affairs had greatly deteriorated. Everywhere, his garrisons were being expelled from the towns in which he had stationed them and the whole region was going over to his enemies. He therefore left Pyrrhus of Epirus to act as his lieutenant in Greece, while he himself put to sea and sailed for the Thracian Chersonese. There he plundered the territory of Lysimachus and out of the spoils he collected was able to maintain and hold together his army, which was now beginning to recover its spirits, and to build up a force of formidable strength. The other kings made no attempt to help Lysimachus: they considered that he was by no means more reasonable than Demetrius, and that because he possessed more power, he was more to be feared.

Not long after this Seleucus approached Demetrius to ask

for the hand of Stratonice,[68] who was his daughter by Phila. Seleucus already had one son, Antiochus, by his Persian wife, Apame, but he considered that his empire had room in it for more than one heir, and he was anxious to form an alliance with Demetrius because he saw that Lysimachus had already married one of Ptolemy's daughters himself and had taken the other for his son Agathocles. For Demetrius a marriage alliance with Seleucus was an unexpected stroke of good fortune, and so he took his daughter on board ship and sailed with his whole fleet to Syria. In the course of his voyage he was forced to put in at a number of places, and in particular he landed on the coast of Cilicia, a province ruled by Pleistarchus, the brother of Cassander, who had been given it by the kings after their victory over Antigonus. Pleistarchus regarded Demetrius' arrival in his territory as a violation of his sovereignty; besides this, he wished to protest to Seleucus against his having made an alliance with their common enemy without consulting the other kings, and so he went up to see him.

32. When Demetrius learnt of this, he marched inland to the city of Cyinda. There he found 1,200 talents of the public treasury still intact,[69] and so he collected this, embarked without any hindrance and quickly put to sea. His wife Phila had by then joined him and at Rhosus he met Seleucus. No sooner had the two men come together than they received one another in princely style without the least deception or suspicion. First Seleucus gave a banquet for Demetrius in his camp, and then Demetrius in his turn received Seleucus on board his galley with the thirteen rows of oarsmen. There were entertainments and the two rulers conversed at leisure and spent whole days in one another's company without either guards or arms, until at length Seleucus took Stratonice and escorted her in great state to Antioch. But Demetrius made himself master of Cilicia and sent his wife Phila to Cassander, who was also her brother, to answer the accusations which had been made against him by Pleistarchus. In the meantime, his wife Deidameia, whom he had married at Argos, arrived by sea, but they had only been together for a short while before she fell sick and died. Then,

through Seleucus' good offices, Demetrius was reconciled with Ptolemy, and it was arranged that he should marry the king's daughter, Ptolemaïs.

So far Seleucus had behaved with the utmost courtesy, but he also requested Demetrius to cede Cilicia to him in return for a sum of money, and when Demetrius refused he angrily insisted that Tyre and Sidon should be handed over to him. This seemed a violent and quite unjustifiable demand. Seleucus had become the ruler of the whole region from India to the coast of Syria. Why should he be so needy or so mean in spirit as to quarrel with a man who had just become related to him by marriage and who had suffered a great reversal in his fortunes, all for the sake of two cities? In short, Seleucus was a conspicuous example of the wisdom that Plato showed when he argued that the man who wishes to be really rich should seek not to increase his possessions but to decrease his desires. For he who can never restrain his avarice will never be free from the sense of poverty and want.[70]

33. Demetrius, however, was not cowed. He declared that even if he should lose ten thousand more battles at Ipsus, he would never consent to pay for the privilege of having Seleucus as his son-in-law. He strengthened his cities with garrisons, but when he had news that Lachares had taken advantage of the civil dissensions which had occurred in Athens and made himself tyrant there, Demetrius hoped that if he suddenly appeared on the scene he could take the city with ease. He crossed the Aegean safely with a large fleet, but as he was sailing along the coast of Attica he ran into a storm in which most of his ships were destroyed and a great number of his men were drowned. He himself escaped and opened a petty campaign against the Athenians, but when he found he was getting no results, he dispatched officers to assemble another fleet for him; meanwhile, he marched into the Peloponnese and laid siege to Messene. Here during an assault on the walls, he was nearly killed, for he was struck in the face by a bolt from a catapult which pierced his jaw and entered his mouth. But he recovered from the wound, and after receiving the submission of a number of cities

that had revolted from him, he again invaded Attica, captured
Eleusis and Rhamnus and devastated the countryside. He also
seized a ship loaded with grain that was bound for Athens, and
hanged the pilot and the owner of the cargo. This action so
frightened other vessels that they turned away from the city,
which was reduced to a state of famine and a great shortage
of other commodities. At any rate, the price of a bushel of salt
rose to 40 drachmas and a peck of wheat to 300. The Athenians gained a short respite from their sufferings when a fleet of
a hundred and fifty ships sent to help them by Ptolemy was
sighted off the coast of Aegina. But then Demetrius was reinforced by a strong naval contingent from the Peloponnese and
by another from Cyprus, so that he was able to concentrate a
fleet of three hundred vessels. In consequence, Ptolemy's ships
hoisted sail and fled, and Lachares the tyrant abandoned the
city and ran away.

34. Earlier, the Athenians had passed a resolution decreeing the
death penalty for anyone who even mentioned the possibility
of negotiating a peace or an agreement with Demetrius, but
now they at once opened the nearest gates and sent a delegation to his camp. They had been forced into this action by sheer
destitution and so did not expect any favours. Among many
examples of the extremities to which they had been reduced, it
happened that a father and son were sitting in a room and had
abandoned all hope of survival. Suddenly, a dead mouse fell
from the ceiling and as soon as the two saw it they sprang up
and began to fight for the prize. It was at this time, too, we are
told, that the philosopher Epicurus kept his disciples alive with
beans, counting out and distributing a ration for them each day.

Such was the condition of the city when Demetrius entered
it.[71] He ordered the whole population to assemble in the theatre,
surrounded the rear and sides with troops and lined the stage
with his bodyguards, while he himself, just like a tragic actor,
made his appearance down one of the stairways which led
through the auditorium. This frightened the Athenians more
than ever, but with the very first words that he uttered Demetrius
dispelled their fears. For he avoided any hint of bitterness,

either in his tone or his words, but he reproached them in a gentle and friendly fashion for their behaviour towards him and showed that he was reconciled to them. He presented them with 100,000 bushels of wheat and appointed as magistrates the leaders who were most acceptable to the people.[72] At this Dromocleides the orator,[73] when he saw that the populace could hardly find words to express their joy and wished to eclipse the panegyrics which the demagogues were accustomed to lavish on Demetrius, put down a motion that Piraeus and Munychia should be handed over to King Demetrius. This resolution was passed, but Demetrius went further still by posting another garrison on the Hill of Muses:[74] he did this to prevent the Athenians from shaking off his yoke yet again and distracting his attention from his other enterprises.

35. Now that he had possession of Athens, he at once laid plans against Sparta. He engaged Archidamus, the king of Sparta, near Mantineia, defeated him, routed his army and then invaded Laconia.[75] Next, he fought a second pitched battle near Sparta itself in which he killed two hundred men and took five hundred prisoner and seemed to have the city within his grasp, although up to that moment no enemy had ever captured it.[76] But no other king seems to have undergone such huge and sudden reversals of fortune; and in the career of no other does fortune seem to have been so often transformed, from obscurity to renown, from triumph to humiliation and from abasement to the heights of power. It was for this reason, so we are told, that when he was in the depths of adversity, Demetrius would call upon Fortune in the words of Aeschylus: '*It is you who fan my flame, and you who seem to burn me!*'[77] And so just when the whole course of events seemed to be moving in conjunction to increase his power and sovereignty, the news reached him that Lysimachus had seized the cities in Asia which had belonged to him, and that Ptolemy had captured the whole of Cyprus except for the city of Salamis, where Demetrius' mother and children were now besieged. But like the woman in Archilochus' poem, who '*treacherously offered water in one hand while she bore fire in the other*',[78] so Fortune drew him

away from Sparta with this dire and threatening news and at the same instant kindled his hopes of fresh achievements on the grandest scale. This was how it happened.

36. After the death of Cassander,[79] his eldest son Philip ruled the Macedonians for a short while, and then died, whereupon Philip's two surviving brothers contested the succession. One of these, Antipater, murdered his mother Thessalonice,[80] while the other, Alexander, appealed to Pyrrhus to come to his help from Epirus and Demetrius from the Peloponnese. Pyrrhus arrived first, and as he promptly annexed a large slice of Macedonia as the reward for his help, he at once became a neighbour whom Alexander dreaded. Demetrius, as soon as he had received Alexander's letter, set out for Macedonia with his army and frightened the young man even more because of his power and reputation. The result was that Alexander met Demetrius at the town of Dium, received him as an honoured guest and then told him that the situation no longer required his presence. This was enough to arouse suspicions on both sides; moreover, when Demetrius was on his way to a banquet to which the young prince had invited him, he was warned that there was a plot to kill him in the midst of the drinking. Demetrius was not at all disconcerted and merely delayed his arrival a little, gave orders to his officers to keep their men under arms and arranged that his personal attendants and pages, who far outnumbered Alexander's retinue, should accompany him into the banqueting room and remain there until he rose from the table. Alexander and his followers were alarmed by these precautions and did not dare to attempt any violence, while Demetrius for his part excused himself on the ground that his health forbade him to drink wine, and took his leave early in the evening. The next day he began making preparations to depart, explaining that fresh emergencies had arisen which called him away. He asked Alexander to excuse him for leaving so soon and assured him that he would make a longer stay when he was more at leisure. Alexander was delighted at this, since he imagined that Demetrius was leaving of his own free will and without any hostile intentions, and escorted him on his way to Thessaly.

When they reached Larissa, they once more exchanged invitations to a banquet and plotted to kill one another. It was this fact more than any other which delivered Alexander into Demetrius' power, as he hesitated to take precautions for fear of provoking a similar action on Demetrius' part; but in the event, he was the first to suffer the fate he had intended for his enemy, because he delayed taking steps to prevent the other from escaping. He accepted Demetrius' invitation to a banquet, in the middle of which his host suddenly rose from the table. Alexander was filled with alarm, started to his feet and, following close behind, made for the door. Demetrius' bodyguards were standing beside it, and as he reached them Demetrius merely said, 'Kill the man who follows me.' He passed through by himself, but Alexander was cut down by the guards, together with those of his friends who rushed up to help him. One of these is said to have cried out as he was killed that Demetrius had been too quick for them by just one day.

37. The night following was one of disorder and alarm, as might be expected. The next day found the Macedonians in a state of confusion and fearful of Demetrius' army, but when instead of an attack there came a message from Demetrius proposing that he should meet them and explain what had been done, they took heart and decided to receive him in a friendly spirit. When he appeared, there was no need for him to make a long speech. The Macedonians hated Antipater for having murdered his mother, and, as they were at a loss to find a better ruler, they hailed Demetrius as king and at once escorted him back to Macedonia.[81] At home, too, the people were ready to welcome the change, for they still remembered and detested the crimes which Cassander had committed against the family of Alexander the Great.[82] If there remained any regard for the moderation and justice with which the elder Antipater had ruled, it was Demetrius who profited from it since he had married Antipater's daughter Phila, and their son, Antigonus Gonatas, who was almost grown up and was serving with his father in this campaign, could be regarded as the heir to the throne.

38. In the midst of this spectacular revival of his fortunes, Demetrius received the news that his mother and his children had been set free by Ptolemy and that he had pressed gifts and honours upon them; in addition, he also learnt that his daughter Stratonice, who had been married to Seleucus, had now become the wife of Seleucus' son Antiochus and bore the title of Queen of the barbarians of the interior.[83] It appeared that Antiochus had fallen in love with Stratonice, who was still a young girl, although she had already borne a child to Seleucus. Antiochus was distressed and for a time he struggled to conceal his passion. But at last, he decided that his malady was incurable, his desires sinful and his reason too weak to resist them; he therefore determined to make his escape from life and to destroy himself gradually by neglecting his body and refusing all nourishment, under the pretext that he was suffering from some disease. Erasistratus, his physician, found no difficulty in diagnosing his condition, namely that he was in love, but it was less easy to discover with whom. He made a habit of spending day after day in the young prince's room, and when any particularly good-looking girl or young man entered, he would study his patient's face minutely and watch those parts and movements of the body which nature has formed so as to reflect and share the emotions of the soul. Sure enough, when anybody else came in, Antiochus remained unmoved, but whenever Stratonice visited him, as she often did, either alone or with Seleucus, all the symptoms which Sappho describes immediately showed themselves: his voice faltered, his face began to flush, his eye became languid, a sudden sweat broke out on his skin, his heart began to beat violently and irregularly, and finally, as if his soul were overpowered by his passions, he would sink into a state of helplessness, prostration and pallor.[84]

Besides all this, Erasistratus reflected, it was most unlikely that the king's son, if he had fallen in love with any other woman, would have persisted to the point of death in saying nothing about it. He saw the difficulty of revealing a secret of this nature to Seleucus, but still, trusting in the king's affection for his son, he ventured to tell him one day that love was the disorder from which Antiochus was suffering, a love that could neither be satisfied nor cured. 'How is it incurable?' the king asked him in astonishment. 'Because', Erasistratus replied, 'he is in love with my wife.' 'Well then, Erasistratus,' said the king, 'since you are my son's friend, could you not give up your wife and let him marry her, especially when you see that he is my only son, the only anchor in my sea of troubles?' 'You would not do such a thing,' the physician answered, 'though you are his father, if Antiochus were in love with Stratonice?' 'My friend,' replied Seleucus, 'I only wish that someone, whether a god or a man, could turn this passion of his towards her. I should be happy to give up my kingdom if only I could save Antiochus.'

Seleucus uttered these words with deep emotion, and wept as he spoke, and thereupon the physician clasped him by the hand and said, 'Then you have no need of Erasistratus; you, sire, are a father, a husband and a king, and you are also the best physician for your own household.' After this, Seleucus summoned the people to meet in full assembly and announced that it was his will and pleasure that Antiochus should marry Stratonice, and that they should be proclaimed King and Queen of all the provinces of the interior. He believed, he said, that his son, who had always been accustomed to obey his father, would not oppose his desire, and that if his wife should be unwilling to take this extraordinary step he would appeal to his friends to persuade her to accept as just and honourable whatever seemed right to the king and advantageous to the kingdom. This is how Antiochus came to be married to Stratonice, so we are told.

39. After taking over Macedonia, Demetrius had also received Thessaly. As he already controlled the greater part of the Peloponnese and, on this side of the Isthmus, Megara and Athens, he marched against Boeotia. At first the Boeotians made a pact of friendship with him on reasonable terms. But then Cleonymus the Spartan approached Thebes with an army, and the Thebans, full of enthusiasm and urged on by Pisis of Thespiae – one of the most prominent and influential men of the time – rose in revolt. But when Demetrius brought up his siege-engines and surrounded Thebes,[85] Cleonymus took fright and stole away,

and the Boeotians were likewise overawed and surrendered. Demetrius stationed garrisons in the Boeotian cities, levied large sums of money from the people and installed the historian Hieronymus[86] as governor and commander; by these measures and most of all by his treatment of Pisis, he earned a reputation for clemency. For when this man was brought before him as a prisoner, Demetrius did him no harm, but even greeted him, treated him courteously and appointed him polemarch in Thespiae. But not long after, Lysimachus was taken prisoner by Dromichaetes, and Demetrius marched with all speed to Thrace, hoping to find it undefended. The Boeotians took this opportunity to rise yet again and at the same time the news was brought that Lysimachus had been released. Enraged at these events, Demetrius quickly retraced his steps southwards, and finding that the Boeotians had been defeated by his son Antigonus, he again laid siege to Thebes.

40. However, when Pyrrhus moved to overrun Thessaly and advanced as far as Thermopylae, Demetrius left his son Antigonus to carry on the siege and he himself marched against Pyrrhus.[87] Pyrrhus quickly withdrew, and Demetrius, leaving a force of 10,000 hoplites and 1,000 cavalry in Thessaly, returned to press the siege of Thebes. He brought up his famous 'city-taker' for the assault but, because of its huge size and weight, the machine was so slowly and laboriously propelled that in the space of two months it hardly advanced a quarter of a mile. The Boeotians defended their city bravely and Demetrius often forced his soldiers to risk their lives in assaulting the city, though he did this out of sheer exasperation rather than any real necessity for fighting. Antigonus, when he saw them losing so many men, was distressed and asked him, 'Why, father, do we allow these lives to be thrown away so unnecessarily?' Demetrius was angry and retorted, 'Why do you trouble yourself about that? Do you have to find rations for the dead?' However, Demetrius was anxious to prove that he was not careless only of other men's lives and careful of his own, but that he was ready to share the dangers of battle, and exposing himself in the siege he was pierced through the neck by a bolt

from a catapult. He suffered great pain from this wound, but he refused to relax his efforts and finally captured Thebes a second time. When he entered the city, the Thebans were filled with fear and expected that he would carry out the most terrible reprisals, but Demetrius only put to death thirteen of the rebels, banished a few more and pardoned the remainder. Thus it was the fate of Thebes to be captured twice within ten years[88] of its being resettled.

The time was now approaching when the Pythian Games were due to be held[89] and Demetrius took it upon himself to introduce an extraordinary innovation. Since the Aetolians held the passes which led to Delphi, he himself presided over the celebration of the games and other festivities at Athens and proclaimed that it was especially appropriate for Apollo to be honoured there because he was a patron deity of the Athenians and was reputed to be a founder of their race.

41. From Athens he returned to Macedonia. His temperament made it impossible for him to lead a quiet life, and since he had discovered that his Macedonian subjects were easy for him to control when they were on a campaign, but restless and troublesome whenever they stayed at home, he led out an expedition against the Aetolians.[90] After ravaging the country, he left a large part of his army under Pantauchus while he himself marched against Pyrrhus. Pyrrhus, at the same time, advanced to meet him, but the two armies missed each other, with the result that Demetrius went on to plunder Epirus, while Pyrrhus fell upon Pantauchus. A pitched battle followed in the course of which the two commanders fought hand to hand and wounded one another, but Pyrrhus routed his adversary, killed many of his soldiers and took 5,000 prisoners. This battle played a great part in weakening Demetrius' cause: the Macedonians did not feel hostile to Pyrrhus for the harm he had done them, but rather admired him because his victories owed so much to his personal prowess. The action earned him a great and glorious reputation among them, and many declared that Pyrrhus was the only king in whom they could see an image of the great Alexander's courage; the others, and especially Demetrius, only

imitated Alexander in the pomp and outward show of majesty, like actors on a stage.[91]

It is true that there was something intensely theatrical about Demetrius. He possessed an elaborate wardrobe of hats and cloaks, caps with double mitres and robes of purple interwoven with gold, while his feet were clad in shoes of the richest purple felt embroidered with gold. One of his robes had taken many months to weave on the looms: it was a superb piece of work, in which the world and the heavenly bodies were represented. It was still only half finished at the time of Demetrius' downfall, and none of the later kings of Macedon ever presumed to wear it, although several of them had a taste for pomp and ceremony.

42. Demetrius' ostentatious tastes offended the Macedonians, who were not accustomed to see their kings dressed in this fashion, and so did the luxury and extravagance of his way of living, but what annoyed them most of all was the difficulty of speaking to him or even coming into his presence. Sometimes he would refuse to see anybody at all, and on other occasions he would behave harshly and discourteously even to those who had been granted an audience. For example, he kept an Athenian embassy waiting for two years, even though he favoured Athens more than any other Greek city, and another time he considered himself insulted and lost his temper when a deputation arrived from Sparta which consisted of only one envoy. When Demetrius demanded, 'What do you mean, have the Spartans sent no more than one?' he received the neat and laconic reply, 'Yes, sire, one ambassador to one king.'

One day, when Demetrius was riding abroad and appeared to be in a more obliging mood than usual, and more willing to converse with his subjects, a large crowd gathered to present him with written petitions, all of which he accepted and placed in the fold of his cloak. The people were delighted and followed him on his way, but when he came to the bridge over the River Axius,[92] he shook out the fold and emptied all the petitions into the water. This infuriated the Macedonians, who felt that Demetrius was insulting them, rather than ruling them, and they recalled or listened to those who were old enough to remember how accessible Philip had been and how considerate in such matters. On another occasion, an old woman accosted Demetrius and kept asking him to give her an audience. Demetrius replied that he could not spare the time, whereupon the old woman screamed at him, 'Then don't be king!' This rebuke stung Demetrius to the quick. He went back to his house, put off all other business and for many days gave audience to everybody who asked for it, beginning with the old woman.

For indeed there is nothing that becomes a king so much as the task of dispensing justice. Ares, the god of war, is a tyrant, as Timotheus tells us,[93] but Law, in Pindar's words, is the monarch of all things.[94] Homer tells us that Zeus entrusts kings not with 'city-takers' or bronze-beaked ships, but with the decrees of Justice, which are to be protected and kept inviolate,[95] and it is not the most warlike or unjust or murderous of kings but the most righteous to whom he gives the title of Zeus' confidant and disciple.[96] Demetrius, on the other hand, took pleasure in being given a nickname which is the opposite of the one bestowed on the king of the gods, for Zeus is known as 'the Protector' or 'Defender' of cities but Demetrius as 'the Besieger'. It is through such an attitude that naked power, if it lacks wisdom, allows evil actions to usurp the place of good, and glorious achievements to be associated with injustice, and so it happened with Demetrius.

43. When Demetrius became dangerously ill at Pella, he almost lost Macedonia, as Pyrrhus made a rapid incursion and advanced as far as Edessa. But as soon as Demetrius had recovered, he easily drove Pyrrhus out and came to terms with him, for he was anxious not to be distracted by continual petty entanglements and border warfare from his main objective, which was nothing less than to recover the whole of the empire which had been ruled by his father. And his preparations were in no way inferior to his hopes and designs. He had already mustered a force of 98,000 infantry and just under 12,000 cavalry. Besides this he had the keels laid for a fleet of 500 ships, some of which were being constructed at Piraeus, some at Corinth, some at Chalcis and some at Pella. He visited each of these places in

person, giving instructions to the artificers and even taking part
in the work, and there was general wonder not only at the
number but at the size of the vessels that were being constructed. Until then nobody had even seen a ship of fifteen or
sixteen rows of oarsmen, although it is true that at a later date
Ptolemy Philopator[97] built a vessel of forty rows of oarsmen,
which was 420 feet long and 72 feet high to the top of her
stern. She was manned by 400 sailors who did not row and
4,000 at the oars, and apart from these she could carry on her
decks and gangways nearly 3,000 hoplites. But this vessel was
only intended for show: she differed little from a stationary
building on land, and since she was designed for exhibition
rather than for use, she could only be moved with great difficulty and danger. But in the case of Demetrius' ships, their
beauty did not at all detract from their fighting qualities, nor
did the magnificence of their equipment make them any less
operational; on the contrary, their speed and their performance
were even more remarkable than their size.

44. Nothing comparable to this great expedition against Asia
had been assembled by any man since the days of Alexander, but
as it was preparing to sail, the three kings, Seleucus, Ptolemy and
Lysimachus, formed an alliance against Demetrius. Next, they
sent a combined delegation to Pyrrhus, urging him to attack
Macedonia. He should consider himself at liberty to disregard
his treaty with Demetrius, in which the latter had given no
guarantee of leaving him unmolested, but had claimed for himself the right to make war upon the enemy of his choice. Pyrrhus
responded to their appeal, and Demetrius thus found himself
drawn into a war on several fronts before his preparations
were complete.[98] For while Ptolemy sailed to Greece with a
powerful fleet and incited various cities to revolt, Lysimachus
invaded Macedonia from Thrace and Pyrrhus from Epirus, each
of them plundering the country as he advanced. Demetrius left
his son in command in Greece, while he hurried back to relieve
Macedonia and marched against Lysimachus. On his way, news
reached him that Pyrrhus had captured Beroea. The report
quickly spread to the Macedonians and Demetrius could no

longer control his army. The whole camp resounded with tears
and lamentations, mingled with shouts of anger and execration
against their commander. The men refused to stay with Demetrius
and insisted on dispersing, ostensibly to return to their homes,
but in reality to desert to Lysimachus. In this situation, Demetrius
determined to remove himself as far from Lysimachus as he could
and to march against Pyrrhus. He reckoned that Lysimachus
might be popular with the Macedonians because he was a fellow-
countryman and on account of his association with Alexander,
while Pyrrhus was a newcomer and a foreigner whom they would
be unlikely to prefer to himself. But these calculations proved
quite unfounded. When he approached his adversary's camp and
pitched his own close by, the admiration which his men had felt
in the past for Pyrrhus' brilliant feats of arms quickly revived, and
besides this their traditions had accustomed them to believe that
the man who proved himself the best fighter was also the most
kingly. Besides, the soldiers also now learnt that Pyrrhus dealt
leniently with his prisoners, and since they were anxious to transfer their allegiance either to Pyrrhus or to another master, but in
any event to rid themselves of Demetrius, they began to desert
him. At first they came over stealthily and in small groups, but
presently the climate of disorder and sedition spread through the
whole camp. At last, some of the soldiers plucked up courage to
go to Demetrius and told him to clear out and save himself, for
the Macedonians were tired of fighting wars to pay for his extrav-
agances. Demetrius thought this very reasonable advice compared
to the hostility shown him by the others, and so he went to his
tent, and just as if he were an actor rather than a real king, he put
on a dark cloak in place of his royal robe and slipped away
unnoticed. Most of his men at once fell to tearing down his tent,
and while they were looting it and fighting over the spoils, Pyrrhus came up and, finding that he met no resistance, immediately
took possession of the camp. And so the whole kingdom of Macedonia, which Demetrius had ruled securely for seven years,[99]
was divided between Lysimachus and Pyrrhus.

45. When Demetrius had thus completely lost his power, he
took refuge in the city of Cassandreia.[100] His wife Phila was

quite overwhelmed by his misfortunes and could not bear to
see her husband, the most unlucky of kings, reduced once more
to the condition of a private citizen and an exile. Henceforth,
she gave up all hope, and in her bitter resentment of a destiny
which seemed to be far more consistent in adversity than in
prosperity, she took poison and died. But Demetrius was still
determined to save what he could from the wreck of his fortunes, and so he went to Greece and tried to rally those of his
generals and supporters who were still there. In one of Sophocles'
plays, Menelaus uses this image to describe the vicissitudes of
his destiny:

> But my fate on the turning wheel of heaven
> Forever whirls, forever changes shape,
> Even as the face of the inconstant moon
> That never keeps her form two nights the same;
> Out of the dark she rises, young and new,
> Her countenance grows fairer, fills with light,
> Until, the moment of her glory past,
> She turns away and shrinks to nothingness.[101]

This image seems even more apt to describe the fortunes of
Demetrius, as they waxed and waned, and appeared at one
moment at the full and at the next dejected. For at this point
too, just as he seemed to be completely spent and extinguished,
his power began to shine forth again and the addition of new
forces made his hope gradually wax full once more. At first, he
visited the various states as a private citizen and dressed without any of the insignia of royalty, and somebody who saw him
in Thebes in this condition very aptly quoted these verses of
Euripides: 'Changing his godhead into mortal guise, He comes
to Ismene's waters and Dirce's stream.'[102]

46. But no sooner had he stepped back on to the path of hope,
as it were upon a royal highway, and had gathered around him
something of the form and substance of sovereignty, than he
restored to the Thebans their constitution.[103] The Athenians,
on the other hand, revolted from him.[104] They had the name of

Diphilus erased from the public registers. It was he who as the priest of the saviour-gods had been granted the privilege of giving his name to the current year; it was now decreed, instead, that archons should be elected for this purpose according to the traditional Athenian custom. But when the Athenians saw that Demetrius was becoming more powerful than they had expected, they sent for Pyrrhus to come down from Macedonia and protect them. This action angered Demetrius and he marched against Athens and laid the city under close siege. However, the people sent Crates the philosopher, a man of high reputation and authority, to plead with him, and Demetrius raised the siege,[105] partly because he was persuaded by the ambassador's appeal and partly because Crates was able to suggest to him courses that were to his own advantage. He therefore assembled all the ships he possessed,[106] embarked 11,000 soldiers and all his cavalry and sailed for Asia[107] with the object of winning over the provinces of Caria and Lydia from Lysimachus.

At Miletus, he was met by Eurydice, a sister of Phila, who brought with her Ptolemaïs, one of her daughters by Ptolemy. The girl had been betrothed to Demetrius several years before[108] through the mediation of Seleucus. Demetrius now married her, and Eurydice gave the bride away. Immediately after the wedding, Demetrius set himself to win over the cities of Ionia. Many joined him of their own accord, while others were compelled to submit. He also captured Sardis and several of Lysimachus' officers deserted to him, bringing with them both money and troops. But when Lysimachus' son Agathocles took the field against him with a strong force, Demetrius withdrew into Phrygia. His plan was to make his way to Armenia, stir up a revolt in Media and from there gain control of the provinces of the interior, where a commander who was on the run could always find places of refuge and lines of retreat. Agathocles pursued him and although Demetrius came off the better in their skirmishes, his troops were reduced to desperate straits because he was cut off from his supplies of provisions and forage, and worse still, his soldiers began to suspect his intention of leading them into Armenia and Media. And not only was famine getting worse, but when they attempted to cross the

River Lycus, a serious mistake resulted in many of his men being swept away by the current and drowned. In spite of this, the men did not cease to joke, and one of them wrote in front of Demetrius' tent the opening lines of Sophocles' *Oedipus at Colonus*, which he altered a little so that they read

> Child of the blind old man Antigonus,
> What is this region where we find ourselves?[109]

47. But at last the army began to be attacked by disease as well as by hunger, as so often happens when men are forced to subsist on whatever food they can find, and after Demetrius had lost no fewer than 8,000 men he turned back with the remainder and descended from the interior to Tarsus. Here he would gladly have refrained from living on the country, which belonged to Seleucus, and so avoided giving the king any excuse to attack him, but this was impossible since his troops had by then been reduced to great privations, and Agathocles had fortified the passes of the Taurus mountains against him. So he wrote a long letter to Seleucus, in which he gave a pathetic account of his misfortunes and implored him as a kinsman by marriage to take pity on one who had suffered enough to deserve compassion even from his enemies.

Seleucus was to some extent touched by this appeal and wrote to his generals in that province that they should supply Demetrius on the scale that was due to a king and make generous provision for his army. But then Patrocles, a man whose judgement was greatly valued and who was a trusted friend of Seleucus, came to him and pointed out that although the expense of maintaining Demetrius and his troops was small enough, it would be a great mistake to allow him to remain in the country. Demetrius, he reminded Seleucus, had always been the most violent of the kings and the one most addicted to ambitious and daring enterprises, and his fortunes had now sunk to a point at which even the most moderate of men might be tempted to embark on some desperate and unlawful course of action. Seleucus was put on his guard by this advice and marched into Cilicia at the head of a large army, and Demetrius, surprised and alarmed at the sudden change in the king's attitude, retreated into the fastnesses of the Taurus range. He sent messengers to Seleucus and asked to be allowed to carve out a realm for himself among the independent barbarian tribes, where he could live out the rest of his days without further wandering and flight; if this could not be allowed him, he begged the king to supply his troops with food for the winter where they were and not to drive him out of the country in such an exposed and helpless condition that he would be completely at the mercy of his enemies.

48. Seleucus treated all these proposals with suspicion. He told Demetrius that he would be allowed, if he wished, to spend two months of the winter in Cataonia,[110] on condition that his principal officers should be handed over as hostages; at the same time he gave orders to fortify against him the passes leading into Syria. Then Demetrius, feeling himself trapped like a wild beast and surrounded on all sides, was driven to use force. He overran the country, and each time Seleucus attacked him, he gained the upper hand. Once, in particular, when Seleucus' scythe-carrying chariots bore down on him, he avoided the charge and put the enemy to flight, and he also succeeded in dislodging the garrison from one of the passes and gaining control of the road into Syria. These successes greatly raised his spirits, and when he saw that his soldiers had recovered their courage, he prepared to engage Seleucus and put the issue to the supreme test. For his part, Seleucus was at a loss as to what to do. He had refused an offer of help from Lysimachus, because he both distrusted and feared him; on the other hand, he shrank from engaging Demetrius, partly because his opponent now seemed to be buoyed up by the courage of despair, and partly because he dreaded those sudden vicissitudes of fortune which in the past had so often swung Demetrius from the depths of failure to the heights of success.

But at this moment, Demetrius fell victim to a dangerous sickness which not only undermined his physical strength but completely ruined his cause, for its consequence was that some of his soldiers immediately deserted to the enemy, while others scattered. After forty days he recovered his strength with difficulty and, taking with him the remnant of his army, he set out – as far as his enemies could see or guess – for Cilicia. But during the night and without sounding his trumpets, Demetrius set out in the opposite direction, crossed the pass of Amanus and ravaged the plains below as far as Cyrrhestica.[111]

49. When Seleucus appeared on the scene and encamped close by, Demetrius got his men on the march at night and advanced against him. For a long while, Seleucus had no warning of his approach and his troops were asleep. But then some deserters arrived and warned him of the danger, and at this he started up in alarm and ordered his trumpets to be sounded, while at the same time he pulled on his boots and shouted to his companions that a terrible wild beast was about to attack them. Demetrius at once understood from the noise in the enemy's camp that they had been forewarned of his attack and pulled back his troops as quickly as he could. When daylight came, he found that Seleucus was pressing him hard, and so he sent one of his officers to the other wing, while he drove back the one that faced him. But then Seleucus dismounted, took off his helmet and carrying only a light shield went up to hail Demetrius' mercenaries; he showed them who he was and appealed to them to come over to him, since they must have known for a long while that it was for their sake, not Demetrius', that he had refrained from attacking them. At this they all greeted him, acclaimed him as their king and went over to his side.

Demetrius, who had experienced so many shifts of good and bad fortune in his career, understood that this reverse was final. He turned his back on the field and fled to the passes of Amanus, where he took refuge with a small company of friends and attendants and waited for nightfall. His plan was to reach the road to Caunus[112] if possible, and from there make his way to the sea, where he hoped to find his fleet. But when he discovered that his party did not have enough food even for the next day, he cast around for other plans. At that point, one of his comrades named Sosigenes came up, who had 400 gold pieces in his belt. With this money they hoped to get through to the sea, and under cover of darkness they started in the direction of the passes. But when they found the enemy's watch-fires blazing all along the heights, they despaired of breaking through that way and returned to their hiding-place in the forest. By then they were fewer in number, for some had already deserted, and much of the spirit had gone out of them. One of them then ventured to suggest that Demetrius should surrender himself to Seleucus. At this, Demetrius unsheathed his sword and would have killed himself, but his friends surrounded him, did their best to comfort him and finally persuaded him to do as the man had proposed. So he sent a messenger to Seleucus and put himself into his hands.[113]

50. When Seleucus heard of this, he declared that it was his own good fortune, and not his opponent's, which had saved Demetrius' life, since in addition to its other blessings it was affording him the opportunity to show humanity and kindness. He sent for the officers of his household and ordered them to pitch a royal tent and to make all other arrangements to receive and entertain Demetrius in magnificent style. There was also at Seleucus' court a man named Apollonides, who had been a close friend of Demetrius, and Seleucus at once sent him to help put Demetrius at his ease and reassure him that he was coming into the presence of a man who was a friend and a relative. When Seleucus' intentions became clear, first of all a few of Demetrius' followers and then the great majority hurried to rejoin him, vying with one another in their efforts to reach him first, for they now expected that he would become a man of great influence at Seleucus' court.

But these actions soon transformed Seleucus' compassion into jealousy and gave the more skilful of the courtiers and those who were ill-disposed to Demetrius the opportunity to thwart and defeat the king's generosity. They alarmed him by suggesting that the first moment Demetrius was seen in Seleucus' camp, all the troops would go over to him. By this time, Apollonides had already arrived in high spirits and others of Demetrius' followers were joining him with wonderful tales of Seleucus' kindness. And Demetrius himself, after all his reverses and misfortunes, even if he had at first regarded his surrender as a disgrace, had changed his mind as a result of recovering his spirits and beginning to feel some hope for the future. But then, suddenly, Pausanias appeared at the head of a detachment of a thousand soldiers and horsemen. He immediately surrounded Demetrius, sent away all his followers and escorted him not into the presence of Seleucus but away to the Syrian Chersonese.[114] Here, for the rest of his life Demetrius was placed under a strong guard, but was granted attendance suitable to his rank: generous funds and provisions were supplied from day to day, and he was allowed to walk or ride in the royal estates and hunt game in the parks. He was free to enjoy the company of any of his comrades in exile who wished to join him, and a number of people contrived to visit him from Seleucus' court; they brought encouraging messages, urged him to keep up his spirits and hinted that as soon as Antiochus arrived with Demetrius' daughter Stratonice,[115] he would be set free.

51. But Demetrius, once he found himself in this situation, sent word to his son and his commanders in Athens and Corinth that henceforth they should pay no attention to any letters written in his name or under his seal, but should regard him as a dead man and hold in trust his cities and the rest of his possessions for his son Antigonus. When Antigonus learnt of his father's capture, he was deeply grieved and put on mourning. He wrote to the other kings, and in particular to Seleucus, entreating him, offering to give up all that was left of his own and Demetrius' possessions, and above all proposing himself as a hostage for his father. Many cities and their rulers supported this appeal, with the exception of Lysimachus, who even approached Seleucus with the offer of a large sum of money if he would put Demetrius to death. Seleucus had always felt a sense of revulsion against Lysimachus, and after this proposal regarded him as even more foul and barbaric. But he continued to delay things and to keep Demetrius under guard for Antiochus and Stratonice, so that the favour of his release might come from their intercession.

52. Demetrius at the start endured the misfortune that had befallen him, and gradually became accustomed to it and learnt

to put up with it more easily. At first, he exercised his body as well as he could and made use of his privileges of riding or hunting, but then little by little he became indifferent and, at last, positively averse to such pastimes. Instead, he took to drinking and playing dice and spent most of his leisure in this way. This may have been because he wished to escape from any thought of his condition, the consciousness of which so haunted him when he was sober that he tried to drown such reflections in liquor. Or perhaps he had come to the conclusion that this was the kind of life he had really desired all along, but had missed through folly and the pursuit of empty ambition. In this way, he had brought many troubles both on himself and on others, by using weapons and fleets and armies to chase after the happiness he had now unexpectedly discovered in idleness, leisure and relaxation. And in fact, for all these wretched kings, after all the risks they run and the wars they fight, what other goal is there than this? Truly these men are both wicked and stupid, not merely because they strive after luxury and pleasure rather than virtue and honour, but because they do not even know how to enjoy the real thing[116] in either case.

After he had lived for three years in confinement in the Syrian Chersonese, Demetrius fell sick through inactivity and over-indulgence in food and wine and died in his fifty-fifth year.[117] Seleucus was generally blamed, and he bitterly reproached himself for having harboured such suspicions against Demetrius and for having fallen so far below the standards even of Dromichaetes, a barbarous Thracian, who, when Lysimachus was his prisoner, had treated him in a manner that was far more humane and worthy of a king.

53. There was, however, something dramatic and theatrical even in the funeral ceremonies which were arranged in Demetrius' honour. When Antigonus learnt that his father's remains were being brought to him, he put to sea with his whole fleet and met Seleucus' ships at the islands. The relics were presented to him in a golden urn and he placed them in the largest of his admiral's galleys. Then at the various cities where the fleet touched land during its passage, some brought

garlands to adorn the urn, others sent representatives dressed in mourning to escort it home and bury it. When the fleet put in at Corinth, the urn was placed in full view on the stern of the flagship, covered with royal purple, crowned with a king's diadem and surrounded by an armed bodyguard of young men. Close to it was seated Xenophantus, the most celebrated flute-player of the time, who played a sacred hymn; the rowers kept time with the music and the rhythmical splashing of their oars matched the cadences of the flute and sounded like a mourner's beating of the breast. But it was the sight of Antigonus, his head bowed with grief and his eyes filled with tears, which excited most pity among the crowds who flocked to the sea-shore. After the remains had been crowned with garlands and other honours had been paid at Corinth, Antigonus brought them to Demetrias[118] to be buried. This was the town named after his father, who had settled in it the inhabitants from a number of villages round Iolcus.

Demetrius left the following descendants. Antigonus and Stratonice were his children by Phila. There were two sons named Demetrius, one known as 'the Thin', by a woman of Illyria, the other, who became the ruler of Cyrene, by Ptolemaïs. Alexander, who lived out his life in Egypt, was his son by Deidameia. Demetrius is also said to have had a son by Eurydice, named Corrhagus. His descendants continued to rule over Macedonia in succession, down to Perseus, the last, in whose reign the Romans subdued Macedonia.[119]

Now that the Macedonian drama has been performed, it is time to bring the Roman on to the stage too.[120]

PYRRHUS

INTRODUCTION TO
PYRRHUS

[319–272 BC]

Pyrrhus was king of Epirus, in north-western Greece. Epirus had been disunited and played little part in wider affairs during the Classical period. Its inhabitants spoke a dialect of Greek, but the system of city-states which was characteristic of southern Greece had not developed here. Instead, the tribe was the basis for political organization. By the mid-fourth century, however, the Molossian tribes, together with several other tribal groups, had formed a federal state with a Molossian king at its head, though Epirus remained generally subordinate to Macedonia. By Pyrrhus' time, a larger Epirot alliance was in existence, under the leadership of the Molossian king.

Pyrrhus came to the Molossian throne when he was twelve in 307 BC, but was driven out in 302 by a rival member of the royal family, Neoptolemus. He took refuge with Demetrius Poliorcetes and fought at his side at the battle of Ipsus in 301. Later, Pyrrhus was sent by Demetrius as a hostage to Ptolemy in Egypt. There he prospered, and in 297 Ptolemy restored Pyrrhus to his throne in Epirus, initially as joint-ruler with Neoptolemus. But Pyrrhus soon had Neoptolemus removed and ruled alone. He proceeded to annex various territories neighbouring Epirus, partly by force of arms and partly through his numerous dynastic marriages. In 288, he even managed to expel Demetrius and establish himself as king of Macedon, but was himself expelled a few years later.

Pyrrhus now turned his attention across the Adriatic Sea. Rome had been rapidly expanding its power in the Italian peninsula, and in 281 the people of the Greek city of Tarentum, in the heel of Italy, appealed to Pyrrhus for help. Pyrrhus crossed to Italy and defeated the Romans in two battles, but suffered very heavy casualties in the process and was unable to take Rome or to bring the Romans, whose huge resources of man-power showed no signs of abating, to the negotiating table. Soon afterwards, he crossed over to Sicily at the invitation of the Syracusans and campaigned against the Carthaginians. He fell out with the Sicilians, however, and returned to Italy, where he was defeated in 275 by the Romans at the battle of Beneven-tum in Campania. He limped back to Epirus with his forces seriously diminished and little to show for it. The final years of his life were dominated by war with Antigonus II Gonatas, the son of Demetrius Poliorcetes, who had by now established himself securely in Macedonia and who maintained garrisons in various strategic cities in Greece. In 272 Pyrrhus was killed in street-fighting in Argos in the Peloponnese.

Pyrrhus has sometimes been compared to the *condottieri* of fourteenth- and fifteenth-century Italy, and the comparison is apt. In many of his campaigns, especially those in Italy and Sicily, Pyrrhus was acting in effect as a mercenary commander, hiring his services out both for pay and for the glory of con-quest. Plutarch's Life is the only extant narrative source for most of Pyrrhus' career. Plutarch mentions several of his sources. One is Hieronymus of Cardia, who was a contemporary of Pyrrhus and whose work on the successors of Alexander was used by Plutarch for his *Eumenes* and *Demetrius*, though sadly it does not survive. For Pyrrhus' wars with the Romans, Plu-tarch cites Dionysius of Halicarnassus, a Greek who worked in Rome in the time of Augustus and whose *Roman antiquities* traced the history of Rome down to the 260s BC. Although much of Dionysius' work survives, all that remains of those portions which dealt with Pyrrhus (Books 19–20) are excerpts. Plutarch may also have used Timaeus for the Sicilian section. For the narrative of Pyrrhus' last campaign in the Peloponnese, Plutarch cites the lost third-century BC historian Phylarchus.

The loss of most other sources for this period means that Plutarch's *Pyrrhus* is of great historical importance. However, *Pyrrhus* is more than just a repository of factual information: it is a carefully composed and structured whole, with a clear moral message. For Plutarch, Pyrrhus is an example of discontent and greed – greed not for wealth but for conquest. Unable to bring himself to enjoy the blessings of his power, wealth and success, Pyrrhus is driven, in Plutarch's telling, by an unreasoning and insatiable desire for more, which leads him into constant and pointless warfare. Thus, when Pyrrhus is driven out of Macedonia in 285, Plutarch comments that he could have chosen to live in peace, 'But for Pyrrhus, life became tedious to the point of nausea, unless he could stir up trouble for others, or have it stirred up for him' (ch. 13). This inability to refrain from war is dramatized in a dialogue with Pyrrhus' adviser Cineas. Acting rather as Socrates does in the Platonic dialogues, Cineas questions Pyrrhus on the aims of his intervention in Italy. By the end of the conversation, Cineas has demonstrated that further campaigns, even further victories, would not add to the happiness of Pyrrhus or his men. Why not stay at home and enjoy the land they rule? 'These arguments', Plutarch concludes, 'disturbed Pyrrhus but did not convert him. He could see clearly enough the happiness he was leaving behind, but he could not give up his hopes for what he desired' (ch. 14).

Alongside this concern with the psychological motivation for Pyrrhus' campaigning, which casts him in a distinctly negative light, are other factors which emphasize his courage and martial qualities. Two figures loom large as models. The first is Achilles, an important symbol in the self-legitimation of the Molossian royal house, which claimed to be descended from him (ch. 1). Plutarch twice compares Pyrrhus with Achilles or points out Pyrrhus' own desire to imitate him (chs. 7 and 13). Another model for Pyrrhus is Alexander the Great, who had himself claimed descent from Achilles. Plutarch comments on how the Macedonians saw in Pyrrhus the likeness of Alexander (ch. 8); and Plutarch has Pyrrhus dream that Alexander appears to him (ch. 11). Various scenes, such as his scaling the walls of Eryx (ch. 22), are reminiscent of scenes in the *Life of Alexander*. These parallels with both Achilles and Alexander give Pyrrhus a heroic quality and suggest a more positive interpretation of his constant warfare.

Plutarch and his readers were living in a world in which

Greece had long been subject to Roman rule. Pyrrhus' campaigns in Italy would have had special meaning as the first point of contact, the first of a series of wars which would lead in the end to the Roman conquest of the Hellenistic kingdoms. It is therefore significant that Plutarch portrays the Roman commanders with whom Pyrrhus had to deal as upright and incorruptible. Indeed, compared with Pyrrhus, the Romans emerge as the more virtuous and the more noble. Furthermore, when Pyrrhus first catches sight of the Roman army, Plutarch has him declare memorably: 'These may be barbarians, but there is nothing barbarous about their discipline' (ch. 16) – a phrase which neatly deconstructs traditional Greek notions of a world divided into Greeks and barbarians. In Plutarch's *Pyrrhus* there is no room for a simple belief in the superiority of Greek over Roman.

The *Life of Pyrrhus* is paired with the *Life of Marius*. The Roman general Marius (*c.* 157–86 BC) won a series of victories in Africa, Gaul and Italy before rivalry with his one-time lieutenant Sulla thrust Rome into almost a decade of civil strife. Plutarch presents Marius, like Pyrrhus, as a victim of a pathological discontent, which showed itself in endless warfare. Even on his deathbed, Marius imagines he is on campaign, crying out and shouting as though in battle (*Marius* 45). There is no closing Comparison of Pyrrhus and Marius, nor is there any prologue. But Plutarch concludes *Marius* with a diagnosis, couched in general terms, and which could apply to Pyrrhus just as much as to Marius: 'Forgetful and foolish people let what happens flow away with time. Therefore since they contain and hold nothing, always empty of good things but full of hopes, they look away to the future and reject the present . . .' (*Marius* 46).

LIFE OF PYRRHUS[1]

1. Tradition has it that the first king of the Thesprotians and Molossians[2] after the great flood was Phaethon: he was one of those who came to Epirus with Pelasgus. But there is also a tradition that Deucalion and Pyrrha[3] founded the sanctuary at Dodona[4] and lived there among the Molossians. In later times, Neoptolemus, the son of Achilles, brought a whole people with him to Epirus, conquered the country and founded a dynasty. These were named 'the sons of Pyrrhus' after him because he bore the name of Pyrrhus in his boyhood, and he afterwards also gave it to one of his legitimate children by Lanassa, who was the daughter of Cleodaeus, son of Hyllus. This was how it came about that Achilles was granted divine honours in Epirus and was known as Aspetus in the nomenclature of that region. However, the later kings of this line sank into barbarism, and the dynasty lapsed into obscurity both in its power and in its way of life. It was Tharrhypas,[5] so it is recorded, who was the first of their successors to make himself famous by introducing Greek customs and letters and who imposed order on the life of his cities by promulgating humane laws. Tharrhypas was the father of Alcetas, whose son, Arybas, married Troas, who bore him Aeacides. This king married Phthia, the daughter of Menon of Thessaly, who earned a high reputation in the Lamian War and gained the highest rank after Leosthenes among the allies.[6] Phthia bore Aeacides two daughters, Deidameia and Troas, and a son, Pyrrhus.

2. After a time, civil strife broke out among the Molossians, Aeacides was driven out and the descendants of Neoptolemus

were restored to power.[7] The friends of Aeacides were captured
and put to death; his enemies also made a search for Pyrrhus,
who was still an infant, but Androcleides and Angelus contrived to escape and carried off the young prince with them.
They were obliged to take a few servants and women to nurse
the child, with the result that they could only travel slowly and
laboriously and soon found themselves being overtaken. They,
therefore, entrusted Pyrrhus to three strong and reliable young
men, Androcleion, Hippias and Neander, whom they ordered
to press ahead as quickly as they could and make for Megara,
a town in Macedonia; meanwhile, they themselves, partly by
entreaty and partly by force, contrived to hold up the pursuers
until late in the evening. They succeeded at last in driving off
their enemies and then hurried on to join the men who were
carrying Pyrrhus. The sun had already set and the party had
begun to hope that they were within reach of safety, when they
suddenly found themselves cut off by the river which flowed
between them and the town. The stream looked wild and dangerous, and when they attempted to cross they found this was
impossible, for the rains had swollen the waters to a rushing
torrent, and the gathering darkness increased the terror of the
scene. They decided that they would never be able to cross by
their own efforts, since they had to carry both the child and the
women who were looking after it, but when they saw several of
the people of the locality standing on the opposite shore they
called out for help to cross and made gestures of entreaty,
pointing at the infant Pyrrhus. Those on the far side could not
hear what they were saying because of the dashing and the roar
of the water, and much time was lost with one group shouting
and the other unable to understand them, until one of the fugitives hit on a solution. He tore off a strip of bark from a tree
and wrote on it, with the pin of a brooch, a few words explaining their predicament and who the child was. Then he wrapped
the piece of bark round a stone to give weight to his throw and
flung it over the torrent. According to another version of the
story, he wrapped the bark around a javelin and hurled this
across the stream. At any rate, when the people on the other
side read the message and understood that there was no time to

be lost, they cut down some trees, lashed them together and thus made the crossing. As chance would have it, the man who first came ashore and took Pyrrhus in his arms was named Achilles, and his companions ferried over the rest of the party in one way or another.

3. Having thus escaped the pursuit and reached safety, the fugitives proceeded to Glaucias, the king of the Illyrians. They found him sitting at home with his wife and they laid the baby on the ground between them. The king was obliged to weigh the matter carefully. He was afraid of Cassander, the ruler of Macedon, who was an enemy of Aeacides, and for a long while he said nothing as he turned the problem over in his mind. Meanwhile, Pyrrhus of his own accord crawled along the floor, took hold of the king's robe and pulled himself up at Glaucias' knees; the king at first burst out laughing, and then was moved to pity, as he saw the child standing there like a suppliant, clasping his knees and sobbing. According to one account, Pyrrhus did not throw himself before Glaucias but seized hold of an altar, and clasping his hands round it, raised himself to his feet, and this the king regarded as a sign from heaven. For this reason, he at once placed Pyrrhus in the arms of his wife and gave orders that he should be brought up with their own children. Then a little later, when Pyrrhus' enemies demanded that he should be handed over to them and Cassander offered 200 talents for him, Glaucias refused to give him up. Indeed, after Pyrrhus had reached the age of twelve, Glaucias actually invaded Epirus with an army and set him on the throne there.[8]

Pyrrhus' features were more likely to inspire fear in the beholder than to impress him with a sense of majesty. He did not have a regular set of teeth, but his upper jaw was formed of one continuous bone with small depressions in it, which resembled the intervals between a row of teeth. He was believed to have the power to cure diseases of the spleen. He would sacrifice a white cock and then, while the patient lay flat on his back, he would gently press upon the region of the spleen with his right foot. There was nobody so poor or obscure that Pyrrhus would refuse him this healing touch, if he were asked for it. He would accept the cock as a reward after he had sacrificed it, and was always very pleased with this gift. The great toe of his right foot was also said to possess a divine power, so that when the rest of his body was burned after his death, this was found unharmed and untouched by the fire. These details, however, belong to a later period.

4. When he had reached the age of seventeen[9] and appeared to be firmly established on the throne, he left Epirus to attend the wedding of one of Glaucias' sons, with whom he had been brought up. Thereupon, the Molossians again took the opportunity to rise in revolt: they drove out Pyrrhus' supporters, plundered his property and made Neoptolemus their king.[10] In this way, Pyrrhus lost his kingdom, and since he was now completely destitute, he attached himself to Demetrius, the son of Antigonus, who had married his sister Deidameia. While she was still a young girl, she had nominally been married to Alexander, the son of Alexander the Great and Roxane, but after the misfortunes that befell them, and since she was of a suitable age, Demetrius married her.[11] Pyrrhus served under Demetrius at the great battle of Ipsus,[12] in which all the kings took part. He was only eighteen at the time, but he routed the contingent that was opposed to him and distinguished himself brilliantly in the fighting. He did not desert Demetrius after his defeat but kept guard over the cities in Greece which were entrusted to his command,[13] and when Demetrius made a treaty with Ptolemy, Pyrrhus sailed to Egypt as a hostage. In Egypt, he gave Ptolemy ample proof of his prowess and endurance both in hunting and in military exercises. He noticed that among Ptolemy's wives it was Berenice who enjoyed the highest esteem for her virtue and her intelligence, and also who exercised the greatest influence, and so he went out of his way to court her favour. He was particularly skilful at winning over his superiors to his own interest, just as, on the other hand, he looked down on his inferiors, and since he was temperate and decorous in his private life he was singled out from among many other young princes as a suitable husband for Antigone, who was one of the daughters of Berenice by her first husband Philip,[14] before she married Ptolemy.

5. After this marriage, Pyrrhus' reputation rose still higher, and since Antigone proved an excellent wife to him, he contrived to procure money and troops and to get himself sent to Epirus to recover his kingdom.[15] Most of the Epirots welcomed his arrival, for they had come to hate Neoptolemus, who had proved himself a harsh and repressive ruler. Nevertheless, Pyrrhus was afraid that Neoptolemus might turn for help to one of the other successors of Alexander, and so he made a pact with him whereby they agreed to share the royal power. But as time went on, some of their partisans secretly provoked friction between them and fomented their suspicions of one another. However, the event which did most to arouse Pyrrhus to action is said to have originated as follows.

It was the custom for the kings of Epirus to offer sacrifice to Zeus Areius at Passaron, a place in Molossian territory, and there to exchange solemn oaths with their subjects: the kings swore to govern according to the laws and the people to support the kingdom as it had been established by the laws. This ceremony was duly performed, both the kings were present and conversed with one another together with their adherents, and many gifts were exchanged. On this occasion Gelon, a faithful supporter of Neoptolemus, greeted Pyrrhus warmly and presented him with two yoke of oxen for ploughing. Myrtilus, Pyrrhus' cup-bearer, asked him for these, and was deeply offended when the king refused him and gave them to somebody else. Gelon noticed this and invited Myrtilus to dine with him, and, according to some accounts, enjoyed his youthful beauty as he drank; then he began to talk seriously to him, and urged him to throw in his lot with Neoptolemus and dispatch Pyrrhus by poison. Myrtilus listened to the suggestion, pretended to approve and agree to it, but privately informed Pyrrhus. In addition, on the king's instructions, he introduced Alexicrates, Pyrrhus' chief cup-bearer, to Gelon, making out that he was willing to take part in the plot, for Pyrrhus was anxious to have several witnesses to testify to the intended crime. In this way, Gelon was completely deceived, and he in turn deceived Neoptolemus, who imagined that the plot was developing smoothly and could not restrain his delight but kept talking about it to his friends. On one particular occasion, after a drinking-party at the house of his sister Cadmeia, he let his tongue run away with him: he imagined that he could not be heard, since there seemed to be nobody near them, except for Phaenarete, the wife of a man named Samon, Neoptolemus' chief herdsman, and she was lying on a couch, apparently asleep with her face to the wall. But in fact, while she took care not to arouse their suspicions, she had heard everything that was said, and next day she went to Antigone, Pyrrhus' wife, and reported the whole conversation. When Pyrrhus heard this, he took no action for the moment, but on a day when a sacrifice was due to be offered he invited Neoptolemus to supper and killed him. For he knew that the leading men in Epirus were on his side and were eager to see him rid himself of Neoptolemus. He was also aware of their desire that he should not content himself with a petty share in the government, but should follow his natural bent and engage in far more ambitious designs; moreover, now that his suspicion of Neoptolemus' treachery provided yet another motive for the deed, they were content for him to forestall Neoptolemus by putting him out of the way first.

6. Pyrrhus honoured Ptolemy and Berenice by giving the name of Ptolemy to the infant son whom Antigone bore him, and Berenicis to the city which he had built on the peninsula of Epirus.[16] Next, he began to ponder a number of ambitious schemes, in particular designs directed against the territories of his neighbours, and he found an opportunity to intervene in the affairs of Macedon upon the following pretext.

Of Cassander's two sons, Antipater, the elder, had his mother, Thessalonice, put to death and tried to drive his brother, Alexander, into exile.[17] Alexander appealed for help to Demetrius and also addressed himself to Pyrrhus. Demetrius' attention was taken up with other matters and he was slow to respond, but Pyrrhus came to Macedonia and demanded as the price of his alliance Stymphaea and Paravaea within Macedonia itself and, of the acquired peoples, Ambracia, Acarnania and Amphilochia.[18] The young man agreed to the terms, and Pyrrhus occupied these areas and secured them for himself by posting garrisons there; he also proceeded to wrest the remaining parts of the kingdom from Antipater and handed them over to Alexander. King Lysimachus,[19] who was anxious to send help to Antipater, found himself too much occupied with other matters to come to Macedonia in person. But as he knew that Pyrrhus would never disoblige Ptolemy or refuse him anything, he sent him a forged letter which purported to come from Ptolemy and which ordered him to abandon his expedition on receipt of 300 talents from Antipater. However, as soon as Pyrrhus opened the letter, he discovered Lysimachus' trick, because it did not begin with Ptolemy's usual greeting to him, which ran, 'The father to the son, greetings', but instead with the words 'King Ptolemy to King Pyrrhus, greetings'. Pyrrhus reproached Lysimachus for the deception, but he nevertheless made peace, and the three rulers met to confirm the agreement and swear a solemn oath at a sacrifice. A bull, a boar and a ram were led up for the ceremony, and the ram of its own accord suddenly fell down dead. The rest of the spectators burst out laughing, but Theodotus the diviner prevented Pyrrhus from taking the oath: he declared that through this portent, the divine was foretelling the death of one of the three kings. For this reason, then, Pyrrhus withdrew from the pact.

7. Alexander's affairs had in fact already been settled with Pyrrhus' help, but this did not deter Demetrius from coming to Macedonia. As soon as he arrived, it became clear that not only was his presence unnecessary, but that it alarmed the young king, and the two had only been together for a few days before their mutual distrust led them to plot against one another. Demetrius seized the opportunity to strike first against his youthful opponent and had Alexander murdered and himself proclaimed king of Macedon.[20]

Even before this Demetrius had had grounds for complaint against Pyrrhus, and Pyrrhus had made incursions into Thessaly. Greed, the congenital disease of dynasties, made the two men distrustful and suspicious neighbours, and their fears of one another were intensified by the death of Deidameia.[21] But now since they had also both annexed parts of Macedonia, their interests frequently collided and the occasions for quarrelling were multiplied still further. Demetrius made an expedition against the Aetolians and subdued them; then, leaving his general Pantauchus there with a strong force, he set out to attack Pyrrhus,[22] while Pyrrhus, as soon as he learnt the news, marched against him. Somehow, they mistook their way and their armies passed one another without meeting. Demetrius went on to invade Epirus and plunder the country, while Pyrrhus came upon Pantauchus and promptly engaged him. A fierce battle ensued and the fighting was especially violent around the two commanders. For Pantauchus was by general consent the best fighting-man of all Demetrius' generals. He combined courage, strength and skill in arms with a lofty and resolute spirit, and he challenged Pyrrhus to a hand-to-hand combat. Pyrrhus, for his part, yielded to none of the kings in valour and daring: he was determined to earn the fame of Achilles, not merely through his ancestry but through his prowess in the field, and he advanced beyond the front rank of his troops to face Pantauchus.[23] First they hurled their javelins at one another, and then coming to close quarters they drew their swords and fought with all their strength and skill. Pyrrhus received one wound, but inflicted two on Pantauchus, one in the thigh and one along the neck. He drove his opponent back and forced him to the ground, but could not kill him outright, as his friends came to the rescue and dragged him away. This victory of their king's uplifted the Epirots' spirits and, inspired by his courage, they succeeded in overwhelming and breaking up the Macedonian phalanx; then, they pursued their enemies as they fled, killed great numbers of them and took 5,000 prisoners.

8. This battle, so far from filling the Macedonians with anger or hatred against Pyrrhus for having defeated them, caused all those who had fought in it and witnessed his exploits to talk about him, admire him and marvel at his courage. They compared his appearance, his speed and his movements to those of Alexander the Great,[24] and felt that they saw in him an image and a reflection of the latter's impetuosity and violence in the

field. The other kings, they said, could only imitate Alexander in superficial details, with their scarlet cloaks, their bodyguards, the angle at which they held their heads, or the lofty tone of their speech: it was Pyrrhus alone who could remind them of him in arms and in action.

As for Pyrrhus' knowledge and mastery of military tactics and the art of generalship, proof is to be found in the writings he left on those subjects. It is said also that when Antigonus was asked who the best general was, he replied, 'Pyrrhus, if he lives to be old' (an opinion which applied only to the generals of his own time). Hannibal's verdict was that the greatest of all generals in experience and ability was Pyrrhus, that next to him came Scipio, and after that himself, as I have written in my *Life of Scipio*.[25] In a word, Pyrrhus seems to have continually studied and reflected upon this one subject, which he considered the most kingly of all branches of learning; the others he regarded as mere accomplishments and set little store by them. We are told that on one occasion he was asked at a drinking-party whether he preferred Python to Cephisias as a flute-player: his reply was that Polyperchon was a good general – so much as to say that this was the only subject on which a king needed to inform himself and pass judgement.

Towards his close friends he was considerate and not easily moved to anger; he was also appreciative of any favours that were done him and eager to repay them. Certainly, when Aeropus died, he was deeply distressed: he remarked that Aeropus had only suffered what was the common lot of humanity, but he reproached himself, because he had been dilatory and had put off what he had intended doing and so had not repaid his friend's kindness. Debts of money can be repaid to the creditor's heirs, but a just and upright man will be tormented by his conscience if he does not repay debts of kindness to his friends at a time when they can feel his gratitude. In Ambracia, there was a man who constantly abused and spoke ill of Pyrrhus, and many people considered that he should be banished. 'No,' declared Pyrrhus, 'he had better stay here, where he can only speak ill of me to a few people, rather than spread his slanders all round the world.' Again, when some young men had insulted him in their cups and were later brought before him, Pyrrhus asked them whether they had uttered the abuse of which they were accused. 'We did, sire,' replied one of the youths, 'but we should have said worse things still if we had had more wine.' At this Pyrrhus burst out laughing and sent them away.

9. After Antigone's death,[26] he married several wives so as to increase his power and further his political interests. One of these was the daughter of Autoleon, king of the Paeonians,[27] another was Bircenna, the daughter of Bardyllis, king of the Illyrians, and a third was Lanassa, daughter of Agathocles, the ruler of Syracuse, who brought to him as her dowry the city of Corcyra which Agathocles had captured. By Antigone he had had a son Ptolemy, by Lanassa Alexander and by Bircenna his youngest son, Helenus. He brought up all three to be fine soldiers, young men of fiery temperament who were well trained in arms, and he whetted their appetite for fighting from their earliest childhood. The story goes that one of them, while he was still a boy, asked him to whom he intended to leave his kingdom, to which Pyrrhus replied, 'To whichever of you keeps his sword the sharpest.' In fact, this saying differs very little from the tragic curse which Oedipus pronounced on his sons, to the effect that the brothers *would divide their inheritance by whetted steel, not by lot*',[28] so savage and ferocious a thing is greed.

10. After this battle,[29] Pyrrhus returned home exulting in the glory and prestige he had won. When the Epirots gave him the title 'the Eagle', he told them, 'It is through you that I am an eagle: how should I not be, when I am borne up by your arms as if they were wings?' A little later, when he heard that Demetrius had fallen dangerously ill, he suddenly led an army into Macedonia.[30] He had not intended to do more than make a swift raid and plunder a few districts, but he came near to subduing the whole country and gaining possession of the kingdom without striking a blow, for he advanced as far as Edessa without meeting any resistance, and many of the Macedonians flocked to his army and joined his expedition. At last, the danger aroused Demetrius to leave his bed and disregard

his sickness, while his friends quickly gathered a strong force
and set out to offer a determined resistance to Pyrrhus. As Pyrrhus' plan had been mainly to plunder the country, he did not
stand his ground but hastily withdrew and suffered considerable losses as the Macedonians harried his retreat.

However, although Demetrius had so easily and quickly
driven Pyrrhus out of the country, he did not leave him out of
his calculations. He had determined to embark on a great
enterprise, nothing less than to win back his father Antigonus'
dominions, for which he had collected a force of 100,000 soldiers and 500 ships; in consequence, he had no wish to embroil
himself with Pyrrhus, nor to leave behind a restless and hostile
neighbour on the frontier of Macedonia. But as he had no time
to fight a campaign against Pyrrhus, he was anxious to come to
terms with him and make peace, and thus free himself to turn
his arms against the other kings. Once he had readied an agreement with Pyrrhus, the size of his preparations revealed the
true nature of his plans, and at this the kings became alarmed
and began sending messengers and letters to Pyrrhus.[31] They
were amazed, they said, that Pyrrhus should let slip the moment
when it was most favourable for him to make war, but allow
Demetrius to choose his own time. Just now, Pyrrhus was well
placed to drive Demetrius out of Macedonia, while his opponent was fully occupied and extended elsewhere. Did he intend
to do nothing and wait for the time when Demetrius had grown
strong again, and could then at his leisure make Pyrrhus fight
for the temples and the tombs of Molossia, and would he allow
all this to be done by a man who had lately taken Corcyra from
him, not to mention his wife? For Lanassa had quarrelled with
him because he paid more attention to his barbarian wives than
to her, and had gone off to Corcyra. There she had invited
Demetrius, since she was ambitious to make a royal match and
had learnt that he was the most ready of all the kings to entertain offers of marriage. So Demetrius sailed there, married
Lanassa and left a garrison in the city.

11. At the same time that they were writing to Pyrrhus in this
strain, the kings did their utmost to distract Demetrius while he

was completing his preparations for the campaign. Ptolemy sailed to Greece with a great fleet and set to work to persuade the cities there to revolt, while Lysimachus invaded upper Macedonia from Thrace and pillaged the country.[32] Pyrrhus chose the same moment to take the field and marched upon the city of Beroea; he calculated, rightly as it turned out, that Demetrius would march to meet Lysimachus and would thus leave southern Macedonia undefended. That night, Pyrrhus dreamt that Alexander the Great sent for him, and that when he answered the summons he found the king lying on a couch. Alexander welcomed him in a friendly fashion and promised his help, whereupon Pyrrhus ventured to ask him, 'How, sire, can you help me, when you are sick yourself?' 'With my name!' replied Alexander, and, mounting a horse from Nisaea, he seemed to show Pyrrhus the way.

This vision gave Pyrrhus great confidence. He led his army by forced marches over the intervening country and occupied the city of Beroea. There, he stationed the main body of his troops and sent out his commanders to subdue the remainder of the region. When Demetrius heard this news and became aware that a terrible commotion was taking place among the Macedonians in his camp, he halted his advance because he was afraid that if his troops came any closer to a Macedonian king of such renown as Lysimachus, they would immediately go over to him. He, therefore, turned back and marched against Pyrrhus, calculating that he would be hated by the Macedonians because he was a foreigner. But no sooner had he pitched his camp in Pyrrhus' neighbourhood than many of the citizens of Beroea came out to visit him. They were loud in their praises of Pyrrhus, described him as an invincible soldier and a man of inspiring courage, and added that he treated his prisoners with kindness and consideration. Some of these visitors were Pyrrhus' agents: they were disguised as Macedonians and spread the word that now was the time to get rid of Demetrius and his overbearing rule by going over to Pyrrhus, a man who possessed the common touch and was devoted to his soldiers. In this way, the majority of Demetrius' troops were roused to a high pitch of excitement and began to look everywhere for

Pyrrhus. For it so happened that he had taken off his helmet. Then he remembered that the soldiers did not know him, and so he put it on again and was instantly recognized by its imposing crest and its goat's horns. Some of the Macedonians ran up and asked him for the password of his army, and others, when they saw that his guards wore crowns of oak-leaves, garlanded their heads in the same way. Meanwhile, some of Demetrius' followers had already summoned up courage to tell him that his best course would be to give up his ambitious plans and slip quietly away. Demetrius saw that this advice reflected only too clearly the mutinous state of his troops, and he took fright, put on a flat cap and a simple cloak and stole off unnoticed. Pyrrhus came up, made himself master of the camp without a blow and was proclaimed king of Macedon.

12. When Lysimachus appeared upon the scene, he claimed that he had done as much as Pyrrhus to overthrow Demetrius and demanded that the kingdom should be partitioned between them. Pyrrhus was by no means certain of the loyalty of the Macedonians, and so he accepted Lysimachus' terms and they divided the cities and the territory. This compromise served its purpose for the moment and prevented them from fighting one another, but it was not long before they recognized that the division of territories, so far from allaying their mutual hostility, was a source of endless quarrels and disputes. For if two rulers are so greedy that neither the sea nor the mountains nor the uninhabitable desert can limit their appetite, nor the boundaries which divide Europe and Asia serve as a barrier to their ambitions, it can hardly be expected when their frontiers actually run side by side that they will stay contented with what they have and do one another no wrong. On the contrary, they are continually at war, because to envy and to plot against one another becomes second nature, and they make use of the words 'war' and 'peace' just like current coin, to serve their purpose as the needs of the moment may demand, but quite regardless of justice. Indeed, they are really better men when they openly admit that they are at war with one another than when they disguise, under the names of justice and friendship,

those periods of leisure or inactivity which punctuate their acts of wrongdoing.

Pyrrhus demonstrated this very clearly. In an effort to check the growing power of Demetrius, and prevent its recovering, as it were, from a serious illness, he began helping the Greeks and entered Athens.[33] There he climbed the Acropolis and offered sacrifice to Athena, and on the same day came down again and addressed the people. He expressed his pleasure at the confidence and goodwill they had shown him, but warned them for the future that if they knew what was best for them, they would never open their gates to any of the kings nor admit them into the city. Later, he actually made peace with Demetrius, but a little later, after Demetrius had set out for Asia, he attempted, again at Lysimachus' instigation, to stir up a revolt in Thessaly, and he attacked the garrisons which Demetrius had left in various Greek cities. This was partly because he had discovered that the Macedonians were easier to manage when they were at war than when they were idle, and partly because his own nature could not endure inaction.

Finally, however, after Demetrius had suffered a crushing defeat in Syria,[34] Lysimachus, who by then felt himself secure and had no other distractions, lost no time in marching against Pyrrhus. He found his opponent encamped at Edessa; there he attacked him, captured his supply columns and caused his troops to suffer great hardship. Next, by writing letters to the leading Macedonians and spreading rumours, he set about weakening their loyalty to Pyrrhus. He reproached them for having chosen as their master a man who was a foreigner and whose ancestors had always been vassals of the Macedonians, and for having driven from their country the men who had been the friends and comrades of Alexander. When Pyrrhus discovered that many of the Macedonians were being won over, he took fright and withdrew, taking with him his Epirot troops and his allies, and in this way he lost Macedonia[35] in exactly the same way that he had seized it. It follows that kings have no reason to blame the mass of humanity if it changes sides to suit its own interests, for the people are only imitating the kings themselves, who set them an example of bad faith and treachery, and who believe that the man who shows least regard for justice will always reap the greatest advantage.

13. At this time, then, when Pyrrhus had been forced to give up Macedonia and retire to Epirus, Fortune gave him the opportunity to enjoy what he had without interference, and to live at peace ruling over his own subjects. But for Pyrrhus, life became tedious to the point of nausea, unless he could stir up trouble for others, or have it stirred up for him. Like Achilles, he could not endure inaction, *'but heartsick he brooded waiting there, pining for the war-cry and the battle'*.[36] So yearning as he did for new adventures, he found his opportunity in the following circumstances.

The Romans were at war with the people of Tarentum,[37] who were neither strong enough to carry on the struggle, nor, because of the reckless and unprincipled nature of their demagogues, inclined to put an end to it. The Tarentines, therefore, conceived the idea of making Pyrrhus their leader and inviting him to take part in the war, since they believed that of all the kings he had the most free time and was the most formidable general. Among the older and more prudent citizens, some, who were directly opposed to the plan, were silenced by the clamour and vehemence of the warmongers, while others, seeing the way that matters were going, stayed away from the assembly. However, there was a moderate man named Meton. When the day arrived on which the decree inviting Pyrrhus was to be confirmed, and while the people were taking their seats in the assembly, he snatched up a withered garland and a torch, as drunken revellers do, and came prancing and reeling into the assembly, accompanied by a flute-girl who led the way for him. At this, as might be expected in a democratic mob which possessed little idea of decorum, some of the audience applauded and others laughed, but nobody made any move to stop him; instead, they shouted to the girl to go on playing the flute and to Meton to come forward and give them a song, whereupon he made as if to obey them. But when silence had been restored, he spoke as follows: 'Men of Tarentum, you are right not to hinder those who wish to make merry and enjoy themselves while they can. And if you are wise, you will make the most of your present freedom, for you may be sure that you will have other things to think of, and your way of life will be very different once Pyrrhus arrives in the city.' These words made an impression on the majority and a murmur of applause ran through the assembly. But those who were afraid that if peace were concluded they would be handed over to the Romans, rebuked the people for tamely allowing a drunken reveller to insult them by such a disgraceful exhibition; then they banded together and drove Meton out of the assembly.[38]

In this way, the decree was ratified and the Tarentines sent a delegation to Pyrrhus, which included representatives of other Greek cities in Italy. They took with them gifts for the king, and explained to him that they needed an experienced commander, who had already earned a reputation. They also told him that they could provide large forces drawn from Lucania, Messapia, Samnium and Tarentum, which would total 20,000 cavalry and 350,000 infantry. These promises not only stirred Pyrrhus' enthusiasm, but made the Epirots eager to take part in the expedition.

14. There was a man named Cineas, a Thessalian in Pyrrhus' entourage, whose judgement was greatly respected. He had been a pupil of the orator Demosthenes and was considered to be the only public-speaker of his time who could revive in his audience's minds, as a statue might do, the memory of the latter's power and eloquence. He was in Pyrrhus' service and was often sent as his representative to various cities, where he proved the truth of Euripides' saying, 'Words can achieve all that an enemy's sword can hope to win.'[39] At any rate, Pyrrhus used to say that Cineas had conquered more cities by his oratory than he himself by force of arms, and he continued to pay him exceptional honours and to make use of his services. This man noticed that Pyrrhus was eagerly preparing for his expedition to Italy, and, finding him at leisure for the moment, he started the following conversation:[40]

'Pyrrhus,' he said, 'everyone tells me that the Romans are good soldiers and that they rule over many warlike nations. Now, if the gods allow us to defeat them, how shall we use our victory?' 'The answer is obvious,' Pyrrhus told him. 'If we can conquer the Romans, there is no other Greek or barbarian city which is a match for us. We shall straightaway become the masters of the whole of Italy, and nobody knows the size and the strength and the resources of the country better than yourself.' There was a moment's pause before Cineas went on. 'Then, sire, after we have conquered Italy, what shall we do next?' Pyrrhus did not yet see where the argument was leading. 'After Italy, Sicily, of course,' he said. 'The place positively beckons to us. It is rich, well-populated and easy to capture. Now that Agathocles is dead,[41] the whole island is torn by factions, there is no stable government in the cities and the demagogues have it all their own way.' 'No doubt what you say is true,' Cineas answered, 'but is our campaign to end with the capture of Sicily?' 'If the gods grant us victory and success in this campaign,' Pyrrhus told him, 'we can make it the springboard for much greater enterprises. How could we resist making an attempt upon Libya and Carthage, once we came within reach of them? Even Agathocles very nearly succeeded in capturing them when he slipped out of Syracuse with only a handful of ships. And when we have conquered these countries, none of our enemies who are so insolent to us now will be able to stand up to us. I do not have to emphasize that.' 'Certainly not,' replied Cineas. 'There is no doubt that when we have achieved that position of strength, we shall be able to recover Macedonia and have the rest of Greece at our feet. But after all these countries are in our power, what shall we do then?' Pyrrhus smiled benevolently and replied, 'Why, then we shall relax. We shall drink, my dear fellow, every day, and talk and amuse one another to our hearts' content.' Now that he had brought Pyrrhus to this point, Cineas had only to ask him, 'Then what prevents us from relaxing and drinking and entertaining each other now? We have the means to do that all around us. So the very prizes which we propose to win with all this bloodshed and toil and danger, and all the suffering inflicted on other people and ourselves, we could enjoy without taking another step!'

These arguments disturbed Pyrrhus but did not convert him. He could see clearly enough the happiness he was leaving behind, but he could not give up his hopes for what he desired.

15. First, then, he sent Cineas ahead to Tarentum with 3,000 soldiers.[42] Next, he assembled from Tarentum a large fleet of cavalry transports, decked ships and ferry boats of every kind, and on them he embarked twenty elephants, 3,000 cavalry, 20,000 infantry, 2,000 archers and 500 slingers. When all these were ready he set sail, but when he was halfway across the Ionian sea, the fleet was struck by a north wind which sprang up without warning and out of season. Although his ship was hard pressed, Pyrrhus himself, thanks to the courage and resolution of his sailors and helmsmen, was able to recover his course and after great labour and peril to make landfall, but the rest were thrown into confusion and scattered. Some were driven away from the Italian coast altogether and on into Sicilian and Libyan waters; other vessels, which failed to round the Iapygian cape[43] before dark, were hurled by heavy and boisterous seas onto the rocky and harbourless coast, with the result that all were destroyed except the royal galley. This ship was so large and solidly constructed that she could hold out against the pounding of the water from the seaward side, but when the wind veered round and began to blow from the shore, she was in danger of breaking up if she met the waves bows on, while to let her wallow in the rough open sea, battered by squalls which came from all directions, seemed the most dangerous course of all. At last, Pyrrhus leapt to his feet and dived into the sea, and his friends and bodyguard vied with one another to follow him. But the darkness and the roar of the waves and the undertow made it difficult to help him, and it was not until daybreak, by which time the wind had begun to die down, that he was able to struggle ashore. By then his strength was almost gone, but his courage and determination sustained him, even in this extremity. The Messapians, on whose coast he had been wrecked, quickly gathered and eagerly offered him all the help they could muster; meanwhile, some of his ships that had escaped the storm put in. These brought with them only a few

cavalrymen, fewer than two thousand infantry and two elephants.

16. With this force, Pyrrhus set out for Tarentum, and Cineas, as soon as he learnt of the king's arrival, led out his contingent to meet him. When Pyrrhus entered the city, he did nothing without the consent of the Tarentines, nor did he try to coerce them into any action, but waited until his fleet had safely reassembled and the greater part of his army had regrouped. By then he had discovered that the people were quite incapable of helping him or themselves, unless circumstances compelled them. Their inclination was to allow him to do their fighting for them, while they stayed at home enjoying their baths and social entertainments. Accordingly, Pyrrhus closed the gymnasia and public walks, where the citizens were in the habit of strolling about and fighting battles against the Romans with words. He also banned drinking-parties, banquets and festivals as unseasonable, conscripted the male population and showed himself strict and inflexible in mobilizing all those required for military service. As a result, many of the Tarentines left the city; they were so unaccustomed to discipline that they regarded it as slavery not to be allowed to live as they pleased.

The news now reached Pyrrhus that Laevinus, the Roman consul, was advancing on the city with a large army, plundering Lucania as he came. Pyrrhus' allies had not yet arrived, but he thought it disgraceful to remain inactive and allow the enemy to advance any nearer, and so he marched out with his troops. He had first dispatched a herald to the Romans to ask whether they would agree to receive satisfaction from the Italian Greeks before resorting to arms, and he offered his services as arbitrator and mediator. Laevinus' reply was that the Romans neither accepted Pyrrhus as a mediator nor feared him as an enemy, whereupon Pyrrhus advanced and pitched his camp in the plain between the cities of Pandosia and Heracleia.

When he discovered that the Romans were close by and had encamped on the other side of the River Siris, he rode up to reconnoitre the position. Their discipline, the arrangement of their watches, their orderly movements and the planning of their camp all impressed and astonished him, and he remarked to the friend nearest him, 'These may be barbarians, but there is nothing barbarous about their discipline; however, we shall see in action what it is worth.' He had already begun to feel some uncertainty as to the outcome, and he now determined to wait for his allies to arrive. At the same time, he posted a guard on the bank of the river to oppose the Romans if they tried to cross it. The Romans, however, were anxious to forestall the arrival of the forces for which Pyrrhus had decided to wait, and immediately attempted the crossing. Their infantry made the passage at a ford, while the cavalry galloped through the water at many different points, and thereupon the Greeks who were on guard retreated from the bank, for fear that they might be encircled.

Pyrrhus was disturbed by this, so he ordered his infantry officers to take up their battle formation at once and wait under arms, while he himself advanced with his force of 3,000 cavalry: he hoped to catch the Romans while they were still engaged in crossing the river and before they could regain their formation. But when he saw the glittering line of shields of the Roman infantry stretching along the bank, while their cavalry advanced against him in good order, he closed up his own ranks and led them in a charge. He stood out at once among his men for the beauty and brilliance of his elaborately ornamented armour, and he proved by his exploits that his reputation for valour was well deserved. Above all, although he exposed himself in personal combat and drove back all who encountered him, he kept throughout a complete grasp of the progress of the battle and never lost his presence of mind. He directed the action as though he were watching it from a distance, yet he was everywhere himself, and always managed to be at hand to support his troops wherever the pressure was greatest.

During the fighting, Leonnatus the Macedonian[44] noticed that one of the Italians had singled out Pyrrhus and was riding towards him, following his every movement. At length he said to the king, 'Do you see, sire, that barbarian who is riding the black horse with white feet? He looks like a man who is planning some desperate action. He never takes his eyes off you, he pays no attention to anybody else and it looks as though he is reserving all his strength to attack you. You must be on your guard against him.' Pyrrhus replied, 'Leonnatus, no man can avoid his fate. But neither he nor any other Italian will find it an easy task once they get to close quarters with me.' Even as they were speaking, the Italian wheeled his horse, levelled his spear and charged at Pyrrhus. Then, in the same instant that the Italian's lance struck the king's horse, his own was trans-fixed by Leonnatus. Both horses fell, but Pyrrhus was snatched up and saved by his friends, while the Italian, fighting desper-ately, was killed. His name was Oplax: he was captain of a troop of horse and a Frentanian by race.

17. This episode taught Pyrrhus to be more cautious in future. He saw that his cavalry were now giving ground and so sum-moned his phalanx and ordered them to take up formation. Then he gave his cloak and armour to Megacles, one of his companions, concealed himself after a fashion among Mega-cles' men and with them he charged the Romans. The Romans resisted their onslaught bravely and for a long while the issue hung in the balance. It is said that the mastery of the field changed hands no less than seven times, as each side gave ground in turn or advanced. The king's change of armour, although well-timed for his personal safety, came near to losing him the battle. Many of the enemy attacked Megacles, and the man who first struck him to the ground, called Dexius, seized his cloak and helmet and rode up with them to Laevinus; as he did so, he brandished them aloft and shouted out that he had killed Pyrrhus. The Romans, when they saw these trophies exultantly displayed and carried along their ranks, shouted aloud in triumph; the Greeks, on the other hand, were disheartened and dejected until Pyrrhus, discovering what had happened, rode along his line with bared head stretching out his hand to his allies and making himself known to them by his voice. At last, as the Romans began to be driven back by the elephants, and their horses, before they could get near the great beasts, started to panic and bolt, Pyrrhus seized his opportunity: as the Romans faltered, he launched a charge with his Thessalian cav-alry and routed the enemy with great slaughter.

According to Dionysius,[45] the Romans lost nearly 15,000 men and Pyrrhus 13,000, while Hieronymus[46] reduces these figures to 7,000 on the Roman side and 4,000 on the Greek. But these were some of Pyrrhus' best troops, and in addition he lost many of the friends and commanders whom he trusted and employed the most. However, he captured the Roman camp, which they had abandoned, and he persuaded some cities previously allied to Rome to come over to his side. He also ravaged a large area and advanced to a point less than 35 miles distant from Rome. After the battle, many of the Lucanians and Samnites flocked to join him. He reproached these peoples for coming so late, but it was clear that he was delighted and took especial pride in the fact that he had defeated such a great army of the Romans without any help but that of his own troops and the Tarentines.

18. The Romans did not remove Laevinus from his office as consul, and yet Gaius Fabricius is reported to have said that it was not the Epirots who had defeated the Romans, but Pyrrhus who had defeated Laevinus. Fabricius took the view that the Romans had been beaten through the fault of their general, not of the army. Meanwhile, the fact that the Romans immediately brought the depleted legions back to full strength, raised others and spoke of the war only in a spirit of undaunted confidence, filled Pyrrhus with consternation. He decided therefore to make an approach to them first and discover whether they would come to terms, for he thought that to storm the city and subdue the whole Roman people would be an immense task and quite beyond the strength of his present force, whereas a pact of friendship and a settlement negotiated after his victory would greatly enhance his prestige. So Cineas was dispatched to Rome, where he conferred with the leading officials and brought gifts for their wives and children in Pyrrhus' name. Nobody was willing to accept his gifts, but they all declared, women and children alike, that if a peace were concluded by the will of the people, they for their part would show their regard and goodwill for the king. Again, when Cineas laid a number of tempting proposals before the senate, not one of them was taken up with the least

pleasure or enthusiasm: this in spite of the fact that Pyrrhus offered to release without any ransom all the prisoners he had taken in the battle, and undertook to help the Romans to subdue the rest of Italy. All he asked in return was that he should be treated as a friend and the Tarentines left unmolested.

Nevertheless, it was clear that the majority of the senators were inclined towards peace, for they recognized that they had been defeated in a great battle and must expect to have to fight another against an even stronger army, now that the Italian Greeks had joined Pyrrhus. It was at this point that Appius Claudius, a man of great distinction but one who had been prevented by old age and blindness from playing an active part in politics, learnt that the king's terms had been presented to the senate, and that they were about to vote on the proposed cessation of hostilities. He could no longer bear to remain at home, but ordered his attendants to take him up and had himself carried through the forum to the senate-house on a litter. When he arrived at the doors, his sons and sons-in-law supported him and guided him to his seat, while the senators honoured him by preserving a respectful silence.

19. Speaking from where he stood, Appius then addressed them as follows: 'Previously, my countrymen, I had felt the loss of my sight as a heavy affliction. But now it grieves me that I have not lost my hearing as well when I learn of the shameful motions and decrees with which you propose to dishonour the great name of Rome. What has become of that boast which you have made famous throughout the world, that if the great Alexander had invaded Italy and encountered us when we were young men, or our fathers in their prime, he would not now be celebrated as invincible, but would either have fled or perhaps have fallen, and thus left Rome more glorious than ever before? Now, it seems to me, you are proving that this was mere bravado and empty boasting, since you shrink from these Chaonians and Molossians who have always been the prey and the spoil of the Macedonians, and you tremble before this Pyrrhus, who has spent most of his life dancing attendance on one or other of Alexander's bodyguards.[47] Now he comes wandering around

Italy, not so much to help the Greeks here as to escape from his own enemies at home, and he has the insolence to offer to help us subdue the country with this army which was not good enough to hold even a fraction of Macedonia for him. Do not imagine that you will get rid of this fellow by making him your friend. You will only bring other invaders after him, and they will despise you as a people whom anybody can subdue. This is what you can expect if you allow Pyrrhus to leave Italy not merely unpunished for the outrages he has committed against you, but actually rewarded for having made Rome a laughing-stock to the Tarentines and the Samnites.'

By the time Appius had finished, his audience were filled with the desire to continue the war and Cineas was dismissed with the reply that Pyrrhus must first leave Italy, and only then, if he still wished it, would the Romans discuss the question of an alliance and a pact of friendship. So long as he remained on their soil in arms, they would fight him to the death, even if he routed 10,000 more men like Laevinus in battle. It is reported that in the course of his mission, Cineas took especial care to study the life and customs of the Romans and to acquaint himself with the peculiar virtues of their form of government, and he also conversed with their most prominent men. On his return, he had much to report to Pyrrhus. Among other things, he told him that the senate impressed him as an assembly of many kings, and as for the people, he feared that to fight against them would be like fighting the Lernaean Hydra.[48] The consul had already raised an army twice the strength of the one which had faced Pyrrhus, and there were still many times this number of Romans who were able to bear arms.

20. After this, a Roman delegation visited Pyrrhus to discuss the subject of the prisoners of war. It was headed by Gaius Fabricius, who, as Cineas advised the king, enjoyed the highest reputation among the Romans both as a fine soldier and as a man of honour, but who was also extremely poor. Pyrrhus entertained him privately and tried to persuade him to accept a present of money. He did not offer this for any dishonourable reason, he explained, but simply as a token of friendship and

hospitality. Fabricius refused the gift, and for the moment Pyrrhus said nothing more. The next day, as he wished to startle a man who had never before seen an elephant, he ordered the largest he had to be placed behind a curtain while they conversed on the other side. This was done and then, at a given signal, the curtain was drawn aside, the animal suddenly raised its trunk, held it over Fabricius' head and trumpeted with a loud and terrifying noise. Fabricius turned, smiled serenely at Pyrrhus and said, 'Your gold made no impression on me yesterday, and neither does your beast today.'

When they dined together, they discussed many different topics, and in particular the subject of Greece and Greek philosophers. Cineas happened to mention Epicurus, and expounded the theories of the Epicurean school concerning the gods, the conduct of politics and the question of what is the highest good. He explained that the Epicureans considered pleasure to be the greatest good, but refrained from taking any active part in politics on the ground that it was injurious to and confused the pursuit of happiness; also, that the Epicureans believed the deity to be completely remote from feelings of benevolence, anger or concern for humanity, and conceived of the gods as leading a life which was devoid of cares and filled with comfort and enjoyment. Before Cineas could finish, Fabricius interrupted him. 'Heracles,' he exclaimed, 'pray grant that Pyrrhus and the Samnites continue to take these doctrines seriously so long as they are at war with us!'

After these encounters, Pyrrhus was filled with admiration for Fabricius' spirit and character, and he desired more than ever to make the Romans his friends instead of his enemies. He even went so far as to invite Fabricius privately, if he could bring about a settlement between the two peoples, to throw in his lot and live with him as the chief of his companions and generals. But Fabricius, so the story goes, quietly said to him, 'This arrangement, sire, would not be to your advantage. The same men who now admire and honour you, if they came to know me, would rather have me to rule them than yourself.' Such a man was Fabricius. For his part, Pyrrhus did not take offence at this speech nor behave like a tyrant; he even told his

friends of Fabricius' magnanimity and entrusted the Roman
prisoners of war to his charge alone. He did this on condition
that if the senate voted against making peace, the prisoners
should be returned to Pyrrhus, though they were allowed first
to greet their friends and spend the festival of Saturn with them.
This was how matters turned out. The prisoners were sent back
after the festival, and the senate passed a decree that any who
remained behind should be put to death.

21. Afterwards, when Fabricius had become consul, a man
arrived in the Roman camp with a letter for him. The writer
was Pyrrhus' physician, who offered to poison the king, provided that the Romans would pay him a sufficient reward for
putting an end to the war without any further danger to them.
But Fabricius was disgusted at the man's treachery and persuaded his fellow-consul to take the same view: he immediately
sent a letter to Pyrrhus, warning him to be on his guard against
this plot. The letter ran as follows:

'Gaius Fabricius and Quintus Aemilius, consuls of Rome,[49]
greet King Pyrrhus. It seems that you are a poor judge both of
your friends and of your enemies. You will see when you read
the letter I have sent you that you choose to make war against
just and virtuous men and put your faith in rogues and traitors.
We do not send you this information to do you a service but
because we do not wish your downfall to bring any reproach
upon us, nor to have men say of us that we brought this war to
an end by treachery because we could not do so by our own
valour.'

When Pyrrhus had read the letter and made further inquiries
into the plot, he punished the physician and, by way of return
to the Romans, delivered up his prisoners to them without ransom; he also, once more, sent Cineas to try to negotiate a peace
for him. However, the Romans refused to take back the prisoners without payment; they were unwilling to accept a favour
from an enemy or to be rewarded for having refrained from
using treachery against him. As for Cineas' overtures concerning a treaty of peace and friendship, they declined to enter into
any further discussion until Pyrrhus had removed his arms and

his troops from Italy and returned to Epirus in the ships which had brought him.

Pyrrhus' affairs thus compelled him to fight another battle, and after he had rested his troops he marched to the city of Asculum and attacked the Romans. Here, he was obliged to manoeuvre on rough ground where his cavalry could not operate and along the wooded banks of a swiftly flowing river where his elephants could not charge the enemy's phalanx. There was fierce fighting in which both sides suffered heavy losses before night put an end to the engagement. The next day, Pyrrhus regrouped his forces so as to fight on even terrain, where his elephants could be used against the enemy's line. He detached troops to occupy the difficult ground, posted strong contingents of archers and slingers in the spaces between the elephants and then launched his main body into the attack in close order and with an irresistible impetus. The Romans could not employ their tactics of withdrawing and attacking from the side which they had used on the previous day and were compelled to engage Pyrrhus on level ground and head on. They were anxious to repulse Pyrrhus' hoplites before the elephants came up, and so they fought desperately with their swords against the enemy pikes, exposing themselves recklessly, thinking only of killing and wounding the enemy and caring nothing for their own losses. After a long struggle, so it is said, the Roman line began to give way at the point where Pyrrhus himself was pressing his opponents hardest, but the factor which did most to enable his men to prevail was the weight and fury of the elephants' charge. Against this, even the Romans' courage was of little avail: they felt as they might have done before the rush of a tidal wave or the shock of an earthquake, that it was better to give way than to stand their ground to no purpose and suffer a terrible fate without gaining the least advantage.

The Romans had only a short distance to flee before they reached their camp. Hieronymus reports that they lost 6,000 men killed and that Pyrrhus' casualties, according to the royal journals, were 3,505. In Dionysius' account,[50] on the other hand, there is no mention of two battles having been fought at

Asculum, nor that the Romans acknowledged any defeat: he says that the two armies fought on one occasion only and that this battle lasted until sunset, when they at last broke off the action with difficulty; he tells us that Pyrrhus was wounded in the arm by a javelin, that his baggage was plundered by the Daunians[51] and that the losses of Pyrrhus and the Romans combined amounted to 15,000 men.

The two armies disengaged, and the story goes that when one of Pyrrhus' friends congratulated him on his victory, he replied, 'One more victory like that over the Romans will destroy us completely!' He had lost a great part of the force he had brought with him, with a few exceptions almost all his friends and commanders had been killed and there were no reinforcements which he could summon. At the same time, he could see that his allies in Italy were losing their enthusiasm, while the Roman army, by contrast, was fed, as though from a spring gushing forth at home, by a constant stream of recruits, from which they could quickly and easily replace their losses. Defeat never seemed to undermine their self-confidence; instead, their anger only gave them fresh strength and determination to pursue the war.

22. Even while he laboured under these difficulties, new prospects and fresh hopes presented themselves to divert him from his original purpose. News now reached him from two different quarters simultaneously. From Sicily there arrived a delegation which offered to put him in control of the cities of Acragas, Syracuse and Leontini, and begged him to help them expel the Carthaginians and free the island from its tyrants. And from Greece messengers reported that Ptolemy Ceraunus[52] had been killed in a battle with the Gauls and his army annihilated, and that this was the moment for Pyrrhus to return to Macedonia, where the people needed a king. He railed against Fortune for presenting him with two opportunities of such importance at the same moment, and for a long while he hesitated in his choice, since he assumed that to take up the one would compel him to abandon the other. In the end, it seemed to him that Sicily offered the more promising prospects, espe-

cially since Libya was so close at hand, and he immediately dispatched Cineas, as was his habit, to open preliminary negotiations with the cities, while he placed a garrison in Tarentum. The Tarentines were angry at this and demanded that he should either devote his efforts to the task for which he had been invited, that is to help them fight the Romans, or else go away and leave their country as he had found it. He answered them roughly by telling them to keep quiet until he had time to attend to their affairs, and then sailed away.

When he landed in Sicily,[53] his hopes started at once to be realized. The cities came over to him with enthusiasm, and wherever force and conflict were necessary nothing was able to hold out against him at first. He advanced with a combined expedition of 30,000 infantry, 2,500 cavalry and 200 ships, and with these forces he routed the Carthaginians and overran the part of Sicily which had been under their rule. Next, he decided to assault the walls of Eryx,[54] which was the strongest of their fortresses and was held by a large garrison. When his army was ready for the attack, he donned his armour, appeared before his troops and made a vow to Heracles that he would hold public games and offer sacrifice in his honour if the god would allow him on that day to prove himself before the Sicilian Greeks as a champion who was worthy of his ancestors and fit to command an allied army of this size. Then he ordered the trumpet to sound the attack, drove the barbarians back from the battlements with a hail of missiles, had the scaling-ladders brought forward and was the first to climb the wall. There he engaged great numbers of the enemy. Some he forced off the wall and hurled to the ground on either side, but most of them he attacked with his sword so that he was soon standing amid a heap of dead bodies.[55] He himself was unscathed, but his appearance filled the enemy with terror, thus proving that Homer was right and was speaking from experience when he says that it is courage alone of all the virtues which often manifests itself in states of divine possession and frenzy.[56] After the city had been captured, he offered up sacrifices to the god on a magnificent scale and organized spectacles of many different kinds of contests.

23. The barbarians who lived in the neighbourhood of Messana had been the cause of many troubles to the Greeks and had compelled some of them to pay tribute. They formed a large and warlike population and so had been given the name of Mamertines, which in the Latin language means 'devoted to Ares', the god of war. Pyrrhus first arrested their collectors of tribute and put them to death, and then he defeated the Mamertines in battle and destroyed many of their strongholds. The Carthaginians showed themselves ready to come to terms with him, and they offered to pay a sum of money and provide him with ships if a treaty were concluded between them. But Pyrrhus, who cherished much larger ambitions than these, replied that he could not consider the idea of a settlement or a pact of friendship between them except on one condition, namely that they should evacuate the whole of western Sicily and make the Libyan Sea the frontier between themselves and the Greeks. Pyrrhus by now felt so elated by his success and the strength of his resources that he determined to pursue the ambitions with which he had originally sailed from Epirus and make Libya his prime objective. Accordingly, since many of the ships of his fleet were undermanned, he began to conscript rowers. However, he set about this in a thoroughly autocratic fashion: he made no attempt to treat the Greek cities with tact or consideration, but angrily resorted to force and punishments. He had not acted in this fashion at first, indeed, he had gone out of his way to win friends by the courtesy of his manner, by his readiness to trust everybody and by his anxiety to do no harm. Now, however, he ceased to behave as a popular leader and became a tyrant, and besides the reputation for severity which he already possessed he acquired another for ingratitude and bad faith.

The Sicilians murmured against these impositions, but nevertheless put up with them as necessary evils; it was his treatment of Thoenon and Sosistratus which proved the turning-point in his dealings with the islanders. These two men were prominent citizens of Syracuse; they had been among the first to invite Pyrrhus to come to Sicily, and as soon as he had arrived they had placed the city in his hands and given him the greatest help in all he had achieved in Sicilian affairs. In spite of this, however,

Pyrrhus would neither take them with him on his campaigns nor leave them behind, but treated them with suspicion. Sosistratus became alarmed at this behaviour and escaped, but Thoenon was accused by Pyrrhus of plotting with Sosistratus against him, and was put to death. From this moment, the attitude of the Sicilians towards him was transformed, and not only in Syracuse. All the cities now regarded him with feelings of mortal hatred, and some of them joined the Carthaginians, while others appealed to the Mamertines to help them. But at this moment, when Pyrrhus was faced on all sides with disaffection, insurrections against his authority and a strongly united opposition, he received letters from the Tarentines and the Samnites, who begged for his help since they had been driven from their outlying territories, were confined to the boundaries of their cities and could scarcely carry on the war even from within their own walls. This gave him a plausible excuse to sail away, so that his departure should not appear to be a flight or the result of his having despaired of his prospects on the island. But the truth was that he had failed to master Sicily, which was like a storm-tossed ship, and it was because he was anxious to escape that he once more threw himself into Italy. The story goes that as he was leaving, he looked back at the island and remarked to his companions, 'My friends, what a wrestling ground we are leaving behind us for the Romans and the Carthaginians.' And certainly it was not long before this prophecy of his was fulfilled.[57]

24. The barbarians combined to attack him while he was crossing to Italy. He fought a sea-battle with the Carthaginians in the straits and lost many of his ships, but escaped with the rest to Italy. Meanwhile, a Mamertine army at least ten thousand strong had already crossed ahead of him. The Mamertines were afraid to face him in a pitched battle, but they harassed his march and caused great confusion to his army by attacking him at difficult points on his route. Two of his elephants were killed in these actions and his rearguard suffered heavy losses. Pyrrhus had been at the head of his column, but he rode to the rear, helped to drive off the enemy and exposed himself

fearlessly in fighting against men who were not only courageous but well trained in battle. The enemy became all the more elated when Pyrrhus was struck on the head with a sword and retired a little way from the fighting. One of the Mamertines, a man of giant stature clad in shining armour, ran out in front of their ranks and in an arrogant voice challenged Pyrrhus to come forward if he were still alive. This infuriated Pyrrhus, and in spite of the efforts of his guards to protect him, he wheeled round and forced his way through them. His face was smeared with blood and his features contorted into a terrible expression of rage. Then, before the barbarian could strike, he dealt him a tremendous blow on the head with his sword. So great was the strength of his arm and the keenness of the blade that it cleft the man from head to foot, and in an instant the two halves of his body fell apart. The barbarians immediately halted and came on no further, for they were amazed and bewildered at Pyrrhus and believed him to be superhuman. He was able to continue his march unopposed and arrived at Tarentum with a force of 20,000 infantry and 3,000 cavalry. He reinforced his army with the best of the Tarentine troops and immediately led them out against the Romans, who were encamped in the territory of the Samnites.

25. But the many defeats which the Romans had inflicted on the Samnites had broken their power and subdued their spirit. They also harboured a grudge against Pyrrhus for having left them and sailed away to Sicily, and in consequence few of them joined him. Pyrrhus divided his army into two parts. He sent one into Lucania to engage the other consul and prevent him from joining forces with his colleague; he himself led the main body of his forces against Manius Curius, who was encamped in a strong position near the city of Beneventum.[58] Here, the consul placed himself on the defensive: this was partly because he was waiting for the troops in Lucania, and partly because the soothsayers had advised against action on account of unfavourable omens from the sacrifices. Pyrrhus was eager to attack this force before their comrades could arrive, and so he took his best troops and his most warlike elephants and set out on a night march to the camp. But as he had chosen a long

roundabout route, which led through wooded country, his torches went out and the soldiers lost their way in the darkness and were thrown into confusion. Much time was lost in this way, the night passed and daylight revealed his position to the Romans as he bore down upon them from the heights.

The sight of the enemy created a great stir and commotion in the Roman camp, but the sacrifices now turned out to be favourable, and, since action was forced upon him, Manius led out his troops and attacked the enemy's advance guard. He routed these and also succeeded in putting the main body to flight; many of them were killed and several of the elephants were left behind and captured. This success encouraged Manius to come down into the plain and engage the enemy there. In this action, on open ground, he drove back one wing of his opponent's army, but in another sector his own men were overwhelmed by the elephants and forced back to their camp. Manius now threw into the battle the troops who had been left to guard the camp and who were standing in great numbers along the ramparts, all under arms and fresh for the battle. They came down at the run from their strong position, flung their javelins at the elephants and forced them to wheel about, thus causing great confusion and dismay as they trampled on their own troops in their flight. This manoeuvre gave the victory to the Romans and at the same time established their superiority in the struggle with Pyrrhus. These battles not only steeled their courage and their fighting qualities, but also earned them the reputation of being invincible: the result was that they at once brought the rest of Italy under their sway and soon after Sicily as well.[59]

26. In this way, Pyrrhus' hopes of the conquest of Italy and Sicily were banished. He had squandered six years[60] in his campaigns in these regions, but although he had been worsted in all his attempts, his spirit remained undaunted in the midst of defeat. The general opinion of him was that for warlike experience, daring and personal valour he had no equal among the kings of his time; but what he won through his feats of arms, he lost by indulging in vain hopes, and through his obsessive desire to seize what lay beyond his grasp he constantly failed to

secure what lay within it. For this reason, Antigonus used to compare him to a player at dice who makes many good throws but does not understand how to exploit them when they are made.

Pyrrhus brought back to Epirus an army of 8,000 infantry and 500 cavalry, and, since he had no money, he looked about for a campaign to enable him to support this force. A number of Gauls joined him and he made a raid on Macedonia, originally intending only to strip and plunder the country, which was now ruled by Antigonus, the son of Demetrius.[61] However, after he had captured a number of cities and a force of 2,000 Macedonians had come over to his side, his hopes began once more to rise. He marched against Antigonus, and, making a surprise attack on him at the entrance to a narrow defile, threw his whole army into confusion. A strong contingent of Gauls who formed the rearguard of Antigonus' force stood their ground bravely, but after fierce fighting most of them were cut down, while the division of the army which contained the elephants was hemmed in and the drivers surrendered themselves and their animals. With this addition to his strength, Pyrrhus decided to trust to his luck rather than his judgement, and, disregarding the superior numbers against him, advanced to attack the Macedonian phalanx, which was already disorganized and demoralized because of the defeat of the rearguard. For this reason, they made no attempt to engage or resist their adversaries, and when Pyrrhus stretched out his right hand and called upon the commanders and captains by name, the whole of Antigonus' infantry went over to him. Antigonus escaped and managed to secure some of the coastal cities, while Pyrrhus, who considered that of all his successes the victory over the Gauls was the one which added the most to his reputation, dedicated the finest and richest of the spoils to the temple of Athena Itonis. This was the inscription in elegiac verses which he had placed over them:

> Pyrrhus the Molossian hung up as a gift to Athena Itonis
> These shields which he took from valiant Gauls
> When he destroyed the entire army of Antigonus. That was no
> great wonder:
> Now too, as of old, the Aeacidae[62] are brave spearmen.[63]

After the battle he immediately moved to occupy the cities of Macedonia.[64] He captured Aegae,[65] where he treated the inhabitants harshly and left a contingent of Gauls who were campaigning with him to garrison the city. As a race, the Gauls possess an insatiable appetite for money, and they now dug up the tombs of the rulers of Macedon who are buried there, plundering the treasure and insolently scattering the bones. This outrage Pyrrhus treated with indifference: he either postponed action because he had too many urgent matters on his hands, or decided not to take any because he was afraid of punishing the barbarians. In any event, the episode did much harm to his reputation with the Macedonians. Then, while his affairs were still unsettled and before his position in Macedonia had been established, Pyrrhus' hopes suddenly veered in a new direction. He abused Antigonus and called him shameless because he continued to wear his royal robe of purple and had not yet exchanged it for a commoner's dress, and when Cleonymus the Spartan arrived and appealed to him to come to Lacedaemon, he sprang at the offer with enthusiasm.

Cleonymus was of royal descent but was considered to possess a violent and autocratic disposition; he had therefore failed to win the confidence or the goodwill of his people and the country was ruled by Areus.[66] This was the cause of a long-standing grudge which Cleonymus bore against his fellow-citizens. In addition, in his later years he had married Chilonis, the daughter of Leotychidas, a beautiful woman who also belonged to the Spartan royal family, but who had fallen passionately in love with Acrotatus, the son of Areus. Acrotatus was in the flower of his manhood, and so their relationship not only tormented Cleonymus, who loved his wife, but also dishonoured him, since every Spartan knew that she despised her husband. In this way, Cleonymus' private troubles and his political grievances exacerbated one another, and it was these feelings of anger which had led him to bring Pyrrhus to Sparta.[67] Pyrrhus had with him 25,000 infantry, 2,000 cavalry and twenty-four elephants, and it was at once clear from the scale of his preparations that his aim was not to conquer Sparta for Cleonymus but the Peloponnese for himself. Of course, he expressly denied any such intention, above all when the Spartan ambassadors met him at Megalopolis. He declared to them that he had come to liberate the cities which Antigonus was holding in subjection,[68] and added that he planned to send his own sons to Sparta, if nothing prevented this, to be brought up according to the Lacedaemonian traditions, which would make them superior to all the other rulers of their time. These inventions were fed to all those who came to meet him on his march, but no sooner had he reached Lacedaemonian territory than he began to ravage and plunder it. When the Spartan envoys complained that he was attacking their country without having declared war, he retorted, 'But neither do you Spartans, as we know very well, give any warning to others of what you are going to do.' At this, one of the envoys named Mandricleidas remarked in the Spartan dialect, 'If you are a god, you will do us no harm, for we have done none to you. But if you are a man, you may meet one who is stronger than you are.'

27. After this, Pyrrhus marched southward against the city of Sparta. Cleonymus strongly urged him to attack the city on the very first evening that he arrived. But Pyrrhus was afraid, it is said, that his troops would sack the city if they attacked it by night, and so he held them back, telling Cleonymus that they could achieve the same result by day. The town was only thinly defended and the speed of Pyrrhus' advance had taken the Spartans unawares, for Areus was in Crete on an expedition to help the people of Gortyn. As events turned out, it was precisely the fact that Pyrrhus despised the city's apparent weakness and lack of defenders which proved to be its salvation. Pyrrhus assumed that there would be no resistance and pitched camp for the night, while Cleonymus' friends and helots prepared his house and decorated it, expecting that Pyrrhus would dine there with him.

When it was dark, the Lacedaemonians at first debated the possibility of sending their womenfolk to Crete, but the women opposed this, and Archidamia walked into the Council of Elders with a sword in her hand and reproached the men on their behalf for proposing that their wives and daughters should

survive while Sparta itself perished. Next, it was resolved to dig
a trench parallel with the enemy's camp and to place at each
end wagons buried up to their axles, so that once embedded in
this way they could resist the charge of the elephants.[69] As soon
as this work began, the women, both married and unmarried,
arrived on the scene, some of them in their robes with their
tunics knotted round the waist, others dressed only in their
tunics, and all joined in to help the older men. The younger
males who had been assigned to the defence were ordered to
rest, and the women dug a third of the trench with their hands.
According to Phylarchus, the trench was 800 feet long, 9 feet
wide and 6 feet deep, although Hieronymus says that its dimensions were rather smaller. When day dawned and the enemy
began to move, the women brought the young men their arms,
handed over the trench to them and urged them to guard and
keep it safe. They reminded them that it would be sweet to conquer in sight of the whole country and glorious to die in the
arms of their wives and mothers, laying down their lives in a
manner that was worthy of Sparta. As for Chilonis, she retired
by herself and had a noose ready round her neck, so that she
would not fall into Cleonymus' hands if the city were captured.

28. Pyrrhus was engaged in a frontal attack with his hoplites.
He strove to force a way through the wall of shields presented
by the Spartans who were drawn up against him, and to cross
the trench, but this proved difficult because the freshly turned
earth gave his soldiers no firm footing. His son Ptolemy had led
a picked force of Chaonians and 2,000 Gauls round the end of
the trench and was trying to break through the barricade of
wagons. These had been dug in so deeply and so close together
that they not only obstructed his advance but made it difficult
for the Lacedaemonians to reach the point he was attacking.
The Gauls succeeded in pulling the wheels up, but as they began
to haul the wagons down to the river the young Acrotatus saw
the danger and, running through the city with three hundred
men, managed to get behind Ptolemy, from whom he was concealed by some depressions in the ground; from here he attacked
the rear of Ptolemy's detachment and forced them to turn and

defend themselves. In this way, the barbarians were crowded against one another so that they fell into the trench and among the wagons, and at last they were driven back with great slaughter. The older men and the crowd of women all witnessed Acrotatus' gallant exploit, and as he returned through the city to his appointed post, covered with blood but triumphant and exulting in his victory, it seemed to the Spartan women that he had grown even taller and more handsome than before and they envied Chilonis her lover; some of the old men even followed him and shouted, 'Go, Acrotatus, and mount Chilonis, but be sure that you beget brave sons for Sparta!' Meanwhile, a fierce battle was also raging around Pyrrhus, and many fought magnificently, especially a man named Phyllius who surpassed all his comrades in the stubbornness of his resistance and the numbers of the attackers whom he laid low. When he found that his strength was ebbing away, on account of all the wounds he had received, he made way for one of his comrades to take his place and fell dead inside the line of shields, so as to be sure that his body should not fall into enemy hands.

29. As darkness fell, the fighting died down, and that night while Pyrrhus slept he saw the following vision. He dreamt that Sparta was stricken with thunderbolts hurled from his own hand, that the whole countryside was ablaze and that he was filled with rejoicing. This feeling of delight woke him and he gave orders to his commanders for the army to prepare for action; meanwhile, he described his dream to his friends, for he was convinced that they would capture the city by storm. Most of them agreed with this interpretation and were full of admiration, except only for Lysimachus,[70] who found the dream disturbing: he explained he was afraid that as places which have been struck by thunderbolts are held to be sacred, and may not be trodden by the foot of man, so the gods might be warning Pyrrhus that the city was not for him to enter. But Pyrrhus declared that this was idle chatter invented for those who knew no better, and he called upon his listeners to take up their weapons and repeat to themselves '*One omen is best, to fight for Pyrrhus!*'[71] Then he rose at daybreak and began bringing up his army for the attack.

The Spartans defended themselves with a resolution and courage out of all proportion to their numbers. The women, too, were in the thick of the action, handing the men arrows and javelins, bringing food and drink wherever they were needed and carrying away the wounded. The Macedonians tried to fill up the trench, bringing up great quantities of material and throwing it over the weapons and the corpses which lay at the bottom, and when the Lacedaemonians tried to prevent these tactics, Pyrrhus appeared on horseback, fighting his way past the trench and the wagons and into the city. Those who were defending this part of the Spartan line raised a shout and came running, and the women began to shriek, but just as Pyrrhus was breaking through and attacking the men in front of him, his horse was wounded in the belly by a Cretan javelin, and, rearing up in its death agony, threw the king on to the steep and slippery slope. This accident caused dismay and confusion among his companions, and the Spartans seized the moment to charge, and making good use of their missiles drove the enemy back. After this, Pyrrhus gave the order to halt the fighting elsewhere on the battlefield; he believed that the Spartans were on the point of surrendering, since many of them had been killed and almost all were wounded. But at that moment, the city's good fortune came to her rescue. It may be that she was satisfied that the courage of her citizens had been proven, or perhaps wished to show her own power to save the day when all seemed lost. At any rate, Ameinias the Phocian, one of Antigonus' generals, suddenly appeared from Corinth with a contingent of mercenaries, and no sooner had he been admitted into the city than Areus arrived from Crete with his army of 2,000 soldiers. Thereupon, the women returned to their homes since they no longer thought it necessary to take part in the defence, and the soldiers relieved those who, despite their age, had been obliged in the emergency to arm themselves, and drew themselves up for battle.

30. For his part, Pyrrhus was spurred on to make an even fiercer effort to capture the city now that it had been reinforced. But as his renewed attacks met with no success and his losses

mounted, he abandoned the assault, took to plundering the countryside and planned to spend the winter there. But his fate was inescapable. For at Argos civil war had broken out between Aristeas and Aristippus, and, since Aristippus was believed to be supported by Antigonus, Aristeas promptly invited Pyrrhus to Argos. Pyrrhus was always entertaining one hope after another, and since he made every success serve as the starting-point for a new enterprise, and was determined that every failure could be retrieved by a fresh start, he allowed neither defeat nor victory to limit his capacity to make trouble for himself or for others. So no sooner had he received this offer than he broke camp and set off for Argos. Areus, however, posted a number of ambushes, and by occupying the most difficult points on Pyrrhus' line of march he succeeded several times in cutting off the Gauls and the Molossians who formed Pyrrhus' rearguard.

Pyrrhus had been warned by his seer that, since the liver of his sacrificial victims lacked a lobe, he would lose a relative.[72] But unluckily, because of the commotion and disorder created by the ambush, he forgot this warning and ordered his son Ptolemy to go with his companions[73] to relieve the rearguard, while he himself hastened the advance of the main body and led them out of the defile. When Ptolemy arrived, a fierce battle developed, and while a picked company of Spartans commanded by Evalcus engaged the troops who were fighting immediately in front of Ptolemy, a Cretan named Oryssus from Aptera, a man who combined exceptional strength of arm and speed of foot, sprinted round the flank, approached the young prince where he was fighting bravely, flung a javelin and struck him down. When Ptolemy fell, the rest of his troops turned in flight and the Spartans followed in headlong pursuit, until before they knew where they were they had broken out into the plain and were cut off by Pyrrhus' hoplites. Pyrrhus himself had just learnt of his son's death, and in an agony of grief ordered his Molossian cavalry to charge the Spartans. He rode at their head and sated himself with Spartan blood. He had always shown himself to be an irresistible and terrifying fighter, but this time his daring and his fury surpassed anything that had been seen before. When he rode at Evalcus, the Spartan side-stepped his charge and aimed a blow with his sword that just missed Pyrrhus' bridle-hand and sheared through the reins. Pyrrhus ran him through with his lance, but in the same moment fell from his horse; he went on fighting on foot and cut to pieces the picked company of Spartans who were fighting round the body of Evalcus. This was a great loss to Sparta: the campaign against Pyrrhus was effectively over and the deaths of these men were really due to the desire of their commanders to distinguish themselves.

31. In this way, Pyrrhus had offered up a sacrifice, so to speak, to the ghost of his son, and had made his death the occasion for a glorious victory. He had also found relief from much of his grief in the fury with which he had attacked the enemy, and he proceeded to lead on his army towards Argos. He learnt that Antigonus had already occupied the heights which commanded the plain, and so he pitched his own camp close to Nauplia. The following day, he sent a herald to Antigonus, denouncing him as a robber and challenging him to come down into the plain and fight for the throne.[74] Antigonus replied that his generalship was a matter not of force of arms but of timing, and that if Pyrrhus was weary of life he could find many ways to die. Meanwhile, the two kings were visited by deputations from Argos, who begged them to go away and allow the city to remain neutral but on friendly terms with them both. Antigonus agreed to this and handed over his son to the Argives as a hostage. Pyrrhus, likewise, agreed to go, but as he gave no pledge he was regarded with even greater suspicion than before.

Pyrrhus was himself the witness of a remarkable portent. The heads of the cattle which he had sacrificed were seen, as they lay apart from the bodies, to put out their tongues and lap up their own blood, and besides this the priestess of the temple of Lycian Apollo in the city of Argos ran out of the shrine in a frenzy, crying that she saw the city full of carnage and dead bodies, and that there was an eagle which was advancing for battle, and then was gone.[75]

32. At dead of night, Pyrrhus marched his troops up to the walls, found that the gate known as Diemperes had been opened for him by Aristeas, and so his Gauls were able to enter the city and seize the market-place before the alarm was raised. But the gate was too small to let his elephants through, and the towers which they carried on their backs had to be unfastened and then put on again when the animals were inside. All these manoeuvres had to be carried out in the darkness and so caused confusion and delay, and at length the alarm was given and the Argives roused. They hurried to the place known as 'the Shield' and to other strong-points in the city, and sent messengers to Antigonus calling on him to help. Antigonus marched up close to the walls, halted there and sent his generals and his son inside with a strong relieving force. Areus also came up with a detachment consisting of a thousand Cretans and the most agile of the Spartans. These troops joined forces, attacked the Gauls and threw them into great confusion. Meanwhile Pyrrhus, with loud shouts, was entering the city in the neighbourhood of Cylarabis. But he noticed that the answering shouts from the Gauls in the market-place sounded weak and undecided, and he guessed that they were hard pressed. He therefore tried to quicken his pace and urged on the horsemen ahead of him; they were picking their way with great difficulty among the water-conduits with which the whole city is intersected and which endangered their advance. All the while, in this night action, there was great confusion as to what orders were being given and how they were being carried out. Men wandered about and lost their direction in the narrow alleyways, and amid the darkness, the confused noise and the confined spaces, generalship was helpless. In consequence, both sides found they could achieve little under these conditions and waited for the dawn.

As it began to grow light, Pyrrhus was disturbed to see that the whole of the open square known as the Shield was filled with enemy troops, and then among the many votive offerings in the market-place he caught sight of the statue of a wolf and a bull carved in bronze and about to attack one another. He remembered with sudden dread an oracle which had predicted many years before that he was fated to die when he saw a wolf fighting with a bull. According to the Argives, these figures were set up to commemorate a very early event in their history. When Danaus had first landed in the country near Pyramia, in the district of Thyreatis, and was on his way to Argos, he saw a wolf fighting with a bull. He supposed that the wolf must represent himself, since he like the wolf was a foreigner and had come like it to attack the native inhabitants. He watched the contest, and when he saw that the wolf had gained the day he offered his prayers to Apollo Lyceius the wolf-god, attacked the city and was victorious, after Gelanor who was then the king had been driven into exile by a rival party. This, then, is the account the Argives give of how Danaus came to dedicate the statue.

33. The sight of these animals, combined with the evident failure of his plans, disheartened Pyrrhus and he decided to retreat. But remembering how narrow the gates were, and fearing that he might be trapped behind them, he sent a message to his son Helenus, who had been left outside the city with the main body of the army: the orders were that he should break down the wall and cover the retreat of Pyrrhus and his men as they passed through the breach, in case they were being hard pressed by the enemy. But in the haste and confusion, the messenger failed to convey these instructions clearly, and a mistake was made with the result that the young man, taking the remainder of the elephants and the best of the troops, marched through the gate into the city to rescue his father. By this time, Pyrrhus was already beginning to withdraw. As long as the action remained in the main square where there was plenty of room to fight and give ground, he could retreat in good order, turning every now and then to drive off his attackers. But after he had been forced out of the market-place into the narrow street which led to the gate, he met the reinforcements who were hurrying to the rescue from the opposite direction. Some of these troops could not hear Pyrrhus when he shouted to them to retire, while those who were only too anxious to obey him were prevented from doing so by the men who kept pouring in behind them through

the gate. For the largest of the elephants had fallen across the gateway and lay there bellowing and blocking the way for those who were struggling to get out. Another elephant named Nicon, one of those which had advanced further into the city, was trying to find its rider who had been wounded and fallen off its back, and was battling against the tide of fugitives who were trying to escape. The beast crushed friend and foe together indiscriminately until, having found its master's dead body, it lifted the corpse with its trunk, laid it across its tusks and, wheeling round in a frenzy of grief, turned back, trampling and killing all who stood in its path. The crowd of soldiers was so tightly pressed and jammed side by side that nobody could help himself: the whole mass, which appeared to be bolted together into a single body, kept surging and swaying this way and that. They could scarcely move to fight those of the enemy who, from time to time, were caught up in their ranks or attacked them from the rear, and, indeed, it was to themselves that they did most harm. Once a man had drawn his sword or aimed his spear, it was impossible for him to sheathe or put it up again, but it would pierce whoever stood in its way, and so many men died from these accidental thrusts that they gave one another.

34. Pyrrhus, seeing the stormy sea that surged about him, took off the diadem which distinguished his helmet and handed it to one of his companions. Then, trusting to his horse, he plunged in among the enemy who were following him and was wounded by a spear which pierced his breast-plate. This was not a mortal wound, nor even a serious one, and Pyrrhus at once turned to attack the man who had struck him. This was an Argive, not a man of noble birth but the son of a poor old woman, who like the rest was watching the battle from the roof of her house. When she saw that her son was engaged in combat with Pyrrhus, she was filled with fear and rage at the danger to him, and picking up a tile with both her hands she hurled it at Pyrrhus. It struck him below the helmet and bruised the vertebrae at the base of his neck, so that his sight grew dim, his hands dropped the reins and he sank down from his horse and collapsed on the ground near the tomb of Licymnius. Most of those who saw

him had no idea who he was, but a man named Zopyrus who was serving with Antigonus ran up to him, recognized him and dragged him into a doorway just as he was beginning to recover his senses. When Zopyrus drew an Illyrian short-sword to cut off his head, Pyrrhus gazed at him with such a terrible look that Zopyrus lost his nerve. His hands trembled but he forced himself to make the attempt. However, as he was half paralysed with fear and excitement, his blow was badly aimed. The first stroke fell on Pyrrhus' mouth and chin, and it was only slowly and with difficulty that he cut off the head.

The news spread quickly, and presently Alcyoneus[76] ran up and demanded to see the head so as to identify it. He took hold of it, rode off to where his father was sitting among his friends and threw it at his feet. When he recognized it, Antigonus struck his son with his staff and drove him out of his presence, telling him that he was accursed and a barbarian. He covered his face with his cloak and burst into tears as he thought of his grandfather Antigonus and his father Demetrius, who in his own family had suffered just such vicissitudes of fortune.[77] Then he had Pyrrhus' body prepared for burial and burned with due ceremony.[78] However, when Alcyoneus found Pyrrhus' son Helenus disguised in mean and threadbare clothes, he treated him kindly and brought him to Antigonus. When he saw him, Antigonus said, 'This is better, my son, than what you did before, but even now you have not done well to leave him in these clothes, which are a disgrace rather to us who seem to be the victors.' After this, he looked after Helenus, dressed him decently and sent him back to Epirus. He also treated Pyrrhus' friends with consideration, when the whole of his opponent's army and their camp fell into his hands.

Chronology

It should be noted that although the *sequence* of events in relation to each other is reasonably certain, and although there is good evidence for the absolute dating of most of these events, the dating of others remains uncertain. In particular, for the period between 322 and 310 there are two possible chronological sequences which differ by a year or so (the 'high' and 'low' chronologies). All dates are BC.

405	Athenian fleet defeated at Aegospotami. Dionysius I seizes power in Syracuse. Accession of Artaxerxes II of Persia.
404	Surrender of Athens. The Long Walls demolished. Rule of the Thirty Tyrants begins.
403	Revolution of Thrasybulus. Fall of the Thirty Tyrants and democracy restored at Athens.
401	Rebellion of Cyrus against Artaxerxes. Battle of Cunaxa.
400	Sparta begins fighting Persians in Asia Minor.
396	Agesilaus begins campaign in Asia Minor.
395	Beginning of the Corinthian War. Coalition of Athens, Corinth and Thebes against Sparta. Battle of Haliartus.
394	Agesilaus recalled from Asia. Sparta defeats the opposing alliance at battles of Nemea and Coroneia. Persian fleet defeats Spartans at Cnidus.
392	End of Carthaginian War with Syracuse. Sparta at war with Corinth and Argos. Diplomatic mission of the Spartan Antalcidas to Sardis.
389	Thrasybulus sails to Hellespont and wins over Byzantium and Chalcedon to alliance with Athens.
388	Plato's first visit to Syracuse.
386	The Peace of Antalcidas (or King's Peace). Dionysius I captures Rhegium.
382	The Cadmeia, acropolis of Thebes, seized by Phoebidas.

379	Liberation of Thebes by Pelopidas and others.
378	Failure of Sphodrias' raid on Piraeus. Alliance between Athens and Thebes. Agesilaus invades Boeotia. Second Athenian Confederacy founded.
377	Second invasion of Thebes by Agesilaus.
376	Athenian fleet under Chabrias defeats Spartans off Naxos.
375	Spartan force defeated by Thebans at Tegyra.
374	Persia attempts to retake Egypt.
372	Alliance between Thebes and Jason of Pherae.
371	Peace agreed between Sparta, Athens and other Greek states (except Thebes). Spartans defeated at Leuctra by Boeotian forces.
370	Assassination of Jason of Pherae. *Autumn/winter* Allied army under Pelopidas and Epaminondas invades Laconia.
369	Founding of Messene despite Spartan opposition. *Summer* Second allied invasion of Laconia. Pelopidas' first expedition to Thessaly. The young Philip of Macedon in Thebes as hostage.
368	Pelopidas' second expedition to Thessaly; imprisoned by Alexander of Pherae. War between Syracuse and Carthage.
367	Epaminondas sent to Thessaly; secures release of Pelopidas. Death of Dionysius I. Plato's second visit to Syracuse begins. Return of Philistus to Syracuse. Embassies from Sparta, Athens and Thebes in Persia.
366	Dion exiled from Syracuse by Dionysius II. Thebes takes Oropus from Athens.
365	Plato expelled from Syracuse.
364	Pelopidas' third expedition to Thessaly; killed at battle of Cynoscephalae.
362	Battle of Mantineia; Epaminondas killed.
361	Plato's final visit to Syracuse. Agesilaus in Egypt.
360	Death of Agesilaus in Egypt.
359	Death of Artaxerxes II. Accession of Philip II of Macedonia.
357	Outbreak of Social War between Athens and her allies. Dion's expedition to Sicily. Dionysius II besieged in Ortygia. Philip takes Amphipolis.
356	The new Syracusan fleet defeats Dionysius II's ships; Philistus killed. Birth of Alexander the Great. Outbreak of Third Sacred War. Dionysius escapes from Syracuse. His son Apollocrates surrenders.

355	End of Social War.
354	Murder of Dion.
348	Phocion's campaign in Euboea. Philip takes Olynthus.
346	Peace of Philocrates between Athens and Philip of Macedon. Dionysius II regains power in Syracuse.
344	Timoleon's expedition to Sicily. Dionysius II surrenders.
343	Repopulation of Syracuse begins. Aristotle becomes Alexander's tutor.
342	Timoleon expels Leptines from Apollonia.
c. 340	Carthaginian expedition arrives at Lilybaeum. Timoleon defeats Carthaginians at battle of Crimisus (exact date uncertain).
340	Athenian expedition to assist Byzantium and Perinthus against Philip of Macedon.
339	Timoleon makes peace with Carthage.
338	Philip defeats Athens, Thebes and their allies at Chaeronea.
337	League of Corinth supports Philip's plans for invasion of Persia.
336	Accession of Darius III in Persia. Assassination of Philip and accession of Alexander in Macedonia. Alexander establishes control of Macedonia.
335	Thebes is destroyed by Alexander.
334	*Spring* Alexander invades Asia Minor. *May* Wins battle of the Granicus. Receives surrender of Sardis. Captures Miletus. *Autumn* Siege of Halicarnassus begins. *Winter* Alexander advances through Lydia and Pamphylia.
333	Alexander marches on Celaenae; cuts the knot at Gordium. *Summer* Advances to the Cilician Gates. *November* Victory over Darius at Issus. Advances through Phoenicia. First peace offer by Darius.
332	*January–February* Surrender of Byblos and Sidon; siege of Tyre begun; second peace offer from Darius. *August* Fall of Tyre. *October* Gaza captured. Alexander crowned as Pharaoh at Memphis.
331	Alexander visits oracle of Zeus Ammon at Siwa. *April* Founds Alexandria; marches north through Syria. *1 October* Defeats Darius at Gaugamela. *Winter* Enters Babylon and Susa. Defeat of Agis by Antipater in the Peloponnese (or early 330).
330	*January* Alexander enters and sacks Persepolis. *Spring* Sets out for Ecbatana and renews pursuit of Darius. *July* Murder of Darius. *August* Alexander advances to Drangiana. *Autumn* Conspiracy of Philotas discovered;

execution of Philotas and Parmenio. *Winter* Alexander advances through Arachosia. Demosthenes delivers his speech *On the crown*.

329   *Spring* Alexander turns north and crosses Hindu Kush. *May* Advances north into Bactria in pursuit of Bessus; Macedonian veterans and Thessalian volunteers posted home. Bessus captured. *Summer* Alexander advances to Samarkand. Battle of Jaxartes. Revolt of Spitamenes in Sogdiana. *Winter* Alexander takes up winter-quarters in Bactria.

328   Execution of Bessus. Campaign against Spitamenes. *Summer* Killing of Cleitus at Samarkand.

327   *Winter* Alexander married to Roxane. Recruitment of young Persians; conspiracy of the pages; execution of Callisthenes. Invasion of India.

326   *March* Alexander regroups in Taxila. *July* Defeats Porus at the Hydaspes river; army mutinies at the Hyphasis river and refuses to go further east. *November* Fleet and army sail down the Indus.

325   Alexander campaigns against the Brahman cities. Severely wounded by the Mallians. *July* Reaches the Indus delta. *August* Army begins march through the Gedrosian desert. *Winter* Alexander is rejoined by Nearchus with the fleet.

324   Alexander returns to Susa; restoration of order and re-organization of army and administration. Alexander declares that exiles must be allowed to return to the Greek cities. *Summer* Army rebels at Opis against scheme for partial demobilization. Craterus appointed regent in Greece to replace Antipater, and entrusted with leading Macedonian veterans home. Harpalus arrives in Athens. Death of Hephaestion.

323   *Winter* Campaign against the Cossaeans. *Spring* Alexander returns to Babylon. *May* Contracts fever. *June* Dies in Babylon. Coalition of Greek states formed against Macedon. *Autumn* Antipater besieged in Lamia (Lamian War).

322   *Spring* Leonnatus reaches Antipater with reinforcements but is killed. *Summer* Battles of Crannon and Amorgos; Greek coalition collapses. *October* Surrender of Athens; flight and (*November*) suicide of Demosthenes. Perdiccas and Eumenes conquer Cappadocia.

321 or 320 *Summer* Craterus killed in battle with Eumenes. Perdiccas invades Egypt but is killed by his troops. *Winter* Conference at Triparadeisus in Syria; Antipater becomes regent.

319 *Spring* Eumenes besieged in Nora. *Autumn* Death of Antipater. Polyperchon proclaimed regent. War breaks out between Polyperchon and Cassander, Antipater's son. Polyperchon supports the democratic, Cassander the oligarchic factions throughout Greece.

318 *Spring* Eumenes withdraws from Nora. Democratic regime seizes power in Athens. Execution of Phocion. *Autumn* Eumenes withdraws to Babylonia.

317 *Winter* Cassander occupies Athens; limits the franchise; installs Demetrius of Phaleron as governor. *Autumn* Antigonus attacks Eumenes in Asia; battle of Paraetacene (or 316). Olympias, Alexander's mother, executes Philip Arrhidaeus and Philip's wife, Eurydice.

316 *January* Eumenes defeated by Antigonus at the battle of Gabiene and is murdered (or 315). *Spring* Cassander expels Polyperchon from Macedonia. Cassander captures and executes Olympias. Antigonus occupies Syria and expels Seleucus from Babylon (or 315).

315 Coalition of Cassander, Lysimachus, Seleucus and Ptolemy against Antigonus. Both Ptolemy and Antigonus proclaim freedom for the Greeks.

312 *Autumn* (or *Spring*) Ptolemy and Seleucus defeat Demetrius at Gaza. Demetrius defeats Ptolemy's army at Myus.

311 Seleucus returns to Babylon (or 312). Peace settlement reached: Cassander regent in Greece, Lysimachus in control of Thrace, Ptolemy of Egypt, Antigonus of Asia Minor.

310 Cassander murders Roxane and her son, Alexander IV (or 309). Ptolemy occupies Cyprus. Agathocles invades Africa.

307 *June* Demetrius expels Demetrius of Phaleron and 'liberates' Athens.

306 Demetrius defeats Ptolemy's fleet off Salamis in Cyprus. Antigonus and Demetrius assume the title of kings; their example is soon followed by Ptolemy, Seleucus and Lysimachus. *Winter* Antigonus' and Demetrius' failed invasion of Egypt.

305/4	Demetrius besieges Rhodes.
304	Demetrius raises Cassander's siege of Athens.
303	Demetrius invades the Peloponnese.
302	Demetrius re-forms Alexander's Hellenic League at Corinth. Fresh coalition of Cassander, Ptolemy, Seleucus and Lysimachus against Antigonus and Demetrius. Pyrrhus expelled from Epirus.
301	'Battle of the Kings' at Ipsus; Antigonus defeated and killed; Demetrius escapes but, finding little support in Athens or Greece, withdraws to the Hellespont to rebuild his forces.
299	Seleucus marries Demetrius' daughter Stratonice. Demetrius' fortunes revive. Pyrrhus sent to Egypt as hostage.
297	*May* Death of Cassander. Pyrrhus restored in Epirus.
295	Demetrius besieges and captures Athens.
294	*Autumn* Demetrius enters Macedonia; kills Alexander, Cassander's successor; assumes the crown.
291	Demetrius captures Thebes.
289	Demetrius campaigns in Aetolia and Epirus against Pyrrhus. Begins to build large fleet.
288	New coalition of Lysimachus, Seleucus, Ptolemy and Pyrrhus against Demetrius. *Autumn* Pyrrhus invades Macedonia; Demetrius' troops go over to him and he withdraws from Macedonia.
287	*Spring* Athens revolts from Demetrius.
286	Demetrius raises troops in Greece; crosses to Miletus; attacks Lysimachus' territories in Caria and Lydia.
285	*January* Demetrius' guerrilla campaigns terminated by sickness; surrenders to Seleucus; is kept in open captivity in Syria. Pyrrhus withdraws from Macedonia.
282	Demetrius dies in captivity.
281	Seleucus defeats and kills Lysimachus at the battle of Corupedium, but is assassinated soon after.
280	Pyrrhus crosses to Italy at the invitation of Tarentum and defeats Romans in first battle at Heracleia; advances on Rome and attempts to negotiate through Cineas; his terms rejected. Gauls invade Macedonia and Greece.
279	Romans renew the war; inconclusive and costly battle at Asculum.
278	Pyrrhus crosses to Sicily at the islanders' invitation to help them against the Carthaginians.

277	Antigonus Gonatas defeats the Gauls and takes Macedonia.
275	Pyrrhus defeated by the Romans at Beneventum.
274	Pyrrhus returns to Epirus with barely a third of his original army.
273	Pyrrhus invades Macedonia and defeats Antigonus Gonatas.
272	Fall of Tarentum to the Romans. Pyrrhus accepts invitation to help Cleonymus regain throne of Sparta. Repulsed from Sparta, he attempts to capture Argos; engaging the Argives and Antigonus, he is killed in street-fighting.

Historical Events After the Death
of Alexander (323–301 BC)

The events of the two decades which followed the death of Alexander can be particularly difficult to make sense of. Five of the subjects of this volume are involved in this epoch of Greek history – Demosthenes, Phocion, Eumenes, Demetrius and Pyrrhus – but Plutarch's account of their individual lives necessarily leaves many blank spaces in the surrounding picture. This section and the Biographical Notes which follow it attempt to fill in some of the gaps and to provide some points of reference.

Alexander died in Babylon in June 323 without naming an heir. The choice of one thus devolved upon the Macedonian nobles and army, and it so happened that the court and the majority of the troops then in Asia were concentrated at Babylon when Alexander died. In the struggle for power which developed, the infantry and the cavalry, which broadly speaking represented the peasantry and the aristocracy respectively, were at first ranged on opposing sides. At the council of generals Perdiccas, the senior cavalry commander, proposed that they should await the birth of Alexander's child by Roxane, his Bactrian wife, and that if this was a male he should be made king. But Meleager, one of the infantry generals, argued that the king should be a Macedonian, not the son of a barbarian woman. The only candidate who satisfied these conditions was Arrhidaeus, Alexander's half-brother, but he suffered from some form of mental disability. A compromise was finally reached whereby Arrhidaeus was renamed Philip and proclaimed king without delay, and in late summer, when Roxane's child proved to be a boy, the young Alexander was also proclaimed as joint king with Philip. Perdiccas assumed command of the empire and of the royal armies in the name of the two kings, with Meleager as his deputy. Meanwhile Antipater, who had been left behind in Macedonia as Alexander's regent, had his powers there confirmed, and Craterus, who was in Cilicia with a veteran army, was given the vague title of protector of the kings. This arrangement left Perdiccas with the initiative and one of his first actions was to execute his rival Meleager.

The death of Alexander encouraged the Greek city-states in the hope that they could throw off the Macedonian yoke. A revolt of the Greek troops whom Alexander had settled in the eastern provinces was put down, but the rising on the Greek mainland was a more serious threat. It was led by the Athenians, who quickly mobilized a strong fleet and joined forces with their allies and other mercenary troops to besiege Antipater in Lamia. But this success was short lived. In the winter of 323/2 Leosthenes, the Athenian commander, was killed outside Lamia, and in the summer the Athenian fleet was defeated and lost control of the Aegean. This enabled Craterus to cross from Asia and relieve the beleaguered troops in Lamia. Thus reinforced, he and Antipater met the Greek army at Crannon in Thessaly, and although the battle was militarily inconclusive, its political consequence was that the anti-Macedonian coalition melted away. Thereafter, Antipater imposed garrisons and pro-Macedonian governments on many of the Greek cities and curbed the Athenian democracy by reforming the constitution and limiting the franchise.

Meanwhile, in Asia the struggle for power developed into a contest between Perdiccas, who aspired to hold Alexander's empire together and impose a central authority, and those generals who believed that the empire must be broken up and wished to establish themselves as local dynasts. One of the most active of these was Ptolemy, who had begun to carve out a kingdom for himself in Egypt and the surrounding territories. In 321 or 320 Perdiccas marched against him, leaving Eumenes to contain the forces of Antipater and Craterus who were moving into Asia Minor from Greece against him. Eumenes carried out this task successfully and at their first encounter near the Hellespont Craterus was killed. Meanwhile, after Perdiccas had failed to force the crossing of the Nile and suffered heavy losses, his troops mutinied and murdered him. Antipater then succeeded in rallying the Macedonian army and imposing a settlement at Triparadeisus in Syria. Antipater became regent of the empire and guardian of the kings, and Antigonus was appointed senior commander in Asia Minor with orders to suppress Eumenes and the troops loyal to Perdiccas there. Antipater later returned to Macedonia, taking the kings Philip and Alexander with him; there he died in 319 at the age of seventy-nine.

Before his death Antipater had delegated his authority as regent to one of his generals, Polyperchon, but this arrangement was promptly challenged by Antipater's son Cassander, who had expected to succeed his father. Polyperchon lacked the stature to dominate the difficult situation which he had inherited. He was unable to impose his authority over either Ptolemy or Antigonus, to whom Cassander at once appealed for help. In an effort to win the support of the Greek city-states, Polyperchon reversed Antipater's treatment of them by removing the occupying garrisons, encouraging many of the cities to bring back those driven into exile by Antipater. Cassander, on the other hand, upheld his father's repressive policy. This was the situation in which Phocion found himself. His friend Nicanor, the garrison commander of Munychia, was a supporter of Cassander, but it was the democrats encouraged by Polyperchon who succeeded in seizing power in Athens, and who took their revenge by putting Phocion to death.

In 317, however, Polyperchon's fleet was defeated off the Bosphorus, and the Athenians, recognizing that they must come to terms with whoever controlled the seas, opened negotiations with Cassander. He came to Athens, reimposed Antipater's limitation of the franchise and installed as autocrat Demetrius of Phaleron, whose rule lasted for the next ten years. Cassander then proceeded to Macedonia, persuaded King Philip to appoint him regent in place of Polyperchon, and went on to consolidate his control of the Greek mainland.

Meanwhile Polyperchon sought out Olympias, Alexander the Great's mother, who was then in Epirus, and persuaded her that she must join forces with him if her grandson, Alexander, were to have any hope of the succession. Such was the magic of Alexander's name that when she entered Macedonia the Macedonian troops at once deserted Philip and went over to her. Philip was executed and Olympias went on to order a massacre of Cassander's supporters. But here she overreached herself and so alienated the sympathies of the Macedonians that, when Cassander returned, he was able to shut her up in the city of Pydna. In the spring of 316 she surrendered on an undertaking that her life would be spared, but soon afterwards Cassander, yielding to the pressure of the relatives of her victims, allowed the Macedonian army to sentence her to death. At the same time he kept Roxane and Alexander in close imprisonment, and thus, seven years after Alexander's death, his heirs had effectively ceased to exist.

It remained to be seen whether any of Alexander's military successors could take up his mantle, and the history of the next fifteen years is dominated by the struggle of the three most powerful of the Macedonian marshals, Ptolemy, Cassander and Antigonus. Of these, Ptolemy was comparatively weak in manpower and Cassander in financial strength. Both men lacked the expansionist outlook which the role required and were content to secure the possessions they already held; only Antigonus combined the resources and the ambition to reunite the empire under his rule.

While Cassander was campaigning against Polyperchon, Antigonus took the offensive against Eumenes, whom he rightly regarded as his most formidable opponent. Eumenes put up a gallant resistance first in Asia Minor and then further east in present-day Iran but he was betrayed by his troops, captured and executed. Strengthened by this success, Antigonus proceeded to assert his authority over the satraps of Asia and their troops, and took possession of a large quantity of Alexander's treasure; in the process he drove out Seleucus, the satrap of Babylonia, who took refuge with Ptolemy. But the result of this action was to bring about an alliance between Ptolemy, Seleucus, Cassander and Lysimachus, the governor of Thrace. They demanded a redistribution both of territories and of the imperial treasure, and when these were refused they declared war in 315.

For this contest Antigonus by now possessed great financial resources and also the advantage of interior lines of communication. He invaded Syria, stirred up trouble for Cassander in Macedonia and for Lysimachus in Thrace and strove to win over the Greek city-states, as Polyperchon had done, by offering them self-government and freedom from Macedonian garrisons. However, on each of these fronts he was able to achieve only limited success and in 311 the five belligerents made peace: this settlement, it was generally recognized, served merely as a breathing-space to enable them to regroup and recover their strength. Cassander took advantage of this pause to end the long imprisonment of Roxane and her son Alexander by executing them.

The next four years witnessed a succession of minor campaigns and political manoeuvrings. But in 307 Antigonus' son Demetrius suddenly seized the initiative: crossing from Ephesus to Athens he expelled Demetrius of Phaleron, Cassander's autocratic governor, and restored to the Athenians the outward forms at least of their democratic freedoms. Many of the institutions abolished by Demetrius of Phaleron were restored, and the Athenians voted Antigonus and his son Demetrius extravagant honours.

The liberation of Athens dealt a serious blow to Cassander's prestige in mainland Greece and accordingly Antigonus felt free to turn against Ptolemy. His first objective was the destruction of his opponent's fleet, which since Ptolemy's annexation of Phoenicia some years before had been built up to a formidable strength, and Demetrius was sent to attack its base on Cyprus. Demetrius, although outnumbered, won a decisive victory off Cyprus at the battle of Salamis in 306. Antigonus followed up this success by conferring the title of King upon himself and Demetrius: by this action he placed his family in the direct line of succession to Alexander, thus implying his intention of establishing a dynasty which would reunite the empire.

With Ptolemy's fleet virtually annihilated, the way seemed clear for a combined invasion of Egypt by land and sea, and in the winter of 306/5 Antigonus marched with a large army. But this time the weather came to Ptolemy's rescue. A succession of storms made it impossible for Demetrius to land, and Antigonus, unable to force the crossing of the Nile, was compelled to retire to Asia Minor. At this point and as a countermove in the diplomatic war, Ptolemy and the other rulers of the coalition followed Antigonus' example and proclaimed themselves kings: this had the opposite effect to that of Antigonus' action, namely of denying the existence of a single imperial house and affirming the rule of a group of lesser monarchies.

Soon afterwards in 305 Demetrius was despatched to besiege Rhodes. This operation was one of the most famous sieges of antiquity and earned Demetrius his title of Poliorcetes ('the Besieger'). The object was to force democratic Rhodes, with her great shipbuilding capacity and strategic position, to abandon her neutrality in the war between Antigonus and Ptolemy. But Demetrius was unable to achieve quick results and the Rhodians finally obtained a negotiated peace. In 304 Antigonus resumed the strategic offensive and sent Demetrius to Greece. Here his campaign was so successful that he regained control of Attica, Central Greece and the Peloponnese and by 302 had compelled Cassander to sue for peace. Antigonus' terms, however, were so harsh that Cassander appealed to his allies for help. The coalition was once more mobilized; Seleucus invaded Asia Minor from the East and Lysimachus from the west, and Antigonus in his turn was forced to recall Demetrius from Greece. The opposing forces met at full strength at Ipsus in Phrygia in 301. Here, thanks to Demetrius' impetuosity, the cause of Antigonus was lost and the prospect of the reunification of Alexander's empire under a single ruler was finally extinguished.

Biographical Notes on Alexander's Generals and Successors

Antigonus *c.* 382–301 Nicknamed Monophthalmus ('One-Eyed'). One of the oldest and ablest of Alexander's generals. He took part in Alexander's invasion of Asia Minor and in 333 was made satrap of Phrygia; after Alexander's death, Pamphylia and Lycia were added to his province. Unwilling to accept the authority of Perdiccas, he avoided Meleager's error of risking a trial of strength and sought refuge in Greece. There he gained the favour of Antipater and later took the field with him against Perdiccas and Eumenes. After the death of Antipater in 319 Antigonus supported the former's son Cassander against Polyperchon. He concentrated his efforts first at dealing with his most dangerous local opponent, Eumenes, who upheld Polyperchon's cause in Asia Minor, and, having eliminated him, tried to bring Seleucus, then governor of Babylon, under his authority. At this point his growing power and the prospect that he might reconstitute the empire under his rule alarmed Ptolemy, Seleucus, Cassander and Lysimachus sufficiently to make them combine in a coalition against him. As a part of his diplomatic warfare against them, Antigonus adopted Polyperchon's tactics of offering self-government and the removal of the occupying garrisons to the Greek cities, including those in the territories of Cassander and Lysimachus. He was the first of the generals to take the royal title (306). In 302 Antigonus' son Demetrius on his behalf revived the League of Corinth created by Philip and Alexander in 337: its aim was to harness the Greeks in an alliance which preserved the forms of their independence. After Antigonus' death at Ipsus in 301 no Greek ruler remained who possessed the power to revive the project.

Antipater *c.* 398–319 Like Parmenion, his near contemporary, Antipater was older than Philip of Macedon and one of his most valued generals. He was sent to Athens as ambassador in 346 and negotiated peace with the Athenians after Chaeronea in 338. When Alexander set out for Asia he left Antipater in charge of Macedonia and Greece.

Here Antipater frequently found himself opposed by Olympias, Alexander's mother, who undermined his position first with Alexander and later with Perdiccas. In 331 he defeated Agis in the Peloponnese. After Alexander's death, Antipater commanded Macedonian troops against the Greeks in the Lamian War of 323–2. At the conference at Triparadeisus in 321 or 320 he assumed the regency. His authority was accepted by the Macedonian troops in Asia, command of whom he entrusted to Antigonus, while he himself brought back the kings, Philip and Alexander, to Macedonia. His alliance with Antigonus was cemented by the marriage of his daughter Phila (the widow of Craterus) to Antigonus' son Demetrius. But by then Antipater was nearing eighty and this period of stability was cut short by his death.

Cassander *c.* 355–297 Son of Antipater, he did not accompany the Macedonian army on its invasion of Asia but remained in Macedonia during his father's regency. He was sent to Babylon in 324 but did not find favour with Alexander. Displeased at his father's choice of Polyperchon for his successor, he set himself to oust his rival from the regency and sought help from Antigonus in Asia Minor. In 317, following the defeat of Polyperchon's fleet by that of Antigonus off the Bosphorus, Cassander returned to Macedonia. In 316 he had Olympias executed and the young Alexander IV and his mother Roxane imprisoned (they were murdered some years later). In the following year, alarmed by the growth of Antigonus' power, he joined the coalition of Ptolemy, Seleucus and Lysimachus against him. His power in Europe was confirmed in the settlement of 311 and in *c.* 305 he assumed the title of king of Macedonia. In mainland Greece, Cassander continued the policy pursued by his father, Antipater, of treating the city-states as subjects rather than allies, in contrast to the policy of Antigonus and Demetrius. In Macedonia his rule was more beneficial, in that by refraining from expansionist aims he reduced the strain upon the country's manpower and financial resources. The Macedonians experienced the exact opposite of this policy during the short reign of Demetrius.

Craterus died 321 or 320 Outstanding among the younger Macedonian generals with Alexander, he came to occupy the place which Parmenion had held in the early years. Alexander trusted him thoroughly: in 324 he was charged with the task of bringing back a large corps of veterans to Macedonia and soon afterwards was appointed to replace Antipater in Europe. Immediately after Alexander's death he was appointed guardian of Arrhidaeus. In the summer of 322 he crossed to Greece to relieve Antipater, who was then besieged in

Lamia, and later engaged the Greek rebel forces at Crannon. His alliance with Antipater was confirmed by his marriage to the latter's daughter Phila. In 321 or 320 he joined Antipater in the war against Perdiccas and at a battle near the Hellespont was defeated and killed by Perdiccas' lieutenant Eumenes.

Lysimachus died 281 An elite bodyguard (*somatophylax*) of Alexander, he was wounded in India in 326. Following Alexander's death he became governor of Thrace, and married Antipater's daughter Nicaea. In 315 he joined the coalition of Ptolemy, Seleucus and Cassander against Antigonus. For many years he was obliged to occupy himself in pacifying his territory and consolidating his authority; he declared himself king *c.* 305. In 302 he launched a perfectly timed surprise invasion of Asia Minor, and in the following year effected a junction of his forces with Seleucus to defeat and kill Antigonus at Ipsus. Lysimachus was the principal beneficiary of the partition of Antigonus' territories which followed the battle. His newly acquired dominions stretched from the north to south of Asia Minor, shut out Seleucus from the western seaboard and thus sowed the seeds of future conflict. He and Pyrrhus expelled Demetrius from Macedonia in 288 and shortly afterwards he occupied the whole country. In the last years of his reign Lysimachus' autocratic and extortionate methods of government became intensely unpopular, and when Seleucus invaded his territory he met little resistance. Lysimachus made a stand at Corupedium near Magnesia in 281 and was killed in the battle.

Perdiccas *c.* 360–321 A member of a princely family of the province of Orestis in upper Macedonia. He served with distinction under Alexander, whose leading general he became after the death of Hephaestion and the return of Craterus to Europe. The dying Alexander entrusted him with the royal seal, and shortly afterwards at the conference in Babylon he was confirmed as supreme commander of the royal armies in the name of the Kings (Alexander IV and Philip III Arrhidaeus). In 322 he successfully invaded Asia Minor and requested the hand in marriage of Antipater's daughter Nicaea, but then rejected it in favour of Alexander's sister Cleopatra, a match offered him by Olympias. Although the marriage never took place, this action was represented by Antigonus as implying that Perdiccas aimed at usurping the crown and caused an irreparable breach with Antipater. In 321 or 320 Antipater, Antigonus and Craterus invaded Asia Minor, while Perdiccas had already marched south to attack Ptolemy in Egypt. He failed to force the crossing of the Nile and lost many men in the attempt, whereupon his troops mutinied and he was murdered.

Polyperchon c. 385–c. 300? A contemporary of Philip, he was a divisional commander under Alexander, and in 324 returned to Macedonia with Craterus and the demobilized veterans. He served with Antipater in the Lamian War, and in 319 Antipater named him as regent and his own son Cassander as second in command, an arrangement which the latter deeply resented. Compelled to seek support against Cassander and Antigonus, Polyperchon reversed Antipater's repressive policy towards the Greek city-states, removing the occupying garrisons and permitting the return of many of the exiles. The effect of this action was to range himself with the democratic factions and Cassander with the oligarchic. In 317 Cassander landed in Macedonia: thereafter Polyperchon's position deteriorated to that of a mere soldier of fortune. In 315 he accepted service under Antigonus, for whom he held the Peloponnese against Cassander's forces, and in 309 he invaded Macedonia, again at Antigonus' instigation, to support a pretender to the throne: this was one Heracles, a supposed son of Alexander and the Persian princess Barsine. Cassander bribed him to change sides, whereupon Polyperchon had the young pretender murdered. He is last heard of campaigning in the Peloponnese for Cassander in 304.

Ptolemy I c. 360–282 Son of the Macedonian nobleman Lagus, and one of the inner circle of Alexander's commanders and advisers. He fought with distinction in India and wrote a history of Alexander's campaigns which was an important source for Arrian's *Anabasis*. After Alexander's death he was appointed satrap of Egypt and determined to maintain his independence of the central authority of Perdiccas. One of his first actions to this end was to divert to Egypt the cortège bearing the body of Alexander, which the army had intended to be buried in Macedonia. Ptolemy justified his acquisition of this precious relic, which was first interred with great magnificence at Memphis and subsequently at Alexandria, on the grounds that Alexander had wished to be buried in Egypt. In 322 he allied himself with Antipater, and in 321 or 320 he defeated an invasion of Egypt by Perdiccas; the pact with Antipater was consolidated by his marriage to Antipater's daughter Eurydice. In 315 he joined forces with Cassander, Seleucus and Lysimachus to resist Antigonus' ambition to reconstitute the empire under his rule. In 306 his fleet was almost wiped out off Cyprus at the battle of Salamis, but Antigonus' and Demetrius' subsequent attempt to invade Egypt was foiled by bad weather. Ptolemy took no part in the battle of Ipsus and hence received little in the subsequent division of the spoils, but he arranged dynastic alliances by marrying his daughters, Arsinoe to Lysimachus and Lysandra to Cassander's son Alexander and then to Lysimachus' son Agathocles, and his stepdaughter Antigone to Pyrrhus of Epirus. More successful as a statesman than as a soldier, he left behind him a kingdom which was to prove the most enduring of the Hellenistic monarchies. He founded the Library of Alexandria and was one of the few Macedonian generals of his generation to patronize literature and the arts.

Seleucus *c.* 358–281 Son of Antiochus, one of Philip's generals, and a near contemporary of Alexander, he became in about 330 commander of the crack infantry formation, the Hypaspists. He took Perdiccas' side immediately after Alexander's death, but was later instrumental in his murder following the failure of the Egyptian campaign. At the conference at Triparadeisus he was appointed to the satrapy of Babylonia. In 316 he was expelled by Antigonus, whereupon he fled to Egypt, joined Ptolemy in the war against Antigonus and commanded Egyptian squadrons in the Aegean. He returned to Babylon in 311 and steadily extended his authority over the eastern provinces. He declared himself king in 306/5. After campaigning in India, he made peace with the Indian ruler Chandragupta, receiving in return a corps of elephants which played a part in his victory at Ipsus in 301. At the partition of Antigonus' domains, Seleucus added Syria to his territories and founded his western capital at Antioch. In 285 his most threatening rival Demetrius surrendered and in 281 he turned on his former ally Lysimachus, invaded his territories in western Asia Minor and defeated and killed him at Corupedium. But when he crossed to Europe to claim Lysimachus' Thracian kingdom, he was assassinated by Ptolemy Ceraunus, the disinherited son of Ptolemy I.

Maps

Map 1. Attica and Boeotia

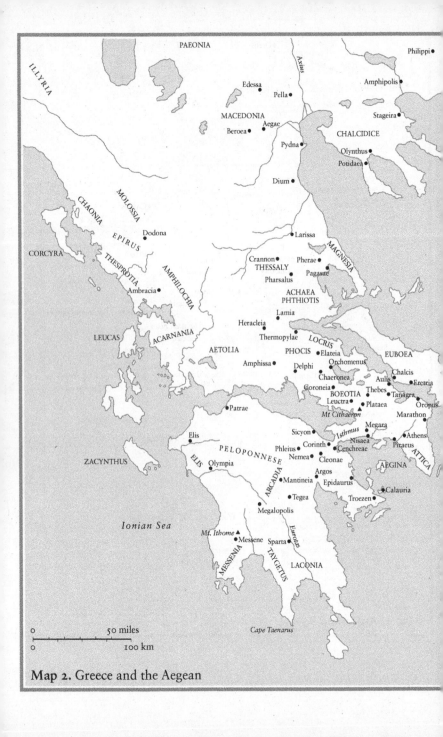

Map 2. Greece and the Aegean

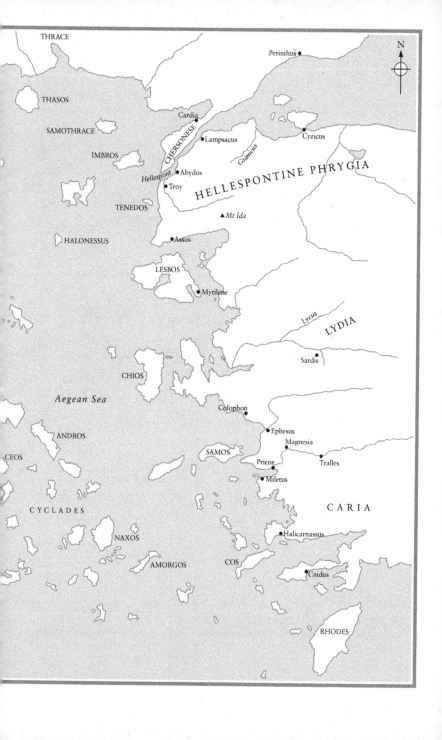

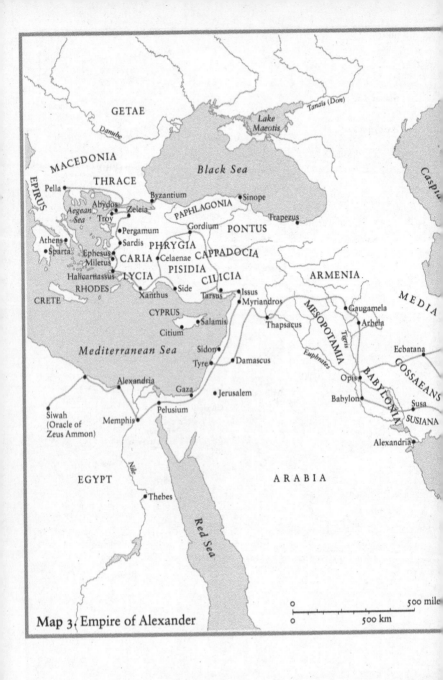

Map 3. Empire of Alexander

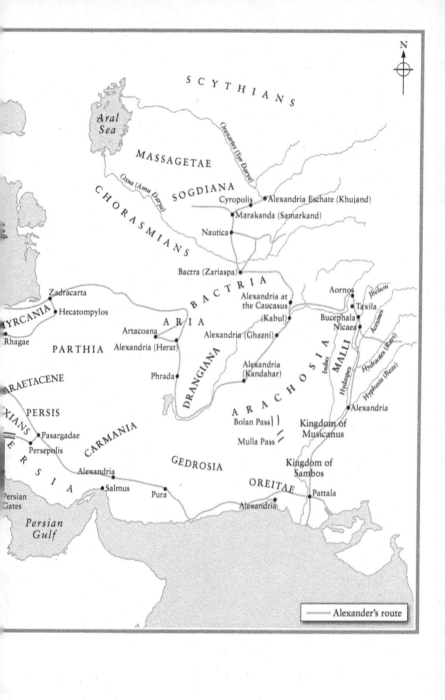

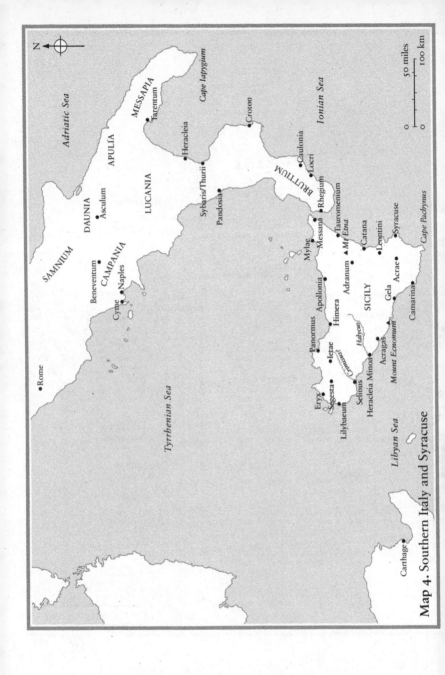

Map 4. Southern Italy and Syracuse

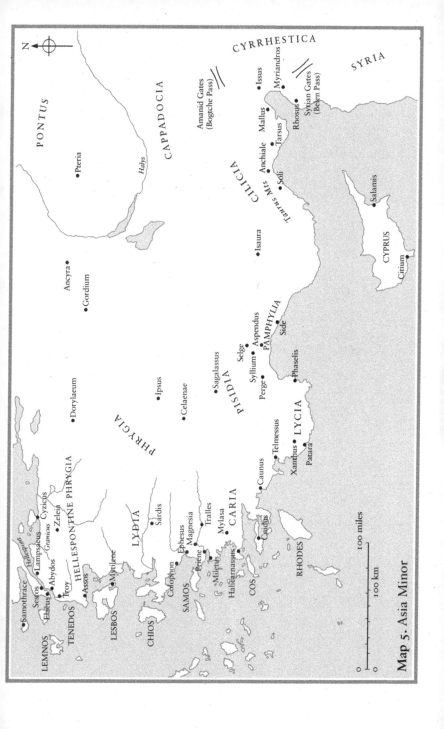

Map 5 · Asia Minor

Notes

All dates are BC unless stated otherwise. Dates expressed in the form 323/2 refer to the single administrative year running from, in this case, summer 323 to summer 322.

ARTAXERXES

Further Reading

Plutarch's Artaxerxes

Antelami, V., Manfredini, M., Orsi, D. P. (eds.), *Plutarco. Le Vite di Arato e di Artaserse* (Milan: Mondadori, Fondazione Lorenzo Valla, 1987).

Binder, C., *Plutarchs Vita des Artaxerxes: ein historischer Kommentar* (Berlin: De Gruyter, 2008).

Mossman, J., 'A life unparalleled: *Artaxerxes*', in N. Humble (ed.), *Plutarch's Lives: Parallelism and Purpose* (Swansea: Classical Press of Wales, 2010), pp. 145–68.

History

Briant, P., *From Cyrus to Alexander: History of the Persian Empire* (Winona Lake, Ind.: Eisenbrauns, 2002).

Cook, J. M., *The Persian Empire* (London: Dent, 1983).

Hornblower, S., 'Persia', in *CAH* vi, pp. 45–96.

Kuhrt, A., *The Persian Empire: A Corpus of Sources from the Achaemenid Period* (London: Routledge, 2007).

Waterfield, R., *Xenophon's Retreat: Greece, Persia and the End of the Golden Age* (Cambridge, Mass.: Harvard University Press, 2006).

Notes to the Life of Artaxerxes

1. *Artaxerxes*: Artaxerxes I, who reigned from 465 to 424/3 BC.

2. *Xerxes*: Xerxes I, who reigned from 486 to 465 BC. He led a failed attempt to conquer Greece in 480.

3. *Darius*: Darius II, illegitimate son of Artaxerxes I, reigned from 423 to 405 BC. He came to the throne after a power-struggle with his brother, Sogdianus.

4. *For Darius and Parysatis had four sons ... Oxathres*: This sentence is almost a verbatim quotation of the opening of Xenophon's *Anabasis*, but Xenophon mentioned only two sons, and Plutarch corrects him.

5. *Cyrus ... Persian word for sun*: This is almost certainly incorrect, though the sun was important in Persian court rituals. The earlier Cyrus is Cyrus II the Great, who ruled from about 559 to 530 BC and founded the Persian empire.

6. *Deinon*: A Greek historian of the fourth century BC, who wrote a history of Persia. His work does not survive, though Plutarch refers to it often in *Artaxerxes*.

7. *Ctesias*: A Greek who served at the Persian court under Artaxerxes. He wrote a long work on Persia, famous in antiquity for portraying the Persian court as rife with intrigue, jealousy and cruelty (see chs. 6, 11, 13, 18).

8. *expectation ... successor to the throne*: Cyrus had since 407 or 408 been supreme commander in western Asia Minor, where he outranked the existing local Persian governors, including Tissaphernes, satrap of Sardis, and Pharnabazus, satrap of Hellespontine Phrygia. He pursued a policy of support for Sparta in its war with Athens and provided her with much-needed financial aid (see Xenophon, *Hellenica* 1.4.1–7 and *Anabasis* 1.9.7).

9. *she had given birth ... a king*: Plutarch is alluding to a story recorded in Herodotus 7.3: Demaratus, the exiled king of Sparta, advised Xerxes to argue that he should take the throne rather than his older brother, because, unlike his brother, he had been born after his father, Darius I, had become king. Herodotus adds, 'But it seems to me that he would have become king even without this advice, for Atossa [Xerxes' mother] held complete sway.'

10. *Artaxerxes*: Artaxerxes II, the subject of this Life, acceded to the throne in 405 BC.

11. *commander of the coastal provinces*: That is, Cyrus' earlier command in western Asia Minor was confirmed.

12. *warrior goddess ... liken to Athena*: Anahita, whose worship seems to have come to special prominence under Artaxerxes.

13. *figs ... terebinth ... sour milk*: The food taken at this initiation rite was perhaps meant to symbolize the frugal, pastoral life of the Persians of old under the elder Cyrus (cf. Strabo 15.3.18). Terebinth is probably the fruit of the *Pistacia atlantica* (not to be confused with the modern pistachio).

14. *Persian education*: Described by Strabo as consisting in, among other things, archery, throwing the javelin, riding and speaking the truth (15.3.18–19). Xenophon imagines the young Cyrus as excelling in these lessons and in self-control and hunting (*Cyropaedia* 1.2; cf. also *Anabasis* 1.9).

15. *the Magi*: Perhaps originally a Median tribe, who appear in Greek sources as Persian teachers and advisers, experts in Persian lore and in interpreting dreams. They seem also to have had a religious function. The figures Plutarch here calls priests are probably to be seen as Magi.

16. *revenue ... for his daily meals*: Satraps levied a tax to supply them with food, which they then in turn used to feed troops and retainers and reward subordinates (see n. 59).

17. *as Xenophon has reported*: Anabasis 1.1.6–11. Xenophon himself served as a mercenary commander with Cyrus on his ill-fated expedition to unseat Artaxerxes.

18. *gave greater honours ... deserved*: The giving and receiving of gifts was central to the ideology of Persian kingship. The gifts of the king, conferred as rewards for services rendered, were expected to outdo in value the service so rewarded; on the other hand, tribute or tax was often seen in terms of gift-giving.

19. *when a certain Omises ... offered it to him*: These two anecdotes also appear in Aelian's *Historical miscellany* 1.31–3, where he comments that it was a rule that peasants present the king with gifts when he travelled, according to their means.

20. *darics*: Persian gold coins, so called probably because they were thought to have been first minted by Darius the Great.

21. *king's robe ... golden necklaces ... not permitted*: Robes and jewellery of different colours and kinds both bestowed and declared status and were frequently given as rewards or tokens of favour by Persian kings. The king's own attire, including his robe (*kandys*), was, of course, distinctive, hence the onlookers' anger at Tiribazus' donning of it.

22. *with the curtains open ... great affection by the masses*: The issue here may be that Stateira could receive petitions and pleas.

Xenophon, *Cyropaedia* 8.3.19, describes petitions being brought to Cyrus as he travelled. For the usual picture of female seclusion while travelling, see *Artaxerxes* 27.

23. *dispatch-roll*: A narrow strip of leather, called in Greek a *scytale*, wound round a stick and used by the Spartans for sending messages; the recipient would have to have a stick of the same size to read the message (see *Lysander* 19).

24. *Clearchus*: Plutarch here presents Clearchus as the official Spartan representative, but both Xenophon (*Anabasis* 2.6) and Diodorus (14.12) claim that, on the contrary, Clearchus was a rebel under sentence of death; Xenophon (1.4) and Diodorus (14.19) name the official Spartan commander as one Cheirisophus. Clearchus commanded the Greek mercenaries in Cyrus' pay.

25. *Cyrus . . . expedition*: Cyrus began his expedition in spring 401; the battle of Cunaxa took place in the same year. Cyrus was born after his father acceded to the throne in 424 and so was now at most twenty-three years old.

26. *this event . . . by Ctesias*: See *Artaxerxes* 19.

27. *ditch . . . Babylon itself*: Xenophon describes these defences in *Anabasis* 1.7.14–17, which linked up with an older construction that he calls the Median wall. Artaxerxes had in effect pursued a scorched-earth policy up to this point. Xenophon describes Cyrus' confidence that, having passed the ditch, the king would not attack.

28. *take refuge in Persia*: I.e., withdraw south-eastwards, into the heart of the old Persian empire, in what is now southern Iran.

29. *scythed chariots*: I.e., with scythes attached to the axles and underneath (see Xenophon, *Anabasis* 1.8.10). In *Hellenica* 4.1.17, Xenophon describes an incident in 395 when a charge by two hundred Persian scythed chariots scattered Greek infantry and left them prey to cavalry.

30. *Xenophon's account*: *Anabasis* 1.8.

31. *actually happening before their eyes*: The notion that events might be made to appear 'as though actually happening before the eyes' was standard in Greek discussions of vividness of writing.

32. *eunuchs*: This term is used by Greek writers in two senses: either for castrated men, who served as palace servants, or for certain high-ranking officials, who bore the title but may not have been castrated.

33. *King's Eye*: Apparently a high-ranking Persian official who observed and reported on the satraps and other officials. The term is known only from Greek sources.

34. *foul, dirty water . . . tasted so pleasant*: Usually the king only

drank water from one river, the Choaspes, and it was boiled before use; supplies of it in silver vessels were taken along wherever he went, including on campaign (see, e.g., Herodotus 1.188).

35. *Persian law*: Strabo 15.3.17 records in his discussion of Persia that 'They are ruled by hereditary kings, and anyone disobedient has his head and arms cut off and his body cast out'.

36. *Xenophon . . . much higher*: Anabasis (1.7) talks of Artaxerxes' forces numbering 900,000, the figure which Plutarch uses in *Artaxerxes* 7.

37. *dagger*: Akinakes, a long dagger or short-sword with decorated scabbard. It was awarded by the king as a sign of favour, and worn by the king or noblemen.

38. *there is truth in wine*: A well-known Greek proverbial saying, sometimes in the form 'There is truth in wine and in children', i.e., when men drink they tend to be less guarded in what they say – as are children (see, e.g., Alcaeus, fragment 366 Voigt; Theocritus, *Idylls* 29.1; Plato, *Symposium* 217e).

39. *guardian spirit*: Plutarch uses the Greek term *daimon* ('spirit', 'god') to represent a Persian term which implies the good fortune or splendour of the king. Athenaeus 252b also suggests that Persians might do obeisance to the king's good fortune at banquets, even setting a separate place at table for it.

40. *tricked by Tissaphernes*: Xenophon in *Anabasis* 2.5 describes how, after Cyrus' defeat at Cunaxa, Clearchus and other Greek commanders who had marched with Cyrus were tricked into coming to the Persian camp under truce, and there captured.

41. *a comb*: The Spartans were famous for their long hair, which they combed before battle (see Herodotus 7.208 and Plutarch, *Lycurgus* 22).

42. *Caryatids dancing*: Caryae was a town near Sparta, where maidens danced in honour of Artemis (Pausanias, *Guide to Greece* 3.10).

43. *managed to escape*: The story of the escape of the surviving Greek forces from Persian territory is told by Xenophon, who participated himself, in Books 3–7 of the *Anabasis*.

44. *arrogant façade with no substance*: Plutarch looks forward here to Alexander the Great's invasion in 334 BC. He may be influenced by Isocrates (*Panegyric* 145–9), who used the fact that the Greek forces hired by Cyrus were able to make it back home safely to argue that a Greek invasion of Asia would be successful. Arrian in his *Anabasis* (2.7.8–9) puts the same thought in Alexander's mouth in a speech to his men before the battle of Issus. Cf. Xenophon, *Cyropaedia* 8.7 and 26, and Polybius 3.6.10–11.

45. *Thibron ... Greek cities*: Thibron commanded Spartan forces in Asia Minor from 400 to 399 and Dercyllidas from 399 to 396, when he was relieved by Agesilaus. The battle referred to here took place at Sardis in spring 395 (see *Agesilaus* 10; Xenophon, *Hellenica* 3.4.20–24; Diodorus 14.80; *Hellenica Oxyrhynchia* 11).

46. *Timocrates of Rhodes ... into turmoil*: Timocrates arrived in Greece in 396. The following year hostilities broke out between Sparta on the one side and an alliance of Athens, Thebes, Corinth and various smaller states on the other. The funds distributed by Persia may have played a role, but the most important cause of the war, known to modern historians as the Corinthian War, was resentment at Spartan aggression.

47. *recall Agesilaus from Asia*: Agesilaus, king of Sparta between 400 and 359 BC, was on campaign against Persia in Asia Minor from 396 to 394. On his return to Greece, he won a strategically indecisive victory over Sparta's Greek enemies at Coroneia in Boeotia in 394 (see *Agesilaus* 6–19).

48. *Conon ... sea-battle at Aegospotami*: The Athenian fleet had been annihilated at Aegospotami by the Spartans in 405, an event which led directly to Athens' surrender the following year. Conon, one of the Athenian commanders, escaped with a few ships to Cyprus (Xenophon, *Hellenica* 2.1.29); there he was appointed commander of the Persian fleet in 398 or 397 (Diodorus 14.39).

49. *sea-battle off Cnidus ... at sea*: In 394.

50. *the Peace of Antalcidas*: Also known as the King's Peace, concluded in 387/6. The treaty involved the surrender of the Greek cities in Asia Minor to Persia, and stipulated that all Greek cities should be autonomous. Crucially, this did not apply to Sparta's control of Messenia, and the Peace in effect underwrote Spartan dominance of mainland Greece.

51. *abandon to Artaxerxes ... islands off the Asian coast*: This is exaggerated for effect. As Plutarch knew from Xenophon, *Hellenica* 5.1.31, of the islands only Cyprus and the small island of Clazomenae were to be under Persian control.

52. *danced away ... Callicratidas*: Leonidas, king of Sparta (490–480 BC), led the Greek defence against the Persian invasion of 480, and died fighting at Thermopylae. Callicratidas, as commander in the Aegean in 406/5, famously refused to pay court to Cyrus; he died in the battle of Arginusae against Athens (*Lysander* 5–7). The phrase 'danced away' alludes to Herodotus 6.129, where Hippocleides of Athens is said to have 'danced away' his chance of marriage with the daughter of the tyrant of

Sicyon by his unbecoming conduct at the marriage banquet. Antalcidas' conduct was, it is implied, equally unbecoming.

53. *battle of Leuctra ... Spartans lost their hegemony*: Sparta was decisively defeated by Thebes at Leuctra in Boeotia in 371, a blow from which she never recovered (see *Pelopidas* 20–23). 'Medizing' was a common Greek term meaning 'collaborate with the Medes' (i.e. with the Persians). 'Laconizing' was coined on the basis of 'medize', and meant either 'imitate the Spartans' or, as here, 'support' them.

54. *Antalcidas travelled ... to help the Spartans*: It is not clear whether Antalcidas' mission to Persia was related to the conference of 367/6 (described in the next chapter) or, more likely, whether this is a separate, later mission to be dated to 361. Agesilaus' mercenary service in Egypt (*Agesilaus* 28, 36–40), which took place in the context of Sparta's backing of the so-called Satraps' Revolt, certainly took place after 367, when Persia had switched its support to Thebes.

55. *ephors*: The five ephors were annually elected Spartan officials, who had wide powers which included negotiating with foreign states and the ability to prosecute other officials in trials over which they presided (see, e.g., *Agesilaus* 5).

56. *travelled up to the king*: Sparta, Athens and Thebes all sent envoys to Persia in 367; the terms of the draft treaty, effectively dictated by Persia, were favourable to Thebes. See *Pelopidas* 30, where some of the same material is repeated, and Xenophon, *Hellenica* 7.1.33–8.

57. *obeisance*: Persian court ritual involved *proskynesis* ('obeisance') before the king, which seems, depending on relative social status, to have ranged from a kiss to a bow to full prostration (Herodotus 1.134). The Greeks interpreted this (wrongly) as worship, such as one should do only before a god (cf. *Alexander* 45).

58. *Timagoras the Athenian*: Athenian envoy to Persia in 367; his fellow-envoy Leon accused him of treason and corruption on their return to Athens.

59. *Artaxerxes was so pleased ... banquets sent to him*: Persian kings conferred and displayed status and favour by giving gifts, sometimes of great value. High-ranking officials might be invited to eat at the king's table; food, sometimes in massive quantities, might also be sent to those favoured, along with valuable accoutrements.

60. *executed Tissaphernes ... which his mother ... seconded*: This was in 395 (see Xenophon, *Hellenica* 2.4.25, and Diodorus 14.80.6–8).

61. *waged war on Egypt ... one another*: Egypt was in constant
    revolt throughout Artaxerxes' reign. In 374/3 the Persians
    attempted to retake it and Athens sent its commander Iphicrates
    to fight on the Persian side at the head of a force of mercenaries.
    Note that Plutarch does not follow chronological order here.

62. *expedition against the Cadusii ... cavalry*: In 385. The Cadusii
    lived to the south-west of the Caspian Sea. They provided Arta-
    xerxes with troops at Cunaxa (*Artaxerxes* 9). Persian kings
    frequently campaigned against them, but this may have been
    more about reaffirming alliances than putting down revolts. Dio-
    dorus (15.8.5) mentions an expedition in 385, but there may
    have been several in Artaxerxes' reign.

63. *Tiribazus ... overlooked*: After his service at Cunaxa (see chs. 7
    and 10), Tiribazus had been commander of Persian forces in
    Asia Minor in the late 390s and then in Cyprus. However,
    according to Diodorus 15.8, shortly before the war with the
    Cadusii, an accusation against him by Orontes over his conduct
    in Cyprus had led to his fall from favour.

64. *parks*: Persian royal parks (in Greek, *paradeisoi*) were used for hunt-
    ing and recreation, and contained lodges at which the king stayed
    when on journeys. Parks and their trees were considered inviolable.

65. *fifty years old*: This seems to date Darius' designation as succes-
    sor to around 375. However, the story that follows, which
    concerns a concubine captured soon after Cunaxa, suggests an
    earlier date.

66. *wear upright the so-called 'tiara'*: The tiara (*kitaris*) was a sort of
    turban, usually worn flat, but worn upright and pointed by the
    Persian king (see Xenophon, *Anabasis* 2.5.23 and *Cyropaedia*
    8.3.13, and Plutarch, *Themistocles* 29). Darius is here in effect
    appointed king-designate.

67. *Aspasia*: In *Pericles* 24, Plutarch says that her real name was
    Milto but that Cyrus named her Aspasia after Pericles' famous
    mistress of that name. Her story is told in much greater depth by
    Aelian, *Historical miscellany* 12.1.

68. *royal concubines ... conveyed*: Plutarch makes this point in
    Themistocles 26, where he describes the covered carriages used
    to prevent concubines from being seen while travelling. Cf.
    Artaxerxes 5 where Stateira does not travel in the seclusion
    Plutarch here describes. In actual fact, aristocratic Persian women
    probably had more freedom than Greek prejudices allowed.

69. *360 concubines of surpassing beauty*: The figure for the number
    of royal concubines is recorded in, e.g., Diodorus 17.77. The

number 360 (sometimes 365) seems to have had special significance in Persian religion, in which the sun played a central role.

70. *Artemis . . . whom they call Anaïtis*: Anahita (see n. 12).

71. *Tiribazus . . . impetuous*: See *Artaxerxes* 5.

72. *young Darius*: Darius can only be called young in comparison with his father; in *Artaxerxes* 26 he is said to be fifty years old.

73. *'Swiftly treads persuasion unto evil conduct'*: From an unknown Sophoclean tragedy (*TrGF* IV fragment 870).

74. *For smooth . . . desire*: Probably an allusion to Hesiod, *Works and days* 288.

75. *Cypriote Aphrodite . . . blameless*: This seems to be part of a poetic quotation, perhaps from an epic poem.

76. *Oromazes*: I.e., Ahura-Mazda (also Ahurumazda, Auramazda), the supreme god of the Persians.

77. *had lived ninety-four years and reigned for sixty-two*: Plutarch's figures seem to be taken from Deinon (see pseudo-Lucian, *On long lives* 15) and are incorrect, as Artaxerxes ascended to the throne in 405 and died in late 359 or early 358, a reign of forty-six years. But he may be counting from the date when he was designated future king by his father (cf. *Artaxerxes* 26).

78. *Ochus*: Artaxerxes III Ochus, who reigned from 359/8 until 338 BC.

PELOPIDAS

Further Reading

Plutarch's Pelopidas

Buckler, J., 'Plutarch on the trials of Pelopidas and Epaminondas (369 BC)', *Classical Philology* 73 (1978), pp. 36–42.

Georgiadou, A., 'Bias and character-portrayal in Plutarch's Lives of Pelopidas and Marcellus', *ANRW* 2.33.6 (1992), pp. 4222–57.

Georgiadou, A., *Plutarch's Pelopidas: A Historical and Philological Commentary* (Beiträge zur klassischen Altertumskunde 105) (Stuttgart and Leipzig: Teubner, 1997).

Pelling, C. B. R., 'Parallel narratives: the liberation of Thebes in *De Genio Socratis* and in *Pelopidas*', in A. G. Nikolaidis (ed.), *The Unity of Plutarch's Work* (Berlin and New York: De Gruyter, 2008), pp. 539–56.

Westlake, H. D., 'The Sources of Plutarch's *Pelopidas*', *CQ* 33 (1939), pp. 11–22.

History

Buck, R. J., *Boiotia and the Boiotian League, 432–371 BC* (Edmonton, Alta.: University of Alberta Press, 1994).

Buckler, J., *The Theban Hegemony, 371–362* (Cambridge, Mass., and London: Harvard University Press, 1980).

Buckler, J., and Beck, H., *Central Greece and the Politics of Power in the Fourth Century BC* (Cambridge: Cambridge University Press, 2008).

Cawkwell, G., 'Epaminondas and Thebes', *CQ* NS 22 (1972), pp. 254–78.

Munn, M. H., 'Thebes and Central Greece', in L. A. Tritle (ed.), *The Greek World in the Fourth Century: From the Fall of the Athenian Empire to the Successors of Alexander* (London: Routledge, 1997), pp. 66–106.

Roy, J., 'Thebes in the 360s BC', in *CAH* vi, pp. 187–208.

Seager, R. J., 'The King's Peace and the Second Athenian Confederacy', in *CAH* vi, pp. 156–186.

Notes to the Prologue to the Lives
of Pelopidas and Marcellus

1. *elder Cato*: M. Porcius Cato, or 'Cato the Censor' (234–149 BC).

2. *Antigonus' soldiers*: It is not clear which Antigonus is intended here: Antigonus I Monophthalmus ('The One-eyed', *c.* 382–301 BC), general of Alexander the Great, major participant in the wars following Alexander's death, and father of Demetrius Poliorcetes; or Antigonus II Gonatas (*c.* 320–239), Demetrius' son, who established the Antigonid dynasty in Macedonia. The precise identification is irrelevant for the point of the story: true courage does not consist in being reckless with one's life because one has little desire to go on living.

3. *Sybaris*: Greek city in southern Italy, often used as a byword for luxury and soft-living.

4. *Not seeing . . . honour*: Plutarch quotes the same epitaph in his *Consolation to Apollonius* 110c. The location of the monument on which this epitaph was inscribed, and its author, are unknown.

5. *Iphicrates*: Athenian general active in the first half of the fourth century. He was famous for employing light troops much more aggressively than had been customary (Xenophon, *Hellenica* 4.5.11–18; Diodorus 15.44).

6. *Callicratidas . . . 'Sparta . . . does not depend on one man!'*: Callicratidas was a Spartan commander who died in the sea-battle off Arginusae in 406. A slightly different version of the incident men-

tioned here is given by Xenophon (*Hellenica* 1.6.22): the helmsman of his ship warned Callicratidas not to fight while outnumbered; he replied that his death would cause Sparta no harm, but flight would be a disgrace. In *Spartan sayings* 122e–f Plutarch has both the helmsman and the seer warn him, and he actually hands over command to a subordinate so that he can fight. More information on Callicratidas is given in *Lysander* 6–7.

7. *Antigonus the old . . . sea-battle off Andros*: This is almost certainly Antigonus II Gonatas. Plutarch tells the same story about this king in *Sayings of kings and commanders* 183c–d, though there talking of a battle off Cos (Antigonus' defeat of the fleet of Ptolemy II either in *c.* 261 in the Chremonidean War or in *c.* 255). It is possible that there was also a battle off Andros, but this may well be a mistake.

8. *Chares . . . great force*: Chares and Timotheus were both successful fourth-century Athenian generals. Timotheus, acting in support of the rebel satrap Ariobarzanes, took Samos and expelled a Persian garrison after a ten-month siege in 366/5.

Notes to the Life of Pelopidas

9. *Most rich men . . . pleasures*: The saying is from a lost work of Aristotle (fragment 56 Rose). Plutarch seems to draw on the same passage in his *On the love of wealth* 527a.

10. *'Abundant . . . pride'*: *Suppliant women* 861–2. The quotation is not merely ornamental. In the play Adrastus is describing Capaneus' character as he stands over Capaneus' corpse: Capaneus died in battle, just as Pelopidas will. Adrastus continues in words which, Plutarch implies, might be applicable to Pelopidas too: 'He was a true friend to his friends, whether they were present or absent . . . He had a guileless character, was approachable in speech, and behaved with moderation to servants and citizens' (867–71).

11. *Themistocles and Aristides . . . Cimon and Pericles . . . Nicias and Alcibiades*: Pairs of fifth-century BC Athenian generals and statesmen who famously clashed with each other; Plutarch wrote Lives of them all. He expands on the importance of harmony and cooperation among statesmen in his treatise *Political advice*.

12. *campaign at Mantineia*: Presumably in 385, when Sparta attacked Mantineia to punish it for not providing adequate support in the Corinthian War; the city was broken up and its democracy dismantled (Xenophon, *Hellenica* 5.2; Pausanias, *Guide to Greece* 9.13.1).

13. *Phoebidas . . . with a body of troops*: Phoebidas was on his way to northern Greece to campaign against the city of Olynthus in the Chalcide in 382.

14. *the Cadmeia*: The acropolis of Thebes.

15. *festival of the Thesmophoria . . . seized the acropolis*: The Thesmophoria was a festival in honour of the goddess Demeter and was celebrated exclusively by women. Xenophon, *Hellenica* 5.2.29, says that Phoebidas' coup took place in the summer (of 382), and that the acropolis was deserted except for the women celebrating the festival.

16. *deprive Phoebidas of his command . . . approving the offence*: Plutarch makes the same point in *Agesilaus* 23 (see also Xenophon, *Hellenica* 5.2.32; Diodorus 15.20). Phoebidas was in fact later appointed harmost, or governor, of Thespiae, where he was killed (ch. 15).

17. *jointly responsible . . . on their way to attack the tyrants*: In 403 the Athenian Thrasybulus had taken refuge with a small group of supporters on Theban territory. It was from here that he launched the expedition which led to the unseating of the so-called Thirty Tyrants, the oligarchs imposed upon Athens by the Spartans.

18. *no Boeotian should see or hear them*: I.e., the Athenian exiles should be allowed to operate from Boeotian territory against the Spartan-backed oligarchy in Athens without hindrance from the Thebans or other Boeotians.

19. *Thriasian plain*: The plain north-west of Athens on the direct route to Thebes.

20. *set out*: Winter 379/8. Plutarch gives a longer narrative of the liberation of Thebes in his *On the sign of Socrates*.

21. *This phrase has become a proverb . . . to this day*: Plutarch mentions Archias' remark in *On the sign of Socrates* 596f and *Table talk* 619e. It is not found elsewhere.

22. *women's gowns . . . garlands of pine and fir which shaded their faces*: Garlands were often worn for parties. In *On the sign of Socrates* 595d, Plutarch speaks of *two* groups of conspirators: those disguised as women and those dressed for a party.

23. *Boeotarch*: An elected federal official, who commanded the Boeotian army and served for one year. At this period there were probably seven in number.

24. *liberation of Athens*: See ch. 6.

25. *invaded Boeotia*: In winter 379/8.

26. *capture Piraeus*: Sphodrias' attack on Piraeus took place in 378. Plutarch describes it in more detail in *Agesilaus* 24. See also Xenophon's *Hellenica* 5.4.

27. *accepted the alliance . . . to revolt*: Plutarch is here referring to the Second Athenian Confederacy, a network of alliances begun early in the 370s and aimed at combating Spartan power (see *Phocion*, n. 20).

28. *the Sacred Band*: An elite, professional Theban infantry unit, three hundred strong, formed soon after the liberation of Thebes (see ch. 18).

29. *battle of Tegyra*: In 375.

30. *Orchomenus*: In Boeotia, like Tegyra. It was often antipathetic to Thebes and now resisted Theban domination of the newly re-formed Boeotian League.

31. *battalions*: *Morai*, a Spartan term for the six units into which the Spartan army was divided, each commanded by a polemarch (see the next chapter and Xenophon, *Constitution of the Spartans* 11).

32. *Leto . . . between two trees*: As in the story of the birth of Apollo and Artemis on the island of Delos (see Callimachus, *Hymn to Delos* 210, 262).

33. *dragon Python and the giant Tityus*: Legends had it that the giant Tityus was sent by Hera to kill Leto after she had given birth to Apollo and Artemis, and that Apollo killed the dragon Python when he founded his oracle at Delphi. Plutarch discusses the second story at *On the decline of oracles* 417f–418d.

34. *a trophy*: A display of captured weapons and armour set up by a victorious army on the battlefield.

35. *Eurotas . . . Babyce and Cnacion*: The Eurotas was the river of Sparta; Babyce and Cnacion may have been tributaries of it (see *Lycurgus* 6).

36. *That clans . . . aid one another*: Homer, *Iliad* 2.363. Plutarch also quotes Pammenes' criticism of the Homeric line at *Table talk* 618d and *Dialogue on love* 761b. Pammenes was an important Theban general, active in the period after Leuctra.

37. *Aristotle says*: In a lost work, perhaps his *Eroticus* (this is fragment 97 Rose).

38. *'inspired by God'*: Plato, *Symposium* 179a and *Phaedrus* 255b.

39. *battle of Chaeronea*: In 338, when Philip of Macedon inflicted a crushing defeat on Thebes and Athens (see *Demosthenes* 19–20, *Alexander* 9).

40. *passion of Laius . . . Thebes*: Laius was a mythical king of Thebes, and father of Oedipus. One tradition had him fall in love with Chrysippus, the son of Pelops.

41. *common peace with the rest of Greece*: Concluded at a conference in Sparta in the summer of 371. Thebes was excluded from the

treaty because, against Spartan demands, Epaminondas insisted that he was representing Boeotia and not merely the city of Thebes. The Spartan invasion of Boeotia was aimed at breaking up the Boeotian League and punishing Thebes (see *Agesilaus* 27–8).

42. *Menoeceus ... Salamis*: The sacrifices of Menoeceus and Macaria are related in Euripides' *Phoenician women* and *Children of Heracles* respectively. It is not clear who the Pherecydes mentioned here is. Leonidas died at the battle of Thermopylae in 480. Themistocles' sacrifice of Persian youths was said to have taken place shortly before the battle of Salamis in the same year. Plutarch records the story in *Themistocles* 13, where he ascribes it to Phanias of Lesbos, and *Aristides* 9; Herodotus does not mention it.

43. *Artemis demanded his daughter as a sacrifice ... ingloriously*: See *Agesilaus* 6, though there Plutarch does not attribute the ultimate failure of Agesilaus' expedition to Asia (396–394) to his failure to sacrifice a virgin.

44. *when the Thebans invaded the Peloponnese*: Winter 370/69.

45. *united the whole of Arcadia into one state*: The Arcadian League, a federation of various Arcadian cities, including Mantineia and Tegea, which was set up after Leuctra.

46. *freed the territory of Messenia ... Ithome*: Messenia had been subjugated by the Spartans in the eighth century BC, and its inhabitants were forced as helots to work the land for their Spartan masters. The liberation of Messenia, which deprived Sparta of a large proportion of its fertile land, was a decisive blow from which Sparta never fully recovered. The city of Messene was built on Mt Ithome, scene of several attempts in the previous centuries to throw off Spartan rule.

47. *Cenchreae*: The port of Corinth situated on the Saronic Gulf. The Athenians, who had made an alliance with Sparta soon after Leuctra, tried, perhaps half-heartedly, to block the Boeotian route back to the Peloponnese (see Xenophon, *Hellenica* 6.5.51–2).

48. *Pherae*: City in eastern Thessaly. Jason, the first tyrant of Pherae, had dominated much of Thessaly. His assassination in 370, and the subsequent seizure of power by his nephew Alexander of Pherae, had thrown the region into confusion.

49. *Epaminondas was fully occupied in the Peloponnese*: In 369.

50. *Alexander, the king of Macedon*: Alexander II of Macedon succeeded his father Amyntas in 370. His brother-in-law, Ptolemy of Alorus, led an uprising against him and had him murdered, probably in 368.

51. *Philip*: Later Philip II of Macedon, father of Alexander the Great.

52. *After this*: That is, in the following year, i.e., 368.

53. *dispatched Epaminondas with another army*: In 367.

54. *'Tychon'*: Luck.

55. *'He cowered ... feathers droop'*: The reference is to cock-fighting. The author of this iambic trimeter (*TrGF* I 3 fragment 17 = *TrGF* II fragment 408a) may be Phrynichus (see Aristophanes, *Wasps* 1490). Plutarch also quotes it in *Alcibiades* 4 and *Dialogue on love* 762e.

56. *dispatched Pelopidas on a similar mission*: In winter 367/6 (see *Artaxerxes* 22).

57. *Mount Taygetus*: The Taygetus range formed Sparta's western boundary and the limit of its power after the loss of Messenia.

58. *made war ... for the possession of Susa and Ecbatana*: An exaggerated way of talking about Agesilaus' campaign in Asia in 396–394; it was not aimed at overthrowing Persia but at excluding Persian power from the seaboard of Asia Minor.

59. *Antalcidas*: Chief Spartan negotiator at the conference of 387/6 where the King's Peace, or Peace of Antalcidas, which was highly favourable to Sparta, was agreed. The incident described here probably relates to that earlier conference (see *Artaxerxes* 22).

60. *the Greeks should be left independent ... Messene ... king's hereditary friends*: This meant the Greeks of the mainland and Aegean islands not those of Asia Minor or Cyprus, which were to be under Persian control. This Theban proposal was in effect to renew the Peace of Antalcidas, with the crucial difference that it insisted on the independence of Messenia, as well as the beaching of the Athenian navy. It was not ratified by Sparta or Athens.

61. *marched at once against Alexander*: Pelopidas marched against Alexander of Pherae for the last time in 364.

62. *the Thessalians ... went further than this*: In fact the Thessalians set up, perhaps after his death, a statue of Pelopidas at Delphi, the base of which survives (Harding 49).

63. *Philistus*: Sicilian Greek historian. His work is now lost, though it was regarded with great respect in antiquity. He was a supporter of Dionysius I and II of Syracuse, the former of whom died in 367 (see *Dion*, esp. 35–6).

64. *Alexander the Great, when Hephaestion died ... former beauty*: See *Alexander* 72.

65. *To die in the hour of triumph ... beyond the reach of fortune*: Plutarch here alludes to the Greek saying, 'call no man happy until his death'. It was given its most famous expression in Herodotus 1.30–32, where Solon declares the most blessed man of all to be Tellus of Athens, who, after living a happy life, died fight-

ing bravely on the battle-field and was buried at public expense where he fell.

66. *Diagoras . . . Olympus*: Diagoras of Rhodes was an athlete, and the subject of Pindar's Seventh Olympian ode. Mount Olympus in northern Greece (to be distinguished from Olympia in the Peloponnese) was held to be the home of the gods; the Spartan meant, 'You cannot become a god'.

67. *suffered a fate to match his own lawless crimes*: Alexander of Pherae was murdered in 358.

DION

Further Reading

Plutarch's Dion

Brenk, F. E., *In Mist Apparelled: Religious Themes in Plutarch's Moralia and Lives* (Leiden: Brill, 1977), pp. 106–11.

De Blois, L., 'Political concepts in Plutarch's *Dion* and *Timoleon*', *Ancient Society* 28 (1997), pp. 209–24.

Dillon, J., 'Dion and Brutus: philosopher kings adrift in a hostile world', in A. G. Nikolaidis (ed.), *The unity of Plutarch's Work* (Berlin: De Gruyter, 2008), pp. 351–64.

Dreher, M., and Scardigli, B. (eds.), *Plutarco. Vite Parallele: Dione–Bruto* (Milan: Biblioteca Universale Rizzoli, 2000).

Pelling, C. B. R., 'Do Plutarch's politicians never learn?', in L. De Blois, J. Bons, T. Kessels and D. M. Schenkeveld (eds.), *The Statesman in Plutarch's Works* (Leiden: Brill, 2004), vol. 1, pp. 87–103.

Porter, W. H. (ed.), *Plutarch: Life of Dion* (Dublin: Hodges, Figgis and Co., 1952).

History

Finley, M. I., *A History of Sicily: Ancient Sicily to the Arab Conquest* (London: Chatto and Windus, 1968; rev. edn, 1979), chs. 6–7.

Lintott, A. W., *Violence, Civil Strife and Revolution in the Classical City* (London: Croom Helm, 1982), ch. 5.

Sanders, L. J., *The Legend of Dion* (Toronto: Edgar Kent, 2008).

Talbert, R. J. A., 'The Greeks in Sicily and South Italy', in L. A. Tritle (ed.), *The Greek World in the Fourth Century: From the Fall of the Athenian Empire to the Successors of Alexander* (London: Routledge, 1997), pp. 167–88.

Westlake, H. D., 'Dion and Timoleon', in *CAH* vi, pp. 592–622.

Notes to the Prologue to the Lives of Dion and Brutus

1. *Sosius Senecio*: The dedicatee of the *Parallel Lives*. He was an important Roman, known to have held the 'ordinary' consulship in 99 and 107 AD. Plutarch mentions him in the opening sentences of *Theseus* and in both the opening and closing sentences of *Demosthenes*, as well as in several works of the *Moralia*.

2. *Simonides tells us . . . Corinthian*: Simonides, fragment 572 Page. Simonides (*c.* 555–467) was one of the most famous Greek poets. His work survives only in fragments, so we do not know the context in which he made this remark. The details about the Trojan War are based on Homer, *Iliad* 2.570 and 6.145–211.

3. *wisdom and justice must be accompanied by power . . . substance*: A reference to Plato's theory that good government would only be brought about when philosophers have power (see, e.g., *Republic* 473c; *Epistle* 7, 326a–c).

4. *Those who utterly deny the existence of such phenomena . . . superstition*: This is a summary of Epicurean doctrine. Plutarch wrote a treatise entitled *On superstition* in which he attacks both those overly frightened of the divine and those who do not believe in the divine at all.

5. *warned by the gods of their approaching death . . . envious spirits themselves*: This passage, in which Plutarch seems to accept the existence of malevolent spirits (*daimonia*), has puzzled scholars, as it does not seem to accord with his views as expressed elsewhere, especially in *On the decline of oracles*. Phantoms do indeed appear to both Dion (ch. 55) and Brutus (*Brutus* 36 and 48); in Brutus' case the phantom predicts his death in the battle of Philippi. But they do not seem to play the role described here, of diverting the two men from virtue. In each passage Plutarch emphasizes the lateness of the hour or the viewer's lack of sleep, leaving it unclear whether the phenomenon might have been imagined. At any rate, Plutarch uses the notion of the spectres to add an undefined supernatural element to both Lives, as well as perhaps to characterize the emotional state of the two men. See also *Alexander* 50 and n. 126.

6. *twelfth book*: Elsewhere Plutarch says that *Demosthenes–Cicero* was the fifth book (*Demosthenes* 3) and *Pericles–Fabius* the tenth (*Pericles* 2).

Notes to the Life of Dion

7. *Dionysius the elder . . . master of Syracuse*: In 405. Syracuse had been a democracy until Dionysius made himself tyrant.

8. *eldest son*: Dionysius II, who was born *c.* 396 and later suc-
    ceeded to the tyranny (ch. 6).

9. *Plato arrived in Sicily*: About 388.

10. *Plato himself has written . . . judgement*: Plato, *Epistle* 7, 327a.
    A little earlier in the same letter Plato talks of his arrival in Syra-
    cuse as having come about 'possibly by luck, but it seems likely
    that one of the greater powers was contriving to lay the founda-
    tion for what happened with Dion and Syracuse' (326d–e).

11. *life of the just . . . misery*: A common philosophical doctrine,
    expounded in, for example, Book 1 of Plato's *Republic*.

12. *as a just man . . . slave*: Dionysius thus took Plato's doctrine that
    the good man is always happy to its logical extreme. It was in
    Plutarch's time a common philosophical conceit that the wise
    man would be happy, even if he were a slave.

13. *Aegina . . . at war with Athens*: Between 389 and 387; hostilities
    were ended by the Peace of Antalcidas. Sparta was also at war
    with Athens in this period.

14. *Gelon*: One of the most illustrious of the Greek tyrants of Sicily.
    He became tyrant of Gela in *c.* 491 and of Syracuse shortly after-
    wards, and inflicted a crushing defeat on the Carthaginians in
    480, which brought him immense prestige. He was succeeded by
    his brother Hieron.

15. *Gelon . . . laughing-stock*: A pun on Gelon and the Greek word
    for laughter, *gelos*.

16. *Timaeus*: Timaeus (*c.* 350–260 BC) was a Sicilian himself (*Timo-
    leon* 10) and wrote a long work on Sicilian history, which now
    survives only in quotations in later writers. He was an important
    source for Diodorus in his Sicilian books and for Plutarch in
    both *Dion* and *Timoleon*. He was critical of tyrants, including
    the two Dionysii.

17. *Dionysius . . . died without ever regaining consciousness*: In 367.

18. *danger from Carthage*: After a long war in the 390s, a peace
    treaty of 392 had limited Carthaginian dominance to the west of
    Sicily. Dionysius I led an unsuccessful offensive against Carthage
    in 368, the year before he died.

19. *'adamantine chains'*: Perhaps an allusion to Aeschylus' *Prometh-
    eus bound* 7, where Power gives Hephaestus, the god of fire, the
    task of keeping Prometheus bound with 'adamantine chains'.
    The phrase, which is found also in Diodorus 16.5, may go back
    to Dionysius himself. He certainly had pretensions as a tragic
    poet, and was said to have bought the writing-tablet on which
    Aeschylus composed in the hope of drawing inspiration from it

(Lucian, *To an uneducated book collector* 15). If so, Dionysius I seems to have implicitly compared himself with Hephaestus and presented his task of ruling Syracuse as divinely inspired.

20. *seem offensive . . . youthful folly*: This is what Plato says in *Epistle* 7, 327b, though he dates the poor reception of Dion's virtue to before Dionysius I's death.

21. *guard against stubbornness, the companion of solitude*: Plato, *Epistle* 4, 321b (see also ch. 52). Plutarch also applies Plato's advice to Coriolanus (*Coriolanus* 15 and *Comparison of Coriolanus and Alcibiades* 3), and mentions it in *Political advice* 808d, where he discusses the importance of a statesman's helping his friends.

22. *Plato . . . bravest man alive*: See ch. 5.

23. *fatherly mode of government*: Possibly an allusion to Plato, *Laws* 680e.

24. *king . . . tyrant*: Technically, kings were monarchs who came to power constitutionally, while tyrants were monarchs, or the successors of monarchs, who seized power unconstitutionally. But by Plutarch's period, and already in Plato, the two words were being used in a moral sense: the king was a virtuous monarch, the tyrant a wicked one.

25. *as he has written*: Plato, *Epistle* 7, 328a–c.

26. *theory . . . action*: Plato argued that a monarch, imbued with correct philosophical thinking, would be an ideal ruler (see n. 3).

27. *Philistus*: Philistus of Syracuse (*c.* 430–356 BC) had been exiled in *c.* 386. He was recalled in the same year that Plato arrived for the second time (367 or 366). He wrote a history of Sicily down to 363 in thirteen books; this has not survived but was highly regarded in antiquity.

28. *Leptines' wife*: Some editors argue that the text here is corrupt, and that Plutarch must mean Leptines' *daughter*, who had married Philistus (see *Timoleon* 15).

29. *when Plato arrived in Sicily*: Plato arrived on his second visit in 367 or 366. He stayed until 365.

30. *dust*: Geometry was practised by drawing with sand on the floor, as happens, for example, in Plato's dialogue *Meno*. Cf. *Nicias* 12, where some Athenians, before the invasion of Sicily, draw maps of the island in the sand.

31. *Athenians . . . invaded Sicily . . . take Syracuse*: The Athenians invaded in 415 and were annihilated in 413.

32. *tyranny of Dionysius*: Dionysius had greatly extended his power and that of Syracuse during his reign. He controlled most of

Sicily except for the small Carthaginian enclave in the west; he also dominated much of the heel and south-eastern coast of Italy and planted colonies across the Adriatic.

33. *ineffable good*: This notion may be derived partly from Plato's *Epistle* 7, 341b–e, where he talks about the impossibility of expressing his doctrines in words.

34. *put ... ashore on the Italian coast*: In 366.

35. *demanded that Plato should respond to his love alone ... corrupt him*: Based partly on Plato, *Epistle* 7, 330a–b.

36. *war had broken out ... summer*: Plato was sent away in 365. The war is perhaps that against the Lucanians in southern Italy mentioned in Diodorus 16.5. Plutarch's source here is Plato, *Epistle* 3, 317a; *Epistle* 7, 338a.

37. *Speusippus*: Plato's nephew, who later succeeded his uncle as head of the Academy.

38. *Timon's Lampoons*: Timon of Phlius (*c.* 320–230) was a sceptic philosopher and poet. In his *Lampoons* (*Silloi*) he ridiculed all other philosophers except Pyrrhon, the founder of Scepticism.

39. *staunch ally against the Thebans*: Xenophon (*Hellenica* 7.4.12) talks of Sicilian troops sent by Dionysius to assist the Spartans in 365.

40. *Archytas*: Archytas of Tarentum was the leader of the Pythagorean philosophical school; he was also a powerful political figure in his own right.

41. *gathered at his court ... much could be expected if he did*: This whole section is based heavily on Plato, *Epistle* 7, 338b–340a.

42. *Scylla ... Charybdis*: Mythical sea-monsters said to guard the straits between Sicily and Italy. Avoiding one meant sailing too close to the other. The quotation, from *Odyssey* 12.428, is taken over from Plato, *Epistle* 7, 345d–e. Plato's third visit to Sicily was in 361/0.

43. *Aristippus of Cyrene*: A former associate of Socrates and supposed founder of the Cyrenaic school of philosophy. Xenophon represents him as loving the life of pleasure.

44. *eclipse of the sun*: Securely dated to 12 May 361.

45. *Plato's own version ... this account*: Plato, *Epistle* 7, 350a–b, which does not really contradict what Plutarch says, but neither does it contain Dionysius' remark or Plato's reply.

46. *letter to Dionysius*: *Epistle* 13 (362e) of the Platonic corpus; modern scholars generally doubt its authenticity, but Plutarch seems to have accepted it as genuine.

47. *prepare for war*: In 360. The expedition finally sailed in 357.

48. *Plato himself refused ... because of his age*: Plato, *Epistle* 7, 350b–d.

49. *On the soul*: This work, often known as *Eudemus*, is lost, though Cicero in his *On divination* 1.25 summarizes some material from it. It should not be confused with another work by Aristotle of the same title, the extant *On the soul* (*De anima*).

50. *only twenty-five joined the expedition ... shrank from it*: In fact, as Plutarch admits later (ch. 32), another force was led by Heracleides.

51. *soldiers assembled*: Plutarch avoids stating here that these were hired mercenaries.

52. *midsummer*: 357 BC. The eclipse mentioned in the next chapter took place on 9 August 357.

53. *Etesian winds*: Seasonal winds which blow from the north in summer in the Mediterranean.

54. *past middle life, as in Dion's case*: He was by then around fifty-one.

55. *Dion and his friends found nothing surprising in this ... sun*: Dion's rational attitude to eclipses is, in Plutarch's view, to his credit. Contrast Nicias, who in his expedition to Sicily had reacted superstitiously to an eclipse in 413 (*Nicias* 23).

56. *Theopompus*: An important fourth-century historian, author of a work called *Philippica* (*History of Philip*), which seems to have been a more general history of the fourth century than the name implies. Diodorus 16.71 tells us that Theopompus devoted three books to Sicily, which covered the period of the reigns of the two Dionysii.

57. *lying in wait ... off Iapygia*: That is, off Apulia in the heel of Italy.

58. *Arcturus*: A bright star which becomes visible in September and was associated by the Greeks with storms.

59. *Cercina*: Situated off the coast of Tunisia, opposite the modern Sfax, and under Carthaginian control.

60. *Great Syrtis*: The bay of Benghazi.

61. *guest-friend*: (Greek, *xenos*) A person in a foreign city with whom one has formed a bond of ritualized friendship, which brought with it obligations of hospitality, loyalty and support. These obligations would be passed to one's heirs.

62. *acropolis ... wall*: The acropolis was on Ortygia, a virtual island connected to the rest of Syracuse by a narrow causeway, which could easily be walled off.

63. *barbarians*: The Greek term *barbaros* originally meant simply non-Greek, but by Plutarch's time it might, as here, have had distinctly negative connotations, similar to English 'barbarian'.

64. *a hundred minas*: A mina was a unit of weight and of coinage. Its

exact value differed from city to city, but one mina often equated to 100 drachmas or almost a pound of silver.

65. *fallen out ... command*: This is probably unfair to Heracleides. Diodorus 16.16.2 says that Dion left him in the Peloponnese as commander of the fleet but he was delayed by bad weather.

66. *they defeated Philistus*: Spring or early summer 356.

67. *Ephorus*: Ephorus (*c.* 405–330 BC) wrote a history of the world from earliest times to his own day. It was arranged geographically, and several books seem to have been devoted to Sicily. Ephorus' work survives only in quotations in later authors.

68. *Gyarta*: The place is unknown and the name may be corrupt.

69. *midsummer*: Of 356.

70. *allies*: It is not entirely clear who these allies were; perhaps they were citizens of other Sicilian Greek states recently liberated. Plutarch also talks of allies loyal to the Syracusans in ch. 42, so his claim here that all the allies supported Dion is misleading (cf. also ch. 49).

71. *Nypsius of Naples*: Perhaps a mercenary commander.

72. *founded by ... fellow-countrymen*: Syracuse was originally a colony of Corinth.

73. *Dionysius*: Some editors emend here to 'Dionysius' son'.

74. *their saviour and their god*: It is possible that we should read here '*their father*, their saviour and their god' to match the address to the mercenaries as 'brothers'. Cf. ch. 39 ('in a paternal fashion') and *Pelopidas* 33 ('their father, their saviour and their teacher'). In Diodorus 16.20 the Syracusans grant Dion honours as a hero and address him as 'saviour'.

75. *sully his virtue by giving way to anger ... weakness*: The criticism here of acting in anger can be paralleled elsewhere in Plutarch's work, especially in his treatise *On control of anger*, where he argues that anger must be controlled by reason. See also *Coriolanus* 15 and *Comparison of Coriolanus and Alcibiade*s 2.

76. *Gylippus ... before him*: The Spartans sent Gylippus in 414 to direct the defence of Syracuse against the Athenians (see Thucydides 6.93; Plutarch, *Nicias* 18–19).

77. *Plato ... eyes of the whole world were now fixed upon him*: Plutarch has in mind Plato, *Epistle* 4, 320d.

78. *'stubbornness is the companion of solitude'*: See ch. 8 and n. 21.

79. *for not having demolished the acropolis ... casting out his body*: See *Timoleon* 22 and *Comparison of Dion and Brutus* 2.

80. *to use Plato's phrase*: *Republic* 8, 557d, where Plato is criticizing democracy.

81. *blend of democracy and monarchy ... model*: The idea is Platonic (see, e.g., Plato, *Laws* 6, 756e–757a; *Epistle* 8, 356b–357a).

82. *according to Plato*: *Epistle* 7, 333e.

83. *the Mysteries*: An Attic cult based at Eleusis, into which individuals, both Athenian and foreign, might be initiated in a secret ceremony. See also *Phocion*, n. 18.

84. *Furies on the stage*: In Aeschylus' *Eumenides*, the Furies, or avenging spirits, pursue Orestes for murdering his mother. Plato talks of Furies in his *Epistle* 8, 357a, apparently referring to Dion's murderers. The appearance of a Fury here suggests Dion's coming doom (see prologue, ch. 2).

85. *committed the murder*: June 354.

86. *Catana ... cheese-grater*: A pun on *katane*, which is both the name of the city of Catana and the Sicilian word for cheese-grater.

87. *These events I have described ... in my Life of Timoleon*: *Timoleon* 33.

TIMOLEON

Further Reading

Plutarch's Timoleon

Barzanò, A., Sordi, M., and Pennati, A. (eds.), *Plutarco. Vite Parallele: Emilio Paolo–Timoleonte* (Milan: Biblioteca Universale Rizzoli, 1996).

De Blois, L., 'Political concepts in Plutarch's *Dion* and *Timoleon*', *Ancient Society* 28 (1997), pp. 209–24.

Holden, H. A., *Plutarch's Life of Timoleon with Introduction, Notes and Lexicon* (Cambridge: Cambridge University Press, 1889).

Swain, S. C. R., 'Plutarch's Aemilius and Timoleon', *Historia* 38 (1989), pp. 314–34.

Teodorsson, S.-T., 'Timoleon, the fortunate general', in L. De Blois, J. Bons, T. Kessels and D. M. Schenkeveld (eds.), *The Statesman in Plutarch's Works* (Leiden: Brill, 2005), vol. 2, pp. 215–26.

Westlake, H. D., 'The Sources of Plutarch's Timoleon', *CQ* 32 (1938), pp. 65–74 (though his conclusions are unconvincing).

History

Finley, M. I., *A History of Sicily: Ancient Sicily to the Arab Conquest* (London: Chatto and Windus, 1968; rev. edn, 1979), ch. 8.

Lintott, A. W., *Violence, Civil Strife and Revolution in the Classical City* (London: Croom Helm, 1982), pp. 213–17.

Talbert, R. J. A., *Timoleon and the Revival of Greek Sicily* (Cambridge: Cambridge University Press, 1974). Ch. 1 discusses Plutarch's *Timoleon* specifically.

Talbert, R. J. A., 'The Greeks in Sicily and South Italy', in L. A. Tritle (ed.), *The Greek World in the Fourth Century: From the Fall of the Athenian Empire to the Successors of Alexander* (London: Routledge, 1997), pp. 167–88.

Westlake, H. D., 'Dion and Timoleon', in *CAH* vi, pp. 693–722.

Notes to the Life of Timoleon

1. *Life of Timoleon*: The second in its pair of Lives. A prologue to the *Lives of Aemilius and Timoleon* precedes *Aemilius*.

2. *Dion ... treacherously murdered*: In 354 (see *Dion* 57).

3. *exchanged one tyrant for another*: The tyrant Dionysius II was expelled by Dion in 356. After Dion's murder his assassin, the Athenian Callippus, held power from 354 to 353, when he was ousted by Dionysius II's half-brother Hipparinus. He in turn was assassinated in 351 and succeeded by his brother Nisaeus, who was driven out in 346, when Dionysius II returned to power.

4. *by a very small force*: I.e., by Dion's expedition.

5. *kinship with the Corinthians*: Syracuse had been founded by Corinth in *c.* 734 BC.

6. *Corinth ... cause of freedom ... liberty of Greece*: An exaggeration, perhaps reflecting a pro-oligarchic bias in Plutarch or his source.

7. *troubled state of Greece ... commitments at home*: The Third Sacred War had been fought between 356 and 346 (see n. 43). Corinth was not directly involved in it.

8. *Cleonae*: Small city between Corinth and Argos. In the battle of Cleonae (*c.* 369), Corinth was allied with Sparta and Athens against Argos and Thebes. Dionysius I sent troops to fight on the Spartan side at this time (Xenophon, *Hellenica* 7.1.20).

9. *treachery of their allies*: The earlier incident of treachery refers to the union of Corinth and Argos in the late 390s to form a short-lived democratic state; Plutarch thus presents here the view-point of the oligarchs.

10. *decree ... Timophanes in command of it*: In *c.* 366. According to Xenophon, *Hellenica* 7.4, the Corinthians also asked the Athenian troops then present on Corinthian territory to leave, as they feared the Athenians were about to stage a coup.

11. *Phocion ... given the advice that he did*: See *Phocion* 23.

12. *twenty years ... enterprise*: That is, he stayed out of politics from *c.* 366 until *c.* 346.

13. *Timoleon set sail*: In 344.

14. *'the island'*: Ortygia, which was joined to the mainland by a narrow causeway.

15. *filled with indignation at the insult they had suffered*: Syracuse had been founded by Corinth, and so the Corinthians felt some right to intervene. Cf. the Corinthians' sensitivity in the run-up to the Peloponnesian War over Athens' interference in the Corinthian colonies of Corcyra, Epidamnus and Potidaea (described in Thucydides 1.24–88).

16. *He had made himself ... hostile to tyrants*: The extravagant praise of Andromachus here is almost certainly derived from the account of his son Timaeus, who was one of Plutarch's sources for both *Dion* and *Timoleon* (*Dion*, n. 16). In reality, Andromachus' position was probably much like that of a tyrant, but he secured his own future by supporting Timoleon.

17. *despite being Phoenicians*: Carthage was originally founded by Phoenician settlers. Both Phoenicians and Carthaginians are stereotyped as untrustworthy and treacherous in many Greek and Roman writers.

18. *Callippus*: See *Dion* 54–8.

19. *Pharax*: See *Dion* 48–9.

20. *Adranum*: This city had been founded in the late fifth century by Dionysius I. It was situated on the south-westerly slope of Mt Etna.

21. *Dionysius had been born and bred ... acts of tyranny*: Dionysius II succeeded his father in 367. He abandoned Syracuse in *c.* 356, leaving behind a garrison in Ortygia commanded by his son Apollocrates, which withdrew soon after. Dionysius was at some point expelled from Locri, where he had been living, and his wife and children were murdered. But in 346 he staged a return to Syracuse. He surrendered the city to Timoleon *c.* 344.

22. *fully described in my Life of Dion*: This seems to be a mistake. Plutarch does describe similar events in *Dion* 58, but they concern Aristomache and Arete, the wife and daughter of Dionysius I. The fate of the wife and children of Dionysius II is described in Plutarch, *Political advice* 821d, Aelian, *Historical miscellany* 6.12, and Strabo 6.259–60.

23. *Philip of Macedon ... 'He can do it ... wine-bowl'*: Philip was notorious for his fondness for drinking (see *Alexander* 9).

24. *Plato ... arrived in Corinth*: Plato died in 347. Dionysius arrived in Corinth in *c.* 344 or 343.

25. *Diogenes of Sinope*: A cynic philosopher, who spent most of his life in Corinth and Athens. He rejected convention and lived a life of poverty Many of the statements attributed to him attack, as this one does, the wealthy and powerful (see, e.g., *Alexander* 14).

26. *Philistus . . . daughters of Leptines . . . life*: See *Dion* 11.

27. *This stroke of fortune . . . Sicily*: The motif of Timoleon's good fortune is prominent throughout the Life, often linked, as here, to the notion of divine protection or sanction (see p. 147).

28. *Pillars of Heracles*: The land on either side of the Straits of Gibraltar.

29. *Dion's mistake . . . cost to build*: See *Dion* 53.

30. *sailed for Syracuse*: In 343. Diodorus does not mention the arrival of colonists from Greece at this time. It is probable that most of these early settlers came from other parts of Sicily rather than, as in the second round of colonization after the battle of Crimisus, from Corinth and elsewhere in Greece.

31. *Athanis*: He seems to have been a contemporary Syracusan historian and statesman. Only a few fragments of his work survive. Archaeological evidence suggests that his figure for the number of settlers here ('60,000') is probably on the low side.

32. *victory . . . at Himera*: In 480 BC.

33. *invaded the territory of these rulers*: In the summer of 342.

34. *Leptines*: Different from the Leptines (brother of Dionysius II) mentioned in ch. 15.

35. *Meanwhile*: The date is uncertain. The landing, and the subsequent battle of Crimisus, took place sometime between 342 and 339.

36. *Lilybaeum*: A port on the extreme west of Sicily.

37. *Crimisus*: Near Segesta, deep into territory long dominated by Carthage in the west of Sicily.

38. *Isthmian . . . Nemean Games*: Athletic contests, held as part of a religious festival every other year. The former were controlled by Corinth, the latter by the small neighbouring city of Cleonae.

39. *two eagles . . . flew*: Cf. a similar portent in *Iliad* 12.200–229, though there the fact that the eagle drops the snake is a sign that initial success would not lead to ultimate victory.

40. *many prisoners were secreted away by the soldiers*: As Plutarch said happened after the defeat of the Athenians in 413 (*Nicias* 27). His wording here recalls that earlier Syracusan victory.

41. *trophy*: A display of captured weapons and armour set up by a victorious army on the battlefield.

42. *the memorial proclaimed . . . to the gods*: Part of what may be this inscription, although it does not name Timoleon in the

extant section, has been found at Corinth (R&O 74). Another inscription found at Delphi records Timoleon's dedication of a chariot to Apollo (cf. ch. 8).

43. *seized Delphi ... sacred treasures*: In the Third Sacred War (356–346 BC). The war began with the refusal of the Phocians to pay a fine imposed by the Delphic authorities on the grounds that they had tilled land sacred to Apollo. The Phocians, who received financial support from the Athenians and Spartans and were opposed by the Thebans, Locrians and Thessalians, plundered the Delphic treasury, an act of gross sacrilege.

44. *justice exacted her penalty ... stroke of retribution*: The text may be corrupt here.

45. *ensured that no harm ... wicked*: The fact that God may sometimes delay punishment of the wicked in order to achieve some wider goal is discussed in Plutarch's *On God's slowness to punish*.

46. *These gilded ... shields*: TrGF I 87 Mamercus.

47. *Calauria*: The text is uncertain at this point and the identity of the place mentioned unclear.

48. *Damurias*: Once again, the text is uncertain here.

49. *'Corinthian women ... from their homes'*: A parody of Euripides' *Medea* 214, where the heroine says to the chorus, 'Corinthian Women, I have come out from my home.'

50. *as I have related in my Life of Dion*: Dion 58.

51. *treaty was negotiated*: Perhaps in 339.

52. *Lycus*: This is probably the River Halycus, which had earlier been the boundary of Carthaginian territory agreed in a treaty made with Dionysius I.

53. *the war with Athens*: Referring to the Athenian expedition to Sicily in 415–413. The Carthaginians had taken Acragas and Gela in 406/5.

54. *master-craftsman*: Possibly an allusion to the picture in Plato's *Republic* (500b ff.) of the philosopher who, if he turns his attention to politics, would prove an excellent craftsmen in moulding the constitution and the characters of men, in accordance with the divine models which he perceives.

55. *Timotheus*: Distinguished Athenian commander of the first half of the fourth century.

56. *Agesilaus*: Spartan king who ruled between 398 and *c*. 360. Plutarch wrote a *Life of Agesilaus*, whom he paired with Pompey.

57. *'O gods ... in this?'*: From an unidentified tragedy (*TrGF* IV fragment 874).

58. *Antimachus ... Dionysius ... Nicomachus*: Respectively, an epic

poet and elegist of the later fifth and early fourth centuries BC, much admired by Plato; a portrait-painter of the fifth century; and a painter of the fourth century.

59. *insatiable pursuit of honours and power*: Plutarch often criticizes excessive and uncontrolled ambition, especially where it leads to disharmony and conflict between statesmen (e.g., *Lysander* 23 and *Sulla* 4). See his comments in *Pelopidas* 4, *Flamininus* 11 and *Political advice* 805e–810a.

60. *every lark . . . crest*: Simonides fragment 538 Page. Plutarch cites the same passage in *How to profit from one's enemies* 91e and *Political advice* 809b.

61. *speeches at the great festivals . . . exhorting his countrymen to attempt*: Plutarch is probably thinking particularly of the speech delivered by Lysias at the Olympic Games of 388, in which he urged the Greeks to unite against Dionysius I and Artaxerxes II. Several years after that, also at the Olympic Games, Isocrates urged the Greeks to unite in a war against Persia.

62. *end his life*: In the mid or late 330s.

63. *buried him in the market-place*: An exceptional privilege, showing that Timoleon was accorded honours reserved for heroes, that is, a class of individuals regarded as semi-divine. The Greeks usually buried their dead outside the city.

64. *lived for a long time*: For about twenty years, after which Agathocles overthrew the oligarchy left behind by Timoleon and made himself tyrant in all but name in 316.

Notes to the Comparison of Aemilius and Timoleon

65. *putting an end . . . in its seventh generation*: Aemilius Paulus defeated Perseus of Macedon, son of Philip V and descendant of Antigonus I Monophthalmus, at the battle of Pydna in 168 (see *Demetrius* 53).

66. *dismissed Gylippus . . . avarice and greed in command*: See *Nicias* 28. Gylippus was the Spartan commander sent out in 414 to assist the Syracusans to resist the Athenian siege. He was later banished from Sparta for embezzlement of state funds (see *Lysander* 16–17 and *Pericles* 22).

67. *Pharax . . . Callippus*: See ch. 11 and the passages cited in the notes there.

68. *neither looked upon . . . treasures . . . bestowed large amounts on others*: See *Aemilius* 28.

69. *over-sensitivity . . . not truly great*: Plutarch elsewhere expresses

the belief that a statesman should not be overwhelmed by private grief (see *Demosthenes* 22 and n. 74). He also criticizes statesmen who enter public life without sufficient thought and are then put off by disgrace or danger (*Political advice* 798c–799a).

DEMOSTHENES

Further Reading

Plutarch's Demosthenes

Geiger, J., Ghilli, L., Mugelli, B., and Pecorella Longo, C. (eds.), *Plutarco. Vite Parallele: Demostene–Cicero* (Milan: Biblioteca Universale Rizzoli, 1995).

Holden, H. A., *Plutarch's Life of Demosthenes with Introduction, Notes and Lexicon* (Cambridge: Cambridge University Press, 1893).

Moles, J. L. (ed.), *Plutarch: The Life of Cicero* (Warminster: Aris and Philips, 1988), pp. 19–26 on the pairing of Demosthenes and Cicero.

Mossman, J. M., 'Is the pen mightier than the sword? The failure of rhetoric in Plutarch's *Demosthenes*', *Histos* 3 (1999), pp. 77–101.

Zadorojnyi, A., 'King of his castle: Plutarch, *Demosthenes* 1–2', *Proceedings of the Cambridge Philological Society* 52 (2006), pp. 102–27.

History

Cawkwell, G., 'Demosthenes' policy after the peace of Philokrates', *CQ* NS 13 (1963), pp. 120–38; reprinted in S. Perlman (ed.), *Philip and Athens* (Cambridge: Heffer; New York: Barnes and Noble, 1973), pp. 145–78.

Pickard-Cambridge, A. W., *Demosthenes and the Last Days of Greek Freedom 384–322 BC* (New York: G. P. Putnam's and Sons, 1914; reprinted New York: AMS Press, 1978; Piscataway, NJ: Gorgias Press, 2003).

Sealey, R., *Demosthenes and his Time* (Oxford: Oxford University Press, 1993).

Worthington, I. (ed.), *Demosthenes: Statesman and Orator* (London: Routledge, 2000).

Notes to the Prologue to the Lives of Demosthenes and Cicero

1. *Sosius Senecio*: The dedicatee of the *Parallel Lives* (see *Dion* 1 and n. 1 there).

2. *'famous city'*: In *Alcibiades* 11 Plutarch quotes more of the poem and attributes it to Euripides. The mention of Alcibiades in the opening words of Demosthenes' Life is significant, as Plutarch will twice compare Demosthenes to Alcibiades (ch. 27 and *Comparison of Demosthenes and Cicero* 4).

3. *'the eyesore of Piraeus'*: Elsewhere (*Pericles* 8) Plutarch attributes this saying to Pericles.

4. *Iulis . . . Ceos . . . Aegina . . . poet*: Iulis in Ceos was the birthplace of the lyric poets Simonides and Bacchylides, Aegina of the actor Polus.

5. *small city . . . smaller*: Plutarch lived in Chaeronea in Boeotia, some 60 miles north-west of Athens. The battle of Chaeronea is central to this Life (chs. 19–20).

6. *fifth book*: See *Dion* 2 and the note there.

7. *As Ion puts it*: Ion of Chios, a poet and prose writer of the fifth century BC. This is *TrGF* I 19 fragments 55 and 58.

8. *'The dolphin's strength . . . dry land'*: In other words, one should not venture out of one's natural element.

9. *Caecilius*: Caecilius of Cale Acte, a Greek orator and critic who worked in Rome in the time of Augustus.

10. *'Know yourself'*: A famous maxim, inscribed on the temple of Apollo at Delphi.

Notes to the Life of Demosthenes

11. *as Theopompus tells us*: See *Dion*, n. 56. Book 10 of Theopompus' *Philippica* was an excursus on the demagogues of Athens, and this piece of information may be derived from that.

12. *As for the charge . . . slander*: Aeschines' story was that Gylon had betrayed Nymphaeum, an Athenian possession on the Chersonese, and had become an exile from Athens; he married a Scythian woman, whose daughter was Demosthenes' mother (*Against Ctesiphon* 171–2). The accusation, which would cast doubt on Demosthenes' own citizenship, is unlikely to be true.

13. *Demosthenes' father died . . . tutors*: This and much of what follows is derived from Demosthenes' own speeches, e.g., the first speech *Against Aphobus* 4 and 46.

14. *Batalus*: Demosthenes, in his *On the crown* 180, refers to this nickname as one given him by Aeschines; Aeschines uses it several times in his extant works. It probably referred to Demosthenes' lisp, but there may be an obscene meaning.

15. *Antiphanes*: A comic poet of the fourth century BC. Plutarch cites him in ch. 9.

16. *the question of Oropus*: In 366 Athens lost control of Oropus to Thebes owing to the intervention of Themison, tyrant of Eretria. The Athenian commanders, Chabrias and Callistratus, seeing the strength of Theban forces, agreed to put the matter to arbitration; they were later prosecuted for misleading the people (see Demosthenes, *Against Meidias* 64). If, as Plutarch seems to imply, Demosthenes, who was born *c*. 384, was still a child at the time of the trial, the case must have been heard very soon after the event.

17. *Isaeus ... Hermippus ... Isocrates ... Alcidamas*: Isaeus and Isocrates were important Athenian speech-writers of the first half of the fourth century BC; the latter was also famous as a teacher of rhetoric. Alcidamas, from the same period, taught rhetoric and wrote about the art of speech-making. Hermippus of Smyrna lived in the third century and wrote, among other things, biographies of literary and intellectual figures. His work on Demosthenes seems to have been a source for Plutarch's *Life*.

18. *come of age*: Athenian young men became adults when they were eighteen, at which point they had to undertake two years' military service as 'ephebes'. Demosthenes' cases first came to trial *c*. 364/3.

19. *speeches attacking them*: Five of these speeches survive: three against Aphobus (*Orations* 27–9) and two against Onetor (*Orations* 30–31).

20. *'by running risks ... effort'*: A very loose quotation of Thucydides 1.18.3.

21. *left the assembly ... met another orator ... gifts wither away*: Plutarch records a briefer version of this incident in *Old men in politics* 795d, where the interlocutor is an unnamed old man who had once heard Pericles speak (some seventy years earlier); his words there are also more encouraging to Demosthenes. The story also occurs in *Lives of the ten orators* 845a.

22. *On another occasion ...* : Much of the material in chs. 7–11 is also found in Plutarch's general discussion of political speeches in *Political advice* 801c–804b. The two passages are probably based on the same sources, though Plutarch does not seem to have had access to Demetrius of Phaleron's work when composing *Political advice*.

23. *drunken sailors*: Possibly a reference to Demades, who had been a sailor (see n. 25).

24. *underground study ... even if he wanted to*: Other, similar
    stories, such as that he used to practise speaking on the seashore
    above the sound of the waves, are recorded in *Lives of the ten
    orators* 844d–f; cf. the story that Euripides used to retreat to a
    cave by the sea (Satyrus of Callatis, *Life of Euripides* 62–4),
    though this is put down to his wish to avoid the public.

25. *Demades*: A powerful orator and contemporary of Demosthenes.
    After Athens' defeat at the battle of Chaeronea in 338 he
    favoured cooperation with Macedonia. He was famous for his
    skills in improvisation, and a collection of witty sayings ascribed
    to him has survived (see *Phocion* 1).

26. *Python of Byzantium ... abuse against them*: A quotation from
    On the crown 136. In 343 Philip sent Python to Athens with the
    offer to renegotiate the Peace of Philocrates which had been
    agreed between Athens and Macedon three years earlier. Python's
    speech in the assembly included attacks on Philip's opponents in
    Athens; in the debate which followed Demosthenes replied by
    opposing both Python and Philip. Persuaded by Demosthenes
    the Athenian assembly approved an amendment to the Peace
    which demanded Philip's surrender of Amphipolis, and sent an
    embassy to Philip to inform him. Philip rejected it out of hand.
    See the speech preserved as *Oration* 7 in the Demosthenic corpus
    (*On Halonnesus*), 18–26.

27. *Lamachus of Myrrhine ... from the festival*: The incident took
    place in 324 at Olympia when Nicanor, Alexander's envoy, con-
    veyed the latter's wishes that the Greek cities take back their
    exiles.

28. *Eratosthenes*: Eratosthenes of Cyrene was a prominent scientist
    and intellectual active in Alexandria in the third century BC.
    Among his interests was literary criticism.

29. *Demetrius of Phaleron*: A Peripatetic philosopher (i.e., a fol-
    lower of the school of Aristotle) and governor of Athens on
    behalf of Cassander from 317 to 307 (see *Demetrius* 8). He
    wrote numerous literary works and is frequently cited in *Dem-
    osthenes*.

30. *'By earth ... floods'*: This line is also quoted in *Lives of the ten
    orators* 845b, where the writers of Middle Comedy Antiphanes
    and Timocles (fragments 288 and 41 K–A respectively) are said
    to have used it to make fun of Demosthenes' habit of swearing
    pompous oaths. The oath may originally have been taken from a
    tragedy or satyr play (it is listed as *TrGF* II fragment 123a). A
    similar oath is found in Aristophanes, *Birds* 194.

31. *'In taking ... take up'*: Antiphanes (see n. 15) fragment 167 K–A.

32. *speech on Halonnesus ... 'retake' it as a right*: *On Halonnesus* 7, though the speech, which is preserved in the Demosthenic corpus (*Oration* 7), is not in fact by Demosthenes. Halonessus (now Agios Efstratios) was a small island lying south-west of Lemnos (not to be confused with modern Alonnisos).

33. *'Athena ... lessons from a sow!'*: Apparently this was a proverbial expression (see Theocritus 5.23).

34. *Phocian War*: That is, the Third Sacred War (356–346), in which Athens and Sparta backed Phocis against Thebes, the Delphic Amphictyony (a group of states in central Greece that controlled the sanctuary) and, eventually, Philip of Macedon. Athens narrowly prevented Philip from seizing Thermopylae in 352. Plutarch's phrasing here is drawn from Demosthenes, *On the crown* 18.

35. *speeches he made against Philip ... connected with it*: Plutarch is thinking especially of the *Olynthiacs* and the *Philippics*, as well as *On the peace* and *On the Chersonese*.

36. *prosecution of Meidias ... thirty-two*: The speech *Against Meidias* survives and contains the information about Demosthenes' age (section 154). The alleged crime, Meidias' assault of Demosthenes, took place in 348.

37. *'He was not ... opponents'*: *Iliad* 20.467, where Homer describes Achilles' refusal to spare or have pity on his defeated opponents.

38. *king of Persia ... King Philip ... distinction*: See chs. 16 and 20 for the respect of Philip and Darius for Demosthenes.

39. *Cassander ... Demetrius*: Cassander, son of Antipater, controlled Athens from 317 to 307 by installing Demetrius of Phaleron as governor. In 307 Demetrius Poliorcetes, the Demetrius mentioned here and the subject of a Life by Plutarch, took Athens and claimed to have liberated it (see *Demetrius* 8).

40. *unchangeable harmony ... start*: For a similar musical metaphor, see *Pericles* 15.

41. *in the one ... taxation*: That is, the speech *Against Leptines* (*Oration* 20).

42. *Thucydides*: Not Thucydides son of Olorus, the historian, but Thucydides son of Melesias, the aristocratic statesman and opponent of Pericles (see *Pericles* 11 and 14).

43. *Ephialtes ... Aristides ... Cimon*: Fifth-century Athenian leaders, famous for their integrity. Plutarch wrote Lives of the latter two. Cf. *Cimon* 10, where the same three men are mentioned as uncorrupted.

44. *overwhelmed by the Persian gold . . . torrent*: See chs. 20 and 25. Plutarch's phrasing here perhaps echoes Aeschines 3.173.

45. *Theopompus*: See *Dion*, n. 56. One manuscript here has 'Theophrastus', but 'Theopompus', the reading of most manuscripts, makes perfectly good sense. Theopompus' Book 10 focused on Athenian demagogues, whom he tended to present in a negative way.

46. *in the case of Antiphon*: According to Demosthenes (*On the crown* 132–3), a certain Antiphon had been bribed by Philip to burn the Athenian dockyards in the late 340s.

47. *Council of the Areopagus*: After the reforms of Ephialtes (462), the council which met on the Areopagus functioned only as a court dealing with cases of homicide, arson and wounding, and some religious matters. In the 340s it seems to have gained greater influence and powers. It should not be confused with the democratic Council of 500 mentioned in ch. 22.

48. *Apollodorus . . . against Stephanus and Phormion*: Apollodorus was the son of the banker Pasion and was extremely wealthy. The speech *Against Timotheus in a matter of debt* (*Oration* 49) is now thought to have been composed by Apollodorus himself. He brought several suits against Phormion, the man who had managed his father's business after his death. Demosthenes wrote one speech in defence of Phormion (*Oration* 36), but later wrote for, or assisted Apollodorus to write, two speeches *Against Stephanus*, in which the real target was Phormion (*Orations* 44 and 45).

49. *from the same knife-shop*: Apparently a punning reference to the family business (see ch. 4).

50. *thirty-two or thirty-three years of age*: The best manuscripts give Demosthenes' age here as twenty-seven or twenty-eight. But the older age, recorded in another manuscript, fits better with what we know of the chronology of the speeches.

51. *Idomeneus*: Idomeneus of Lampsacus, a philosopher of the late fourth and early third centuries BC, who wrote a work, now lost, *On popular leaders*.

52. *visited Macedonia as one of a delegation of ten*: There were in fact two embassies, with the same participants, both in 346. The peace-treaty that was negotiated with Philip was known as the Peace of Philocrates, after one of its main Athenian proponents. The peace was later seen as a disaster at Athens and Philocrates fled into exile. Demosthenes in his *On the false embassy* and Aeschines in his *On the embassy* later traded accusations over their respective roles in the negotiations.

53. *Demosthenes could not refrain from belittling ... a king*: This seems to be derived from Aeschines, *On the embassy* 51–2 and esp. 112, where, according to Aeschines, Demosthenes made some such remark before the assembly in Athens, but denied it to Philip's face.

54. *he urged ... invade Euboea*: The speech in question is Demosthenes' *Third Philippic* of 341. The Athenians intervened in Euboea in 341 and deposed Philistides, tyrant of Oreus, and Cleitarchus, tyrant of Eretria.

55. *the Social War*: 357–355, when Chios, Cos, Rhodes and Byzantium revolted against Athens.

56. *relieving both cities*: In 340.

57. *an army of 15,000 infantry ... to pay these soldiers*: Closely based on Demosthenes, *On the crown* 237.

58. *persuade Thebes to join the alliance*: Theban territory also lay on the direct route to Athens; securing her alliance meant that the war might be kept out of Attica.

59. *Phocian War*: That is, the Third Sacred War (n. 34).

60. *petty quarrels ... between the two cities*: Plutarch may have in mind the dispute over possession of Oropus, which had been taken by Thebes in 366 (ch. 5 and n. 16).

61. *Amphissa*: The Delphic Amphictyony had accused Amphissa of cultivating sacred land and in winter 340/39 declared war (known to modern historians as the Fourth Sacred War). When Amphissa refused to comply, Philip was delegated to use force. This enabled him to occupy Amphissa and Elateia in the autumn of 339.

62. *Elateia*: The principal town of Phocis, which controlled the route south to Boeotia and central Greece. Its fall to Philip in 339 was a decisive moment. In his speech *On the crown* Demosthenes describes the mood in Athens when news arrived that Elateia had been taken by Philip; this paragraph is partly based on sections 169–79 of that speech, as is much of chs. 17–21.

63. *making overtures for peace*: Spring 338.

64. *Sibylline books*: Collections of prophecies of various dates, ascribed to a legendary prophetess or prophetesses called Sibyl. Sibylline prophecies are referred to as early as the fifth century BC, and were well known in Rome.

65. *Douris*: Douris of Samos (*c.* 340–270 BC), philosopher and historian, and also tyrant of Samos. His huge *Macedonian history* survives only in quotations in later authors. Plutarch cites him frequently in his Greek Lives, sometimes criticizing him for an over-dramatic approach, e.g., *Pericles* 28 and *Alcibiades* 32.

66. *Thermodon . . . Amazon in his arms*: In mythology the Amazons were said to have invaded Greece and been defeated by Theseus. This Thermodon must be the personification of the River Thermodon in the country of the Amazons (cf. *Pompey* 35).

67. *the battle*: At Chaeronea, in summer 338. Philip won a decisive victory over the forces of Thebes and Athens.

68. *to risk . . . single day*: Based on Aeschines, *Against Ctesiphon* 148.

69. *Philip died soon afterwards*: He was assassinated in 336 (see *Alexander* 10).

70. *Council*: The democratic Council of 500, whose members were chosen by lot from the demes (districts) of Attica.

71. *reported by Aeschines*: In *Against Ctesiphon* 77.

72. *treated them with such tolerance and humanity*: After his victory Philip had freed his Athenian prisoners without ransom and had offered the city generous peace terms.

73. *find consolation . . . dignity*: Some editors think that there is a lacuna in the text at this point.

74. *I believe . . . misfortunes of the individual*: Plutarch commends statesmen who do not show emotion in the face of private grief (see, e.g., *Pericles* 36, *Brutus* 15, *Aemilius* 36 and *Comparison of Aemilius and Timoleon* 2). In his treatise *On tranquillity of mind* (469a ff.), Plutarch advises that one should, when in misfortune, focus one's mind on the good things that one still possesses.

75. *attacked the Macedonian garrison . . . killed many of them*: In 335. The Macedonian garrison had been installed on the Cadmeia after the battle of Chaeronea.

76. *wrote letters to the Macedonian king's generals in Asia . . . declare war on Alexander*: Diodorus 17.3 and 5 records that the Athenians entered into secret communication with Attalus, one of the two generals commanding Macedonian forces in northwestern Asia Minor. Attalus was assassinated soon after on Alexander's orders.

77. *Margites*: An idiot, the hero of a mock epic. The remark may have been intended to puncture Alexander's own self-identification with the Homeric hero Achilles. Plutarch's source is Aeschines, *Against Ctesiphon* 160.

78. *Thebans . . . lost their city*: Thebes was razed to the ground in October 335 (see *Alexander* 11).

79. *Polyeuctus, Ephialtes, Lycurgus, Moerocles, Damon, Callisthenes and Charidemus*: The best known of these to posterity were Lycurgus the famous orator, and Charidemus and Ephialtes, both

soldiers who were banished from Athens and later took service under Darius. The latter was killed at the siege of Halicarnassus, the former executed by Darius before the battle of Issus for opposing offensive operations.

80. *lone wolf of Macedon*: Lone wolves, as opposed to those that hunt in packs, were considered particularly dangerous (see Aristotle, *History of animals* 594a). The term was evidently used here as an insult.

81. *Aristobulus of Cassandreia*: Aristobulus accompanied Alexander on his campaigns in the East and later wrote a history about him, which is now lost. Plutarch used it in his *Life of Alexander*.

82. *eight men . . . terms of peace for the city*: See *Phocion* 17 and n. 40 there.

83. *when Agis the Spartan organized a revolt against Macedonia*: While Alexander was fighting in Asia, Agis III, king of Sparta, launched a war against Macedonia (331), with funds from Persia. He was defeated by Antipater and killed at Megalopolis in the Peloponnese.

84. *indictment against Ctesiphon . . . archonship of Aristophon*: In spring 336 Ctesiphon had proposed that Demosthenes should be awarded a golden crown for public services. Aeschines denounced the proposal as illlegal and instituted a prosecution of Ctesiphon. But the case remained in abeyance for over six years (not ten, as Plutarch says), and it was possibly the defeat of Agis which encouraged Demosthenes' enemies to proceed in late summer 330, during the archonship of Aristophon (that is, in the year when Aristophon held the office of 'eponymous' archon, one of the chief magistracies of Athens). The trial was the occasion for one of Demosthenes' most famous orations, *On the crown*, in which he defended his own record. In dating the initial indictment to the archonship of Chaerondas (338/7), Plutarch has followed the spurious version of the indictment transmitted with Demosthenes' speech (*On the crown* 54); the indictment was in fact made in the archonship of Phrynichus (337/6).

85. *a fifth of their votes*: Accusers in public trials who did not obtain at least a fifth of the votes had to pay a fine of 1,000 drachmas and were debarred from bringing similar cases. Aeschines went into voluntary exile.

86. *Harpalus*: A Macedonian nobleman who was in charge of Alexander's treasury. In 324, expecting punishment for embezzlement, he fled Asia, taking with him a huge sum of money and a force of mercenaries. He had earlier been granted Athenian citizenship

for lavish gifts to the city but was now at first refused entry to Athens. Later, however, when he appeared as a suppliant, he was allowed in. When envoys from Antipater and Olympias demanded his surrender, Harpalus was arrested on Demosthenes' proposal and his money deposited for safe-keeping in the acropolis. He escaped soon after and fled, whereupon it was discovered that half the treasure was missing.

87. *'won't you give a hearing . . . cup in his hand?'*: The joke alludes to the custom at Greek drinking-parties whereby the cup was passed from hand to hand, and the person holding it had the right to speak or sing a song.

88. *He tells us*: In the second of the letters attributed to Demosthenes (*Epistle* 2.17).

89. *owl . . . snake*: Both sacred to Athena.

90. *if . . . he had been offered . . . death*: This recalls the well-known story of the 'choice of Heracles', where the hero must choose between the easy path that leads to destruction and the hard path to virtue.

91. *Alexander died*: In Babylon in June 323. See *Alexander* 75–6.

92. *Phylarchus*: A third-century historian. Polybius (2.56) criticized him for love of the sensational in his work.

93. *more honourably than Alcibiades . . . welcome him back*: In 408 or 407, as the tide of the Peloponnesian War flowed against Athens, the Athenian general Alcibiades was recalled from exile. After having first aided the Spartans and Persians against Athens, he had later taken command of the fleet, and had won a series of much needed victories; Demosthenes implies here that the Athenians really had no choice but to recall such a successful commander (see *Alcibiades* 32–3). In the *Comparison of Demosthenes and Cicero* 4, Plutarch notes that Demosthenes behaved better in exile than Alcibiades, who betrayed his country.

94. *battle of Crannon*: The forces of Athens, Aetolia and their allies were decisively defeated in Thessaly by the Macedonian generals Antipater and Craterus. A passage in the *Life of Camillus* (ch. 19) dates the battle to 7th Metageitnion (i.e., August) 322. The Athenian fleet was defeated at Amorgos around the same time. Even before Crannon the tide had turned against the Greeks, as Macedonian reinforcements had crossed from Asia and raised the siege of Lamia (see *Phocion* 26).

95. *Boedromion . . . garrison entered Munychia . . . in Pyanepsion Demosthenes met his death*: In *Phocion* 28 Plutarch dates the entry of the garrison into Munychia, a strategic hill overlooking

the Piraeus, to the 20th of Boedromion, that is, October 322. Demosthenes' death took place just under one month later, on the 16th of Pyanepsion (see ch. 30).

96. *Cleonae*: For the location, see *Timoleon*, n. 8.

97. *Calauria*: An island in the Saronic Gulf (the modern Poros); it is some 12 miles from the island of Aegina. The temple of Poseidon there seems to have been considered particularly inviolable.

98. *speaking like the . . . oracle*: In other words, expressing your real sentiments.

99. *Creon . . . without burying it*: The allusion is to Sophocles' *Antigone*, in which Creon decrees that the body of Polynices, Antigone's brother, is to be left unburied.

100. *breathed his last*: The phrase probably contains an allusion to Orestes' words in Euripides, *Orestes* 1171. Readers who knew the play would find significance in this quotation: Orestes was vowing to do what was right (take vengeance on the murderers of his father), even if it should cost him his life. If not, he claimed, 'I will breathe my last *as a free man*.' By recalling this speech of Orestes, then, Plutarch suggests the nobility of Demosthenes' death.

101. *what he had swallowed was gold*: The notion that Demosthenes might have swallowed gold reinforces the sense of his love of wealth and corruptibility. Swallowing gold need not be fatal.

102. *Thesmophoria*: An annual festival dedicated to the goddess Demeter and celebrated exclusively by women. At Athens the festival was held in the autumn and lasted three days. The second of the three days involved fasting.

103. *statue in bronze*: In the Athenian agora. Pausanias, writing later in the second century AD, mentions seeing the statue (*Guide to Greece* 1.8).

104. *prytaneum . . . public expense*: The *prytaneum* was the official building of the *prytaneis*, the executive committee of the Council of 500. The grant of the privilege to dine here regularly at public expense (*sitesis*) was a great honour, given to victorious athletes and generals and, from the fourth century, to benefactors of the city. This is the first certain example of the award of *sitesis* on a *hereditary* basis since it had been granted to the descendants of the tyrannicides Harmodius and Aristogeiton some time after the establishment of democracy in 508/7.

105. *If only . . . Ares*: In *Lives of the ten orators* 847a, these lines are ascribed to Demetrius of Magnesia.

106. *arrived in Athens*: Plutarch studied in Athens, probably in the 70s AD. He must subsequently have visited frequently.

107. *Demades ... Perdiccas ... Antipater*: Perdiccas, who had been
     designated supreme commander of Alexander's armies in 323,
     had fought Antipater and others for mastery of the empire, and
     been killed in 321 or 320 (see *Eumenes* 3–8). Demades' embassy
     to Antipater took place in late summer 319. Plutarch gives a
     slightly different version of Demades' death in *Phocion* 30.

PHOCION

Further Reading

Plutarch's Phocion

Bearzot, C., Geiger, J., and Ghilli, L. (eds.), *Plutarco. Vite Parallele:
    Focione–Catone Uticense* (Milan: Biblioteca Universale Rizzoli,
    1993).
Duff, T. E., *Plutarch's Lives: Exploring Virtue and Vice* (Oxford:
    Oxford University Press, 1999), ch. 5.
Lamberton, R., 'Plutarch's Phocion: melodrama of mob and elite in
    occupied Athens', in O. Palagia and S. V. Tracey (eds.), *The Mace-
    donians in Athens 322–229 BC* (Oxford: Oxbow, 2003), pp. 8–13.
Trapp, M. B., 'Socrates, the *Phaedo* and the *Lives* of Phocion and
    Cato the Younger', in A. Pérez Jiménez, J. García López and R.
    Mª Aguilar (eds.), *Plutarco, Platón y Aristóteles* (Madrid: Ediciones
    Clásicas, 1999), pp. 487–99.
Tritle, L. A., 'Plutarch's *Life of Phocion*: An Analysis and Critical
    Report', *ANRW* 2.33.6 (1992), pp. 4258–97.

History

Bearzot, C., *Focione tra storia e trasfigurazione ideale* (Milan: Pub-
    blicazioni dell' Università Cattolica di Milano del Sacro Cuore 37,
    1985).
Gehrke, H.-J., *Phokion. Studien zur Erfassung seiner historischen
    Gestalt* (Zetemata 64) (Munich: Beck, 1976).
Tritle, L. A., *Phocion the Good* (London, New York and Sydney:
    Croom Helm, 1987).

Notes to the Prologue to the Lives of Phocion
and Cato the Younger

1. *Demades the orator*: See *Demosthenes*, n. 25. Demades is often
    contrasted with Phocion in this Life. The saying 'by the time he

came to the helm, the ship of state was already a wreck' (Demades fragment 17 De Falco) is also recorded in *Political advice* 803a.

2. *tongue and stomach*: I.e., Demades was only interested in giving speeches and eating. The comparison of Demades to a dismembered, slaughtered animal is highly charged, as it looks forward to his brutal death in ch. 30.

3. *'Reason ... troubles come'*: Sophocles, *Antigone* 563–4. The speaker is Ismene addressing Creon.

4. *menoeikes*: See, e.g., Homer, *Odyssey* 5.165–6, where the word is applied to wine 'which gladdens the heart'.

5. *Cicero tells us ... dregs of Romulus*: Cicero, *Letter to Atticus* 2.1.8, though Cicero's comment is not directed specifically to Cato's campaign for election to the consulship.

6. *two men may possess the same attribute in different forms*: Plutarch makes this point in *Virtues of women* 243c–d, though with a different set of examples. Here, while accepting the general validity of the proposition that the same virtue may be manifested in different ways in different people, he claims that, in fact, Phocion and Cato were particularly similar.

Notes to the Life of Phocion

7. *Cato's origins ... as shall be described later*: At the start of *Cato the Younger*, which was paired with *Phocion* and immediately followed it.

8. *Idomeneus*: See *Demosthenes*, n. 51. References to his work in Plutarch and elsewhere show that he was fond of this kind of anecdotal material.

9. *Douris*: A historian of the late fourth and early third century (see *Demosthenes*, n. 65).

10. *take his hand from under his cloak*: Keeping one's hands inside the cloak seems to have been seen as a mark of dignity and self-control. Spartan youths were expected to walk this way (Xenophon, *Constitution of the Spartans* 3.4), and a statue of Solon was famously shown in this pose (Demosthenes 19.251, Aeschines 1.25).

11. *public bath ... hard winter*: Phocion's habits are meant to be reminiscent of those of Socrates, who did not normally bathe, wear shoes, or dress warmly (see Plato, *Symposium* 174a and 220b).

12. *Zeno*: Zeno of Citium (335–263 BC), the founder of Stoic philosophy.

13. *Chabrias*: One of Athens' most successful fourth-century generals, active from at least the early 370s to his death at Chios in 357.

14. *what happened at Chios*: In 356 during the Social War (357–355), when Chios, Cos, Rhodes and Byzantium revolted from Athens' Second Confederacy.

15. *sea-battle off Naxos*: In 376. The Athenians under Chabrias defeated a Spartan fleet.

16. *command of the left wing . . . decided*: The role of Phocion, who would only have been twenty-six at the time of the battle of Naxos, may be exaggerated here. Diodorus 15.34.5 names Cedon as the commander of the left wing, and does not mention Phocion. But Cedon was killed in the battle, and it is possible that Phocion, who may have captained a trireme, distinguished himself.

17. *first sea-battle . . . capture of their city*: On Athens' surrender in 404 at the end of the Peloponnesian War, her fleet had been reduced to twelve ships. The Athenian general Conon had defeated the Spartans off Cnidus in 394, but he was then acting as commander of the Persian fleet. Shortly after Naxos the Athenians defeated the Spartans again at sea off Alyzia near Leucas (375).

18. *Great Mysteries*: An initiation festival which began in Athens and ended in Eleusis and took place over nine days between the 15th and 23rd of Boedromion. It included a public procession of initiates in which the god Iacchus was escorted from Athens to Eleusis (see ch. 28).

19. *The battle . . . Boedromion*: September 376. In *Camillus* 19 Plutarch gives the date of the battle of Naxos as 'about the full moon of Boedromion'.

20. *contributions . . . due . . . islands*: From 379/8 onwards Athens built on its bilateral alliances with individual allies to form an organized alliance, known to modern scholars as the Second Athenian Confederacy. An inscription of 377 records a promise not to levy tribute on allies, as the Athenians had done in the fifth century (Harding 35 = R&O 22); instead, sources talk of allied states making voluntary 'contributions' for common defence.

21. '*both a servant . . . Muses*': Archilochus, fragment 1 West. Plutarch has adapted the quotation for his own use; in the original poem, which is quoted also in Athenaeus 627c, Archilochus was talking about himself ('*I am a servant . . .*').

22. *both war and politics . . . addressed as such*: Athena, the patron deity of Athens, had the epithets 'Promachos' (champion) and 'Polias' (guardian of the *polis*).

23. '*A cowardly man . . . "You may croak . . . meal of me"*': This story is also found in Aesop, *Fables* 47 (the coward and the crows).

24. *territorial dispute with Boeotia*: The dispute in question is prob-
    ably that of 366 over Oropus (see the note on *Demosthenes* 5).
    Phocion's reply here exploits the well-known Athenian prejudice
    that Boeotians were stupid.

25. *'The Athenians . . . again'*: Plutarch records the same story in
    Political advice 811a, but there it is Demades, not Demosthenes,
    who is Phocion's interlocutor.

26. *Alexander . . . ten orators should be surrendered to him . . .
    request*: See ch. 17 and *Demosthenes* 23. The episode took place
    in 335 after the sack of Thebes by Alexander.

27. *Archibiades . . . his face*: This description of Archibiades is based
    on Demosthenes' description of him in his speech *Against Conon*
    34.

28. *'you might just as well have shaved this off'*: I.e., not tried to
    cultivate a Spartan appearance if he was not willing to adopt
    their toughness and straightforward way of speaking, but pre-
    ferred to pander to the people.

29. *Phocion was sent out . . . support*: In 348. In response to the
    appeal by Plutarch, tyrant of Eretria, the Athenians sent out an
    expedition to assist him against Cleitarchus, exiled tyrant of
    Eretria, and Callias of Chalcis (see Aeschines, *Against Ctesiphon*
    86–8). It is doubtful whether the expedition was really aimed at
    countering Philip: Plutarch or his source may have projected the
    motivation for the later expedition to Euboea in 341 back to this
    earlier one.

30. *captured by the enemy*: In 348. The Athenians were forced to
    pay 50 talents to ransom the soldiers taken captive, and lost con-
    trol of almost the whole of Euboea.

31. *Philip reached the Hellespont*: In 340.

32. *people of Megara appealed . . . for help*: About 344 or 343. The
    only other evidence for this episode is a brief statement in Dem-
    osthenes' *Fourth Philippic* 8 that at some unspecified date
    'Megara was almost captured'. Cf. also Demosthenes 19.87 and
    295.

33. *two long walls . . . from the city*: Like the Long Walls at Athens.
    Megara had had such walls in the fifth century, but they were
    destroyed in 424 in the Peloponnesian War.

34. *as far away from Athens as possible*: That is, in Boeotia rather
    than in Attica. Demosthenes himself took pride in this (see his
    speech *On the crown*, 195 and 230).

35. *when Athens was defeated*: At Chaeronea in Boeotia in 338,
    when Philip crushed the armies of Athens and Thebes.

36. *congress for all the states*: Philip organized a meeting in Corinth, in which he set up an alliance, known to modern scholars as the League of Corinth; members swore not to oppose Macedonia and not to alter the constitution of other members.

37. *When Philip was assassinated*: In 336 (see *Alexander* 10). For Athenian rejoicing at the news, see *Demosthenes* 22.

38. *'Foolhardy man ... savage?'*: *Odyssey* 9.494, where Odysseus' comrades urge him not to insult the Cyclops as they make their escape.

39. *After Thebes had been destroyed*: By Alexander in 335 (see *Alexander* 11).

40. *Phocion then rose to his feet ... resentment against the Athenians*: Contrast *Demosthenes* 23, where it is Demades who goes to Alexander and, on the basis of personal friendship with him, successfully pleads for the lives of the orators. In Arrian, *Anabasis* 1.10.3, and Diodorus 15.15 it is Demades who proposes the motion to send an embassy; in Diodorus, Phocion is actually ejected from the assembly for saying that the orators ought to sacrifice themselves for the city. In *Phocion* Plutarch consistently chooses the version more favourable to the subject of the Life.

41. *chairein*: Literally, 'rejoice', a common way to start a letter, in the form, e.g., 'X [bids] Y rejoice'.

42. *Chares*: Originally from Mytilene, he was prominent at Alexander's court, and later his master of ceremonies. He wrote a work entitled *Histories of Alexander*, which seems to have contained anecdotes of court life. He is not to be confused with the Athenian general, Chares, mentioned in chs. 5 and 14.

43. *sent Craterus back to Macedonia*: In 324. Craterus had been ordered to bring back some of Alexander's veterans to Macedonia.

44. *revenue ... he might choose*: A gift typical of a Persian king and reminiscent of the gift of three cities made to Themistocles (see *Themistocles* 29).

45. *Spartan discipline*: Spartan males underwent a tough programme of state-regulated education, known as the *agoge*, from the age of seven, designed to prepare them for life as a soldier. Plutarch discusses it in *Lycurgus* 16–21. Xenophon's sons are the only other known examples of foreigners allowed entry to the *agoge*.

46. *Lycurgus ... state-controlled dining halls*: Lycurgus was the semi-mythical founder of the Spartan constitution. (He is to be distinguished from the Athenian politician of the same name, who is mentioned in this Life.) One of the features of the Spartan

system was that all adult male citizens, including the two kings, had to eat in common messes.

47. *send him triremes*: Probably in 333, when Alexander was campaigning in Asia Minor and the Persian fleet was active in the Aegean (see Curtius Rufus 3.1.19–20).

48. *Harpalus, Alexander's treasurer*: He absconded in 324 with large sums of money and sought refuge in Athens. The problem of what to do with him caused great debate (see *Demosthenes* 25 and the note there).

49. *When Pythonice died*: In fact, Pythonice's death occurred while Harpalus was still in Asia.

50. *broke the news of Alexander's death in Athens*: In 323.

51. *the Greek War*: Of 323–2 BC, often known as the Lamian War because the allied Greek forces besieged Antipater, Alexander's regent, in the town of Lamia in south-eastern Thessaly (see *Demosthenes* 27–8). The term 'Greek War' would normally mean 'war against the Greeks' (cf. 'Peloponnesian War', 'Persian War'), but its use here, paralleled in inscriptions and in Diodorus, reflects contemporary Athenian attempts to present the war as Panhellenic and so induce Sparta to join in.

52. *the force which Leosthenes had assembled*: Acting as a private citizen, Leosthenes had taken command of 8,000 mercenaries who had returned from Asia to the Peloponnese. He was elected Athenian general for 324/3 and 323/2, and on Alexander's death successfully advanced into central Greece, where the Aetolians supplied another 7,000 troops. The Athenians dispatched more troops to him, including both citizen hoplites and mercenaries.

53. *'good enough for a sprint . . . hoplites'*: In the pseudo-Plutarchan *Lives of the ten orators* 846e, the same statement is attributed to Demosthenes.

54. *when Leosthenes was killed*: In winter 323/2, while laying siege to Lamia.

55. *When the Athenians were eager to invade Boeotia*: It is not clear when exactly this was; the period after the battle of Crannon is perhaps more plausible than the period before.

56. *under the age of sixty . . . disagreement*: Citizens between the ages of fifty and sixty were liable for military service, but only in defence of Attica itself.

57. *Micion . . . Rhamnus*: It is not clear whether Micion's landing was made before or after the defeat of the Greek allied army at the battle of Crannon, which Plutarch mentions in the next

chapter. Plutarch's *Sayings of kings and commanders* 188e–f places it before.

58. *battle was fought at Crannon ... Greeks were beaten*: In Thessaly in August 322 (see *Demosthenes* 28). The Greek fleet was also defeated at Amorgos around the same time.

59. *Phocion was sent to Antipater*: In fact, we know from Diodorus 18.18 that Demades also took part in the delegation to Antipater; in that account, it is to Demades that the people turn, and Phocion is mentioned only as an afterthought.

60. *Cadmeia*: The acropolis of Thebes.

61. *Antipater told the Athenians ... Lamia*: Antipater's statement is also recorded by Diodorus 18.18.3.

62. *Xenocrates*: Then head of the Academy where he had succeeded Plato and Speusippus.

63. *property qualification*: Diodorus 18.18.4 records that the property qualification was set at 2,000 drachmas. This severely restricted the influence of the poor, but democratic institutions were not abolished.

64. *Munychia*: A strategically important hill to the east of the main harbour of Piraeus. The Macedonian garrison fortified it, perhaps for the first time.

65. *Callimedon*: See *Demosthenes* 27.

66. *twentieth day of ... Boedromion ... celebrated*: October 322.

67. *Mysteries ... Iacchus ... Eleusis*: See n. 18.

68. *mystic apparitions ... into the hearts of their enemies*: E.g., before the victory over the Persians at Salamis (*Themistocles* 15, itself based on Herodotus 8.65).

69. *'heights of Artemis'*: There was a sanctuary of Artemis at Munychia.

70. *Cantharus*: The main harbour of Piraeus. Candidates for initiation in the Mysteries had to offer piglets, presumably for sacrifice; both candidate and piglet were ritually purified in the sea. Cf. Aeschines, *Against Ctesiphon* 130, which refers to the death of an initiate in 339; the ancient scholiast explains that he was killed by a shark while undergoing purification.

71. *twelve thousand*: Diodorus 18.18.5 gives a figure of 22,000 poor Athenians deprived of their citizen rights.

72. *which I have described elsewhere*: Demosthenes 28–30.

73. *Ceraunian mountains or Cape Taenarus ... Greek cities*: Cape Taenarus is at the southern tip of the Peloponnese and the Ceraunian mountains are in Epirus; these exiles were, then, in effect banned from mainland Greece.

74. *Antigonus*: In the version in *Demosthenes* 31, it is Perdiccas to whom Demades' letter had been addressed.

75. *blood ... filled them*: The image of the blood of his murdered son drenching Demades' clothing suggests the image of perverted sacrifice as in, e.g., Aeschylus' *Oresteia*, and fulfils the notion, introduced in ch. 1, of Demades as a sacrificial victim.

76. *Antipater appointed Polyperchon ... Cassander second in command*: Antipater died in 319 at the age of seventy-nine. Cassander was his son; Polyperchon was a contemporary of Antipater and had held command under Alexander.

77. *Nicanor*: Possibly identical with the Nicanor who commanded Alexander's fleet in 334, or with a relative of Aristotle of the same name, who proclaimed Alexander's Exiles Decree in 324.

78. *president of the games*: In Greek, *agonothetes*. The exact role envisaged here is unclear, but the funding of festivals by a foreign general was unprecedented.

79. *the king*: That is, Philip III Arrhidaeus, who succeeded Alexander in 323, together with Alexander's infant son, Alexander IV, though neither exercised power. Philip suffered from some kind of mental disability and was used as a pawn by those pressing competing claims to Alexander's empire until his murder in 317 (see *Alexander* 10, 77 and *Eumenes* 3, 12 and 13).

80. *Nicanor ... began to surround Piraeus with a trench*: Winter 319/18.

81. *Hagnonides*: On whose behalf Phocion had earlier intervened with Antipater: see ch. 29.

82. *Callimedon and Charicles*: Supporters of Antipater, and therefore hostile to Polyperchon (see chs. 21–2, 27 and *Demosthenes* 27).

83. *Deinarchus of Corinth*: Denounced by Demosthenes as a traitor who supported Philip (*On the crown* 295). He should be distinguished from the Deinarchus, originally from Corinth, who was an orator and speech-writer in Athens and a supporter of Cassander's agent, Demetrius of Phaleron, and who died *c*. 290. There is a third Deinarchus of Corinth mentioned in *Timoleon* 21 and 24.

84. *Hegemon*: Probably to be identified with the Hegemon mentioned by Demosthenes (*On the crown* 285), alongside Demades, as an advocate of accommodation with Macedonia at the time of Chaeronea.

85. *Cerameicus*: An area of Athens, north-west of the Agora, through which the road from the north-west passed.

86. *'I propose the penalty of death for my political actions'*: According to Athenian law, in cases where the penalty was not legally

fixed, the accuser proposed a penalty and the accused had the right to propose a counter-penalty; the court then chose between them. This was the procedure which was followed at the trial of Socrates. In general, Plutarch constructs the death of Phocion in such a way as to recall that of Socrates.

87. *when they were in the prison . . . the fee*: The scene of Phocion's death by hemlock while in prison, surrounded by his friends, is reminiscent of that of Socrates, as described in Plato's *Phaedo*.

88. *Phocion's death . . . Munychion*: May, probably 318.

89. *not to postpone the execution . . . while a festival was being cele-brated*: There is an unspoken contrast here with Socrates' execution, which, barbaric as it was, was delayed for thirty days to avoid a festival (in that case, the visit of the sacred delegation to Delos). See Plato, *Phaedo* 58a–c, and Xenophon, *Memorabilia* 4.8.

90. *set up a statue of him and gave his bones a public burial*: In 317, the year after Phocion's death, when Demetrius of Phaleron had been installed in Athens by Cassander. The poorest Athenians were again excluded from citizen rights (the property qualifica-tion was now set at 1,000 drachmas).

91. *reminded the Greeks . . . of Socrates . . . almost identical*: See nn. 86, 87 and 89. In the *Life of Cato the Younger*, which is paired with *Phocion*, parallels with Socrates' death are developed fur-ther.

ALEXANDER

Further Reading

Plutarch's Alexander

Buszard, B., 'Caesar's ambition: a combined reading of Plutarch's *Alexander–Caesar* and *Pyrrhus–Marius*', *Transactions of the Ameri-can Philological Association* 138 (2008), pp. 185–215.

Cook, B., 'Plutarch's use of λέγεται: narrative design and source in *Alexander*', *Greek, Roman and Byzantine Studies* 42 (2001), pp. 329–60.

Duff, T. E., *Plutarch's Lives: Exploring Virtue and Vice* (Oxford: Oxford University Press, 1999), pp. 14–22.

Hamilton, J. R., *Plutarch, Alexander: A Commentary* (Oxford: Oxford University Press, 1969; 2nd edn, London: Bristol Classical Press 1999).

Hammond, N. G. L., *Sources for Alexander the Great: An Analysis of Plutarch's 'Life' and Arrian's 'Anabasis Alexandrou'* (Cambridge: Cambridge University Press, 1993).

Mossman, J. M., 'Tragedy and epic in Plutarch's *Alexander*', *Journal of Hellenic Studies* 108 (1988), pp. 83–93; reprinted in B. Scardigli (ed.), *Essays on Plutarch's Lives* (Oxford: Oxford University Press, 1995), pp. 209–28.

Pelling, C. B. R., 'Plutarch, *Alexander* and *Caesar*: Two New Fragments', *CQ* NS 23 (1973), pp. 343–4.

Sansone, D., 'Plutarch, Alexander and the Discovery of Naphtha', *Greek, Roman and Byzantine Studies* 21 (1980), pp. 63–74.

Stadter, P. A., 'Anecdotes and the thematic structure of Plutarchean biography', in T. E. Duff (ed.), *Oxford Readings in Ancient Biography* (Oxford: Oxford University Press, forthcoming).

Wardman, A. E., 'Plutarch and Alexander', *CQ* NS 5 (1955), pp. 96–107.

Whitmarsh, T., 'Alexander's Hellenism and Plutarch's textualism', *CQ* NS 52 (2002), pp. 174–92.

History

Bosworth, A. B., *Conquest and Empire: The Reign of Alexander the Great* (Cambridge: Cambridge University Press, 1988).

Bosworth, A. B., and Baynham, E. J. (eds.), *Alexander the Great in Fact and Fiction* (Oxford: Oxford University Press, 2000).

Green, P., *Alexander of Macedon, 356–323 BC: A Historical Biography* (Berkeley: University of California Press, 1991).

Hammond, N. G. L., *Alexander the Great: King, Commander and Statesman* (Bristol: Bristol Classical Press, 1981; 2nd edn 1989).

Hammond, N. G. L., *The Genius of Alexander the Great* (London: Duckworth, 1997).

Heckel, W., *The Conquests of Alexander the Great* (Cambridge: Cambridge University Press, 2008).

Heckel, W., and Yardley, J. C., *Alexander the Great: Historical Sources in Translation* (Oxford: Blackwell, 2004).

Lane-Fox, R., *Alexander the Great* (London: Allen Lane, 1973).

O'Brien, J. M., *Alexander the Great, The Invisible Enemy: A Biography* (London and New York: Routledge, 1992).

Pearson, L., *The Lost Histories of Alexander the Great* (American Philological Association: Philological Monographs, 1960).

Roisman, J. (ed.), *Brill's Companion to Alexander the Great* (Leiden and Boston: Brill, 2002).

Stoneman, R., *Alexander the Great* (London: Routledge, 1997).

Worthington, I. (ed.), *Alexander the Great: A Reader* (London: Routledge, 2003).

Notes to the Life of Alexander

1. *Caranus*: The legendary first king of Macedonia according to one tradition (e.g., Theopompus, *FGrHist* 115 F 393).
2. *Aeacus*: The legendary king of Aegina and grandfather of Achilles.
3. *betrothed himself to her*: The marriage took place in 357 or earlier. Philip was polygamous and had already been married several times before. His marriages served dynastic purposes; the one with Olympias cemented an alliance with the Molossian royal house in Epirus.
4. *Aristander of Telmessus*: Prominent later as a seer (see chs. 14, 25, 33, 50, 52, 57).
5. *Klodones and Mimallones*: These seem to be Macedonian names for Bacchantes, female followers of Dionysus. See Callimachus fragment 503 Pfeiffer; Strabo 10.3.10; and Ovid, *Art of love* 1.541.
6. *threskeuein*: Plutarch associates the Greek verb *threskeuein* ('worship') with *Thressai* ('Thracian women').
7. *'making Hera jealous of me'*: I.e., implying that Alexander's father was the god Zeus. Hera was Zeus' wife.
8. *sixth day ... temple of Artemis at Ephesus was burned down*: That is, 20 July 356 BC. Miraculous stories were often attached to the births of great men in antiquity; at any rate, it will have suited Macedonian propaganda to associate Alexander's birth with the fire which destroyed the temple of Artemis. Cf. the notes on chs. 4 and 35.
9. *goddess ... birth of Alexander*: The goddess Artemis was thought to preside over childbirth.
10. *Magi*: See *Artaxerxes*, n. 15.
11. *poise of the neck ... face and chest*: Plutarch seems to assume knowledge here of what was known as 'physiognomics', that is, the theory that character could be deduced from appearance.
12. *sweet-smelling ... permeated the clothes he wore*: A sweet smell was regarded as a mark of divinity (e.g., Euripides, *Hippolytus* 1392); this detail probably derives from pro-Alexander propaganda. Aristoxenus was a pupil of Aristotle, and so roughly contemporary with Alexander.
13. *Theophrastus' ideas*: Theophrastus was a pupil of Aristotle and author of numerous scientific treatises, including two on botany.

14. *heat . . . fond of drinking*: Plutarch is here drawing on the theory that the body's mix ('temperament') of the elements of cold and dry, hot and wet, affected character. Alexander, whose birth was announced by fire (chs. 2–3), will later in the Life be particularly associated with heat (chs. 35, 38, 77) and with excessive drinking, which Plutarch links to the god Dionysus (ch. 13).

15. *energetic*: The term translated 'energetic' here (*thymoeides*) is Platonic. It refers to that part of the soul which is unreasoning but from which necessary emotions arise; it suggests energy, ambition and also anger – passions that are vital spurs to action but which, when not controlled by reason, can lead to megalomania and obsession.

16. *pancration*: A violent form of athletic contest combining wrestling and boxing, in which only biting and scratching were banned.

17. *attendant*: In Greek *paidagogos*; normally a servant or slave who accompanied and watched over a child, though Leonidas was plainly of higher status than the word implies.

18. *Peleus . . . Achilles . . . Phoenix*: Peleus was Achilles' father and Phoenix helped bring him up. Phoenix is called Achilles' *paidagogos* in, e.g., Plato, *Republic* 390e, but he was, like Leonidas, of noble birth.

19. *13 talents*: Thessaly was known for its fine horses, but this is a stupendous sum.

20. *'The rudder's guidance and the bit's restraint'*: From an unknown play by Sophocles (*TrGF* IV fragment 869). Plutarch cites the same line in *Dialogue on love* 767e, and seems to allude to it in *On Isis and Osiris* 369c and *Political advice* 801d.

21. *sent for Aristotle*: In 343, when Alexander was thirteen. Aristotle was in fact not yet very well known.

22. *'casket copy'*: See ch. 26.

23. *Philistus*: Author of a history of Sicily (see *Pelopidas* 34 and n. 63, *Dion* 11 and n. 27).

24. *Anaxarchus*: Cf. ch. 28.

25. *Xenocrates*: He became head of the Academy at Athens in 339 but declined to accompany Alexander on his expedition to Asia. See also *Phocion* 4 and 27.

26. *Dandamis and Calanus*: See chs. 65 and 69.

27. *expedition against Byzantium*: In 340 BC (see *Phocion* 14).

28. *Maedi*: A Thracian tribe.

29. *battle of Chaeronea*: In 338, where Philip smashed Theban and Athenian resistance, and thereby established control of most of mainland Greece(see *Demosthenes* 20 and *Phocion* 16).

30. *Sacred Band*: An elite Theban infantry unit (see *Pelopidas* 18–19).

31. *decided to marry*: The marriage probably took place in 337. Philip had not divorced Alexander's mother, Olympias: Macedonian tradition did not require the king to be monogamous.

32. *legitimate heir to the throne*: This probably means one born of a Macedonian mother, unlike Alexander, whose mother, Olympias, came from Epirus. At any rate, a marriage with Cleopatra threatened Alexander's prospects of succession.

33. *Demaratus*: He had recently been sent by the Corinthians to assist Timoleon in Sicily (see *Timoleon* 21, 24, 27, where Plutarch calls him Demaretus).

34. *persuaded him to return*: It is not clear how long Alexander remained in exile. It may have been several years.

35. *Pixodarus ... military alliance*: Pixodarus may have wanted to ally himself to Philip in view of the latter's planned invasion. He later withdrew his marriage offer and married his daughter to a Persian, Orontopates. Pixodarus died in 335, before Alexander's invasion, and was succeeded by Orontopates.

36. *Arrhidaeus*: An illegitimate son of Philip by Philinna of Larissa. He later succeeded Alexander (see *Alexander* 77 and *Eumenes* 3). The fact that Alexander could believe the story suggests how precarious he thought his position had become. Philip's wife Cleopatra gave birth to a girl shortly before his death.

37. *went to Alexander's room*: The text is in doubt here.

38. *humiliated by Attalus*: Attalus was the uncle of Philip's new bride, Cleopatra (see ch. 9). Diodorus 16.93–4 explains how eight years earlier Attalus had arranged for Pausanias to be assaulted by his muleteers, in revenge for his having brought about the death of a kinsman of Attalus.

39. *'The father, bride and bridegroom all at once'*: Quoting *Medea* 288 and implying that Alexander should kill Attalus, Cleopatra and Philip. In the play, Medea wishes to murder Creon, Creon's daughter, and her own husband Jason, who now planned to marry Creon's daughter. The murder of Philip took place on the day of the wedding of Philip's own daughter, also named Cleopatra, to Alexander of Epirus in October 336.

40. *horrible revenge which she took upon Cleopatra*: That is, on Cleopatra, Philip's widow. According to the second-century AD writer Pausanias (*Guide to Greece* 8.7), Olympias had Cleopatra and her infant child roasted over a brazier. Alexander himself ordered the execution of Attalus, who was then one of the com-

manders of Philip's expeditionary force to Asia, for allegedly treasonable correspondence with Athens (*Demosthenes* 23).

41. *arrived before Thebes*: In September 335.

42. *actions of the Thebans against them*: Thebes had attacked and destroyed Plataea in the Peloponnesian War in 427, and again in 373. Thebes and Phocis had clashed in the Third Sacred War (356–346), which ended in Phocian humiliation.

43. *murder of Cleitus ... refusal of the Macedonians to cross the Ganges*: See chs. 50–51 and 62.

44. *Dionysus*: The god of wine was supposedly born in Thebes. In *Alexander*, Dionysus and drink are often associated with negative traits of Alexander's character, or with his destruction (chs. 4, 50, 67, 75).

45. *The Greeks gathered at the Isthmus of Corinth*: The congress at Corinth took place the year before the revolt of Thebes, that is, in 336; Philip had set up the League of Corinth in 337, and it had declared him its leader and its general for an attack on Persia. The decisions of the representatives were hardly free, as after Chaeronea opposition in Greece had been effectively subdued.

46. *set out*: In early spring 334.

47. *Orpheus*: A mythical figure associated with song and music. Pindar called him 'the father of songs' (*Pythian ode* 4.176–7).

48. *size of his army ... cavalry*: Similar figures are given by Plutarch in *On the fortune or virtue of Alexander* 327d–e and by Polybius 12.19, Diodorus 17.17.3–5 and Arrian, *Anabasis* 1.11.3. From these other passages it appears that the lower figure Plutarch quotes was probably given by Aristobulus, the higher by Anaximenes. The difference between the higher and lower figures could be partly explained by conjecturing that the lower figure did not include the 10,000 men sent by Philip as an advance force.

49. *companions*: An elite group who acted as the Macedonian king's advisers and entourage and who were often appointed to high office. On the battlefield they formed a cavalry unit, known as the royal squadron. The term 'companion' was also used to designate a member of a larger cavalry unit, of which the royal squadron formed a part.

50. *faithful friend ... great poet to sing of his deeds after his death*: Achilles' friend was Patroclus, whose death was mourned deeply by him. Homer sang of Achilles' deeds in the *Iliad*.

51. *Alexander of Troy*: That is, Alexander, son of Priam, who is portrayed in the *Iliad*; he was also known as Paris.

52. *sang of the glorious deeds of brave men*: A paraphrase of *Iliad*
     9.189. Alexander thus identifies himself not with his Asian
     namesake, who was associated in the Greek tradition with soft-
     living and womanizing, but with his enemy, the Greek Achilles,
     whom Homer presents as the fiercer fighter and more noble fig-
     ure and from whom Alexander's family claimed ancestry.
     Alexander certainly cultivated a connection between himself and
     Achilles (see, e.g., ch. 5), and Plutarch introduces other parallels
     as well as stressing Alexander's love for Homer (chs. 8, 26, 63,
     72). The comparison is in Alexander's favour, and suggests his
     bravery and martial prowess, his semi-divine status and his
     Greekness.

53. *Darius' generals had gathered a large army*: Arrian, *Anabasis*
     1.14, says that the Persian forces at Granicus numbered about
     20,000 cavalry and slightly fewer foreign-mercenary infantry.
     There must have been locally levied infantry too, but Diodorus'
     figure (17.19) of at least 100,000, along with 10,000 cavalry, is
     too high.

54. *never made war during the month of Daesius ... Artemisius*:
     Daesius in the Macedonian calendar is roughly May/June;
     Artemisius immediately preceded it. The original reason for
     avoiding fighting in that month may have been the need to gather
     the harvest.

55. *crossing at such a late hour of the day*: Diodorus (17.19) gives a
     different version, in which Alexander crossed the river at dawn
     before the enemy could stop him and was only then engaged by
     the Persians.

56. *'Black' Cleitus*: Commander of the royal squadron of Compan-
     ion Cavalry, called 'Black' to distinguish him from Cleitus the
     White, an infantry commander.

57. *only thirty-four soldiers ... infantry*: According to Arrian, *Ana-
     basis* 1.16.4, the overall losses were somewhat higher, but
     twenty-five of the companions fell in the first charge; it was these
     men, he says, whose statues, carved by Lysippus, were set up at
     Dion in Macedonia.

58. *except the Spartans*: Sparta had refused to send delegates to the
     congress at Corinth. In 331 the Spartans, under the leadership of
     Agis III, and with financial support from Persia, would launch a
     war against Macedonia and be quickly defeated by Antipater.

59. *Halicarnassus*: An important Persian naval base (modern Bod-
     rum). Both it and Miletus were defended by large numbers of
     Greek mercenaries. Unlike Miletus, Halicarnassus was not

entirely subdued at this point, as a Persian garrison held out in two fortified citadels until early 332 (see Arrian, *Anabasis* 1.20–23, 2.5.7, 2.13.4).

60. *His advance through Pamphylia . . . waves receded to make way for him*: Such accounts may go back in part to Callisthenes, who accompanied Alexander and was later executed by him (chs. 53–5). He wrote an extremely laudatory account of Alexander which included such miraculous tales.

61. *Like Alexander . . . path for me*: Menander fragment 598 K–A. The play is lost and the title unknown.

62. *Climax*: 'Ladder', through the mountains north of Phaselis. Arrian, *Anabasis* 1.26.1, mentions the construction of the road and says that one part of the army used it but that Alexander himself led another part along the sea-shore.

63. *Theodectas*: A successful tragic poet at Athens. His relationship with Aristotle is unclear.

64. *captured Gordium*: Spring 333.

65. *Memnon*: A Greek commander from Rhodes who had long experience in Persian service and was now commander of Persian operations in the Aegean. In 333 he captured Chios, overran most of Lesbos and laid siege to Mitylene, where he died (Arrian, *Anabasis* 2.1).

66. *this battle*: The battle of Issus in November 333.

67. *'So this . . . is what it is to be a king'*: An ironic remark intended to express not admiration but pity for Darius, for thinking that royalty consisted of mere wealth and luxury.

68. *'These Persian women are a torment for the eyes'*: I.e., because they incite the body to rebel against the discipline imposed by reason. The story recalls an incident in Herodotus 5.18 where Persian ambassadors to Macedonia call the royal Macedonian women 'torments to their eyes' and proceed to lay hands on them. Alexander's restraint stands in contrast.

69. *Ada*: The sister of Pixodarus, former satrap of Caria (see ch. 10). Pixodarus had in fact ousted her from power but he had died by the time Alexander arrived and she submitted to him and was reinstated. She made Alexander her heir.

70. *sitting down*: That is, not reclining as was the custom for a banquet.

71. *battle of Issus*: November 333 (see ch. 20).

72. *besieged Tyre for seven months*: February to August 332.

73. *satyr*: Satyrs were mythological male creatures, often represented as half-man and half-horse or -goat. The commonest place to

meet them was at fountains or wells. The god Dionysus was often depicted as accompanied by revelling satyrs, and these associations with Dionysus and with drink may be intended here (see chs. 4 and 13).

74. *laid siege to Gaza*: September to October 332.

75. *to found a . . . Greek city there, to be called after him*: The modern Alexandria, which, like many of the cities Alexander founded, was named after Alexander himself. Alexandria in Egypt grew in the centuries after Alexander's death to be one of the largest and most prosperous cities in the Mediterranean world.

76. *Out of . . . Pharos*: Homer, *Odyssey* 4.354–5.

77. *Pharos . . . an island*: It was later the site of a famous octagonal lighthouse connected to the city by a causeway.

78. *temple of Ammon*: At the oasis of Siwah, 350 miles south-west of Alexandria. The local god Ammon was identified with the Egyptian sun-god Amun-Ra, and with the Greek Zeus. The temple of Ammon had been known to the Greeks for several centuries, and was considered an important oracular shrine.

79. *Cambyses*: The son of Cyrus the Great, and king of Persia 530–522 BC. He reconquered Egypt in 525 after it had revolted. Herodotus 3.26 records the disappearance of the expedition sent by Cambyses to Siwah.

80. *welcomed him . . . as a father greeting his son*: I.e., implying that Alexander was the son of Zeus-Ammon. Cf. the portents indicating Alexander's divine birth in chs. 2–3.

81. *wrote to the Athenians on the subject of Samos*: Since 365 the Athenians had held Samos and had installed a large number of settlers there. This letter may have been written after Alexander's conquest of the coast of Asia Minor. Some scholars date it instead to the last year of Alexander's life, when he decreed that all Greek cities must receive back their exiles: this would have meant the evacuation of Athenian settlers from Samos, as well as the return to Samos of those expelled by the Athenians.

82. *'who was called my father'*: There is some debate about the meaning of Alexander's words. Plutarch takes it that Alexander was implying that his father was not Philip but, presumably, Zeus. But, if the letter is genuine, it is possible that Alexander meant merely 'the one you refer to [rightly] as my father'.

83. *'ichor, which flows in the veins of the blessed gods'*: Homer, *Iliad* 5.340. Aphrodite has been wounded in battle: 'The immortal blood of the goddess flowed, *ichor*, which flows in the veins of the blessed gods. For they do not eat bread nor drink shining

wine, so they are bloodless and called immortal.' Alexander
implies that he is mortal and not immune to harm.

84. *Hephaestion*: A childhood friend of Alexander, and particularly
close to him (see, e.g., chs. 39, 41, 72; *Eumenes* 1–2).

85. *enslave others*: Presumably, the barbarians.

86. *On his return from Egypt to Phoenicia*: In 331 BC.

87. *Darius wrote Alexander a letter*: Plutarch gives no chronological
context for this incident. According to Arrian (*Anabasis* 2.25), it
had taken place at the time of the siege of Tyre, and Alexander's
reply was the conclusion of a more arrogantly phrased letter.

88. *evil god of the Persians*: Persian religion was in some sense dual-
istic. In *On Isis and Osiris* 369d, Plutarch talks of a good and an
evil force in the universe, called by the Persians Ahura-Mazda
and Areimanus respectively; he claims that some people called
the latter a *daimon* – the Greek word Plutarch uses here. On the
other hand, in *On the fortune of the Romans*, he talks of 'the
daimon of the Romans', which seems more akin to providential
protection.

89. *Lord Oromazes*: That is, Ahura-Mazda, the supreme god of the
Persians (see *Artaxerxes* 29).

90. *'how can a young man's treatment of his enemy's wife be virtuous . . . such tributes?'*: I.e., Darius assumes that Alexander must
have seduced or raped his wife.

91. *a million men*: The figure here is almost certainly inflated, though
the Persian army at this point did undoubtedly outnumber Alexander's.

92. *Boedromion . . . eclipse of the moon*: The eclipse is securely
dated to 20 September 331 BC. Plutarch therefore dates the battle at Gaugamela to 1 October, as he does also at *Camillus* 19.

93. *all tyrannies . . . under their own laws*: A misleading statement,
as Macedonian-backed tyrannies existed in various states in
mainland Greece.

94. *To the Plataeans . . . common freedom*: In the Persian Wars. The
combined Greek forces won a decisive victory near Plataea in
479 BC. On Plataea's subsequent fate, see n. 42.

95. *Phaÿllus . . . danger*: The story is told in Herodotus 8.47.

96. *Ecbatana*: The name is almost certainly corrupt, as Ecbatana is
in Media not Babylonia.

97. *naphtha . . . afterwards*: The digression on naphtha is probably
meant to express something about Alexander's 'fiery' nature (ch.
4). He, like it, is brilliant, fast-moving and destructive.

98. *Medea . . . Creon's daughter*: See n. 39.

99. *Greek plants ... all except ivy ... killed it*: The successes and failures of transplanting Greek plants to Babylonia are probably meant to be symbolic of the successes and difficulties in transplanting Greek customs to Asia. In addition, the fiery soil of Babylonia may also suggest Alexander's fiery nature (ch. 4); the inability of ivy, the plant of Dionysus, to grow there suggests Dionysus' hostility to Alexander (ch. 13).

100. *purple from Hermione ... 190 years*: Cloth dyed with purple, obtained from the sea-snail (murex), was extremely expensive; assuming talents here refers to weight, this is an incredible amount of it (*c.* 130 tonnes). The cloth mentioned here would have been obtained around the time when Darius I came to the throne in 522 BC. Hermione was a city in the eastern Peloponnese.

101. *Deinon*: See *Artaxerxes*, n. 6.

102. *Persis*: The old Persian homeland, across the Zagros mountains in modern Iran (Fars province).

103. *a guide ... short diversion*: Plutarch does not narrate here the forcing of the pass known as the Persian Gates, which was guarded by a large army (see Arrian, *Anabasis* 3.18).

104. *fire to be put out*: For Alexander's fiery nature, and its ambiguities, see chs. 4 and 35.

105. *Paeonians*: Cavalry from Paeonia, which lay to the north of Macedonia.

106. *wrote to Phocion ... favours*: See *Phocion* 18.

107. *bodyguards*: Perhaps referring here to the high-ranking noblemen, seven in number, who received the title of bodyguards (*somatophylakes*) from the Macedonian king and formed an inner circle of trusted officers.

108. *Mazaeus ... governor of a province ... add an even larger one to it*: Mazaeus, who had been satrap of Cilicia and Syria under the previous Persian kings and had fought at Gaugamela, had been appointed by Alexander to the satrapy of Babylon. This marked a new policy: henceforth, Alexander appointed or confirmed in their old appointments members of the Persian nobility, though in each satrapy Macedonians were also appointed to command the army. One of Mazaeus' sons surrendered to Alexander in 330 (Arrian, *Anabasis* 3.21.1; Curtius 5.13.11); two others were admitted to the Companion Cavalry in 324 (Arrian 7.6.4).

109. *wrote to Antipater ... plots against his life*: Antipater had been left behind to govern Macedon. Plutarch does not specify whom Alexander suspected of plotting against Antipater, but it may have been his mother Olympias, who was on bad terms with Antipater.

110. *Craterus*: One of Alexander's most important generals and, with Hephaestion, his second-in-command after the execution of Philotas. Following Alexander's death he was killed in battle against Eumenes (see *Eumenes* 5–7 and Biographical Notes).

111. *hunting scene represented in bronze ... at Delphi*: The base of the statue group, which measures more than 45 feet in length, and the dedicatory inscription which accompanied it, have been found at Delphi.

112. *Harpalus had deserted*: See *Demosthenes* 25.

113. *He was marching against Darius at this time*: In spring 330. Plutarch here takes up the chronological narrative again which he had left off in ch. 38. Darius retreated east from Ecbatana, but was assassinated in a coup led by several of the eastern satraps.

114. *2,000 talents, besides their regular pay*: Other sources explain that he gave one talent to each man – a huge sum.

115. *Lake Maeotis*: The Sea of Azov, linked to the Black Sea by a narrow channel.

116. *outer sea*: According to the beliefs of Plutarch's time, the 'outer sea' encircled the world. Alexander planned an expedition to determine whether the Caspian Sea was a gulf of this ocean, but did not live to carry it out (Arrian, *Anabasis* 7.16).

117. *obeisance*: See *Artaxerxes* 22 and n. 57. Alexander was seen by many of his non-Greek subjects as the successor to the kings of Persia, and adopted this and other aspects of Persian court procedure and dress, much to the annoyance of some of his Macedonian officers.

118. *tiara*: On the Persian tiara, see *Artaxerxes*, n. 66.

119. *Lysimachus*: Not Alexander's tutor, but one of Alexander's generals, who later declared himself king (see *Demetrius*, n. 34, and Biographical Notes).

120. *Philotas, the son of Parmenion ... Macedonians*: Parmenion had served Philip, and was one of Alexander's most experienced generals. Philotas, his son, commanded the Companion Cavalry.

121. *Dimnus*: The manuscripts of Plutarch have Limnus, but Dimnus is the spelling used by Arrian and Curtius Rufus.

122. *put to death*: Parmenion and Philotas were killed in the autumn of 330.

123. *dreaded ... above all by Antipater*: Antipater's son-in-law, Alexander, of the royal house of Lyncestis, had been arrested in 333 and was now put to death.

124. *Aetolians ... not by the sons of the Oeniadae but by him*: Alexander's threat to Aetolia for occupying Oeniadae, a town in

Acarnania, was contained in the Exiles' Decree of 324. Antipater's negotiations with them, forestalled by Alexander's death, should be dated to around that time.

125. *Not long after this*: Two years later, in the autumn of 328, at Marakanda (Samarkand).

126. *evil genius*: Plutarch occasionally elsewhere speaks of spirits (*daimones* or *daimonia*) associated with each individual (see *Caesar* 69; *Dion* 2, 55; *Brutus* 36, 48; *On the decline of oracles* 593d–594a; and *On tranquillity of mind* 474b–c).

127. *Spithridates' sword*: See ch. 16.

128. *Aristophanes*: Perhaps Aristonous is meant, as no bodyguard called Aristophanes is attested. On the bodyguards (*somatophylakes*), see n. 107.

129. *corps of guards*: Hypaspists (literally, shield-bearers), an elite infantry unit responsible for guarding the king.

130. *in Macedonian . . . a signal that this was an extreme emergency*: The detail that Alexander shouted in Macedonian (rather than standard, Attic Greek) would have been suggestive for Plutarch's original readers: when in the grip of emotion he is portrayed as reverting to a less sophisticated self.

131. *'Alas, what evil customs reign in Greece'*: *Andromache* 693. The context of the quotation is significant: in the play, Peleus is lamenting that Menelaus, the commander, is taking the honour won by the army at large. The passage continues: 'When the army sets up victory-trophies over the enemy, people do not regard this as the deed of those who have done the work, but rather the general receives the honour. He brandished his spear as one man amongst ten thousand others and did no more than a single man, yet he gets more credit' (694–8).

132. *Olynthus*: A Greek city in the Chalcidice, which had been destroyed by Philip in 348.

133. *'A wise man . . . own interests'*: A line from an unknown play of Euripides (*TrGF* V fragment 905).

134. *'On noble subjects . . . speak well'*: *Bacchae* 267. In the play, these words are addressed by Teiresias, the seer, to Pentheus, the tyrannical king of Thebes, who has been insulting and deriding the worship of Dionysus. Readers who remember the play may wonder whether Alexander is acting more like the tyrant than the prophet.

135. *'Once civil strife . . . honoured'*: This line is quoted also in *Nicias* 11 and *Sulla* 39, but its provenance is not known (Adespota elegiaca fragment 12 West).

136. *'Braver by far ... death did not spare him'*: Homer, *Iliad* 21.107, where Achilles is speaking to Hector. Elsewhere in the Life, Alexander is associated with Achilles; Callisthenes' point here is that Alexander is not immortal.

137. *Demaratus of Corinth*: On Demaratus, who had fought at the Granicus, see ch. 9 and n. 33. The placing of this episode here contrasts Alexander's treatment of him with his treatment of Callisthenes.

138. *cross into India*: Late spring 327.

139. *refreshment for their labours*: A quotation of Plato, *Menexenus* 238a.

140. *besieging the fortress ... Sisimithres*: This operation took place in the winter of 328/7. In this chapter Plutarch describes various incidents without chronological link in order to illustrate Alexander's character.

141. *Taxiles*: The ruler of the great city of Taxila about 20 miles north-west of the modern Rawalpindi.

142. *the philosophers*: The Brahmans of Sind.

143. *campaign against Porus*: In 326.

144. *crossing the Ganges*: Alexander did not in fact reach the Ganges. The river where the troops mutinied was the Hyphasis; the upper Ganges was some 250 miles further east. There is much dispute as to his real intention: in Arrian, *Anabasis* 5.25–6, Alexander gives a speech at the Hyphasis where he talks of pressing on to the Ganges and the 'eastern sea', which he assumes is part of the outer sea (see n. 116).

145. *Sandrocottus*: The Hellenized form of Chandragupta, whose accession probably took place around 322. He later wiped out the Macedonian garrisons in India.

146. *altars for the gods of Greece*: Arrian, *Anabasis* 5.29.1–2, specifies that there were twelve huge altars (i.e., one for each of the twelve Olympian gods) and Diodorus 17.95 that they were 75 feet high.

147. *a dazzling sheet of flame ... his body*: This suggests Achilles' shining armour in *Iliad* 19.369–83. For Alexander's association with Achilles in Plutarch, see ch. 15, and with fire, chs. 4 and 35.

148. *reached the ocean*: In July 325.

149. *ordered them ... keeping India on their right*: The plan was that the fleet should sail up the Persian Gulf and rejoin Alexander at the mouth of the Euphrates.

150. *terrible privations ... 15,000 cavalry*: Alexander may well have chosen this route to enhance his reputation by surpassing earlier

rulers (Cyrus and the mythical queen Semiramis) who had famously failed to cross the Gedrosian desert with an army (Arrian, *Anabasis* 6.24.2–3, and Strabo 15.1.5). The troop numbers given here are exaggerated, and anyway represent the total Alexander had earlier on his campaigns, not on his march through Gedrosia.

151. *as though the god himself were present to lead the revels*: Plutarch's description of the revels in Carmania in fact recalls the myth of the triumphant return of Dionysus from India. This may have been Alexander's own purpose, but for Plutarch Dionysus represents a threat to Alexander (ch. 13).

152. *Gedrosia*: Probably a mistake for Carmania.

153. *Nearchus . . . voyage*: Arrian's *Indica* describes Nearchus' voyage. In December 325 he landed at Harmozeia, near the strait of Hormuz on the Persian Gulf, and joined Alexander after five days' march inland.

154. *fill the whole coastline with cities*: Or 'with wars'. The text is uncertain here.

155. *the custom of the Persian kings*: In *Virtues of women* 246a–b, Plutarch records that Cyrus the Great instituted the custom when, after a defeat, the Persian women had shamed the troops into fighting again and winning. See also Xenophon, *Cyropaedia* 8.5.21.

156. *Ochus never set foot there at all*: On Ochus, see *Artaxerxes*, n. 78. The claim that Ochus never entered Persis is unlikely to be true.

157. *whom . . . he would soon see in Babylon*: A prophecy of Alexander's death.

158. *the so-called Indian's tomb can be seen there to this day*: Strabo 15.886 describes the tomb and its inscription, which Plutarch had probably seen. The Indian had come as an ambassador to Augustus, *c.* 20 BC.

159. *marriages of his companions at Susa*: In April 324. According to Athenaeus 538b, Chares, Alexander's chamberlain, claimed that ninety-two of the companions married Persian women. Many repudiated them after Alexander's death.

160. *arranged to send . . . to the sea-coast*: I.e., in order to return them to Macedonia.

161. *arrived in Ecbatana in Media*: In late summer 324.

162. *horses should be shorn*: Arrian, *Anabasis* 7.14.4, claims Alexander cut his own hair too; cutting the hair of horses or humans as a sign of mourning was a Persian practice (Herodotus 9.22) but also apparently a Thessalian one (see *Pelopidas* 33–4 on mourn-

ing for Pelopidas, where Plutarch criticizes Alexander's actions). Alexander may here also, as Arrian claims, be imitating Achilles' mourning for Patroclus in the *Iliad*, which involved cutting the hair (23.135).

163. *sacrifice to him as a hero*: 'Heroes' were mortals who were thought to have become semi-divine and who were honoured after death (see *Timoleon* 39 and n. 63).

164. *Cossaeans*: A mountain tribe who made their livelihood from brigandage. They had not been subdued by the Persians.

165. *grief was uncontrollable ... sacrifice to the spirit of Hephaestion*: This recalls Achilles' mourning for Patroclus in *Iliad* 23.175–83, and his sacrifice of twelve Trojans at Patroclus' tomb.

166. *on the way to Babylon*: Spring 323.

167. *ravens ... pecking one another*: The fighting of birds was customarily regarded as an ominous sign.

168. *called Dionysius*: The name of this man, whose mysterious appearance seems to predict Alexander's death, suggests the god Dionysus (see n. 44).

169. *the palace was filled ... slave to his fears*: The text is corrupt at this point. Plutarch wrote a work entitled *On superstition*, which criticizes both atheism and (more strongly) superstition, and advocates a middle course of traditional piety.

170. *Heracles' cup ... to embellish the occasion*: Plutarch is here arguing against a version preserved in Diodorus 17.117 in which Alexander had been engaged in heavy drinking to commemorate the death of Heracles, and was finally taken ill after drinking a huge cup of unmixed wine; 'suddenly he groaned loudly,' Diodorus claims, 'as though struck a hefty blow.'

171. *thirtieth day of the month of Daesius*: Daesius corresponds with May/June. In the next chapter, Plutarch reports that the royal journal gave the date of Alexander's death as the twenty-eighth of Daesius. A Babylonian astronomical tablet establishes the date of Alexander's death as 11 June 323.

172. *ice-cold water ... Nonacris*: Nonacris was a city in northern Arcadia in the Peloponnese. The river that flowed near the town was called the Styx and seems to have been thought to have had deadly powers (Herodotus 6.74). The reference to the coldness of the water is significant: Alexander's nature has been described as fiery (ch. 4) and he has been consistently associated with heat (e.g., chs. 4, 35).

173. *her accomplice was Perdiccas*: Perdiccas was himself killed by

his own officers a few years later as he marched against Alexander's former general Ptolemy (*Eumenes* 8).

174. It is possible that the *Life of Alexander* did not originally end here and that the final part of it has been lost. It is also possible that the Byzantine writer Zonaras (4.14) preserves a summary of that lost ending:

> It is said that, when he realized that his life was leaving him, he wanted to drown himself secretly in the Euphrates, in order that by disappearing he might cause a rumour that he had gone to live with the gods, since he had come from them. But Roxane found this out and prevented the attempt, and he said with a groan, 'So you begrudged me the reputation of having become a god and not died.'

EUMENES

Further Reading

Plutarch's Eumenes

Bosworth, A. B., 'History and Artifice in Plutarch's *Eumenes*', in P. A. Stadter (ed.), *Plutarch and the Historical Tradition* (London and New York: Routledge, 1992), pp. 56–89.

Geiger, J., 'Plutarch on Hellenistic politics: the case of Eumenes of Cardia', in I. Gallo and B. Scardigli (eds.), *Teoria e prassi politica nelle opere di Plutarco* (Naples: M. D'Auria, 1995), pp. 173–85.

Landucci Gattinoni, F., and Konrad, C. F. (eds.), *Plutarco. Vite Parallele: Sertorio–Eumene* (Milan: Biblioteca Universale Rizzoli, 2004).

History

Anson, E. M., *Eumenes of Cardia: A Greek Among Macedonians* (Boston and Leiden: Brill, 2004).

Bosworth, A. B., *The Legacy of Alexander: Politics, Warfare and Propaganda under the Successors* (Oxford: Oxford University Press, 1992).

Heckel. W., 'The politics of distrust: Alexander and his successors', in D. Ogden (ed.), *The Hellenistic World: New Perspectives* (London: Duckworth, and Swansea: Classical Press of Wales, 2002), pp. 81–95.

Schäfer, C., *Eumenes von Kardia und der Kampf um die Macht im Alexanderreich* (Frankfurt am Main: Buchverlag Marthe Claus, 2005).

Westlake, H. D., 'Eumenes of Cardia', *Hellenica, Bulletin of the John Rylands Library* 37 (1954), pp. 309–27; reprinted in *idem, Essays on the Greek Historians and Greek History* (Manchester and New York: Manchester University Press, 1969), pp. 313–30.

Wheatley, P., 'An introduction to the chronological problems in early diadoch sources and scholarship', in W. Heckel, L. Tritle and P. Wheatley (eds.), *Alexander's Empire: Formulation to Decay* (Claremont, CA: Regina Books, 2007), pp. 179–92.

Notes to the Life of Eumenes

1. *Life of Eumenes*: The second in its pair of Lives. A prologue to the *Lives of Sertorius and Eumenes* precedes the *Sertorius*.
2. *Cardia*: A Greek city on the Thracian Chersonese (the Gallipoli peninsula).
3. *Douris*: See *Demosthenes*, n. 65.
4. *cart-driver*: Given Eumenes' education, and the antipathy between his family and that of Hecataeus, the tyrant of Cardia (ch. 3), it seems unlikely that his father was a mere cart-driver. The detail may come from hostile propaganda.
5. *Philip . . . in the vicinity*: Possibly in 342, when Philip was campaigning in Thrace, and when Cardia received a Macedonian garrison.
6. *After Philip's death . . . force under his own command*: Philip was assassinated in 336, and succeeded by his son Alexander (*Alexander* 10). Eumenes served under Alexander in his Asian campaigns.
7. *Hephaestion's position on the latter's death*: Hephaestion, one of Alexander's most trusted friends, died of fever in 324 (*Alexander* 72).
8. *Artonis*: The manuscripts say 'Barsine', which is almost certainly a mistake. 'Artonis' is the name found in Arrian, *Anabasis* 7.4.
9. *distributed the other Persian women . . . to his companions*: See *Alexander* 70.
10. *disputes with Hephaestion*: Arrian also comments on the enmity between the two men at *Anabasis* 7.13–14.
11. *Nearchus . . . outer sea*: See *Alexander* 66 and 68 and n. 116.
12. *honours . . . construction of his tomb*: For the honours paid to Hephaestion after his death, see *Alexander* 72.
13. *When Alexander died . . . companions*: Alexander died in Babylon in June 323 without an heir. The Macedonian nobles, here designated 'companions', wished to wait for the birth of Alexander's child to see if it were male; the rank and file, on the other hand, preferred to designate as king Alexander's half-brother

Arrhidaeus, who suffered from some kind of mental disability (see *Phocion* 33, *Alexander* 77). In the end, a compromise was reached whereby both would be designated king, and Perdiccas assume command of the empire and of the royal armies in their names (see Introduction to *Eumenes*).

14. *as a foreigner ... disputes of Macedonians*: Eumenes was not a Macedonian. Diodorus (18.60.1–3, 62.7; 19.13.1) and Nepos (*Eumenes* 1) make the point that Eumenes' Greek origins were a disadvantage to him in dealing with his Macedonian troops, as does Plutarch in the Comparison with Sertorius, ch. 20(1). This may have meant that he was unable to address his troops in their native Macedonian language. Cf. ch. 18, where the Silver Shields call him a 'pest from the Chersonese'.

15. *Leonnatus*: He had accompanied Alexander in Asia (*Alexander* 21 and 40), and is said by Arrian (*Anabasis* 6.9, 6.11, 7.5), by Curtius Rufus (9.5.15) and by Plutarch (*On the fortune or virtue of Alexander* 344d) to have saved Alexander's life among the Malli (cf. *Alexander* 63). He was now satrap of Hellespontine Phrygia.

16. *Antigonus*: Antigonus Monophthalmus, one of Alexander's most trusted generals, had under Alexander been satrap of Phrygia; he now governed much of western Asia Minor.

17. *escort ... region*: In 322 BC.

18. *Antigonus took no notice of Perdiccas' written instructions*: In fact, Antigonus joined Craterus and Antipater in Europe after disobeying Perdiccas' instructions to cooperate with Eumenes in the conquest of Cappadocia.

19. *besieged in Lamia*: On Alexander's death the forces of Athens, Aetolia and several other states attacked Antipater, who had been left by Alexander as his regent in Macedonia, and besieged him in Lamia. He was relieved by Leonnatus, and, with reinforcements from Craterus, defeated Athens at the battle of Crannon in 322 (see *Phocion* 23–6).

20. *Cleopatra*: Alexander's sister (*Alexander* 68), who was now a widow after the death of her husband, Alexander of Epirus; her hand was eagerly sought by various of the competing generals.

21. *the kings*: That is, the infant Alexander IV and Philip III Arrhidaeus.

22. *Neoptolemus*: He had received Armenia in the distribution of provinces but it was probably not fully under Macedonian control.

23. *Craterus*: Sent by Alexander back to Europe with the veterans

who wanted to return home in 324, though on Alexander's death he was still in Cilicia. He had then crossed over to Greece and assisted Antipater in the Lamian War.

24. *planning to invade Cappadocia*: In 321 or 320. Perdiccas was now faced with an alliance of Craterus, Antipater, Antigonus, Lysimachus and Ptolemy.

25. *on campaign against Ptolemy*: In Egypt, where Ptolemy was satrap. Perdiccas had with him Philip Arrhidaeus and Alexander's infant son, Alexander.

26. *Alcetas*: Perdiccas' brother.

27. *deploying . . . for battle*: Summer 321 or 320 BC.

28. *oaths . . . serve under him*: A papyrus fragment (*PSI* xii, 1951, 1284), perhaps from Arrian's *History of the Successors*, may describe negotiations after this battle.

29. *enmity with Antipater was long standing*: The quarrel with Antipater is also mentioned in ch. 3. We have no evidence for its cause.

30. *If either one became greedy*: The Greek is odd here and there may be a lacuna in the manuscripts. One editor suggests '<As long as they kept their oaths he would eagerly fight as an ally to both, but> if either one . . .'

31. *flat cap*: The *kausia*, a distinctive hat worn by Macedonian soldiers from at least this period onwards.

32. *opposing him in his rush to imitate Persian manners . . . pride*: See *Alexander* 47.

33. *like triremes ramming*: A similar metaphor is found at Xenophon, *Hellenica* 7.5.23: 'Epaminondas led his army forward, prow-on, like a trireme, thinking that wherever he rammed and broke through . . .'

34. *Meanwhile, Neoptolemus encountered Eumenes . . . harm*: Plutarch's description of the duel between Neoptolemus and Eumenes has many elements reminiscent of such scenes in the *Iliad*. Eumenes is thus presented here in a heroic light.

35. *Perdiccas had been killed . . . Antipater*: In 321 or 320. Eumenes was condemned by the army in Egypt, partly because he was responsible for Craterus' death, and partly because of his alliance with Perdiccas. The new distribution of powers took place at Triparadeisus in Syria. Antipater became regent of the whole empire and guardian of the kings.

36. *Mount Ida*: In Hellespontine Phrygia, in the north-west corner of Asia Minor.

37. *Cleopatra*: Alexander's sister, who was now living in Sardis,

having refused offers of marriage from Cassander, Lysimachus and Antigonus.

38. *He promised ... arrears of pay*: These efforts of Eumenes to pay his men are described in the Göteborg Palimpsest, which first came to light in the 1970s and appears to be a fragment of Arrian's *Events after Alexander*.

39. *able to distribute purple caps ... royal gift*: Probably because Eumenes presented himself as acting in the name of the kings and with the blessing of Cleopatra.

40. *where the battle ... ashes*: Possession of the battlefield after a battle, and the ability to bury one's dead without having to seek a truce or ask permission from the opponent, was considered a sign of victory.

41. *Eumenes kept on the move ... unnoticed*: Plutarch ignores here the major defeat inflicted on Eumenes by Antigonus (described in Diodorus 18.40), after which many of his men deserted him.

42. *took refuge in Nora*: Spring 319 BC.

43. *'I count no man ... sword'*: An ominous statement which looks forward to his betrayal by his troops (ch. 17), when his dagger is snatched from him.

44. *Ptolemaeus*: Also known as Polemaeus. He is not to be confused with Alexander's general Ptolemy, who was now satrap of Egypt.

45. *Antipater had died ... hostility between Cassander and Polyperchon*: Antipater died of illness in autumn 319. He named Polyperchon as regent, not his son, Cassander. In the war which followed (the Second War of the Diadochi), Eumenes supported Polyperchon, as did Olympias, Alexander the Great's mother, whereas Antigonus, Ptolemy and Lysander supported Cassander (see *Phocion* 31).

46. *Hieronymus*: Hieronymus of Cardia (*c.* 364–260 BC) came from Eumenes' own city. He was the author of a historical work on the period after Alexander's death, which was an important source for Plutarch in *Eumenes*, *Demetrius* and *Pyrrhus*. See Introduction to *Eumenes*, and cf. *Demetrius* 39 and *Pyrrhus* 17.

47. *He left ... siege continued*: Eumenes left Nora in spring 318. Plutarch's account implies that no sooner was the siege lifted than he fled, but Diodorus 18.53 and 58 suggests there was a period when Eumenes was at peace with Antigonus; the latter only marched against him once Eumenes had been appointed commander of the royal armies.

48. *Alexander's son*: He must now have been five years old.

49. *Antigenes*: Since Triparadeisus, satrap of the province of Susa.

50. *Silver Shields*: An elite infantry unit, originally known as Hypaspists, but renamed Silver Shields (*Argyraspides*) because Alexander, shortly before the invasion of India, had awarded them armour and weapons decorated with silver (Diodorus 17.57.2, Justin 12.7.5, Curtius Rufus 8.5.4).

51. *As they advanced ... joined forces with them*: The date is now autumn 318 and Eumenes is moving inland towards Babylon. Peucestas was satrap of Persis; the other satraps mentioned here were in charge of other eastern provinces. They had formed a coalition against Peithon, the satrap of Media, who seems to have been trying to extend his domains. They turned to Eumenes for support, and Peithon to Seleucus (Diodorus 19.14).

52. *just like in a democracy*: This derogatory comparison with a democracy may have originated in Plutarch's source, Hieronymus. But it is just as likely Plutarch's own comment. Plutarch was suspicious of democracy and of unfettered popular power; a firm leader like Pericles or Phocion might assert his moral authority and control the people, but there was always, in Plutarch's view, the risk that demagogues might manipulate them through pandering to their desires.

53. *Antigonus ... with a large force*: He had moved inland into Mesopotamia in the winter of probably 318/17; in summer 317 he entered Babylonia at the invitation of Peithon and Seleucus.

54. *Pasitigris*: Now known as the Karun, east of Susa, which Eumenes had evacuated as Antigonus advanced on it. After his failure to cross the Pasitigris, Antigonus pushed north-eastwards into Media. Diodorus 19.21 records that Eumenes wished now to march back to the Mediterranean, but had to give way to the wishes of the satraps of the interior who wanted to defend their possessions, and so marched instead to Persepolis. Diodorus also claims that on the march Peucestas provided the army with generous provisions, as well as giving a magnificent feast in Persepolis.

55. *a few days later*: This and the next episodes took place after Antigonus had moved south from Media, in the days leading up to the battle of Paraetacene in probably late 317 (though some scholars place it in 316), which is not itself described by Plutarch. A fuller account can be found in Diodorus, 19.24–32.

56. *dangerously ill*: According to Diodorus 19.24, after drinking heavily.

57. *golden weapons*: Alexander had begun the practice of awarding elite troops weapons decorated with precious metals (see n. 50).

58. *elephants*: The Macedonians first encountered elephants on the battlefield at Gaugamela in 331. They were subsequently utilized in the armies of the successors.

59. *Gabiene*: In the hills of central Persia, south-west of modern Isfahan.

60. *his mind remained versatile ... reverses of fortune ... suffered*: The description here, especially the use of the word 'versatile' (*polytropos*), suggests a comparison with Odysseus, whose cunning as well as his long wanderings were famous.

61. *draw up his forces*: The battle of Gabiene took place in January of probably 316 (though some scholars date it one year later). It is described in Diodorus 19.39–43.

62. *'It is against your fathers ... you scum!'*: Diodorus 19.41 records, perhaps more plausibly, that this message was shouted to Antigonus' Macedonian infantry by a single cavalryman sent for the purpose.

63. *pest*: The term translated as 'pest' here (*olethros*, literally, 'ruin, destruction') is the same as that used by Eumenes himself in ch. 8 when he quotes the proverb 'No account is made of ruin'. His words are here fulfilled.

64. *sleep for the third night in a row with the enemy*: Eumenes' baggage train had been captured in the battle a few days before (ch. 16), and with it not only his men's possessions but their families had fallen into the hands of Antigonus' army.

65. *Demetrius*: Demetrius Poliorcetes (see the next Life in this volume).

66. *Nearchus the Cretan*: Alexander's admiral (ch. 2).

67. *murder him*: Probably early in 316, though some scholars date it to 315.

68. *Arachosia*: In the far east of Alexander's empire, in what is now south-east Afghanistan, the area around Kandahar.

69. *exterminate and destroy them ... behold the Greek sea*: Plutarch, like Diodorus, makes the fate of the Silver Shields a moral lesson about betrayal and punishment; in fact, the truth is likely to be more mundane: that as elite troops they were sent east where their presence was now needed.

Notes to the Comparison of Sertorius and Eumenes

70. *Sertorius*: See Introduction to *Eumenes*.

71. *in command of Macedonians*: See n. 14.

72. *begging and pleading for his life ... his body*: This judgement on Eumenes' death is much less favourable to Eumenes than the

narrative in chs. 17–19 had been. In several other Comparisons, deaths are treated rather less favourably than they had been in the Life itself: cf., e.g., *Nicias* 26 with the *Comparison of Nicias and Crassus* 5, and *Antony* 77 with the *Comparison of Demetrius and Antony* 6.

DEMETRIUS

Further Reading

Plutarch's Demetrius

Andrei, O., and Scuderi, R. (eds.), *Plutarco. Vite Parallele: Demetrio–Antonio* (Milan: Biblioteca Universale Rizzoli, 1989).

De Lacy, P., 'Biography and tragedy in Plutarch', *American Journal of Philology* 73 (1952), pp. 159–71; reprinted in T. E. Duff (ed.), *Oxford Readings in Ancient Biography* (Oxford: Oxford University Press, forthcoming).

Duff, T. E., 'Plato, tragedy, the ideal reader and Plutarch's *Demetrios and Antony*', *Hermes* 132 (2004), pp. 271–91.

Harris, B. F., 'The Portrayal of Aristocratic Power in Plutarch's *Lives*', in *idem* (ed.), *Auckland Classical Essays Presented to E. M. Blaiklock* (Auckland: Auckland University Press, and Wellington: Oxford University Press, 1970), pp. 185–202.

Pelling, C. B. R. (ed.), *Plutarch: Life of Antony* (Cambridge: Cambridge University Press, 1988), pp. 18–26 on the pairing of Demetrius and Antony.

Santi Amantini, L. C., Carena, C., and Manfredini, M. (eds.), *Plutarco. Le Vite di Demetrio e di Antonio* (Milan: Mondadori, Fondazione Lorenzo Valla, 1995).

Sweet, W. E., 'Sources of Plutarch's *Demetrius*', *Classical Weekly* 44 (1981), pp. 177–81.

History

Billows, R., *Antigonus the One-eyed and the Creation of the Hellenistic state* (Berkeley: University of California Press, 1990).

Hammond, N. G. L., and Walbank, F. W., *History of Macedonia*, vol. 3: 336–167 BC (Oxford: Clarendon Press, 1988).

Wheatley, P., 'The lifespan of Demetrius Poliorcetes', *Historia* 46 (1997), pp. 19–27.

Wheatley, P., 'The young Demetrius Poliorcetes', *Ancient History Bulletin* 13.1 (1999), pp. 1–13.

Will, É. 'The succession to Alexander', in *CAH* vii, pp. 23–61.
Will, É. 'The formation of the Hellenistic Kingdoms', in *CAH* vii, pp. 101–17.

Notes to the Prologue to the Lives of Demetrius and Antony

1. *the ancient Spartans . . . to be drunk*: See, e.g., *Lycurgus* 28. Helots were inhabitants of Laconia, and especially Messenia, who had been reduced to a form of slavery or serfdom by the Spartans.
2. *Antony the Imperator*: Mark Antony, Julius Caesar's lieutenant. He was finally defeated by Octavian in 31 BC.
3. *Plato's saying that great natures . . . great virtues*: Plato, *Republic* 6, 491b–495b. Plutarch alludes to the same passage in *Coriolanus* 1 and *On God's slowness to punish* 522c–d.

Notes to the Life of Demetrius

4. *Antigonus*: Antigonus I Monophthalmus, general of Alexander and major player in the power-struggles after Alexander's death.
5. *Philip*: Philip V of Macedon, who killed his son Demetrius in 180 BC (see *Aratus* 54 and *Aemilius* 8).
6. *eight generations later by the Romans*: In 66–63 BC, when Pompey campaigned against Mithridates VI Eupator of Pontus, who was finally forced to commit suicide by his son (see *Pompey* 30–41).
7. *Empedocles*: A pre-Socratic philosopher (fifth century BC), who saw the universe as made up of four elements: fire, air, water and earth. He explained the attraction and repulsion of these elements by forces which he called respectively 'love' and 'strife'. Plutarch refers to him frequently; a list of Plutarch's works from the fourth century AD called the Lamprias Catalogue mentions a long treatise in ten books on Empedocles, though this is now lost (Lamp. Cat. no. 43).
8. *sent his son Demetrius . . . as the supreme commander . . . at stake*: In 314/13. Demetrius had in fact already participated in his father's campaign against Eumenes several years earlier, though had not there held absolute command.
9. *Demetrius was crushingly defeated near the city of Gaza*: In 312 BC.
10. *reversals of fortune*: The theme of the mutability of fortune

recurs frequently in *Demetrius* (see Introduction and chs. 1, 5, 31, 35, 38, 42, 45, 47–50 and 52).

11. *Celaenae*: A city in southern Phrygia, Antigonus' base at this time.
12. *Nabataeans*: The Nabataeans occupied a region in Arabia Petraea, south of Petra and east of the Gulf of Aqaba.
13. *Seleucus*: (*c*. 358–281 BC) Founder of the Seleucid dynasty, who had accompanied Alexander to Asia and distinguished himself in the expedition to India. He became governor of the province of Babylonia in 321 but was driven out of it in 316 or 315. He then took refuge with Ptolemy, returning to Babylon in 312 or 311.
14. *liberate the whole of Greece*: The notion of 'liberating' Greece from Cassander, the son of Antipater, was a key part of Antigonid propaganda, already declared in 315 (Diodorus 19.61). Cassander had installed garrisons in Piraeus and Munychia, and Ptolemy in Corinth and Sicyon; the two agreed a peace treaty in 308.
15. *Demetrius of Phaleron*: Demetrius, of the deme of Phaleron in Attica, governed Athens from 317 to 307 on behalf of Cassander. He was also a Peripatetic philosopher and a historian. When Demetrius Poliorcetes took Athens in 307, Demetrius of Phaleron took refuge with Ptolemy in Egypt.
16. *twenty-fifth . . . of Thargelion*: June 307 BC.
17. *ancestral constitution*: Used in this case to mean full democracy, in contrast to the restricted franchise set up by Cassander under Demetrius of Phaleron.
18. *Cratesipolis*: A powerful figure in her own right. After the death of her husband in 314, she maintained control of Sicyon and Corinth with the support of Polyperchon. In 308 she surrendered them to Ptolemy.
19. *Patrae*: This should possibly be emended to Pagae.
20. *When Megara was captured*: In 307. It had been taken by Ptolemy the previous year.
21. *Munychia . . . demolished the fortress*: In August 307.
22. *Lamian War and the battle of Crannon*: After Alexander's death, Athens fought a short but disastrous war, known as the Lamian War after one of its main theatres, in an attempt to free itself from Macedonian control (323–2). It ended with defeat on land at Crannon in Thessaly and at sea off Amorgos and the installation of a Macedonian garrison (see *Demosthenes* 27–8 and *Phocion* 23–8). Plutarch here ignores the oligarchy led by Phocion (321–318) and the short-lived restoration of democracy in 318–17.
23. *the Phalerean*: That is, Demetrius of Phaleron (see ch. 8). Plu-

tarch's phraseology here recalls Thucydides' famous statement, said with approval, that in the time of Pericles, Athens was 'in theory a democracy but in reality ruled by its first citizen' (Thucydides 2.65).

24. *confer ... title of king*: Perhaps in 306, after the battle of Salamis in Cyprus (ch. 18).

25. *saviour-gods ... 'eponymous' archon*: An exaggeration. Athenian inscriptions of this time refer to them as saviours, not saviour-gods, and continue to give the names of the eponymous archons.

26. *sacred robe of Athena*: At the Panathenaic festival, which took place every four years, a sacred robe was carried in procession as an offering to Athena.

27. *the Descending*: An epithet of Zeus and Hermes, who 'came down' from heaven. These last honours were probably not granted to Demetrius until 304.

28. *created two new tribes ... fifty councillors*: Athenaeus 252f–254c lists various other extravagant honours voted to Demetrius by the Athenians, including addressing him as a god, and quotes the text of a hymn sung to him.

29. *Cleon*: A popular leader in the period of the Peloponnesian War, and much satirized by the comic poet Aristophanes, especially in the *Knights*. He died in 422 BC.

30. *naval battle off Amorgos*: In 322, during the Lamian War. The defeat marked the end of Athenian naval resistance to Antipater and Craterus.

31. *'there are some things even hotter than fire'*: Aristophanes, *Knights* 382. The quotation continues, 'and speeches more shameless than the most shameless of speeches'. In the play, this line is said by the chorus and refers to the fact that the 'Paphlagonian', a thinly disguised alias for Cleon, has been outdone in a shouting-match by the 'Sausage-seller', both of whom are presented as shameless, corrupt and vulgar demagogues. Plutarch has already compared Stratocles with Cleon in the previous chapter; now, just as Cleon was outdone by the 'Sausage-seller' in the *Knights*, so Stratocles is outdone by this demagogue, likewise unnamed.

32. *changed the name of the month Munychion ... renamed the festival of the Dionysia the Demetria*: In fact inscriptions show that the festival entitled the Dionysia did not disappear, and the Demetria occurs only after 294 BC; it was only from that date that the month Demetrion appeared. But Plutarch is working thematically here, and does not claim that all these events took place in 307.

33. *It was because ... people*: Philippides fragment 25 K–A; more of
    the same passage is quoted in ch. 26. A comedy by Philippides
    had won the competition at the City Dionysia in 311. See *Dia-
    logue on love* 750f for another attack by him on Stratocles.

34. *Lysimachus*: One of Alexander's generals, who had received
    Thrace as his province after Alexander's death and was con-
    firmed in it in 311; in the settlement after the battle of Ipsus in
    301 he received much of Asia Minor. He declared himself king
    c. 305, and had close ties with Athens. He was defeated and
    killed by Seleucus at Corupedium in 281.

35. *favours from the king*: An Athenian decree of 283/2 (after
    Demetrius' surrender) honours Philippides for obtaining various
    favours for Athens from Lysimachus in the previous decade and
    a half, including a gift of grain, and the release of Athenian pris-
    oners taken at Ipsus (Austin fragment 54).

36. *consecration of the shields ... oracular response from Demetrius*:
    The date is unknown. The shields may possibly be from the
    spoils mentioned in ch. 17. Plutarch refers to the fact that
    Demetrius' replies were treated as oracles in *On the fortune or
    virtue of Alexander* 338a.

37. *May it be propitious*: A formula prefixed to official inscriptions.

38. *Craterus ... greatest affection by the Macedonians*: See *Eumenes*
    6. Craterus died in 321 or 320; Demetrius married Phila shortly
    afterwards, when he was fifteen.

39. *Euripides' words*: *Phoenician Women* 395. Polynices, the
    speaker, is describing the ills that exile brings. Readers who
    know the play may therefore see this quotation as suggesting
    Demetrius' troubled years after being expelled from Athens.

40. *battle which then followed*: The battle of Salamis in Cyprus,
    which took place in 306.

41. *Lamia*: She is discussed in Athenaeus 577c–f; cf. also 253a–b.

42. *acclaimed Antigonus and Demetrius as kings*: In 306 BC.

43. *tragic actors ... address*: Demetrius is often compared to a tragic
    actor in this Life (see Introduction and chs. 25, 34, 41, 44 and
    53).

44. *launched another expedition against Ptolemy*: In winter 306/5.
    The intention was to invade Egypt.

45. *Chios ... Thasos*: Two islands famous for their wine.

46. *'city-takers'*: Siege-engines.

47. *besieging ... Soli in Cilicia*: Possibly in 299 (see ch. 32).

48. *war with the people of Rhodes*: In 305–4 BC.

49. *the greatest of his 'city-takers'*: Diodorus 20.91 gives a detailed

description. He claims that the siege-engine was nine storeys high and was moved by 3,400 men.

50. *Ialysus ... destroyed by fire*: Ialysus was one of the legendary heroes of Rhodes. The painting was brought to Rome by Cassius, one of the assassins of Julius Caesar, and placed in the Temple of Peace.

51. *Athenians ... besieged by Cassander*: In 304. Cassander had since 307 been waging war on Antigonid interests in Greece.

52. *Demetrius marched into the Peloponnese*: In 303 BC.

53. *married Deidameia ... sister of Pyrrhus*: See *Pyrrhus* 4.

54. *congress ... at the Isthmus*: In 302 at Corinth, during the celebration of the Isthmian Games.

55. *proclaimed commander-in-chief of the Greeks, as Philip and Alexander had been before him*: See *Alexander* 14.

56. *'Penelope'*: In Homer, the wife of Odysseus, who was said to have waited faithfully for his return. Lysimachus' wife was Arsinoe II Philadelphe, daughter of Ptolemy I; unlike the loyal Penelope, she intrigued against her husband with her half-brother Ptolemy Ceraunus.

57. *Mysteries ... Epopteia*: There were several stages of initiation into the Eleusinian Mysteries: first one attended the Lesser Mysteries in the spring; ordinary initiation followed at the Great Mysteries in the autumn; initiation into the final stage, the *epopteia* ('seeing'), was completed a full year later at the next Great Mysteries.

58. *torch-bearer*: One of the leading priests responsible for the Mysteries at Eleusis.

59. *'Who cut the year ... virgin-goddess'*: Fragment 25 K–A (see ch. 12).

60. *Lynceus of Samos*: Brother of Douris of Samos, and a comic writer. Athenaeus 128a–b also refers to Lynceus' account of this extravagant dinner.

61. *'city-taker'*: See ch. 20–21, and n. 46.

62. *like the myth ... Lamia*: Lamia was also the name of a mythical female monster, supposed to eat children.

63. *Bocchoris*: That is, Bakanrenef, pharaoh of Egypt in the eighth century BC, famous for his wisdom and justice.

64. *alliance against Antigonus ... forces*: In 302 BC.

65. *not chosen 'Alexander and victory' for his password*: Cf. *Eumenes* 6.

66. *the battle began*: The battle of Ipsus, in which Antigonus and Demetrius were defeated by Seleucus, Cassander and Lysima-

chus. The battle took place in 301 in Phrygia (western Asia Minor).

67. *Antiochus, Seleucus' son*: The future Antiochus I Soter. He would be co-regent with his father Seleucus from 292 BC and accede to the Seleucid throne in his own right in 281.

68. *Not long after this . . . Stratonice*: *c.* 300 BC. The marriage took place in 299.

69. *1,200 talents . . . still intact*: The remains of a royal treasury, probably sent there for safe-keeping from Susa. It had fallen into Antigonus' hands after Eumenes' defeat in 316 (see *Eumenes* 13).

70. *the man who wishes to be really rich . . . poverty and want*: Plato, *Laws* 5, 736e.

71. *when Demetrius entered it*: In 295 or 294 BC.

72. *appointed as magistrates . . . most acceptable to the people*: Plutarch's wording here may reflect Demetrius' propaganda. In fact, he made Athens less democratic by changing the Council from a body chosen by lot to an elected one.

73. *Dromocleides the orator*: See ch. 13.

74. *Hill of Muses*: The Mouseion, a hill overlooking the city of Athens; control of it gave Demetrius a firmer hold on Athens than the garrisons at Piraeus and Munychia did.

75. *Mantineia . . . invaded Laconia*: Probably in 294 BC.

76. *no enemy had ever captured it*: Sparta had for the first time in its history been hastily fortified with a ditch and palisade in *c.* 317 against a feared attack by Cassander. The defences had now been repaired against Demetrius' attack.

77. *'It is you who fan . . . burn me!'*: Or, *'It was you who sired me, and now . . .'*. The quotation is from an unknown play of Aeschylus (*TrGF* III fragment 359). Plutarch also quotes it as a saying of Demetrius in his *On democracy, monarchy and oligarchy* 827c.

78. *'treacherously . . . other'*: Archilochus, fragment 184 West. The same passage is also quoted in *On the principle of cold* 950f and *Against the Stoics on common perceptions* 1070a.

79. *death of Cassander*: In 297. His son Philip reigned for four months.

80. *Thessalonice*: She had acted as regent after the death of her and Cassander's eldest son, Philip. She had divided the kingdom into two for her remaining sons; the elder, Antipater, killed her, drove his brother Alexander out and seized power in 294 (see *Pyrrhus* 6).

81. *hailed Demetrius as king . . . to Macedonia*: In 294 BC.

82. *crimes . . . against the family of Alexander the Great*: Cassander had put to death Alexander the Great's mother Olympias in 316

and the young king Alexander IV and his mother Roxane in 310/9.

83. *barbarians of the interior*: That is, the satrapies of the Iranian plateau and Central Asia (the 'Upper Satrapies').

84. *the symptoms which Sappho describes . . . pallor*: Sappho, fragment 31 Voigt. Plutarch paraphrases the same poem in his *Dialogue on love*, 763a, and quotes part of it in *Progress in virtue* 81d.

85. *when Demetrius . . . surrounded the city*: In 293 BC.

86. *the historian Hieronymus*: See *Eumenes*, n. 46.

87. *marched against Pyrrhus*: See *Pyrrhus* 7.

88. *twice within ten years*: Demetrius captured Thebes in 293 (ch. 39) and 291. Plutarch's calculation seems erroneous here, as Cassander began rebuilding Thebes in *c.* 316, after its destruction by Alexander (335). But the process may have taken a number of years.

89. *Pythian Games . . . held*: In 290 BC. The Pythian Games, which included contests in music and athletics, were held every four years at Delphi, in honour of Apollo.

90. *expedition against the Aetolians*: Probably in 289 BC.

91. *Pyrrhus fell upon Pantauchus . . . like actors on a stage*: See *Pyrrhus* 7–8.

92. *River Axius*: The Axius flows past Pella, capital of Macedonia.

93. *as Timotheus tells us*: Timotheus of Miletus (*c.* 450–360 BC) was a lyric poet. Plutarch quotes more of the same line (fragment 790 Page) in *Agesilaus* 14: 'Ares is a tyrant, but Greece does not fear gold.'

94. *Law . . . is the monarch of all things*: Pindar fragment 169.1 Maehler. The same line is also quoted in *To an uneducated ruler* 780c and in Plato's *Gorgias* 484b.

95. *Zeus entrusts kings . . . inviolate*: Homer, *Iliad* 1.238–9.

96. *Zeus' confidant and disciple*: Homer, *Odyssey* 19.179.

97. *Ptolemy Philopator*: Ptolemy IV Philopator, ruler of Egypt from 222 to 204 BC.

98. *drawn into a war . . . complete*: In 288 BC. See *Pyrrhus* 10–12.

99. *ruled securely for seven years*: Demetrius had ruled Macedonia from autumn 294 to perhaps autumn 288. Plutarch may have arrived at seven years by counting the archon years with which his reign overlapped. Eusebius has Demetrius ruling for six years (*FGrHist* 260 F 3).

100. *Cassandreia*: Situated on the westernmost of the three peninsulas

of Chalcidice; it had earlier been known as Potidaea. It was refounded, with its new name, by Cassander in 316.

101. *But my fate . . . nothingness*: The quotation is from an unknown play (*TrGF* IV fragment 871). Plutarch uses the second half of the passage quoted in *Roman questions* 282b and *On talkativeness* 517d.

102. *'Changing his godhead . . . Dirce's stream'*: Euripides, *Bacchae* 4–5, except that 'I come' has been changed to 'He comes'. The lines described the arrival of the god Dionysus in Thebes, disguised as a man.

103. *restored to the Thebans their constitution*: That is, Thebes was made autonomous, i.e., self-governing (287 BC). This marks a return to Demetrius' earlier declared policy of allowing the Greek cities to be 'free'.

104. *Athenians . . . revolted from him*: Spring 287 BC.

105. *Demetrius raised the siege*: In fact, Ptolemy had sent troops to Attica to support the Athenians, and was involved in the negotiations. Demetrius left Attica but retained his garrisons in Piraeus and Munychia.

106. *assembled all the ships he possessed*: See ch. 43.

107. *sailed for Asia*: Probably 286 or winter 286/5 BC.

108. *betrothed . . . several years before*: See ch. 32.

109. *Child of the blind old man . . . find ourselves?*: These are the opening words of *Oedipus at Colonus*. In the original, the question is put *to* Antigone, the daughter of the blind Oedipus, as they wander in exile. Plutarch has cleverly transformed this so that it refers to Demetrius as *son of* Antigonus, likewise now wandering about. Antigonus was blind in one eye.

110. *Cataonia*: A region north of Cilicia, in the south-eastern part of Cappadocia. It had been granted to Seleucus after the battle of Ipsus.

111. *Cyrrhestica*: In northern Syria. The mountains of the Amanus range separate Cilicia and Syria.

112. *Caunus*: In western Asia Minor, opposite Rhodes.

113. *put himself into his hands*: Probably early 285 BC.

114. *Syrian Chersonese*: Probably situated in a bend of the River Orontes in the neighbourhood of Antioch, and later known as Apameia.

115. *Demetrius' daughter Stratonice*: She had earlier been married to Seleucus and was now married to Seleucus' son, Antiochus (ch. 38).

116. *this was the kind of life he had really desired . . . real thing*:

Plutarch wrote a treatise advocating contentment with what one has called *On tranquillity of mind*. He also explores the danger of discontent in the *Lives of Pyrrhus and Marius* (see especially *Pyrrhus* 14).

117. *died in his fifty-fifth year*: Probably early in 282 BC.

118. *Demetrias*: A city in Thessaly, on the Gulf of Pagasae, founded by Demetrius *c.* 290.

119. *Romans subdued Macedonia*: In 168 BC, when Aemilius Paulus defeated Perseus at the battle of Pydna.

120. *bring the Roman on to the stage too*: That is, to begin the *Life of Antony*, which is paired with that of Demetrius.

PYRRHUS

Further Reading

Plutarch's Pyrrhus

Braund, D., 'Plutarch's *Pyrrhus* and Euripides' *Phoenician Women*: biography and tragedy on pleonectic parenting', *Histos* 1 (1997), pp. 1–8.

Buszard, B., 'The decline of Roman statesmanship in Plutarch's *Pyrrhus–Marius*', *CQ* NS 55 (2005), pp. 481–97.

Buszard, B., 'Caesar's ambition: a combined reading of Plutarch's *Alexander–Caesar* and *Pyrrhus–Marius*', *Transactions of the American Philological Association* 138 (2008), pp. 185–215.

Duff, T. E., *Plutarch's Lives: Exploring Virtue and Vice* (Oxford: Oxford University Press, 1999), ch. 4.

Mossman, J. M., 'Plutarch, Pyrrhus and Alexander', in P. A. Stadter (ed.), *Plutarch and the Historical Tradition* (London and New York: Routledge, 1992), pp. 90–108.

Mossman, J. M., '*Taxis ou barbaros*: Greek and Roman in Plutarch's *Pyrrhus*', *CQ* NS 55 (2005), pp. 498–517.

Nederlof, A. B., *Plutarchus' Leven van Pyrrhus: Historische Commentaar* (Amsterdam: H. J. Paris, 1940).

Schepens, G., 'Plutarch's view of Ancient Rome: some remarks on the *Life of Pyrrhus*', in L. Mooren (ed.), *Politics, Administration and Society in the Hellenistic and Roman World* (Leuven: Peeters, 2000), pp. 349–64.

Schepens, G., 'Rhetoric in Plutarch's *Life of Pyrrhus*', in L. Van der Stockt (ed.), *Rhetorical Theory and Praxis in Plutarch* (Leuven: Peeters, 2000), pp. 413–42.

History

Garoufalias, A. P., *Pyrrhus King of Epirus* (London: Stacey International, 1979).

Lévêque, P., *Pyrrhos* (Paris: E. de Boccard, 1957).

Franke, P. R., 'Pyrrhus', in *CAH* vii, pp. 456–85.

Notes to the Life of Pyrrhus

1. *Life of Pyrrhus*: There is no common prologue to the *Lives of Pyrrhus and Marius* of the kind that begins many books of *Parallel Lives*.

2. *Thesprotians and Molossians*: Two of the most powerful tribes that inhabited Epirus in north-west Greece.

3. *Deucalion and Pyrrha*: The mythical survivors of the great flood, which, according to Greek legend, overwhelmed the world.

4. *Dodona*: A famous sanctuary and oracle of Zeus, located in Epirus, near the modern Ioannina.

5. *Tharrhypas*: A Molossian king in the late fifth century BC.

6. *Menon ... Lamian War ... Leosthenes among the allies*: The Lamian War, which broke out on the news of Alexander's death in Asia, was fought in 323–2 BC between various Greek states and the forces of Antipater of Macedon. The most important Athenian commander was Leosthenes; the Thessalian cavalry was led by Menon of Pharsalus (see *Demosthenes* 27–8 and *Phocion* 23–6).

7. *Aeacides was driven out ... restored to power*: Aeacides supported Polyperchon against Cassander in the war which broke out after Antipater's death in 319. He was driven from power in 317 or 316, and Neoptolemus II was put on the throne.

8. *set him on the throne there*: In 307 or 306 BC. Aeacides had regained the throne in 313 but had been defeated and killed by Cassander shortly afterwards.

9. *reached the age of seventeen*: In 302.

10. *made Neoptolemus their king*: Neoptolemus II, who had already ruled from *c.* 317 to 307, with an interlude in 313 when Aeacides was in power.

11. *nominally been married to Alexander ... Demetrius married her*: See *Demetrius* 25. Alexander's son Alexander IV, who was born after his death in 323, was murdered in 310 or 309, at the age of thirteen or fourteen. Although nominally joint-king with his uncle Philip Arrhidaeus, he never exercised power.

12. *battle of Ipsus*: In 301 (see *Demetrius* 28–30).

13. *cities ... entrusted to his command*: See *Demetrius* 31.
14. *Philip*: This Philip is otherwise unknown.
15. *sent to Epirus to recover his kingdom*: In 297, when Pyrrhus was twenty-two. Pyrrhus had support from Ptolemy.
16. *city ... Epirus*: Near the modern Preveza, on the site of the future Nicopolis.
17. *Cassander's two sons ... into exile*: Cassander died in 297. For the power-struggle after his death, see *Demetrius* 36.
18. *Ambracia, Acarnania and Amphilochia*: Ambracia (modern Arta) was a city in southern Epirus, north of the Ambracian Gulf; Pyrrhus made it his capital. Amphilochia and Acarnania were regions to the south of Epirus, east and south respectively of the Ambracian Gulf.
19. *Lysimachus*: See *Demetrius*, n. 34, and Biographical Notes.
20. *proclaimed king of Macedonia*: In 294 BC (see *Demetrius* 36).
21. *death of Deidameia*: In 299.
22. *set out to attack Pyrrhus*: Probably in 289 (see *Demetrius* 41).
23. *hand-to-hand combat ... face Pantauchus*: Descriptions of single combat or of exchanges of insults before battle are common in the *Iliad*, but the practice was rare in the Classical and Hellenistic periods. Plutarch's Pyrrhus engages in both (chs. 16, 24, 30 and 31). This may be the result of Epirot custom or of a deliberate policy of presenting himself as heir to his supposed ancestor, Achilles. But by describing such episodes at length, Plutarch suggests a comparison with the Homeric heroes, and also that Pyrrhus failed to act with reason and forethought.
24. *compared ... Alexander the Great*: Cf. *Demetrius* 41.
25. *Hannibal's verdict ... Life of Scipio*: Scipio Africanus the elder (consul in 205 BC), who fought Hannibal. Plutarch records a slightly different version of Hannibal's comment in *Flamininus* 21, where he names as the best generals Alexander, Pyrrhus and himself, in that order. According to a fourth-century AD list of Plutarch's works (the Lamprias Catalogue), Plutarch wrote Lives of two Scipios, one paired with the lost *Epaminondas*, and one free-standing.
26. *Antigone's death*: In 295 BC.
27. *Paeonians*: The northern neighbours of Macedonia.
28. *'would divide ... not by lot'*: Euripides, *Phoenician women* 67–8.
29. *After this battle*: That is, the battle described in ch. 7. The material in chs. 8–9 is not a chronological narrative but, rather, designed to illustrate Pyrrhus' character.
30. *led an army into Macedonia*: See *Demetrius* 43.

31. *began sending . . . .letters to Pyrrhus*: For the alliance between Pyrrhus, Seleucus, Ptolemy and Lysimachus, and Demetrius' expulsion from Macedonia, see *Demetrius* 44.

32. *Ptolemy sailed to Greece . . . Lysimachus . . . pillaged the country*: In 288 BC.

33. *Pyrrhus . . . entered Athens*: In 287. The Athenians had revolted from Demetrius. Pyrrhus' arrival and pressure from Ptolemy caused Demetrius to lift his siege (see *Demetrius* 46 and n. 105).

34. *Demetrius . . . defeat in Syria*: Winter 286/5 (see *Demetrius* 49).

35. *lost Macedonia*: In 285.

36. *'but heartsick . . . battle'*: Homer, *Iliad* 1.491–2.

37. *Romans . . . Tarentum*: From 281, when Tarentum had attacked a Roman naval flotilla and then the city of Thurii. The Tarentines had shortly before assisted Pyrrhus in recovering Corcyra (Pausanias 1.12).

38. *moderate man named Meton . . . assembly*: This incident has a parallel with the attempt of another Meton to prevent the Athenians from attacking Sicily in 415 BC or to have his son released from military service (*Nicias* 13 and *Alcibiades* 17). It is possible that the incident described in *Pyrrhus* was invented with that earlier one in mind. At any rate, Plutarch exploits the parallel to suggest that disaster will follow for Pyrrhus and the Tarentines, just as it did for the Athenians.

39. *'Words . . . hope to win'*: Euripides, *Phoenician women* 517–18.

40. *started the following conversation . . .* : Cineas is presented here in the role of a 'wise adviser', a wise man who gives advice to a tyrant, often on where happiness lies, but is ignored (e.g., Solon and Croesus in Herodotus Book 1, or Artabanus, who warns Xerxes not to invade Greece, in Book 7). Disaster always follows. The Cineas episode thus suggests Pyrrhus' ignorance and arrogance, and leads one to expect that no good result will come of his overseas ventures.

41. *Agathocles is dead*: Agathocles, tyrant of Syracuse, died in 288. Pyrrhus had married his daughter Lanassa, and so may have considered that he had some claim on Sicily (ch. 9). As Pyrrhus himself notes later in this chapter, Agathocles had landed in Africa in 310, while Syracuse was itself under attack by the Carthaginians.

42. *sent Cineas . . . with 3,000 soldiers*: In 280. Pyrrhus followed in the same year.

43. *Iapygian cape*: Probably the modern Cape Leuca in south-eastern Apulia.

44. *Leonnatus the Macedonian*: Possibly the son of Alexander's

general Leonnatus (on whom, see *Phocion* 25; *Alexander* 21, 40; *Eumenes* 3).

45. *Dionysius*: Dionysius of Halicarnassus, who wrote in Greek in the first century BC. Books 19 and 20 of his historical work, *Roman antiquities*, were an important source for Plutarch in *Pyrrhus*, though they survive now only in excerpts. One of these excerpts contains part of Dionysius' account of this battle (Dionysius 19.12).

46. *Hieronymus*: On Hieronymus of Cardia, see *Eumenes*, n. 46.

47. *dancing attendance on . . . Alexander's bodyguards*: A sarcastic allusion to Pyrrhus' dealings with Ptolemy, Demetrius and Lysimachus.

48. *Lernaean Hydra*: A mythical many-headed monster, killed by Heracles. When one head was cut off, two more would grow back.

49. *consuls of Rome*: In 278. Later in the chapter Plutarch narrates the battle of Asculum which took place in the previous year, that is, in 279.

50. *Dionysius' account*: His detailed account of this battle survives (20.1–3).

51. *Daunians*: The manuscripts of Plutarch here read 'Samnites', but the passage of Dionysius which Plutarch is summarizing (20.3) has 'Daunians' and that is probably what Plutarch wrote.

52. *Ptolemy Ceraunus*: Ptolemy 'the Thunderbolt' was the son of Ptolemy I Soter of Egypt. After the defeat of Lysimachus by Seleucus at the battle of Corupedium in Lydia in 281 BC, he murdered Seleucus and was proclaimed by the army king of Macedon. He was killed in battle against the Gauls, who launched an invasion of mainland Greece in 280. The Gauls attempted to take Delphi, but were defeated by the Aetolians in perhaps 279 and by Antigonus Gonatas in Thrace in 277.

53. *landed in Sicily*: In 278 BC.

54. *Eryx*: In the extreme west of Sicily, near the modern Trapani.

55. *drove the barbarians back . . . dead bodies*: This episode seems to recall Alexander's similar feat in the country of the Malli (*Alexander* 63).

56. *Homer . . . divine possession and frenzy*: See *Iliad* 5.185, 6.101 and 9.238, where Homer seems to connect rage in battle with divine inspiration.

57. *not long before . . . fulfilled*: Pyrrhus left Sicily in 276 or 275. The First Punic War began eight or so years later in 264.

58. *Beneventum*: The battle of Beneventum took place in 275. Part of Dionysius' account is preserved (20.10–12).

59. *rest of Italy ... Sicily as well*: The fall of Tarentum in 272 marked the completion of the Roman conquest of Italy. After defeating Carthage in the First Punic War of 264–241, Rome turned most of Sicily into a Roman province.

60. *squandered six years*: 280–274 BC.

61. *Antigonus, the son of Demetrius*: Antigonus II Gonatas, who reigned in Macedonia *c.* 277–239 BC.

62. *Aeacidae*: The 'sons of Aeacus', the ancestor of Achilles from whom Pyrrhus claimed descent.

63. *Pyrrhus ... with the spear*: The *Palatine anthology* 6.130 ascribes this epigram to Leonidas of Tarentum.

64. *moved to occupy the cities of Macedonia*: In 273 BC.

65. *Aegae*: Modern Vergina, near Beroea, and the site of the Macedonian royal tombs.

66. *Cleonymus ... Areus*: Areus I was one of the two kings of Sparta from 309 to *c.* 265 BC. Cleonymus was Areus' uncle, and the son of Cleomenes II, but had been bypassed in the succession to the throne.

67. *led him to bring Pyrrhus to Sparta*: In 272.

68. *cities which Antigonus was holding in subjection*: Antigonus II Gonatas, son of Demetrius Poliorcetes, had taken control of Macedonia in 277 and maintained a firm hold on mainland Greece by means of garrisons in Corinth, Megara, Troezen, Epidaurus, Piraeus, Chalcis, and elsewhere. His supporters were in power in other Peloponnesian cities.

69. *trench ... elephants*: A palisade and ditch had in fact already been thrown around Sparta *c.* 317 and repaired, probably in 294, to resist an attack by Demetrius (*Demetrius* 35).

70. *Lysimachus*: Not the well-known Lysimachus, one of the successor kings.

71. *'One omen is best, to fight for Pyrrhus!'*: The line is adapted from Hector's words at *Iliad* 12.243, 'One omen is best, to fight for one's country.' In the *Iliad*, Hector has just disregarded a portent which prophesied disaster and has refused to heed the words of his comrade Polydamas, who urged him not to go on fighting. His own death follows. Plutarch's use of this quotation here suggests Pyrrhus' noble qualities, but that he, too, will soon be killed.

72. *liver ... lose a relative*: The entrails, especially the liver, of animals killed in sacrifice were examined for omens about the future. This was done especially on campaign and immediately before battles, where signs of the gods' favour were sought (see, e.g.,

Phocion 13 and *Alexander* 25). The lack of a liver was considered particularly portentous (e.g., *Agesilaus* 9 and *Alexander* 73).

73. *his companions*: Perhaps designating the 'Companion Cavalry', companions being a term used by Hellenistic kings for their elite cavalry corps. Cf. *Alexander*, n. 49.

74. *challenging . . . for the throne*: Pyrrhus has already fought several times in single combat (chs. 7 and 24).

75. *an eagle . . . was gone*: Cf. ch. 10, where Pyrrhus was given the name 'the Eagle'.

76. *Alcyoneus*: The son of Antigonus II Gonatas.

77. *grandfather Antigonus and his father Demetrius . . . just such vicissitudes of fortune*: Antigonus I Monophthalmus died in 301 at the battle of Ipsus. Plutarch presents the life of his son Demetrius, who died in 282, as a case-study in the ups and downs of fortune (see p. 400 and *Demetrius*, n. 10).

78. *burned with due ceremony*: But see the end of ch. 3, on how part of his body survived the flames.

The New Penguin Plutarch

The Lives are arranged as follows:

FALL OF THE ROMAN REPUBLIC

Marius
Sulla
Comparison of Lysander and Sulla
Crassus
Comparison of Nicias and Crassus
Pompey
Comparison of Agesilaus and Pompey
Caesar
Cicero
Comparison of Demosthenes and Cicero

RISE AND FALL OF ATHENS

Theseus
Solon
Themistocles
Aristides
Cimon
Pericles
Nicias
Alcibiades
Comparison of Coriolanus and Alcibiades
Lysander
On the Malice of Herodotus

RISE OF ROME

Romulus
Comparison of Theseus and Romulus
Numa
Comparison of Lycurgus and Numa
Poplicola
Comparison of Solon and Poplicola
Camillus
Coriolanus
Fabius Maximus
Comparison of Pericles and Fabius Maximus
Marcellus
Comparison of Pelopidas and Marcellus
Cato the Elder
Comparison of Aristides and Cato the Elder
Aemilius Paullus
Philopoemen
Flamininus
Comparison of Philopoemen and Flamininus
Aratus

THE AGE OF ALEXANDER

Artaxerxes
Pelopidas
Dion
Timoleon
Comparison of Aemilius and Timoleon
Demosthenes
Phocion
Alexander
Eumenes
Comparison of Sertorius and Eumenes
Demetrius
Pyrrhus

PLUTARCH ON SPARTA

Lycurgus
Agesilaus
Agis and Cleomenes

PENGUIN CLASSICS

THE CAMPAIGNS OF ALEXANDER
ARRIAN

'His passion was for glory only, and in that he was insatiable'

Although written over four hundred years after Alexander's death, Arrian's
Campaigns of Alexander is the most reliable account of the man and his
achievements we have. Arrian's own experience as a military commander gave
him unique insights into the life of the world's greatest conqueror. He tells of
Alexander's violent suppression of the Theban rebellion, his total defeat of Persia,
and his campaigns through Egypt, India and Babylon – establishing new cities
and destroying others in his path. While Alexander emerges from this record as
an unparalleled and charismatic leader, Arrian succeeds brilliantly in creating an
objective and fully rounded portrait of a man of boundless ambition, who was
exposed to the temptations of power and worshipped as a god in his own lifetime.

Aubrey de Sélincourt's vivid translation is accompanied by J. R. Hamilton's
introduction, which discusses Arrian's life and times, his synthesis of other
classical sources and the composition of Alexander's army. This edition also
includes maps, a list for further reading and a detailed index.

Translated by Aubrey de Sélincourt
Revised, with a new introduction and notes by J. R. Hamilton

PENGUIN CLASSICS

THE CONQUEST OF GAUL
CAESAR

'The enemy were overpowered and took to flight.
The Romans pursued as far as their strength enabled them to run'

Between 58 and 50 BC Julius Caesar conquered most of the area now covered by France, Belgium and Switzerland, and invaded Britain twice, and *The Conquest of Gaul* is his record of these campaigns. Caesar's narrative offers insights into his military strategy and paints a fascinating picture of his encounters with the inhabitants of Gaul and Britain, as well as lively portraits of the rebel leader Vercingetorix and other Gallic chieftains. *The Conquest of Gaul* can also be read as a piece of political propaganda, as Caesar sets down his version of events for the Roman public, knowing he faces civil war on his return to Rome.

Revised and updated by Jane Gardner, S. A. Handford's translation brings Caesar's lucid and exciting account to life for modern readers. This volume includes a glossary of persons and places, maps, appendices and suggestions for further reading.

Translated by S. A. Handford

Revised with a new introduction by Jane F. Gardner

PENGUIN CLASSICS

THE RISE OF THE ROMAN EMPIRE
POLYBIUS

> 'If history is deprived of the truth,
> we are left with nothing but an idle, unprofitable tale'

In writing his account of the relentless growth of the Roman Empire, the Greek statesman Polybius (*c.* 200–118 BC) set out to help his fellow-countrymen understand how their world came to be dominated by Rome. Opening with the Punic War in 264 BC, he vividly records the critical stages of Roman expansion: its campaigns throughout the Mediterranean, the temporary setbacks inflicted by Hannibal and the final destruction of Carthage in 146 BC. An active participant in contemporary politics, as well as a friend of many prominent Roman citizens, Polybius was able to draw on a range of eyewitness accounts and on his own experiences of many of the central events, giving his work immediacy and authority.

Ian Scott-Kilvert's translation fully preserves the clarity of Polybius' narrative. This substantial selection of the surviving volumes is accompanied by an introduction by F. W. Walbank, which examines Polybius' life and times, and the sources and technique he employed in writing his history.

Translated by Ian Scott-Kilvert

Selected with an introduction by F. W. Walbank

Penguin Classics

THE POLITICS
ARISTOTLE

'Man is by nature a political animal'

In *The Politics* Aristotle addresses the questions that lie at the heart of political science. How should society be ordered to ensure the happiness of the individual? Which forms of government are best and how should they be maintained? By analysing a range of city constitutions – oligarchies, democracies and tyrannies – he seeks to establish the strengths and weaknesses of each system to decide which are the most effective, in theory and in practice. A hugely significant work, which has influenced thinkers as diverse as Aquinas and Machiavelli, *The Politics* remains an outstanding commentary on fundamental political issues and concerns, and provides fascinating insights into the workings and attitudes of the Greek city-state.

The introductions by T. A. Sinclair and Trevor J. Saunders discuss the influence of *The Politics* on philosophers, its modern relevance and Aristotle's political beliefs. This edition contains Greek and English glossaries, and a bibliography for further reading.

Translated by T. A. Sinclair
Revised and re-presented by Trevor J. Saunders

PENGUIN CLASSICS

THE BIRDS AND OTHER PLAYS
ARISTOPHANES

The Knights/Peace/The Birds/The Assemblywomen/Wealth

> 'Oh wings are splendid things, make no mistake:
> they really help you rise in the world'

The plays collected in this volume, written at different times in Aristophanes'
forty-year career as a dramatist, all contain his trademark bawdy comedy and
dazzling verbal agility. In *The Birds*, two frustrated Athenians join with the birds to
build the utopian city of 'Much Cuckoo in the Clouds'. *The Knights* is a venomous
satire on Cleon, the prominent Athenian demagogue, while *The Assemblywomen*
considers the war of the sexes, as the women of Athens infiltrate the all-male
Assembly in disguise. The lengthy conflict with Sparta is the subject of *Peace*,
inspired by the hope of a settlement in 421 BC, and *Wealth* reflects the economic
catastrophe that hit Athens after the war, as the god of riches is depicted as a
ragged, blind old man.

The lively translations by David Barrett and Alan H. Sommerstein capture the full
humour of the plays. The introduction examines Aristophanes' life and times, and
the comedy and poetry of his works. This volume also includes an introductory
note for each play.

Translated with an introduction by David Barrett and Alan H. Sommerstein

PENGUIN CLASSICS

CONVERSATIONS OF SOCRATES
XENOPHON

Socrates' Defence/Memoirs of Socrates/The Estate-Manager/The Dinner-Party

'He seemed to me to be the perfect example of goodness and happiness'

After the execution of Socrates in 399 BC, a number of his followers wrote dialogues featuring him as the protagonist and, in so doing, transformed the great philosopher into a legendary figure. Xenophon's portrait is the only one other than Plato's to survive, and while it offers a very personal interpretation of Socratic thought, it also reveals much about the man and his philosophical views. In 'Socrates' Defence' Xenophon defends his mentor against charges of arrogance made at his trial, while the 'Memoirs of Socrates' also starts with an impassioned plea for the rehabilitation of a wronged reputation. Along with 'The Estate-Manager', a practical economic treatise, and 'The Dinner-Party', a sparkling exploration of love, Xenophon's dialogues offer fascinating insights into the Socratic world and into the intellectual atmosphere and daily life of ancient Greece.

Xenophon's complete Socratic works are translated in this volume. In his introduction, Robin Waterfield illuminates the significance of these four books, showing how perfectly they embody the founding principles of Socratic thought.

Translated by Hugh Tredennick and Robin Waterfield and edited with new material by Robin Waterfield

PENGUIN CLASSICS

HOMERIC HYMNS

> 'It is of you the poet sings ...
> at the beginning and at the end
> it is always of you'

Written by unknown poets in the sixth and seventh centuries BC, the thirty-three
Homeric Hymns were recited at festivals to honour the Olympian goddesses and
gods and to pray for divine favour or for victory in singing contests. They stand
now as works of great poetic force, full of grace and lyricism, and ranging in tone
from irony to solemnity, ebullience to grandeur. Recounting significant episodes
from mythology, such as the abduction of Persephone by Hades and Hermes' theft
of Apollo's cattle, the *Hymns* also provide fascinating insights into cults, rituals
and holy sanctuaries, giving us an intriguing view of the ancient Greek relationship
between humans and the divine.

This translation of the *Homeric Hymns* is new to Penguin Classics, providing a key text
for understanding ancient Greek mythology and religion. The introduction explores
their authorship, performance, literary qualities and influence on later writers.

'The purest expressions of ancient Greek religion we possess ... Jules Cashford is
attuned to the poetry of the Hymns' Nigel Spivey, University of Cambridge

A new translation by Jules Cashford with an introduction by Nicholas Richardson

PENGUIN CLASSICS

THE ANNALS OF IMPERIAL ROME
TACITUS

'Nero was already corrupted by every lust, natural and unnatural'

The Annals of Imperial Rome recount the major historical events from the years shortly before the death of Augustus to the death of Nero in AD 68. With clarity and vivid intensity Tacitus describes the reign of terror under the corrupt Tiberius, the great fire of Rome during the time of Nero and the wars, poisonings, scandals, conspiracies and murders that were part of imperial life. Despite his claim that the *Annals* were written objectively, Tacitus' account is sharply critical of the emperors' excesses and fearful for the future of imperial Rome, while also filled with a longing for its past glories.

Michael Grant's fine translation captures the moral tone, astringent wit and stylish vigour of the original. His introduction discusses the life and works of Tacitus and the historical context of the *Annals*. This edition also contains a key to place names and technical terms, maps, tables and suggestions for further reading.

Translated with an introduction by Michael Grant

THE STORY OF PENGUIN CLASSICS

Before 1946 ... 'Classics' are mainly the domain of academics and students; readable editions for everyone else are almost unheard of. This all changes when a little-known classicist, E. V. Rieu, presents Penguin founder Allen Lane with the translation of Homer's *Odyssey* that he has been working on in his spare time.

1946 Penguin Classics debuts with *The Odyssey*, which promptly sells three million copies. Suddenly, classics are no longer for the privileged few.

1950s Rieu, now series editor, turns to professional writers for the best modern, readable translations, including Dorothy L. Sayers's *Inferno* and Robert Graves's unexpurgated *Twelve Caesars*.

1960s The Classics are given the distinctive black covers that have remained a constant throughout the life of the series. Rieu retires in 1964, hailing the Penguin Classics list as 'the greatest educative force of the twentieth century.'

1970s A new generation of translators swells the Penguin Classics ranks, introducing readers of English to classics of world literature from more than twenty languages. The list grows to encompass more history, philosophy, science, religion and politics.

1980s The Penguin American Library launches with titles such as *Uncle Tom's Cabin*, and joins forces with Penguin Classics to provide the most comprehensive library of world literature available from any paperback publisher.

1990s The launch of Penguin Audiobooks brings the classics to a listening audience for the first time, and in 1999 the worldwide launch of the Penguin Classics website extends their reach to the global online community.

The 21st Century Penguin Classics are completely redesigned for the first time in nearly twenty years. This world-famous series now consists of more than 1300 titles, making the widest range of the best books ever written available to millions – and constantly redefining what makes a 'classic'.

The Odyssey continues ...

The best books ever written

PENGUIN CLASSICS

SINCE 1946

Find out more at www.penguinclassics.com